MW00611598

Meade's Army

Meade's Army

THE PRIVATE NOTEBOOKS *of* LT. COL. THEODORE LYMAN

Edited by David W. Lowe

The Kent State
University Press
Kent, Ohio

© 2007 by
The Kent State University Press,
Kent, Ohio 44242
All rights reserved
Library of Congress Catalog Card
Number 2006028372
ISBN: 978-0-87338-901-3
Manufactured in the United States of America

11 10 09 08 07   5 4 3 2 1

The Theodore Lyman Notebook, 1863–1865, and Lyman family papers
and photographs are reprinted with permission of the Massachusetts Historical Society.

Library of Congress Cataloging-in-Publication Data

Lyman, Theodore, 1833–1897.
Meade's army : the private notebooks of Lt. Col. Theodore Lyman / edited by David W. Lowe.
p. cm.
Includes bibliographical references and index.
ISBN-13: 978-0-87338-901-3 (hardcover : alk. paper) ∞
ISBN-10: 0-87338-901-8 (hardcover : alk. paper) ∞
1. United States—History—Civil War, 1861–1865—Personal narratives.
2. Virginia—History—Civil War, 1861–1865—Personal narratives.
3. Lyman, Theodore, 1833–1897—Diaries.
4. United States. Army—Staffs—Diaries.
5. Meade, George Gordon, 1815–1872—Friends and associates.
6. United States. Army of the Potomac.
7. Virginia—History—Civil War, 1861–1865—Campaigns.
8. United States—History—Civil War, 1861–1865—Campaigns.
I. Lowe, David W., 1951–.
II. Title.
E601.L978   2007
973.7'3092—dc22   2006028372

British Library Cataloging-in-Publication data are available.

For George B. Lowe

Orange Combat Team, 5307th Composite Unit (Provisional)

and Dave Richardson, combat correspondent

Burma 1944

Lyman was a keen, discreet observer; and moreover, realizing to the full the importance of what was transpiring, he kept a careful private record of all he saw and heard—a record still in existence, and which will probably some day see the light. When it does—perhaps half a century hence—I do not hesitate now to put on record my belief that it will prove the most valuable, as well as the most graphic, of all the inside views of the memorable Virginia campaigns of 1863, 1864, and 1865.

—CHARLES FRANCIS ADAMS JR., 1897

near Petersburg.   A R Waud

Sketch of Theodore Lyman by A. R. Waud.
Theodore Lyman to Elizabeth Lyman, 5 August 1864.
Lyman Family Papers. *Massachusetts Historical Society.*

Contents

———∞∞∞———

Foreword

———◦∞∞◦———

THEODORE LYMAN COULD EASILY have avoided serving in the Civil War.
Born into a fabulously wealthy family, he was educated privately and at Harvard, determined upon a scientific career, and when the war began was newly
married and traveling in Europe. Although his father, while serving as mayor
of Boston, had been involved in the rescue of William Lloyd Garrison from
an angry mob, Lyman had little sympathy for Republicans, whom he believed
responsible for the conflict. Yet he felt uncomfortable with a life of comfort and
privilege when a wide array of family, friends, and classmates had engaged in
battle and some had already died. Private wealth required public service.

As a prewar scientist studying starfish in Florida, Lyman had already met
George Gordon Meade, who by the midpoint of the war became the commander of the North's largest army and the celebrated victor of the Battle of
Gettysburg. Meade and Lyman had become friends, so when Lyman asked
for a staff position, Meade replied encouragingly. Although Lyman began the
correspondence in 1862 from Europe, problems of communicating, returning
from abroad, and settling his family in Brookline kept Lyman from actual
service until late the following year.

Readers of Lyman's letters to his wife and his journals can only regret the
delay. Lyman brought to the headquarters of the Army of the Potomac a practice
of detached observation quite unusual for the situation. Carefully trained in
scientific procedure by the renowned Louis Agassiz, Lyman brought skills as

a naturalist to wartime scenes. Family background also set him apart and led to a cool appraisal of excited men amid tumultuous events.

In 1922 George R. Agassiz published *Meade's Headquarters: Letters of Colonel Theodore Lyman from the Wilderness to Appomattox*, a collection of letters to his wife that became a Civil War classic. Incisive and readable throughout, Lyman provides a vivid picture of one of the focal points of Union command. *Meade's Headquarters* serves as counterpoint to a comparable account by Horace Porter, *Campaigning with Grant*, also remarkable for clarity of vision and sharpness of detail.

During the final year of the Civil War, Meade and Ulysses S. Grant had a peculiar relationship. Grant received command of all the Union armies in March 1864 with a presumption that he would coordinate operations from Washington. Although urged by Gen. William Tecumseh Sherman to remain with the western armies that he had previously commanded, Grant decided to leave Henry W. Halleck, his predecessor as general in chief, in Washington as chief of staff and to accompany the Army of the Potomac on the spring campaign without displacing Meade. Initially, Meade and his staff welcomed Grant's decision. Meade now had the support of his commander amid a flurry of objections to his conduct of the Battle of Gettysburg, objections strengthened by the subsequent lackluster performance of his army. Lyman used every opportunity to train a careful eye on Grant, a man whose apparent simplicity concealed complexity of thought.

As a relationship that began auspiciously deteriorated during the Overland campaign against Robert E. Lee's Army of Northern Virginia, Lyman's observations prove especially valuable. Although a close friend and an increasingly valuable assistant to Meade, Lyman's sharp eye did not overlook the faults of his commander. Meade's touchiness and insistence on his own worth, his scorn for newspaper reporters, his tendency to give unintentional offence, his inability to dominate subordinates, and his basic lack of battlefield aggressiveness would eventually lead him to occupy the role of forgotten man at Appomattox. Lyman left the victorious armies in 1865 with his friendship with Meade intact and enhanced respect for Grant.

But the upward view is not all that is valuable in Lyman's observations. He assessed the common soldier, and gradually some of his Boston Brahmin prejudices softened. Above all, he grew and matured amid the vicissitudes of military service. He presents a remarkable self-portrait as well as a view of battles and leaders.

Since 1922 *Meade's Headquarters* has been all that readers expected to have of Lyman's Civil War experience. Now David W. Lowe has uncovered private notebooks that Lyman maintained contemporaneously. Lowe presents the text faithfully and annotates with scholarly zeal. Agassiz occasionally tapped the notebooks for background in transcribing Lyman's letters to his wife, but modern readers will find them fresh, original, and a valuable enhancement to a Civil War classic.

JOHN Y. SIMON
Southern Illinois University Carbondale

Acknowledgments

—∞—

I appreciate the encouragement and tutelage of Dr. Joseph L. Harsh throughout this project. I thank Peter Drummey, Massachusetts Historical Society librarian Stephen T. Riley, reference librarians Nicholas Graham and Kimberly Nusco, and their staff for making my research at MHS a pleasurable experience. J. David Bohl of Hull, Massachusetts, masterfully photographed Lyman's sketch maps and illustrations. Colleague Bonnie Burns turned up relevant materials at the Harvard Map Collection and in the Harvard University Archives and critiqued early drafts of the transcription. My wife, Lynne, and her mother, Rosalyn White, undertook the final proofreading. I must acknowledge Zoe for patiently awaiting the long walks that were promised. Errors and omissions that remain are mine.

Editorial Note

‒‒‒⦿⦿⦿‒‒‒

THE SWIFT PENCIL OF *HARPER'S* special artist Alfred Waud captured Lt. Col. Theodore Lyman seated on a hardtack box, hunched over a sheet of paper with pen in hand, with balding head, sleeves rolled up, and a look of intense concentration. It must have been Lyman's familiar pose at army headquarters, as he was an obsessive correspondent. Every few days he mailed long letters—each a gem of description—to his wife, Mimi. In 1922, Lyman's nephew, George Russell Agassiz, collected these letters in *Meade's Headquarters 1863–1865: Letters of Colonel Theodore Lyman from the Wilderness to Appomattox*, a book that has been a staple for historians writing about the Army of the Potomac. The letters, clear and concise as they were, were not Lyman's magnum opus.

During his tenure at Meade's headquarters, Lyman kept a series of private notebooks written for a most discriminating audience—himself—and therein he found his voice as a military historian. It seems strange that his notebooks languished so long unpublished in the collections of the Massachusetts Historical Society (MHS). Editor Agassiz quoted some 3,500 words from Lyman's notebooks in *Meade's Headquarters*, and I refer the reader to these passages to encourage comparison between the published letters and the notebooks. Although there is inevitable overlap in subject matter, there are many significant differences. The two volumes should be studied together.

In his letters to Mimi, Lyman often emphasized the humor or irony in events and sometimes illustrated his anecdotes with a silly drawing or a caricature of one of the staff officers. He downplayed the dangers and spared her gory, frightening, or overly technical details. Following the conventions of his time, editor Agassiz excised the cloying, sometimes racy endearments with which Lyman opened and closed most letters. Perhaps it was for the best, as a generation of historians might have taken Lyman less seriously than he deserved.

Theodore Lyman kept a notebook for many years. I have retained the original structure of his writings and reference both his given volume numbers and the accession numbers of the MHS. Lyman recorded his volumes 12, 13 (parts one and two), 14, and 15 as events transpired. Volumes 13A and 13B covering the Virginia campaign of 1864 were completed at war's end. Lyman continued to scrawl hasty notes during this hectic time, but he was a stickler for putting things in "finished form." He finished these two books in his office at Singletree. The draft entries were not uncovered if indeed these still exist. Throughout, Lyman maintained the tone of his contemporaneous writings as though reliving events, and his occasional asides with the benefit of hindsight are useful to the historian and student of the war.

At some point editor Agassiz prepared a typescript af the notebooks. These pages and OCR saved me untold hours of transcription. The scanned text was then compared word by word with the originals and corrected. I have appended selected entries from Lyman's volume 16 to the end of volume 15 to carry the reader through General Meade's postwar visit to Boston and his induction into the Porcellian Club. Nothing else has been abridged. I have tampered with the text of Lyman's notebooks as little as possible. His dates were standardized. A number of silent corrections were made to Lyman's punctuation. His sometimes "excentric" spellings and his use of "&" and "&c." have been retained for their flavor. His misspellings of proper names, such as "Stewart" for "Stuart," are clarified in the notes.

Lyman befriended the army's topographic engineers and proved a skilled mapmaker. Many of his more finished maps remain buried within his letters home or to friends and, for the time being, remain unpublished. The sketch maps and other drawings in the notebooks served as a form of shorthand and were an integral part of his narrative. In my editing, I took care to place these sketches as closely as possible to their original locations relative to the text. Since Lyman identified most items himself, there seemed to be little need to duplicate his efforts or disrupt the visual flow of the page with additional caption text. The interested reader may locate specific items in the index under the entry "maps and drawings."

Introduction
Something for the Cause

———— ❦ ————

THEODORE LYMAN III JOINED the headquarters staff of Maj. Gen. George Gordon Meade as a volunteer aide-de-camp in September 1863, by which time the American Civil War had raged for two and a half years. Ted Lyman had spent much of that time on a grand tour of Europe, where he could have ridden out the war in safety. His wife's cousin Robert Gould Shaw, colonel of the 54th Massachusetts, advised him to stay in Europe to avoid conscription or, upon his return, to join his own regiment as a chaplain. In retrospect, Shaw's well-meant offer was demeaning, as Lyman had more to offer the Cause than sermons.[1]

Ted Lyman was thirty years old when he commenced soldiering. Up until then he had played his role among Boston's gentry, tied by birth, education, and marriage into an intricate, aristocratic web. His grandfather—the first Theodore—was a sixth-generation New Englander, one of a group of hardy sea captains who cast their lot with ocean commerce. Captain Lyman had built a trading and shipping firm that cornered a third of the fur trade with the tribal nations of the Pacific Northwest. In the early 1790s, Captain Lyman relocated from York, Maine, to Boston and acquired a four-hundred-acre estate in Waltham. The captain sought out noted Salem architect Samuel McIntire to build a twenty-four-room residence that he called the Vale. He transformed the property into the image of an English country home with tree-lined country lanes and grounds landscaped with plants collected during his seafaring years.

At a time when Boston's mast-filled harbor was the center of an expanding mercantile empire, Captain Lyman allied his affairs with other merchant

Lt. Col. Theodore Lyman, ca. 1865. Carte de visite by A. Sonrel, Boston, Mass. Carte de visite collection. *Massachusetts Historical Society.*

families—Perkins, Cabot, Forbes, Sturgis, and Russell—to invest in the China trade. For a dozen years, Captain Lyman's ships carried their furs from the American Northwest to Canton where the cargo was exchanged for tea, silk, and chinaware to sell in Boston and New York. In 1807, with furbearing animals on the decline, the captain sold off his China interests to J. & T. H. Perkins Company. By this shrewd move, he avoided much opprobrium. Boston merchants who stayed in the China trade turned to selling Smyrna opium in Canton and Shanghai—a highly lucrative, if morally ambiguous, business that continued until the eve of the Civil War.[2]

In retirement, Captain Lyman cultivated bananas, pineapples, and more exotic tropical fruits in his greenhouses to the delight of neighbors and friends. (The oldest greenhouse in the country today stands on the grounds of the Vale.) Along with his associates in the Massachusetts Horticultural Society, he cultivated an exuberance of ruby-red *Camellia japonica*, cross-fertilizing his specimens, and carefully recording each plant's attributes. He and wife, Lydia, had three children—George Williams, Mary, and Theodore II. George followed his father's footsteps as a merchant and married Elizabeth Gray Otis, daughter of Harrison Gray Otis, U.S. senator and Boston's mayor from 1829 to 1831. Mary Lyman wed statesman and orator Samuel Atkins Eliot, who would be mayor of Boston from 1836 to 1850.

Theodore Lyman II studied literature at the University of Edinburgh and afterward authored volumes on international diplomacy. As young men, he and Edward Everett (later Boston mayor, U.S. senator, and Harvard president) traveled through countries in Europe, such as Turkey and Bulgaria, that were not on the typical grand tour itinerary. Theodore kept a full and detailed journal of his travels, a habit that he would pass on to his son.

Theodore Lyman II returned to Boston, studied law, and entered the state legislature. He married Mary Henderson, of a prominent New York shipping family, and settled comfortably into business, investing in one of the country's first water-powered mechanized looms at Waltham. He joined Francis Cabot Lowell, Patrick Tracy Jackson, Nathan Appleton, and Amos and Abbott Lawrence in the Boston Associates to develop mass-production textile mills at Lowell, Springfield, and elsewhere in New England. Although lacking any formal military education, he was appointed a general in the Massachusetts militia, a mostly honorary position, and occasionally signed himself "General Lyman."

In 1834, Theodore Lyman II was elected mayor of Boston. His backers—among the city's most influential citizens—called themselves "silk-stocking Democrats" to differentiate themselves from the Jacksonian "rabble." Mayor Lyman's tenure was noted for the Garrison Mob, a riot in which angry textile mill owners and their Southern cotton agents nearly lynched abolitionist William Lloyd Garrison. Mayor Lyman did not much care for the growing antislavery movement, but he abhorred social unrest on his watch. The mayor and a few constables rescued Garrison at considerable risk to themselves and then saw him quietly escorted out of the city to ease tensions. As early as the 1830s, the politics of cotton and slavery had become a divisive issue in Boston. Abolitionists were considered bad for the textile business, which was, after all, the business of New England. The perpetrators of the riot—all well known—were never brought to justice. Despite this oversight, or perhaps because of it, Mayor Lyman was considered "very popular as mayor," wrote one of his colleagues, "and could have held the office for years—if he had chosen to do so."[3]

Mayor Lyman and Mary had two children who lived to adulthood—Cora, born in 1828, and Theodore III, born in 1833. Mary lived but three more years after her son "Dory's" birth, and her passing left the mayor grief stricken. He withdrew from politics (after serving two terms as mayor) and abandoned Waltham for a farm in Brookline because, he said, the Vale reminded him too much of Mary. Mayor Lyman devoted himself to horticulture and the welfare of his children for his remaining years. In 1849, the mayor returned from a European trip complaining of exhaustion. He lingered in a feeble state for a week before succumbing to what may have been a stroke. The mayor was remembered for generous donations to the horticultural society and to the state reform school, which was renamed the Lyman School in his honor.

By the terms of the will, the mayor's brother, George Williams Lyman, took possession of the Vale, and daughter Cora received title to the family's city house at 8 Mount Vernon Street on Beacon Hill. Young Ted Lyman inherited the sixty-acre working farm in Brookline called Singletree. He and his sister divided more than $430,000 in assets and a sizable investment income derived from banking, mills, canals, and railroads.[4]

Despite its rural pretensions, Brookline had grown into a rather exclusive enclave. Business magnate Augustus Lowell and the near-legendary Thomas Handasyd Perkins of Perkins & Company owned estates nearby. Perkins's business partner and son-in-law, Samuel Cabot Jr., purchased hundreds of acres adjacent to the Lyman property, which his widow inherited and she and several of her children occupied. Prominent businessman Henry Lee Jr. married one of the Cabot daughters and moved in next door. There were few locales around Boston on the eve of civil war, other than Beacon Hill, with more concentrated wealth and influence than Brookline.

In the year before Mayor Lyman's death, merchant Gardner Howland Shaw married Ted's older sister, Cora, and enfolded his brother-in-law into the extensive Shaw clan. Howland (as he was known to the family) would remain Lyman's confidant and financial adviser throughout his life. Among Howland's brothers were Quincy Adams Shaw, who in 1846 conducted historian Francis Parkman on his storied trip along the Oregon Trail. "Uncle Quin" also was known as one of the finest horse breeders in New England. Another brother was Francis Shaw, Staten Island businessman and father of Robert Gould Shaw, future colonel of the 54th Massachusetts Infantry.

Because of childhood ailments and extended overseas travel with his father, Ted Lyman had missed the opportunity to enroll in the preparatory academies such as Boston Latin, but he had been extensively drilled by private tutors. At the urging of his Uncle George, he enrolled in Harvard University, where he was a popular fellow. As befitted a social extrovert, he filled his first year more with socializing than with study. He tugged an oar for a college rowing team, composed witty chorales for the Hasty Pudding Club, and was tapped for the exclusive Porcellian Club—the "Porc" or "P.C.," as he called it. Along the way, he began to apply his considerable intellectual talents and in 1855 graduated near the top of his class.

Ted Lyman delivered the commencement address, titled "Influence of the Passion for the Marvellous on the Truth of History." This was a lighthearted but barbed indictment of historians who refused to let facts get in the way of a good story. The *Boston Herald* wrote that Lyman "exhibited a rare satirical talent and fund of humor, and richly deserved the hearty applause he elicited." The *Boston Telegraph* described his performance as "an able production both in substance and delivery," but went on to say that Lyman "went out of his way to bow to slavery, by a fling at 'abolitionists'—the only *strain* of this kind of attempted wit which was observed through the whole day." Lyman's attempted wit was not out of line with the conservative politics inherited from his father.[5]

Ted Lyman was by inclination an academic, and having the education and wherewithal, he gravitated toward the study of science. Under the tutelage of Professor Jean Louis Rodolphe Agassiz, one of the preeminent natural scientists of the nineteenth century, he pursued an advanced degree at the Lawrence Scientific School at Harvard. His area of expertise was peculiar for a would-be soldier. He specialized in taxonomic classification of the *Ophiuridae* and *Astrophytidae*—the starfish families—but this interest in starfish led him into a significant military relationship.

In 1856, Professor Agassiz dispatched his pupil to Florida to collect specimens for Harvard's newly established Museum of Comparative Zoology. Agassiz's scientific colleague, Alexander Dallas Bache, superintendent of the U.S. Coastal Survey, all but ordered his subordinates—officers of the U.S. Army Corps of Topographical Engineers—to extend Lyman every courtesy, including "any facilities which you may be able to command for purposes which he may specify, subject to the usual discretion in regard to the interests of your regular duty."[6]

During this expedition, Lyman met 1st Lt. George Gordon Meade of Philadelphia, who was supervising the construction of lighthouses along the Florida coast. Meade provided quarters, boats, and soldiers to aid Lyman's reef-scouring but also proved a hospitable companion. During the day, Lyman dredged along the reefs, examined sea creatures with an optical lens, and bagged and labeled specimens. In the evenings, he and Meade discussed their diverse adventures and talked of Europe, politics, common acquaintances, and science.[7]

"I have just returned," Lyman reported to Howland, "from a fortnight's cruise with Lieut. Meade of the Topog. Engineers. We went as far as Cape Florida, which is on Key Biscayne, and taking there a sail boat, went about 8 miles to the mouth of the Miami. The government have about two dozen men at Cape Florida, enlarging the present light-house. Mr. M. is the head of this."

Here Lyman experienced Meade's infamous "irascibility" for the first time. Lyman wrote to Howland: "As soon as he was ashore—'Now Mr. Masters (a meek superintendent), why in the world did you put such a little watch box on top that temporary tower? All the rest ought to have been a chamber for the light keeper!' In less than a minute he had ascended several very dizzy ladders and was criticizing the unfortunate watch box, while the superintendent followed humbly behind and said 'Yes, sir,' at intervals." "These people," Meade afterward complained to Lyman, "even with the most exact instructions, seemed to be all very stupid." Meade's impatience with subordinates who proved incapable of following his orders would be a source of friction within his future command relationships.[8]

To express gratitude for Meade's hospitality, Lyman shipped "delicacies and freight" after his return to Brookline. The delicacies likely included, among other items, jars of pickles cured from a family recipe, of which Meade grew fond. The freight, undoubtedly, was one of Lyman's customary gifts, a case of vintage Madeira wine. Meade and Lyman continued to correspond, always warmly, after their shared experience in the wilderness of Florida.

Lyman wrote up his discoveries from the Florida reefs, and in 1858 the Lawrence Scientific School awarded him an advanced degree summa cum laude. He emerged a qualified natural scientist, trained by the finest minds of the era to observe detail, question anomalies, organize observations, and above all record these observations systematically—skills that would serve him well as a staff officer in the Army of the Potomac.

With his profession on track, Lyman turned to marriage. For several years, Lyman's sister and brother-in-law, Cora and Howland, had encouraged a relationship with Howland's niece, Elizabeth Russell, and they were gratified when flirtation developed into romance. Elizabeth, whom Lyman always called "Mimi" or "his Mimette" was the oldest daughter of Howland's sister Sarah Parkman Shaw and George Robert Russell. Mimi's father, George Russell, had labored overseas for fifteen years in the East India and China trade, and, in the idiom of the time, had been "very fortunate." He retired from Russell & Company to West Roxbury, still a young man, and devoted himself to literature, philosophy, and philanthropy. In the 1840s, Russell helped underwrite the Brook Farm Institute of Agriculture and Education, a spiritual/intellectual commune that attracted such supporters as Ralph Waldo Emerson and Nathaniel Hawthorne.

Elizabeth "Mimi" Russell Lyman
and Cora, ca. 1863. Photograph
by A. Sonrel, Boston, Mass.
Lyman family photographs.
Massachusetts Historical Society.

Ted Lyman and Mimi married in 1858, cementing the Lyman-Shaw-Russell connections. Mimi's sister, Anna, married a Curtis. Mimi's brother, Henry Sturgis Russell, wed a Forbes, considered one of the great Boston families. On the eve of civil war, Lyman counted as near relatives any number of Shaws, Hendersons, Parkmans, Pratts, Eliots, and others—all among the most prominent families of Boston.[9]

Readers of our century often find such distinctions tedious, but for members of Boston's highly stratified antebellum society, pedigree determined the course of life. Those born into wealth and position exacted daily deference from their social inferiors. If it came to war, few questioned the assumption that the upper classes would furnish officers, and the lower classes, the rank and file.

In the 1860 presidential election, Lyman voted for his father's friend and the former president of his university, State Party candidate Edward Everett, casting what he called a "thinking man's vote." Lyman felt little loyalty toward the Republicans, which he viewed as a sectional party. "All sectional parties are *bad*," he once wrote, "bad in principle and bad in practice. The leaders of the Republicans say, in substance 'You of the South have had your own way and kicked us; now we are going to have our own way and kick *you!*'"[10]

Less than two weeks before Confederate artillery opened fire in Charleston Harbor, Lyman and his Mimi embarked on a long-planned European tour. The

Russells—Mimi's parents and sisters—awaited them in Paris. Ted Lyman's life was following the well-trodden path of wealthy Bostonians—engagement, marriage, and a tour of the capitals of Europe—Paris, Stockholm, Copenhagen, Brussels, Berlin, Zurich, Vienna, and Rome. While traversing the south of France, Mimi announced to the family that she was pregnant. All the while, news of the war at home dogged their steps. Lyman, like most Bostonians, expected a short war, its outcome likely decided before he could return.

From the first report of the bombardment of Fort Sumter, Ted Lyman swallowed his disapproval of the Republican Party and pledged himself a fervent Union man. For timely news of the war, Lyman was forced to rely on the London *Times*, which he came to despise for its arrogant treatment of President Lincoln and the Union cause. A *Times* account detailed the Federal advance on Manassas Junction from Washington in July 1861 but left the outcome of the battle in suspense. Lyman wrote, "Perhaps before this a battle has been fought, never mind whether it has turned for or against us, [it is clear] that the South has got to go down! I read Russell's letter to the *Times*, describing the rebels around [Fort] Pickens; and when I saw that, instead of working, they were lying under trees and smoking, I saw that the Southron had not changed his nature."[11]

Responding to lurid descriptions in the *Times* that followed the rout of the Federal army at Bull Run, Lyman wrote, "Even to this moment I have hardly dared to look in the face all the probable consequences of this dreadful failure— the loss of prestige abroad, the encouragement of rebellion in Tennessee, Maryland, and Missouri, the destruction of reasonable confidence in our troops, and the prospect of a war of indefinite length." He assured Howland that he was not discouraged or in favor of peace or "in favor of anything but going on fighting till we at least have shown that our men can become soldiers worthy of the name."[12]

Howland dutifully shipped bundles of Boston newspapers to a new hotel in a different European city every month to be eagerly devoured. In November, a U.S. Navy warship overhauled the British mail packet *Trent* in the Atlantic and took into custody Confederate commissioners James Mason and John Slidell on a diplomatic mission to London. The British House of Commons threatened armed intervention, and for several months it appeared, at least on the Continent, that Britain might go to war on the side of the Confederacy. Lyman, then in Italy, began publicly to challenge Brits he encountered. He recounted the incident of one chap who loudly mocked the Union navy and its ragtag blockade with drink in hand. Lyman then demanded to know if the British were getting all the cotton they needed to run their mills. The "Bull" began to "sputter," at which

Lyman declared himself "winner" of the exchange. But Lyman's verbal tit for tat sounded hollow to his own ears when his friends were placing their lives on the line. Mason and Slidell were eventually released from their confinement in Boston Harbor, and tensions eased between the countries.

The amount of correspondence between Boston and Europe that passed among the Lyman and Russell relatives was staggering, averaging perhaps a dozen letters a week. Mimi's sister Anna Curtis and her cousin Anna Shaw sent weekly letters full of war news and accounts gleaned from gossip and from soldiers' letters home. "Did it occur to you when you [first] wrote," Anna Shaw asked Mimi, "that we shall have civil war? That Bob and Harry & all our friends were going to fight?" Anna referred to her brother, Robert Gould Shaw, and Mimi's brother, Henry Russell, who had joined the officer corps of the 2d Massachusetts Infantry along with friends Ed Abbott, Charlie Mudge, Jim Savage, Stevie Perkins, Dick Goodwin, and Charlie Morse. Commissioned into the 1st Massachusetts Cavalry were Greely Curtis, Henry Higginson, and Luke Sargent. The 20th Massachusetts Infantry (dubbed the Harvard Regiment, because its roster of officers read like a page from the alumni rolls) boasted Frank Palfrey, Paul Revere, Wendell Holmes, Henry Patten, Ed and Hal Sturgis, Henry Bond, Henry Abbott, Arthur Curtis, George Macy, and Jimmy Lowell. Lyman's classmate Frank Barlow made lieutenant colonel of the 61st New York and would rise to major general. Most of these twenty-three men made fine officers; ten would die in battle or from their wounds.

By New Year's Day 1862, the Lymans had rejoined the Russells in Florence, and Mimi soon after took to her bed, tended by a nurse, who supervised Mimi's confinement in rapid-fire Italian. Little Cora, "Co-co," was born on March 9. The baby was healthy—"ten fingers and ten toes," as Lyman reported—but it was a hard birth, and Mimi recovered slowly. The family stayed in Florence until June and, when Mimi at last was up and around, continued to Venice and thence to Austria. Ted Lyman climbed an Alpine mountain alone. Although not an overtly religious man, he likely gazed over the mountains and pondered what the Fates intended for him and for his family. Would the war continue unabated as he made his leisurely way across Europe?

In July, Gen. George B. McClellan's vaunted campaign to take Richmond was thrown down at great cost. Sister Cora reported the death of Jimmy Lowell, killed at Glendale. Cora's "first pages are devoted to excellent arguments against my coming home," wrote Lyman, "while her last turn with wishes that she were a man, to enlist, and with denunciations of those who don't serve their country. *Now these stones hit my glass house.* As before stated, I am troubled from time to time, with fits of conscience in the matter of fighting in so good a cause, and shall feel in the future days quite mean in the presence of Revere, Palfrey, Hal, and 50 others I could name. However . . . I shall *not* return this autumn. With the Baby on hand it won't do."[13]

A few days later, he wrote, "I see the death in battle of How, Major of the Mass. 19th. He entered college the year I graduated! *Such notices stick fires in me. I feel my life is going along and I doing nothing.* Not that I want to be killed, only here is a young man who risked himself with the rest, and a bullet was a bullet."[14] How's death may have tipped the scale of Lyman's inner debate. On August 19, he composed a letter to friend Meade, then commanding a division in the Army of the Potomac (soon to be boosted to corps command) and enclosed it with his next letter to Cora. Lyman wrote of Europe and fatherhood and asked if Meade could use him on his staff.

In early September 1862, news of the battle of Cedar Mountain reached the Lymans in Berlin. The 2d Massachusetts had been badly cut up on August 12. Many close friends had fallen. Mimi's brother, Henry Sturgis Russell, was captured while trying to stem the bleeding of classmate Jim Savage's severed leg and sent to Libby Prison. The anger from the home front was palpable. "I hope I shall live to see the rebels lying before us & cut into little pieces," wrote Anna Curtis, who added stingingly, "oh, why do not all the men come down here? Why does not Uncle Quin & Uncle Howland come? They can go on someone's staff and have an easy berth." Lyman made light of Anna's suggestion that Howland and Quincy should "come down," considering their age, but stressed his own qualifications. "I would go, if I were now at home, because campaigning agrees with me," he wrote, "and I could stand it." Mimi now wanted to return to Boston "as much as she did before to stay abroad." Lyman disagreed. He would not return until spring. "Baby & Baby only stands firmly in the way." Letters arrived from Mimi's brother Hal reporting that he would soon be exchanged.[15]

In October, news reached the Lymans' hotel in Brussels of McClellan's victory at Antietam and of the president's statement that he would issue a proclamation of emancipation on New Year's Day 1863. For Lyman, the victory—such as it was—was long overdue, but he thought emancipation a "blow." He responded with a diatribe to his sister: "Lincoln is a man of excellent judgment, uncommon common sense, very broad statesmanlike views, and perfectly honest and courageous. But I begin to see he has not enough steel in his backbone. He cannot make up his mind to see with his own eyes & with nobody else's." In Lyman's eyes, Lincoln had fallen under the hypnotic sway of the radicals in his cabinet. "It is the old story," he continued, "the abolitionists dragged us into this war, and left the conservative men to fight it; now they will drag us into emancipation and again leave the conservatives to take care of the vagrant negroes." He added, "I see that my friend Meade was in the thick of it again; did you send him my letter?"[16]

Ted Lyman had already immersed himself in reading books on strategy, tactics, and fortifications. It was time to return home to what may await. Crossing the English Channel toward the end of their journey, Lyman could not resist a jab at John Bull, who had so belittled Lincoln: "Yes, there were the White Cliffs of Dover—cuss 'em! And the British flag—cuss it! And the beastly British generally with them!"[17] Ted, Mimi, and little Cora took passage from England on a steamer and reached Boston Harbor by the end of May 1863 as the American Civil War approached a crisis.

Meade's reply to Lyman's letter awaited him at Brookline, dated December 22, 1862, written less than two weeks after the disastrous Federal defeat at Fredericksburg. Meade did his best to discourage Lyman and made it clear that staff duty was no "easy berth," as Lyman's sister Cora had described it. "I have had two aides killed," he wrote, "one, Hamilton Kuhn, a most excellent young man of family & future from Philadelphia—the other, Arthur, son of Theodore Dehon of your city, whom you doubtless know by reputation. Dehon was a fine fellow to whom [I] was very much attached. He fell in the last battle. Three other aides have been wounded, and any number of orderlies have been wounded and had their horses shot. . . . If you join my staff, which I would be most delighted were you to, you must make up your mind to see the elephant in his most formidable proportions."

After detailing the dangers, Meade advised Lyman how to proceed. "I have now," he wrote,

> two young gentlemen from Philadelphia who like yourself deemed it necessary, for their well being & comfort at home, that they should smell a little powder. They are on my staff as volunteer aides—receiving no compensation from the Government beyond the forage for their horses. They have commissions from the Gov. of the state, and are recognized & respected as members of my staff. The advantage of this mode of proceeding is that you are not bound by any obligations to the Government, and when you have seen . . . war & its horrors, you can return to the bosom of your family, without consulting any but yourself, a decided convenience.[18]

In short, come for a month or two if you need to "smell a little powder." But if you are up to it, Meade implied, come help me.

Ted Lyman's friend, Henry Lee Higginson, fell wounded at Aldie, Virginia, on June 17, when his regiment attempted to uncover the Confederate movements that led to the Battle of Gettysburg. Lee's army had started north, and the invasion of Pennsylvania unfolded in the newspapers. At this critical moment, Lincoln lost confidence in army commander Joseph Hooker, dismissed him, and after consulting the army's corps commanders, placed George Gordon Meade at the head of the Army of the Potomac. Meade assumed command on June 28, three days before the decisive battle.

After days of suspense, news of Meade's Gettysburg victory reached Brookline, tempered at once by the cost. Lyman wrote,

> We have the sad, sad news that Paul Revere is dead! He was struck by a fragment of shell while commanding his regiment (20th) on the 2d of July, and died on the 4th at Westminster, Md. No one's death has struck me like his; he was a man superior in all respects, of undaunted courage, and that of the best kind; very intelligent and of a ready wit. As a member of our club he was very well & intimately known by me. It is too much! Now we have lost men enough, and have suffered enough from these southern villains. Nothing will ever break them, till their *rich* are made poor and reduced to weakness. I am in favor of confiscating their property to the last man of them!

On July 14, Lyman recorded: "Lieut. Ropes (a good oar once in the *Harvard*) and Lieut. Col. Charlie Mudge were likewise killed. Barlow was recaptured after the battle."[19]

Further bitter news arrived on July 24. "We were this morning shocked by a report," Lyman wrote, "founded on a paragraph in the Richmond papers that Bob Shaw had fallen in a battle before Charleston." Confirmation arrived three days later. "We definitely ascertained that the mournful report about Bob Shaw is only too true! In the desperate assault on Fort Wagner, he was shot dead as he stood on top the parapet, cheering on his men."[20]

With Mimi and Co-co settled at Singletree, Lyman replied to Meade:

> I arrived here, from Europe with my family some weeks since; all well. In your letter . . . you were kind enough to say: "I shall be delighted to have you on my staff." . . . I clearly understand that this is *no promise*,

only an expression of good will. Therefore, I ask you frankly if you are now able and willing to take me as a volunteer aide. I am assured that Governor Andrew would, for his part, give me a commission. My military accomplishments are most scanty. I can ride, shoot & fence most tolerably, speak French fluently and German a little, have seen many thousands of troops of most of the nations of central Europe, and have read two or three elementary books. After all, I fear my sole recommendation is my wish to do *something for the Cause.*[21]

Meade responded within a week telling Lyman to bring two good horses and a man to care for them and little else, "as our transportation is limited." "I beg that you will let Mrs. Lyman understand," wrote Meade, "that this is all *your doing*, and that she must not hold me responsible for anything beyond not throwing obstacles in your way, which in view of your very agreeable company, she could hardly expect me to do."[22]

Meade later would describe Lyman as "a true friend" with a "healthy mental organization, which induces him to look on all matters in the most favorable light."[23] At the same time, Meade was aware that Lyman's connections with the governor of Massachusetts might serve him well. On at least one occasion, Lyman would appeal directly to Governor Andrew and other influential Bostonians when he thought his general unfairly treated at the hands of Washington politicians. In the midst of war, the interests of the lighthouse lieutenant—now a major general—and the scientist—a lieutenant colonel— coincided once more.

With Meade's letter in hand, Lyman approached his friend John Quincy Adams (grandson and great-grandson of presidents), who served on Governor Andrew's staff. "Jack Adams," wrote Lyman, "went to the Governor and got me a commission as a Lieut. Colonel in the Massachusetts Militia, in a very short time! Et Voila! God give me proper qualities to discharge my duty!"

The following Monday, Lyman was in Boston "in great gog and up to the State House where took the oath in the Service of the State and received a special order giving me a furlough for a year and detailing me to serve on the staff of General Meade, all before the impressive Gen'l Schouler, Adj't Gen'l of the State."[24]

Ted Lyman filled his remaining days at home with errands and obligations. He dashed off to Huntington's—an exclusive clothier—to be measured for uniforms, and then to Baker's for saddlery and military accoutrements. He posed in his new uniform for photographs at Sonrel's studio "with my

Meade and personal staff, September 1863. Left to right: Capt. Meade, Bache, Rosenkrantz (seated), Bates, Mitchell, Humphreys, General Meade (seated), Biddle, Cadwalader, Ludlow (seated), and Lyman. *Library of Congress.*

hair cropped close, and almost stewed to a jelly under his skylight." "My big photograph was much abused," he confessed, "but the smaller met with more favor." Lyman issued detailed instructions to caretakers Silas and Eben for Singletree in his absence and completed a final draft for a catalog of the Ophiuridae collection for the Museum of Comparative Zoology.

The decision to go to war was personal, but "going to war" was a social event. Lyman's classmate, lawyer Ned Browne, prepared a codicil for his will and with the papers presented a silver whiskey flask as a parting gift. Howland and Cora gave him a handsome sword; his neighbors, the Cabots, added a pocket compass, and the Brimmers, an officer's sash. Col. Frank Palfrey, convalescing from his Antietam wound, sold him a warhorse, but within a few days it turned up lame. Palfrey refunded the purchase price, but Lyman, in turn, sent a hundred dollars back to Palfrey, saying he had ruined the horse's value by rejecting it. Mimi's mother found a replacement mare, "Culpeper," that served Lyman with strength and patience. The housekeeper's son, sixteen-year-old Albert Woods, agreed to act as Lyman's groom and reported for duty in a blue uniform and cavalry boots. As he packed, Ted Lyman thrust into his bag a small notebook bound in chocolate buckram that he had purchased from J. L. Fairbanks Stationer. In it, he intended to record his military experiences.

Years later, Charles Francis Adams Jr., with that unmistakable Cambridge cockiness, wrote of Lyman that "the previous training of the typical Harvard man specially qualified him for efficient work on the staff. He had but to familiarize himself with his duties." Ted Lyman reached army headquarters in Virginia on September 3, 1863, after riding the train from Washington. General Meade stuck out his hand and said simply, "Hullo. How are you, Lyman?"[25]

One of Lieutenant Colonel Lyman's first duties at headquarters was to prepare "a sort of résumé of Gen. Meade's official report of the battle of Gettysburg, to be sent to Mr. Everett, who is to deliver an oration at the cemetery, to be made at that place." In this role, Lyman served as a ghostwriter for Edward Everett's less-remembered Gettysburg address. In fall 1863 and in winter quarters at Brandy Station, Lyman hosted foreign military observers, trading fluent *français* with the French delegations and leading British officers (some of whom he mocked on the side) on tours of the army. Then there arrived a clutch of Russian naval officers, whom the staff placed on horseback and watched scatter across the countryside, all in good fun one must presume.

Lyman encountered Harvard men at headquarters on a daily basis. Meade's adjutant, Maj. Simon Forrester Barstow, welcomed Lyman to camp on his first day and made him comfortable as befitted a fellow Porcellian Club brother. Thomas Greely Stevenson, Ninth Corps division commander, and Wendell Holmes of the 20th Massachusetts were P.C. brothers. Notable among many was classmate Francis Channing Barlow, who led a division in Second Corps. Horace Sargent led the 1st Massachusetts Cavalry, and "Charlie" Lowell, the 2d Massachusetts Cavalry. Classmate Edward Barry "Ned" Dalton, who was afterward appointed chief surgeon of the general hospital at City Point, was with Lyman in the Wilderness when classmate Joe Hayes, 18th Massachusetts Infantry, was carried in seriously wounded. He waved to Henry Abbott who was leading the 20th Massachusetts into battle and watched him return minutes later with a mortal wound. Harvard men James Starr, Edward Flint, and Charlie Adams commanded squadrons of the army headquarters escort.[26] Classmate Channing Clapp turned up unexpectedly as an aide-de-camp to General Benham. When one counts other Harvard men, Boston acquaintances, and officers in Massachusetts regiments, it is clear that Lyman's circle formed a sizable clique within the Army of the Potomac.

Socializing was one of Lyman's habits throughout his life. He used his notebooks to track those he met, to fix names and faces in his memory, to assign a person's position in the social order, to record, for example, the names and ranks of corps and divisional staff officers with whom he would need to interact on the battlefield. He just as meticulously recorded the names of dinner guests when home on leave, knowing that he might need to reciprocate an invitation.

Social duties aside, when hard campaigning began in 1864, Meade dispatched Lyman to the front lines. Lyman sent hourly reports and sketches back to headquarters at the Wilderness, Spotsylvania, Cold Harbor, Petersburg, and beyond. He regularly came under fire with minié balls zinging past his head and bore it well for a scientist and bon vivant. It seemed to surprise him, but at times he displayed extraordinary courage. At Cold Harbor and again at Petersburg, he braved sharpshooters to carry all-important flags of truce into enemy lines that allowed wounded soldiers trapped in no-man's-land to receive medical attention.

Lyman's most important contribution at army headquarters was as archivist and campaign historian. His powers of observation and recall of detail were exceptional. Using skills derived from his academic training, Lyman worked systematically at his composition. He first listed the notable events of the day then neatly struck through each one as he recorded it. In some cases, he scrawled a rough draft before putting his thoughts in "finished" form. Many of his vignettes are structured with a narrative introduction, a main body, a climax, and a summation—evidence of a highly organized mind. When Meade sat down to write his report of the Virginia campaign in October 1864, he threw up his hands and turned to Lyman. "Hence it came," wrote Lyman in a letter home, "that I was requested to give him some extracts from my valuable archives, and I since have written a lot of notes for him, extending from May 4th to August 28th."[27]

If Lyman had one failing as a military historian, it was an unswerving loyalty to his general. Only occasionally does he provide Meade's critics with any fodder. Charles Dana, assistant secretary of war, wrote that Meade was "totally lacking in cordiality toward those with whom he had business, and in consequence was generally disliked by his subordinates." Grant's aide-de-camp, Cyrus Comstock, described Meade as a "bear to his subordinates. I have heard him abuse Burnside, Hancock & Warren to their faces." Fifth Corps commander Gouverneur Warren had a bitter falling out with his commanding general on the eve of the grand assault at Cold Harbor. "A rupture is probable between me and Gen'l Meade," he confided to his journal. "[Meade] has become very irritable and unreasonable of late and with whom I had a square understanding today

Meade and staff at Cold Harbor, June 1864. Identified by Lyman, left to right: 1. Craig; 2. Berlin; 5. Bache; 6. Dr. McParlin; 8. Burton; 10. Patrick (seated); 11. Wilson; 12. Mason; 13. Humphreys (seated); 14. Sanders; 15. Captain Meade; 16. General Meade (seated); 17. Riddle; 18. Biddle; 19. Pease; 20. Ingalls; 21. Lyman; 22. Barstow; 23. Sharpe; 24. Hunt; 26. Edie; 27. Jay; 28. Worth; 30. Bissell; 32. Rosenkrantz; 34. Captain Page. Theodore Lyman photographs, "Souvenirs of the Rebellion," 23. *Massachusetts Historical Society.*

to the effect that *I was no creature of his*." Lyman rarely portrayed Meade in a bad light, although he did acknowledge in his notebook, "He is a slasher, is the General, and cuts up people without much mercy. His family is celebrated for fierceness of temper and a sardonic sort of way that makes them uncomfortable people; but the General is the best of them, and exhausts his temper in saying sharp things."[28]

In March 1864, Lt. Gen. Ulysses S. Grant made his appearance in Virginia as commander-in-chief of the armies and established his headquarters in the field with the Army of the Potomac. From this day forward, it was inevitable that George Gordon Meade's importance as an independent commander would be eclipsed. Grant had a moral authority and a stoic charisma derived from his victories in the Western Theater. Meade could by no stretch of the imagination be deemed a charismatic leader. He was more often described as an officer who valued efficiency and deemed obedience to orders his highest demand and duty.

A newspaperman at the time described Meade as "tall, thin, a little stooping in the shoulders, quick, comprehending the situation of affairs in an instant, energetic—an officer of excellent executive ability." Historian Richard Sauers summed up Meade as "a reliable, capable officer whose attention was fixed on his duty, with no concern for posterity or how others saw him."[29] These descriptions might as easily apply to a mid-century railroad executive whose focus was logistics, timetables, and the bottom line. In some ways, this is an apt analogy for Meade's approach to command. He was a "corporate" general whose energies were expended on making sure that the trains ran on time. In his mind, failure on the battlefield resulted from his subordinates running behind schedule or on the wrong tracks. If Meade could not get his carefully crafted orders obeyed, then outbursts of anger against disobedient or foot-dragging subordinates might well have been justified. Lyman recognized these traits as strengths.

Meade also suffered at the hands of politicians. Maj. Gen. Daniel Sickles, the former congressman and Tammany Hall lawyer who commanded the Third Army Corps at Gettysburg, ignored Meade's orders for the placement of his troops there and endangered the safety of the Army of the Potomac. Instead of fading into the shadows of military history, the politically connected Sickles sought first to retrieve command of his corps after recovering from his Gettysburg wound. Failing that, Sickles and his cronies impugned Meade's reputation in testimony before the Congressional Committee on the Conduct of the War, claiming that Meade had been set to retreat at Gettysburg before Sickles forced the issue through his disobedience. Hearing these accusations, committee members Senators Chandler and Wade demanded that Pres. Lincoln relieve Meade and return Hooker to command of the army. This "cabal," as Lyman called it, was followed by leaks of committee proceedings to the press and two disparaging letters in the *New York Herald*, penned by one "Historicus," who in all likelihood was Sickles's chief of staff. Meade wanted an official inquiry into Sickles's "libel," but Henry Halleck advised against taking the New York politician head-on. "Nothing would suit him better," wrote Halleck, "than to get you into a personal or newspaper controversy. He would there be perfectly at home." Although Meade ably defended himself before the committee, accusations of cowardice or incompetence during the Gettysburg, Bristoe, and Mine Run campaigns continued to follow him through the war, and Senators Chandler and Wade sought to block Meade's promotion to major general in the regular army. Ultimately, Meade was promoted because Grant demanded it.[30]

Meade compounded his difficulties by his patrician disdain for war correspondents in an era when newspaper editors and journalists were learning to mold and sway public opinion. In June 1864, Edward Crapsey of the *Philadelphia Enquirer* was expelled from the army for writing that Meade had counseled retreat from the Wilderness and that if it were not for Grant, Meade would have retreated. Meade's provost marshal, Marsena Patrick, carried out the expulsion order in such a way as to humiliate the correspondent as much as possible. Meade was blamed also for expelling Swinton of the *New York Times* some weeks later, although this largely was the work of Burnside and Grant.

The correspondents were outraged by this high-handed treatment of their colleagues. In truth, few of the army's leading generals cared much for journalists, but Meade was singled out for their disdain. The *New York Herald*'s Cadwallader wrote that "after the 'Crapsey' affair at Cold Harbor all newspaper correspondents with the army (excepting myself) and those in Washington City united in ignoring Gen. Meade's official existence. His name never appeared in print if they could prevent it."[31] Other names, prominently Grant's, were swept into the vacuum of Meade's omission. It was during this period that the heading "News from Grant's Army" replaced "News from Meade's Army" on the front pages. Capt. George Meade, his father's aide-de-camp, complained, "I see the papers persist in not mentioning Meade's name, and that Grant has done all the fighting. The army, I think, can tell a different story. It is perfectly disgusting if Grant is running the Army I wish to Heavens he would use his own staff officers. I notice, we are all kept running continually."[32]

Meade and Grant for their part developed an efficient command relationship that was in some ways ahead of its time. Military critic Henry Coppée wrote that the Army of the Potomac was "directed by Grant, commanded by Meade, and led by Hancock, Sedgwick, and Warren," which Meade confirmed "about hits the nail on the head." Officers of the modern military who have had the three levels of command—strategy, operations, and tactics—drilled into their heads immediately recognize the system. Meade directed army operations, while Grant focused on grand strategy. The arrangement suited both men's temperaments.[33]

Perhaps the greatest outrage perpetrated by history against Meade's reputation, according to Lyman, was the elevation of Sheridan to preeminence in the war's final campaign that he almost certainly did not deserve. "Little Phil" deserved a share of credit, certainly, but he seemed to demand it all. After returning home to Brookline, Ted Lyman summarized his opinions in the Boston Daily Advertiser: "In no one engagement did General Sheridan handle one-half as many troops as were commanded by General Meade. It was Meade's troops that carried the rebel lines by assault [at Petersburg], and it was his troops again that made the decisive charge at Sailor's Run. At no period during the toilsome pursuit were they wanting in the right place and at the right moment. But General Sheridan is fortunate in his arm of the service, the swift-moving cavalry; and the cavalry are fortunate in their music—the trumpet." Lyman noted that Sheridan's self-serving reports of the campaign reached the newspapers long before any official reports from Meade's headquarters.[34]

George Gordon Meade retained command of the Army of the Potomac until the end of the war and for longer than any of its previous commanders, a fact of which he was duly proud. Yet his name has been divorced from its greatest operations—Wilderness, Spotsylvania, Cold Harbor, Petersburg, and Appomattox. In the drama of the war, in its contemporary reporting and narrative simplification by historians, the final apocalyptic struggle was reduced to personal combat between Grant and Lee. Meade and his army had a great deal to do with the victory, and it is difficult to come away from Lyman's notebooks without concluding that history may have slighted his general.

Within days after the surrender of the Army of Northern Virginia, Lyman was en route to Brookline where he slipped back into civil society apparently as seamlessly as he left it. Meade wrote to his wife upon his departure: "Lyman, much to my sorrow and regret, leaves me today, he considering the destruction of Lee's army as justifying his return home. Lyman is such a good fellow, and has been so intimately connected personally with me, that I feel his separation as the loss of an old and valued friend."[35]

Lyman accepted a position on the Massachusetts Commission of Inland Fisheries, offered by Governor Andrew, and pursued his duties with habitual thoroughness. He was an early proponent of aquaculture (then called pisciculture) and recommended installing fishways to pass spawning shad and salmon upstream beyond the ubiquitous milldams. Readers interested in the early history of ecology should delve into an article Lyman wrote for the *Atlantic Monthly.* In "De Piscium Natura," he first disarmed his readers with wit and humor, before driving home the effects of the annihilation of the Atlantic salmon by greedy mill owners. "If you would have fish," he proclaimed, "you must extend their breeding-grounds. Open then the ten thousand dams that bar our streams."[36] Lyman was afterward appointed to the U.S. Fish Commission on which he served for many years.

In July 1865, Ted Lyman secured General Meade's appearance as principal speaker at Harvard's commencement, a grand event that was reported in detail in newspapers in Boston, Philadelphia, and New York City. Lyman hosted his general at Singletree, organized the welcoming dinner with Governor Andrew, and oversaw Meade's induction as an honorary member into the Porcellian Club. A newspaper account noted that Meade signed the club's constitution "and is hereafter one of the gods."[37]

In April 1866, Lyman and his friend (soon to be brother-in-law) Charles Peirson revisited Virginia and wandered over the silent campgrounds and battlefields from Brandy Station to Petersburg, analyzing the earthworks, detritus of battle, and skeletal remains that were yet strewn across the ground. At the Wilderness, Lyman wrote, "We were following a low, rude breastwork of logs among a growth of scrub oaks when Peirson exclaimed 'Just look at the trees!' I did look and saw that not one was standing, for a distance of some hundreds of yards in length—to an unpracticed eye it was just as if a whirlwind had twisted off each trunk and left the top hanging by the torn fibres. But it was the whirlwind of musket balls." Everywhere they went, they saw groups of men lounging idly about "still wearing the familiar gray jacket and metal buttons," while industrious emancipated slaves grubbed in the fields and labored to rebuild fences that had disappeared into the armies' campfires. It was a bittersweet pilgrimage.[38]

Lyman was elected to the board of overseers of Harvard College in 1868 and was influential in the selection of his cousin, Charles W. Eliot, as Harvard's president, a position Eliot held for forty years. Lyman was inducted as a resident member of the Massachusetts Historical Society and was active in the Society of the Army of the Potomac and the Military Historical Society of Massachusetts. He corresponded frequently with former officers, in particular

Gouverneur Warren, John Gibbon, Frank Palfrey, and Morris Schaff. When his general, George Gordon Meade, died in 1872, Lyman attended the funeral in Philadelphia and was instrumental in raising subscriptions to establish a trust of $106,000 to support the widow and her family.

Ted Lyman's beloved little Cora, born in *Firenze la bella*, died in 1869 of a "lung fever." For Ted Lyman, wrote Charlie Adams, "the light had gone out of life." He and Mimi subsequently had two sons, Theodore and Henry. Theodore IV would grow up to become a physicist of some renown.[39]

Ted Lyman visited Washington, D.C., in February 1881 for a meeting of Smithsonian trustees, and he described it as a "quasi Siberian experience." "It was an appropriate exhibition," he wrote Mimi, "that of a long-legged gentleman, with a new silk hat, a closed umbrella, and two worked boys, hurrying through the icy streets in face of gale of zero wind which flung a fine snow in his face!" At the Riggs house, he met Pres. Grant for the first time since the end of the war. "Grant is a good deal changed," he wrote, "and, in a front view, at some distance, for the worse. It is entirely because he has grown fat, and his eyes, rather small, are made still smaller, and his face, naturally stolid, is still moreso. But close to, he looks quite natural except that he seems very content and even merry; constantly joking, smiling, and even laughing. . . . By dint of long practice he has learned to make a kind of fashionable bow, but it is quite a gymnastic feat. On the whole he is the same cast iron, kind-hearted honest man."[40]

By the end of 1881, Ted Lyman began to complain of numbness in his arm and sought treatment by the latest scientific methods. He traveled to New York City where a Dr. Morton "examined the offending right arm with care and affirmed his idea that the trouble was an early stage of writer's cramp" that had somehow crept up the nerves of his arm to the central nervous system. The "learned medico" sat him upon an insulated chair and attached him by wires to a generator. "Immediately," he wrote, "my scanty hairs began to stand up!" Then the doctor reached a metallic ball toward his arm and "there flew out a spark with a loud crack and there was a feeling as if a little sharp hammer had hit me."[41]

Boosted by his father's reputation and family connections, Col. Theodore Lyman was drafted as an independent civil service reform candidate, and he returned to Washington in 1883 as representative to the U.S. Congress, Ninth District. He seemed surprised to find himself there and was soon disillusioned as to what he could accomplish. "As to the House," he wrote, "it is simply an incomprehensible babel! Not a third of the members present; some talking to

Sketch of Theodore
Lyman by A. R. Waud.
Theodore Lyman to
Elizabeth Lyman, 5 August
1864. Lyman Family
Papers. *Massachusetts
Historical Society.*

each other loudly; some clapping their hands for pages; some writing; and a
few gathered about some member who is shouting out a speech at the top of
his voice in a vain attempt to make himself heard."[42] The Honorable Theodore
Lyman did not consider his service in the esteemed chamber all that esteemed.
Nonetheless, many of his colleagues respected his principled stands on reform
issues, and he was considered a persuasive orator. Representative Lyman stood
for a second term, but the coalition of Democrats and Independent Republicans
that had supported him collapsed, and he was not renominated. For his part,
Lyman seemed happy enough to return to Mimi and his two boys at Brookline.
By this time, his always immaculate handwriting was shaky and taking on a
backward slant.

Jolts of electricity and a range of other procedures that included leeches,
suction cups, and a futuristic vacuum chamber, did not prevent the crippling

debilitation from creeping into his other limbs. He grudgingly took up a cane to get around. In March 1887, he wrote, "I have come to have such poor use of my hands that I can no longer work at the [Zoological] Museum." He ordered a collection of West Coast Ophiurans on which he had been working to be packed up and shipped back to the Smithsonian Institution. "After thirty-one years," he added, "it is hard to give up my old surroundings, but disease is stronger than will."[43] Within a few years, Ted Lyman was bedridden, but he continued to greet his constant stream of visitors with a warmth and quiet humor that all found inspiring. He died on September 9, 1897, and was buried in Mount Auburn Cemetery. Mimi, who always had embellished her personal stationary with a sketch of a leafy elm in the upper-left-hand corner to represent their Singletree estate, now drew a lifeless snag standing starkly against the sky.[44]

Theodore Lyman made many contributions to natural science in the years following the war, but his scientific legacy may best be preserved on Buttermilk Bay, Cape Cod. On a visit there as fish commissioner, he became interested in the Red Brook watershed, one of the last remaining habitats for the sea-run brook trout, a rare trout that breeds in freshwater, but like a salmon lives much of its life in the ocean. He built a cottage there as a retreat and over a period of thirty years bought land along both banks of the stream. Today, the 600-acre Lyman Reserve and adjacent wildlife management area protect the surviving sea-run brook trout. The Lyman cottage still stands.

Theodore Lyman III was best remembered in Boston for his military service to his country. Until he was no longer physically able, Lyman hosted a monthly dinner for the "old sojers" of Boston. "There never was such a splendid staff officer," wrote Charles Peirson of Lyman, "of great courage & proved bravery, with ready wit and quick intelligence, he was capable of commanding troops anywhere. General Morris Schaff, a West Point man, calls him the best educated officer upon any staff in the Army of the Potomac and of this I have no doubt."[45]

August 31, 1863–
March 9, 1864

Private Notebook, Washington, Sep. 2, 1863

Note: In case of my death I ask that this book may be sent
unread to my wife.

———— ❦ ————

August 31, 1863, Monday.

This was the black Monday for starting; packed up and was all ready. Little Wife, poor child, was really a heroine, and did try hard to keep up a good heart! She cried moderately and was very brave. At noon the waggon was ready. I kissed her and my poor little Baby too (who was sleeping away like a wee top) and so good bye my dear Mimi! Dined with Howland at the Somerset, where poor Mr. Mudge, who so recently lost his son, wished me all fortune with tears in his eyes; and many more friends said good bye. Ah, Beverly is a pleasant place; it hardly bears thinking of. Howland, who goes to New York with me, went in company to the Old Colony [& Newport Railroad] where we soon were on our way to Fall River where we took a tremendously crowded boat to New York. Monty Ritchie was aboard and Ned Dexter.[1] At 11 ocl' next morn [September 1, Tuesday] we got in, late for all the morning trains! So there was nothing for it, but the hardship of a good breakfast at Delmonico's. After which we called on Uncle Frank who was well, though serious. Col. Hallowell came up, still lame from his Charleston wound. Then parted from good Howland, who was choky withal. Went and found Heywood at 11 Wall St., he more Heywoody than ever. He has a good house (taken with 3 others) at 21 St. Mark's Pl. Has written a "pome," Salome, well spoken of. Dined with me. At 7.30 took the night train for Washington; getting a sleeping car at Philadelphia. Arrived at 6.30 in the morn.[2]

September 2, Wednesday.

Room at Willard's, where are lots of officers; the streets full of soldiers, many sloutchy, some dirty; but nearly all, tough and strong looking. For that matter New York is full of troops, there for the draft. There are the 1st & 2d Mass. and the soldiers are encamped all about the public squares & on the islands. With militia there are doubtless over 20,000. Saw Capt. Horton, who is on Heinzelman's staff. Also beheld a gorgeous & gray-haired Major, who turned out to be Mr. Mallet, whom saw in Florence. He is only a talkative pay-master. After some enquiry got a pass from Col. Conrad (Penn. Ave. near 19th St.) and information from Capt. Curtis (G St. near 18th) as to transportation. Weather not hot or depressing; fine overhead. Walked up the Capitol steps—the interior an incongruous mixture of fine marble, common plaster, and tobacco juice. Introduced to Lieut. Col. Morse of the 2d Mass., a fine soldierly young man, also to Capt. Amory, 16th Mass., who has been in the war since the beginning. He looks like his Bro' George, but much smaller. Silas & Albert got along with the horses and put them up at Chapin & Mattock's 450 G St.[3]

September 3, Thursday.

Up betimes and aboard the Alexandria boat, which takes only 20 minutes to that rubbish of an old town. The depot, on the other side of the place, is merely a wooden shed for an office, with a brick engine house &c. Was in company with Mr. Stephen H. Phillips, formerly Att'y Gen. of the state; and he presented me to Col. Devereux Chief of Transportation and head of the R.R.[4] Thereupon was made comfortable and placed first in the car, with a female doctor, Mr. P[hillips] and other honored guests! The car soon filled with officers, among them Capt. Amory who joins his regiment, & at 11 ocl' we were under way. On top the train were perched, like roosting pigeons, a hundred or two infantry as a guard. Most of the officers with us were nicely dressed enough & looked well, one however had overcharged himself at Washington, and was silly; and there were one or two most extraordinary combinations of brigand & dust-man. We proceeded slowly, but without accident, through a miserable country, full of ridges, sandy in soil and mostly given over to low woods where these had not been cut away by passing troops. Everywhere the houses had been burned or gutted, and the frequent pickets, under bough shelters, were the only living creatures to be seen. At about half way we passed the sadly famed Bull Run, a broad brook, much surrounded by woods, and steep ridges. The great fighting was north of this, some 3 miles; we shortly, however, passed Kettle Run and here Capt. Amory showed me the battle ground of Hooker's

Division, previous to the second battle of Bull Run. Here begin the plains of Manassas, which are sandy, with scanty vegetation and not much wood, and an undulating surface, mostly accessible for cavalry. The R.R. here bends to the southward and takes its course through a similar country to Warrington Junction where we got about 3 P.M. There is nothing here but a shanty & a lot of shelter tents for the guard, together with a great heap of army stores.[5] Got a place in an ambulance with a Quartermaster Capt. Howell for headquarters while Albert & an employed nigger[6] got on the horses, and so we started on a dusty wood-road for the Chief's tent. This was about 2½ miles away & lies close to the R.R. not ½ a mile, and to the west of it.[7] The camp consists of a street, with a double row of side tents to the east and a single row to the west. To the north lies a cross row, of the Tent of the Commander in Chief and the Chief of Staff, Gen. Humphreys in front of which is the large camp flag. Was accosted by the Officer of the day, Lieut. Rosencranz, a Swede, to whom did speak of Stockholm,[8] while waiting for the General, who presently came back from a ride and greeted me, just as of yore, with "Hullo! how are you Lyman?" —He looks a little thinner but otherwise the same. He was as kind as possible and asked me to mess with him! the only other man being Gen. A. A. Humphreys, a very neat, studious looking man, with a soft, gentlemanly way. Unto us enter Maj. Simon Barstow who did all hospitable acts, and gave me a temporary tent, while another was getting ready, which can have in a day or two. Here was a camp cot, belonging to Col. Platt, Judge Advocate General whereon obtained a very good sleep, Albert snoring on the ground beside me.[9]

September 4, Friday.

The springs are low hereabout, the horses having to go 1½ miles to water, which takes time. Mine are picketed in a grove, say 250 yards away. About noon, the General with Gen. H[umphreys] and an escort of dragoons, with self in company, started for Gen. Sykes' headquarters (5th Corps). We rode about 7 miles southward, to the north branch of the Rappahannock, nearly, passing Gen. Crawford's Headquarters, where the 5th Corps presented a sword recently to Gen. Meade.[10] Everywhere the country is cut up with cross roads, or rather trails, made by the army waggons, which, with ambulances and Sanitary Commission teams, were camped here and there. Gen. Sykes is *at* a house, but not *in* it; his tent being outside. It protects a house from damage to camp a general thus near it. The Gen. is a pleasant, calm looking man, a little like the photographs of Lyon. He has a very thick head of brown hair, standing up very stiffly. Saw also Lt. Col. Locke, his Adj. Gen. and some other officers.[11]

The river is here very narrow and on the fords, not over 4 or 4½ feet. We hold the opposite bank with posts & pickets, and have made a tête-de-pont for the bridge. The enemy's pickets are occasionally seen, but not very often. Then we rode somewhat to the N.E. to see Gen. Newton, who holds the river on Sykes['s] left (1st Corps). Newton has an intelligent face and is a somewhat tall, strongly built man, with a good deal of light hair, and a gentle way of talking, somewhat like Gen. Humphreys. He offered us much drink, of sundry kinds, which temperately did refuse. His quarters were also at a house, but his tent outside. And so we trotted home, with our escort of dusty, harum-scarum dragoons. The general goes at a most aggravating pace, a kind of lope or amble, which bumps one confoundedly and is neither fish, flesh nor fowl! Two officers came in tonight (one Maj. Ludlow of the Staff) who have been with an expedition on Port Royal, to destroy the two boats taken from us by the enemy. This they did, with the loss of a Lieut. killed and two men wounded.[12]

September 5, Saturday.

A deserter was brought in this morning, a stout fellow in spectacles! He was well dressed and of a very undisturbed demeanor. Today we rode say 4½ miles to Gen. Howard's Headquarters (11th Corps). He is near Catlett's Station above Warrenton Junction. He would be a decidedly handsome man, were he a little taller, having a high, projecting forehead, with a comely beard and a very thick head of hair, just now turning to gray. His eyes are large and of a mild but firm look. He has been placed in an unfortunate position, being given the 11th Corps, a body of very inferior material, and full of insubordinate Germans &c. They ran at Chancellorsville, but behaved much better at Gettysburg. This general has had much abuse, naturally, which he takes with dignity & patience.[13] We were invited to quite an elaborate "spread" under a tent, where the General asked grace, with the true New England style. Gen. Meade read a severe attack on himself in Wilkes' Spirit of the Times, and made running comments, with that close sense of justice, for which he is very remarkable. Sometimes he would say "Well, that's true, I *did* think so, and was mistaken." In the country hereabouts game has been *so* undisturbed as to be quite plenty. Especially noticed flocks of quails & doves. Our tents are protected from the sun by a platform covered with pine branches. Since have been here have seen the following staff officers, besides those mentioned already. Gen. Hunt, Chief of Artillery; Lieut. Edie, Ordnance; Gen. Patrick, Provost Marshal; Capt. Paige, Quartermaster; Capt. Starr, Chief of Escort (Harvard Class of '57), Capt. Pease, Assistant Adjutant General; Maj.

Biddle, Capt. Cadwalader, Capt. A. G. Mason, Capt. George Meade (Gen's Son) & Lieut. C. W. Woolsey. Also, at Gen. Howard's, Lt. Col. Leduc.[14]

September 6, Sunday.

Sunday & nothing doing. Went to church at the 93d N. York, encamped in a grove close by. This regiment has done the duty of Headquarter Guard since the War, and has never smelt powder! They sung, but not so well as New Englanders would have done, and the Chaplain delivered a sermon, suitable enough for the soldiers. Several Generals paid visits to the Headquarters, and Gen. Warren (commander of the 2d Corps) staid to dinner. He strikes me as the most original officer that have seen; a small, dried up, pointed nosed, though still young man, with a restless black eye, like a weasel's, and a body & mind that seem full of watch-maker's springs. He has a broad New York accent and is by no means particular in grammar. His conversation shows that his mind is extremely ready and sure, on all points. The reputation of a great fighter goes with him.[15] Gen'l Seth Williams came back. He is an odd looking man, with close-cut sandy red hair, a large, massive head & jaw and a face that looks as if it loved a joke. His aspect is not at all military, and reminds one rather of an expressman. His ability is said to be very great, which seems entirely probable. When he heard of Gen. Gilmore's successes, he remarked "Those 300-pounder Parrotts are an article that no family should be without."—[16]

September 7, Monday.

Grand review today of the 3d Corps, Gen. French. We mounted at 8.30 & rode 6 miles, about S.E. to a point near Fayetteville where are the Headquarters, at the house of a Mrs. Dulaney. This Corps joins the right of Sykes and continues the line of the Rappahannock. Our cavalcade was quite extensive; perhaps 30 staff officers, including Gens. Humphreys, Pleasonton, & Hunt—also an escort of cavalry under Starr, carrying the flag. Maj. Ludlow & self were the two aides who rode just behind the General and were well out of the dust, which sadly covered those behind. As we drew near we beheld a distant slope quite black with the troops, and the artillery could be seen filing along to take position. After dismounting a few moments, Gen. French came up, a large, stout man, with a face that looked on the point of apoplexy, and reminding one precisely of one of those plethoric French colonels.[17] Then we all mounted, Gens. Meade & French in front, then Ludlow & self, and then the staff. The troops were drawn up in three lines, according to the 3 divisions, which, in all corps, are

1. red. 2. white. 3. blue.[18] On the left flank the artillery, in two lines, 42 pieces, mostly 3-inch rifles and brass Napoleon guns, which are a sort of howitzer, and said to be very effective at short distances, or moderate ones.[19] We rode up & down the lines; first along the front from right to left, then round the left flank and along the rear; then down the next line and so on; the bands playing "Hail to the Chief" and the drums rolling; as the General passed each regiment the colors were drooped and the Gen. saluted the chief officer. The Major Gen. of each division accompanied the Commander to the end of his line. Gen. Birney 1st Div., Gen. Elliot 2d Div., Gen. Prince 3d Div. Gen. Birney is a serious, soldierly looking man with light beard & hair. Gen. Elliot is also light haired; Gen. Prince (who was taken at Cedar Mt.) had perhaps the best division of all. He is a stout, dark-eyed man with a black beard, mixed with gray.[20] Having taken position, Generals in front & staff in two lines to the rear, the troops marched past, with division front. They marched well, but, among all these veterans, there wasn't a platoon that had the air & carriage of a parcel of negro soldiers that saw, the other day, in Washington! It is clear to me that the nature of the American is such that some modifications must take place in the way of treating him as a soldier. Here were men who have performed feats in marching and in fighting, on a par with the best armies of the world; but each man looked just as before he was a soldier, only browner and more trained. It was pathetic to see these regiments some reduced to less than 200 men, with their travel stained uniforms and their firm, patient air. Their weapons were in perfect order, & one or two regiments had even got gloves. The appearance of the artillery was admirable, though the horses seemed rather light. Among it was the 10th Mass. Battery, Capt. Sleeper, a tall, soldierly looking young man, with a very careful toilette and, in the infantry, the 11th & 16th Reg's Mass. Vol. the latter commanded by Lieut. Col. Meriam, whom used to see about. The poor tattered flags of both were covered with the names of battles. Here too were the men of the celebrated Excelsior Brigade, distinguished for its fighting qualities; also Berdan's sharpshooters, a body of very superior looking men. There were 8,000 or 9,000 men in all—a part of the corps is at N. York, including the 1st Massachusetts.[21] The knapsacks struck me as very poor, being without stiffness, so that they must drag; but the bayonet and cartridge box, slung with a belt & one cross-belt of black leather, were very practical; besides these, they have a haversack and a flat canteen. Most men wore either a cap or a small round felt. The meanest looking regiments were from Pennsylvania; though others, from the same state, looked very well. After the defiling we went to the Headquarters where the officers of rank had champagne in a bower and

the Staff were regaled with punch & sandwiches in the open air. Met here little Ordway, who is now on Prince's staff. He is still a Lieutenant, but looks for a place in the Regular Army. The plucky fellow has been gone two years, without a day's leave of absence! He should have got higher. The black mare showed off nicely and did not mind the guns or drums. And so home, the staff arriving in a very perspiry condition (some of them) which did attribute somewhat to punch, as stood it entirely well, myself, who took only water. Introduced to Col. Howard.[22]

September 8, Tuesday.

Nothing doing, weather sultry, and some diarrhoea about camp. Saw today Capt. Graham whom knew as a little Lieutenant in Florida, at the mouth of the Miami (Ft. Dallas). He now has really a General's command, of six batteries, and is camped near us. He is married & has a baby of 9 months.[23]

September 9, Wednesday.

Trained my black horse a little, who is not taught to guide by the rein. Hoorey! At last got an epistle from Mrs. Mimette, after thinking that never should. All well. Sam Cabot dead; a merciful deliverance for him. Ned Hooper engaged to a Miss Chapin. The children's fair, for the Sanitary [Commission], netted $300, quite a wonder! My poor little Baby has cried for Papa; she will forget me, the little chicken, alas! Barstow says Ned Jeffries' failure has ruined the poor old Doctor, and cut $40,000 out of John; and that his assets are some horses & champagne—engagement broken off—he with brain fever; some of which, do think, must be exaggerated. Poor Ned, you always were a humbug, though withal a kind hearted man![24] Went, with Maj. Ludlow, & visited the camp of Provost Marshal. Here, under a cover of boughs, some 30 feet square were grouped perhaps 40 of the most forlorn looking objects possible. They were deserters, bushwhackers, stray rebel soldiers, &c. &c. Among them was a well dressed man, an illegal sutler, who had been seized, waggon & all. The most of them were "white trash," dressed in all kinds of battered hats & dirty coats, their faces displaying every grade of low cunning & brute passion. Among them was an extraordinary *metis*, a negro with sandy red hair. He seemed partly idiotic, but was said to be a rebel soldier, or bushwhacker.

There was a sentry on each side of the place, and a picket guard by them. Made the acquaintance of Gen. Patrick, Provost Marshal General, a gray haired old soldier, who had a most artistic bower, made by some grateful mutineers. Also have come to know Maj. Duane, Chief Engineer, a railroad looking man

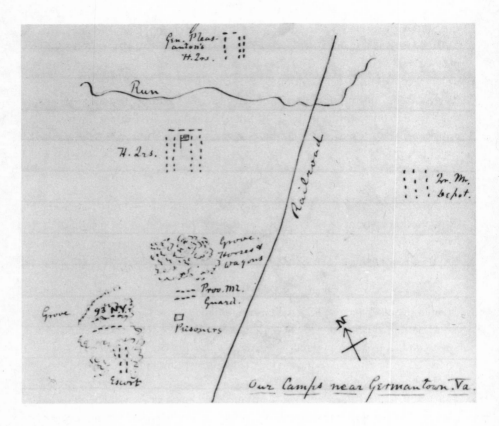

with a long beard, whose clothes would be improved by a brush. A young Lt. Col. Kingsbury dined today with the General. Our Commissary here of Capt. Coxe, a jovial & stout party, whose reputation as a patriot is well founded on the fact that he made a strong union speech in the La. Legislature, by which he was kicked out of the state.[25] The army is now cantoned in a sort of triangle.

Telegraphs run to all the Headquarters. The army of Lee, according to the best information, is widely scattered; a part at Richmond, and a part from Port Royal to above Rappahannock Station. His own headq'rs said to be at Orange C[ourt] H[ouse].[26] Deserters are brought in nearly every day. They look well fed, and have usually very fair clothes, either of a coarse, bluish gray cloth, or of an iron-rust color. Gen. Meade showed me a letter from a spy within the enemy's lines. He says the cavalry are much demoralized; and states the general positions. It was written in pencil, the spelling most extraordinary, but the language very good. Fitz Hugh Lee appeared as "fizyewlee" or something of the sort. Maj. Ludlow told me some interesting military anecdotes; how Gen.

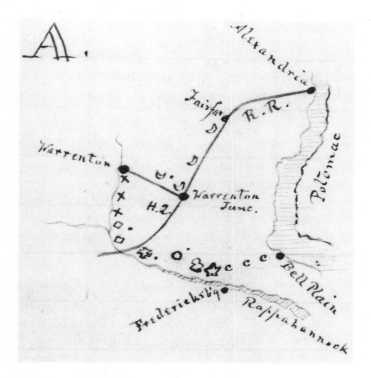

Meade, at the battle of Gettysburg, came out of the house where his quarters were, while the shells were flying very thick, and saw his staff sitting under the lee of the house, upon which he laughed and said "That reminds me of the feller that got behind the baggage waggon and told General Taylor, he knew it warn't much protection but it kind 'er felt *as if it was!*" Major L[udlow] stood beside Gen. Hooker when a shot struck the pillar of the portico, between them, and a splinter stunned the General—this was at Chancellorsville.[27]

September 10, Thursday.

By the papers see the death of Mr. Timmins, also of Powers' eldest daughter, which must be the pretty, gentle Loulie. She was to be confined about this time, and doubtless that was the sad cause. Mr. William Perkins' son James, in the 24th Mass. has fallen before Wagner, of whose capture we, at the same time, get news; Fort Gregg is likewise evacuated and thus we hold Morris' Island, to Cumming's Point, a mile nearer Charleston! The eastern part of Tenn. is now free! Burnside at Knoxville, Rosecranz occupying Chattanooga. *Tandem triumphans!*[28] Had an attack of diarrhoea, not bad however, and doubtless owing to change of living & the water here.

September 11, Friday.

This evening important rumors about that Lee is falling back! The General said to me: "how would you like to go out with 5,000 or 6,000 cavalry & 20 pieces of artillery, to see a shindy?" Suppose had better go, as it would instruct me.[29] Two scouts came in this eve and were examined, in the General's tent. The weather drier and drier!

September 12, Saturday.

It was generally understood that the cavalry were gathering for the reconnaissance in force, and the 2d Corps under marching orders, to support. Got my orders to report to Gen. Pleasonton and to report back to him, from time to time. Capts. Mason, Mitchell & Starr, and Lieuts. Woolsey & Worth went, as volunteers. Packed up my things, suspecting that Headq'rs might be moved, before my return.[30]

September 13, Sunday.

At 4.30 got up, for had to ride 8 miles yet, to join Gen. Pleasonton at Rappahannock Station. Rain, in sheets. Starr & Woolsey were also nearly ready, and we got some tea and bread & meat, midst dripping India rubber coats. However, the rain presently held up & about 6 or 6.30, departed with 6 orderlies in the train. Went slipping and sliding, in the red mud, towards the river; and, as we approached it, there were long trains of ambulances, artillery, & waggons, & columns of infantry moving slowly forward. Gen. Pleasonton was just over the bridge, when got there. So joined him at once. He was accompanied by a staff & escort and was then moving to the front to reconnoitre. Our forces, at this place, hold the right bank of the stream and the pickets lay some two miles out; arrived at this point, we beheld an expanse of country partly open & partly wooded & generally of a rolling character. Within ⅓ mile stood the rebel videttes, and, behind them, a small cavalry reserve. Meanwhile our cavalry was concealed in the woods, behind us. We waited some time for Gen'l Gregg, 1st Div., and Kilpatrick to get across and in position, the one on the right near Sulphur Springs, the other on the left at Kelly's Ford.[31] Then our skirmishers advanced & deployed, at a brisk trot, Col. Devin commanding the right, Col. Chapman the left, and all under orders of Gen. Buford. To this officer the young hair-brains of our Headq'rs attached themselves, as he has a great reputation for cool daring, and is good hearted withal. He is a man of middle height with a yellow moustache, and a small, triangular gray eye; his expression is sinister, though his reputation is the contrary.[32] The sun was now out & it was a picturesque spectacle to see the long chains of skirmishers in front, followed by the regiments of support & the batteries. The enemy's outposts retired very coolly, till near Brandy Station (we following the R.R. line) when we could hear them engaging Gen. Kilpatrick, on the left, with artillery.[33] Presently a puff of smoke, in the distance, was followed by the whiz of a shell, which struck by Gen. Buford's staff, a little ahead of us, and took the leg off an Orderly. Several more soon followed, coming close to us, and this was my first introduction to artillery fire, a very disagreeable thing! But stood it better than expected and succeeding in taking the shots, without ducking. There is a certain discipline & a sense of necessity that bear you up. One of our batteries drove back that of the enemy before long, and we kept on till within a couple of miles of Culpeper Court House, where in a densely wooded tract, northeast of the town, the Rebels made a determined stand, wishing to cover the removal of stores from the town. Our men were dismounted and thrown into the wood, and the cracking of carbines soon became general, while the Rebels began a great yelling. Pretty soon they fell back and we rode out on the open hills in full sight of Culpeper, whence a R.R. train was just going out; our guns shelled it, but did not succeed in disabling the engine. Meanwhile Gen. Custer, having got round on the left, made a brilliant dash at three guns and took them, with their caissons, his horse being shot under him. All of which we saw from the hill to great advantage. The enemy now hastily evacuated the town and we rode in, finding some stores, arms & accoutrements in the depot. Culpeper stands on the top & side of a hill, in fine view of the Blue Ridge, whose highest peak here rises 2800 feet. There are a good number of fair brick houses, whereof some have garden patches in front, now full of roses in bloom. The inhabitants had, in large part, fled, and the rest regarded us with little favor, but were silent. The conduct of the troops was excellent, & they contented themselves with some contraband apples and the green peaches on the trees. Here all the generals rode up. Custer is a sight to behold, looking like a crazy circus rider! He has a faded velvet suit, with tarnished lace trimmings, a little gray felt hat and long boots. His head is garnished with short flaxen curls, and he has a devil-may-care blue eye, very appropriate to his style. Gen. Kilpatrick is a spare, nervous, jerky man, with a long, thin, aquiline nose, no upper lip, to speak of, and light hair. Gen. Gregg has a long, tawny beard & a clear, dark blue eye; he has less of dash in his expression, but more of judgment & sense than the others.[34] Attached to Gen. Pleasonton's staff are the Chief, Col. Smith, a very fine looking man, of quiet & pleasing demeanor; Doctor Pancoast, the medical director; Lieut. Yates (who was continually discovering new batteries) and Lieut. Hutchins, a wee, hunched up man, without body or legs. Also two extremely intelligent signal officers were along, Jerome & Castel;[35] the feats of the signal corps are quite surprising. They go boldly ahead with the skirmishers and examine everything with their glasses. Behind follows a man with a flag, who therewith signals to the nearest station on the neighboring hills, and this again is sent to some telegraph station, or direct to Headquarters. The telegraph operations are not far behind, as the waggons follow on and make connections, wherever it is possible, with all the Corps' Headquarters. After a little rest at Culpeper, we pushed on; Gen. Gregg following along the railroad, towards Cedar Mt. while we bore S. towards Raccoon Ford. At Pony Mountain there was again resistance, along its wooded slopes.[36] Also they filled a brick house with sharpshooters, whereupon Gen. Pleasonton ordered the battery next us to fire through it, which was done, the Rebels thereupon running, as fast as possible away, but most unfortunately some of the people had hid in the cellar and, of these, an old man and a child were killed! Hence we pursued to a point 5 m. south of Culpeper, where, as it was late, a halt was sounded, and pickets thrown out. Our Headq'rs were a wretched house inhabited by an old woman called Ross. She was as poor as poor could be, absolutely nothing in the house to eat. The General gave them some coffee, and I a dollar. They took the spoiling of their little corn crop without complaint, and were very pleasant, poor old things (for there was old woman No. 2). At Culpeper had bought some corn for my horses, of a man who seemed a little better off. A grape shot had passed into his house, coming within two feet of killing his wife! Bought the shot as a souvenir. Had some bread & sausage in my saddle-bags, wherewith did feed the staff, making them tea also; and producing the only candle on hand.[37] It came on to rain hard now, but that continued not long. Had sent back one or two despatches that day to Gen. Meade. Then rolled myself in my big coat and so to sleep, on the bare floor.

September 14, Monday.

Our losses yesterday were 3 killed and some 50 wounded. We took about 150 prisoners and 3 cannon, with their caissons. Early this morn' sent over 4 of my orderlies (whom do not need) giving them a letter to Gen. Meade and orders to report to Capt. Starr, whose horse fell on his leg, and who is therefore obliged to return. At about 8 we proceeded again to advance encountering, as we passed through the oak woods, only a few pickets, till we got to within a short space of Raccoon Ford, on the Rapidan, when *bang!* a shell exploded in the road, a little way in front of us. Riding a bit to the right, into an open field, to reconnoitre, we were presently greeted by several more, which came very near us. The enemy's position now became apparent. On the opposite side of the river, the land rises in steep banks, or hills, quite commanding this side, which presents only gentle undulations. In some 25 minutes a battery was got in position & drove off the rebel guns, but the opposite shore was garnished with rifle-pits, and we could see a force of infantry. Gen. Kilpatrick was therefore despatched with orders to try and get across at Somerville Ford, about 2 miles above. This he did, but the Rebels brought down a dozen guns, and, after 2 hours cannonading, drove back his artillery. So, at 2.30 P.M. the fords were voted not practicable, a line of skirmishers (dismounted) was established along the bank; artillery was placed in position to command the crossings and the main cavalry was concealed in the woods, to the rear. Then, away went our staff to the house of one Horton, on a cross road, much more comfortable than the one of last night. The General, for some reason, insisted on galloping, through direful holes of mud and big stones, in consequence whereof, the horse of an orderly fell and broke its neck and little Lieut. Hutchins enjoyed a roll in the sacred soil. The only two women left in the house were rabid Secesh, but very good natured about it. Here we got some mutton, a very agreeable change, after sempiternal beef! The nights being decidedly mild, many of the officers slept on the piazza, while I got a hard sort of settle, with a large History of the Bible for a pillow.

September 15, Tuesday.

All quiet, except skirmishing and an occasional cannon. We rode to the right, 6 miles by the road, to Gen. Gregg, at Cedar Mountain. Alas! what remembrances cluster round that name. A year and a month ago the Second Massachusetts Infantry marched a full regiment into the fight and, in 30 minutes returned, less one half their number. Close by that mountain fell Savage, Cary, Goodwin, Abbott and Perkins. There Harry fell a prisoner into the rebel hands. And now, in 13 months, we only reappear at the same spot, the foe still in our front![38]— We ascended the S.W., bare hill, and thence obtained an excellent view of this fine valley. It so happened that the 1st Mass. Cavalry were encamped at the foot. So rode down and saw Col. Sargent & Charlie Adams. The Colonel lay on a mass of dirty straw, with a protection over him, consisting of some rails and old rubber blankets; he looked wild and bearded, and has, apparently, some of the flightiness of his family. As to Charlie, he was a spectacle of forlornness; as he reclined, under a poor shelter tent, in his shirt and trowsers and with sad, heelless stockings on. *Au reste* he had a tawny brown beard and his thin hair was cropped close to his head! They both said, with much sincerity, that I was a "ray of sunshine."—Poor fellows! Two years at this thankless job![39]

September 16, Wednesday.

Received a telegram, that Gen. Meade advanced, last night, with all but the 11th Corps, and ordered his Aides to report at Culpeper, whither he would come at noon. So Gen. P[leasonton] with the rest of us got to horse and rode up, but our Chief did not get in till about 2.30. The town was swarming with troops, being occupied chiefly by the 2d Corps. Gen. Webb (a handsome man, with regular features, and very neatly dressed) was Governor of the town and engaged in various explanations with persons who had lost their cows, or wanted to prove themselves loyal, &c. &c.[40] Gen. Meade looked haggard and worried, for he had no sleep last night, and is bothered with abundance of good advice from Washington. Then his forces are scanty, the six corps with him numbering some 50,000 infantry, then the cavalry perhaps 8,000, and with artillery &c, perhaps 60,000 strong, altogether. (Note: vide, September 20) Then Lee's forces are very uncertain but it looks as if Longstreet's Corps had gone south, while those of A. P. Hill and Ewell with the cavalry under Stewart may be from 45,000 to 50,000.[41] For offensive moves, against strong positions the disparity is not enough. The Headq'rs were established at the house of a Unionist, Mr. Wallach, within a mile east of the town & close to the R.R. The waggon train did not arrive till dark, and then there was grief to Gen. Seth Williams, for his waggon had been upset in a creek and all his books & papers soaked with muddy water!

September 17, Thursday.

Got my tent up & things in position. Mr. Wallach, a fat, talkative gent, with the profession of editor of the Washington Star, was taking advantage of our occupation to move his family and furniture to Washington.[42]

September 18, Friday.

This morning the rain descended in a perfect deluge, with a N.W. gale from the mountains. Down went Maj. Barstow's tent! And all the tent pins rather got shaky. Gen. Humphreys, just back, was quite floated out of house & home. Nothing, indeed, can be more dismal! However, the flood held up after a while, to our relief.

September 19, Saturday.

Two letters lately from Little Wife, the bud writes nice epistles, with accounts of all she does. Remarkable change in the weather last night, it turning so cool with a wind from the mountains, that we were fain to lay hands on all available

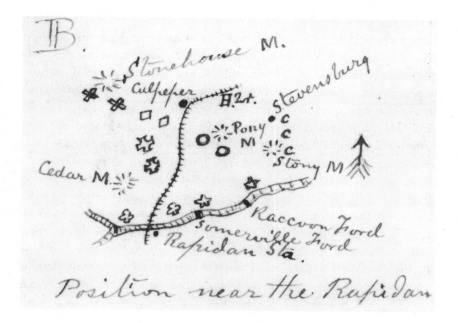

blankets & great coats. There did appear at our gate no less a personage than John Minor Botts, who has been paroled by the Reb's to give no information. He is a fat man, with a mild blue eye, and his clothing seemed to show the world had gone hard with him; his companion, an old withered man was a foil to him, however and looked as if he had had neither clothing nor food, since the War broke out. He went up to see Gen. Meade. Also we have as a visitor, an Austrian officer, Capt. G. Boleslawski, who comes to look at pontoons & telegraphs & signals. Also is he an excellent selection, as he speaks no word of English and is exceeding deaf! Likewise there transitorily appeared one Stevens, a fellow of Trinity College, an Englishman repeated for the millionth time, with the satisfactory difference that he is on our side.[43]

September 20, Sunday.

A very fine day, with a cool, bracing breeze. Saw actual return of our forces (7 corps) on the 10th inst. there being ready for battle about 58,000 infantry; 10,500 cavalry; & 2,500 artillery, officers & men, being a total = 71,000. The largest corps is between 10,000 & 11,000 (6th) the smallest about 4,800 (11th). Gen. Meade is much troubled & anxious. He said once, "I wish I were at home"; and another time, "Lyman, I wish *you* had command, instead of me!" Tonight he showed such confidence as to give me to read his despatch just sent to Gen. Halleck and the answer of H[alleck] and a letter sent by the President. These are worthy of record. Gen. Meade first stated his position; that Lee had some 40,000 or 50,000 men, while he himself had, now available, some 65,000 for action in the front. He supposed the Rapidan could be forced, but it would be at a great loss, so that, after such a passage the superiority, counting position, might rest with Lee. If a victory resulted, it would not probably destroy Lee's army, which could retreat on the fortifications of Richmond whither it was of no use to pursue, his forces being insufficient to lay the required siege. On the other hand a reverse might accrue, with new loss of life and less than no good done. At the same time he suggested a move on Fredericksburg, whence the enemy would be compelled to fall back, without a fight, giving all the moral result to be hoped for. To this he would call attention and would ask Gen. H[alleck]'s opinion whether it were better or not to fight a battle! Halleck replied in an exordium that he was not an Aulic Councillor, and would by no means thrust in dogmatic advice. He must leave to the General in the field *plein pouvoir* to do as he saw fit. Could not a threatening attitude be held, raids made in the enemy's rear, provisions collected? If he could not get across, perhaps it might be well to fall back, but of the Fredericksburg move he was not in favor. He must remember that *Lee's army, not Richmond* was the object of the campaign! (i.e. to fend off from Washington or to destroy said army.) In fact he did not answer Meade's question at all.[44] Mr. Lincoln said: "Gen. Meade with 90,000 men (should be 70,000) says he is held at bay by 40,000, or even call it 60,000. If then 2 can hold back 3, why should there be so many men in the Potomac army? Why not take the surplus & send elsewhere? Since the idea of capturing Richmond is not on the cards!" In which observation there is a gist of common sense, and, if such be the policy I don't myself see the policy of having such armies in and below Washington.[45]

September 21, Monday.

The climate here does not give the idea of being in advance of that of Boston; i.e. the peaches are not ripe, and the white corn, though too old to cook is still milky. This morning was quite cool, so that there was very likely a white frost in the low grounds. Have seen Gen. Wright, who is as smiling as of yore and looks very young. Last Friday there were 7 more deserters shot.[46]

September 22, Tuesday.

Prof. Eustis was over the other day. His nose indicated much sun or more whisky. He has just got his Brigadiership. A cavalry reconnoissance was today sent out, to the right, to look after the region near Madison Court House by the upper Rapidan, and its tributary Robertson River. Buford had command, with 2 brigades. My home letters say that Henry Higginson, the patient waiter, has possessed at last Miss Ida Agassiz! Had a letter from Alex; one too from Palfrey, and one from Em', enclosing photographs of herself. Poor Ned Mason has died of his hurts.[47]

September 23, Wednesday.

Gen. Meade left for Washington yesterday evening, and returned this afternoon. He went to consult the authorities. Oh, dear, dear! Geniuses do not grow on every bush; and I know not when I have been so struck with it as here in the army. There are the finest tools for a genius to work with; men by the thousand who are brave, hard working, honest, even able; but, of that rapidity & originality that mark the leading control of great minds, there is nothing, or almost nothing. Gen. Warren is the only man of inborn originality, and even he is perhaps at his maximum with a Corps. Such are the impressions of an outsider who has had good chances for seeing. There seems little doubt that Halleck is a mediocre man. Mr. Lincoln thinks he knows a great deal about War. We have fuller advices of our disaster in Tennessee. Rosecrans was attacked south of Chattanooga by Bragg, reinforced by Longstreet and a certain part of Johnston's command. They fought the 19th, 20th, and a little the 21st. Rosecrans was driven back, with considerable losses in guns & prisoners, and is now in or near Chattanooga, waiting for Burnside. If he can hold on there, it does not seem to me that the Rebels have carried their point, and he has, it would appear, inflicted terrible losses on them in killed & wounded.[48] Sir Henry Holland the Queen's Dr. a brisk, rather conceited old gent of 75, came down to visit us; he said he was greatly pleased by the Washington hospitals. We jolted him down to the front & showed him a review of horse batteries, a peep at the Rebels, and the camps of the 12th Corps. Gen. Slocum is a man of middle height, rather slender, with a face of a soldierly mould, cheek bones rather high, eyes gray. Also saw there Brigadiers Williams (of Cedar Mt.) & Kneipe; whereupon there was much introduction all round.[49] Buford came back, drove the Rebs across the Rapidan, took 100, killed 20 &c, &c. Got a letter from Mimette.

September 24, Thursday.

The General, honest old soldier, burst out laughing, at breakfast, and read a paragraph from the Richmond paper; "With Meade 'I would' still waits on 'I dare not.'" "Ha! ha! ha!" said he, "sharp fellers, they have hit it precisely!"[50]— At dinner time, out came big news, that the 11th & 12th Corps, with their artillery are to be immediately sent west! Some 17,000 men in all. They will probably get them there in time to be of good in neither place. The Rebels whistle and we follow. By the papers it would seem that Maj. Coolidge was killed at the Tennessee battle.[51] Gen. Meade was to move to the attack *tomorrow*; but it is too late now. Alas! It looks to me as if we had lost a week for naught. The move was to be a flank by Madison Court House, and this was even more feasible a week since than now. Our reconnoissance should have left the army prepared for a spring, with plans duly digested, in case the enemy were in retreat; but, as a fact, the army was not so ready and plans remained to be made and Mr. Halleck & Mr. Stanton and Mr. Lincoln were to have their opinion. Gen. Warren, who dined here, implied we could at once have moved to the right.[52]

September 25, Friday.

The 11th Corps have got to Alexandria, Gregg's cavalry relieving. The 12th Corps are at Brandy Station, whither we rode to see them. Found the whole body of officers quite furious; not only disgusted at leaving the Army of the Potomac, but indignant at being placed under Hooker, whom they despise. Gen. Slocum was resigned and seemed chipper, for they say he wants to leave the service. Gen's Williams, Greene, Ruger & Kneipe were quite boiling over.[53]

September 26, Saturday.

Rode down, with the Gen. & Gen. Humphreys, to examine the positions of the 5th Corps; for this now is necessary in view of the men taken from us. The troops occupy a ridge of which the body trends about W. & S. and which lies the other (S) side of the town, along the railroad. This corps embraces a Division with a brigade of regulars in it, Gen. Ayres; a Division of volunteers under Gen. Griffin; and the Division of Pennsylvania reserves under Gen. Crawford. Gen. Meade rode about criticizing the positions with a very sharp eye. "Confound the fellers," said he "they think no position *is* a position unless it is a right line! The object of a position is to hold the ground, no matter where you put the men."[54]

September 27, Sunday.

We took another reconnoitre on the ridges close to headquarters. Then passed beyond the town and stopped at Gen. French's, where saw Capt. Hill (English) and Zerbad (Hungarian) also Capt's Russell & French. There was great pleasantry between the imperfect English of Zerbad & the Cockneyisms of Hill.[55] (*Nota bene*. Called yesterday on Joe Hayes, Col. of the 18th Mass. Poor fellow he threw out his shoulder the other day, but is getting along well and was very glad to see me.) Today appeared Gen. Benham, a very dirty slip-shod, looking big man, and, in his wake, followed a broad-shouldered soldierly officer with a fine moustache & imperial.— I gazed and beheld Channing Clapp! but more altered than any man have seen here. He was a stout, thick necked, martial looking fellow, nothing left of his ancient quiet self, but the quietness. Very gladly did we greet and have a friendly chat.[56] The news from Chattanooga is, strategically considered, favorably to be thought of. For Bragg, though he has inflicted a severe defeat (36 cannon; 7000 prisoners; 15000 small arms &c. &c.!!) has not gained his point at all; and still stands at the gate. Also has he lost 3 generals killed & 4 wounded, besides a great mass of men. It is extraordinary! This Army of the Cumberland of which we heard so much, and of its discipline, perfections, and confidence, being tried, shows no homogeneity. Thomas' Corps makes a magnificent fight; those of McCook & Crittenden stampede without any good cause.[57] This eve came more distinguished foreigners, Mexican critters, Gen. Jose Cortez; Sen. Mariano Degollado; & Sen. Francisco deP. Suarez. We got them 2 stretchers, a cot, and a wash basin, which was all we had, for each has but for himself.[58]

September 28, Monday.

A couple of cavalry regiments, together with the reserve artillery and the 5th Corps were ordered to be ready, & we reviewed the lot. Of the Reserve Artillery there are 18 batteries, of from 4 to 6 pieces, including some 20- & 30-pounders. The troops presented a fine appearance, especially the Divisions of Gens. Ayres & Griffin. In the latter were the 18th, 22d, & 32d Mass. the 22d under Lieut. Col. Sherwin a classmate of Hal's. This corps is the old one of Meade, and includes the Division of Pennsylvania Reserves, a solid looking body, but much more slovenly than the two other divisions.[59]

September 29, Tuesday.

Mrs. Lovely writes me every two or three days; a letter came today, for example. Little Baby learns many new words & asks for "Cologne"; and says, "Papa all gone—'Or!" Philo Shelton engaged to Miss Carrie Bigelow— Ah! important, very, and Miss Lilie Lodge to Mr. James, a certain Ohio demi Secesh.— Well, one sees the sad side of this war from time to time. There came a certain Dr. Foster, an old man, but hale and dried withal. He was a type of the best class of those wealthy high-toned, semi-civilized Southern planters—serious, proud, self reliant and gentlemanly; while his dress was slovenly and his mouth crammed with tobacco. He had come from Natchez to take care of his son, wounded in a cavalry fight; and was surprised by the sudden advance of our troops; when asked how his son was, he quietly said "He died last night." "I have not much left," he continued; "the Confederates burned 1,400 bales of cotton for me, and your troops have taken 384 negroes."[60]

September 30, Wednesday.

A letter from Em' tells me of the death of Sturgis Hooper, of consumption. Poor man, some fall in war, some by disease.[61] The losses of this army, from the outset, are set at not less than 90,000 in killed and wounded! Of course its depletion from disease has been still greater. Dr. Letterman told me that, within the year (including Antietam) 60,000 wounded had been in his department! Voila!— As there is nothing else to do, swords are presented. This time to Gen. Warren at his Headquarters at Mitchell's station.[62] Lately an attempt was made to get up a testimonial to McClellan, each soldier to give ten cents & officers in proportion. The Government got wind and stopped it, and has ordered Col. Davis to New Mexico, who was concerned in the matter. The testimonial was doubtless ill timed; still more the interference, which reminds one of the action of a second-rate parietal board.[63] Gen. Warren was lodged in a miserable farm-house; whether he has better clothes or not I don't know, but he, at any rate appeared in his little, old, straw hat. There came a band; likewise a *centaine* of officers. Our staff had come down by the R.R. with dignity, on a grain car; including Gen. Meade; Gens. Humphreys & Pleasonton; Gens. Hunt & Tyler of the artillery & a lot of staff. Also there came Gens. French, Griffin, Kilpatrick, and a lot more. Gen. Warren stood on the porch, and Dr. Young over against him; thereupon each read a three-minute speech from a paper, and the thing was done. The sword was a good one, handsomely mounted with gold, on a bronze ground & with an amethyst in the guard. After which there was a spread of roast beef, baked ham, pickles and bread. While, in the other room, buckets of "commissary" punch was prepared; whereby two or three of the Aides got the worse, especially young Geo. Meade whom we were at pains to shield from Papa. We were within long range of the Reb's, who might have made a practical joke with a Parrot[t] shell.[64]

October 1, Thursday.

Accompanied Gen. Humphreys and Capts. McClellan & Cavada to visit Mr. Botts, who dined with us yesterday. His house is over against Brandy Station and some 3 miles from these Headq'rs. Botts is a ready witted, clear headed man, and entertaining to hear. He is a great talker and very much on himself, which is natural. The Rebel Secretary of State having asked him what he thought of the prospects, he took an apple and said: "This slice I take off from your Confederacy, for Kentucky; this for west Va.; this for Tenn.; this for La.; this for Mo.; &c. &c. and now, when you get all those slices to make one apple again, I will believe in the future, wholeness of your Confederacy!" He has 2,000 acres here for which he gave $103,000 when the Rebel money was worth about 33/0. The carpeted house, & the cows feeding about it are a great contrast to the surrounding desolation. His daughters were pleasing, somewhat countryfied young ladies.[65] There was a race today, between the Cavalry Corps and the 3d Corps, on the Brandy Station road. Two days since Albert was quite sick—a very severe pain through the right side. It seems to have been something rheumatic. Having a silk handkerchief round my leg, to avoid a chafe, was rewarded by an inflamed vein, which, luckily seems to have gone away.

October 2, Friday.

Big rain. Mimette back in Brookline, which she declares dull, poor child. She groans over her Teddie who is away—it is very hard for her! A certain Englander, Gillie, came down, who is an owl, with a tongue hung in the middle and a talking devil.[66]

October 3, Saturday.

Splendid day again. Yesterday 3d Div. VI Corps marched to the Rappahannock, to defend the chief bridges between there and Manassas. Conscripts and returned men arrive, some hundreds daily. The General has prepared his report, on Gettysburg; and the Corps & Div' Commanders sent in theirs, which is a signal for the latter to go together by the ears! Especially Gen. Humphreys got indignant with Gen. Hancock for saying he abandoned his guns; and quite furious with Birney, for something of the same sort but stronger; the usually nicely courteous H[umphreys] called B[irney] "a damned lying dog!"[67]— There came a farmer from Indiana, to get the body of his only son, slain in our fight of the 13th Sep. He had journeyed a thousand miles, and had succeeded in his mission, and even had his son's horse; "for which" said he, "I wouldn't take a thousand dollars." When a country has such men as this among its common people, it can scarcely have a higher boast.

October 4, Sunday.

A quiet Sunday. As always after our battles, there is a lull; so now in the West. Maj. Riddle appeared for the first time on the Staff, having been off on leave for sickness.[68]

October 5, Monday.

The 2d Corps was relieved by 2 divisions of the 6th and moved up to the ridge north & west of this house, creating much alarm in the Reb' ranks, who thought that we were falling back, advancing and all sorts of things; and telegraphed wildly, with their signal flags! Rode with Gens. M[eade] & H[umphreys] to Pony Mt. whence we got a fine view of the whole country and of the Blue Ridge. Opposite we could see extensive camp smokes from the Rebs; while northward the country was patched over with white tents and waggon parks. Coming up, the General got quite indignant with some army people who were perversely pulling the boards of some deserted houses; and took the names of the persons in command. Prepared, by order, a sort of résumé of Gen. Meade's official report of the battle of Gettysburg, to be sent to Mr. Everett, who is to deliver an oration at the cemetery, to be made at that place.[69] An index of the campaign is as follows—June 28. Gen. Meade takes command. Ewell at Susquehanna, near Harrisburg & Columbia. Longstreet & Hill at Chambersburg & on Cashtown road. Our army, in all about 100,000 between Harper's Ferry & Frederick. 29th, Army moved; left to Emmetsburg, right to N. Windsor. French was left to Guard [Baltimore & Ohio] R.R. & conduct stores from Harpers Ferry to Washington. Buford's Cav' at Gettysburg; Kilpatrick's at Hanover, where he beat Stuart's rear; Gregg's passing to the right. 30th, the right moved to Manchester, the left (1st, 3d, 11th Corps) remained still. July 1. Reynold's (1st Corps) on news from Buford, attacks Hill's advance, beyond Gettysburg. 11.30 Howard supports with 2 divisions of 11th C. leaving one div' on cemetery ridge, south of town. At 4 P.M. our men driven back to the ridge. Slocum, 12th C. and Sickles (part of 3d) come at 7 P.M. Gen. Meade orders all corps at once on Gettysburg, and arrives from Taneytown at 1 A.M. July 2d. At 2 P.M. 6th Corps comes, with a march of 32 miles since 9 of the day before. The position this:

The enemy on parallel ridge, 1 to 1½ m. off. At 3 P.M. Sickles, going too far in front, was attacked and forced back; but, supported by 5th & 6th and parts of 1st & 2d Corps, the enemy were, at sunset, repulsed in confusion. At 8 P.M. an assault on 11th Corps repulsed, with loss. 3d early, Geary returned from assisting the right, and drove off the enemy, who had occupied his line. At 1 P.M. enemy opened, for two hours, with over 125 guns, and then delivered a grand assault, on left and centre, which was repulsed, with terrible slaughter, and the fight was done. Kilpatrick worked on the left, & Geary on the right with cavalry against the rear & flanks. 5th, Enemy in full retreat by Fairfield & Cashtown roads. Army followed, by Middleton, and on 12th got to the Marsh Run heights, held by the enemy, before Williamsport. 13th, Reconnoissances. 14th, Enemy found to have

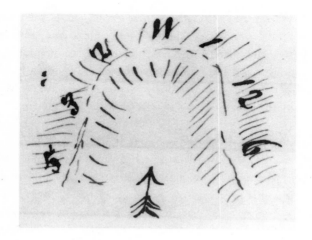

gone across the river. The pursuit was continued to the Rappahannock via Berlin
& Loudon Valley. *Losses* in campaign. Killed 2,834. Wounded 13,709. Missing
6,643. Total 23,186. Gens. Reynolds, Zook, Farnsworth, and Weed, killed. Gens.
Warren, Paul, Barlow, Doubleday, Barnes, Butterfield, Graham, Sickles, Hancock
& Gibbon = 14 wounded. Rebels. Prisoners 13,621. Killed 5,000. Wounded 13,000.
Stragglers. Total, about 36,000. Gens. Barksdale, Pettigrew, Pender, Armistead,
Garnett & Semmes, killed. Hood, Trimble, Heth, Kemper, Scales, Anderson,
Hampton, Jones, Archer and Jenkins, wounded = 16.[70]

October 6, Tuesday.

Baby is most improper, she places her doll, whom she calls "Budger" on the
little "chair," and says "Budger, Sts! Sts!" A cool snap, which gave me an attack of
diarrhoea and pain, the most common trouble in camps. The last return since
departure of 11th & 12th Corps, gives about 56,000 infantry, 10,000 cavalry &
2,500 artillery = 68,500 ready for action.[71]

October 7, Wednesday.

Quite an excitement in the way of a box of grapes and pears from Mimi, which
came in good condition, in company of some warm things for winter.

October 9, Friday.

We took a long ride to Cedar Mt., stopping on the way at Gen. Sedgwick's,
whom saw for the first time, a stout, sturdy man, with a bright kindly eye, and
a face full of intelligence. He looks like a reliable officer, but those who most

impress me are Warren and Sykes, the former for his genius, the latter for his cold, steady, air and his thorough soldierly look. He accompanied us, with Lieut. Col. Kent, to the quarters of Gen. Howe, who commands a division, and thence to the signal station, where they were of the opinion that the Rebs were moving, either in retreat, or in flank by Madison C. H. We could see some cavalry moving by the distant road. There & back is some 23 miles.[72]

October 10, Saturday.

There arrived (yesterday) an Englisher Capt. E[dward H.] Schenley (14 Prince's Gate, Hyde Park) who ran away with a young heiress in this country and made a great [. . .] but seems to have proved a good husband, now rejoicing in 7 children! He is a Peninsular & Waterloo man, now 64 yrs. old. Was deputed to show him round, for he hath brought a telescope for the Gen'l and insisted on giving me a pair of spurs and indeed was a most liberal old cock. Took him to Pony Mt. where learned that the enemy, in heavy force, were passing round by our right flank! Then took him to see the 2d Corps, marching out to support the 3d Corps on our right. Whereat he was much pleased; and departed in peace at 2.30. Behold the Rebs are in motion sure enough! Nobody knows whither and tomorrow, before light, we break up camp! All night the trains were in motion towards the Rappahannock, 3,500 waggons! No joke——

October 11, Sunday.

We were up before daylight and had a meagre breakfast; all was busy, packing and striking tents. All the waggons went ahead, the 1st & 6th Corps followed on the south side of the railroad and the 2d and 5th on the north, while the 3d went more to the north still, crossing at Freeman's Ford. Of course the trains perversely endeavored all to go on one side of the road, and so there was delay, the Staff never getting off till 11 o'cl, when we looked back on the Wallach house, after a sojourn of nearly 4 weeks, and wended our way back, over familiar ground. Rappahannock Station is ornamented with an earthwork on each side of the river. The bridge was crowded with infantry, and we forded just below, the water coming about to the girths. Our camps were pitched near a brick house (Anderson) once headquarters of Gen. Crawford, and still displaying the fancy bowers and pavilions of now faded evergreens, that had graced Gen. Meade's sword presentation.[73] This river country is of a gray clay; but little undulating—water poor. It is quite extraordinary what little information is to be had. The idea of the enemy, 50,000 or 60,000 strong, marching about, and we not know whether they were going one way or another, seems incredible; but then it is to be observed that 1st the woods & hills greatly conceal distant moves; and 2d by an outlying cavalry, a move may either be covered or simulated.— Buford had crossed at Germanna Ford to the south side of the Rapidan, and gone along to Morton's Ford, finding the country nearly deserted; there, under Orders, he recrossed & with Kilpatrick, covered our rear. In the afternoon they had a severe fight with Stuart supported by infantry, with considerable loss on each side. 1 Major & 4 captains being lost on ours, in killed. Their large force led to the belief that their whole army was coming down to Culpeper by the Madison Court House road; so *Oct.* 12 [Monday]. the 2d, 5th & 6th Corps were ordered to recross and advance, but found only one regiment of cavalry and a gun or two; so Buford in the advance, went close to Culpeper & halted for the night. But, in the evening, there came a despatch from Sulphur Springs, from Gregg, saying he had been fighting all day, trying to prevent the columns of the enemy from crossing at that point, but had been driven back, with heavy loss to some regiments, and that now they were opening on him with 20 cannon! So it was plain they were marching on Warrenton & thence probably on Centreville.[74] Orders were immediately despatched to the 2d, 5th & 6th Corps to counter-march & recross, that night, and to continue their march in the direction of the railroad; while the 3d marched from Freeman's Fd. and bore on Greenwich, keeping well north, and the 1st took the lead south of the R.R. with orders to keep on to Bristoe Station, the 6th to bivouac in their rear at Kettle Run; and the 5th at Catlett's house close to the Junction (where Howard was); while the 2d would stop at Auburn Mills, on Cedar Run.

October 13, Tuesday.

The distances on the rail are Brandy Sta. to Rappahannock 4½. Bealton 4. Warrenton Junc. 6½. Catlett's 2. Bristoe 8½. Manassas Junction 3. The first Corps marched some 22 miles. Our Headquarter Baggage was cut down to a roll of bedding & some simple mess arrangements, with a tent to each 3 or 4. We were up betimes but did not start till 9, when we followed the north side of the road, till we got to Warrenton Junc. passing the old camping ground, on Licking Run, a dry & desert country, as before. The General (who is a man full of sense of responsibility; who takes things uneasily; and who has the most singular patches of gunpowder in his disposition, which exploding suddenly, are then gone) kept getting fierce at the waggons, his particular detestation—: "My God: General Ingalls, what is that enormous train doing there; it can't belong there?" To which I[ngalls] would reply in mild explanation.[75]

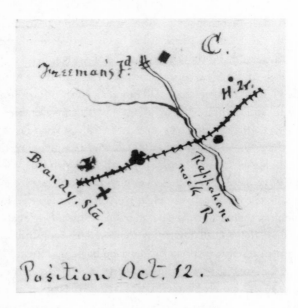

By Cedar Run we found the 1st Corps halted & halted ourselves. One or two spies came in, but only brought negative evidence that the enemy had not yet got along by Warrenton (yesterday). We are puzzled to know their whereabouts. As we pushed on, we saw a most singular sight, at the point where the Brentsville road branches off, namely, on an open undulating space, of some hundreds of acres, a vast park of 2,500 waggons; these are all ordered to Fairfax Station, under escort of Buford, the Army keeping only ammunition, trenching tools, & ambulances, while the soldiers have each 3 days' rations in haversacks & 5 days' hard bread & small stores in knapsacks, together with 40 rounds in the boxes. At a point close to Catlett's house we camped for the night and were near the 5th Corps.

This night all doubt as to the passage of the enemy was removed. There came a dragoon who, having his horse killed, had lain concealed all Monday night (12th), near Sulphur Springs; and there saw the enemy's columns of infantry passing rapidly. Also came an intelligent Captain of 1st Maine Cavalry, who, cut off with his men, from Gregg, made a detour, to come in by Warrenton, where he rode into a cavalry camp, at night, and boldly asked the name; to which they replied "12th Virginia!" — On our march these two days have seen three or four buildings on fire, from the carelessness or the intention of the men.[76]

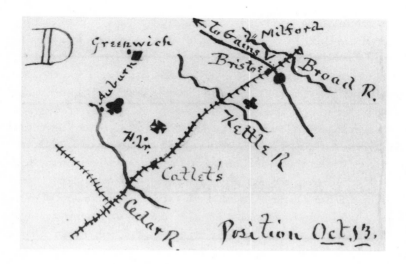

October 14, Wednesday.

All off at daylight, marching in haste on Centreville; the Corps to centre on Bristoe and on Milford (1 m. north of it); thence on Manassas, and so to Centreville heights by Blackburn's and Mitchel's Fords on Bull Run; the 1st Corps holding the redoubts; the 6th on its right; the 3d & 5th on the left; the 2d in rear. Reserve artillery still in rear. We of the staff were all waiting for the 2d [Corps] to pass our camp, coming from Auburn, when, crack, cr-cr-crack went the cavalry carbines, in a wood, not a mile distant, where, it would appear, a force of the Reb' horse had coolly camped all night! and our men were now driving them off. Some cannonading also could be heard towards Auburn Mills.[77] At 9.30 A.M. appeared the head of Warren's column; consisting of the two divisions en route; he staying behind to check the Reb's, who were pressing in on the Warrenton road. 1½ miles beyond Catlett's, a division was halted in line of battle to await & cover the rear corps coming up. The General left camp at 10.30 & we all got to Bristoe at noon. The General ordered me to hasten on and tell Gen. Sykes that his rear had outmarched his waggons, which were exposed on the left flank. His corps forded Broad Run at Milford and massed on the high ground beyond. Bristoe Sta. is on a naked swell of land, which then descends rapidly to Broad Run, hard by, and again rises the other side; the railroad passes through a cut & then over a high bridge, across the run. Keeping on, 3 miles brought us to famed Manassas Junction, where the Rebels lay all the winter of 61–62. It is an elevated, undulating, arid water-ridge, sloping gradually N.E. to Bull Run, & S.E. to Broad Run. There are some small redoubts still left. Hence we passed down to Mitchel's Ford, where Gen. French was crossing his corps; and received orders to leave two brigades behind, to cover Manassas. From the ford, the ground rises in a steep, naked ridge, to the well-known Heights of Centreville, a long, high, bare ridge, running about N & S, and offering a position for the largest army. Centreville is a hamlet, lying at the crossing of the Warrenton pike & other roads; and near by is a line of redoubts & breastworks. About 1.30 we halted on the crest, above the Run. At 3 P.M. cannon were heard in the direction of Bristoe; and, from the high ground the heavy smoke was seen, rising over the trees. The firing increased, and, about 3.30, very heavy volleys of musketry came in. Heth and Anderson's divisions (as we knew that night) coming down the ~~Gainsville~~ [TL corrected to] Greenwich road, attacked Warren in flank; but he, putting his line in the railroad cut, poured musketry with great destruction upon them, and repulsed them handsomely, taking 5 guns 2 colors and some 500 prisoners. The heavy fight was from 3–4, but cannonading held on till after dark. His loss was not heavy, only some 200, including Col. Mallon, killed. The 5th Corps was sent back to support, but was not needed.[78] At dark we reached Headquarters, some 2 miles in rear of Centreville and on the pike. The General felt anxious about the 2d Corps; but, about 1 h. before day-light, Warren came himself and reported all over safely. Gave him some brandy; he lay down in our tent, and in a minute, was asleep.

October 15, Thursday.

Cloudy. 6th Corps sent up to Chantilly, to hold that road; 5th back to Fairfax. Got whole heap of letters, from Mimi, Em', Tint, Howland &c. Today came over Crowninshield, Lowell, Forbes, & Windsor, all looking well.[79]

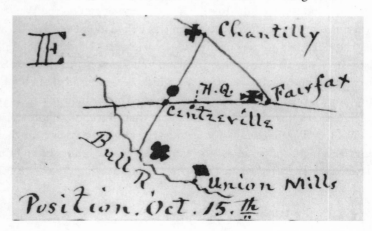

2d Mass. Cav. is at Vienna. Windsor is with his reg. 6th Penn. Cav. to which Starr, Meade, & Mitchell belong. Starr is going to join; his escort squadron being relieved by one of the 5th dragoons. The "regular" cavalry Brigade has come down from W[ashington] about 1,800; and infantry belonging to us, are also en route, say 3,000. Gen. Halleck, who, when asked for an opinion, said he "was no Aulic Councillor." Now sends a despatch asking if Lee is not trying to bully us; and advising a battle! which is just the little thing we are trying to get. Advice gratis![80]

October 16, Friday.

After a threatening day the rain came in a deluge, with much wind, in the eve', just as the 5th Corps was moving up to Centreville, on a report of an advance of the Rebs. This swells the Bull Run so much that we shall not be able tomorrow to cross and attack the enemy at Bristoe, where he is supposed to be. But our information is indeed meagre, particularly of Ewell's Corps. Gen. Sickles came down, a well looking man, with a brisk gray eye, and a good tempered, dashing air. He does not look his antecedents. Gen. M[eade] told him he was not well enough, with his lost leg, for active service, which he took in good part and cleared out.[81] Tonight Buford got in to Fairfax Sta., bringing in the rear of the waggons in safety. We had to burn 5 pontoons of which the mules gave out. B[uford] skirmished the last of the way, killing many with his artillery.— The elections in Ohio and Penn. on Tuesday went heavily Republican; a relief! Maj. Ludlow had a horse shot on the 14th, while on a message to Gen. Warren. Yesterday some 600 prisoners were marched through on the way to Washington. Many were boys, who looked much the worse for the hard marching. They looked not very badly clad, but had no knapsacks, or had lost them. Poor Gen. Meade! Said he, "I used to think how nice it would be to be Commander in Chief; now, at this moment I would sooner go, with a division, under the heaviest musketry fire, than hold my place!"[82]

October 17, Saturday.

The enemy's position is still uncertain; too much so for attack, though Kilpatrick & other cavalry have tried hard to get definite information. Yesterday came a letter from the President, saying 1. Lee had but 60,000. 2. That Lee thought we had lost *four* corps. 3. Now was the time to fight; if with success Gen. Meade should have the glory; if with failure, he, the President, would bear the blame. To which Gen. Meade replied his whole object was to fight, could he but get a decent chance. Gen. Merritt, a very young man, one of the cavalry batch with Custer & Kilpatrick, came down, and went out to command the regular brigade reconnoitring towards Manassas. The prevalent impression is he (Lee) has gone to the Shenandoah Valley.[83]

October 18, Sunday.

A boy was brought in early, a deserter from Rhodes Division; once a drummer boy, lately a vendor of papers & tobacco. He said the Rebels were going back to the Rappahannock, leaving a covering force at Bristoe; and were tearing up the track & burning the bridges; that Hill was rumored under arrest, for not getting first to Centreville heights; that the brigade of Cooke was much cut up at Bristoe. C[ooke] having expostulated against the order to charge. Gen. Merritt on to at or near Bristoe where 8 guns opened on him.— Stuart is known to have passed round our right, say with 4,000 cavalry and some artillery. President's proclamation came out with a call for 300,000 volunteers for old regiments, or, in default, a draft Jan. 4th, 1864. That sounds right.[84]

October 19, Monday.

We were up and off betimes, after the Rebels. The morning, at first threatening, was presently fine, with a gentle N.W. wind. The 5th Corps marched on Groveton, on the Warrenton pike; the 2d moved to Milford, the 3d to Bristoe; the 1st to Haymarket & the 6th to Gainsville. For our part, we proceeded to

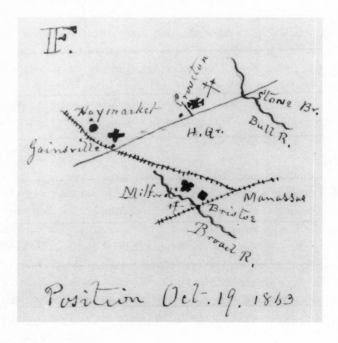

Groveton, some 8 miles, and pitched camp in a field, just south of the road. This so-called pike is a made road, once very likely good, but now consisting of holes & gullies of hard gravel; still, the waggons got briskly on, along it and there was room enough for the infantry.[85]

The land is somewhat regularly hilly, with much good, open, field; and extensive groves, or patches, of large trees; a really good country. There are frequent "runs" of which the first is the stream called Cub Run, which, after the rain of last night, was up to the horses bellies, and perhaps 40 feet wide. The classic Bull Run is beyond this, & a larger stream, running through a sandstone bed, some 30 feet below the road. A sort of tête-de-pont and some rifle pits are still there. Beyond this lies the battlefield, among the woods & the cultivated ridges. A Lieut. Berlin is with me temporarily; having come here with a cavalry [regiment] & wishing to join Gen. Hunt's staff, as an artillerist. He is a Swede.[86] The quails are exceeding plenty. A soldier today caught two in his hand, and some frightened young ones even came in the tents. All through this region the persimmon tree is common, and is now charged with round, yellow fruit, the size of a plum; its taste is remarkably astringent, making the whole mouth contract. When well frost bitten it gets sweet. This afternoon Kilpatrick ran into a hornets' nest of cavalry, near Buckland Mills in the front, and came near getting used up, but escaped with a loss of 100 or 200 men. He is a brave, vigorous man, but apparently deficient in judgment, a fault in which his two Brigadiers, Davies & Custer do not much help him.[87] Hoof disease has appeared among our horses, making great ravages; it is epidemic, & will strike nearly all the horses in a battery, at once. It is a suppurating sore, above the hoof.

October 20, Tuesday.

By reason of Kilpatrick's report we looked this day for a great battle near Warrenton; but our advance found nothing at all; and a squad of cavalry entered Warrenton unopposed. Night before last, at Centreville, we had a set-to between Meade & Halleck. Meade had asked, by telegraph, for some advice, and stated that he was not sufficiently assured of the enemy's position to risk an advance; so conflicting were the reports. Halleck, apparently after dinner, replied in substance "Lee is plainly bullying you. If you can't find him, I can't. If you go and fight him you will probably find him!" Gen. Meade, much offended, prepared a reply in some such words, "If you have any orders, I am ready to obey them; but I must insist on being spared the infliction of such truisms in guise of Opinions as I have recently been favored with. If my course is not satisfactory I ought to be & I desire to be relieved." He had written "Bunsby opinions" and consulted me as to whether it would do; to which replied that the joke was capital, but not in accordance with the etiquette of a commander-in-chief; so he substituted the other. At Groveton came H[alleck]'s answer, wherein he completely apologized![88] The Sixth Corps moved to Warrenton; the 5th halted at Buckland Mills; the 1st marched through Thorofare Gap to Georgetown, & the 2d & 3d moved respectively to Auburn & Greenwich. Our Headquarters stayed at Gainsville, where passes the Manassas R.R. and where we soon got a wire to Washington. There are 3 or 4 houses in the "ville" and hence branches the road and leading to Thorofare Gap, which is to be recognized by a bare hill beyond, & which is 6 miles beyond.

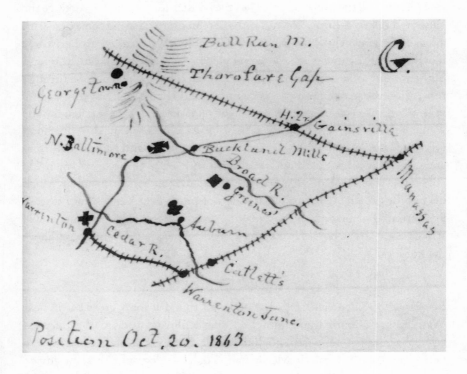

Bull Run Mt. is an out-lying parallel ridge to the Blue Ridge and is now rich brown with the changing forests.[89] The enemy have completely destroyed every thing on the R.R., at least to the Rappahannock; burning the sleepers with the rails on top; & blowing up culverts. Their object is to keep Meade at arms' length; so as to send reinforcements to Bragg. At Gainsville some petty troubles with certain of the Staff culminated; the troubles were two: 1st Gen. M[eade] did not know (nor I, of course) that Volunteer Aides were illegal; therefore my rank was no rank at all so far as concerned the U.S. service. 2d the fact of my messing, and being intimate with the General roused the jealousy of certain small gentlemen, more especially of Capt. Bache, a remarkably empty-headed and ill-bred young man (the General's nephew) who considers himself the Ζεὺς Βροντίζων of the place. And so they made the most childish fuss about the position of my tent in the line; in vain I said I would take any place that was in reason. They seemed to imply that there was no place in particular for me. As to Bache he was right down rude, but was so absurd that I could not argue with him, and shall give him the cold shoulder for the future. As the position was a reflection on the General as well as on myself, I told him that, if my position was not one capable of good, it was a damage to him & to me. He had up Gen. "Seth" [Williams] and consulted; & said he would apply for a commission for me from the President.[90]

October 21, Wednesday.

The Corps stood still, but we advanced the Headquarters 12 miles to Warrenton. Here found a town the most civilized that have seen in Va. There were many really good, modern houses, a few with some show of architecture; some sidewalks, of flat stones, like the Florentine pavement; a certain number of tolerable shops (closed) and two or three hotels. It lies on high ground with a distant view, from the higher parts, of the Blue Ridge; the surrounding country is prettily hilly and is much cultivated. Near by is Watery Mountain, a continuation of the Bull Run ridge, and comparable to Pony Mt. but not so rough. On the road at the point where it crosses Broad Run is a poor hamlet, Buckland Mills, but prettily situated in a swale; the pike goes mostly through a hilly region, of good farms. Our Warrenton camp, pitched on a smooth slope of greensward, just beyond the town is the pleasantest we have had, and our cook John Skarren gloried in a brick outhouse wherein to prepare our diet, which much improved in consequence.

October 22, Thursday.

Early in the morning the orderly put in his head & said "Breakfast at 7, this morning, Sir." I smelt a rat; for we had waited the day previous till 1 P.M. at Gainsville, hoping to get a despatch by telegraph from Halleck, in answer to a general statement of the position. So, as had anticipated, a telegraph had come summoning Gen. Meade to Washington; and he asked me to go also, to which assented, though in sooth, would as lief stick by my old tent, till that hoped for day when I can go even to Mimette. We mounted after breakfast (8 o'cl) and

rode to Gen. Sedgwick, hard by, who takes the command. Then we continued
our 12 miles, briskly, to Gainsville; where the General threw himself into a room
and put on a clean uniform with such velocity that was forced to pursue him
to the car with many of my fine garments still in my hand! It took only some
25 minutes to Manassas, whence we passed through Alexandria, crossed the
long bridge, and got to Washington at 2 P.M. Gen. Humphreys & Capt. Meade
were with us. We drove first to Halleck's office, where the two had a pow-wow,
then to the President's, where was more pow-wow. It was understood that the
President said he had certainly hoped for a decisive battle out of Lee; but now
he thought nothing more could be done this season; as it would take 30 or 40
days to repair the railroads. Halleck thought some could be done. He is a stout
man, somewhat stooping, about 5 feet 9, with a big head & bright black eyes; but
is not impressive looking. By the time we two had waited 2 hours, the *concilia*
got over, and we had a fine dinner at Willard's, though somewhat bothered with
dirty politicians who kept boring the Commander. Saw Staunton Blake there;
also Dunster, who seemed smaller than ever. After getting my head shampood,
got to bed, which seemed strange. (Weighed in common clothes 163½.)[91]

October 23, Friday.

Up early & back, as we came, getting to camp at 1 P.M. having left at 8. Garrison
duty is done at W[ashington], by the Invalid Corps who are the least invalid
looking men that have seen; a fine strapping set of fellows, wearing a light blue
uniform. Certain of the enemy have crossed near Rappahannock Station and
our forces are concentrating more in that direction.[92]

October 24, Saturday.

Mr. Stanton will return today to Washington and we hope for some information soon, as to the determinations of the Areopagus. A wretched weather!
N.E. wind with cold, intermittent rain. The First Corps, with painful splashing
marched from Georgetown to Bristoe; the 2d went forward to Turkey Run; the
5th took its place at Auburn; and the 3d has advanced to Catlett's. There has
been slight skirmishing. Saw the death of Mr. Wm. Sturgis in the paper.[93]

October 25, Sunday.

Weather clear & cool. There are fine varieties of roses blooming in the fields,
or rather plots, in front of the best houses. They say the clergyman prayed for
"all constituted magistrates" & so got out of the scrape!

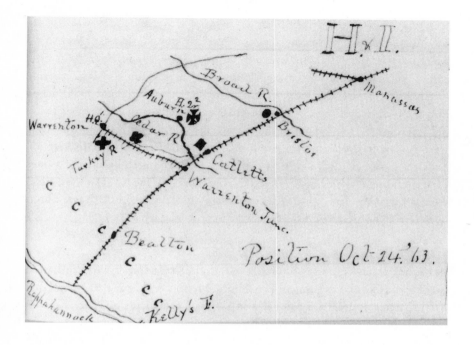

October 26, Monday.

Got a letter from Mr. Everett asking some further information of the Gettysburg campaign. The which answered to best of my ability. Old Mr. Wm. Sturgis is dead. Ned Jeffries is in jail for getting money on false pretenses! It seems as if he must have had some monomania!— The guerillas are most daring. They pounced last night on a train, and took 119 mules & horses. These they sell to the Confed' Gov' at fixed rates. The waggons they commonly leave, for want of time. These men get no pay, but are regularly enlisted and are entitled to all booty, except animals, which they must sell, getting the money for themselves. The Rebels advanced infantry in some force, from Rappahannock Station, to this side of Bealton, Buford checking, and skirmishing with them. There was also a report of infantry advancing from Kelly's Ford. These signs led the Commander to look for an attack, so the camp was ordered moved to Auburn, next day, at 8 A.M.

October 27, Tuesday.

My acquaintance Capt. Zerbad, the Hungarian, was "gobbled" near Bealton, lately, while on staff duty for Gen. French. Our train left the pleasant grass slope at Warrenton betimes. While we followed the Warrenton R.R. to Turkey

Run where are Gen. Warren's Headq'rs, who gave us a fine lunch, whereof ate too much and gave myself an elegant turn of dyspepsia, that eve. And so we waited a good bit, till 2 P.M., when, thinking the telegraph must by this time run to our new Headq'rs we rode over to a spot near Auburn's Mills, crossing Cedar Run, on the way, Gen. Warren showing the way the enemy attacked him the morning of the 14th. It would appear Ewell's whole corps was there, but their numbers stood in their own way, and Warren slipped off, while they were getting in position. Our camp had been pitched by Inspector General Schriver (a rather thick old betty) on a slope covered with briars and stones & terminating in a clay bog![94] A letter from Alex tells me he has the star-fish embryology from the egg to 11 years old; very nice. Papa [Louis Agassiz] has been having a shindy with the Scientific School Faculty, *de re* Clark.[95]

October 28, Wednesday.

No attack at all—oh fiddle! Halleck telegraphed that spies gave information that Ewell's Corps was going to Lynchburg. Meade's reply was that he had that day prisoners & deserters from E[well]'s Corps, of which 2 divisions were on this side of the river! H[alleck] (who had given orders for immediate attack) said he would speak to the President, since which—*nichts!* Lieut. Appleton came over & saw me.[96] Ice thicker than plate glass, these last two nights.

October 29, Thursday.

Railroad repaired to Catlett's.

October 30, Friday.

As the railroad will be done tonight to Warrenton Junction, Headq'rs were moved more to the front. The 3d Corps was pushed a couple of miles beyond Warrenton Junction; and the 5th to the south side of the Warrenton Branch R.R. We got off by 10 A.M. & passing by way of Catlett's to see the progress in the R.R. proceeded to Headq'rs which are near Col. Murray's between Turkey Run & 3-Mile Station. The house is a large rambling building, with fine bushes of box, and luxurious ivy growing, the latter took me with a sudden jump to Florence & to Rome; and almost brought tears to my eyes. I cut two little roots and sent them, in an envelope, to Mimi.[97]

October 31, Saturday.

In case my horses should be stolen, made an examination of their marks. The horse is all black, except a white spot on the forehead as big as a ten-cent piece, also scars of scratches on off hind fetlock. The mare has a white forehead

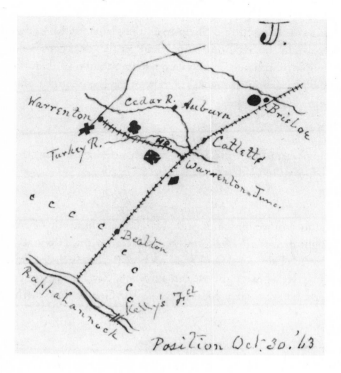

mark & the near hind foot white, as above; the rest black, inclining to brown round the nostrils.

November 2, Monday.

My little Wife's birthday; she 27 and no hub' to give her a present. Twenty-five pontoons, additional came down today, which looks like going round.

November 4, Wednesday.

Weather exceeding fine. Indian summer; in the day quite warm. There is a hitch somewhere! Humphreys said, very discontentedly, that the Washington Government had disapproved their plan, which would have succeeded. Judge that it was to cross on our left, possibly below the junction of the 2 rivers, and turn their right. Oh Lord! I don't wonder the General feels blue.[98] By letters from home see that Col. Lowell was married to Effie Shaw on the last day of Oct., gone to live at Vienna; rather an excess of mud & guerillas, one would say. These last murdered (or rather killed) an officer of the 6th Penn. Cavalry today, lots of engagements keep going. Lieut. Dabney to Miss Clara Bigelow, Ned Grew to Miss Clark (must be a sister of my classmate R. M.) then the other Miss

Bigelow has made happy Philo Shelton; and my friend Alice Crowninshield, Joe Bradlee; would she had done better than get this deaf gentleman without brains! A couple of military Britons came down today, on a flying visit; one, a little engineer Harrison, was not lacking; the other, Lieut. Smith, of the guards, was 7 feet high & nearly idiotic.[99]

November 5, Thursday.

An enervating, warm west wind. Cora writes that they are moving from Beverly. First Corps moved to Catlett's.

November 6, Friday.

There is plainly a move on hand; probably of attack by Kelly's Ford or there-about. Tonight orders are out to move camp tomorrow, at 9 A.M. Kilpatrick has been towards Falmouth, but know not how far, or much about it. Perhaps tomorrow may see a great fight; we can never tell. Got a letter from dear Mimi a good cheerer before a fight; if it is to come. The General busy with maps and officers.

November 7, Saturday.

At daylight, all the corps were in motion; the 6th and 5th on Rappahannock Station, where Gen. Sedgwick took chief command; the 2d, 3d, and all of the 1st, but 3 brigades left on the R.R., on Kelly's Ford, where Gen. French had the command. We mounted at 9.30, getting to Warrenton Junction at 10 where we staid some little time and then continued to Bealton, passing many troops, chiefly 2d Corps, on the way, along the railroad.[100] The weather mild & fine, though windy. Gen. Warren was there, and presently up rode Gen. Webb, fol-lowed by two persons in plain clothes, who turned out to be one Atkinson, a Bull, in company of Hon. Yorke, who was of our company aboard the "Africa" and left us at Halifax to join his regiment. He had a couple of letters for Maj. Biddle and greeted me kindly.[101]

Thence we struck off to the left (S.E.) over a country new to me, much of it considerably wooded, both with oak & pine. Keeping on the Morrisville road nearly to that place, we struck off to the right to the house of one Carter, situ-ated on an open of farming land. Before arriving there, however (say at 1.30) we heard firing towards Rappahannock Station, and, a few minutes after, guns in the direction of Kelly's Ford. Arriving at Carter's we could see the smoke of Gen. French's firing, floating chiefly over Mt. Holly, about 2½ miles off. Very soon there came an officer, to say that, after a cannonade, one division had forded and effected a lodgment, the Rebels then advanced a division to an

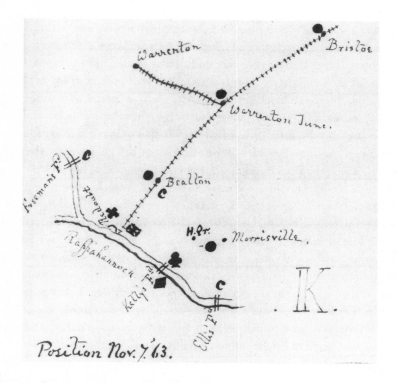

Position Nov. 7 '63.

extensive rifle-pit but our guns at once opened with grape and shell, driving them back at once. We took some 300 prisoners. This man Carter has more stock than one often sees in this unfortunate country, a dozen very nice sheep, some chickens, several cows, and something of a vegetable garden. Towards sundown came a despatch from Gen. Sedgwick, that he had taken all the rifle-pits and established his pickets on each side of the redoubt, resting on the river; but had not yet got the redoubt itself. Later, however, in the night, came intelligence that he had stormed the work and taken it, with prisoners & four cannon; which put us all in good spirits.[102]

November 8, Sunday.

Last night the woods got on fire, to the south & east, and burned somewhat the whole night through, looking very brilliant. It was supposed that we should have today a heavy action and everything was arranged accordingly. We were up by the light of the stars which was extraordinary fine; Venus, especially stood out, over a small moon, with the brilliancy of a fire-ball. Breakfast at early daylight and then waited till perhaps 7.30, to see if any news would come in; but, all remaining quiet, we rode on, to Mt. Holly; this is a somewhat steep hill, of not much height, but so placed as completely to command, and almost to enfilade, the crossing at Kelly's Ford from its southern slope. Between it & the ford is a stretch of good, open, undulating ground. The other side of the river is a flat, rising presently into a ridge which, however, is lower than the other side. There is a brick church on Mt. Holly, now full of wounded. At a poor house, hard by, we staid some time, while the troops crossed, apparently in countless numbers, for orders had been issued to bring up Sykes' Corps & cross it here, also two brigades of the 6th, for a bridge guard, while the bulk of the forces would advance and attack the enemy whom we hoped to find near Brandy Sta. But, behold, no enemy! Groups of stragglers were brought in, all of whom concurred in stating that their army had put, in all haste, for the Rapidan, the night before. Gen. Birney, who had the advance, reported only a weak line of dismounted cavalry in his front. While waiting we got more precise information of our successes; the number of prisoners, on all hands, reaches nearly 2,000 (chiefly of N.C. & Va. reg'ts. but also of La., Al. & Ga.). There are, besides, 4 guns, 8 colors, and a pontoon bridge. The prisoners that have seen are very thin, but still healthy looking, their clothes are of a gray cloth. Have seen none with overcoats, but most have a blanket, and a good proportion, excellent English shoes. Finally we crossed the river on a pontoon bridge, perhaps 35 yards long, and moved through the masses of the 5th Corps, who cheered vociferously. Thence we bore west, over a flat bottom land of gray clay, to a rising ground where is Thom's house, last night the Headq'rs of Ewell; and where Gen. Warren then was. Thence we passed N.W. to near Brandy Station and found Gen. Sedgwick, who received his congratulations in his usual quiet, smiling way. As we descended to Brandy Sta., the 3d and 2d Corps were pouring in, to bivouac, and the way some ruined framed buildings went to pieces and walked off on men's shoulders, was marvelous! The men were in fine spirits and yelled and whooped merrily. And so, towards sunset, we made for the Rappahannock en route for the old Headq'rs of Oct. 12 at Anderson's house. The way led over the redoubt on the hill, on the north side, the river being crossed by pontoons. This work, originally of our make, had been turned inside out by the Rebs (so as to face up the railroad & from the river) and had been greatly strengthened with breast works & with rife-pits running parallel to the river, on each side. These pits were constructed with traverses and carefully laid out.

Below the redoubt is a long, naked slope, perhaps ¼ or ½ of a mile, to the edge of the woods. Up this the 6th Maine and 5th Wisconsin charged, just at sundown and captured the work at the point of the bayonet; a most daring

act! Our camp was the other side of the house this time; but, *Nov. 9* [Monday] as we only came to be near the telegraph, we today recrossed the river, on the captured bridge ½ mile below the R.R. bridge.

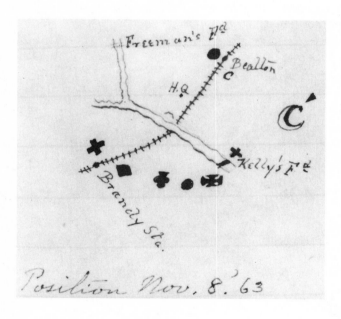

Kilpatrick came up yesterday from Kelly's Ford seeing nobody. Buford came down from Rixieville and was stopped by a division of infantry, with whom he skirmished. At a ruined house this side of Brandy Sta., we stopped for some time, while a new camp was selecting. The wind really cold & raw, from the north. The 1st Corps was filing off to occupy the north side of the River; its brigades still guard the upper railroad. Our camp was at a deserted brick house ½ mile N. of R.R., and 2 m. N.E. of Brandy Sta.

November 10, Tuesday.

As this is a bad ground we moved ¾ m. W. to a nice pine wood, and there
pitched, in a semi-circle, near "St. James Church." The President sent a telegraph,
saying, "Well done!" to our movement. In the afternoon came a detachment from
each regiment that distinguished itself in the 6th Corps bearing the 7 captured
colors, and the staff of the 8th. The General made them a neat speech of praise.
These so called "battle-flags" are a red ground with a blue cross, from corner
to corner, bearing 13 stars; some had the names of many battles. This was the
coldest night we have had, and a little ice made in the bucket inside my tent.

November 11, Wednesday.

Henry Sturgis is married, according to letters from home. The alabaster vase
has been unpacked and excited great admiration; Agassiz could not get over
my having dug it up.[103]

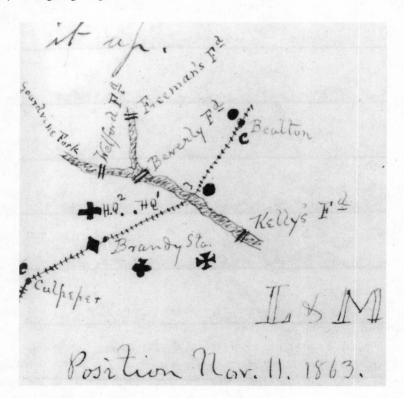

November 12, Thursday.

Poor John M. Botts made his appearance. The Rebs stripped him pretty much of everything, all his corn, much of his fences, &c. They took him to Culpeper, but there released him. Rode today to look at the country near Welford Ford; this side of which is Dr. Welford's house, now Headq'rs of 6th Corps. This house was framed in *England*, and is very old. The workmen in the absence of the owner, put the frame up with the *front to the rear*. It is very large, but merely an oblong building with a bead cornice.[104]

November 14, Saturday.

At midday came a telegram that 4 English officers were coming down, and Barstow asked if would like to bring them from Bealton. So went, with Lieut. Hagen and an escort. We got there a few minutes before the train. These Britons are the best lot that have seen. Names: Lieut. Col. Earle; Lord Castlecuffe (Grenadier Guards), Capt'ns Stephenson & Peel (Scotch Fusileer Guards). We rode through that picture of desolation, the country between this & Rappahannock Station, where everything is worn to dust by the waggons; the trees are cut away, in good part, and the air is tainted by dead horses. Showed them the work we took and then got speedily to headq'rs, just in time to avoid a drenching shower which continued, with thunder, a good part of the night. Early this morning, Gen. Meade went to Washington, taking Mitchell, Meade, & Biddle; where, suppose, he will much pow-wow with the Big Indians.[105]

November 15, Sunday.

Gen. Sedgwick came, as Vice Roy, and gladdened the camp, with his kind face.[106] But mice play when the cat is too good natured! Last night punch was in order, and behold Barstow, who, since have been here, has been the most temperate soul about, showed the old colors, by brewing a famous jorum, and taking too much of it! "Uncle John" sat in the tent with the rest of the youngsters, smoking a quiet cigar. This evening we rode over to Sleeper's 9th [10th] Mass. Battery, the Englanders being the guests. Our way lay through the woods & in passing Gen. [Marsena] Patrick's tent, we were brought up by a stentorian "Halt!" which made all jump in our boots. The kind general laughed, when he found his mistake in taking us for evil-doers! We had much punch & singing at S[leeper]'s; not very appropriate for Sunday, particularly as do not join in the liquids. Barstow got a heavy load on, and pitched into everybody.

November 16, Monday.

Yesterday morning we heard heavy artillery fire, apparently not over two miles away! It proved to be a reconnoissance by Custer at Raccoon Ford, 10 miles away. The damp air probably conveyed the sound; but there was some singular reflection, for, at Stevensburg it was not heard at all. Very positive information had come in, that the enemy were falling back on Richmond; but this reconnoissance seemed entirely to disprove it.[107] Today was celebrated by a review of the 3d Corps. The 1st & 3d Divisions, under Birney & Carr were reviewed first, with some 48 guns; and then the 2d, Gen. Prince. After which we took a lunch at Gen. French's, whereat was Gen. Prince, despite his bitter quarrel with F[rench].[108] Nothing would do then but a review of Graham's horse-batteries, and another lunch at Gen. Pleasonton's. Whereupon it became evident to me that some active operations would highly benefit the army; for whiskey drinking is taken to as a defence against nothing to do. Have not seen so many people for a long while, who have got too much; for this there are two reasons; first the great strength of the liquor; second the nervous temperament of the Americans, that often renders them more susceptible to liquor than the English. Nothing can be worse, for the men than to be deprived of drink themselves, yet see their officers with too much! Poor Barstow made a sad spectacle of himself, by appearing, in a prominent way, before French, Sedgwick & Pleasonton, in a decidedly boozy condition, and with his saddle girth broken. At Pleasonton's he got much worse, and finally barely got home. The General appeared, some time after dark, having seen *his* wife in Washington. The enthusiastic Biddle, too, got his wife on, & was allowed an extra day of felicity.

November 17, Tuesday.

By invitation of Robertson, we went to Stevensburg, to see a drill of a horse-battery. We passed by Thom's house, where introduced the Britons to Gen. Warren; and so on to Gen. Custer's Headquarters, in a well built modern house, between Stevensburg & Pony Mtn. The great C[uster] appeared in his ordinary gold & black velvet; and accompanied us, to see the drill; after which a review of two little regiments of cavalry, which, with us, is but a poor show; for the very essence of such things is fine horses and well trained men. The weather continues remarkable and the country is everywhere passable. Have here seen a younger brother of Ned Dalton; also Lieut. Blücher (a Holsteiner in the artillery).[109]

November 18, Wednesday.

Never did 4 guardsmen get greater chances & turn-outs. Gen. Warren had some manoeuvres by two divisions, before which we all rode to Buford's

Headq'rs, beyond Culpeper, and near where Sykes was. It seemed familiar to pass Wallach's old house and the streets of Culpeper. After a talk with the cavalry chief, who was laid up with rheumatism, we rode, in all haste, to Gen. Warren's Headquarters. That morning the enemy's cavalry, under Hampton, had crossed and stampeded a cavalry regiment, but with what loss did not hear. On the plain, north of Thom's house there was a manouvre of two divisions ending by a bayonet charge, at the double quick, up the hill; all extremely well done, and very beautiful to see.

November 20, Friday.

Today a grand review of the 6th Corps for the Englanders. This was by far the best review that have seen. As we rode along the rear of the line, not a head was turned; everyone steady. The men were clean; the cannon burnished. Line formed by columns of regiments. In breaking into column to pass in review, the regiments changed direction by left face, file right; which, executed at a double quick, is very pretty. Saw there Gens. Wright, Wheaton, Terry, Howe, Neil, Shaler, &c.[110] A most sumptuous lunch (for which General Sedgwick is noted) finished the day. There was a huge amount of champagne & punch; and fancy the Welford house, despite its reputation for ancient hospitality, never saw a bigger bend. Stephenson performed an extraordinary amount of health-drinking, but returned in a state of entire calm!— Ah! I am better off, not to take anything.

November 21, Saturday.

The clouds, which last night were gathering, came down today in a heavy rain, though a quiet one, lasting some 20 hours. The General, with Gens. Humphreys & Hunt went to dine with John Minor Botts, where were several other Generals. The old chap is bound to have an out and out declaration. The four English officers were all at the mess and we sat a long time after, in pleasant converse, with many good stories.

November 22, Sunday.

Explained today a remarkable phenomenon, viz: that lately all my clothes have been getting too tight, on weighing myself, found that weighed 170 lbs., a gain of 6½ in 30 days. Master Castlecuffe paid a visit to Gen. Webb where he got terribly tight and afterwards went to see Gen. Warren. Coming home he fell off his horse and lost his watch. McClellan, in a similar plight, got off to help him and both their horses ran away!

November 23, Monday.

Willie Paige made his appearance, coming forward with some of the Sanitary Commission things for the expected battle. He seems smaller than ever, the useful little man![111]

November 24, Tuesday.

We were to move today, having sent the baggage of an extra sort to Alexandria. Each has a roll of bedding, necessary mess arrangements & a minimum wardrobe. But it rained, so the move was deferred. Castlecuffe went back to Washington.

November 25, Wednesday.

The day was lowering but clear at eve. Great news came from Grant, that he had driven Bragg from his fortified positions, capturing 48 guns & 6,000 prisoners![112]

November 26, Thursday.

Thanksgiving day, when the fat turkey is served in state. And this was appointed for our flank move on Orange Court House, via our left. At 7¾ A.M. we started. The order of march was 5th followed by 1st Corps to cross by pontoon at Culpeper Mine Ford, advance by a cross road to the Orange C.H. plank road and keep on to "Parker's Store." The 3d followed by the 6th, cross at Jacob's Mills and keep on to form on right of 2d, which crossed at Germanna Mills took a cross road to the Orange Court House turnpike and then keep on to Robertson's Tavern, or, if possible, to Verdiersville.

The [3d] Div. of 1st Corps left to guard railroad. Reserve Artillery [to] follow 1st Corps. Waggon train park at Richardsville, under guard of Merritt's (Buford's) division of cavalry, Custer's division (Kilpatrick's) to hold Raccoon & Morton's Fords. Gregg's Div. to cross at Ely's Ford and cover the advance & left of Sykes.[113] Owing, apparently, to some dullness on part of Gen. Prince, this division did not start till say 7.30, which delayed the rest of the 3d Corps; moreover they had not properly reconnoitred the roads or repaired them, so they took the wrong road, this side of the river, and got their artillery stalled into the bargain! At about 10.30 we got within ½ mile of Germanna Ford & there found the troops massed and the batteries placed, ready to run up and shell the crossing. The Rapidan there runs between high, steep banks whereof the northern dominates the southern, the reverse of what happens at the fords above. Officers were sent to French & Sykes, to find whether they had got up;

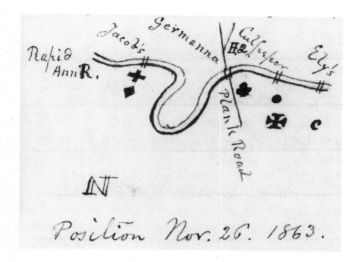

because it was deemed important to force the river, at the same moment. The communications were difficult, and so the officers did not get back till late, so that our troops (2d Corps) began to cross at about 2 P.M., Sykes having begun at 12, and French not till later. The artillery of the 3d & 6th had finally to come to Germanna and was not over till 5 next morning. We camped at the junction of the plank and dirt roads on the north side of the river. It was quite cold and the water froze in the tent.[114]

November 27, Friday.

We were up before daylight, with a magnificent moon glittering on the hoar frost, but the Staff did not move till 8.45 A.M. Then we crossed on the pontoons and kept down the plank road, to a point some 2 or 3 miles from the river where we struck off, more to the S.W. to make a short cut for the Orange court house turnpike. Before this turn-off we got to the artillery of the 6th Corps, to whom the General gave a good blowing up, for not knowing their precise road. On this side of the river, the country is, for some distance, open farming land; then succeeds dense, scrub-oak wood, penetrated only by farm roads, narrow and intricate, at best, and in wet weather, impossible for artillery. Near the river had been made long rifle-pits, with some entrenched epaulements for guns, but they were quite unoccupied. About midday through the woods we came on the rear of the 2d Corps, moving briskly, and we filed past them, with some difficulty. At 9.30 we heard cannon ahead and, at 10.45 struck the turnpike, along which we advanced to within say 1¼ miles of Robertson's Tavern, and there halted by the roadside, at which time (11) there was brisk skirmishing by Warren, who had gained the ridge of Robertson's Tavern and pushed back the Rebel advance (part of Ewell's Corps.) And now we found ourselves with a weak centre, on the pike and the strong right not heard from, and inexplicably behind-hand! Aides were sent to French, under guidance of natives & niggers. Ludlow, sent to Sykes, reported him well up on the left. About 12.45 we heard cannon off on our right, which seemed from the 3d Corps. McBlair came, but he, honest soul, did display his usual muddleheadedness, as to time & place, and could only make out, that French was going along somewhere in the thick woods. At length Cadwalader returned, who had taken an order to French to attack & smash through to Warren, and reported French's left some 2 miles from Warren's right. Meanwhile Gregg, in the left advance, had a sharp fight with the enemy's infantry, in which the cavalry did excellently and, among them, the 1st Mass. Longfellow and Bowditch were here wounded.[115] An aide from Custer stated he had made a good diversion at Raccoon & Morton's Fords, by charging across both, and forcing the enemy to detach a large force to drive him back again. Meanwhile Warren had received orders to attack without French, or not, at his discretion. He concluded it would not be safe; and so we pitched camp where we stood. After dark came a despatch from French that he had had a sharp action, with very heavy musketry (none of which we had heard) and had driven the enemy from the field, taking 900 prisoners (a number which proved greatly exaggerated) and losing some 900 himself in killed, wounded, &c. His fight, also, was with a portion of Ewell's Corps.[116]

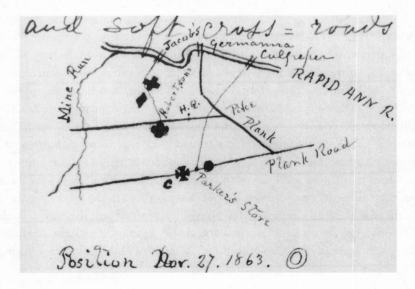

November 28, Saturday.

A pretty place to pass my Wedding-day! Twelve months ago we were in Paris, and enjoying the quiets of the Hotel Wagram. And this morning, behold me, with little Wife hundreds of miles away and a cheery prospect of mud and intermittent rain! At 7.45 we rode to Robertson's Tavern 1¼ m. which stands on a ridge along which the 2d Corps was in line of battle and just advancing. The enemy had disappeared from our front, and many thought them in full retreat. After some talk with Gen. Warren, Gen. Meade went to the tavern, and sat by the fire. However, say at 10.15 there was a report that we had come on the enemy in entrenchments; and we all rode to the front, slop, slop in the mud, and amid infantry, artillery & ambulances going to the front, also. A little behind the crest of the next ridge, and about 1 m. from the tavern the General halted us, and rode alone to reconnoitre. At 11, a battery opened and fired some time, posted just on the left of the 'pike. They were in entrenchments, sure enough, and we had only to wait for other troops to come along. The rest of the day was occupied by the corps getting into position, a very laborious thing, midst mud and soft cross-roads. The day previous Meade, anxious for his centre, had brought over both Sykes & Newton, from the plank road; and the 5th Corps was now in reserve at Robertson's Tavern, while the First [Corps] took position in line.

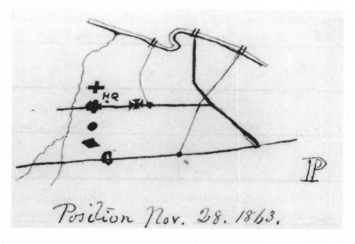

Position Nov. 28. 1863.

November 29, Sunday.

The enemy's position was found to be a very strong one. Along a bold ridge, running nearly north & south across both turn-pike and plank road, rising from Mine Run by a steep slope, which in many parts was quite naked, and in others partially wooded, they had thrown up a heavy and continuous breast-work, supported by batteries, for which they had made epaulements. The corresponding high ground east of the Run, and occupied by us, was at least a mile in average distance, so that artillery would be deprived of much of its strong effect, and canister & spherical case pretty much out of the question. Then, at most points the attacking force would be exposed over nearly the whole stretch, to artillery fire, followed by musketry. It was a bad look out! From our ridge we could see the Rebs in hundreds, standing on top their works, or enlarging some portion of them, with logs and earth. The thing was, if possible, to flank. So Warren, with his own corps & a division of the 6th, marched in the morning and passed towards our left, hoping to get beyond the plank road and attack that afternoon; the rest of the line be ready to support. However, the column was delayed by a report of entrenchments that had no existence, and by some skirmishing, so that they did not get on the enemy's flank till too late for an attack. As it was they created great excitement & a brigade was brought on the double-quick to resist an attack. Major Ludlow came back with fine accounts of the prospect in the morning. The General, much encouraged, made immediate disposition for the attack and put French's two flank (left) divisions under Warren (Prince & Carr) greatly to F[rench]'s indignation. Sykes had already occupied Warren's vacant position. At 8, or earlier, a general cannonade was to open, for an hour, and then the assault to take place. The grand attack on the left, and others, according to opportunity, along the whole line. One division of the 5th Corps occupied the extreme right. Gregg had continued skirmishing, on the left. The day Sykes & Newton moved along the plank road (27th) the enemy's cavalry performed a feat of extraordinary daring. They dashed on the trains, between the tail of the 5th and head of the 1st Corps, cut out a dozen or more waggons and made off with them. They were chiefly ammunition, but one was a Headquarter waggon, so there was Capt. Barnard, quite without blankets or any comfort, poor man; and his general Bartlett, in a similar fix.[117] A brigade from Merritt was sent to reinforce Gregg.

November 30, Monday.

We were up bright & early, for it was necessary to get the trains out of the way about sunrise, as they would be exposed to shell, when the cannonade opened. All was expectation. Yet such is the force of your surroundings that I felt no particular nervousness—to be sure I did not have to lead an assault—which makes a wide difference. The soldiers of the 2d Corps, that morning pinned bits of paper on their clothes, with their names on them! As for Col. Farnum (he of yacht *Wanderer* fame) he said he considered himself under sentence of death, that morning, for an hour![118] A little before 8 General Meade mounted & went a

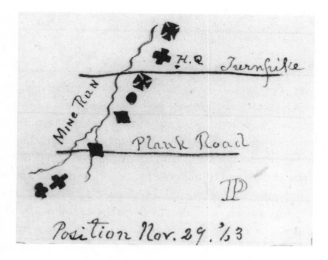

Position Nov. 29. /'63

little way in search of Gen. Newton; while we rode, at 8.10, a single gun sounded from the right, and then a cannonade, not very heavy, opened along the line, as far as Newton's part. We returned to Headquarters. At 8.30 came Robling with a note from Gen. Warren, saying the enemy had arrived in great force, during the night, had thrown up more rifle pits, and that, on reexamination of the ground he considered an attack there as hopeless!! The General simply turned to Gen. Humphreys, saying "Read that," and exclaimed to Robling "My God! Gen. Warren has half my army."[119] He then issued orders to cease firing; and soon all was still, save an occasional gun. Disappointment was on every face. For about an hour Gen. Meade remained in consultation with Gens. Sedgwick and Humphreys. Then at 9.45, he rode, with Gen. H[umphreys], Major Biddle [possibly Riddle], Mitchell & myself, to Gen. Warren's. We passed along the front, in rear of our batteries, proceeded through a wood and emerged on a bare plateau where was Gen. French's command, then through another pine wood and came out on the plank road. We stopped at a run (a branch of Mine Run) and Gen. Warren rode up and dismounted to talk with the two other Generals; and there they sadly stood, over a fire the orderlies had made them, for it was sharp, and thin ice was on the pools. It was then 10.15. After a very long talk, at noon we rode back, stopping at Gen. French's house. He was very mad and talked loudly. He had pushed his skirmishers to within 300 yards of their works, and his troops had counted on success. Warren's troops were in three lines by the Run; French's were on the plateau, behind earthworks. It was of no use! We came back; the moment had passed, the assault was countermanded and the 2d Corps might unpin their bits of paper. That night was cold; 5 of our men on picket, who had been obliged to wade the stream to get to their places, were frozen to death, and the same fate, it is said, befell some rebels.

December 1, Tuesday.

As I looked out of my tent, at daylight, there were the 4½ inch big guns going to the rear, which argued we were soon to follow. It came out shortly that the generals were unanimous in thinking the moment for the assault had passed; and the order was out to fall back. The 1st Corps would start that afternoon, proceeding to Germanna Ford, and halt, to cover the crossing. The 5th Corps would withdraw at dark and be followed by the 6th, marching for Germanna Ford via the Turnpike & the cross wood-road. The 3d would march at dark, on the plank road, and cross at Culpeper Ford; the 2d following. The pickets would be withdrawn at 3 in the morning and, assembling at Robertson's Tavern, march under Col. Hayes (Joe).[120] Some pickets of the 5th Corps had been 3 days on duty without relief! At sunset, went and took a farewell look at Jonny Reb. They were standing in groups on their parapet, while some were walking about in front. At dark we rode as far as Robertson's Tavern, where we built good fires and kept warm, till the 5th Corps should get past. It was a picturesque sight, so many officers, in their long coats, standing, sitting, or lying on the bare floor. Thereto also enter T. F. Meagher "of the Sword" *ci-devant* commander of the Irish Brigade; was in mufti and very drunk![121] He talked thickly with the English officers (who, by the by, established themselves in a seemingly safe place this morning, but got shelled for their pains, whereat Stephenson returned with a bit of spherical case, as a trophy). We started immediately in rear of the corps, but could go but at a snail's gain; broken bridge ahead and a slough, which kept checking the column. Of the many neglected details in the army none are worse than the repair of essential roads. A slight slough, e.g. makes each rank hesitate as it crosses, and almost stops the column. A working party of 10 men would repair such a place in ½ an hour. A whole corps had preceded, but nothing done! We got mightily cold crawling along this way, but at last got past, and then the General broke into a smart trot and we clattered along the most infernal of pikes, in holes and over rocks till we got to the plank road and turned up, to the left, where we found the holes, if possible worse, among the broken boards. We soon came on a train which had missed the way and we set it right. Then we passed the turn-off to Mine Ford (Culpeper) and, immediately after, came on the head of the 5th Corps, debouching from the woods, on the left and striking the plank road for Germanna Ford, which we reached, crossed by the pontoon bridge, and found our camp pitched at the old spot, at juncture of dirt & plank roads; 2 A.M. of *Dec. 2,* [Wednesday]. Gregg had followed the army, covering both columns. The enemy made no attempt to follow, not even attacking the rear cavalry. In the afternoon we returned to our old camp in the woods, not getting tents pitched till late at night.

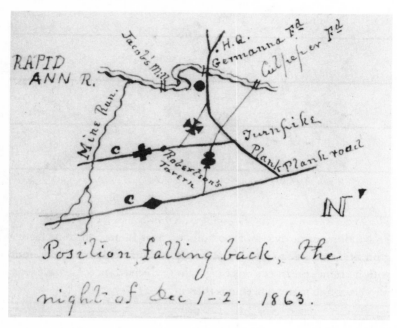

All corps returned to their positions, except the 1st & 5th which exchanged places. Got a good stock of letters from Deary Mimi and from others. Mrs. Paige is dead. The firm of Paige & Co. is dissolved, which throws out Arthur.[122] It has been very mild north, moving trees as late as the last of November, which is unheard of, almost.

December 3, Thursday.

Our British officers who really were an exceptionally good crowd took their departure. Towards evening we had an alarm that the enemy were crossing, which troubled me not a whit, seeing they fought so shy before. It turned out only a reestablishing of their pickets, this side. Sent my Mimette, yesterday, a perfect book of a letter, with a manuscript map.[123]

December 4, Friday.

Weather very fine & bracing; making things comfortable, about camp.

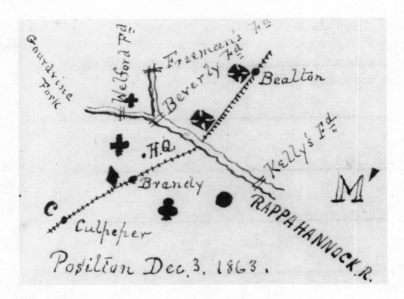

December 5, Saturday.

John M. Botts came over and took dinner, & as Louis had come from Washington, we were able to give him a turkey and other luxuries. Not, indeed, to mention a mince pie from a box of "goodies" which Mimi & Co have sent; cakes & preserves and many fine things therein![124]

December 7, Monday.

Sent Botts yesterday a case of claret, the General adding a turkey. Made myself a board floor from the goody box. To me enter Charlie Adams, who was forlorner than ever, with loss of a saddle, blankets, &c., which fell a prey to Hampton when they cleaned their camp out at Parker's Store. Gave him a treat of cake, claret and cigars and lent him Ellis' great coat, which more than covered him all over.[125]

December 8, Tuesday.

Took a ride to the Cavalry Headquarters, which are in Dr. Greene's large brick house, between here and Beverly Ford. The woodwork is full of bullets from the Beverly Ford fight. Then rode to 1st Mass. Cavalry where found Adams & Flint, also Ben Crowninshield, whom saw for the first time. He looks as beefy as ever, and was in a great rage, because they had declared he had illegally employed a soldier to groom his horse, and so would not give him a cent of two-months' pay due. Gen. Meade's report went to Washington today, in charge of Barstow. The General has been rather sad, of late, but is cheering up now. The report will bring a load on French & Prince and will doubtless make a row in that quarter.[126]

December 9, Wednesday.

By a letter from Mimi see that Ida Agassiz was married on the 6th, Mrs. Dr. Cabot, Mrs. Harriet Gardner &c. have babies. Go it![127]

December 10, Thursday.

Took a ride beyond our outlying pickets with Gen. Humphreys. We went beyond Botts' house and found the picket line near Bennett's house, where they challenged and told us only a written pass from Corps Headq'rs would suffice. To which *should* have been added "from General Headquarters." However, they knew General Humphreys & we passed on. There is much, very much, of detail that is neglected in this army. No offal or dead horses buried. The men usually as raw in manners as if they had never been soldiers. Too much familiarity among officers of different grades, and too much "boyishness," absence of strict accountability as gentlemen. Then the plundering they do, especially cavalry, is not to be excused; buildings are gutted and burned, at once, or piece-meal, without official authority. This would not be if punishment were severe & sure.[128] The men are eminently tractable and reasonable, and can be managed easily. One has only to look at the 6th Corps to see how neatness among officers & men may be made a general thing. One has only to look at the cavalry to see, how, (in most cases) slovenliness and want of order may become the rule. These details, trifling in appearance, assume great importance when added together. When officers buy clothing, not regulation, soldiers do the same, and soon a regiment gets to look mottled; then the men lose pride in their uniform, then in the cleanness of their weapons, & so they go. All this need not be. We cannot ask a European standard; it is not necessary; but these are things practicable. On the other hand there are great features that are admirable. The thorough manliness of the men; their extreme patience; their courage; their intelligence; their real skill in the military work of a campaign; their civilization, as shown in the respect for the Dead, and kindness to women & children; and an absence of anything like ferocity.

December 11, Friday.

A letter from Mimi says that Hal has half accepted a commission in a Negro cavalry regiment, as Colonel! *C'est mauvais!* The Negro cannot change his nature; thus hath God made him. As a rule he cannot fight against the White.

This is leaning on a broken reed. There is no general historical precedent for their being efficient troops.[129]

December 12, Saturday.

Leave has been given to Corps commanders to grant "10 day leaves," and, in some cases, 15-day. Lots do avail thereof. Mitchell, Mason, Ludlow, Sleeper (10th Bat.), Pease, &c. are on the wing.

December 13, Sunday.

Anniversary of Fredericksburg. We were too wise to repeat it, this year, on the 1st. Heavy showers last night; and today almost summer warm, with fine weather & fine mud. Read the report of Chase, Sec. of Treas.; to me a most able document. He points out the great success of the "national currency" and of the "5-20 loan." Our debt, 30th of June last ('63) about $1,100,000,000; estimated for next 30th June ('64) about $1,650,000,000; and 30th June, 1865, $2,200,000,000. Big figures! But our strength, when thus organized, has proved amazing. These figures of course suppose the war to continue at its present proportions.[130] Per contra, have just read Jef. Davis' message to the Rebel Congress—a strikingly good piece of English composition. But not in the New York Tribune have I seen a piece that so plainly assorted the desperate condition of the South! $600,000,000 of paper currency afloat which the people dislike to receive. More severe conscription, without substitutes, called for. Every measure to increase the men in the field. The semi-official Chronicle stated that Gen. Meade would be continued in command of this Army. *Bon!* The General is in much better spirits thereat.

December 14, Monday.

Capt. Bache, to whom have not spoken for two months, came up of his own accord and said he thought he had been rude to me & owed me an *amende*; upon which we were very friendly! Appleton & Geo. Barstow came over from the artillery of the 5th Corps and so rode back with them to the River. Day fine but country sloppy.[131]

December 15, Tuesday.

Went out to take a walk and saw a very fine covey of quails, just by the railroad. Coming back found the whole camp in a commotion with the sudden news that 24 Russian officers were bearing down on us; all from the vessels that are now on our coast. We had but a couple of hours notice, but sent down a lot of ambulances and got them up from the railroad, at same time giving the order to Gen. Sedgwick to turn out his corps. A certain Capt. Bootekaff, or such a name, was chief and a very well looking, intelligent man, with somewhat of a Sclavic face, short nose, round countenance, and eyes rather small & sunken. Most of the rest were quite ordinary, seemingly. There was an appearance of weakness, a want of hardihood, and a sort of half oriental listlessness that gave them a common air. Two or three were palpable Jews. In one or two you could see that uncouth, barbaric air, often attributed to the most educated, even.[132] They were presently put on horses and (except some who went in ambulances) we all rode to near the parade-ground beyond the 6th Corps' headquarters. Here the ambulancers were fired with a desire to mount, so the escort gave them horses & I lent mine to the Captain. But, lo! the troop horses, finding a new load, which held by the pommel & not by the bridle, started at full gallop with three or four of them! Away went caps & all sorts of odd articles; they clinging like sailors reefing a topsail, and pursued by officers & orderlies! Some were caught, one or two tumbled, and some disappeared & never turned up till night. The rest viewed the troops with such ease as they could. Then they were treated to crackers & cheese and to wine, at Gen. Sedgwick's; then to dinner at headquarters, and finally they were bundled on the cars, at 9 P.M. and sent to Alexandria.[133]

December 16, Wednesday.

Woolsey got back a few days since, after a pretty severe course of rheumatism at home. Took a ride to Welford's Ford, on the Hazel River (or "Gourdvine Fork" on the map). This is rather picturesque, resembling the Rapidan at Germanna Mills, running, the same way, between high banks, close to the bank on one side, separated from it on the other by a stretch of flat. We received today the surprising intelligence of Buford's death at Washington, of typhus fever. Our best cavalry officer and a great loss! He was but 38 years old, and entered as a Lieutenant in the 3d regular cavalry.[134]

December 17, Thursday.

A note from Mimi gave me the most sorrowful news that has fallen on me for many, many a day, the death of Perrin Ellis. This man was perhaps my nearest friend in the world, beyond my own family. Nobody can tell why he truly loves a man, or is indifferent to him; it is so, and thus it is. Perrin was a man of many human weaknesses, but of a soul above every sort of meanness. From the first days I knew him, a Freshman in college, our friendship has been unbroken, and growing constantly. Often have I looked forward to the time when he would come back, and we should see each other socially, as of old; but it was not to be; and he is now only one of the pleasant memories of the past. Peace to his soul! He died at Shanghai, September 26th 1863, of dysentery.—[135]

December 18, Friday.

The last two days we have had rain and sleet, and oceans of mud, with a cold, north-east wind; very disagreeable. Meanwhile, though our stay just here is questionable, all hands are making comfortable; some have board floors, and all are furnished with a stove. Then a log sidewalk has been made the length of the camp, and the Chief Quartermaster, like a true officer of his army, has had a log hut made, about as big as a hospital tent, with a brick chimney. Also the horses have bough shelters provided.

December 20, Sunday.

The air was today cold, about ⅓ of an inch of ice made in the buckets of water, standing last night outside. Came there a certain Englander, savoring of Liverpool, one Blackmoor, who was given to me to toot round. Carried to General Sedgwick's the same, thence, with Major Whittier and Lieut. Farrar, we visited the camp of the Vermont Brigade—here Col. Grant showed me round; the hospitals where were very few patients, were in hospital tents, heated by chimneys, which smoke however sometimes.[136] Dr. Letterman approves a "California" fireplace, the fire made *outside*, and the flue conducted under the floor and a chimney built, also outside, at the opposite end. The men were in cots, clean & comfortable. Thence we crossed the pontoon at Welford Ford, and so to the Headquarters of Upton's Brigade 6th Corps at the house of one Major, a fine, brick farm house & many outbuildings, the best that have seen in these parts, as a farm establishment. About it are fine farm lands, and the river runs near at hand. In a great, oak wood the brigade was hutted, in model style. We specially examined the camp of the 5th Maine. This was laid out, according to rule; the huts were of logs, four men to a hut, the roof of shelter tents, at one end the fire-place, at the other two double bunks, like berths, one over the other. The officers were each accommodated, each with a hut.[137] A more hardy or intelligent set of men, it would be hard to find. Then took B[lackmoor] across the country and introduced him to Gen. Pleasonton. And so home. Yesterday rode to J. M. Botts, whom found, and who groaned over his destroyed timber, which is natural, though he is well paid therefor. Also read me much of his speeches, for the brave old cock is vain.

December 21, Monday.

Hoorey! Tomorrow I will start for home, on a leave of say 20 days, for as a Volunteer Aide I can go when I please, but have asked Gen. Meade, who is willing. Ha! Ha!— Got a pass from Gen. Patrick. Packed up and got ready to leave. Gave Albert all directions and arranged with tentmate Rosencrantz.

December 22, Tuesday.

Up before daylight and departed in the mail-waggon at 7.15, having made my bow to Gens. Meade & Humphreys last night. The ancient, polite and cheaty French cook John has retired sick, and is to be succeeded by a wee Gaul, Mercier, at $64.00 a month for self & servant. The morning was cold, ground hard frozen. At 8.15 left Brandy Sta. accommodated in a grain car, with a lot of officers, soldiers, & nig's. Capt. Page and Capt. Mendel were along.[138] We passed over the Great Desert with the usual bumps, delays & jolts, and got at 1.50 to Alexandria, where we ran for the boat, which took us by 2.45 to Washington, passing the Russian Frigates. As the express did not leave till 8.30 there was plenty of time to tittivate, in the way of a comfortable shave, followed by a warm bath and a good dinner, chez Willard, whose hostelrie was crowded with officers, congressmen and shoals of rascals. Took a place in a sleeping-car where found Monty Ritchie, likewise Col. McCallum, who is going with his construction corps to the west, to repair the Chattanooga R.R.[139]

December 23, Wednesday.

Got to the Brooklyn ferry, just in time to take a carriage and race to the New Haven station for the 8 ocl' train. The day was really cold and last night must have been near zero. Gen. Corcoran was killed yesterday by a fall from his horse, know not whether because he had bid too much good bye to "Meagher of the sword" (who came up with us from Rappahannock) or from an unfortunate mishap. He had deserved sympathy for his sufferings in the Southern prisons, but was nothing of an officer. On the cars was Dr. Geo. H. Lyman, who has been to Grant's army and on the Peninsula and has served throughout the War as a Medical Director, and been sick, and worked very hard.[140] How neat & flourishing and civilized did New England look! The fields were silver with ice, frozen on each blade; the trees were loaded also, and looked like glass chandeliers. I have rarely seen so beautiful frosting. Soon the soldiers will be coming home in droves; every man who reenlists gets 35 days, a free passage, and a large bounty. Those who decline and the soldiers who have joined since July 1 are to stay. Any man having less than a year to serve may avail of this privilege as Veteran Volunteer. The train was long & heavy, so we were near 2 hours late in Boston; arriving at about 1.30 P.M. Took a carriage in all haste and drove to Cora's, where was heartily welcomed by all; who had already given me up for that night. And so briskly to Brookline. The front door was open—marched in and there, in the snug library, were dear Mimi & Emily sitting quite innocent; for they did not expect me till tomorrow! Poor little Wife was too glad to speak, and we were indeed joyful & thankful! She looks very well indeed & blooming as blooming can be. Saw little Baby, fast asleep, in her wee crib.[141]

December 24, Thursday.

The Baby has grown a wonder! so large, fat & rosy; she talks a great deal, and makes sentences of four or five words; also stands & walks, with help of a chair. Silas is as usual, and glad to see me. The Baby did know me, quite a marvel! Went & told Mrs. Woods about Albert. Called on old Mrs. Cabot, who is in good health & in better spirits than had expected. Just staid at home this day and enjoyed myself. There is Story's Boy & Panther, some pictures, & various pretty objects which have been disposed in various places, bringing back Rome & our journeyings. In return for the sum we sent (Cora's present) of less than 100 Francescone, Mr. Alexander has sent us a head & a copy of the Sybil of Guercino; the head *said* to be by Sassoferrato; at any rate very good, which is the principal point.[142]

December 25, Friday.

An enjoyable Christmas indeed! One of the biggest dinners at Cora's that ever saw; there were chicks as follows, Fred & Min' Sears, Willie Greene, Mabel Shaw, Frank, Harry & Amee Shaw, Tina Sears, Bob Russell, Parkie; and of elders Quin & Pauline, Aunt Anna, Mr. & Mrs. Russell, Em' & Tint; Hal & Mary; Annie & Alex; Mr. & Mrs. Park Shaw, Annie & two boys; Bob Oliver; Bessie Greene; Nellie Shaw; Aunt Mary, Lou, Howland & Co & ourselves, making a grand total of 35! whereof the children ate down stairs. Poor little Sallie Russell had an influenza & couldn't come. We had a gay time; and then a great excitement, in way of presents; the library had been arranged for the purpose, and its large centre table was not big enough to hold the pile of gifts, which was a perfect mountain to behold, the largest lot that ever saw! Got a pair of camp candlesticks from Annie; life of Prescott from Co; slippers from Mimette, & a scarabeus ring from Mrs. Russell. Stepped across the street & called on Uncle George, where found the family, save Arthur, in melancholy conclave! Sich Christmas gravity![143]

December 26, Saturday.

Dined with the Russells at Mrs. Putnam's. Mimi declares that the dining room is so close as to make her sick! In the evening Mr. Hartman Kuhn called, looking just as of yore. Saw Caspar Crowninshield, Blagden & a host of others in town.[144]

December 27, Sunday.

Took a walk to Hammond's Pond, with Mimi, where the ice is ten inches thick. Stopped a moment at Frank Lee's, to shake hands with him & Madame. The success of the Sanitary Fair is now the great theme—not less than $140,000 made, as they say. On the hill the steady Silas has neatly walled off & partly cleared the furthest 4 acres.

December 28, Monday.

Being in town called on Palfrey, who is as usual, but somewhat more so. Mrs. Revere kindly sent me, as a souvenir, Napoleon's Maxims, which had belonged to her husband, poor Paul.[145]

December 29, Tuesday.

Went to Cambridge, where saw Agassiz (on Sunday night we were there to tea [27th] and saw Ida, Mr. & Mrs. Agassiz, old Burkhardt, also Henry Higginson, the happy bridegroom, who is on a sofa, and seems to mend but slowly.) He [Dr. Agassiz] goes tomorrow to lecture throughout the west. The Museum goes on, and has had good things from Stuttgart, Paris, &c. Anthony has done excellent work in neatly arranging the land shells.[146]

December 30, Wednesday.

Quite a family dinner, part invited, part volunteers, Mr. & Mrs. R[ussell] & Bob, Hal & Mary (she is to be a mamma in March), Burkhardt & Cora, & Howland appeared after dinner. In consequence of new rules Putnam refused to hold on longer at the Museum, and will have a place as Curator at Salem. This morning called on Abbott, at his office to enquire what was in the Classbook about poor Perrin. Everything here brings him back to me, and, many times a day, the thought of him is a drawback to my happiness. Met his father in the street, looking old—very old. Took a quiet dinner with Bill Otis, No. 139 Beacon St., Sam Hammond being the only other guest. Bill has 3 children now, Harrison Gray; William Sigourney & Herbert Foster.[147] Brought out a set of sables for Mimi—very fine—cost $500, whereat she was delighted.

January 1, 1864, Friday.

How are you New Year? I *do* hope I may be spared to the next, and that we may eat our New Year's dinner with Peace about us!—We dined at Mr. Horace Gray's; a most unchanged family in an unchanged house. They all look well, and about as they used, a dozen years ago. The real Boston, painted brick house, with its large, comfortable rooms; none of your 23-foot freestone humbugs! Now it is almost overgrown by the Summer Street stores. There were Mr. & Mrs. [Gray], Misses Bessie & Harriet, & Mr. Horace; with Co & Howland & Mimette & self for company.[148]

January 2, Saturday.

A cold day, with a still colder wind. Started, in a sleigh, to go over to Quincy & visit Mrs. Paul Revere to thank her for a little book, with Paul's name, which she sent me. But, when I got to Milton Hill, lo! bare ground everywhere, and so had to go back, with my trouble for my pains. In town, called on poor Mr. Ellis. His fate has been hard, poor man; he has lost a daughter (long since), his favorite son, his wife, and what, as he said, was "worse than death," his other son (who always seemed a simple, respectable man) has left wife & family & gone off with another woman!— The second Mrs. Ellis was there, of the order of country schoolmistresses. He showed me Perrin's last letter, at the end of which he says he had been two days sick, as the tremulous writing showed. As I left the house I could not speak, it was too many for me. Went to the Advertiser & gave a notice of Perrin, which have written, to be printed next Monday. We dined at the Russells. Sallie is better of her influenza.[149]

January 3, Sunday.

Sunday dinner with Cora. Frank Parkman was in, but had to leave with one of his head attacks. Frankie Shaw looks very poorly; white & thin. Ran down & saw Barstow, just in. There was Gov. Andrew, whom good old Mrs. B[arstow] addressed as "Albion."[150]

January 4, Monday.

In town, looking after various things. Intend to take back a small mess-chest whereof our Headq'rs mess hath not yet boasted; so our crockery always get smashed!— Alex & Annie dined with us; and I made one or two suggestions for the Ophiuran catalogue.[151]

January 5, Tuesday.

A quiet dinner, of Clapp, Browne, Barstow & Maj. Whittier. They came in a snowstorm, that threatened to be big, but gave only some 4 inches. Channing is fatter than ever, a miracle of stoutness is old Phleg! and takes his glass of wine in the same quiet way. The best old Madeira was out for the worthies; it is well to get it while you can![152]

January 6, Wednesday.

Met Arthur in town, who seemed glad to see me, & looked crimped up. Governor opened Legislature today; Cadets drumming round; cannon firing, as of yore. Big dinner after, whereto was bidden, but preferred Brookline, thank you! Went to see old Mr. Tom Dexter, father's chum. He is very old to look on, but seems bright; and was most glad to see me.[153]

January 7, Thursday.

Took a most merry dinner with Cora; James Lawrence came too & was great company. He said Lincoln would be next president, sure; though not his first choice withal.[154]

January 8, Friday.

In town on final errands. Oh dear, tomorrow, back again! Said good bye to Co & H[owland]. We have given a silver tea-urn, as a wedding present to Harry; cost $225. Bedad! Sent a long letter to Charles Eliot, No. 4 Rue des Basins, Paris, with a map that had made for him. Next Monday my Mimi goes to stay at Cora's; with the exception of a short visit to Staten Island, she will remain til about March 1. For Mr. Frank Shaw's she starts next Friday. Spent the day in arranging household matters to my satisfaction and in packing up the things for camp. Mrs. Reed died 3 days since; went the same day and visited poor Eben, who looks broken by hard work & trouble. I do so well remember him, a young man, when he first came to work on the place; and I a littlish chap.[155] Howland came out, for a few minutes, and said adieu. At 7.30 in the eve' bid a very sorrowful farewell to my Sweet, & got in the sleigh for town. Had kissed my little Cora, when she went up to her crib, and who said "Papa—go—War!" My sixteen days have gone as one. Enter sleeping-car—exit Boston. Let us see what has happened of late? Thackeray died in England. Then little Jim Sturgis died in New York, of apoplexy. Hard little fellow, it is to be feared. Pretty much everyone engaged to be married. Ah! There was Stanton Blake, also in sleeping, and, when we got to New York[156] at 7 A.M. *Jan. 10.* [Sunday] he invited me to church; so, after taking breakfast at the Astor, went away up town again, and to church at the Calvary—large & gothic—where was Rev. Cox, so to speak expelled loyalist of Baltimore, who gave us an excellent sermon, though afflicted much with the puff Episcopal. There was John Sturgis, he of poor puns & platonic loves. Went, after, to visit Sue Minturn, 16 West 17th. On the way, stumbled on Miss Mary Bowditch, whom was delighted to see, and she seemed very glad to see me. Sue was at home, much grown, as a woman, these last years, and so gentle, ladylike & full of feeling; much the superior of that family. She was very sad over Bob & does not get over it. Was introduced to Monsieur, who is not one to set the great rivers afire, though an amiable man, and one of a certain education. His brother John, there, was like a talking doll that cannot shut its eyes. Mrs. John was much the better half and rather pretty. An Aunt of middle age made up the party.[157] At 6 P.M., took the Jersey ferry for the Philadelphia train; and very nicely we got to Phil', only there they crammed a horse-car, which the horses couldn't draw, so we got late to the train; and this patriot passed the night over a first-class Irish grog-shop. Good sleighing here & in New York.

January 11, Monday.

Took the 8 A.M. train for Baltimore, where got at 1 & took dinner at Barnum's. Alas, for old Baltimore! When I last staid here it was in the time of peace & union, when poor Lanny was alive. Now big guns command the houses from the hills near by and the streets are full of soldiers. At 3 got off for Washington and found that city crowded as an egg, so that had to double in a room with Capt. Stanhope of the 12th Infantry. He is a Rhode Island man & was some time at school at old Greene's on Jamaica Plain. Met Holyoke, who is big on tobacco now; he living in New York and Eckley (who is engaged to a Miss Thwing) in Boston. He said he thought that John Bancroft had been sweet on Effie Shaw, and that Charlie Lowell had *first* been smashed on Sue, and after, gone in for Effie, when Minturn sailed in. *Peutêtre.*[158]—

January 12, Tuesday.

Went to the station, on Maryland Ave. got my pass stamped & put my valise on board; the soldiers guarding the train and the men searching the luggage reminded one of Europe. The train was full of officers, with glum faces; and a contrast to those coming the other way. A good many women also, as officers' wives are now allowed to come down. Lt. Col. Merriam of the Mass. 16th was on board; also Morrow & Kehoe formerly of Buford's staff. K[eogh] is going West with Stoneman, also Wadsworth. At 2.45 (leaving at 10) we got to within 2 miles of Brandy, where, of course, was an engine off, that delayed us ¾ hour. Round Brandy was a thin stratum of mud, where found an ambulance to take me to Headq'rs. There found all natural and was welcomed by Mitchell, Bates &c. &c. Dined with Meade & Cadwalader, Rosencrantz came in the same train with me. He hasn't the tent floored, of course, because he hath no practical turn, the goodly Swede. Most now have double tents, with floorings, and fire places. In place of the bloodless 93d we now have the 114th Penn. Red-legs (Collis' Zouaves).[159]

January 13, Wednesday.

The position of the corps has changed since went away. Now it is as represented on the diagram, nearly. The horses are well & have grown fatter.

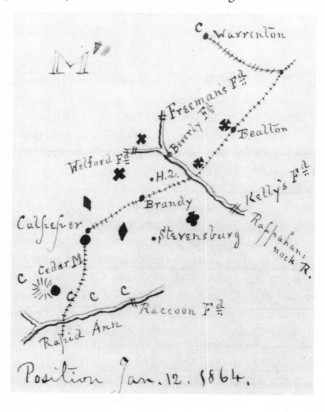

Position Jan. 12. 1864.

January 14, Thursday.

Rode over to Gen. Pleasonton's Headq'rs & paid him my respects. Asked him about an application for a furlough of 70 days to Charlie Adams, to visit his mama in London. It has his approval & has gone up to Gen. Sedgwick; a lucky thing that Gen. Meade is not here.[160] Bestirred myself and got some boards from the Quartermaster and a detail of pioneers from the 114th. Then also a tent, to make a bedroom. This was pitched close behind the first & the two connected by ripping up the back of the front one and looping up the canvas, curtain fashion.

January 15, Friday.

Finished the tent today with a board floor straight through. For myself a board trough on the ground, as a bed; while "Rosy" has his bunk on legs. The fly of the front tent is pulled a little back, so as to cover the joint between the two. A brick hearth, in one corner, makes a base for the stove, and there is a place for a smaller one in the inner tent also. Thus are we quite palatial.

January 16, Saturday.

My big box came today, containing the new mess chest, the wine, cigars &c. *pro bono aliorum.* Also the table, in pieces, was there & straightway put up. Frank Palfrey arrived today, to make a little visit to the army. To meet him came over Macy, now Colonel of his old regiment, and who lost a hand at Gettysburg. Both dined with me, and, afterwards, we had a social gathering of officers at our tent. Gen. Meade was to come this day, but has an extension, by reason of sickness of his son.[161]

January 17, Sunday.

Phil Schuyler, a Capt. now in 14th regulars, was over last night. He has portentous black whiskers and is getting thin on top the pate, the *ci-devant* cockswain of the "Oneida!"[162] Put Frank on my mare, and, getting on black myself, we journeyed to the camp of the Mass. 20th which lies on the left of Stevensburg just across Mountain Run. The hills thereabout, well wooded some months since, are now pretty much bare; nevertheless the *coup d'oeuil* of the camps of the 2d Corps is very pretty. Macy has a good hut, with a big chimney, very comfortable. There did congregate, Holmes, Dr. Hayward, Dr. Perry, Capt. Curtis (Arthur), Bond (Adjutant), Capt. Patten, Major Abbott. Nearly all these young officers, almost boys in look, had been wounded in from one to three places; a sight to be remembered! Abbott has a most extraordinary resemblance to Channing

Clapp when in college, and also speaks and moves like him. After a very good turkey & dumpling rode back again. The country is covered with a sort of thick mush, about 4 inches deep. Palfrey remained with the regiment.[163]

January 18, Monday.

One of the most disagreeable days have seen since have been with the army; a muggy, heavy rain making everything soft & sticky—truly suicidal weather! Not healthy either; it throws the old chills-and-fever fellows on their quinine. To my surprise Palfrey came back this afternoon & passed the night. Felt bilious & poorly. Cuss such a time! The great work of laying down board sidewalks & tinkering canvas doors and board floors continues. It is an unshipshape camp and ill policed, in good sooth.

January 19, Tuesday.

Palfrey insisted on departing by the morning train. There are some commissary changes, of late; Col. Clark as commissary in chief is replaced by Capt. Wilson. Dr. Letterman by Dr. McParlin. Col. Platt, also, intends to try to get out of the Judge Advocate box. Col. Shriver has been ordered west, to be recorder of the court of enquiry on Gens. Crittenden & McCook.[164]

January 20, Wednesday.

Rode out to the picket line of the 6th Corps, beyond the Welford house, perhaps 2 miles. It went to my heart to see the fine oak timber coming down here; whole woods of trees, some of them 2–3 feet in diameter. Wood will be pretty much cut off by spring. Already much country is hard to recognize by reason of the disappearance of groves. The country is dreary with dead horses, butchers' offal and the most stupendous flocks of crows. All unnecessary, even to the birds.

January 21, Thursday.

Gen. Meade has had an attack of inflammation of the lungs, which doubtless will keep him at Philadelphia some time yet.[165] Yesterday Rosencrantz went on a 15-day leave. Told Albert would give him a few days at home; but he said he should want to stay when he *did* go. Pretty sick of it is this once enthusiast for enlistment! Rode with Biddle & Craig, past J. M. Botts nearly to Culpeper, when met [Carswell] McClellan coming back. The night before he had taken over a flag of truce in the night-time (rather hazardous). He was received with courtesy and saw his brother, a Major on the staff of "Jeb" Stuart. They were very uncommunicative; but all asked, "How long do you think this will last?"[166]

January 22, Friday.

Barstow is quite sick & weak, with a cold on the lungs. Gen. Humphreys returned, looking very well, which was quite a relief after my loneliness. His son [H. H. Humphreys], Worth, & self rode down through seas of mud, to meet him. This morning Gen. Sedgwick was over, with Whittier and buzzed a bottle of sherry very gracefully. My small wife is spending her week at Staten Is., says Mrs. Frank Shaw looks a deal older; but is well. Anna's poor little baby has water on the brain, of which they hope to cure it; ma-ma!

January 24, Sunday.

Weather so mild that it seemed like the warmer days of April. Had no fire in my tent, as read a sermon by no less a person than classmate Phillips Brooks, now a clergyman of great renown in Philadelphia.[167]

January 25, Monday.

Little Wife is back again and at No. 1 Joy St. That foot-ball of fortune, Eliot Parkman, was taken prisoner, with a boat's crew, on the coast of N. Carolina. Abby Lyman has lost her second child, of croup; and Charlie Eliot's oldest boy is desperately ill of typhoid.[168] Gen. Getty reported here today, late of Gen. Butler's Department. He is a military looking man, a Major of Artillery, in regular service. He spoke of Gen. Wild (the doctor) commanding blacks. This man seems to have gone insane through fanaticism. When he came back from his expedition he brought 2,000 to 3,000 negroes, mostly women children & old people, for whom there is no proper accommodation or employment—a dead incubus. This man also brought two women, as hostages, one a girl of 15. The rebels hanged one of his blacks, in return for a "guerilla" he had executed, whom they maintained was a regularly enlisted man. Thereupon he was about to *hang these two women*, when stopped by Gen. Barnes. It would appear that they impress negroes secretly. Hard philanthropy![169] A great ball at the 3d Corps tonight. Tents &c were put up at Gen. Carr's Headq'rs which are at a house, beyond Brandy, on the R.R. (same place where the Rebs dropped a shell in our staff.) There were over a hundred ladies & bushels of officers. Did not go but Gen. Humphreys did, and said it was a success. J. M. Botts was there & in full feather with his daughters.

January 26, Tuesday.

George Barstow came up, with whom returned as far as the fort at Rappahannock river; turning to come back, was riding under a ridge, when ping! went a bullet over my head, apparently close to; and then tsiz! another. Put spurs and ran for it, say 300 yds. when pulled up to see the cause; behold four chaps with muskets the other side of the ridge! Rode up to them, in no pleasant humor, and demanded their authority for firing. They "thought they would just fire at a stump!" Took their names and reported them at their regiment, 6th N. Y. artillery. Then continued, a very pleasant ride, up the river, saw Beverly Ford and tried to cross, but found it rather deep. There is a dam & ruined mill-race just above. All along are more or less rebel rifle-pits, dug in the alluvial gray sand; and, opposite the ford, on the first knoll, say 1,000 yards, is an epaulement for a couple of guns. The junction of the Hazel River is not far; and, in the forks are the camps of Upton's brigade. Just in these parts were several large houses, such as Major Welford's, and one or two more which have been swept away to their very foundation stones. Nothing remains to mark them but the gaping cellars, the shrubbery, and some great buttonwood trees that are blackened by the fire. In the long deserted garden of one, a covey of quails was feeding, and playing hide & seek in the dry, matted weeds! Verily these foolish and headstrong people have reaped the whirlwind!

January 27, Wednesday.

Rode to Culpeper & back, having Lieut. Humphreys & his bro' Charles for company. The houses & churches of the town are full of soldiers—few natives seem left. Wallach's house, also that where Pleasonton's headq'rs were and where Graham's headq'rs were, are all razed. Coming over Mountain Run, my mare, to the huge delight of the other riders, lay down with me! A trick she perhaps got from lying down when taken to drink.

January 28, Thursday.

A pack of 13 women & about 30 officers came as a surprise party to see Gen. Humphreys! Gens. Mott and Carr were along. It was, in the female part, Lowell factories gone mad! To my horror, was sent for to help entertain. Was introduced to a Mrs. Morris, a widow, sister of the General M[ott]. She is a brightish, vulgarish, English looking lady. Then we all went to Gen. Sedgwick's, whither was obliged to go in the train of Gen. H[umphreys] who got perfectly coltish! In riding thence to Headq'rs of 3d Corps, the women of course got racing, and one ran away, and Gen. Humphreys in trying to save her from a limb, was swept thereby smack out of the saddle. After which we must needs go to Carr's and finally to Morris', where we got after dark, and then wearily, home, 2 ½ hours late for dinner. *Par bleu!*—[170]

January 29, Friday.

Maj. Biddle appointed Camp Commandant, whereupon the new broom did in good sooth sweep clean, ordering up a detail of 250 men to police camp, cut away stumps, burn the loose brush &c. &c. It was about time; we were a perfect Augean stable. *Par example,* an order has just gone out to bury all dead horses. Phil Schuyler was at pains to count those in the neighborhood of these Headquarters and counted 94! Chiefly battery and cavalry horses.

January 30, Saturday.

Our fine weather closed today and was followed by a cold drizzle. We have had about 9 days of spring, sunny weather, which is a fair share. Rode down to Thom's house (burnt) towards Kelly's Ford where Warren's Headquarters once were. The woods near there looked rather guerillary! There are no troops in that ilk. However the picket line probably keeps them out; but I am fain to say I shrink from the inglorious death or captivity at the hands of these successors of Lutzow.[171]

January 31, Sunday.

Barstow is about well. It would appear that Mary Arnold, with George, has run the blockade, and Bill is going to Cuba, to see her, before departure for Europe. Let her go![172]

February 4, Thursday.

There suddenly appeared Alonzo Langley who used to work for me. He is now a sergeant in K. 4th U.S. Artillery having originally come out as a private in the 1st Mass. Infantry. He wished a recommendation from me as a commissioned officer in a new Mass. battery, which gave him with pleasure. He has acquitted himself with great courage everywhere & has been in all the battles of this army.

February 5, Friday.

They have convicted Ned Jeffries of buying goods under false pretences, but he has not his sentence yet. It is well and should be more frequently thus pushed home to such persons. Gen. Humphreys sent for me and showed me a cipher correspondence between Butler & Halleck and Halleck and Sedgwick. B[utler] telegraphed that large reinforcements had been sent from the Rapid Ann to North Carolina and that he wished a demonstration to "draw their forces from Richmond."[173] S[edgwick] replied that, with the exception of some two or three brigades, nobody had been sent to that place from the army in our front. B[utler] then said he was going to move on Richmond, or something of the sort, and would like a demonstration not later than Saturday (tomorrow). S[edgwick] said it was too short a time to make any great show and that it would spoil our chances for a surprise on their works, in the future. H[alleck] then telegraphed to do at any rate, what we could. So Kilpatrick has been sent to their right via Mine Ford, and Merritt is to threaten Barnett's Ford; and to threaten Raccoon Ford, while the 2d will make a stronger demonstration at Morton's Ford. Old Sedgwick and Gen. Humphreys are cross at the whole thing, looking on it as childish.

February 6, Saturday.

Foggy & warm with some drizzle, from time to time. We up and had an early breakfast, quite as in old campaigning times; but Gen. Humphreys did not go out, because the news could get him more readily at Headquarters. About 10.30 A.M. there were cannon, which continued intermittently and sometimes with considerable rapidity. After thinking that we should not budge at all, Gen. Humphreys finally mounted at 3 P.M. and started for the front with Biddle, McClellan, Rosencrantz, Christiancy, Cadwalader, Mason and self.[174] It is good 10 miles to the ford, and the going was atrocious! Mud, of all depths and all consistencies, with rills, runs & pools to cross. It was about 5, when we got to Gen. Warren's headquarters, and near sunset, therefore. It was the house of Robinson, a large one, standing some 700 or 800 yards from the river; it was on a high bank of cultivated ground, at whose foot was a wide flat. On the other side the land rose, without much flat, nearly from the river's edge, in two or three rolls, to a high ridge. Dr. Morton's house was on the top of the first roll, say 500 or 600 yards from the bank. Opposite his house (nearly) the river divides round a little wooded island, and just here is Morton's Ford. The river is but a narrow affair and runs in a trench, so that it cannot be seen from the high land; it is perhaps 75 feet wide, at the most. The rebel works ran along the crest of the back ridge and formed a sort of amphitheatre, converging its fire in the direction of the ford. Through a glass, at least two lines could very plainly be seen. To the right the river took a considerable southerly bend and the banks became rapidly more steep and high, tending to the outlines at Raccoon Ford. Our skirmishers had boldly advanced, dashed across the ford and captured 28 of a party, who were coming down to relieve the pickets. Then Hays' division had waded and, us with sharp skirmishing, driven back the enemy to their works, and they now lay under the ridge, near Morton's house; while their skirmish

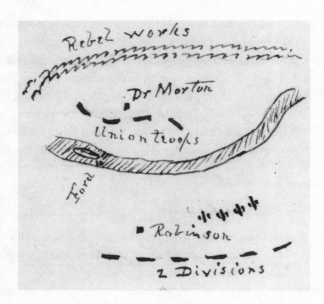

line was close to that of the rebels. Our artillery was on the high ground on this side. Gen. Warren had just crossed to reconnoitre. The 2 remaining divisions were on the edge of the woods, behind Robinson's.[175] Taking Biddle, McClellan, and me, Gen. Humphreys rode down to cross, meeting Gen. Warren on the way, who turned with us. The ford was bad, hard to get in, or out, and about up to the breast of the horses. As we got to a road with a bank, behind the house, we got off and the two generals advanced to look about, and were immediately shot at. We had not been there five minutes when the Rebels opened from a battery on our right throwing spherical case, of which one struck in the infantry, killing a poor man, and another exploded throwing the pieces close to us, and a bullet hit our orderly's scabbard. The generals came back and mounted and rode again towards the river, and shot still coming over. I do confess I dodged them when standing there! a wrong thing. We had got but a little way when a heavy, very heavy, skirmish fire broke out; it was the enemy advancing to retake a fence favorable to us. After halting a moment, we kept on & crossed the river, when Gen. Warren ordered a brigade of Gen. Webb's division to cross in support (a little bridge was now finished). The firing kept on sharp till quite dark, and our cannon opened also. Then the rest of Webb's Div. crossed. Quite a stream of wounded now began to come in, attracted by the fire at the house, wherein a hospital was established. The hit men were most cheerful & brave.

One or two were mortally hit in the head but were happily insensible. On the other side saw a soldier laid out for burial, as sad a sight as could be; his white hands folded across his breast and the cape of his coat folded up over his face. We rode home in the dark, taking over 3 hours and getting in at 11.15 P.M. As we came along the pontoons were going down, with infinite labor. The orders were to withdraw all the troops to this side by the pontoons, which was done by 11, this night, and so finished the "demonstration."

February 7, Sunday.

At 12 the active Humphreys was in the saddle and, with me & Sanders, off for the ford again. We found all the troops safely across and everything quiet. The rebel officers and men were walking about, close to the river edge, and were standing in groups on their works. The officers had coats nearly like our own over-coats. The men were in jackets, gray, blue-gray, or "butternut." They had much the air of our men. There was a better view of them than even at Mine Run. A prisoner there, of the 61st Georgia, had on a jacket of indigo gray, dark, home-spun, trousers and a very good little black felt hat. He was trig & his clothes well mended. Our loss yesterday was a little over 200, of whom only some 15 were killed or mortally hurt. Gen. Humphreys gave orders for the troops to return that eve' to camp, the demonstration being over. We returned by the east side of Stony Mountain and struck the 2d Corps' corduroy road, running several miles to near Brandy.[176]

February 8, Monday.

There came a despatch (unofficial) that Ben Butler's grand move on Richmond was a fiddling thing which was brought to a stand by some trees felled across Bottom Bridge! Gen. Humphreys very mad![177]

February 9, Tuesday.

At 2 P.M. Gen. Humphreys & McClellan went to Washington, for a day. Rode with Sleeper over to Gen. Sedgwick's where we stopped a short while with Whittier. There appeared various women for passes. Among them a wife of one of Mosby's men, who had given himself up, one of the coolest of females (and the most hideous). She enquired for her spouse's horse and equipments, and—was informed they all were stolen from the U.S. Tonight a soldier, an orderly, shot at a negro, directly in camp! A gross outrage, which the Aides seemed to take no trouble about! So childish are they in many things, and loose. But Haycock of the regulars took it up and I also, and blew up the officer of the guard for being away and ordered search to be made for the delinquents.[178]

February 10, Wednesday.

Berlin was here last Friday & Saturday (5th & 6th). The poor chap is at last ordered from the picket line to Washington. We took sundry games of whist. Preferred charges against Geo. Rutherford, Co. I, 1st Md. Cav. for the pistol affair.

February 11, Thursday.

By invitation to dine with Joe Hayes, who now commands 2d Brig. 1st Div. 5th Corps. His Headq'rs are about ½ mile from Rappahannock Station, on the east side of the R.R. Around is a neat hedge of evergreen and the Colonel's reception hut is elegantly papered and the ceiling adorned with the American flag. The arch of the fireplace is made ingeniously from half the cog-wheel of a mill, once standing by the river. Here assembled Mrs. Sykes and the General, Mr. & Mrs. Lieut. Snyder, Dr. Moldan, Dr. & Mrs. Holbrook, Lieut. Appleton, two nephews of Joe, Col. & Mrs. Gwynn, Capt. Judson, Gen. Bartlett, Capt. Tucker and some half-a-dozen more ladies and a dozen more officers. The dinner was laid in two hospital tents, joined, and decorated with flags, greens and bayonet-chandeliers. For dinner had we oyster soup, fish, boiled mutton, roast beef & pig, roast turkey, pies, and dessert. It went very well and we had a band to play outside. Afterwards the tables taken out and a promenade, even with a little polka, in which the genial Sykes (who thawed amazingly) joined. We had songs, whereof sang two comic with great success. Mrs. Gen. S[ykes] is quite a ladylike person and well to look on. Mrs. Snyder also is a pleasant little woman, and both in silk dresses withal. Among the guests was one Ball, a Capt. & Commissary of subsistence. In him recognized a curly headed chap, who, in college days, was ever to be seen at the theatres and was a petty playwright! Ha, ha, how people do turn up. But he is bald now and fatty, and has naught left save his stage accent. Spent the night here.[179]

February 12, Friday.

After a late breakfast hied me home. Hayes has his notch, though not good at his college lessons, he is a most capital officer, so much so that he has a reputation through the corps. Capt. John Fassitt called tonight, quite sprung, as is with him common. Recognized in him, at last, a man of [Harvard] class of '57, noted even then as a hard nut. He now is a tremendous rum barrel, though a good humored fellow; and is on Birney's staff. It was about him that Lane made the joke, when it was objected that F[assitt] in his preparatory examination had been prompted—"Qui fassitt per alium fassitt per se."— Gen. Hunt is back, Bissell also.[180]— Hayes told me he collected the picket line at Robertson's Tavern, and that, in a line of 4 miles, the whole reported within 10 minutes! which is remarkable.

February 14, Sunday.

The General [Meade] was in Washington today, and we expected him by the mail train, but notice came that he would be delayed till tomorrow, so took a ride on the east side of the railroad towards Culpeper. Here are considerable woods, still standing, where observed a good many woodpeckers, among others a great one, black & white, which never saw before (Picius pileatus?), very shy. We have a variety of birds, now for some time past, owing (for some species) to the warm weather. The three most plenty are crows (in vast numbers), meadow larks, and quails; to which may be added hawks (two species of Falco, and two or three of Accipiter & Buteo), owls (barn & screech); a few turkey buzzards; woodpeckers, some 4 or 5 species; red birds; blue birds; nuthatches; snow birds; titmice; sparrows or buntings, one or two species; doves; & one species of wren; also Charadrius vociferus (!) and an officer said he had seen snipe. It is extraordinary how the country has dried up, a week ago the riding was almost unridable, when we went down to Morton's Ford; and now there is good going everywhere & in some places even dust.[181]

February 15, Monday.

A change for the colder and snow, which by evening, whitened the ground, though most melted. Gen. Humphreys has been in the habit of talking much, after breakfast & dinner; often on Europe and light topics, but also on military affairs and the war. Like most old soldiers he is jealous of his reputation and is now particularly indignant that Gen. Barnard of the Engineers, claims to have arranged the army, previous to the battle of Malvern [Hill]. He says McClellan was completely exhausted by two nights without sleep and of intense labor, & told him to go up and place the troops, which he did, and issued all the orders; that he there met Barnard, who had similar orders, but who did nothing. He, on the whole, stands by McClellan, and says he was the best Chief the Army ever had, but wanting in elan and over cautious. Gen. Meade came today. Went to receive him in full tog. He looks much better than had expected, though pale. Shook hands very kindly. With him were Mitchell, Biddle, George M. Bache & Cadwalader.[182] We had the band out for him, who played appropriately & the guard turned out. He was much pleased with his reception in Philadelphia;

his "levee" at a public hall was crowded & jammed. At Washington, Stanton [told] him if a success were not achieved in the spring, our finances would break down; by which he thought S[tanton] meant the prestige of the Republican administration would break down! But, *ma foi!* gold is going steadily up. It is said that they fear the nomination of Grant on an anti-slavery platform; then Chase, Stanton, Banks, Fremont, are all making a point at the White House, & McClellan will probably be put up also. Nevertheless it happens, after all, that the contest is narrowed to one or two prominent men. Gen. Williams & Woolsey went on leave.[183]

February 16, Tuesday.

Poor Abby Lyman has lost her eldest daughter, a very bright good child, according to everyone. George Lyman, celebrated his return, after three years' absence, by coming to Boston on a spree and getting a fit of delirium tremens! Really he is a disgrace to everybody and deserves nothing better than the House of Correction. A heavy wind sprung up today, which soon became a small gale and grew colder and colder, so that it was really bitter by night. Miss Molly Felton engaged to a Mr. ———, a long lovesick swain.[184]

February 17, Wednesday.

Ice on the water bucket, high wind and thermometer at 12°. Letters from Bob Winthrop and from Charlie Thorndike, the latter in Paris. They touched chiefly on the death of poor Perrin.[185] Wrote a number of letters yesterday for the General. To add to the mishap of cold weather the tent of McClellan & Humphreys burnt down—caught from a spark. H[umphreys] returned today from a leave, and was encountered by this dismal spectacle!

February 18, Thursday.

Last night the coldest that have seen in the army; mercury at 6° this morning. (In the night it fell to 0°). We have an Assistant Medical Director here, Dr. Gieselin a very quiet intelligent man.[186] Gens. M[eade] & H[umphreys] had quite a dialogue today on the campaign of the Peninsula. They agreed that McClellan was too slow, making needless lines of works on the Chickahominy, advancing too slowly &c, while the rebels were gathering men each day; but they also agreed that the fatal thing was the most injudicious meddling of the President, when he detached McDowell, with whose help Richmond might doubtless have been captured. They consider the fight at Gain[e]s Mill unnecessary, the enemy being two to one, and no battle desirable on that side of the river. They estimated the rebel army then at 170,000 and ours at 110,000. Gen. Meade is severe, but manly, in his military criticisms; so also is Gen. Humphreys, who has a rather jealous disposition. This I have noticed among most old army officers.[187]

February 19, Friday.

The General ran up to Washington for a day or two, advice perhaps. They are going to put up a chapel tent. Waud having caught a crow, we dressed him up with a white band and put him secretly in Biddle's tent, with a note tied to his wing, saying that Mr. James Crow respectfully applied for the situation as sexton in the new chapel. Which all created great mirth among the idle officers.[188]

February 20, Saturday.

The weather moderated greatly during the day, though there was ice last night, making the fourth successive night that water has frozen in my tent. At the Provost Marshal's saw an examination of the article found on Mosby's men. The small things of value taken from each were put in an envelope marked with their name. U.S. money & other property will be retuned to them, but the Confederate paper money is confiscated, & used for secret service; also postage stamps & their gray paper envelopes. The examination was most amusing. There were almost always rebel bills, one sergeant having $450; another had $7.40 in U.S. silver he had hoarded. Each had a certificate that he belonged to "Mosby's battalion." Many had copies of verses, with a good deal of bad spelling, the poetry sometimes tolerable, often laughable. It was patriotic for the most part and is doubtless earnest stuff to them, for they fight well on it! Only one or two seemed to have testaments, & one man, besides the testament, had a religious paper and a couple of tracts.— Having seen, near the Scouts Camp, hard by, a bunch of quails, got Waud to come out with his gun; he could not fire, but told me to do so; and so fired four shots & got three birds on the wing, to the great advancement of my reputation! Spent the eve at Phil Schuyler's, where was Captain Lyttle of the Provost Marshal Department, also an Irish Captain Coppinger, who, however seemed more of Bull style with long whiskers & part in the middle of his head. He now is in the 14th Reg. Inf. Formerly in the Irish Legion & taken prisoner by the Piedmontese at La Boca not far from Foligno. Think that remember the place, which is mentioned by Murray in connection with the luckless Pats.[189]

February 21, Sunday.

Dr. Rockwell gave us a very good sermon & service, *sub Jove*. It was at Gen. Patrick's. Afterwards rode towards Culpeper with Biddle & Cadwalader, and made some study of the rebel line, flanked by epaulements for guns, which they made the night of Nov. 7th.[190] Gen. Humphreys sent for me to show me a note of a singular kind from Gen. French. H[umphreys] had sent a printed circular from himself to all the Generals, asking their autographs, which were to be forwarded to a Sanitary Fair. To which Gen. French replied, that he "had the impression" that Gen. H[umphreys] had some remote connection with the attempt to "ruin" his reputation, & so must decline &c. Gen. Humphreys was divided between wrath & amusement, and sent an answer in which he said that being ignorant of any such attempt he could not be mixed up with it; and did not see how "impressions" could warrant such a reply to a printed circular &c. &c.[191] Gen. Meade came back with Biddle [possibly Riddle] et al., among others Capt. Mickler. The General said, on authority of Mr. Kennedy, that Negroes in the north died faster than they were born, while in the South they (when free) increased only about 1 pr. ct. in 10 years, but the slaves increased beyond all other classes.[192] Introduced to Mrs. Capt. Coxe, quite a good looking woman. *From the pocket of one of Mosby's men:* "To tell the age of a young horse from an old one. —Jan. the 3, 1864 By W. S. Nuckols, Louisa Co[unty] Va. The eyes of a young horse appear plump, full and lively, the lids with few rinkles; the hollows above the ball small, and no gray hairs upon the brow unless they proceede from the color or mark of the horse. The eye of an old horse appears sleepy dim and sunk and the lids loose and verry much shriveled, with large hollows, and the brow gray. At six years old the grooves and hollows in a horse-mouth begin to fill up a little, and their tuskes have their full growth, with their points sharp and a little concave, or hollow on the insides. At 7 the grooves & hollows will be pretty well filled below, except the corner teeth, leaving where the dark brown hollows formerly were little brown spots. At 8 the whole of the hollows & grooves are filled up, and you see the appearance of what is termed smooth below. At 9 there verry often appears a small bill on the outside corner teeth; the point of the tusk is worn off, and the part that was concave begins to fill up and become rounding. The squares of the middle teeth begin to disappear and the gums leave them small & narrow at top." —

February 22, Monday.

Washington's birth-day, celebrated by a great ball at the 2d Corps. Both Generals Meade & Humphreys went and did not get back till 3 or 4 in the morning. There was a ball room, 90 feet long, and the lighting and decorations were said to be in excellent taste. Vice President Hamlin, with his daughter, were there, Judge & Mrs. Miller, Gov. & Mrs. Sprague &c. &c. The Staff and many other officers were very mad because they were not invited; and it is true that the best taste was not shown in the manner of invitation. There came down Col. Dickinson, a regular *roué*, and he & Rosencrantz went drinking about the country, from which it resulted that Rosy, by night, got completely full, and unfortunately his horse fell with him, and he gave his face an awful smashing which will lay him up for some days.[193]

February 23, Tuesday.

Despite the fatigues of last night the tough old General started out at 11 to review the 2d Corps, away beyond Stevensburg. The whole staff & escort went, besides Gen. Pleasonton & his crowd. So it was quite like old times. Went first to their Headquarters and picked up two ladies on horseback, cutting a harum-scarum figure. The troops were on a great flat, beyond the houses; rather a rough ground. Gov. Sprague was the chief gun there, a small man, with bright black eyes, and a pleased expression, save that it was rather too sharp. Hamlin also there, a most ordinary looking person. Sundry ladies accompanied us down the lines, among them Mrs. Morris. Certainly thought they would break their necks among the ditches & holes! There was Kilpatrick's Div. of cavalry & the corps, besides the artillery of both arms. Kilpatrick is certainly an odd looking specimen. His colorless eye, big nose, and narrow forehead, with an indescribable air between a vulgarian & a crack-brain, combine to render him almost laughable. He is pushing & managing in the extreme, but I don't believe he is worth a fig as a general. The cavalry looked Gipsy as usual, horses in very fair condition. The infantry were unequal, some (as the Mass. 20th) excellent, others marching & looking indifferently. Then we had a cavalry charge of 500 men, which seemed to me mobby, though doubtless they are good dragoon skirmishers. Day really warm, & withal beautiful. Saw "Sprig Carroll" who commands a brigade, and is noted as a great fighter. He is a raw-boned, Scotch looking man, with great, tawny moustache & whiskers.[194] And so home, after a collation at "Kill-Cavalry's," where the Aides were allowed to knock their heels on the porch outside! The General [Meade] none the worse for his fatigue.

February 24, Wednesday.

Saw Phil Schuyler's father today. He told me he bought in 1861 equipment & camp equipage complete (except arms) for 10,000 men, in France; the whole finished in 4 weeks, & making three steamer cargoes. Also he bought over 100,000 rifles, viz: 30,000 at Dresden, and 70,000 at Vienna; the latter he got through the *finance* minister, by offering him a good profit.[195]— My little miss Cora is really cunning; the other evening she laughed & entirely refused to kiss Mamma; so Mamma went down stairs, but presently a little penitent voice was heard "Me torry, me want to tiss Mamma."

February 25, Thursday.

Went out and fired at some quail, with Waud, and missed them, forsooth. Paine of engineers said that in two months, he had gone in and out of the picket lines, and his assistants too, in civil & military dress, and had been stopped but *once*!!![196] I have long thought our picket line was no picket line at all; and there are many army details just as bad! Gen. Meade said there was evidence to show that scarcity of food was growing most alarming, in the south; the flour mills stopped in Richmond for lack of grain; 300 barrels out of 900 seized in Petersburg by the rebel government &c. &c. Am sorry to see the Danes have been defeated, near Flensborg, apparently in a series of engagements, and have retreated with loss to the island of Alsen.[197]

February 27, Saturday.

There was a congregation of high mandarins today, Sedgwick, Warren, Newton, Merritt, Kilpatrick, Chapman &c. For an expedition is plainly on foot. Gen. Humphreys has been writing these last days and enveloped in mystery, and there has been the usual amount of gossip in circulation. At daylight this morn' the 6th Corps moved through Culpeper and Capt. Dalton told me their headquarters that night would be at James City.[198]

February 28, Sunday.

We had the first service in our new Chapel, Dr. Dorr of Philadelphia giving the sermon. He is a very pleasant, modest old gentleman, and a good preacher. He dined with us after; as did Mr. Schuyler yesterday. Birney's Division, 3d Corps, moved out to support Gen. Sedgwick, at Madison Court House.

February 29, Monday.

Bang! The whole plot came out today. Last night Kilpatrick, at the head of 4,000 to 5,000 cavalry, with 8 guns, crossed the Rapid Ann, on our left, at Ely's Ford, and captured 13 men & two officers on picket. Klein, a scout guide, came in today and reported him, at 2 in the morning, past Spotsylvania C. H. making direct for Richmond! At Spotsylvania Col. Dahlgren (who is scarcely well of the loss of his leg) will diverge with 1,000 men, cross the James, at Goochland, and swing round to enter the city from the south side; while Kill-cavalry keeps on straight and enters from the north. Means have been taken to cut the telegraph & railroad from Orange Court House. The idea is to dash into the city (which is supposed to be feebly defended by home guards and a few regulars), liberate the prisoners, grab all the M.C.'s possible and then make the best of their way to the nearest, and safest, part of our lines.[199] I venture beforehand to prophesy that it will fail, for the following reasons: 1st, I believe that Kilpatrick is an incompetent officer for such a thing; he is a great talker & manager, but has no head or skill, so far as proved; as to his dash & physical courage, *peutêtre*. 2d, Geographical difficulties, & rivers, and roads bad or hard to find. 3d, Military difficulties; the home-guards must be poor indeed if, behind some breastwork or stone wall, they fail to drive off our cavalry. Other reasons could be brought forward, but *nous verrons*.[200] Custer left early this morning to make a diversion on the right & cut the rail, if possible, at Charlottesville. Christiancy went with. Behold Leap-year's day, when the lassies should make love to the laddies; whereof there is small chance down here. The wind having shifted to N.E. a light rain fell tonight, but only about ½ inch in all.

March 1, Tuesday.

There began a cold rain, towards noon, which grew quite heavy and, towards evening changed first to hail, then to snow, and then, at midnight lo, it was bright star light! Custer came back in the night; could not get to Charlottesville to cut the road, because of many troops there, but went in sight of it. Surprised & burnt a camp with 7 caissons, got 400 or 500 horses, and destroyed 3 flour mills with grain, and took a few prisoners. Had some skirmishing but lost nobody.

March 2, Wednesday.

Very fine day. Saw in the paper, a day or two since, that my "substitute" James Miles, whom sent, while in Europe, with the 2nd Mass. Cavalry, was killed the other day in that disgraceful affair with Mosby; *requiescat in pace!* He fell to cover the fault of others, like a good soldier. It is strange that, of four men who have gone from my place, three have been killed in action, Barrel, Fernal and Miles.[201]

March 3, Thursday.

Gen. Grant gazetted as Lieutenant General in the regular army.[202]

March 4, Friday.

Scouts that came in last night report that they cut the wire from Lee's army on Sunday night at 11. That the next day Dahlgren came in to Frederickshall, destroyed the rail &c and passed within 500 yards of the Rebel Reserve Artillery without destroying it, or discovering it (!). That he saw large fires towards Hanover Junction &c. Later there came a telegraph from Kilpatrick at Williamsburg (!) saying he had failed in the Grand Object of the expedition, but had driven the enemy through their fortifications to the suburbs; destroyed railroads, mills &c; and *lost*—less than 150 men!! Confound the vaporing braggart! He *proposed* and got up the expedition, & insisted on it with the President; told Pleasonton he would succeed or die; and now runs down to Butler's lines with a loss of 4 men in each 100! After letting those wretched prisoners hear the hopeful sound of his guns. He should be relieved from his command and degraded to his favorite company—newspaper reporters![203]

March 5, Saturday.

Rode down to visit Joe Hayes, whom found at his quarters. Who should appear at Headquarters but Ned Dalton. He is ordered to report here as Acting Medical Inspector. Looks thin but well, with a great pair of red whiskers & a moustache.[204]

March 6, Sunday.

General Meade returned; also Berlin whose patron, Gen. Berry, is relieved, & so B[erlin] comes back to stay, if possible on Gen. Hunt's staff.[205] Gen. Meade has been for a day or two at Washington to conclude the consultation on the consolidation of the corps. There he found a cabal against him, headed by Sickles, who had testified before the Committee on the Conduct of the War that Meade had sent him an "order to retreat," before the battle of Gettysburg!—a shameless perversion of fact, founded on an order, to all corps commanders, cautioning them to be on the look-out, and stating that the concentration for action *might* have to be to the rear, along Pipe-clay Creek. A few hours later (the information of the enemy's position having come in) orders were issued to march in all haste on Gettysburg. The principle of Meade's tactics was, so to direct his march, as to make Lee let go the Susquehanna, and concentrate to give him battle. The General appeared before the Committee and gave a complete sketch of his manoeuvers since having supreme command.[206] Services today by a Vermont clergyman.

March 7, Monday.

They have discovered, in the Provost Marshal's prison a gang of 14 prisoners, regularly organized to garotte and plunder each new comer. These desperate rascals today appeared made fast to a long chain, and doing police work under charge of two sentries. We have news that Dahlgren, in an attempt to cut his way through, was killed, and some 50 of his men captured. The Richmond papers state that on his body were found addresses to his troops exhorting them to fire Richmond, to kill Davis & his cabinet &c. &c. all very improper and un-authorized; but we know not how authentic. Then, what is most tragic if true. He is said to have hanged, on suspicion of treachery, a certain negro, furnished as a guide from these Headquarters. This man was a faithful creature who had protected and nursed for 9 days, one of our officers escaped from Libbey, (and who was sick) and afterwards brought him safe through our lines passing in the midst of the whole Rebel army.— Dahlgren was a boyish looking young man, of middle height, thin, and with light hair, moustache and imperial. He had lost one leg at Gettysburg.[207] Gen. Meade having given me leave, prepared to go home tomorrow—*Gloria!*

March 8, Tuesday.

After breakfast, took the 9.45 train for Washington. Found there Lt. Col. Kingsbury en route for the same. Rain, quite hard. There is a truss bridge for the R.R. now over the Rappahannock; also a new pier bridge (parallel to the long bridge, over the Potomac) nearly done. Got at about 2.30 to the station, whence to Willard's for a warm bath, shave and dinner. While taking dinner, Gen. Grant came in, with his little boy; and was immediately bored by being cheered, and then shaken by the hand by the οἱ πολλοί! He is rather under middle height, of a spare, strong build; light brown hair, and short light brown beard. His eyes of a clear blue; forehead high; nose aquiline; jaw squarely set, but not sensual. His face has three expressions; deep thought; extreme deter-mination; and great simplicity and calmness. "Biggy" Lawrence was there, deaf and clammy, as usual.[208] Took the 7.30 P.M. train for N. York. No sleeping car, great crowd, and the night made hideous by re-enlisting soldiers, who, like Jack ashore, were rather too full of whisky. The most, to do them justice, were quite respectable & sober; but it is indeed shameful to hear them swear—a mere trick and in good part the fault of their officers.

March 9, Wednesday.

Colder & clear. Got to N.Y. at 8 A.M. where, after breakfast at the Astor, went to Trinity building and saw Uncle Frank. He looks old; but, *au reste*, well. And so by the "Shore line" at 12, to Boston; an inferior route, by reason of two ferries, one at Connecticut river and one at New London, albeit the sea shore &c makes the road pleasant. Met Mr. Canterbury, who has got gray since the year '56, when he & I & Clapp the editor made a merry pilgrimage to the Montreal railroad celebration. There too was Dick Fay, at N. London, who told me C. Hammond had bought there a house; a pretty spot, with its deep, river harbor and its fort.[209] Got to Boston at 9 P.M. a proper moment to end this volume, and to start a fresh one.

Finis

March 9–
May 3, 1864

Growl you may. Go you must.

Private Notebook, Brookline, March 9, 1864
Note: In case of my death I ask that this book may be sent
unread to my wife.

March 9, 1864, Wednesday.

Well, there were the drawing-room windows at Howland's all lighted—a festivity, apparently. My appearance at the door was the signal for shouts from the children of "Uncle Theodore! Uncle Theodore!"—and, looking up, there was my Mimi in a best dress, looking over the stairs! For was it not Baby's birthday, and was there not a family party in honor thereof! Annie, Alex, Uncle Park and Aunt Hannah, Mr. Burkhardt, the Russells, all (save Emmie) &c. &c. Two years ago, about this hour, I sat in anxiety with Dr. Wilson, in Firenze la bella, and little Cora had not yet drawn her first breath. Time does go like a mill-race!— Why can't I stay at home and end my days in peace and in their due time? But there is no peace yet for those who would do what they ought. All of which did not prevent great festivity and joyfulness. Poor little wife was really content enough! There is a great piece of family news. Hal hath a son!—born yesterday and to be called James Savage, after poor Jim who fell at Cedar Mountain.[1]

March 10, Thursday.[2]

Drove with Wifekin to Brookline, whither we move next Monday. All looked natural and right. Spoke to Mrs. Woods of Albert and told her would like to have him stay and would raise his wages to $20.00. That eve called on Uncle Charles who looks remarkably well, as does Florence. Fred has whiskers whose longitude is a marvel, and presents rather an excess of *mauvaise graisse*. Old Snelling was there, the same good, simple man.[3]

March 11, Friday.

Running about town on odd errands. Went to see Aunt Eliot at Lizzie's. Kate is going next Wednesday to join Charles in Paris, bravo![4] My little Cora is now a great walker and talks at a great rate, though in a tongue of foreign sound!

March 12, Saturday.

We had one Saturday dinner at Putnam's where appeared Father Hal. Mr. Russell is rather pulled down by colds and a touch of gout. Called with Mimette on Aunt Pratt, now 98. She looks upright and well, though thinner than ever. Her hands are but skin with the purple veins. Went to see Fannie Foote, hoping to find Kate also; but she was at Cambridge. In good sooth, Foote is not a Narcissus: Why don't some one shave him?[5]

March 13, Sunday.

To the Stone Chapel to hear cousin Foote who performs the services well & without affectation. Had hoped to see there Kate, but she remained in Cambridge. There is a sudden current report that Meade will be superseded by "Baldy" Smith, who has been recommended for Maj. Gen. Can't believe it, yet it is possible, if Grant has taken that notion.[6] Went to see Arthur. Ella looks remarkably well; her little girl a fine child, but not to me pretty. Went to see Chas. Codman, also. Called on Mrs. Barstow and told her the Major would try to come on another leave. In the eve came Ned Browne to see me; also Richard Codman Deputy Marshal P[orcellian] C[lub] to consult about the increase of expenses in that ancient establishment.[7]

March 14, Monday.

Saw all three Howes, among whom Jim was the most gratifying specimen. He looks well, has given over drinking, and is at last married to his old love Miss Slater: bravo!— Took a genteel cocktail with Billy in the Somerset Club, where we were joined by Jack Anderson, Charlie Appleton, Ives Bates, &c. John Bates has taken most strangely to soaking whisky and gets boosy night after night. Walked into the Union Club; nobody there, it being early; it is Mr. Abbott Lawrence's old house, fitted up in good taste and in the ordinary way of Clubs. Saw Col. Macy in the street; also Capt. Dalton.[8] Drinking those cocktails this morning reminded me of old days, when we college boys used to gather of Saturdays, in the Albion and take sometimes too many of them. I never had what is known as a "thirst" for strong drink (a rare disease I fancy), but liked the taste of some wines, and drank always for the effect on my spirits. Brandy or any strong liquor, seems, for a short time, to raise the whole of my powers several degrees, and makes me more quick & decided. Strong tea and coffee have a similar effect, but influence chiefly the thinking powers, and have no disagreeable reaction. Tobacco I never tried to adopt, and would simply make me sick if I used it. The curious thing is, that one man, under artificial excitement of this sort, is in the *normal* condition of some other man, whose natural temperament is more excitable. For instance, if I undertake the amount of work and "drive" that some men do *from choice,* I become depressed and tired; still another may become even more tired and depressed, but his mind still drives him on, leaving him no peace. Such are the varied combinations of mind with physical structure, overbalanced sometimes on one side, sometimes on the other; or, again, nicely adjusted. Concerning the existence of mind and the nature of matter, it seems to me impossible to speculate with hope of any clear result. Our beliefs on this topic are natural, and rise from actual intercourse with persons of fine intellect; or rather are made clear by such intercourse. When we see these vast subjects opening out before us into the infinite, it inclines us to take the view of Hamilton that intellectual studies were in the nature of gymnastics, to develop & keep lively the mind, but ended in no solution of the great problems. At any rate, the vegetation of the intellect, or its employment on one small matter, to the exclusion of all others, is a sad affair. (A discourse on the theme "cocktail." N.B. Mostly foolish—don't know what I wrote it for.)[9]

March 15, Tuesday.
A very agreeable dinner at Jim Lawrence's. There were Dr. Mack; Tom Motley; Mr. Geo. Dexter; Mr. Frothingham; Gen. Barlow; Howland; "Jake" Rogers; and Mr. Winthrop Sargent. It was odd to see Frank in his General's shoulder straps, the same old penny. Really nothing could be handsomer than this dinner with fine silver, flowers, and rare wines. Alas! poor Jim would give them all for the health of one of his own servants. Mimi stayed meanwhile at Cora's, where she dined, and I drove her out thereafter. So natural as it seems thus to be at home; and I must go back, in a few days, to witness perhaps one of the bloodiest campaigns, and to share its dangers. Old Tim Lewis is the greatest of philosophers—"Don't borrer no trouble!"[10]

March 16, Wednesday.
To Cambridge, where an examination satisfied me that the Porc Club was carried on too extravagantly. Shall thereon take measures. Saw Ida and her Henry.— Jim Higginson is at last exchanged—good! Alex's boy is grown much

prettier and looks like the Agassiz side. They have elected me a Trustee of the Museum; may your honor live till you sit on the board![11]

March 17, Thursday.

Went, with my Mimette, to see Hal's camp at Readville. The Colonel has a quarters like a tool-house, of which he has not even stopped the cracks—a rather excessive Lacedemonianism.— The troops are in sheds, 1 company to each. His negroes now number over 700 and look very well. They are of all colors from coal black, to palest white. May they do well—but to me they do seem *trop doux.* It was somewhat sad for me to see Harry there in Bob's old room. There are 3 regiments of infantry and 2 of cavalry here camped. To dine came Alex, Annie and Burkhardt, and Frank Lee came in the evening with Madame. Bickmore is collecting Money for a continued expedition to the Spice Islands &c.[12]

March 18, Friday.

Grant issues an order that he will have his headq'rs as General-in-Chief in the field; for the present with Army of Potomac, for which he starts tomorrow from Nashville. We shall see how this affects Meade. Was in town all the morning on small purchases, and opened my eyes not a little at the stupendous prices. Firkin butter 48 cents pr. lb; champagne $30. pr. doz. &c. &c. Poor Mimie had an old fashioned sick headache, whereby we were deprived of seeing the theatricals at Chickerings, for the East Tennesseeans; wherein Em' is said to shine wondrously. Too bad![13]—

March 19, Saturday.

Dined with Pa Russell and family. The Putnam boarding house smells, as Mimi declares, of castor oil! Boarding houses are humbugs.

March 20, Sunday.

Mimi & I took a long Sunday walk away up by Clyde St. and round by Newton Baptist Seminary. Though the land is still gray and the ice even to be seen in shady pools the views were most beautiful and very much removed from poor Virginia. Horace Gray took dinner with us; a bright man who is always pleasant to see.[14]

March 21, Monday.

Having determined to see a half dozen of friends at dinner, today they came. Bill Otis, Bob Winthrop, Jack Adams, Ned Browne, & Frank Palfrey. Moreover, Miss Emmie graced the table, to bear up Madame L. We had flowers,

& Poisson the French cook, who don't pay & costs most infernally! Still the dinner was excellent, viz—Julienne soup; Sandwich trout; Boned turkey; filet sauté; Jaté de cailles; dande trouffeé; omelette souffleé &c. &c. To give an idea of the extravagance and high prices of today, Poisson's bill was $67.00—then 3 bottles of claret $10.50—and these, with other wines, and flowers &c. &c. will run this dinner of 8 persons to about $100.—! It is well to have of the best on rare occasions, when friends come. As to Bill Otis, he pleaseth me not; a bluntness of perception & coarse levity that were amusing and excusable in a very young man, have not worn off in a father of a family. It was this defect that led him to speak of Perrin, in a way that was intended for kind but really entirely misplaced. I now begin to notice many of these men who do not ripen with age, but maintain the raw greenness that once was fitting, but which must in time end in a sort of atrophy.— Old Ned Browne! He is reckoned a bore among the ladies, because of his awkward Chesterfield style; but he is a good crony, is Ned.[15]

March 22, Tuesday.

Accompanied Mimette & Em' part way to Uncle Quin's. On the way visited Billy Greene. His house (Mrs. Sam Eliot's) is a very snug one and fitted in good taste. Brother G. was full of his usual suspicious, half-cracked vanity. He has the offer of a regiment of repentant rebels in Butler's department, and thinks of going. There was Willie, grown a great boy; and Bessie a very good dispositioned girl, apparently. Then to Quin's new place, which overlooks Jamaica Pond and is really an excellent situation. His house, too, is apparently a success, with good pictures hung round. Saw the baby, Pauline and Master Louis. There also were Prof. & Mrs. Agassiz, back from their 3-month lecturing tour. He greeted me warmly and asked advice on Museum Assistants. Advised him to employ paid experts and not students who made more trouble & did not a tithe of the work. Dined with Cora. Howland has bought Gus Lowell's place at Beverly, and his soul has rest.[16]

March 23, Wednesday.

Brother Deputy R. Codman having represented that P.C. bills were getting too heavy, had called a meeting of consultation and so drove over, taking Mimi to leave her at the Agassiz's. On our way we had a breakdown—little horse, scared at the cars, ran us into a post & broke the shaft. What made it laughable was that had a box of wine in which had a bad air to transfer to the waggon that borrowed! However, we got over with little delay and found the Agassiz *famille* all right, viz: Mr. & Mrs. A[gassiz]; ditto junior; Maj. & Mrs. Higginson &

M. Burckhardt. At the Porc' were Br. Deputy Codman; Br. Sec. Tucker; & Brs. Walley, Mifflin, Hunnewell & one more Immediate. Of Honoraries appeared Brs. Burckhardt, Browne, Agassiz, Geo. Chase, Mason, Mifflin, & Quincy making a baker's dozen, or so, for our little consilium. We speedily agreed to get up a subscription of $800 for the lightening of expenses; and did appoint a Committee as follows: Brs. Browne; G. B. Chase; M. Brimmer; H. Quincy; A. Lawrence; H. Ritchie; Aug. Perkins & Henry Whitney. Gave also advice to recommence sociables & avoid extravagance. Then a spread at my cost, which passed off very pleasantly. At a seemly hour drove Mimi home.[17]

March 24, Thursday.

Foster Whitehouse, a corporal of the 2d Mass. is about here,—a fine looking young chap. At Gettysburg he had his musket shot in two, a wound in the arm and, at last, a ball entering in front near & inside the head of the pelvis and coming out behind near the vertebral column; the wound gangrened most terribly; but despite all, he is well again, after 8 months! Alonzo Langley has been here too, seeking a commission. To the opera with Mrs. Wife, the first time in a year and a half. Lucrezzia had we—very good—one Bellini as Duke; Medori for Dutchess—both good; the tenor Mezzolini, really a high baritone.[18]

March 25, Friday.

William Murphy, the new inside man, departed to the hospital, being not well—hopes to get back in a week or so. The carriage driving in with Mimi ran over a boy, John Campbell, but didn't hurt him much. We dined at Howland's who was highly indignant with the horses &c. of a squadron of cavalry, embarking for Hilton Head. And after to Opera—a new one, Faust, by Gounod. It is the familiar story, the music somewhat of Meyerbeer's style, but better, wanting however, in "tunes," which I do insist are essential in opera and in all music. People who are beyond "tunes" in music are parallel with people who are beyond common sense in philosophy. Bob Oliver in his school uniform, dined with us. Mrs. Mimi having had a craving for a "big ring," have had a big—enormous—one made of a crysolite or olivine. It was against my own judgment and she was disappointed in it; but it was not my fault. In Faust we had Miss Kellog as Margerite, with a small but good voice. A certain Hermans sung Mephistopheles in German—rather harsh against the balance of Italian! His conception of the part was the vulgar one, into which even Retoch has partly fallen—grotesqueness. Really, Mephistopheles should be pale, sardonic, terrible.[19]

March 26, Saturday.

Today was remarkable at the family dinner in that all the family were there for Bobbie (looking much improved) was home for holidays. Harry came from his camp; Annie & Alex from Cambridge; Mimi & I from Singletree, and then there were in the house Madre, Padre, Em,' Marian & Sallie. So were we right merry and Cora & Howland came in later. This morning went with little wife and saw Mrs. Cabot's flower houses—remarkably fine this year. How beautiful & luxurious it looked with whole banks of azaleas and roses in full bloom, with many other plants mingled here & there. Mr. Wm. Gray's new house, about on the old site, is nearly done. So far it is hideous! Then he has cut down the wrong trees & scraped the rest. Oh, *Mon Dieu!*[20]

March 27, Sunday.

Alas, my last day at home; how the weeks go! A quiet pleasant Sunday, withal. Harry Lee called, full of pleasant talk and told us Alonzo Langley had a commission in the 16th Mass. battery. Elliot Cabot with Mrs. and two bouncing boys, came also and behold they have a baby at home—*ça va*—Mr. & Mrs. Russell came at midday, and Co & Howland in the evening.[21] They felt sad to take leave of me; for we look for a bloody campaign—I sometimes try to realize a death on the field, but I cannot. My poor mind cannot take in this one great Certainty for us all. One fruit is broken by the wind, green from the tree; another, in its full time, falls, ripe, in the pleasant autumn. All fall. To me all close creeds seem like futile attempts to grasp the infinite; but it cannot be that Life with all its intense *Reality* of Beauty, Goodness, and Religion, should be a thing that passes into nothing.— (Gave Mrs. Campbell $5.00 in full of all demands.)[22]

March 28, Monday.

Poor little dear Wife! It seems almost foolish to come home, so sad is it to see her acrying when I go. Then little Baby, a very pretty child and of an excellent and affectionate disposition. I may never again see them; but it can't be helped. What wicked men have brought on, decent folks must fight out. Had given all necessary farm directions to Silas, and packed up the night before. At 7.45 A.M. kissed poor Mimette, and so off to take the train from the village. It is lonely out there for her, poor child—I would sooner see her staying with Co. Bye bye, little Miss Cora with your rosy cheeks! Howland kindly saw me off at Boston, and looked moist, good man.— There is no green yet but no snow;

nothing but a little ice round the edges of some small ponds. On the train were shoddy old Brewer, Henry Sturgis, Gardner Hammond and flighty pated Mr. Reed, who has lost his nice daughter Meymi, a sad thing indeed.[23] Away went Worcester (with a glimpse of the familiar Westboro Reform School), Springfield, neat Hartford, New Haven, and finally New York; where was plenty of time for a quiet dinner before the 7.30 P.M. train for Washington. In this was in company of a retired Maj. Whittlesea, who was on the Peninsula and who seems rather a betty, inclined to be blue in his public views. A classmate was he of Pleasonton.[24]

March 29, Tuesday.

Got in to Washington at 6.30 A.M. on time, for a marvel! Shave and breakfast at Willard's, to the great refreshment of the inner man. The train for the front left at 9.45 A.M. and got to Brandy at 2.45 P.M. Arrived, as left, in a rain. Much welcome from the staff, who seem all here except Christiancy. "Rosie" was rejoiced again to welcome his tent-mate; found Berlin staying there too, but will presently move to Dr. Wilson's tent where the occupant rarely or never appears, as the Washington quarters suit him better. Gens. Meade & Humphreys were at dinner when saw them; also were three juvenile visitors two sons of the late General Whipple and one of Gen'l Meade (Spencer). The younger Whipple was a very bright, nice boy.[25]

March 30, Wednesday.

Great changes have taken place in this consolidation recently of this army. The whole I Corps (made into two divisions) is put in V Corps. The 1st and 2d divisions, III Corps go in the II Corps; the 3d Div. III Corps in the VI Corps. Hancock has the II, Warren the V, Sedgwick the VI. Gen. Prince (an ordinary têtu man, I think) takes Carr's old div. into the VI Corps, while Carr takes Prince's Div. into the II Corps. Among the returning men, Gen. Getty has a division in the VI Corps; Gens. Barlow & Gibbon in the II; Gen. Wadsworth in the V. Gen. Webb descends to a brigade, (a fine one) in the II Corps; as does Gen. "Alick" Hays.[26] Gens. Sykes, Newton, French, Caldwell, &c. are relieved from duty with this army. Poor Sykes! It was to him a heavy and an unjust blow—a stern, Spartan "regular" he is, not brilliant, but like a good clock, always on time. Then for the cavalry, there is friend Pleasonton blown sky high and sent west. I am sorry. He treated me with courtesy and "baptized" me. He is a singular man, cold-blooded yet kindly; ambitious but not soaring; of a quick, ready brain, though not capable of judging things *en grand*. He has a good mind to command a division of cavalry.[27] Newton is said to be an excellent subordinate and fine engineer; but as a commander he loses all aplomb and is a regular stampeder. Gen. French is a thorough soldier and doubtless an excellent division commander, but his capacity does not rise to a corps, and it is said on good grounds that he sometimes drinks too much. Gen. Humphreys is as much prejudiced against him as in favor of Warren.[28] It is a real comfort to be able to write opinions in one's note-book as make it a rule to speak an opinion never on a superior; though could not help it once or twice about Kilpatrick whom esteem an arrant knave and impostor, not capable of commanding even a battalion! Gen. Meade's place now seems pretty secure. Gen. Grant lives in Culpeper and has nothing to do with the army, except through Gen. M[eade].—He moves from place to place a good deal.—The cabal against Meade continues, though in diminished force, and he goes tomorrow to Wash' to fire a volley more at the committee. Gen. Butterfield is now trying to scrape together some documents to prove *another* attempt to retreat on Meade's part.[29]

March 31, Thursday.

There was a deluge of rain l̶a̶s̶t̶ [TL corrected to] night before last, which swelled the Rappahannock at the rate of 2 feet per hour, and somewhat sprung the R.R. bridge. Rode down to the 2d Corps. The sunny slopes already have a tinge of green, where the young grass is springing here & there. Mountain Run Bridge carried away, so that had to ford on the Stevensburg road. Saw Gen. Webb who is cheery as ever, also the officers of the Mass. 20th. Introduced to Col. Sprigg Carroll, who still has a brigade. Mitchell, who has joined his regiment, was here at Headq'rs. He has taken to work & given over whisky, and looks marvellously improved.[30] Gen. Warren was along in the evening. His Headq'rs are at Culpeper & part of his new corps there; part north of the Rappahannock. He submitted to Gen. Humphreys a plan of putting small redoubts along the railroad, north of the river. So, as he said "that a division could hold it when we are gone." By which inferred that this line was to be persisted in; at least Warren *judice*.[31] He also made suggestions for the shortening of the old 5th Corps picket line. Grant seems to have impressed people favorably. He is plainly sharp. Two of his aides getting past him, he said "What is the new regulation by which aides ride before their General?"—

April 1, Friday.

We had the proverbial showers, which, that night turned to snow. Barstow went off on a 15-day sick-leave, being but poorly. Got my first letter from Deary. Notice Cunningham, Dabney's partner, is dead. Letter also from Capt. Peel, enclosing photogs of Stevenson, Earle & Castlecuffe.[32]

April 2, Saturday.

Gen. Meade came back and with him, came Gen. Gibbon who commands 2d Div. II Corps. He is an off-hand, soldierly man, of middle height; sharp nose, light brown hair, and rather stern of aspect. He is remarkably outspoken. He spoke in light terms of Barlow, and said he feared Hancock could not keep the field, as his bone wound threatened to slough; in this case the corps would fall to Birney, an undesirable result. Gen. M[eade] in good spirits. He has fired a volley into "Dan" Butterfield, before the Committee on Conduct of the War. The old General is a little more chary of his reputation than he was, and a shade more vain, which is no harm as he was too careless. He is a slasher, is the General, and cuts up people without much mercy. His family is celebrated for fierceness of temper and a sardonic sort of way that makes them uncomfortable people; but the General is the best of them, and exhausts his temper in saying sharp things. When it comes to practice he is full of kindness and often lets off men that should be summarily dealt with.[33]

April 3, Sunday.

Rev. Mr. Hall, of Washington, preached for us. It was a mystic sermon on the text that Charity (i.e. Love) was the enduring virtue, on which to count. He is quite eloquent and has a good deal of ability—a positive man also, perhaps rather too much so. He spoke at dinner of the two "thieves" crucified with our Savior, and said they were probably not that, but Siccani, Jewish fanatics who, refusing to pay tribute to Rome, fled to the wilderness and there lived on robbery of the Gentiles.— He is a Georgian by birth and has been suspected of being not entirely sound.

April 4, Monday.

A day of snow, sleet, and cold rain; indeed the last six days have been intermittent storms. Gen. Ricketts came today to get his order for command of 3d Div. 6th Corps. This will knock Prince down to a brigade, whereat P. will be wroth! Gen. Ricketts is a man of gentlemanly manners, stoutly built and with a John Bunyan sort of head. He looks to me like a person of very small ability, but is known as a brave officer. I fancy Prince is a blunderhead, and these two, with a division containing "Milroy's weary boys," may easily bring down some of the reputation of the celebrated 6th Corps.[34] Bought a roan mare of Maj. Robinson, 3rd Penn. Cav. She is some 15½ hands, very strongly built, apparently kind, and say 7 to 8 yrs. old. Saw no blemish but two small wind-galls on the hind fetlocks. Gave $150, which is very cheap if she is as good as she seems.[35]

April 5, Tuesday.

Rain all night and today worse than ever, a perfect type of a north-easter; cold & windy & wet. Took a ride, when it let up a little, and saw the Blue Ridge covered with snow. Muddy Run was running full with red water, and the Hazel River had swept away its bridge, though the pontoons at Welford's [Ford] held fast. The other day at dinner, Gen. Gibbon mentioned that the surgeons said of his Gettysburg wound, that it would have been mortal, had it passed a quarter of an inch more to the left.—"Ah," said Gibbon dryly, "the quarter-inches are in the hands of God!"—The first meeting between Grant and Meade had not much of pomp about it. Grant was driven to Headquarters in a four-horse spring-waggon.—It was raining hard.—Gen. Meade, dressed in a soldiers' knit jacket, the worse for wear, opened the door half way, put out his arm and said "Good Morning, General Grant. Come in."[36]

April 6, Wednesday.

The rain held up; and it cleared. Capt. Jay, lately of Sykes' Staff came to join ours. He was formerly on Meade's Staff. He is an excellent gentleman and *argal* an addition. He tents with Maj. Riddle.[37]

April 7, Thursday.

Rode out with Gen. Meade to a bit beyond Brandy Station, Gen. Rice going with on his way to Culpeper. R[ice] said the 1st Corps was well content to go with the 5th and looked now to some good fighting and implied that "Johnny" Newton did not do much of that sort.[38] The 11th & 12th Corps have been consolidated under title of 20th Corps, and Joe Hooker is in command. Howard takes Granger's corps. Slocum is afloat and will probably be glad of the chance to resign. Some of the 3d Corps (among which are to be found shoals of bowery boys) have made a fuss about going in the 2d Corps, and the merry Excelsiors have sewed the trefoil to the seats of their trowsers! The 3d Div. however is very content to be in the 6th [Corps].[39] On our return found Lt. Col. Gustave de Struve a Russian engineer officer, who was turned over to me to entertain—a young man very gentlemanly, but with that "soft" way peculiar to the Russians. *Au reste*, he is Prussian on the mother's side and a relation of Struve the astronomer.[40] Got a letter from little Mimi that troubled me a good deal. John, the coachman, whom I supposed the slowest & safest of men, drove, or tried to drive her out of town, on a stormy night. She had only little Frankie Shaw with her. John proved to be regularly drunk, and, at last, she had to seize the reins and drive herself, from the village up! Damnation, a pretty affair! At once wrote her to shut up Brookline and go where she would be near protection. It is too much for her to be out there all alone. I have been already uneasy, and now I have my mind made up. I also wrote to Howland and to Mr. Russell, hoping they would ask her to stay at Beverly this summer. Poor child, poor child!

April 8, Friday.

Another fine day; yesterday was really quite warm. Spent the whole day in show‐ing Col. Struve about. The departments first; then the photographs by Sullivan, of which he bought several, and sat for his fereotype for me.[41] Rosencrantz & I then took him and showed him the battery and ammunition, where Torslow, the Swede is serving as Lieut. Then to show him the pontoons at Welford's ford and finally to Robertson's horse artillery brigade. In the evening we had a great collection of staff officers in my tent, and Biddle, who goes over like a child, was very amusing with his accounts of his political & military opinions.— All sutlers ordered to the rear before the 16th, but think we shall not get off before May 1st. Struve said the Polish insurrection was the saving of Russia, which before had been imminently threatened by democratico-military revolution, rising from the ukase releasing the serfs. But the conduct of the Poles was so insulting and finally so violent & cruel, that the whole Russian sentiment was turned against them, a sentiment heightened by the interference of foreign powers.[42]

April 9, Saturday.

Heavy rain storm again.

April 10, Sunday.

Dr. Kirk, with a strong Boston deputation of the Chr. Commission, turned up, and he preached for us a severe but good sermon. He is a man of ability but rather oratorical. Along were Mr. Tobey; also the "Holy" Sturgis, who talked in his usually conceited manner; said he liked military life, having inherited it from his father (!) ha, ha, ha! Poor, vain, cretin! Nevertheless he doubtless does more good than many a more sensible man. There was also Col. Merriam's father, in the cheerful shopkeeper order. The day was fine but with lots of mud. George Scarron who has been our faithful waiter boy thus far, has been spirited away by his pa, the old John, much to our discomfort.[43]

April 11, Monday.

The General with Gen. Humphreys & Col. Struve, went to Culpeper. He found the way pretty good; but, at Mountain Run, the bridge was swept away and we had to go high up, to find another. Some little snow on the Blue Ridge still; but the air warm here, in the plain. We found Grant's Headq'rs at a brick house off the street where the bank was. Tents pitched in the front yard. Grant has a sitting & eating room in the house. Saw Capt. Janes, his Q. Mr., who invited us to his tent. Afterwards was presented to Gen. Grant; also to Lt. Col. Comstock, and Lt. Col. Badeau. Comstock, a Mass. man, is the engineer and much relied on. He resembles a Yankee schoolmaster buttoned up in a double-breaster. Gen. Rawlings, the Ch' of Staff, is one of those black eyed, thick haired, off hand, energetic looking Western men.[44] Grant is a man of considerable rough dignity and as determined looking as well may be.— Arthur Lyman has been dangerously ill of a sort of diphtheria but is now better.[45]

April 12, Tuesday.

Took Col. Struve to Morton's Ford, west to Stony Mountain, whence we got an excellent view of the country the other side of the ford, where we were, the day we crossed for the "demonstration."[46] The Rebs have made a new battery on the bluff towards Raccoon Ford; it mounts about 6 guns and is regularly finished with gabions. We could also see a part of the heavy infantry-parapet, covering their right flank and running off towards Mine Run. This hill seems to be covered with rounded masses of granitic rock; it is very steep and commands a good view. A brigade is still camped here.— Gen. Meade read me the testimony he last gave before the Committee on the War. In which he flatly denies the statement of Gen. Butterfield that he ordered him to write an order for retreat. Also, that he intended, if possible, to fight a defensive battle, which would of course be more advantageous to him. A subscription for the band was got up at Headq'rs so as to raise about $200 per month.

April 13, Wednesday.

McClellan, to our regret, left this today, to become Adjutant Gen. for Torbert's Div. of Cav. We went to a review of Birney's Div. near J. M. Botts' house. The two brigades are under H. Ward and Alex. Hays.[47] About 5,000 men were actually on the ground. Here saw Gen. Hancock for the first time. He is a tall, soldierly man, with light brown hair and a military heavy jaw; and has the massive features and the heavy folds round the eye that often mark a man of ability. Then the officers were asked to take a little whisky chez Botts. Talked there with his niece, a dwarfish little woman of middle age, who seems a great *invalide*. She was all of a tremor, poor woman, by the mere display of troops, being but nervous & associating them with the fighting she had seen round the very house. Then there was a refreshment at Birney's Headq'rs where met Capt. Briscoe (said to be the son of an Irish nobleman &c. &c.) also Major Mitchell on Gen. Hancock's staff. The Russ' was delighted with the politeness & pleased with the troops. Introduced to Gen. Sheridan, the new Chief of Cavalry—a small broad shouldered, squat man, with black hair & a square head. He is of Irish parents, but looks very like a Piedmontese. Gen. Wilson who is probably to have a division, is a slight person of a light complection and with rather a pinched face. Sheridan makes everywhere a favorable impression.[48]— Annie's baby has been christened. Got a letter (in answer to mine) from Howland, in which he says he is of my opinion & will be glad to have Mimi at their house &c.; all most kind, as always.[49]

April 14, Thursday.

The Russian departed this morning, with some maps presented to him. Carr's Div. was reviewed on the other side of Culpeper Creek, near the Stevensburg road. There are two brigades, Mott's and Brewster's. In the former are the Mass. 16th & 1st. Barlow came over, looking as natural as possible despite his sash & military hat with its red trefoil. Here too is the "Excelsior Brigade," quite good fighters, but slovenly & great blackguards. Gen. Hancock reviewed them. Afterwards we rode to Stony Mtn. once more, to show the Reb's to Mr. Smith, a brother of Lt. Col. S[mith] of the Cavalry Corps; also is he the husband of Mrs. Meade's sister.[50]

April 15, Friday.

A review of Gibbon's Div. by Gen. Hancock; on nearly the same ground as Carr's. The brigades were Webb's & Carrol's. It was the finest review yet, marching, deportment and equipments most perfect. Everyone remarked the 20th Mass. as better than anything there, which was true enough. After the review we went [to] Gen. Webb's, where a part of the 19th Mass. went through the manual, in a most perfect manner. After which the 20th Mass. showed a new drill of running in disorder and rallying, each man in his place, on a line established by the color & two guidons. It was pleasant to see the old state stand out so brightly. Lieut. Gale did the honors for the Aides at Gibbon's Headq'rs. Barlow introduced me to Col. Miles commanding one of his brigades. The

General afterwards rode through the woods (now much thinned) to Culpeper, where saw Lt. Col. Duff of Gen. Grant's staff. Gen. G[rant] arrived soon after us, from Washington and pow-wowed with Gen. Meade. Old Robertson was along. A dubious telegraph reports that Forrest has taken Ft. Pillow & Is. No. 10 & reoccupied Paducah! Pretty business. Gen. Rawlins said he thought it would not do to trust negroes without good white support.[51]

April 16, Saturday.

Poor Rosencrantz! His application to be mustered back has been refused by the War Dep. and he ceases to be in the military service. We must try & get him another commission. He is a good soldier, but, like many Continentals, he is a child in affairs temporal.[52] Rain again. Saw yesterday a peach tree in bloom at Culpeper. A letter from Mimette says there fell 10 inches of snow on the 12th!!

April 17, Sunday.

A young man, Dr. Duryea of N. Y. gave us a service in the chapel. He (like many clergymen) handled the Infinite in a rather easy way, but he had a good manner & an excellent voice for singing. The General gave me an important confidential letter to Gen. Grant, to make a fair copy of. It was a statement of preparatory steps taken. By last of this month 1,000,000 rations to be on shipboard at Fortress Monroe, ready to run up the James or Pamunkey; in the same place & manner 100 rounds per man, and 50 rounds per gun; medical supplies for 12,000 wounded; and proportional forage. At Alexandria a *duplicate* medical depot for 12,000, to be sent by rail, in case a battle were fought near the rail communication. In the army, always kept on hand 150 rounds per man, 50 on the person, 100 in train; 12 days' beef on the hoof, 1 day's salt in train, 3 full & 5 small rations on the person, the balance of small rations in the train; 10 days forage for all animals. Siege train & tools ready at (Alexandria) or Washington.[53]

April 18, Monday.

Last night Gen. Meade showed me the photograph copies of the Dahlgren orders, said to have been found on his body. There was an address and a sheet of memoranda. In both, reference was made to killing Davis and cabinet and burning the city. The address was signed "U. Dahlgren." With it was a letter from Lee asking if the U.S. or Gen. Meade gave or approved such orders? The whole was dated Ap. 1 and sent by flag of truce, endorsed by J.E.B. Stuart, that a reply could be sent to Lightfoot Ford. Gen. Meade replied that no such orders had been given or were approved by him or the U.S. & enclosed was a letter from Kilpatrick saying that he had examined the men with Dahlgren who all denied hearing any such address. Gen. K[ilpatrick] further stated that he had endorsed "approved" in red ink on an address similar to this, but *without* the obnoxious passages. Gen. Meade however told me he considered the weight of evidence in favor of the authenticity, and plainly said he did not consider Kilpatrick a trustworthy person. The flag was sent by Cadwalader. Kilpatrick has gone west, gloria!—also Prince has applied to be relieved and also ordered west—no loss.[54] A review of the whole 6th Corps by Gen. Grant. We rode along the R.R. and met him near Birney's Headq'rs. He was mounted on a fine chestnut and was well dressed in a simple uniform of Lt. General. Lt. Cols. Duff, Rowley & Comstock were along. The corps seemed an endless affair; there were upwards of 20,000 men in line, battalions massed. Grant gave some offence by receiving Gen. Sedgwick's salute with a cigar in his mouth, a fault partly to be laid on Gen. Meade's shoulders, who told him there was no harm in it; for the good General has the failing of nine tenths of our officers, a disregard of formal details that brings more trouble than one would think. Afterwards, a lunch at Gen. Sedgwick's and then a review of the Artillery reserve including the Horse Brigade, and Kitchen's and Schirmer's regiments of heavy artillery, both very large and both marching with great steadiness. S[chirmer]'s is composed chiefly of Germans, and many an old Prussian soldier might one recognize, as they marched in review.[55]

April 19, Tuesday.

To my tribulation the Sturgis mare was lame today; 3 day's ago she ran a bit of bone in her foot at Culpeper, and today there is a fester below the pastern. Ned Dalton viewed it and ordered the shoe off. Hope it will get well soon. Barlow's review, on same ground as Gibbon's. He has a big division—7,000 or 8,000 rank & file equipped for duty. There are 4 brigades Brooks', Miles', Franks' (a Saxon), and Smyth (Irish Brigade). In this division about ⅓ are new men, who injured the marching, but all looked remarkably clean and well equipped. The Irish Brigade had the 28th Mass., said now to be a good reg. At Barlow's Headqr's in a hollow beyond Gen. Hancock's, we had champagne & refreshments. Barlow said, in his characteristic way, to the precise Webb: "General, there is punch, if you prefer to get drunk on *that!*" Was introduced to Col. Brooks and Frank. The former had seen Kalapsa in the west, and was much impressed with him. He tried for a commission, but could not get one, and it was rumored that he afterwards went south.[56] Returning, we halted at

Gen. Mott's where waited at the quarters of Lieut. Thompson. They are a dirty minded set those 3d Corps men—of the stamp that keep indecent photographs in their baggage. Some of these nowadays from France, are of an extraordinary depth of foulness. There was a Lt. Col. Burns there, a typical "Excelsior," half drunk & of a general appearance in keeping.[57] By special order, 10 rounds per man are to be expended in target practice, each man firing under guidance of an officer; so, between 10 & 12 on firing days, the echoes resound with popping. This afternoon enter Adams, much altered for the better; all shaved save moustache, and in new clothes! Gave him a blowing for sending his squadron without even a Captain; which he entirely appreciated, and indeed had already written to Flint pitching into *him*.[58]

April 20, Wednesday.

A coldish, raw day. Was much surprised to learn from Barstow that Bill Lyman, was dead! No particulars—It's pretty hard indeed. This winter Uncle George has lost a son and two grandchildren.[59]

April 21, Thursday.

Rosencrantz left for Washington for two or three days.

April 22, Friday.

A grand review of the whole Second Corps, on the right of the Stevensburg road, beyond Culpeper Creek. There were four lines, each of a division in masses of battalions. On the right was Wilson's division of cavalry (*çi-devant* Kilpatrick's) and its horse batteries, also the artillery of the corps and Tidball's regiment of heavy artillery. The appearance was really fine, even the cavalry looked decently. Gen. Grant was there and an immense crowd of mounted officers from all quarters. The marching was excellent, that of Barlow's division especially improved. There was a handsome lunch after, at Hancock's Headq'rs. In the afternoon arrived an England-Oxford man, Exeter Hall Abolitionist—son of Lord Stanley of Alderly—Mr. E. Lyulph Stanley. He looked about idiotic, but was quite bright and very full of information, which was not so singular, seeing that he did nothing but ask questions.[60]

April 23, Saturday.

Rode to Culpeper with the Gen. [Meade] & Stanley, who was introduced to Gen. Grant. We took a one o'clock dinner with the Commander. It was plain but good; soup, fish, 2 meats, 3 vegetables & a pudding with coffee. There were the staff at table, including Capt. Parker the Indian, who is chief of his tribe. Grant drinks no wine or spirit; the moment the last man was through, he rose. He is a very still, steady man, but evidently enjoyed a pleasant joke. He also makes quiet, sarcastic remarks, without moving a line of his face. He said (referring to Bank's late fight on the Red River, where he lost 20 guns and some thousands of prisoners, though he at last drove the enemy back) that "Banks' victories were of a kind that three or four of them would ruin anybody." He added that "there were some Generals who had not enough patriotism to resign." It was warm today—one thermometer said 80° in the shade—with a wind that raised clouds of dust.[61]

April 24, Sunday.

Stanley departed; after succeeding in raising a great ire against himself by declaring his admiration of John Brown! Jay, however, who is a great abolitionist, stood up for him. A Mr. Cram, brother-in-law of Gen. Meade & a N. Y. lawyer, is on a visit with John Cadwalader, cousin of the Captain. Cram is a queer man—never saw one exactly like him. He has a jerky, theatrical style that made me at first suppose he had had a toddy or two.[62]

April 25, Monday.

The enemy have taken Plymouth, N.C. with some 2,000 men & 26 guns. They are said to have committed atrocities there, as at Ft. Pillow, which I do trust is untrue. Mr. Sec. Stanton had a flurry today about army visitors, and stopped everybody at the railroad station from coming down; to the horror of cooks & purveyors who got caught.[63] Burnside has suddenly marched from Annapolis and arrived at Alexandria! *Ecco!* I have a notion that it was intended to have him move by say Tappahannock, but the arrival of Longstreet and of others perhaps has forced Grant to concentrate. B[urnside] is rumored to have 25,000 to 30,000 of whom 7,000 to 12,000 blacks.[64]

April 26, Tuesday.

There is weeping in Headquarters; all detailed men cleared out and their places supplied by men from the regiments attached to the Provost Marshal General, viz 114th Penn., 68th Penn., 3d Penn. Cav., and Adam's squadron. The last supplies the 4 mounted orderlies for the General. The Zouaves, the 4 foot orderlies. The ancient stagers went with wry mouths to their regiments. Rode to Rappahannock Sta. and saw Appleton, still there with his battery.[65]

April 27, Wednesday.

Again to Culpeper, where was introduced to Lt. Col. Babcock of Grant's staff. Gen. Warren took us to Green's house on the ridge beyond the town and showed the redoubts and rifle-pits he has constructed. That active engineer never can let dirt alone, when he is lying still. Got a box of summer clothing, *id est* thin flannels. Have packed and sent home, winter clothes & bedding & all superfluities.

April 28, Thursday.

Turning in extra tents and taking up board floors. The Reserve Artillery was reviewed by Gen. Hunt; Col. Burton commanding.[66] The number of turtle doves hereabout is very great. In Culpeper yesterday, saw the apple trees loaded with blossoms. Weather cooler with wind N.—fair.—The crows, that were in such flocks during winter, are now only here & there in pairs, which exemplifies the fact, that no abundance of food will suspend the instinct of migration.

April 30, Saturday.

Rode to Culpeper with the General. We passed part of the Pennsylvania "Preserves" moving to the front along the railroad. At Headq'rs of Grant was Gen. Burnside, now grown much heavier, these last 3 or 4 years. Lt. Col. Loring, his Insp. Gen'l was also there, & we talked together. Col. Comstock said that, at Vicksburg, we made Cohorn mortars of logs, hooped, and, with an ounce of powder, threw 6 & 12 lb. shells 100 or 150 yds. into the enemy's bastions. Gen. Warren rode with us all the way. He is very hungry always for information, & has actually read Woodward's manual of conchology this winter—pretty dry stuff for an amateur!—[67]

May 1, Sunday.

A fine day, very. The rest of the 5th Corps moved up & camped in the neighborhood of Brandy. Rode down to Rappahannock Sta. and found the redoubt on the north side occupied by the 57th Mass. (Bartlett) while the 14th Mass. battery was in the old camp of the 5th. The next troops are at Bealton, the 26th Mass. with Brig. Gen. Tom Stevenson. Burnside's four divisions are commanded by Gens. Ferrero (black troops), Wilcox, Crittenden, and Parke. Shook hands last eve' with Burnside, who came to our Headq'rs.— Introduced this eve to Capts. Winthrop & Swan, regular infantry. Swan was class of '59. Temple, of the Porc. Club, was in his regiment, and was killed the first day at Chancellorsville.[68]

May 2, Monday.

Each Aide had given him a "manifold letter writer"—which I prophesy few will use. Adams got new horses, to his joy. My mare quite well again. Flint has joined the squadron. He came over to see me.[69] The officers at these Headq'rs now are nearly as follows; Maj. Gen. Meade (Aides) Maj. Biddle & Riddle, Capt. Meade, Bates, Mason, Cadwalader, Bache & Jay, Lieut. Rosencrantz; Maj. Gen. Humphreys, Chief of Staff (Aides) Capt. Cavada, Lieut. Humphreys, Christiancy, Brig. Gen. Williams, Assistant Adjutant General (Aides) Maj. Barstow, Capt. Pease, Lieut. Woolsey; Brig. Gen. Hunt, Chief of Artillery (Aides) Capt. Craig; Lieuts. Berlin, Bissel & Worth, Col. Warner. Brig. Gen. Ingalls, Quarter Master (Aides) Capts. Howell, Pierce; Capt. Paige; Brig. Gen. Patrick, Provost Marshall (Aides) Capts. Schuyler & Beckwith & Col. Sharpe, Clinton (?); Col. Schriver, Inspector General; Lt. Col. Wilson, Chief Commissary; Dr. McParlin, Medical Director, Drs. Ghiselin, Dalton, Asch, McKenzie; Maj. Platt, Judge Advocate; Maj. Duane, Chief Engineer, (Aides) Capt. Mickler, Paine; Capt. Sanders Mustering Officer; Capt. Coxe, Commissary; Lt. Edie Chief of Ordnance; Capt. Stryker, Signal Department.[70]

May 3, Tuesday.

At last the order of march for tomorrow at 5 A.M.! of it more when it is over—if I am here to write.— Only spring wagons go for our little mess kits & baggage; other things go with the main train. May God bless the undertaking at last & give an end to this War!—Made all preparations for the campaign.

May 3–
June 16, 1864

Nota bene. The notes in this book were not written herein on the spot, but taken from letters home & from memoranda written at the time and afterwards enlarged when I wrote out the notes of the Campaign for Gen. Meade's Report.
This book was not begun till June 1865.

———⦿———

Headquarters Army of the Potomac, May 3d, 1864—
evening—Epitome of Order of March.

2d Div. Cav. (Gregg's) to Richardsville with ½ the canvas pontoon train. at 2 A.M. (4th) cross at Ely's Ford, and throw out towards Piney Branch Church, Fredericksburg, &c. and here to remain covering passage of trains, and afterwards to move with them.— 3d Div. Cav. move at midnight (3d), cross at Germanna Ford, and move to Parker's Store, covering both Orange Turnpike and Plank Road.[1] 1st Cav. Div. draws in on morning of 4th and pickets from Rapid Ann Station to Germanna Ford—afterwards to cross at Ely's Fd. and cover left flank of train. 5th Corps to be at Germanna pontoon by 6 A.M. (4th), cross and go to Old Wilderness Tavern (on the 5th to cross Orange Plank [Road] at Parker's Store and cross the head of Catharpin Run)—6th Corps follows 5th, crosses and bivouacs on the other side. Canvas pontoon at Germanna [Ford] will follow 6th Corps. At Culpeper Mine Ford a pontoon will be thrown, and road opened by engineers to Richardsville. 2d Corps to get to Ely's Ford by 6 A.M. (4th), cross and move to near Chancellorsville; its canvas pontoons to follow; wooden ones to stay down. Reserve Artillery to cross after 2d Corps, marching to Hunting Creek Church on Chancellorsville road. Roads to be repaired. Troops crossing at Ely's Ford to look out for their left flank; those at Germanna Ford to look out for their right flank. Corps commanders will frequently communicate with each other. Army Headquarters will be on the Germanna Plank [Road], between 5th & 6th Corps. Main trains will park at Richardsville. 1,200 men to be detached from each corps as train guard. Wooden

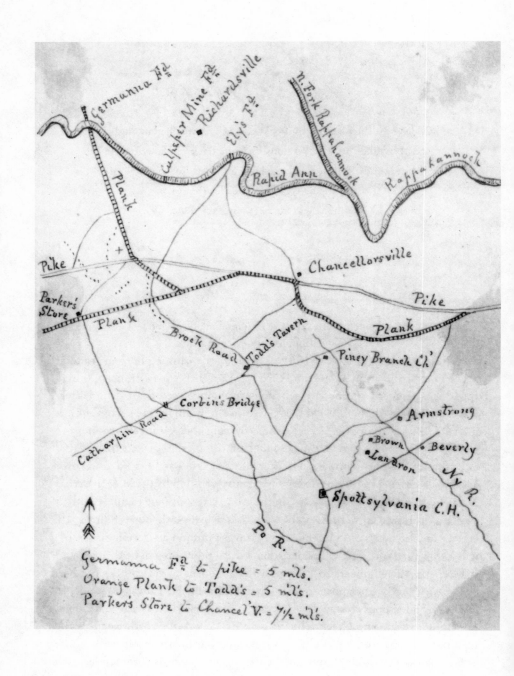

Germanna Fᵈ to pike = 5 mls.
Orange Plank to Todd's = 5 mls.
Parker's Store to Chancel' V. = 7½ mls.

pontoon to stay down at Germanna for Burnside. Signal stations to remain as long as possible, 1 hospital and one medical supply-waggon to accompany each brigade. Only spring-waggons for Headquarters. One half of its ambulances, intrenching tool- & ammunition waggons to accompany each corps. 3 days' full and 3 days' small rations, and 50 rounds on the person, and 3 days' rations on the hoof to accompany the troops.[2]

May 4, 1864, Wednesday.

We all were up by star-light; a warm, clear night; had our breakfast by daybreak, and at 5.25 A.M. turned our backs on our little village of the last six months, and the grove about it, dear even in its desolation! The columns had been moving a good part of the night and we cut a part of the 6th Corps, just at Brandy Station, beyond which point the road was full of waggons and troops. Beyond Stevensburg the road-side was full of violets, and the little leaves of the wood trees were just beginning to unfold, the size of a mouse's ear perhaps. 7 A.M. The General unluckily came up with a cavalry waggon train, out of place; the worst thing for his temper! He sent me after its Quartermaster, Capt. Luddington, whom he gave awful dressing to, and ordered him to get his whole train out of the road and to halt till the other trains had passed.[3] The sun getting well up made the temperature much warmer, as was testified by the castaway packs & blankets with which troops will often at the outset encumber themselves. 8 A.M. Arrived near Germanna Ford and halted just where we had camped the night of the withdrawal from Mine Run. *Sapristi*, it was cold that night! Though here was green grass in place of an half inch of ice, Griffin's division was over and his ammunition was then crossing. 8.30 A.M. News from Hancock that he was crossing, Gregg having had no opposition and having seen only videttes.— Roads everywhere excellent. 9.30. We crossed. There were two pontoons, a wooden & a canvass, the ascent up the opposite high & steep bank was bad, with a difficult turn near the top.[4] We halted just on the other side and Grant & his staff arrived some time after. 12.15 P.M. All the 5th Corps, with its artillery and wheeled vehicles across.— It began at 6.30 A.M. The 6th Corps began to cross at 12.40 and was all over at 5.20 and the canvas pontoon was taken up. A good part of the time, say ½, only one pontoon could be used, because the troops were moving in single column. We may then estimate 15 hours for the passage of 46,000 infantry, with one half of their ambulances and ammunition and intrenching waggons and the whole of their artillery, over a single bridge, with steep, bad approaches on each side; i.e. a little over 3,000 men an hour, with their artillery and wheels. The latter

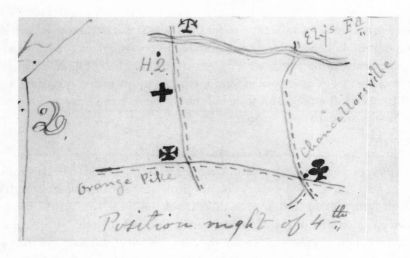

took a good deal of the time because of the delay in getting them up the steep ascent. Sat on the bank and watched the steady stream, as it came over. That eve took a bath in the Rapid Ann and thought that might come sometime to bathe in the James! Our cook, little M. Mercier, came to grief, having been spirited away by the provost guard of the 2d Corps, as a straggler or spy; so our supper was got up by the waiter boy, Marshall. Our camp was near the river, and Grant's was close to us. Some of his officers; Duff & old Jerry Dent e.g. were very flippant and regarded Grant as already routing Lee and utterly breaking up the rebellion!—not so the more sober.—There arrived Gen. Seymour, the unlucky man of Olustee, dark bearded and over given to talk and write; but of well known valor. He was assigned to a brigade 3d Div. 6th Corps, where his command was destined to be of the shortest.[5]

May 5, Thursday.

The head of the 9th Corps got last night as far as Germanna Ford; but the troops extended thence far back. Order of march (epitome) for May 5.[6] (Of course this was but partially carried out, owing to the battle.) Sheridan, with Gregg's and Torbert's Divisions, to attack enemy's cavalry at Hamilton's crossing (towards Fredericksburg). Wilson's Cav. Div. to move out at 5 A.M. to Craig's Meeting House, on Catharpin road, and to throw out on the Catharpin & Pamunkey roads and on the Orange Plank & Pike, &c. 2d Corps move at 5 to Shady Grove Church, and extend its right towards the 5th Corps at Parker's Store. 5th Corps at 5, to Parker's Store and extend its right to 6th Corps at

Wilderness Tavern. 6th Corps to Wilderness Tavern, leaving one Div. at Germanna Fd. till Burnside had got over troops enough to hold it. Reserve Artillery to Corbin's Bridge. Trains to near Todd's Tavern. Headq'rs on Orange Plank near to 5th Corps. When in position the army will be held ready to advance. Right & left flanks to be well watched and pickets thrown well out. (Note. In the first of this order, may be seen already Sheridan's budding ambition for personal and independent distinction. He wanted to do something *separate*, though the interests of the service were plainly against the scattering of forces. The order was countermanded.)[7]— We rode some 4½ miles and arrived at 7.10 A.M. at Old Wilderness Tavern, on the right of the road and near the Orange Pike. Here were Generals Warren & Sedgwick. The 5th Corps was marching past and the 6th was in its rear. Was greeted by Bill Thorndike, Surgeon in the 39th Mass. of Robinson's Div. Told him that Griffin reported the enemy on the Orange Pike, 2 miles west of the Germanna Plank. Wright was ordered to move S.W. from the Germanna Plank and feel for Griffin's right.[8] 10.30 A.M. The 5th New York cavalry, holding the Orange Plank at Parker's store, has been attacked by infantry and driven in, with loss.[9] Enemy reported at Frederickshall, south of the N. Anna (idle story).— 10.45 Getty's Div. of 6th Corps ordered to proceed at once to junction of the cross-road (continuation of the Brock Road) and the Orange Plank, and hold it. One division of Burnside reported across. All expected over by night. Headq'rs move to a piney knoll on the right of the Orange Pike and opposite the Maj. Lacy house.[10] There was a good space of open country just here extending on both sides of the pike, though chiefly on the left; but, about a mile up the road were pine woods, wherein was Griffin's division going south along the Germanna Plank, the low woods began near the junction of the Brock cross-road with this. 12.10.[11] Ordered to go to Gen. Getty and explain to him the position of the army and direct him to seek roads to the right and join with Crawford's left. At the beginning of the cross-road found Gen. Eustis' brigade going into the woods;—told him the orders, and he said he would send 3 regiments instead of 2, to feel to the right. Found Getty sitting on the ground, near the Plank Road, but on the cross-road. He said the whole of Hill's Corps was coming down the plank, and the skirmishers were within 300 yards. They had been fighting, and two or three bodies lay near us, and a wounded man occasionally passed. Getty told me to tell Gen. Meade that he had but 3 brigades, having been ordered to leave one behind.[12] 12.50. Reported back at Headq'rs. Just at this moment, heavy musketry from Griffin and some apparently from Wright, also from Wadsworth on Griffin's left. It lasted, rising & falling, for about 1½ hours. 1.50. Ordered to go to 5th N.Y. Cav. & direct them, as soon as filled up with ammunition, to proceed down the Brock Road and open communication with Gen. Hancock, who was moving up. Found the regiment to the rear of the Germanna Plank; men distributing cartridges; the Colonel having somewhat cooked. Ordered him to report to Gen. Getty, as above. 2. Sent again to countermand the above order, as Hancock was nearly in junction with Getty's left. Returning to Headq'rs found the pike blocked with ambulances and with wounded on foot, who continually enquired "How far to the 5th Corps Hospital?" They were chiefly from Griffin's Div. and also many from Wadsworth's. Met Joe Hayes, supported by Dalton, and by a servant on his horse. He was talking wildly and the blood streamed down his face! A dangerous wound to look at—shot in the head. There we were three classmates together!— Helped him along till assured he had enough assistance, when left him with Dalton.[13] 2.45. Griffin comes in, followed by his mustering officer, Geo. Barnard. He is stern & angry. Says in a loud voice that he drove back the enemy, Ewell, ¾ of a mile, but got no support on the flanks, and had to retreat—the regulars much cut up. Implies censure on Wright and apparently also on his corps commander, Warren. Wadsworth also driven back.— Rawlins got very angry, considered the language mutinous and wished him put in arrest.— Grant seemed of the same mind and asked Meade; "who is this Gen. *Gregg?* You ought to arrest him!" Meade said "It's Griffin, not Gregg; and it's only his way of talking."— Rawlins asked me what he had done; told him his reputation as an officer was good.[14] In this charge Bartlett's brigade, the first line commanded by Hayes, broke and drove the enemy, handsomely.— Bartlett's horse was killed and he badly hurt in the head by his fall. There is little doubt that Wright made slow work in his advance.[15] 3 P.M. Burnside ordered up. 3.15. Sent with a written order to Getty to attack (& Hancock to go in too); but to attack alone if Hancock was not ready. Delivered it at 3.25. Getty in the same spot—very cool—evidently did not think it good strategy to attack till more of the 2d Corps was up; but promptly sent aides to Eustis & Wheaton directing them to prepare at once to advance. 4.15. Ordered to take with me orderlies; report to Hancock and send back reports of progress from time to time. Reported at 4.45 to Hancock, who sat on his horse at the crossing of the Brock and Plank roads. He told me to write to Gen. Meade that it was hard to bring up troops in this wood—only part of corps up, but would do as well as he could.— All this time heavy musketry in our front and stray balls coming over. The country a "Wilderness" indeed!—a thick cover of sapplings, from 15 to 30 feet high with a close under-growth of bushes. Now rides up an officer—Maj. Mundy—"Sir! Gen. Getty is hard pressed and his ammunition nearly out"—"Tell him to hold on, & Gen. Gibbon will be up to help him!" Another officer, from the left, comes up; "Sir! Gen. Mott's division has broken, and is coming back!"—"Tell him to stop them!" roared Hancock, and galloped towards the left and began rallying the retreating troops in the Brock road. "Maj. Mitchell, go to Gen. Gibbon and tell him to come up on the double-quick!"[16] (The bad conduct of this division of Mott's, once renowned as the 2d Division of the 3d Corps, Hooker's old command, was an instance of demoralization. Commanded successively by the dull Prince, the dancing master Carr, and by Mott, a cool, gallant man but without capacity for a large body of troops, its morale was further shaken by the breaking up of the Third Corps and its transfer to the 2d. In this, and the fights just after, its conduct was doubtless on the whole, disgraceful. When reduced to a brigade, under old McAllister, it did once more, good fighting at the Battle of Hatcher's Run &c.) Hancock rode then off to the left. I was in the "cross-road" (continuation of the Brock) when Carroll's & Hay's brigades came up, the former leading (or Hays perhaps was already there and only sent some regiments to assist.)— At any rate Carroll's men formed in the cross-road, and faced left to the front. They were blown by the double-quick. One of their Colonels said; "Now I don't want any hollering;—that's childish!"— Then, prime! Forward!— Soon after heard that Carroll was shot through the arm, and then that Hays was killed. The musketry continued, but the fresh troops had saved the day. Just as the sun was declining Gen. Hays was carried past me, on a stretcher borne on the shoulders of four men. He was shot straight through the head, but still had a mechanical respiration.[17] At dark the fight was a drawn one; the line extending, as before, along the Brock and west of the cross-road. Portions of the 5th, 6th & 2d Corps had been opposed to Hill's & Ewell's Corps. It was after dark when got to Headq'rs, the tents being pitched in a dusty field, east of the Germanna Plank. Had frequently sent reports during the day, as ordered. Wilson's cavalry got cut off today between Parker's Store & Catharpin Road, and had to cut their way through to Sheridan.[18] Grant ordered a general attack tomorrow at 4.30 A.M. but postponed it to 5, because they suggested Burnside would not be up till that time. "He won't be up—I know him well!" said Duane (who hates B.) and so it turned out.[19]

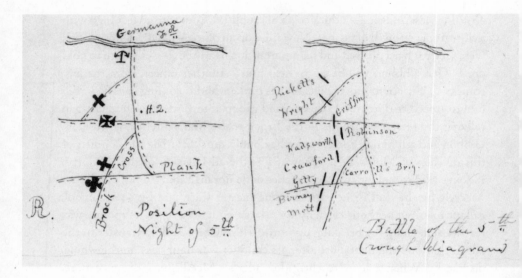

May 6, Friday.

All hands up before daylight. Sunrise was at about 4.50. The General was in the saddle in the gray of the morning. As he sat in the hollow by the Germanna Plank, up comes Capt. Hutton of B[urnside]'s staff and says only one division was up and the road blocked with artillery (part of which was then passing us).— The General uttered some exclamation, and H[utton] said: "if you will authorize me sir, I will take the responsibility of ordering the artillery out of the road, and bring up the infantry at once."—"No Sir" said M[eade] flatly. "I have no command over Gen. Burnside." And here was the first mishap—the fight would have been better if Grant had not been there, for Meade knew B[urnside] well and would have got him on the march at an earlier hour. B[urnside] had been up the night before and had said "Well then my troops shall break camp by half past two." (I think)—But he had a genius of slowness.[20] 5.15. Ordered to ride to Gen. Hancock, remain there during the day, and report back by orderlies.[21] There was skirmishing already and, as rode down the cross road, the volleys began. Found H[ancock] at join of the Brock and Plank. "Tell Gen. Meade" he cried, "we are driving them most beautifully. Birney has gone in and he is just cleaning them out beautifully." I said I was ordered to report only one division of Burnside up; but he would attack as soon as he could.—"I knew it! Just what I expected!" cried Hancock. "If he could attack *now*, we could smash A.P. Hill all to pieces!!"—The musketry was receding.—Squads of prisoners were coming in. We had taken the rifle-pits they had made in the night and now we were straightening the line, previous to pushing on. The fire therefore slackened. 6.45. Gen. Getty rode past me, in the cross-road, looking pale; to my enquiry, he said; "I am shot through the shoulder; I don't know how badly"—a man of indomitable courage and coolness!— One of his aides (the fair haired), shot through the arm, the other with his horse shot. Immortal fighting did that valiant 2d Division 6th Corps, on these two bloody days![22]— About 7 A.M. Webb's brigade moved up the Brock and wheeled into the plank to support Birney. Waved my hand to Abbott, as he rode past at the head of the 20th, smiling gaily. 7.45. Stevenson up with one brigade of his division, sent to reinforce Hancock. The other brigade had lost the road, but was expected soon. There was Charlie Mills, and Stevie Weld, Lt. Col. of the 56th. Told them we were driving them, and they had only to go in & finish up the rebs.[23] 7.50 A.M. One of Barlow's brigades is to go in along the incomplete railroad cut and strike the enemy in flank. 9. Column reported coming up the Brock road and deploying skirmishers. This, in the event, proved only a lot of cavalry, but these demonstrations had a most paralysing effect on our left, and seriously affected the fight. Gibbon was stampeded and made no vigorous handling of Barlow's division and of Carroll's brigade.— Hancock complained after, that Gibbon's feeble command of the left wing of his corps changed the face of the day. 10. These rebel cavalry were beaten by ours, on the Brock road. It must have been about this time that a prisoner of *Longstreet's Corps* was brought to me! This showed the presence of these troops, who had not before been in the fight, being on the march from Orange C. H. Reported this at once to Gen. Meade.[24]— Macy was shot through the leg about this time, the 20th being heavily engaged on the right of the plank. He told me (after) that Gen. Wadsworth was back & forth there a great deal ordering him to the *left* of the plank, whereas Webb had put him where he was. 11. Abbott mortally wounded. Maj. Angel told me he saw him lying on the line; his eyes fixed. There is a great likeness between Angel & Maj. Norval, both Staff officers of 2d Corps; the former being Engineer at Headq'rs.[25] 11.10. The first grand break—said, by the officer who came, to be first the right of Barlow, but think it was the left of Mott. Longstreet had struck heavily there, diagonally towards the Plank (as would appear from rebel accounts).[26]— For a long time the wounded had been coming back rapidly along the road; at one period 2 light twelves had, by order of Gen. Birney, been placed on the plank and had fired solid shot over our men. Gibbon too had opened a battery on the left, but it ceased firing on information that the shot struck in our own lines. The attack became general on the whole front. Stevenson's brigade of raw "Veterans," broke after being under a severe fire for 10 minutes. Col. Griswold of the 56th was

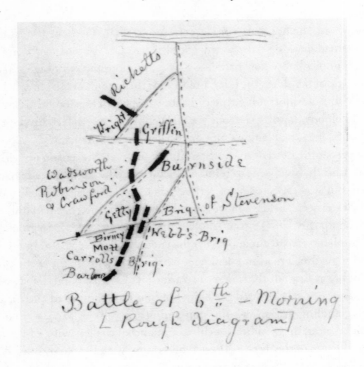

Ricketts
Wright
Griffin
Burnside
Wadsworth
Robinson
& Crawford
Getty
Brig. of Stevenson
Birney
Mott
Webb's Brig
Carrolls Brig.
Barlow

Battle of 6th — Morning
[Rough diagram]

killed. Col. Bartlett, of the 57th, wounded, Gen. Stevenson, nearly surrounded, escaped by the right.[27] A large part of the whole line came back, slowly but mixed up—a hopeless sight! American soldiers, in this condition are enough to sink one's heart! They have no craven terror—they have their arms; but, for the moment, they will not fight, nor even rally. Drew my sword and tried to stop them, but with small success, at the partial rifle-pit that ran along the road. There was no danger, the enemy did not follow. 12. Rode in and reported the state of the case in person to Gen. Meade. Gen. Patrick went out with his brigade, and, as the stream of stragglers came up the cross-road, he stopped them in the open fields & rapidly reorganized them. Artillery had been planted on the ridge near Headq'rs pointing S.W. The General told me to remain a little. Grant, who was smoking stoically under a pine, expressed himself annoyed and surprised that Burnside did not attack, especially as Comstock was with him as engineer & staff officer, to show him the way.[28] 1 P.M. Trains ordered to fall back towards Ely's Ford, as a precautionary measure. 1.15 (about)—Back to Hancock. He alone, in rear of Brock Road; and there he asked me to sit down under the trees, as he was very tired indeed. All his staff were away to set in order the troops. They had now constructed a tolerable rifle-pit extending along the Brock and to the head of the cross-road. He said that his troops were rallied but very tired and mixed up, and not in a condition to advance. He had given orders to have the utmost exertions put forth in putting regiments in order, but many of the field officers were killed & wounded, and it was hard. At 2 P.M. Burnside, after going almost to Parker's Store and again back, made a short attack with loud musketry. Ventured to urge Hancock (who was very pleasant & talkative) to try and attack too, but he said with much regret that it would be to hazard too much, though there was nothing in his immediate front, which had been swept by Stevenson's other brigade, which marched from left to right. He spoke highly of the commander of this brigade.[29] There presently came a note from Gen. Meade that Burnside had attacked and taken a small breastwork, and could Hancock attack also?— Burnside's success was, after all, trifling, if anything. Potter told me (after) that his division like the rest in that corps, was mostly of raw men, that they made a very good rush at first, but were presently driven back as fast as they came. Gen. Wadsworth today was mortally wounded and left in the hands of the enemy, near the Plank Road. The attacks of Griffin and of Sedgwick's two divisions, on the right amounted to nothing. Flint saw (May '65) the place where the 6th Corps charged, and said there were no marks of very hard fighting, but on the left, along the Plank Road, there were places in front of the rebel pits, where the entire growth of saplings was cut down by musketry.[30] Concerning this fight on the Plank Road there has been the greatest discussion between Webb's brigade, Getty's division and the division of Birney and of Wadsworth, especially the two latter. Wadsworth's people, and Cope, of Gen. Warren's staff, state that they drove back the rebels, and got a footing on the Plank Road (attacking the rebel left in that part of the field) and that one brigade swept the whole front of the 2d Corps and came out on the other side, while the 2d Corps were lying behind breastworks doing nothing! Birney's people *per contra* say that Wadsworth's attack amounted to nothing and he was driven back, though personally he came on the Plank Road and interfered with the order of battle, while they did all the successful fighting! The two accounts are entirely unreconcilable, but are not astonishing in a desperate fight in a thick cover, where no one can see 100 feet, and every one is liable to get turned round. Macy told me that, though he lost over ¼ of his men killed and wounded he *never saw a rebel*! In truth this whole Battle of the Wilderness was a scientific "bushwhack" of 200,000 men![31] 3.15 P.M. All being quiet got permission of Hancock to go back to 2d Corps Hospital & look after Abbott. (The hospital was some 2 miles back on a cleared farm, approachable only by a winding wood road, south of the plank. It was excellently arranged, particularly for the small means, but a ghastly sight indeed! Arms & legs lay outside the operating tents, and each table had a bleeding man on it, insensible from ether, and with the surgeons at work on him. As I entered a large tent and asked "Is Maj. Abbott here?"—"Here he is, sir," said a servant.— I should not have recognized the white face & uprolled eyes! He was unconscious and dying fast. Lifted Macy up, and we stood there till he was gone—Macy shedding tears. Took his valuables in charge and a lock of his hair, and got the promise that his body should go home, if possible.— In the embalming place (a negro house) there lay already the body of a Captain of Infantry; the assistant had just cut down on the femoral artery.) Abbott died about 4.[32] As was riding again towards the front, about 4.30, the artillery on Gibbon's left suddenly opened heavily, followed by a sharp musketry. Immediately rode up the Germanna Plank to Gen. Meade, reported the fact and asked if he could not get Burnside ordered in to attack and help Hancock. In spite of this Gen. Meade seemed sceptical of the severity of the attack. Burnside did of his own accord, put in a division, with good effect. "The best thing old Burn' did during the day," said the General afterwards. 5.20 P.M. Rode back to join Gen. H[ancock] but on the road met Maj. Hancock (I think) who said the enemy had broken through at the plank, and there was no communication with the left wing! Found Birney in the cross-road, and he said the same; upon which sent back a note which stampeded the General. All wrong on Birney's part—along came Saunders (I believe) & we rode together down the road & found all open, and that the enemy had only broken through in one small place, but had been driven out, leaving over 50 dead on that spot.[33] Presently found Hancock and remained till about sunset with him. 7 P.M. While at dinner heard a little scattered musketry and presently up gallops Capt. Beaumont, followed by Lt. Col. Kent—in great flurry, saying the 6th Corps was broken and driven back, the enemy on the Germanna Plank & Orange Pike, and that we had better look out not to be captured. They both were quite out of their heads. "And where" said Gen. M[eade] calmly, are Upton's & Shaler's brigades, that Sedgwick said he could spare me, this morning?"—"I don't know Sir."—"Do you mean to tell me that the 6th Corps is not to do any more fighting this campaign?"—"I am fearful not Sir!" quoth Kent.[34] Orders were sent at once for the Pennsylvania Reserves to move to the support, by the Germanna Plank. There were the wildest reports that Gen. Sedgwick was taken &c. &c. Capt. Cadwalader who rode up the plank towards Germanna Ford, was fired on, sure enough, by some rebs! About 7.30 P.M. Ordered to take over a statement of the case to Gen. Grant, in the hollow hard by. He seemed more disturbed than Meade about it, and they afterwards consulted together. In truth they (the enemy) had no idea of their success. They made a dash with Edw. Johnson's division about dusk, or somewhat before, and surprised completely Ricketts' shaky division, which fled at once; but most, or the whole of the first division (and perhaps part of the 3d) stood firm; and the rebels were more than content to get Gens. Seymour & Shaler, and some other prisoners, and a lot of muskets & camp equipage. In consequence of this mishap the right was ordered swung back, so as to slant towards Germanna Plank. That poor 93d N.Y.—the "bloodless," so long the headquarter guard, even from McClellan's day! Today they went in and are bloody enough now; 15 or 16 officers hit in these two days, and men in proportion.[35] Lost my sword today from its scabbard, while galloping in the woods. Some means should be devised to hold in the swords of mounted officers, the number lost is very great. Col. Walker found it & gave it to me; he, by the way, had lost his. Old Washburn, senator & the great friend of Grant, is a companion of the campaign. He came down entirely confident that Grant would at once swallow and annihilate Lee; but he wears another face now! Griffin lost a couple of guns yesterday.— We took some colors today. Grant told Meade that Joe Johnston would have retreated after two such days' punishment. He recognizes the difference of the Western rebel fighting. During this day Sheridan defended our flanks & rear, with considerable fighting.[36]

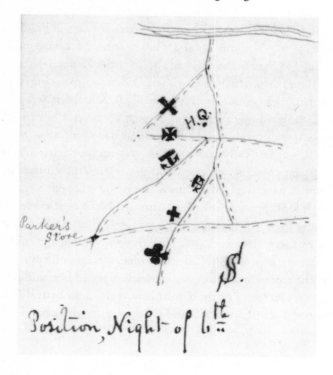

May 7, Saturday.

When we rose this morn we were pretty uncertain what the enemy was about, whether working on our flanks, or fallen back, or stationary.—All was quiet.— 5 A.M. Ferrero's negro div. of the 9th Corps was up and massed in a hollow in the direction of the Lacy house. It made me sad to see them.—Can we not fight our own battles? The General rode through them on his way to Grant.[37] 5.30. Ordered, to write to Gen. Sedgwick and direct him to hold all the ground the enemy would let him; and keep his cavalry & pickets well out. 9. Hancock reports nothing in his immediate front; Wright, from the other wing, reports nothing just in front of him, apparently. Warren reports a force in his front, though perhaps fallen back. 10. Warren sends out a reconnaissance of 1,000 men along the pike, from Griffin.—Heavy skirmish in that direction, and some artillery. 10.45 Ordered to ride out to Griffin and ask the result of the reconnaissance. Rode out to our breastworks on the pike, and found our artillery firing in the road and the enemy firing back, though rather wildly, for the most part. Some shooting in the heavy pine woods in front. There were a good many deep hollows hereabout, quite hilly as compared with the plank-road. Did not find Griffin, but Capt. Martin, his Chief of Artillery, told me the result of the reconnaissance was not yet reported.[38] Rode to the left, then to the rear to Gen. Warren's Headq'rs where stopped and sent a written report to our Headq'rs. Two or three shells fell in the hollow hard by; the place was the Lacy house. 2 P.M. Had returned to Headq'rs.—Meade in an ill humor, had read what Warren sent—"the enemy's shells fall near my Headquarters."—"Well, can't I see that? What's *that* to do with it?" says the General. Was rejoiced & surprised to find tent-mate "Rosie," who had ridden across country, all the way from Rappahannock Station, in company of Mr. Dana, Assist. Sec. of War, a large man, a combination of scholar and newspaper editor, with a dab of amiability, a large dab of conceit, and another large dab of ultraism. He was to be another civil companion of Grant.[39] Rosie was equipped, from Washington, with what we supposed to be a huge field-glass, but which turned out to be a large case-bottle, which banged his ribs whenever he galloped! A scout was now to go through to Rappahannock. Sent (through McGregor, correspondent of the Associated Press) by his hand a telegram to Mimi. 3. The 22d N.Y. Cav., somewhere by Germanna ford, got a shell thrown at them and rushed in wild confusion down the road, led off by the Colonel, an abominable coward and scoundrel. The regiment itself was raw. Meade arrested him and put the Major in his place, remarking tartly, "I don't believe he's a bit better!"[40] Wounded ordered sent to Rappahannock Station. Butler yesterday occupied suddenly

City Point.[41] Went into a hollow behind our knoll, where was a field hospital. There were some rebel wounded there lying. They were loading the wounded in ambulances, to go north, only leaving a few very badly hurt. Now however, came notice that the rebel infantry and cavalry were advancing along the river bank, to occupy all the fords, including Ely's. The cavalry officer who sent this in ought to have been shot! The force the enemy sent along there is pretty known now to have been most trifling and nothing prevented us from driving them off. Alas! for the poor wounded! The train of them was already far on its way, when Gen. Meade had to send word to halt, and subsequently to face it towards Fredericksburg. What delay & suffering! How many men whose vital force was just sufficient to have brought them safely to Washington, were killed by this protraction of their trials! This day Sheridan concentrated near Todd's Tavern and attacked and severely beat Stuart's cavalry.[42] The order of march for eve of May 7th. Reserve Artillery at 7 P.M. via Chancellorsville and Aldrich's to crossing of Alsop and Piney Branch Church roads, 5th Corps to Spottsylvania C.H., via Brock road and by Todd's Tavern. 6th Corps by pike & plank to Chancellorsville and escort trains to cross of Piney Branch & Block house roads. 9th Corps follow 6th. 2d follows 5th to Todd's Tavern.[43] As Grant sat under a pine tree, he said, in his short way: "Tonight Lee will be retreating south!" This showed that he did not yet fully take in Lee's obstinacy & the goodness of his army. Although his remark about Johnston showed that he already began to appreciate them.[44] At 8.45 P.M. we left Headquarters. All the afternoon there had been commotion among the baggage waggons, and the heavy artillery were moving too. The dust was in fine clouds as we rode down the cross-road and halted at Hancock's near the junction of the plank. The General bade us ride on and stop for him at Gibbon's whom we found on the Brock, at a little house. It was a picturesque sight the infantry closely huddled asleep, under the breastwork that followed the road. On top it and outside were sentries with their muskets ready. The officers paced up and down; all were prepared for instant action. We got some iced water from Gibbon, and lay down to take a nap in the dust. By & bye came the General [Meade], with a following of all that cavalry of Gen. Patrick's, which raised such a dust as well nigh to suffocate us. We rode on by the Brock road; then got wrong, in passing some batteries in position; then got straight again. The General told me to make the cavalry in rear go ahead of us; which did, at expense of tearing my blouse to pieces, for the road was narrow with woods each side and was full of cavalry. Could see nobody, so dark was it. At last we struck a cavalry outpost, and, soon after, got to Todd's Tavern, at the crossing of the roads. It is an ordinary old building, of moderate size. There were some women & negroes there. Gen. Gregg came out to welcome us. They have had successful fighting round here for 3 days.[45]

May 8, Sunday.

(Early morning) and yesterday Capt. Ash was killed and Carpenter (6th Penn. Cav.) taken. Starr was wounded. Ash was a slight, black-eyed man, of extraordinary personal gallantry; and well known in the regular cavalry. The cavalry of Custer here got in the way, very much of the 5th Corps, but, nevertheless, at 5.45 A.M. two divisions had passed this point.[46] We got some coffee made by an old nig there and also some hoe-cake, which went well. Meantime the infantry (most now stripped of all luggage save a shelter tent, or rubber blanket) were passing at a very rapid rate. 9.15. The wounded sent to Fredericksburg; 12,000 in number. Rode to near Piney Branch Church.[47] Day warm; country very poor & sandy; part open & part wooded with pine. About half way came on a park of ambulances, in one of which was Starr, with a bullet right through both cheeks, a most distressing wound. He was speechless and could only shake our hands. Last night Cadwalader lost his favorite blood mare, at which he was excessively troubled, for in sooth an officer's horse is here his all. We pitched camp, set the cooks at work. 11.40. A.M. Warren engaged with Longstreet, who has got first to the road and bars the way. Wilson's cavalry is in Spottsylvania Court House itself. Robinson's Division advanced to clear the road, but behaved badly. Robinson himself rode forward, crying to use the bayonet—was shot in the knee and carried off the field.[48] Sheridan came now to Headquarters—we were at dinner. Meade told him sharply that his cavalry was in the way, though he had sent him orders to leave the road clear. S[heridan] replied that he never got the order. Meade then apologized, but Sheridan was plainly full of suppressed anger, and Meade too was in ill temper. S[heridan] went on to say that he could see nothing to oppose the advance of the 5th Corps; that the behavior of the infantry was disgraceful &c. &c. Maybe this was the beginning of his dislike of Warren and ill-feeling against Meade.[49] 12.20 P.M. A great herd of prisoners passed in the hollow—some 1,800, en route for Fredericksburg perhaps. 12.50. Firing towards Catharpin road—a new direction—it was Miles' Brig. of Barlow's Div. which had been posted near Corbyn's bridge.[50] Of course the rebel column, moving on Spottsylvania, brushed it with its flank. The enemy tried, in three charges to repulse it, but were driven back with heavy loss. Hancock then withdrew the brigade, at which Meade said; "Why didn't he reinforce it?—I would as soon fight there as anywhere."— We all were very filthy here, every pore full of dust. Went to the "branch" and managed to give myself a bath. 1.45 P.M. Headq'rs move down Piney Branch Road. As we got to the corner of the woods there was a knot of soldiers, and they said they had just shot a deserter. Halted not far above its junction with Todd's Tavern Road. All our spring-waggons ordered turned in for use of the wounded. 3.30. Ordered to go and find general position of our lines and the enemy's and how far preparations for assault were made. A little below where road opens into an extensive open space found Gens. Sedgwick, Warren & Wright. Was struck by their worn and troubled aspect, more especially in Sedgwick, who showed its effect more from contrast with his usual calmness. In fact the sudden transition from a long winter's rest to hard marching, sleepless nights, and protracted fighting, with no prospect of cessation, produced a powerful effect on the nervous system of the whole army. And never, perhaps, were officers and men more jaded and prostrated than on this very Sunday. Artillery was planted here and there had been some cannonading. Gen. Sedgwick said—"Where is the Vermont brigade?—not up yet—just when I wanted it—everything unlucky!" He nor Warren could give no positive answer when they would assault. Wainwright, Chief of Artillery of 5th Corps, was also there and said he had reconnoitred the enemy's line. He seemed in better spirits than the rest. Reported back at 4.20 P.M. Grant & Meade were now moved forward to the Hart house, which stood west of the Todd's Tavern Road and was surrounded by a wheat field. It commanded an extensive view towards the Po River and beyond.[51] Was sent to see once more how the plan of attack progressed, but met Riddle, coming back with news that Warren had devised a plan which was at once to be carried out. The two generals at once started, with their staffs, down the road passing Alsop's and so through a hollow and up a turn to the right, to a wooded knoll, where nothing was to be seen at all. There was skirmishing just in our front and the balls came clicking among the large trees, while a shell occasionally added its crashing to the general noise. As we sat there Neil's brigade passed to the left, marching by a flank. "Bean Neil" himself rode by the men, attired in a sort of civilian suit of grey brown;—faith he never is dressed like anybody else![52] Gen. Humphreys could not endure sitting there and rode off to the left, and reconnoitred into every sort of dangerous place, quite round the enemy's flank! Grant now turned homeward, and the General appointed me to show him the way to the new Headq'rs, which I did, not loathingly, for the place waxed hot! We pitched our tents in an open place, west of the Todd's Tavern Road, Grant being close to the road, and Meade a little inside of him. Martin, former Chief of Artillery of 5th Corps was today badly shot in the neck by a sharpshooter; and Locke,

A.A.G. of 5th Corps, through both cheeks.[53] 6.30 P.M. Sharp musketry on our left, for a few moments—the only result of Warren's grand plan of attack—an advance of the Pennsylvania Reserves, who came back in a hurry. Duane was there and Gen. Sedgwick, who got hit in the stomach by a spent ball. Duane expected to be blown up by the Commander for not doing more in the way of putting in the troops; but Meade only said, that evening; "I suppose you did all you could."— Duane's horse reared over on him in the Wilderness fight and plastered him with mud, besides hurting him a good deal.[54] 6.30. At this time Hancock, near Todd's Tavern, reported the enemy in his front. (This was only Lee's rear guard and baggage train marching, in all haste on Spottsylvania.) After our late dinner the General let out. Burnside he said was too late, in the Wilderness, to do any good. He wandered down the Parker's Store Road and came in after all the damage was done. Sedgwick was constitutionally slow. The men were now very tired. "I told Warren today" continued he "that he had lost his nerve; at which he professed to be very indignant. Ward, of the 2d Corps, I have been obliged to relieve. They say he was in liquor in the Wilderness and that he rode away from the fight on a caisson."[55]— 10 P.M. Directed to authorize Gen. Patrick to transfer his prisoners to the waggon train. We were much gratified all night by a very rich dead horse. Old Col. Schriver remarking that it was really "impossible to get any spades to bury him!" S[chriver] is the most precise representation of inefficient red-tape, that can be![56]

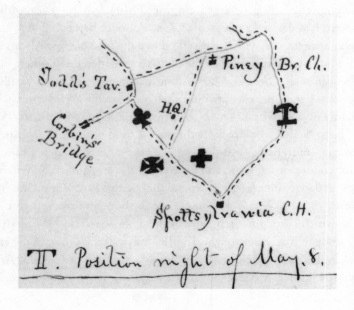

May 9, Monday.

Two divisions of the 9th Corps were to be at the "Gate" on the east road to Spottsylvania C.H. at 6 A.M.[57] 7 A.M. Out with the General up the Todd's Tavern Road. A really hot day with sandy dusty roads. Before getting to Tavern, met Gen. Hancock and his staff. They were under a cherry tree, which was fully leafed out. There were small breastworks along the road in several places; but the troops were more west (left)—except some artillery. Barlow too was there, a queer, lean figure, in a cap, checked shirt and blue pantaloons, mounted on a tall horse! Walker had found my sword, which flew out of its scabbard at the Wilderness, and returned it to me, to my great satisfaction. Birney too rode up, with another checked shirt, a strange contrast to his pale, dry, and rather precise, face. Hancock said the enemy were in his front. After giving some orders Meade again rode towards the front (south). On the way we came on a field hospital in the woods, where lay Gen. Robinson, shot through the knee and in much pain with it. Meade dismounted and went in to see him.[58] He then sent me off on an errand, with orders to follow him to the front, where Warren was. As rode down the wood-road, just where it comes out at the open, met Lt. Col. McMahon, looking haggard and distressed.— He exclaimed "Gen. Sedgwick is shot through the head; and, my God! I'm afraid he is killed!"— He bowed in the saddle and seemed quite unmanned, for he loved Gen. Sedgwick very much. 10 A.M. I followed and got up with Gen. Meade near the wooded knoll, where we went last afternoon. He knew the news, and had sent an order for Wright to take the corps. Believe that Humphreys went in person. Ricketts, who thus was overslaughed took it very kindly. Neil succeeds to W[right]'s division;—Warren was on the knoll, and with him the Gen'l consulted.[59] 10.30 Cannon from Burnside on the left. He moved down the "Gate" road, but, naturally enough, found no place called the "Gate" (though there was a gate there). Encountered the enemy on the north side and, with pretty sharp fighting, drove them across and established himself the other side of the stream. Little Gen. Morris got shot through the leg today. Exit M[orris] to appear no more on the stage of the field! Butler was reported only 11 m. south of Richmond.[60] All the time there was skirmishing and rapid sharpshooting along the lines. There passed an ambulance with the body of Gen. Sedgwick, and followed by his favorite aide, Whittier. He was killed by a sharpshooter; just as he clapped a man on the back and said; "Why, what are you dodging about? They couldn't hit an elephant at that distance!"— He had established his Headq'rs in an exposed spot, partly perhaps because Meade had said to him, with some asperity, that "he desired he would take command of his own corps"—referring to a disposition by Sedgwick to lean on the opinion of Warren, whose corps was first in position. "I feel the more grieved at his death" said the General, that evening "because we had not parted entirely in good feeling."[61] 1.10 P.M. Ordered to go to Wright, and tell him that Gibbon had moved up on the right and that the rest of the 2d Corps was to follow. Found him on the wooded knoll, still. He said the rebels were passing to our left (to oppose Burnside).— 3.10. General & staff near the Hart house with Gibbon, whence we could see the rebel waggon train, moving down towards Spottsylvania, the other side of the Po. He opened upon it, which made the rear of the train hurry up a good deal. There was talk too of attacking it; but it ended in giving and countermanding an order. Doubtless there was a good chance yesterday and today, for Hancock to make a bold dash on our right and rear, to cut off their train and rear guard. The General rode out with Gibbon to reconnoitre, leaving us with Col. Sprigg Carroll, whose brigade lay there with the rest of Gibbon's division. Sprigg had erected a bower, to keep off the hot sun; and had iced water, from the neighboring house, and whiskey from a canteen. His wounded arm, he said, was getting mighty sore, but he "must stay for one more fight!" A man was brought under guard, who had stolen a horse. "I think," quoth Sprigg, with grave facetiousness, "that I will shoot you!" The joke of which the man could not see. At our Headq'rs and under an arbor of pine branches, lay Gen. Sedgwick, in state, with two Zouaves keeping guard, their arms reversed. Dr. Brinton embalmed him, as well as he could, with a solution of an arsenic salt; and the body was sent, in charge of Whittier, to Fredericksburg. Whittier took a note for me, to Mimi. 5.15 An attack on the right centre.[62]

May 10, Tuesday.

7.05 A.M. Ordered to go to Gen. Wright, and remain to send back information; also to carry an order to Gen. Mott. 7.25. Reported to Gen. Wright, who was in a hollow, a little this side of the wooded knoll. 7.45. Took the order to Gen. Mott. Found him by following along Russell's line, to the left. Russell directed me along his skirmish line, still to the left, and, going through a little wood, came out on a cleared ridge, where was the Brown house. Mott's troops were massed, making coffee behind the ridge, while, on the side towards the enemy the skirmishers were deployed.

Explained to Mott his relative position as well as could, and directed him to demonstrate in his front and find a road to his left to Burnside. Mott showed a want of force and intelligence, though always a cool, brave man. He said "Well, my men are making coffee (they had had a night march) and I will push out as soon as they have done." As rode back the batteries were playing

Spottsylvania

Position Night of May 9.

on Russell's right and the pieces of shell from the enemy came close to me as I rode through the pine woods. A number of men were killed there, despite the parapet with which they had covered their front. 8.35 Reported by orderly to Gen. Meade from Wright's. 10.15. Heavy cannonade from batteries on our left; also from a battery on the right, beyond the wooded knoll. The latter drove the rebels from their guns, and continued to fire rapidly by section, hoping to get the pieces, for Neil was driving the enemy's skirmishers. There was a great din with cannon and crackling of rifles. 11. We had news of successful advance by Sherman in the west; also reported success near Petersburg.[63] 11.30. Gen. Meade, who had come down to see the progress, ordered me to again cross to Mott, and get a written report of his position. He was as before, at the Brown house, with no great change since 4 hours, except the skirmishers had apparently been pushed out.— An officer had been through to Burnside and brought back word that Gen. Stevenson was killed this morning by a stray ball; he was sitting after breakfast, in a hollow way and was struck in the head!— The rebel sharpshooters were occasionally firing over, from a very great distance, and the direction of the Landron house.[64] One apparently shot at me, and they had before tried Gen. Mott. There saw Lt. Col. Merriam (for the last time). He had charge of the skirmish line. He was sorely depressed, but pride held him to his duty. He entered this campaign with the fixed presentiment of death, and had tried to resign, after his long service and severe wounds. Mott said he could not make much of a written description of his position (which readily believed). 12.45. Reported back to Gen. Meade, indicating position of Brown house, as well as could. Meade now went back. Kent, Dr. Holman and I made ourselves small in the hollow where we were waiting, hour after hour, while the spent bullets kept dropping in. Holman is a consistent fatalist and was not shaken when a ball struck his coat-tail! Next day about one [P.M.] he was struck on the breast by a bullet and only saved by his note-book.[65] Wright planned an attack, to be made at a point S.W. of the Brown house, and headed by Upton. Warren's Corps and Gibbon's Division (2d Corps) were to go in at the same time, on the right. During the day Barlow's division had crossed the Po, on the extreme right, to feel round the left of the enemy; but they were found there intrenched in force. As B[arlow] was recrossing, Heth came out and attacked his rear, but got repulsed with great loss. The artillerists laughed at Barlow for putting a smooth 12-lbdr. battery behind a 3-inch rifled one, to fire over it![66]— 5–6 P.M. All the batteries opened and roared as hard as they could, particularly on the point for Upton's attack. 6.30. Fine charge by Upton. The columns went up with a rush, the men who faltered were run through by those behind. The works were taken, with 900 prisoners. Upton escaped, with a graze of the arm. Mott's men on his left, behaved abominably. It is represented that they broke almost before getting under fire. Upton's flank being thus exposed he was forced to come back but brought off his prisoners. Among those who fell was the son of Dr. Dorr, who preached for us last winter in camp.[67] The nomadic artist Waud said it was a fine sight to see the prisoners brought in on the double-quick in a great herd. At dusk rode back to near Alsop's, where found the General, with Grant and all the staff. Told him of Upton's feat, at which he exclaimed "Well, that is something good at any rate!" In fact the 5th Corps and Gibbon had been repulsed completely in their attack, and many of the troops had fallen back in confusion to the rear of their former line, as heard staff officers say, then & there. Was puzzled to observe a stampeded look on the faces of some officers and to hear Grant say, in a cool, sarcastic way "*I* don't see any of these Greybacks." Presently up rides old Washburn, looking thoroughly scared, and gobbling something about, "This is not so, is it? There's nothing wrong, is there?" Then learned that Headquarters had been turned out with a scare! It came about thus:—when Barlow recrossed the Po, the rebels pushed out skirmishers round our right flank and Miles sent in word that Headq'rs better be on the look out. This was interpreted by somebody to mean pack up! So the waggons were loaded in haste and Flint was sent out with the escort (under Adams) who pushed as far as he could and lost one or two prisoners. The infantry guard was also deployed, to skirmish with nobody! The result of the whole being the shaking of old W[ashburne]'s nerves and the moving of Headq'rs to the S.E. of the road from Alsop's to Armstrong's. 11 P.M. Grant in consultation with Meade. He said, "Burnside's isolated position alarms me; he is within a mile and a half of Spottsylvania court house."[68] Wright came up also; he uttered no complaints, but said quietly & firmly to Meade; "General, I don't *want* Mott's men on my left—they are not a support; I would rather have no troops there!" (Reflection: Poor troops are better left behind; this is shown here and in the Wilderness. When such soldiers break they make a gap in the line and the regiments on the right and left get flanked. It avails not to put them in three lines of battle. When the first line gives way, the two others will not go in, but fall back and make a mass of confusion!) Warren is not up to a corps command. As in the Mine Run move, so here, he cannot spread himself over three divisions. He cannot do it, and the result is partial and ill-concerted and dilatory movements. This day Sheridan (off on his raid) attacked Beaver Dam Station, destroyed all the stores there and rescued 350 of our prisoners whom they were about to put on the cars for Richmond! The brave Gen. Rice was struck today in the thigh by a ball, and sunk under the amputation. As he lay on the stretcher, he called out to Gen. Meade: "Don't you give up this fight! I am willing to give up my life, if it is to be; but don't you give up the fight!"[69]

May 11, Wednesday.

Mott withdrawn. Wright to push out his left and connect with Burnside.

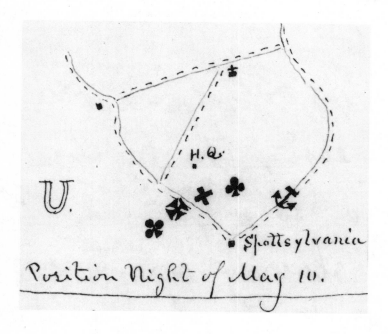

Barlow to cover our right flank with his division intrenched. (*Remark.* The use of these intrenchments—vulgarly called "rifle pits," but really an infantry parapet—is a feature, if not *the* feature in our mode of warfare. The soil, being sandy and free from boulders or hard gravel, may easily be cast up with a simple spade, or even by a wooden shovel, or by a rude scoop made of a split canteen. The straight, "hard pine" furnishes an admirable revetment; so that a breastwork, good against musketry, and tolerably revetted, may, when the men are spurred by impending danger, be thrown up, in an hour or two. Experience has taught us; so that, by the spring of the present year, in both armies, and west as well as east, the practice became universal, and so ingrained that the men began with alacrity to cover their front the moment they halted.) 11.15. Was standing near Grant's tent when word was brought in, that some rebel sharpshooters had got in rear of Wright's picket line connecting with Burnside, and were firing on our men. Grant ordered me to go out to Wright and direct him to send out and hunt them up (getting my order through Gen. Meade). "And let it be understood" said he, "I want no prisoners taken of any such men!" Rode out and found Wright in the skirt of wood just before getting to the Brown house. His troops were moving by the left flank, to extend towards Burnside. The illegitimate sharpshooters seem to have fled, for we heard no more of them. There was now a breastwork along the Brown house ridge, and batteries in position. Indeed, by today, the whole army, along its front of some miles, was strongly intrenched, with the pickets in pits, and the batteries covered by strong epaulements. Thus a diminished force

could hold the line and the whole Second Corps was left with a free foot. The telegraph was got through to Burnside. All available troops are now on their way from Washington to reinforce us. In the afternoon the dust was converted into mud by a heavy thunderstorm. That eve, saw Sleeper making himself as comfortable as might be in his battery ambulance, which already had a bullet through it! He was in the open field near Alsop's and to the right & front of our Headq'rs. In Alsop's was a hospital, with the ambulance station farther down the road, in rear of the hollow where were Wright's Headq'rs. Hancock to move tonight, by the left flank. This day Sheridan destroyed Ashland Station, and defeated and killed "Jeb" Stuart at Yellow Tavern.[70]

May 12, Thursday.

Hancock was massed on the left, to attack, (at 4, or as soon as possible after daylight) the salient S.W. of the Landron house. Warren, assisted by Kitchen's brigade of Heavy Artillery to occupy the former line of the 2d, and his own corps and to hold a reserve column at the cross-road by Alsop's.[71] Burnside to attack also. About daylight, we all stood round Grant's Headq'rs in the woods on the opposite side of the road, anxiously waiting for news. 5.15 A.M. Gen. Williams, (with smiling face, approaches from the telegraph tent—Hancock has carried their first line! 5.20 Ordered to take this news to Gens. Wright and Warren and to order the latter to attack. 5.45. News of the capture of the second line with two or more generals! Hereat Gen. Rawlins, with his hard hollow voice, broke out into loud, coarse exultation "By G—! They are done!—Hancock will just drive them to H—!" He is a man who gives a very disagreeable first impression; loud and profane in talk, fiery and impulsive of temper, and with a general demeanor of the bad "Western" kind. In truth he is a man of a cool, clear judgment, and well gifted with common sense; despite his temper too, he is a good hearted man. His flashes of anger & of over confidence depend perhaps on his pulmonary tendency; for he seems hopelessly consumptive.[72] 5.55. Hancock telegraphed desiring a brisk attack made on his right. 6.10. Burnside has made a junction with Hancock. 6.30. Heard somebody say "Sir, this is General Johnson"—and, turning, saw the rebel officer walk up gravely;—a stout built man, with a coarse stern face. He had on riding boots, a blue-grey, double-breasted coat and a very bad black felt. He was terribly mortified and kept coughing to hide his nervousness. Gens. Meade and Grant shook hands with him and Gen. Williams took him kindly to breakfast. He said to Gen. Williams "Doubtless you have gained an advantage, but you are much mistaken if you think we are beaten yet!"—He was right!—and he was fated to live to be captured once again with his whole division, by Thomas, before Nashville. The other General, a little Baltimore Stewart, behaved like a donkey, refused to shake hands with Hancock and was sent to Fredericksburg on foot, for his pains, with the mud ankle deep![73]— Burnside was meantime heavily engaged and advancing. 6.45 Ordered, to go out and ascertain progress in Wright's front. Found his column going into the pine woods S.W. from Brown house and at the foot of the ridge on which it stands. As returned, met Eustis's brigade (2d Div. 6th Corps) moving on. Told him the good news, and how we had 3,000 prisoners; whereupon cried some sceptic; "And how many did they take from *us?*" 7.15. Ordered to return to Wright & remain to report back progress by orderly. Column still marching into the pine woods in front of the Brown house, and the shells were coming through, as the enemy could probably see some indications of the movement. A little further on there were a good number of bullets flying and clicking among the trees. An aide came back just then and ordered the brigade to advance on the double quick. Asked several officers the whereabouts of Wright. Some said this way, and some that; so at last dismounted, stowed my orderlies and myself behind trees and wrote a despatch to the General, the rain coming down heavily (which it continued to do intermittently during the day). I was on the front edge of the woods, before me an extensive, rolling open; beyond this another skirt of woods, in which was the fighting. Just before me was a battery, at whose caissons the enemy were firing explosive bullets, which hit on all sides of me, going off just like fire-crackers. In a few moments Capt. Arthur McClellan came along behind me and I asked him if he knew the way to Wright, which he showed me.[74] The General [Wright] was close to me and in a little hollow where the road from the wood came into the open, with his staff. They were sitting on the ground. He had been hit, a little before, by a piece of shell, on the leg, making a bad contusion. Just by us lay a dead infantryman, on his back, with his knees drawn up. He seemed a sorry German with a frowsy red beard. Birney rode up presently. He too had been bruised by a fragment of shell. "There are forty guns there," said he: "I have seen them!" Some of them however were not in our hands but between the lines. Meantime the musketry in our front was continuous and heavy and bullets not a few came dropping into our hollow, killing one horse and wounding another. Soon a battery was turned on us (because, perhaps the officer saw so many horsemen coming, and going). "You must cut your fuzes shorter," said Col. Tomkins as a shell came past our ears and exploded beyond. Then came any quantity of them, with fragments of and bullets from spherical case. It was very hot! Ordnance officer Sawin passed, anxious to get up cartridges. "The only way to keep the men there is to let them fire," he said.[75] Gen. Russell ("Old David") rode up, as calm and natural as a May morning (not *this* One!). He sat there and talked pleasantly awhile with Gen. Wright; then said he "would go up and see how they were getting along." — Upton rode with him and had his horse killed under him soon after. 10.25 A.M. Kitchen's brigade up, and formed under the crest, just on our right, ready to advance. Kitchen himself, in a very tall felt, the brim turned down to shed the rain, rode in a cheery manner about, and reported for orders to Gen. Wright. Rickett's division reported coming along. The combat growing hotter & hotter! In some places our men just on one side of the breastwork, and the rebels, 50 feet off, on the other! Kitchen sent up a squad to man some pieces that had been got close in, and whose men were shot off. 12.15. The enemy outflank and force back a small part of the right of the 6th Corps, in the woods. Kitchen advances in support of that point. Meantime, Ricketts had reported for orders, the little sturdy, Puritan looking man! "Do you think the men will go up?" said Wright dubiously ("Milroy's weary boys" had a woeful reputation!). "I think they will" quoth R[icketts] "I have been talking to the officers and I think they will." — "Very well, then, move in by the left flank and attack." The whole 5th Corps is moving to its left. 12.30. Rode in to Gen. Meade and reported the state of the field. Found him at Mrs. Armstrong's, a short mile northerly of Brown, and across the Ny.[76] Before went, Wright had moved to the other side of our little bank; but it was out of the frying pan into the fire; there was no safe place that day! — Told the General how things stood, that the enemy pressed our right pretty strongly, at the salient, & that troops had gone up to support. I was a sorry figure! dripping with wet and bemudded with galloping hither & thither. After asking dubiously if could go back with my tired horse, the General gave me an order telling Wright that Griffin was coming along and he could put him, if necessary, in support of the 6th Corps. On my way learned (1.30 P.M.) that Wright had been fairly shelled out of his hollow and was now at the Landron house with Hancock. Found them sitting in chairs behind a log barn, for the sharpshooters were firing at everything they could see. By the house was a battery.[77] Delivered my order to Wright and staid there some time. Do not remember exactly how long. The position remained about the same till dark with additional carnage. The great historical fight of this day extended over a front of only 1,000 to 1,500 yards, along the faces of the salient, or the "Death-angle" as it was afterwards called. Within that narrow field two corps were piled up to assault and in support. Indeed we had *too many* troops, as the generals justly said. The lines got mixed and jammed together and were hard to handle. For 14 hours the troops were at close quarters, and the amount of bullets fired may be known from the fact, that a red oak, 23 inches in diameter was reduced, about 6 feet from the ground, to a fibrous structure and blew down that night! Bodies that lay between the lines were shot to pieces and could only be raised in a blanket! The result was damaging to the enemy—very—but the army of Lee was not cut in two, an issue clearly looked for by Rawlins and some others of Grant's staff, but not so confidently assumed by those who knew a little more.[78] In this action Lt. Col. Merriam fell, shot through the head, while leading on his skirmishers (16th Mass.). He was a great friend of Sleeper who was much moved at his death, and sent the remains to his father. Gen. Webb was very badly hit, by a musket-shot, in the head, and Briscoe, Mundee and Bingham were all severely wounded.[79] Our captures were over 3,000 prisoners, 19 guns, and 20 colors, with two general officers. On the right Warren made three partial attacks, without success. Burnside, on the left, had heavy fighting but without much advance. There now is regular communication with Fredericksburg. We pitched Headq'rs near the Armstrong house. Mrs. A. is a Union woman; her husband a refugee in the North. She was greatly gratified to have Gens. Grant & Meade to lunch with her; and Meade was highly tickled at the fresh butter, though it was intolerably garlicky to my mind! Barstow came back in the afternoon from leave of absence. He was the happy bearer of a package of good tea.

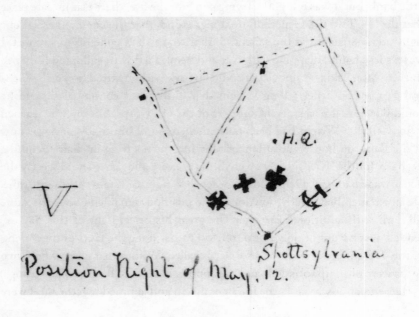

May 13, Friday.

6 A.M. The enemy has abandoned the salient and fallen back, some hundreds of yards, to its base, and straightened his line. 6.30. Gen. Burnside comes over to consult. 7. Special order issued that officers of this staff be ready for duty at daylight, when in presence of the enemy, or incur the displeasure of the Commanding General! This was a raker for some of the young gentlemen who kept too long in their blankets or who hadn't their horses saddled. Officers in from the salient described its awful aspect, this morning; the bodies piled, one on another in heaps and rows! The burial parties are hard at work, but it is dangerous for them, for the rebel sharpshooters fire over from their new front.[80] 8.30 Ordered, to telegraph to corps commanders asking the number of colors captured by their commands, this campaign. A congratulatory address was issued.[81] "May showers" still; first bright, hot sunshine; then a heavy, black rain. The roads a slush of gray sand and water.—The red, Culpeper mud is not here.— Sent Albert to the waggon train to get me some clean flannels; for am in a doleful toilette, with my blouse torn in ribbons with branches & briars!— As we all sat in front of our tents, we were edified by a novel sight, on the Fredericksburg road, which passed just by Armstrong's house. There came a large waggon, marked "Christian Commission," and flanked, skirmisher-wise, by four "philanthropic" looking men, in their shirt sleeves; whereof one cried out; "Where are Meade's Headquarters? We want to do good! We want to do good!"—Biddle, the Warden, issued forth and directed them to the 5th Corps hospital.— Hard by us were a large number of prisoners, from yesterday's fight. Some of them slightly wounded. They were talking briskly among themselves, partly, perhaps, to show their indifference. One Lieutenant said he was taken because a man "was shot off the parapet and sprawled over him!"— There came a letter from Stanton sympathizing with the General in his labors and anxieties.—(S[tanton] can well write such a letter, on occasions). At dark, the 5th, followed by the 6th Corps, are to move to the left and attack on the left of the 9th at 4 A.M. 2d & 9th Corps to stand fast for orders. Waggon train and artillery reserve to Salem Church.[82]

May 14, Saturday.

At 3.30 A.M. in profound darkness, we rode off for the left. There was a long train of army waggons full of wounded, journeying wearily for Fredericksburg. A painful spectacle! As the wheels would jolt into the deep sand holes, we could hear the cries of the poor sufferers mingled with the voices of the drivers shouting to their mules as they struggled through the hard pulling. It was the best we could do—pine branches in army waggons—every spring waggon & ambulance had already gone on. The road, which was circuitous, first to the north & then southerly, was picketed by cavalry. The deep mud impeded the marching of the troops, and, in men so tired, created a vast amount of straggling. In a night march it must be so: for 1st, the men are sleepy; 2d, they stumble and get exhausted; 3d, they can fall out in the darkness. It is a movement to be avoided when possible. Probably not more than one half of Warren's men kept up with the column. 5 A.M. Arrived at the F. Beverly (Gayle) house on the "Gate road" and near the Ny.[83] On the other rising bank of the river the 5th Corps were in position on a line with S. Beverly's. Dr. Adams—a funny little surgeon of the regular army, who much reminds one of the apothecary in Romeo & Juliet, came by & bye and busied himself with caring for a number of stray wounded who had been hid in the woods since the fight of the 12th.[84] Already when we arrived, an infantry lad of ours lay on the piazza shot in the leg, and beside him, a powerful North Carolinian, with light, curly hair, in the half stupor of coming death—a bullet through the upper lung.—When revived by brandy, he said "I was charging one of your batteries, day before yesterday."— Then came, on a stretcher, a tall man, with a canister ball through his thigh—a rebel—his last charge, too; for his mouth was full of foam, and he had no force to stand the amputation. Soon the lower rooms were full of them; but in a pitiful condition; no supplies & only one surgeon just up & without instruments. It was high noon before they could operate on any of them. One man there was a most extraordinary case, at once of escape from death and of cheerful fortitude. A bullet had entered about 2½ inches below the eye, traversed the head diagonally and come out under the opposite ear, cutting off part of its lobe! Yet this man was walking about and positively facetious! His face was black and swelled and he talked thickly, but seemed otherwise vigorous. A singular thing was that he saw & heard perfectly.— This house is on a high roll sloping to the river (really a brook 15 or 20 feet wide). J. Beverly's is opposite on a high roll corresponding. It is all cleared land there. To the left, over the woods, appears the Myers' (Gayle No. 2) house in a small clearing about 1½ miles distant. There was a rebel cavalry regiment there, and we plainly could see them with our glasses, walking about and taking it easy. 8.15 A.M. A regiment sent to dislodge them suddenly charged from the woods, and the cavalry ran for it, despite the gallant exertions of an officer, who galloped about in the most exposed manner. Then we could see our men clustered behind fences and buildings, firing away at the enemy who still hung about; and then the shells exploding from a rebel battery that opened on them. 8.30 Grant & staff come up. Upton's brigade sent to hold the Myer's house.— Rummaged about in the attic, to find something to read. There were a lot of political tracts, as far back as 1839. Also an old & good edition of Johnson's lives of the poets, of which did read a most stilted account of Joseph Addison. Towards afternoon we went to Headq'rs pitched near the Harris house.[85] Presently the General again rode out, with only a couple of aides. 4.15. Sudden musketry on our left! Mounted and rode towards the front. Crossed the Ny and kept to the left, looking for the General, but found him nowhere. Upton's men were coming slowly back, in poor order; a number of wounded among them. It was thus: Gen. Meade on getting to the Myer's house, found Upton's pickets but a few yards out and ordered them at once advanced. This discovered the enemy, close at hand, who charged and drove off our people. Gen. Meade had to gallop for it, and, not being familiar with the paths came quite near enough being cut off! The place was untenable from our artillery fire, and Ayres retook it at 6.15, without trouble. Friend Berlin got into a ludicrous scrape today. In his gray Swedish coat, he was mistaken for a reb and was seized and examined by our infantry! Bache had a great sell played on him by Mason, who poked a bullet through a hole in his jacket, which B[ache] took for a narrow escape from death, when he discovered it in the lining! There was no attack on our part because of the fatigue and straggling of the men. 3,000 fresh troops are expected tonight. Auger, with 10,000 more, is rumored on the way. Train ordered to Fredericksburg. Gens. Humphreys and Wright have been confirmed Maj. Gen'l. of Vols. to our great satisfaction.[86] My choice black mare, poor lady, played out this day completely; worn down by 10 days of galloping, and hot sun, and standing saddled almost day and night. She is so weak & thin that can use her no more just now. Will now take to the roan.[87]

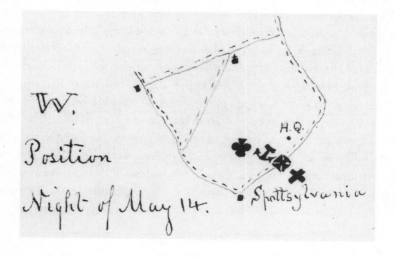

May 15, Sunday.

8 A.M. The 2d Corps was moving from the right and massed not far from our Headq'rs. Burnside holds the right today. 7.45. Ordered, to go to Warren & Wright find out the field return and anything else new. Warren was in the J. Beverly house, which was full of mud & officers. Found Gen. Wright in rear of the Anderson house. Just in front of the Anderson house Gen. Neil was in position with a breastwork. The "Bean" was there in person and in answer to my request for information, replied "Ah! Yes.—My division in position—(a wave of the left hand). Skirmishers (a wave of the right hand)—enemy! (a tremulous flourish of both hands)."— It took much pains to extract, midst bows, flourishes, and promiscuous politeness, that his skirmishers were out 600 yards, finding only rebel videttes; and that he had heard our cavalry skirmishing far on his left. With all this information returned to Headq'rs at 9.20 but found the General had gone out to Wright, and so telegraphed to him. Rain again. This Anderson house is a large brick building, the best that have seen hereabout, with a good bit of a flower garden and many outbuildings. Around was a great, cleared farm, arguing a rich man, for the country.[88] Yesterday Rosser's cavalry came into one of the 5th Corps hospitals, that did not pick up quick enough, and took all stragglers, and everyone who did not belong, as patient or nurse, to the place; also all rebel prisoners well enough to walk. Sprigg Carroll got hit in the *other* arm yesterday, during a skirmish. (This wound afterwards turned very badly; and the surgeon at Washington said, if he did not have the arm cut off, it would come to be a question between suppuration and constitution."—"Well" said, Carroll "I guess old Cons' will carry the day, so we will leave it on!") A surgeon went out with a letter from Gen. Meade, and got the body of Gen. Wadsworth on the field of the Wilderness. He died in the rebel hospital, and was well cared for.[89] Hancock, Gibbon and Barlow came to Headq'rs, and the last took lunch with me and wrote a letter to his wife at Fredericksburg. "Headquarters are a good place," said he "You can get victuals and stationery there." He related many anecdotes of the "Salient." How he whacked one officer with his sabre, for being in a hole. How he had compelled two officers to resign and had endorsed that they were "cowards" on their applications &c. &c. He believes greatly in the close column of attack. Poor Warren was out of all provisions, at his place, except sugar & hard tack; so he sent an orderly whom loaded with the necessary rations. Gibbon has been recommended by Meade for a Maj. Gen. Hancock recommended Barlow, but Meade could not endorse it, because there was no vacancy. Carroll, Miles & Brooke recommended for Brigadiers. 8 P.M. News that

Sheridan has destroyed the railroad in two places and beaten the enemy; and now is near James River. Butler has taken the outworks of Ft. Darling. Johnson has been compelled to evacuate Dalton.[90]

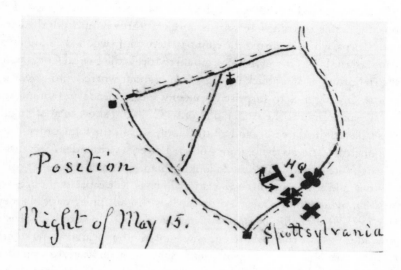

May 16, Monday.

Visitors today, though why anyone who can stay away should come down is not plain! Gov. Sprague of R.I. once a great military bird, in Bull Run days, and Hon. Sherman of Ohio. The former a small headed, black-eyed, sparrow little man, who rode fearlessly about in a straw hat. The latter very tall, as flat as a pancake, and ornamented with a long linen "duster" that made him look 12 feet high. He plainly is a very superior man, as becomes the brother of the General. Here, too, appeared a Fusileer Guard Surgeon, a perky John Bull, one Baker. He bored Med. Director McParlin fearfully; for McP. is not much, on entertaining anyway, and he now is overwhelmed with work![91] Have been able to write, shorter or longer, about 2 days out of three, to Mimi, and have got the history of the campaign as far as Gen. Hay's death; only in the Wilderness yet. It is some comfort to her great anxiety to get letters. Thackeray says truly that it is "the girl we leave behind us" who is the sufferer in War!—Mott's division, which has behaved badly, thus far, (how is this fighting division of Hooker fallen!) was consolidated as a brigade of Birney's division, which now covers the right flank, while the rest of 2d Corps is in reserve. For an exception it was mostly fine weather.

May 17, Tuesday.

Artillery reserve broken up. To the grief of Gen. Hunt and its commander, Col. Burton, who was afterwards appointed Inspector of Artillery.[92] 10.30 A.M. Headquarters moved to the rear of the Anderson house, on the edge of the woods. Early this morning a reconnaissance was thrown out from the left of the 6th Corps, which reported the country there badly wooded and unfavorable for attack. It was therefore determined to throw the free 2d Corps & 6th to the right tonight and attack on old ground (about where Upton went up) at 4. A.M., hoping thus to surprise the enemy. Gens. Meade and Grant went and staid some time at the Anderson house. Old A., a short man of 50 odd, was as sullen as he dared be, and all the family was in the same order. There was a bunch of Generals there, among others Potter & Crittenden (Stevenson's successor). The latter is a stary, wild looking man, with hair to his coat collar; but withal mild & pleasant in conversation. He has little capacity though once a corps commander in the West. Potter is tall, with a full, phlegmatic black eye. He is particular about his dress, of few words, and reputed an excellent division commander.[93] As we rode over to our new camp there appeared a long column of cavalry, streaming into the open. Meade sent me, in all haste, to stop them, as they were exposed to the full observation of the enemy. He afterwards gave the Lt. Col. Com'd'ng a severe blowing up for his want of foresight. (Think it was Chamberlain; 1st Mass. Cav.) This was a mixed remounted force, which accompanied Tyler ("Bob") just now up with 11,000 men, chiefly heavy artillery, but including some Irish zouaves commanded by McMahon's brother. To my great surprise, Channing Clapp appeared in camp and was received heartily. He had some message from old Benham who is flourishing about as usual, somewhere far in the rear.[94]

May 18, Wednesday.

All in the saddle by daylight and got to the Stephenson house (Stevens) by 4 A.M. Only the chimneys stand there, blackened by fire. In front was Sleeper's battery, in position. The artillery, union & rebel was roaring away on our front and to our left, where Warren was; and, in the damp morning air, the hum of the shot was very distinct, though distant. 6.30 A.M. Cannonading mostly done. Burnside, Wright & Hancock (all to right of Warren) had advanced their first line and driven the enemy out of their front pits (probably intrenched skirmishers) but here they were encountered by a wide slashing, on the other side of which was a heavy infantry parapet, well lined with muskets and supported by batteries that threw canister & case-shot into our troops. So far from being surprised, the rebels had spent the last days in strengthening their front and had rendered it impregnable. 8 A.M. News that Sigel, with 5,000 men, had been badly beaten by Breckenridge, losing his artillery. Crook successful. Butler driven from his lines in front of Ft. Darling.[95] 9.45 A.M. Renewed cannonade from Warren & Burnside. 10.30 A.M. The General faced about and rode to camp. It was a depressing day! Ill news from all sides; and the enemy securely on guard, despite our success of the 12th. Went to the 2d Corps hospital, in rear and right of our Headq'rs and saw Curtis off (Capt. A.) in the ambulance. He had been struck in the shoulder by a piece of spherical case. He exhibited great stoicism under the terrible trial of seeing most of his brother officers shot down within these few days; but plainly he was deeply depressed by it. Dr. Perry was there looking after him; there lay there another officer of the 20th—Keltzer—with his whole arm and shoulder torn off by a shell, which exploded upon it. Perry thought he could not live an hour. (However, he *got well* and returned to duty at Petersburg!)[96]— Most wounds today are from artillery and very bad. That eve Lt. Col. Kingsbury once A.A.G. to Newton; now with Sheridan, came in from across country and reported that Sheridan left Haxhall's Landing this morning to return. He said McClellan (who was with Humphreys) was in arrest for intoxication. Poor devil, it required Humphreys to keep him straight. He has served in many fights with credit, but he is a weak man.[97] In the evening the 2d & 6th Corps were moved back to position, as before (see diagram May 15). While his corps was moving, Hancock came into my tent to catch a wink of sleep. Tired as he was he could not rest till he had smoked a short pipe and poured out a volume of energetic conversation, to the delight of chum "Rosie."— After this he laid his big head on his arm and went off like a babe; till waked by his staff officers, when he jumped up (awake as quickly as asleep) and strode out of the tent.

May 19, Thursday.

Last night Torbert burnt Guinea Station and tonight he is ordered to return there, in anticipation of the 2d Corps move thither; but moves do depend on the enemy somewhat, as we shall see.[98] As we were dining, at 5 P.M., we heard sudden & heavy skirmishing on our right flank & even to the rear. It continued, and, by and bye, grew more general and nearer. 5.30. Ordered, to go out and see what was the matter. Galloped towards the "Gate" on the Fredericksburg road and found ambulances & waggons hurrying back, to get out of the way, for stray balls were already coming over the main route. One or two heavy artillery regiments were moving up at the double quick, and the way was strewn with their new baggage with which they had loaded themselves down. On the open, by the Harris house—to the right—were several regiments of them, just advancing into the woods. These were Tyler's division (newly arrived) going in to support Kitchen's brigade, which had been picketing our right, Tyler being massed in support; while the 9th Corps had been transferred last night and this morning, to the left of the 6th. All these moves had excited speculation in Lee, who ordered Ewell to leave his entrenchments and swing on our right flank, for a reconnaissance in force. At the Harris house was a battery, shelling the enemy. In the hollow ground, in front, and not far distant, was a dropping musketry fire, but not heavy. Reported accordingly to Gen. Meade, who ordered me to return and tell Gen. Tyler to drive the enemy back across the Ny, and say that a brigade from Warren and Birney's division would be up at once. Could not hear anything of Tyler, who was riding about somewhere in the thick woods; so gave the order to the Col. of an artillery regiment, and to Roebling who had just come on the ground with a small brigade. Just then the head of Birney's Division arrived. Repeated the order to him and he made preparations to put in his men. "Pat Ryan's" battery (think his name is Ryan) came up just then, and went into position also by the Harris house. This Pat was an artillery driver before the city of Mexico, and won Hunt's attention by the gallantry with which he carried his piece to a place where it was almost sure death.[99] When got back, found Meade sitting in front of Grant's tent. A mounted officer presently brought up two rebel prisoners, one of whom was a rare curiosity—he was a rank coward! "Oh!" he said "*may* I sit down?" (he was entirely blown) "Oh! It's the first battle I ever was in, and I pray God it may be the last!" He was a fat man, and his terror was so funny that Grant burst out laughing in which he was ably seconded by the second prisoner who sat on the ground munching a bit of hard tack, with characteristic *sang froid*. In this demonstration (or perhaps attempt to cut our communication) Ewell got roughly handled, lost 350 prisoners, and was repulsed at all points. His extreme left got on the Fredericksburg road and was repulsed by the negro troops guarding the waggon trains. The heavy artillery behaved well, but from their greenness, lost heavily. They had no idea of covering themselves and even shot each other in the excitement of battle. All of which illustrates that drill is but part of the soldier; for they are the best drilled troops in the army. We lost 1,500 men in the fight.[100] "You were mistaken in saying the affair seemed not serious" said the General that eve; "We had heavy loss and there must have been hard fighting." To which replied that, when was sent, there was certainly very little musketry at any point. At the same time the General said, "Grant has admitted the quality of Lee's fighting. He told me that, after such an engagement as the Wilderness, Bragg or Johnson would have *retreated!*"[101] An admirable thing to see in this army is the management & moving of hospitals. In an army thus constantly fighting and moving the Medical Department is called on for labors almost impossible. With the number of medical supply waggons so limited and even the ambulances reduced as much as possible, the surgeons are still called upon to care for enormous numbers of wounded. By great system and economy of force they accomplish wonders. As soon as the battle opens the main hospitals are established in situations safe, yet accessible, well supplied with water, and sufficiently open. The road thither from the front is marked by little yellow flags, at short distances. Tents and flies are instantly pitched and the operating tables laid out. Nourishing drinks and food are made ready. At some intermediate point, not too much exposed, the ambulances are parked. Thither are brought the wounded, some by stretcher bearers expressly detailed; some walking, and some borne in blankets, or shelter tents, by their comrades. They are rapidly loaded in the ambulances and carried to the main hospitals, after a primary dressing (if necessary) by a surgeon who remains with the ambulance park. At the main hospital the names of the wounded are entered in a record, as they come in. The operations are at once performed, and the patients laid in the tents, where they are cared for by detailed nurses. As soon as safe and practicable (often at once, from necessity) the wounded are put in ambulances or waggons and sent to a base, whence they are shipped to the great hospitals at Washington. During all these movings their sufferings are incredible. No care or labor can prevent those! Often a hospital must be struck and moved, before anything is ready, the wounded half bandaged, and perhaps still coming in. On the sad march of the ambulance train from the Wilderness, which had to turn back from the other side of the Rapid Ann and go all the way to Fredericksburg, they buried a man every mile. This train was 7 miles long. There are now 200 of the Sanitary Commission at Fredericksburg. The feeling between them and the army surgeons is bad. In the early part of the war the Commission in their publications severely criticised the faults of the yet unorganized Medical department. And, since then the writing members of the Commission have been fond of augmenting their own credit by showing what a dreadful state everything was in, when they arrived on the ground. Beyond all this lies the general principle that clashing always follows upon the mixing of members of an organized body with volunteers. The surgeons, on their part, are in fault in not accepting with allowance and good grace, the labors, often officious or clumsy, of men & women who are really patriotic and devoted and humane.

The propriety of allowing them actually at the front is questionable; but their real place of usefulness is at a base, like Fredericksburg, where everything is needed, and nothing is to be had.

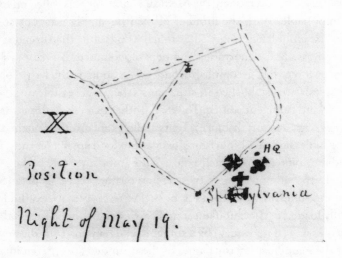

May 20, Friday.

A straggler was today shot in the 2nd Corps as an example. There was issued a complimentary order to the Heavy Artillery for their good conduct yesterday.[102] All very quiet:— Gen. Meade rode out for an examination of his lines, on the centre & left. The Headq'rs of Wright were in the edge of a field, not far from the Myer's house (now burnt). He had ridden out and we found him on the line. He rode with us along his breastwork, whose left rested at Widow Carter's and the right near a little run, and just opposite Spottsylvania Court House, which lay on a gentle swell, across open fields, ¾ of a mile off. The enemy's works ran somewhat in front of it and the pickets were thrown well out, on both sides, & were covered by rail & dirt protections. Not a shot was fired—our men were chiefly busy with their savory messes; the rebels were loitering about in all directions. Near this run was a battery, where the gunners had made themselves little holes to burrow in, for the fire must have been severe there in action. We also visited Burnside, who held a refused flank line. Saw there Gen. Willcox (9th Corps) a negative looking man, with much whisker. There too was Maj. Willie Cutting short, friendly, buckish & bald as to the head; he and other New York birds of the club make a large part of B's staff. Even in this our extreme there was a pair of kid [gloves], or so, to be seen on this staff. Friend Waud is along with us still and sojourns with the Engineers. He draws for Harper's Weekly, very good sketches he sends them, and very poor woodcuts they make thereof. His indignation has, long since given place to sarcasm; for W[aud] is a merry & philosophic Bohemian! Got a letter from poor Judge Abbott acknowledging the little I had been able to do for his poor son. After dark, the Second Corps marches to the left, for a long stretch![103]

May 21, Saturday.

6 A.M. Reports that the enemy also is in motion. 7.15. Griffin pushing out, to demonstrate and reconnoitre. News that, at 4 A.M., the 2d Corps was 1½ miles beyond Guinea Station. 10.15 Gen. Russell is to mass at the Anderson house and allow the 5th Corps to pass in his rear. The General staid some time at this house, superintending the movement. Presently he moved off with the headquarters and, at 11.20, arrived at Massaponax Church. Weather hot, roads dusty; the springs few and small. This church, a plain brick building, stands at the crossing of the direct Telegraph Road from Fredericksburg to Richmond, and the cross-road from above Spottsylvania (by which we had come). Grant also was there; church benches were brought out and we remained till 1.40 P.M. while the 5th Corps passed.[104] As soon as their artillery got along we remounted, went down the Telegraph Road a few hundred yards and turned sharp to the left towards Guinea Station. Soon the country grew more open, with not a few decent houses, and many fields, where the corn now was miles high, & though the soil was light & sandy, with a pebbly foundation, still the contrast to the Wilderness tract was most pleasant. 2.40 P.M. We crossed the Fredericksb'g rail, and, at 3, arrived at Motley's house, which lies on the high swell that overlooks the meadow land where the Po & Ny join, and where is Guinea Station and bridge. It was a good house, with store of fruit trees and rose bushes in flower. The strawberries beginning to ripen and the apples as big as bullets. Old M[otley] was an elderly man of a certain sour dignity; a bitter rebel plainly. He showed us a small house on the flat, where their strong stay "Stonewall" Jackson died from pneumonia brought on by cold water too freely applied to his amputated arm. There is little or no doubt that he was shot by a picket reserve of his own men who fired a volley at him by mistake.[105] Halted in rear of the house was our Headq'rs train, and Quartermaster Page in a deuce of a stew; for the other bank of the Po-Ny was held by the enemy's cavalry and he didn't dare to go on! However, Meade ordered everybody to go in and force the bridge. The "Zou-zous" and 68th Penn. under little Collis, followed by Adams' squadron, went down at once. Also there was a lot of cavalry under Lt. Col. ——— which formed line and contemplated nature! Irresponsible Charlie Turnbull, with

his regular engineers, came up, and was much flustered by my telling him the order was to go in! "I have no officers," quoth he:—as if the globe were resting on his shoulders! Word was sent back to Warren to hurry up, but, meantime the Headquarter infantry forced the bridge and Charlie Adams charged across & triumphantly captured 5 rebs who hadn't enough legs.[106] 3.45 P.M. Warren came up with his staff; and, immediately after, the head of his column (Penn. Reserves) was in sight. They at once crossed and took position on the other bank. Our tents were pitched in rear of Motley's. 6.15 P.M. Heavy & rapid artillery in direction of Anderson house. This gave much anxiety to Meade, who feared the enemy was trying to overwhelm Russell's division left to cover the rear. As the eve wore on his anxiety was increased by the prolonged absence of George, sent to carry an order to Hancock with a strong cavalry escort. Hoke was reported as confronting Hancock, having been newly brought from N. Carolina. Soon intelligence came that Russell repulsed the attempts of the enemy, partly with his entrenched pickets and partly with his artillery, at which we breathed more easily.[107]

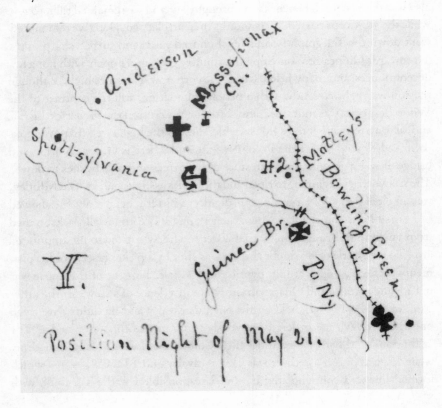

May 22, Sunday.

Order of march:—Trains to Bowling Green. 9th Corps and Headq'rs to near New Bethel Ch. 2d Corps to Milford. 5th Corps to Harris' Station. 6th Corps in rear of 5th. Reviewing the progress of the campaign, Gen. Meade said to me at breakfast; "I am afraid the rebellion cannot be crushed this summer!"— The enemy are reported going down the Telegraph Road.[108] Headquarters left the Secesh Motley about noon and, crossing at Guinea bridge, stopped a little at a shabby house a little the other side, (full of cross women) and then rode on toward the Telegraph Road. After crossing the Ta, a wide clear brook, with a stony bottom, we reached Madison's Ordinary at 1.15 where a road comes in from New Bethel Church on the east. An "ordinary" is a country "variety store" in Virginia. Here the house itself was locked, but empty; on the grass about it were strewn quantities of papers, chiefly orders, sent from far away plantations by the hand of negroes, for everything under the sun, but especially patent pills! There was a breastwork, also, the work of Hancock's Heavy Artillery, who, poor green chaps, reported to him that their protection was only bullet proof and the enemy were shelling them! "Well" quoth he, "tell them to take it comfortably; the Rebs have a way of throwing shells and I am sure I can't stop them!"— The 5th Corps was passing, all this time, en route for the Telegraph Road; into which this runs, not very far off. At 3.15 P.M. we got to New Bethel Church, taking the cross-road, above mentioned. There were fine oak woods a good part of the way, and I never saw their foliage exceeded for size & glossiness of leaf; although the soil is extremely light and sandy, and it is nearly impossible to make a sod on it. The church stands in a fine wood and on the direct road from Guinea Station to the North Anna. Burnside and his staff sat within, in the pews, after the manner of a congregation.[109] The 9th Corps was passing, straggling badly—whole companies fell out and deliberately halted to rest. This is partly accounted for by the rawness of many of the troops. There came news that a line of battle was advancing against Hancock, which turned out to be Birney's division, of his own men! Hoke's division is reported up to help Lee, from North Carolina.[110] 4.30 P.M. In camp in a glorious clover field on this same road, a little north of the church and near the large Tyler house. Immediately made a reconnoissance and bought a lot of fresh vegetables; some eggs; some milk, and a "pone" of hot corn bread! *Par bleu!* that was luxury indeed! The inhabitants were old Mrs. Tyler and her daughter-in-law, both strong rebels, and the younger cried, at first, from fear & anger, but recovered and talked quite reasonably. The older was a simple and narrow person; she had lost a son at

"Sharpsburg" (Antietam). While we dined in plenty, came Torbert and sat down too. He is grown rough, and wears a sailor shirt, since he joined the cavalry. He told the General that Sharpe's "scouts" were not worth a button; that he found them just outside the picket line simply plundering and not scouting at all! Grant's staff have rather western ideas on foraging; Rawlins gave a forage order to their "purveyor" who interpreted it as a privilege to steal every eatable he could see. Gen. Russell caught him at it and gave him a sound caning to the huge amusement of the by-standers.[111] Mr. Dana is back—some regard him as a sort of spy on Grant. He is a good natured man, but vain, bigoted and injudicious. Butler has just bottled himself up in Bermuda Hundreds and has indeed made a nice mess of it! The enemy are thought to be all across the North Anna.

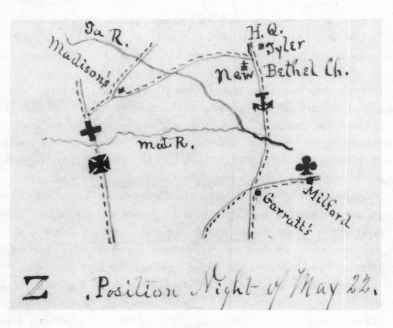

May 23, Monday.

Lawry Motley was reported dead, mortally hurt in a cavalry fight.— Burnside has a short, military jacket, and, with his bell-crowned felt hat, the brim turned down presents an odd figure, the fat man![112] At 7.45 A.M. we left the goodly clover field, to our grief, and to that of the women, who counted on our protection. Stopping for a little at a homely house (Campbell's) we pushed on along the road parallel to the rail, and on which the 9th Corps was marching. Grant went nimbly ahead on his black Mississippi pony which piqued Meade, who pushed on with his big trotter, beating Grant very soon, and followed by staff and orderlies as best they might. Thus riding through and by the column, we pulled up, at 10 A.M. at a side road, beyond Garratt's, turning in to the right, along a pine wood. There was Maj. Morton, the most active engineer of the 9th Corps. He is a tall, light bearded man, with an eccentric blue eye, and a generally "radical" look. He is a son of the famed ethnologist and passes for a man of ability, though queer in his ways. They wished to turn off this corps so as to keep it from interfering with the 5th, where this road strikes the Telegraph Road. Morton thought it could be done by this by way; and so a regiment was sent ahead and we followed close after.[113] 10.45. Dismount at the corner of a wood; everything very dry, and no water that was fit to drink. In the woods were recent signs of rebel cavalry. Wilcox's division passed; a great many men riding on the caissons, under plea of sickness—probably lazy! There are some Indians in one of his Michigan regiments, miserable, sullen looking creatures, who look as if they wished themselves well out of it; and small blame to them! After these troops got by, we rode forward, passed a large house with outbuildings & crossed the Polecat River, a clear brook with a stoney bottom, and overhanging elders. There Riddle & Mason straggled and took a bath. Beyond this we came on Capt. Paine, who had a negro guide, for whom we appropriated an old cream horse from a small house where dwelt four women. We left them a guard for their consolation. Bad times these for lone women, midst a country full of stragglers![114] 1.40. Struck the main road again by the house of a Mrs. Moncoure. She was a vulgar, railing old woman, and talked roundly to us, saying "Ah! we shall soon see you coming back on the double quick!"— Nevertheless she sold the Yanks her sheep with a haggling worthy of New England. "Oh," would she say, "I *would* like to be paid in gold!"[115] At 6.30 P.M. we heard heavy firing to the southward, which gave much anxiety to Meade, whose troops are now much strung out. It was late before we got the satisfactory news that Warren had crossed the North Anna at Jericho Bridge, and repulsed a heavy attack by Longstreet. Old Cutler's people behaved badly and broke, but the light batteries advanced through the fugitives in the handsomest way, at a trot, and repulsed the enemy with canister. At Ox Ford Hancock stormed the enemy's rifle-pits gallantly and held the bridge, at this end, ready to cross. We pitched, long after dark, in the angle of the roads.[116] This country, off the streams, is very dry, sandy & meagre; and the cultivation low. The grand struggle concentrates hither, more and more. We have received, to date, about 14,000 reinforcement.

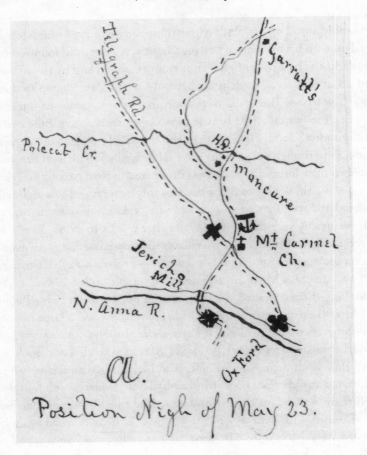

May 24, Tuesday.

Headq'rs moved at 5.45 A.M. Keeping south, we arrived at 6.30 at Mt. Carmel Church where crosses the "Telegraph" road. A most hot, dry, dusty and barren corner it was! where we boiled in a semi idiotic state for hours! Our only excitement was a funny nigger who came in, late a slave of Col. Baldwin rebel chief of artillery. He told of Lee's simple life, of his few waggons and his meals of only corn bread & bacon (which believe to be true).[117] They laid boards across the broad aisle in the mean little church and made a table where sat Grant, Meade, Gen. Williams &c. writing. Pretty soon we had a fine blow-up! There came a cipher despatch from Sherman, in the West, one of the florid style in which he occasionally indulges, wherein he said, that the army of the West had fought enough to be entitled now to "manoeuvre" and that if Grant could inspire the Potomac army to do a proper degree of fighting, the final success could not be doubted. All of which was bad taste and conceited in Sherman, and very broad flattery to Grant. Meade had this read to him by the gossipy Dana, and his grey eyes grew like a rattlesnake's.—"Sir! I consider that despatch an insult to the army I command, and to me personally. The Army of the Potomac does not require General Grant's inspiration or anybody's else inspiration to make it fight!!"—He did not get over it all that day, and, at dinner, spoke of the western troops as "an armed rabble."[118]— 7 A.M. A negro from Hancock reported the enemy retreating on Richmond, but it seemed only to be that some rebel officers had told the inhabitants that their troops would be likely to fall back. 7.15 Capt. "Tick" Wadsworth brought news that Sheridan was at Dunkirk. He had been delayed in crossing by a rise in the Pamunkey.[119] At 6.30 P.M. a brigade of Crittenden's people made an unsuccessful attack (though in good style) on the south side of the river, just where the enemy's works touched the stream, near Ox Ford.[120] At last we crossed the river, about dusk, midst a terrific thunder storm; the flashes seemed verily to hiss! and the situation was not helped by the ammunition train in the road. We crossed the pontoon at Jericho Mills, a romantic spot where the river runs between high steep banks, in a sort of ravine. The stream is say 125 feet wide and the banks often heavily wooded with oak and the most magnificent of tulip trees. We luckily found the camp ready pitched on the bluff just south of the river. They are still joking the Heavy Artillery and now affirm that, near Madison's Ordinary, they called for volunteers to go on picket. The inferiority of the 9th Corps begins now to show a good deal, in the straggling and the general comparative want of tone and discipline.

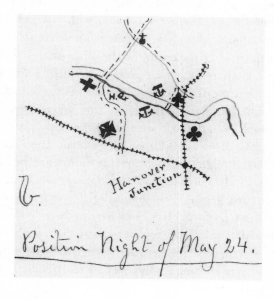

Position Night of May 24.

May 25, Wednesday.

The 9th Corps incorporated with the Army of the Potomac, and brought under Meade's immediate command.[121] 7.45 A.M. Ordered to go to Gen. Warren and stay with him "as long as there was anything going on." Rode off to the S.E. and, after some trouble, found him in a pine wood 2½ mls. from our Headq'rs. Leaving most of his staff, Warren rode off to inspect his line; first to Cutler, who sat on the edge of the wood, to our right (southward). They were skirmishing very hotly in the front. Then we continued to the right, about a half mile, and came to the railroad (from Gordonsville). There was Griffin with Cope, who was drawing a plan of the ground. The skirmishing in his front, also, was heavy and the bullets came through the bunch of bushes behind which we sat. "Spent!" said Roebling, "perhaps so; but they come hard enough to go through if they hit!"—Griffin, as usual, was greatly excited and enthusiastic about putting some batteries which would enfilade this, that and the other! And presently up came the batteries, led by Lt. Natie Appleton, who was to put them in position.[122] About 10, we rode still more to the right, Warren left his officers in the edge of a wood, but invited me to come with him. We rode down a lane, through the open, to Lowery's house, and so further on to a log barn, where a picket reserve of the 22d Mass. was sheltered against sharpshooters. This was far beyond the right of our line of battle. This place we left at a canter to avoid the sharpshooters' attention, and, by the lane before mentioned, met the skirmishers of the 2d Div. 6th Corps, under Maj. Long (the "Sangler") swinging out to join on the right of the 5th; whereupon we repaired to the 6th Corps headq'rs at E. Anderson's.[123] There was Wright and his whole staff, and there was iced water, which tasted good. There was a stream, with very bad banks, running a half mile from the house, and which bothered us much by its bends, and by the uncertainty of the force of the enemy on the other side. (It was Little R[iver] and there was nobody there but outposts & videttes). Old Anderson was a short man, and wore the usual expression of dismal acerbity. 11.45. Once more to Griffin. "I ought, I suppose, to ride faster" said Warren, "but I work so hard I really am not able." On the road we met Griffin's aide, Case, very pale, on a stretcher. His brachial artery had been cut by a ball. There too was a valiant, light blue Zouave stumping to the rear; "He didn't care; he hit five or six of *them* first!"—Griffin had now his batteries blazing away. Natie Appleton was shot through the arm getting them in position.[124] We followed the line to the left till we came to Crawford. His troops were in the woods, and had a heavy breastwork. He himself lay asleep under a neat shelter, which his guard fail not to provide him on short notice. They seemed to be fighting in front, for a few bullets came over, clicking among the pine trees. Still more to the left we struck Crittenden's division of the 9th Corps, which lies on this side of the river. Crittenden had his fly pitched immediately in rear of the breastworks. He was quite offended at being ordered to report to his junior, Warren, but was very pleasant and did not visit his dissatisfaction on W[arren]. Close by, saw Lt. Col. Weld of the 56th Mass. He had a narrow thing in the attack last night; a bullet went through his coat and grazed his side.[125] All along the front of this and Crawford's line are dense woods. 2. P.M. We descended the precipitous bank and crossed the river, by a temporary bridge of trunks of trees and brush. It was a beautiful spot, with fine woods on either side of the ravine. Getting up the opposite steep bank we passed through the scrub pine woods and came out down the river, at some batteries of the 9th Corps, on its bank. Warren's wish was to discover the position of the enemy's line but it was hid completely in the woods, except a battery, distant a fair cannon-shot further down and on the opposite side, of course.— This battery had been silenced, but the rebel flag was still planted on its parapet. Warren asked the Captain to throw a shell through the woods, to enfilade (by guess) the enemy's line, and he proposed to ask his own skirmishers, on Crawford's front, how it seemed to strike. (This was Warren's great way, to go about, looking thus after details and making ingenious plans; but it kept him from generalities, and made it hard to find him, so that he finally came to trouble as much by this as by anything else.)— At 4.15 rode back to Headq'rs (now moved to the north bank, near Quarles' Mill) with Mason's brother, who commands Grant's cavalry escort.[126] A good many of the men were bathing in the river. Went down, after dark, and took a bath in a clear brook, close to the river. Some rebs were brought in,

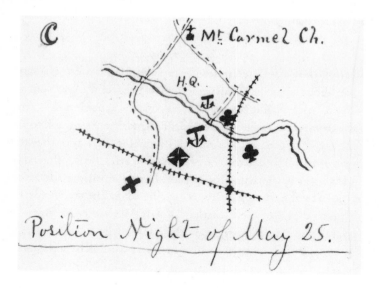

Position Night of May 25.

captured in a curious way. Seeing our cattle on the other side, and not seeing any troops, they swam the river after beef and were taken at once by our people! Saw two Lt. Colonels who were recaptured by Sheridan. They were naturally right merry and remarked that we had got "pretty far down." Cavalry rejoins the army. Having, in their raid taken a line on the Brook Road (pike); destroyed railroad bridge over Chickahominy; arrived May 14 at Haxall's Landing; and destroyed May 21, the rail near Hanover Court House. They are engaged now in destroying the railroads that are within our lines.[127]

May 26, Thursday.

We rode to the left and saw Burnside who had his Headq'rs in a shady pine grove just above a run. He produced ale for the General and Loring, Pell &c. entreated us kindly; after which B[urnside] rode with us to near Chesterfield Sta. where Hancock had pitched, near a house & at the foot of a slope.[128] In their leisure (for there is very little shooting along the lines today) the 2d Corps commanders had turned their attention to the prosecution of stragglers! Barlow, in particular, tied them up in strings and thrashed them, to the great benefit of the service! Got back to camp in time to run over to the 5th Corps hospital and see off Natie Appleton in his ambulance. There too was Case, partly over his loss of blood. They captured a *female* rebel soldier a day or two ago, and now she is here in the Provost Marshal's hands. She was an artillery driver, and had on a common, gray soldier jacket, and a U.S. forage cap. Her hair was long and fell on her shoulders. She seemed a common woman, but not wanting in decent modesty, and said she had enlisted because her only brother had gone. She asked not to be mixed with the prisoners in going to Washington. Thunder every evening now.

May 27, Friday.

6th Corps, followed by 5th recrossed the river last night, the 5th Corps pickets getting over about daylight.[129] Burnside, who is to cover the rear, sent a brigade to the fords at Jericho Mills & Quarles Mill, one to each. Hereat Warren complained the troops cut his march; and Meade sent a hot telegraph to Burnside that his men were not in position and were blocking the way of the 5th Corps. Burnside's troops are to destroy the bridges. The 6th Corps followed by 2d to move on Hanover town; Russell's division having already made a very early start, preceded by the whole cavalry, under Sheridan. The 5th Corps, followed by the 9th is to move on New Castle.[130] 4 A.M. We had to be pretty lively in getting off, for there we were, right on the bank of the river, and the enemy's skirmishers expected down at any moment; so we were all breakfasted, packed and mounted at this hour; but, as it was, before the train could get off, the rebs came down and wounded the telegraph waggon! We stopped at Burnside's as we passed. He came out, pretty angry, and stood by Meade's horse and complained indignantly of being told his men were not in position.—Explanations followed.—My impression is that Burnside was nearly, or quite, right; and that it was impracticable to get a brigade to Jericho Mill without cutting Warren's column.[131] Then on to Gen. Hancock's, and heard what he was going to do; and thence up the road to Mt. Carmel Church, where we turned sharp to the right and went down to Chesterfield Sta. southward.— Ricketts' Division was there getting rations, and he told Gen. Meade he would move on immediately. Sending now some cavalry men ahead, we pushed on, at a steady rate. The road is a ridge road and consequently very dry, with no water save from springs. It was actually strewn with the dead horses from Sheridan's returning column. There was a horse every few rods and the air was tainted with them.[132] By and bye we pulled up, to wait for the infantry, at a mean house, not far from the road. When I asked the thin, ill favored woman if I could buy a bunch of little beets from her garden, her children burst out crying and said "We shall starve!" They had been well scared & cleaned out by the cavalry. The soft-hearted General was thereat so moved that he gave them his whole luncheon & $5.00! Afterwards they said the man was a guerilla because they found some cavalry saddles in his loft. But that don't prove the point though he was indeed not well favored. And so on through more poor country till 9.30 A.M. when we stopped to eat lunch, at one Jeter's, on the left hand of the road. (This habit of eating lunch, is like water drinking, during the day—foolish. When you get up, eat a hearty breakfast and drink plentifully of coffee; or water; then eat and drink no more till the day's work is over. Thus, in hot weather, the course of the blood will remain regular & balanced and the heat will not be felt. Even with the extreme labors of the infantry, it is well known that those, who are always filling their canteens, play out soonest.)—This was a house of good class with a nice vegetable garden. Jeter was an old, simple sort of man. His wife was much younger—one of his daughters pretty, with a sharp tongue—two brothers of hers at the war. The old chap said, with much gravity, "I am much pleased your officers are clean, handsomely dressed, and well mannered! Those that came the other day (Sheridan's) were quite rude and very *dusty!*"—Then he continued in a conclusively argumentative way, "Is it fair now, when we are obliged to contribute a large part of our crops to support *our* army, that you should come and take still more from us?" His remarks were cut short by the discovery of three fowling pieces hid under his barn, which he declared had been loaded to shoot a fox, but which we thought might chance also to shoot a Yankee; and Sharpe took them.[133] Grant & his staff were along and we all sat pleasantly under the trees. 12 M. An orderly came up, as we were riding along, and reported the cavalry across the Pamunkey and the infantry of Russell close to Hanover Ferry and over, probably, by this time. 12.50 P.M. Halted at the house of one Thompson, a singular being, with light hair and a squeaky voice, who talked just like a nigger. He was sharp enow to say he had been completely stripped, but he proved to have a large store of corn. We camped hard by, as there was a spring. Just the other side of us was Mangohick Church, where the road makes a sharp south bend, to go to the Pamunkey. This church was a great rendezvous for rebel volunteers at the beginning of the war. It is built of old bricks brought from England, and laid "header and stretcher" fashion. We came 21 or 22 miles today. Grant with a very bad sick headache, which he has periodically. He had to use chloroform for it.[134]

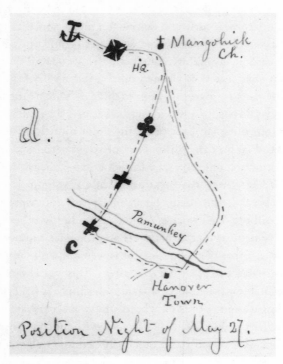

May 28, Saturday.

6.30 A.M. The 5th Corps marching past, with bands playing and men in good spirits cheering. They came by the upper road which comes into this, a little way from here. 7.45. Headquarters move. 8.30. Came on Gen. Hancock at the crossing of the Nelson's Ford road, on which place he was moving, as nearer than Hanover T[own]. 10 A.M. Arrived at Nelson's ford on the Pamunkey. This river flows between low banks, and has, on either side, a stretch of flat, alluvial land, subject to overflow, and bounded by a steep bank some 50 feet high; so that you suddenly descend to the flat and thence pass to the river. The Widow Nelson's stood on the top of this bank, on the right of the road—a large, wooden, tumble-down house with a considerable garden and some fine beech trees near by. Thither was sent back, by Gen. Meade, to tell Grant (who had halted there) of his whereabouts.[135] Cadwalader remembered the spot from McClellan's day, when he came up with "Rush's Lancers" and drove off the enemy and picketed the river, after burning the bridge. He told me Rush was a poltroon, and was scared out of the command by getting a volley from an outpost!— The land was cultivated in wide fields of wheat and corn, but the farming was meagre; there might be excellent crops. The artillery of the 6th Corps was crossing on a canvas pontoon. Tried to find where the General had gone and turned to the right and went up to a large house, Dr. Pollard's, where found Torbert & Russell but no Meade. There was an extraordinary luxuriance of roses in the neglected garden, all in full bloom. Rode to the east, parallel to the river, and came to a large and good house, Mrs. Newton's, where found Gens. Grant & Meade. 12. There was an old lady there and a widow, of say 35, whose husband had been killed in my first fight, at Raccoon Ford. Ordered a civilian out of their garden, which was under guard, and he turned out to be respectable Coffin, the "Carlton" of the Boston Journal; but then he shouldn't steal onions![136] Old Biddle went in, with his accustomed style to prove to them 1st that they were his distant cousins; 2d that they ought to be Unionists! This regular procedure on his part excites much mirth in the staff! Presently arrived an Aunt, a Mrs. Brockenbrough, a conceited, curious, sallow, middle-aged woman itching to "tackle" a Northerner. She said the Cavalry Provost Marshal had been very kind to her. She then began to catechize Grant, with an eager relish, who replied with entire calmness and candor, whereat she was plainly taken aback, as she looked for a volley of gasconade!— The negro houses were full of our wounded cavalry, and some rebels. One man was of the 1st Mass. And told me he knew positively of Motley's death, some day's ago. That afternoon the cavalry cannon began again and a very severe combat followed, in which we drove the enemy at all points, but with a loss to us of 400 or 500 men, including 50 officers killed and wounded. It was near Hawe's Shop, S.W. from here. Christiancy's brother was very badly hit in the thigh and (yesterday) "Tick" Wadsworth's horse was killed under him. Probably it was very needful for Lee to cover his front as long as possible. Afterwards, heard of "Rooney" Lee, that he rode into the field near Ena Church and said "We *must* hold on here! I cannot give up any more ground!" We camped on the river, at Dr. Newton's between this and where we crossed. The river, just there, has a steep bank, 20 feet high, and is overhung with good trees.[137]

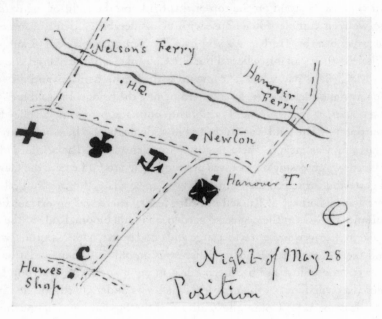

May 29, Sunday.

At 11 A.M. the General rode over to Dr. Pollard's, where Wright was camped by the roadside. Russell's division was moving out with intention of converging on Tolopotomoy Creek; but, for some inexplicable reason, they took the wrong road and marched on Hanover Court House![138] There is an extraordinary box hedge in Pollard's garden, over six feet high and eight feet wide, at the top! Hancock came soon and we all rode to Burnside's Headq'rs at Hawe's House in the direction of Salem Church—a notable place for me, for I bought a rubber blanket full of lettuce and small beets. We are reconnoitering to see if the enemy is in position. Russell has encountered nothing but cavalry (naturally!). Barlow is moving west towards Shady Grove; and Griffin south towards Bethesda Church. 1.45 P.M. Arrive at Salem Church, from which radiate one road, northward, to Hanover Court House; two eastward to the Pamunkey; one south, to Tolopotomoy Creek, and one west, towards Shady Grove. The church was small, rather neatly painted within, but the pulpit and pews were stained with blood. It had been a hospital for the cavalry. At this place is the ruins of Hawes shop, burnt in some former raid. It seemed to have been a steam mill.[139] 4 P.M. Gen. Meade got uneasy at the delay, and rode off, southward, with three of us. At an old mill, on a small brook, we came suddenly on the dead body of a light mulatto, who looked very like a rebel soldier—He was shot.—Mason thereat rode ahead to see what was in the wood, and the General turned up to the left and presently came on old Cutler's division of the 5th Corps, massed. The General rode up to the first brigade commander and asked him, in a stormy voice, why he had no pickets out! Then to Warren, close by, at Norman's house. "Well," said W[arren] "all I can say is this; if Gen. Cutler doesn't know enough to throw out pickets, without my telling him, the only thing is for me to get rid of Gen. Cutler!" Ever since about 4 P.M. we had heard Griffin skirmishing, the other side of the Creek. The enemy at first charged his skirmishers and drove them back, but he seems to have driven them in turn. The General went back then to the church. 5 P.M. Barlow sends back word that he has found the enemy intrenched, with guns in position, over three miles from here, south of the fork in the road.[140] We returned to camp at the same place. Orders out for all the corps to move up, form line of battle, and close in on the enemy. Wendell Holmes came near being captured, carrying a despatch to Wright. Some reb' cavalry came in from a by-road and he had to make a bolt straight through them![141]

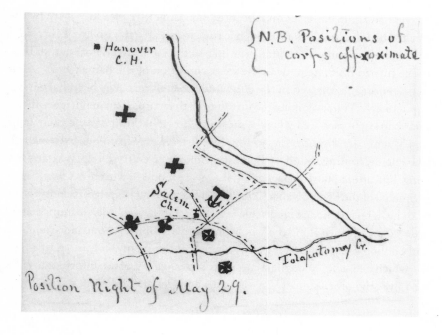

May 30, Monday.

7.30 A.M. Headq'rs got to Salem Ch. again. The 9th Corps passing, and wheeling into the south road, to take position between the 5th and 2d. The trains are now crossing the river. As it was precious hot and nothing to do, lay down flat in a pew, and went to sleep. Was roused by a hand on my shoulder, and, looking up, my eyes encountered a face that recognized at once as that of Richard Barlow, whom have not seen for years, and who was much altered by his beard. Have always quoted this to myself as an instance of my power of remembering faces, though names go from me most treacherously. He had come on some Sanitary Commission business; and was full of the idea that Frank had been commissioned Maj. General, which turned out not so, and made much heart-burning afterwards, for Gibbon *was* commissioned. 12 M. Camped near Ena Church—a dreary, sandy clearing, with scrub pines about it. Three or four dead rebels were found still hid in the bushes, for near here had been a severe fight with the cavalry. Not a tree but had a carbine bullet, and I counted five in one, within the space of a hat.[142] 1.30 P.M. To Hancock, who was near Gentry's, by the Shady Grove Road. He was arrayed, as usual, in an ample white shirt, which must be a trial just now to the astute body servant Shaw! The weary staff were getting a nap in their tents, and the universal Major Mitchell said faintly, "There are a great many wood-ticks eating me, but I haven't the strength to fight them!" Then to the left, and across Tolopotomoy creek to find Burnside. His parapet was on the rise, the other side of the creek, but he had some batteries on the north side, still. His Headq'rs were by the creek, which is a small affair though it runs in an extensive hollow. B[urnside] had ridden out somewhere along the line, so the General did not wait for him. As he turned back, he noticed the weak condition of the battery horses that were standing, harnessed to the guns, and directed that they be unharnessed, if practicable. Whoever is chief of artillery to that corps is an inefficient officer; their battery horses are by far the most run down in the army, and their artillery is generally slovenly.[143] 6.30 P.M. Sharp musketry from our extreme left. The enemy, coming round by Bethesda Church, tried to roll up Warren's left wing; but, after a sharp engagement, they were repulsed with heavy loss. Some regiments of the Pennsylvania Reserves, whose time had expired, gallantly went into the fight and made a creditable last chapter of it. Gen. Meade immediately ordered an advance along the whole line; and a profusion of artillery opened, and Gibbon charged, carrying a large extent of the enemy's advanced rifle pits, the which he held.[144] Bought some beets & peas today, of an unfortunate cuss, who lives the other side of the way, with a parcel of children & a wife. He is

48 years old and crippled with rheumatism, yet they conscripted him and he only escaped by hiding in the bushes. His name, Tyler. Gave him some pork and bread, which he looked at in a way more eloquent than words! The cavalry have reached Cold Harbor.

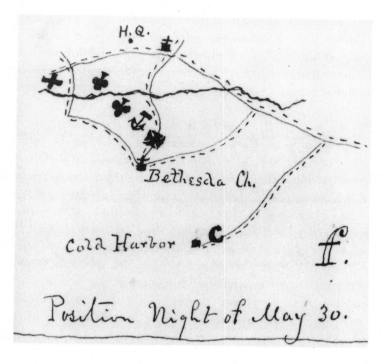

May 31, Tuesday.

Wilson's cavalry division was sent to the right & rear to destroy the two railroad bridges over the South Anna, which he effected (June 1) after brisk fighting. Sheridan with the other two divisions, made an advance towards Shady Grove. All day long there was the heaviest skirmishing on the lines, swelling sometimes into volleys, especially on the right, where Wright, Barlow and Birney pushed in and captured the front line of the enemy crowding close in on their main works. There was much artillery too, especially of coehorn mortars which are very effective, with their vertical shells, against earthworks. The enemy are concentrating hither every available soldier, including Hoke's people, from N. Carolina, and Breckenridge's from the Shenandoah. Gen. "Baldy" Smith is at Whitehouse with the 18th Corps.[145]— Lay still all day in my tent chiefly. A good chance to write out notes and write letters home. The methods of the topographical engineers, in correcting maps and making new ones, during actual warfare, are interesting. They go along all the roads, that are open, take their directions and estimate their length either by the paces of the horse, or by an odometer attached to a waggon or ambulance. At evening they draw out the result, and, if the enemy's position is required, they put that in, by what they can observe from the skirmish line, and by theoretical drawings of those portions that are concealed. They then place the map, which is on tracing muslin, on a sheet of photographic paper and thus reproduce it, in the required number of copies. Gen. Abercrombie reported on his way, with 8,000 reinforcements.[146]

June 1, Wednesday.

At 1.30 last night the 6th Corps marched round our left, on their way to Cold Harbor, where Sheridan had been ordered to hold on with all his might; and he accordingly did so, though it had otherwise been his idea to withdraw. And he had, this morning, a sharp engagement from behind breastworks! A notable fact, as the first instance, that have observed, where the cavalry have used field-works on a large scale. He repulsed the enemy.[147] 8.30 A.M. To Gen. Burnside on Tolopotomoy Cr. and thence to Via's house, whence Gen. Warren was just moving to establish himself at Bethesda Church. Both Meade and Grant halted at Via's. On a large tree in front of the house the cherries were just ripe, and I performed feats in my big boots to get some of them! The house was a pretty good one, with a sandy garden of meagre appearance, and a jingling piano, on which Col. Wilson performed. Hither had come a Mr. & Mrs. Currie, a most laughable couple, despite their tragic situation; for their house being near Bethesda church, where the fight was, our men rushed in and completely gutted it! Mrs. Currie was a young dark-eyed woman, tawdrily dressed, and with a stupendous tongue with which she easily killed all sympathy. She was very violent and common in her language, exclaiming: "A week ago I had no sympathy with the South against the North, but now I wish the ground would open and swallow both me and the Yankee army!"—Nevertheless she was disposed to giggle at the playful observations of some of the young officers. Her husband was a flabby and entirely resigned party, who kept saying, "There, there, hold your tongue.—Don't mind her, gentlemen, it's only her way; she's in a flurry!"— The mulatto that Gen. Meade saw shot near the mill belonged to this Via, who told me he was his favorite and trusted slave. He had gone there out of curiosity, and, seeing our pickets foolishly started to run, was mistaken for a rebel and killed. Old Dr. Winslow was there also, and watched his son's regiment, the 5th N.Y. Zouaves, as they marched past. They are part of the newly arrived reinforcements, and go to Warren, for he was once their Colonel. 12 M. News that Wright has arrived at Cold Harbor, where he was joined by the 18th Corps under "Baldy" Smith, who formed on the right of the 6th and was ordered to report to Gen. Meade.[148] In the afternoon the 6th & 18th Corps attacked and Ricketts' division handsomely carried a line of works & made 500 prisoners, while the 18th Corps charged across an open field and also drove back the enemy. This was the first creditable appearance of Ricketts' troops—"Milroy's weary boys," or as Hancock called them "a weakly child." But the simple-hearted soldier Ricketts by the mere force of his earnestness and bravery, put the fight into these men, and, while other divisions were running down, this one suddenly brightened up. 6.30 P.M. Heavy attacks on Griffin and on Willcox, both severely repulsed. Previously, Birney had been attacked but had also driven back the enemy. All this was partly reconnoissance, on Lee's part, and partly counter fighting, to keep us from marching too fast to the left. After dark they made a strong attempt to get back Smith and Wright but could not succeed at all; for a long time we could hear the roll of the musketry in the still evening. All the small arm firing was heavy during these operations; indeed the enemy was to the highest degree active, knowing the importance of covering the roads to Mechanicsville and of ascertaining very exactly our moves. He must have lost a large number of men in the operations of today, but they were well expended. General Meade was in one of his irascible fits tonight, which are always founded in good reason though they spread themselves over a good deal of ground that is not always in the limits of the question. First he blamed Warren for pushing out without orders; then he said each corps ought to act for itself and not always be leaning on him. Then he called Wright slow (a very true proposition as a general one). In the midst of these night thoughts comes there from Gen. Smith bright, active, self-sufficient Engineer Lieutenant Farquhar who reports that his superior had arrived, fought &c. &c. but that he had brought little ammunition, no transportation and that "he considered his position precarious." "Then, why in Hell did he come at all for?" roared the exasperated Meade with an oath that was rare with him. (Sequel. F[arquar] posted back—he swore by Smith—and reported the General's words. Smith never forgave him and put that sentence, in large letters, in his report, which appeared many months after and amused Meade, for Smith had dished himself then and was nobody).— We camped in a corner, east of Via's, and close by it.

Learned, by home letters, of the death of Mrs. Jas. Lawrence which surprised me extremely; for thought her only an invalid and not dangerously sick. Then poor "Grumpy" Gorham is gone; the Somerset Club will know him no more! His little money and little life are gone together![149]

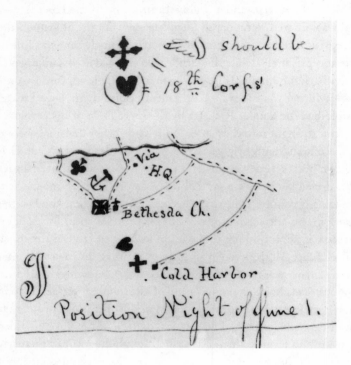

June 2, Thursday.

The 2d Corps marched last night to form on the left of the 6th. Owing to the night march and the faulty guides they made 15 miles, instead of 9, and, with men so exhausted, the fatigue and straggling were very great. The column got at 6.30 A.M. to Cold Harbor. 7.30 A.M. H'dq'rs moved and arrived at 8.30 at Kelly's house just above Cold Harbor. We came a roundabout road, sometimes cutting across fields and finally striking the road by Bosher's house. "—Of all the wastes I have seen this first sight of Cool Arbor was the most dreary! Fancy a baking sun to begin with; then a foreground of breastworks; on the left, Kelly's wretched house, in the front, an open plain, trampled fetlock deep into fine, white dust, and dotted with caissons, regiments of weary soldiers, and dead horses killed in the previous cavalry fight. On the sides and in the distance were pine woods, some red with fires that had run through them, some white with the clouds of dust that rose high in the air. It was a Sahara intensified and was called Cool Arbor!" (Letter T.L.)[150]— Here Wright had pitched his tents and here was "Baldy" Smith, a portly, rather short man, with a large round head and a long, sandy moustache. He had the air of a German officer—one of those uneasy, cross-grained ones. Sheridan has gone towards Bottom's Bridge. 1.30. To see Hancock, who was established a little to the front & left, close to the cross-roads known as Cold Harbor. He stated how his men were weary and getting up slowly. Meade ordered a general assault for 4 P.M. but countermanded it from the exhausted state of the 2d Corps. At 2.30 P.M. camp near Leary house, where, soon after, we had a perfect deluge of rain, which lasted an hour, and sunk immediately into the ground (Note. This was the last rain for *47 days*; viz. till July 19th!) Late in the afternoon the 5th Corps closed in to the left and the 9th Corps swung back, from the neighborhood of Bethesda Church to form a refused flank. Notwithstanding, there was no junction between the right of the 18th & the left of the 5th. They botched it, between Burnside (who was to mass in support) and Warren: for the enemy followed close up, caught a division of 5th Corps "in the air" and severely used up the regulars and the 5th N.Y. Zouaves, before they could be supported and the enemy repulsed. When Grant heard of it; he said to Meade: "We ought to be able to eat them up; they have placed themselves in such a position. Generally I am not in favor of night attacks; but I think one might be justified in such a case as the present."— Indeed it was a wretched affair; and so suddenly did the enemy swing in, by Via's house, that they captured several miles of our telegraph wire and shot one of the men. (Here was wounded Col. Winslow;

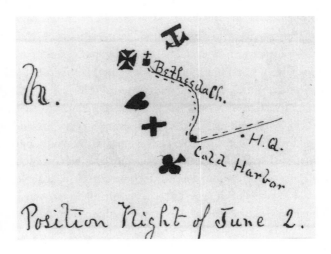

Position Night of June 2.

and his old father, while taking him to Washington, fell overboard and was drowned. The son died of his wound.—A tragic history!) There were lost also, several hundred prisoners. The General is getting more & more discontented with Warren; of Burnside he never, I think, expected much. Roebling the silent (Warren's factotum) came over late that night. He ate of cold meat & pickles in my tent, being half starved.[151]

June 3, Friday.

To be a general assault at daylight. 4.30 A.M. To Kelly's, where Wright's tents were left standing. Cannonading had already begun. Some stray shells and solid shot came over where we were; and one of these, striking near where the Indian, Capt. Parker, was sitting, on an old breastwork, that worthy uttered a loud "Waugh!" and slid down the bank! A comic incident in a very painful drama.[152]— There, too, was a certain Swinton, a sort of Mandarin newspaper correspondent, much more cultivated than most of those gentry, and a clever writer. He did not love danger (small blame to him!) and, when he became aware of the first stray shell, took to diligent composition of his notes, in a tent, and in a recumbent position. In our front, on the open ground below, was a battery, firing; and there came a shell and blew up a caisson, the first that ever saw exploded. A considerable column of white smoke went straight into the air, with but small explosion. 5.15. Despatch that Barlow has carried their line in his front, which for the time encouraged us much, but we presently heard he was driven out again, with loss of a good many prisoners. He struck Breckenridge and smashed him, but reserves of A. P. Hill's men came up, and recovered the line. 6 A.M. Ricketts carries their first line but is in a very exposed position; Russell cannot succeed on his front.—He was wounded in the arm but, with accustomed excentricity, told nobody; and, that evening, got Medical Director Holman to bind it for him, secretly! 9.45 A.M. Despatch from Burnside that he has taken the enemy's first line. (It was for calling this "*vox et preterea nihil*" that S[winton] was afterwards excluded from the army. He hated Burnside, because when in command of the Potomac Army, B. had threatened to buck and gag him for some libelous statements.)[153] The 18th Corps also got the first line but were at last obliged to come back. Finding, after some three hours fighting, that all was in vain, Gen. Meade ordered the whole line to entrench and hold on; and, subsequently, to dig in on the enemy. Our men lay behind little ridges, often within 50 or 100 yards of the enemy's works, and there they entrenched, with such tools as they had, till the trenching tools ordered up from the rear could get to them. All day there was skirmishing, with volleys breaking out here and

there, and much artillery; for the rebels threw canister in plenty, often enfilad-
ing our new position. The placing of the corps was thus: a refused right from
above Bethesda Church, to the E. and N. (9th Corps)—then the 5th Corps,
running from near Bethesda church, East of south to a point say ½ mile N.W.
of Woody's and connecting by a picket line with the 18th Corps which continued
south to a point say ¼ mile west of Woody's, whence the 6th Corps continued
to a point say ½ mile westward of Cold Harbor, and joined the 2d Corps which
trended E. of S. & rested its left (Boston) on the head of the Elder swamp.
Of all this assault saw nothing, by reason of the intervening thick pine wood,
which not only shut off the sight but even the sound of the musketry, except
in the direction of the 18th Corps where it was loud. 11 A.M. Birney ordered to
Warren to fill the gap between the 5th & 18th, which he accomplished, and got
the line arranged and straightened by 4 P.M. In the afternoon came Hancock
and Wright to consult with Meade at the 6th Corps headquarters. The staff
officers made some iced brandy juleps (with whisky and *without* water), the
which, coupled with the heat, so bemuddled Rosie that he lost a day, and could
never after find out how we got from Via's house to this place! 6 P.M. Ordered
to go to Birney, get an explanation of his position, ask if the enemy were strong
in his front, and if he could be spared to return to his corps; and then proceed
to Warren and find if he could not close in to the left, with Burnside, so as to
relieve Birney's division. Found Birney eating tapioca pudding in his tent. His
camp was in a hollow between Woody's and Bosher's, just on the east of the
road. "My people thought it a safe place," said he, with his grim smile, "but three
or four shells have tumbled in here already!" Then he went on to remark that
this campaign, for bloody and continuous fighting, exceeded all his experience.
"The retreat on the Peninsula was nothing to it!" He told me there was a strong
enemy before him and explained how he had gone to work to connect the two
corps and shorten and straighten the line. Then to hunt after Warren. Rode
speedily to Bethesda Church near which, and under a tree, sat Col. Bankhead
and others of the 5th Corps staff.[154] Before them was piled a neat pyramid of
artillery projectiles which had fallen near them during the day and which they
had amused themselves by gathering. "No! The General has ridden out along
the line!" Oh, charming prospect! and dusk near at hand. However, retraced
my steps, following the breastworks part of the way, and, near Birney's, came
upon Gen. Warren, and showed him the way to Headq'rs. He looked haggard;
for one trouble he has a tender heart, which cannot grow used to bloodshed.
He said: "For thirty days, now, it has been one funeral procession past me, and
it is too much! Today I saw a man burying a comrade, and, within half an hour,

he himself was brought in and buried beside him.—The men need some rest!" He had a consultation with Meade.—The friction increases between them. Meade finds fault with Warren's contradictory spirit which loves to do a thing by a different way from the one ordered. At 9 P.M. there was a strong attack on Gibbon which was repulsed, after a great deal of firing which reverberated in the still night. Our men shouted derisively: "Bring on some more Johnnies, there ar'n't enough of you." Also, they leveled their muskets and then got one of their number to shout "Forward! Guide centre!" at which the rebels rose, to repel the assault and received a volley. Capt. Candler was here today, a native of Brookline, and on Hooker's staff, when in the service. Gave him the small articles found on Abbott's person, to take home to his father.[155] So ended the great and disastrous attack on the entrenched lines near Cold Harbor. We lost 8,000 to 9,000 men, including some 2,000 prisoners or missing and, with the dead, a great number of fine officers. Col. Porter, commanding a heavy artillery regiment, and an old friend of Cora's, was slain. Col. Brooke, one of Barlow's brigadiers, was wounded, very badly. Gen. Bob Tyler severely hit in the foot. McMahon, of the 6th Corps staff was anxiously trying to get information of his brother the Colonel of the Irish Zouaves, who was last seen wounded, and was thought to be a prisoner. (In the subsequent truce, he was found dead, beneath a tree.)[156]— "And there the two armies slept—almost within an easy stone's throw of each other; and the separating space ploughed by cannon-shot and dotted with the dead bodies that neither side dared to bury.— I think nothing can give a greater idea of deathless tenacity of purpose, than the picture of those two hosts, after a bloody and nearly continuous struggle of thirty days, thus lying down to sleep with their hands almost on each other's throats!" (Letter T.L.)[157]

June 4, Saturday.

Yesterday afternoon there was an attack on Warren and on Burnside; both repulsed the enemy.— Last night Wilson, returning from his bridge burning, came down from Hawe's shop and suddenly charged the rear of the rebel left, causing a great tumult and getting some prisoners. Thereafter the enemy swung his left back, so that this morning there was nothing in the immediate front of Burnside. 9.30 A.M. The General rode out to visit his corps commanders. After a few moments at Wright he went to Hancock, who had a battery near his headquarters, which was firing furiously. 11 A.M. To Gen. Smith, who had his headquarters between Woody's house and the line of battle, on the edge of a field across which the 18th Corps had charged. Smith's tent is much better than Meade's and he treated his superior to champagne and a fine lunch; also, in sooth, to cannon balls, which occasionally came ripping through the pines or skipped over the open field. There was an artillery Lieutenant whose face seemed familiar and who turned out to be Denning Duer's son, the same that was in the Scientific School. He was sociable with me, but seemed an idle and rather supercilious young gentleman. Farquhar the self-sufficient was also there; and a capable Capt. West, once on the Coast Survey. Finally, raw-boned rattle-brained Elder, of the light battery, now "Baldy's" chief of artillery. Then there was a drunken Doctor (said to be a kindly and energetic man when sober) who said the company needed a prescription of *spiritus frumenti*; and coolly opened a bottle of hospital whisky for his own chief benefit! He had ridden out and captured two rebels, a day or two before. (The sequel of this exploit was that he got captured himself the next time he was drunk.) With the Generals was Gen. (vel "Bully") Brooks, a tall strong man, with a heavy, rather sullen face. He has a great reputation as a valiant man & steady soldier, but seems to quarrel plentifully.[158] 3.30 P.M. Midst the general hilarity enter Gen. Burnside, whereat great fall in the mercury and Brooks & Smith became military icicles! Of this the explanation is that Burnside, when in command of A. of P. had a tremendous row with both these officers, so they don't speak. B. had come to arrange the position of his corps which is to be put on the right of Smith, while Warren is to be refused on the right. 4 P.M. All returned to camp. Birney has been returned to the 2d Corps. Some force of the enemy reported at Bottom's Bridge. Sheridan moves to cover our right flank and, if possible, attack the enemy's rear. I do think there has been too much assaulting this campaign! After our lessons of failure and of success at Spottsylvania we assault here, after the enemy had had 36 hours to intrench, and that time will cover them over their heads and give them slashings and traverses besides! The best officers and men are liable, by their greater gallantry to be first disabled; and, of those that are left, the best become demoralized by the failures, and the loss of good leaders; so that, very soon, the men will no longer charge entrenchments and will only go forward when driven by their officers.[159] Our losses of yesterday must be many times over those of the enemy.

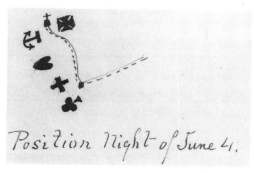

Position Night of June 4.

June 5, Sunday.

The General discoursed on affairs military: "McClellan's line," said he, was the true one. We have received 40,000 reinforcements since starting. If, now, leaving a sufficient garrison in Washington, we had these men, our own army, Butler's troops, and the Shenandoah forces, to throw against Richmond, it would have compelled Lee to retreat on that place, and we could have massed 200,000 men against the city. But here, in this country, I must fight a battle to reconnoitre a position, as in the assault of day before yesterday." He criticized some of his own officers rather harshly, complaining, for example, that Warren was not content, by Bethesda church, when his flank was covered, within two miles, by the cavalry.[160]— At this stage it is noticeable that the enemy's tactics are stubborn, but only defensive; even offensive-defensive attacks are rare and not heavy. 3 P.M. Gen. Meade sent for me. He was lying on his cot, with his riding boots cocked up on the foot-board, and he ordered me to carry a letter, from Gen. Grant to Lee, under flag of truce, asking for a suspension of hostilities for burial of the dead and succour of the wounded. A pretty errand! Heavy firing along the whole line and never carried a flag in my life! Not my business to ask questions, however. Put on all the good clothes I could muster and a pair of white cotton gloves and sent for a trumpeter who could blow a parley, but there was none such! So took a cavalry sergeant and so to Hancock, who *also* was on his cot, and told me it was too hot to get the flag out on the main line, but might try it on the picket line on the left. So the active Shaw found a *pillow-case* and ripped it up, making a nice flag![161] And so to the left, under Major Mitchell's guidance, till we got to Birney, who was on the move. From him we got Capt. McMichael and the corps officer of the day, Col. Hapgood of the 5th N. Hampshire, a black-eyed, active man, who proved a skilled guide.[162] We now struck off to the breastworks—still going to the left—and came on Barlow's division and Miles' brigade. All the officers had their tents with little cellars about 2 feet deep, to avoid the projectiles. At that moment it was nearly quiet. There was a certain Lt. Col. Hamyl, who was picket officer, or something, and he insisted on going along though I made what opposition I could, for it is no way to conduct flags with a whole color-guard of hangers on.[163] We now cut through a bit of woods galloped over a small clearing, so as to avoid the sharpshooters that the enemy had in the tall trees, and came to a poor log house whence we descended to a brook which feeds a mill pond below. We had a German bugler along, by this time, who seemed not to understand either a parley or the king's English. Here we dismounted, in the hollow, just on the other rise ran a wood road, which a sharpshooter of McClellan's time, recognized as the

Mechanicsville road. On this road we had our extreme left, held by a picket line, and beyond was that of the enemy. A brisk little Lieutenant, who was on picket, said he would go out and attract the attention of the enemy & open communication. This proved a hard job; but, at last, we attracted their attention, at 6 P.M. Then there was much delay in arranging, and in hunting up their picket officer. And, finally, the brisk Lieutenant & Mitchell got it right, and at 6.45 I formally met Maj. Wooten of the 14th N.C. with all the formality of Gen. Hancock's pillow-case! It was a picturesque sight, there among the great oaks, on this forest road. The rebel officers in their gray overcoats and slouched hats and a group of their men, stood there, half-seen in the failing light. Wooten was a superior man, with a gentle dignity of carriage that was pleasing to see; and all that he said was becoming. He sent in the letter and we sat down to wait an answer.[164] Meantime word was passed on both picket lines in no event to fire, and, very soon the pickets were together, holding friendly converse, despite constant watching by their officers! There we sat as twilight changed to darkness. There was a lieutenant there who said; "Gentlemen you can *never* whip us!" with a quiet earnestness that showed his belief. From another, heard of the safety of young Clarke, supposed killed at Spottsylvania. He got turned round, rode up to *their* breastworks, and was captured. He was Barlow's green Aide.[165] There had been a heavy cavalry fight in these woods, as our noses soon told us! The place was full of dead horses, which smelt most awfully. The Major said they buried a cavalry officer of ours, and a man or two. Probably an outpost of Sheridan on the last of May. 8.30 P.M. Suddenly there was an augmentation of the distant sharp-shooting then a volley of musketry, and then wr—r—r, the crash of small arms rolled rapidly down both lines, towards us; while the batteries waked up, and, in another minute, the singing of the shells added its ill-toned music. In all haste we sent along the line to warn the pickets from taking up the fire, and there we stayed listening to the crash and roar and to the reverberation in the still, damp, night air. Wooten listened a little and said quietly. "An attack, I suppose.—and on Sunday too!"— By degrees the fight died down and then I waited till 11 o'clock when word came that an answer could not be sent till tomorrow morning, at the same place. So we shook hands and marched off. As we got into the open by the small house there was Mott's brigade moving to extend our left. When I went out I had forbidden an aide of that division to put his men in position while the flag was out, as it would be a violation of the truce to move a hostile force in immediate neighborhood of the picket line. In the moonlight the appearance of the column was most picturesque; only masses of shadow with the gleam of the musket barrels and the tall figures of mounted officers, here & there. They showed me the way to Headquarters or I should not have found it till morning! Passing by Barlow's, stopped in to tell him about Clarke. He was in a merry state; for he had put some hundreds of his stragglers in an open field & left them there while the shells were flying, and one got hit! A shell came into Hancock's camp and took the leg off his Provost Marshal, Macuen. (He died afterwards, of it.)[166]— When I arrived in camp Gen. Meade sung out from his tent: "Hullo Lyman! I thought perhaps the rebs had gobbled you up during that attack!" They had tried to carry a part of the 2d Corps line but had been repulsed, probably, with much waste of ammunition, as is usual, in night fighting.

June 6, Monday.

Birney has extended our left nearly, or quite, opposite the mill-pond, where the flag went out. The 9th Corps is swung back, resting its right on the mill-pond, by Allen's Mill.[167] The 5th Corps has been taken out of the line and massed near Leary house, in rear of our Headq'rs. Rode over there and saw C. D. Smith, of the 18th Mass. He is husband of Cora's nurse, Annie.[168] Dust! dust! everywhere—fetlock deep! At camp was surprised to find that adventurous and restless person, Maj. Ludlow (!) who had ridden all the way from York river here. He is inspector of cavalry for Butler, and had wearied of lying still behind the Bermuda Hundred lines. He reported nothing doing and plenty of strawberries. He pow-wowed over old times, and he took a note from me to Hal (which, of course, he never delivered).[169] No arrangement yet for the armistice.

June 7, Tuesday.

Two divisions of the 5th Corps, under Griffin, extended our left as far as Despatch Station, at the crossing of the railroad on the Chickahominy. Two cavalry divisions, under Sheridan left for a raid on the Va. Cent. R.R. moving westward from near New Castle on the Pamunkey, intending finally to join Hunter in the valley, near Charlottesville.[170] After a delay of 4 days (!) an armistice was concluded from 6–8 P.M. this eve. Nearly all in our front were dead for our men had got in the most of our wounded, during the nights; and those not reached either died from exposure or were relieved by a friendly bullet. The body of Col. McMahon, of the Irish Legion, was found under a tree, pierced by several bullets. Poor McMahon, the Adjutant General, has lost, within a few months, his father, two brothers, and his chief, Gen. Sedgwick, and he now looks quite broken with grief.[171] The position of our front line, especially near the Gaine's Mill road, is very severe. The men have constructed all sorts of traverses and bomb-proofs, to shelter themselves, and still many are hit; some even have been shot vertically in the *top* of the head by glancing bullets. The misery of the men, also, was extreme, exposed to a hot sun, constantly under a searching fire, short of water, and surrounded by the scantily buried dead! Several rebel officers were seized for being within our lines, after the expiration of the truce; but they were liberated on ascertaining that they were not in fault. Crawford came to dine. He plays his cards with the General and is a sharp looker out for himself.

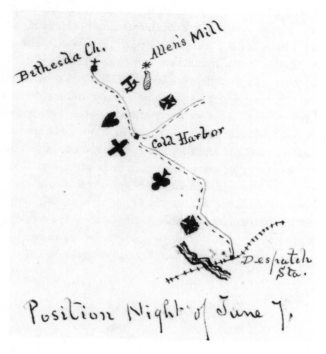

Position Night of June 7.

June 8, Wednesday.

McMahon was over; he has recovered his brother's watch. Weld, Col. of the 56th Mass. and Loring, Insp. Gen. 9th Corps, came also to visit me. Another & entirely new apparition, was Gen. Barnard of the engineers; an ungainly, studious looking man, with a stoop in his shoulders. He is as deaf as a post, extremely ill bred; vastly book learned; and thoroughly unreliable. In fact, a time serving critic, and a military pedant, only fit to write disquisitions. Here he is simply in the way, and he is here, only (as Meade said afterwards) to "make another book" and to try and glean a little credit for himself.[172] 11 A.M. To Grant's, close at hand, and then to Warren's at Leary's, just in rear of us. There then passed an entertaining pageant—a trumpet, followed by the provost-marshal's flag, followed again by a guard in whose midst rode a civilian, sandwiched between two placards "Libeller of the Press!" This man was one Cropsy, correspondent of the Philadelphia Enquirer. He stated, in one of his letters, that the army would have fallen back across the Rapid Ann, after the Wilderness fight, had Grant not withstood the advice of one of his high officers.—He confessed he meant thereby Meade; and had nothing to show but rumor to prove this gross false-hood! Thereat the General, considering this as greatly calculated to shake the confidence of his soldiers in him, ordered him thus publickly exhibited, and then put beyond the lines.[173] (This hurt Meade much, afterwards. The press people rallied on their injured *confrère*, and studiously avoided mentioning Meade in any of their despatches,—to the very last. The General's mistake was, that he was too short with newspaper people to be popular, and not severe enough to be feared. The correspondents are a very ordinary set, as a general rule; vulgar, half-educated, and without discretion or any high trait of character. The good officers usually avoid them, and they become the cronies of ignoble commis-saries or inferior brigade commanders. As exceptions there is one Swinton (Scotch?) a man of good education and a clever writer; also a very respectable Mr. Coffin from Boston, and a black-eyed man with the 6th Corps.)[174]— At Warren's they had a singular heavy shot, with a base-cup of copper, to take the rifling. This cup was fitted on by a single screw in the centre and had radiating shoulders, to keep it from twisting, on the base of the shot.

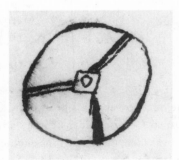

It was thrown from a "railroad monitor" at our troops near Despatch Station. But the gun can only traverse a small angle; for fear of kicking the machine off the track. Gen. Warren accompanied us as far as Allen's Millpond, a pleasant spot with large trees. The soldiers of the 9th Corps were having a famous bath under the water-wheel. At 2.15 P.M. got to Old Church Tavern, where a lot of negro troops were drilling. It seemed strange to see anyone who had enough leisure to drill! A certain fat, and rather unpleasant looking Col. Thomas was in command.[175] Riddle was vastly amused to recognize in the ranks the broad grin of his *quondam* table servant "Mr. Jeff. Mess!" Thence we kept on to Ruffin's house (brother of the venerable Edmund) which stands above the alluvial flat through which runs the Pamunkey. Wilson had there his headquarters and showed us the position of his pickets. A back room was littered up with rubbish, among which found some fossils, which Ruffin had (for he was a writer on agriculture and marls).[176] We took a different road back to the Tavern and saw marks of sharp cavalry fighting and some graves here and there. At the Tavern Warren talked with two girls, who remembered him when he came there in McClellan's day as Colonel of the 5th N.Y. Zouaves.— In digging an entrenchment, the other day, near Tolopotomoy Cr. some of Potter's men found $4,000 or $5,000 in coin. Such is the practice of hoarding now in the south! We found Gen. Martindale at Headq'rs on our return; a black haired talkative man, full of great plans to do great things. News of a victory by Hunter, who has routed the valley rebels and is pressing towards Lynchburg.[177]

June 9, Thursday.

About noon, Gen. Meade rode over to Hancock, (who has been forced to move back out of the way of shells) and confabbed with that commander. He told H. he would give over his pretensions to the Philadelphia Fair sword, if he (Hancock) would send him some fresh bread, which his ingenious cook makes. He rode off, after lunch, to visit the extreme left.— Stopped at Birney's who is in line opposite the millpond, near which I went out with the flag. At the battle of Gaine's Mill, Waterman's battery was here (that must have been on Porter's second position). We could hence see the Dudley house, on the other side of the river, over the tops of the heavy timber that marked the stream. The Trent house, where were McClellan's Headq'rs, was a mile to the west of that.[178] Taking the Despatch Sta. road, which runs parallel to the river, we came to the Tyler house, once Sumner's Headq'rs; now Griffin's. We could see a rebel battery, on the other side, which had killed some of Griffin's men. The house stands on the river bottom, which, along this stream, is very extensive and reckoned extremely unhealthy. Capt. Barnard (Geo. M.) was there and is shortly to leave the service.[179] All along here is a continuous intrenched line, with batteries. 4.15 P.M. Griffin accompanied us towards Despatch Station. From the rise near Savage's large house, (where were Cutler's Headq'rs) we could see the rebel works very well, with a battle-flag on one of them. The main buildings at Savage's were burnt. Some of the opposite line is held by a battalion of Richmond clerks, who amuse our men by their continual, nervous firing! Going through a woody tract and over two or three little runs, we passed St. James' Church and came to the railroad, and got an excellent view, over an extensive bog, of the other side, where we could behold little knots of rebs, standing here and there. But no railroad monitor; which, as it seemed, had retired in disquiet. The track was all up.[180] These swamps are full of small magnolias, (now beginning to flower) and look and smell very sickly. Another thing noticeable is the swamp flies. We returned by cross roads, coming out at 6.30 by Warren's Headq'rs. The country on the way had a few poor log houses and the young crops seemed to promise barely enough to support the scanty population. The hospitals are on these back roads; also we passed a picket of "Dutch" heavy artillery—not a formidable protection! Gibbon is confirmed a Major General. Hayden, Farrar and Rosencrantz also confirmed as Captains.[181]

June 10, Friday.

By order of the Confed. authorities, all people had laid in much ice in this part of the country; and it is a blessing for us now, and for our wounded. Usually it is about 3 inches thick and of poor quality; but we do not stoop to be difficult! Gen. Meade read me, from a Richmond paper, an account of Longstreet's attack, at the Wilderness, which was *diagonal*, it would appear, from the south side of the Plank Road, so that our left flank was struck and doubled up. This explains much of the blind history of that part of the field. The General took occasion to comment on the slowness of our troops, and their want of promptness in pressing a favorable chance. We visited Gen. Burnside's who is camped in a vortex of dust, by Kelly's. "Old B-sides," is one of the "all-will-come-out-right" sort; a sort of faith pleasant to see even when not backed by strong reasoning. They were trying an officer there for self-mutilation to get out of action! a trick not unusual among enlisted men, who frequently blow off a finger in the most deliberate manner. Saw Gen. Parke there—a handsome man, with a very kindly and sensible countenance. There was a negro convicted today of rape.[182]

June 11, Saturday.

Warren this morning marched, with his two remaining divisions, and massed near Moody's, east of Despatch Station. The engineers engaged in marking out an interior line, to be held by two corps, while the other two begin their move by the left flank. Whereupon, of course, succeeded plenty of bickering between Michler and Duane with Wright & Hancock! The two corps commanders insisting that the engineers had laid out their second line in a very exposed style. In the leisure of these last days we have had the apparition of Brady, who photographed the General & whole staff.[183] Col. Burton, now holding the sinecure of Inspector of Artillery (to his disgust) has had leisure to tell us lots of stories of lower California, where he long lived, with his Spanish wife. He's a fine looking old Vermonter, is the Colonel, and has a grandiloquent way that is highly entertaining.[184] Barlow was over, fired by Gibbon's promotion, and conferred with Gen. Meade, who explained that Hancock had certainly recommended B[arlow] for a grade, but as Gibbon had the precedence, and as there was but one vacancy, he could not send the recommendation up. With this Barlow was fain to retire half satisfied (and subsequently rather embroiled himself with Hancock and Meade about it.)— There was a cool wind today, for a contrast; though it is observable that the days are hot and the nights cool, so that a double thickness of blanket does not go amiss. Cora is at Beverly, also the Russells (in the Bancroft house). The Jube's Lane house is sold to one Thompson—more's the pity for I was married there.[185]

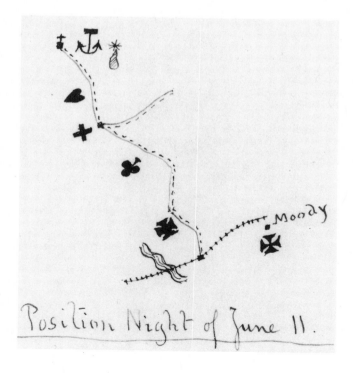

Position Night of June 11.

June 12, Sunday.

"I have been obliged to relieve Gen. Eustis," said the General, this morning; "He could not be found for two or three days, here." The fact seems undoubted that he drinks; and then he is said to be incompetent—sad ending for a man of so much promise as he, when he was chosen Professor at the Scientific School! Barstow is quite melancholy over the loss of two brothers, of whom one, an army surgeon, committed suicide in a fort in Boston Harbor, and the other (the youngest brother) died of typhoid at Newberne.[186] The footing of our killed, wounded, and missing since May 5 is appalling —50,000 to 55,000!— By rebel sources we hear that Crook and Averill's cavalry have joined Hunter in the valley. Old Washburn is down again. Meade feels pretty sure that he is the party who started the story that Meade wanted to recross after the Wilderness![187] 3 P.M. After a stay of 9 days, in this sand field, we broke camp, and

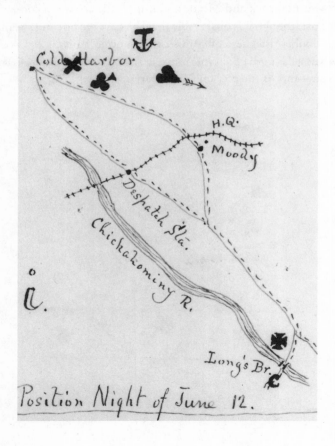

rode, via Despatch Station, to Moody's. The two Generals, with their staffs and escorts, made a long cavalcade, and it is surprising the enemy did not open on us, as we passed near Savage's. Dust worse than ever!— Moody's is a little house, as it were on skids, like a corn-barn, and with several pleasant catalpas round it. We got there at 5, and found Warren just striking his tents to move on. There too was Col. Locke, just back, from his wounded "leave," and with a big scar on his cheek and rather shaky about the grinders.[188] We would fain camp in a flat, near by. It was cool and damp and they built a fire in front of which Grant accommodated himself for a nap on a board. The waggons were not up till 10 P.M. because they undertook to cross a sort of mill dam, and some tumbled off. *Order of march.* At dark 5th Corps to go to Long's bridge, preceded by cavalry, and cross the Chickahominy. 2d & 6th Corps to retire to the inner line. 18th Corps to march to Whitehouse and embark for City Point. During the night, 9th Corps, followed by the 6th to move on Jones' Bridge, via Allen's Mill. 2d Corps, via Despatch Station, to Long's Bridge. 11 P.M. News that our cavalry had forced a passage at Long's Bridge, and that they were now laying a pontoon.[189]

June 13, Monday.

Headquarters moved at 5.30 A.M. and took the nearest road for Long's Br. passing Prospect (Providence?) Church. 6.15. Coming on the main road, we struck Barlow's division which presently massed on the right of the road. 7 A.M. Joined Gen. Hancock, who was sitting on the grass, close to Long's Bridge. His wound, on the inside of the thigh, received at Gettysburg, has reopened and troubles him a good deal.— Rumor that the enemy are at Malvern Hill. The Chickahominy is of small width—3 or 4 pontoons suffice for it, it is more like a sluggish ditch of warm, brown, muddy water, from which rise tall cypresses, with their singular, conical bases. But, when it overflows, it inundates the bottom land on either side, and may then be perhaps 1,000 yards wide, more or less, according to the extent of the bottoms. Hence rose McClellan's troubles. Here we all rested with the infantry, and, when Barlow was over, we crossed also. Noticed Col. Frank go past, whom Barlow relieved for intoxication at the Wilderness. He is a type "Dutchman" and just good for nothing![190] Got over at 10.30 and halted again the other side at a farm. There was a goodly mulberry tree wherein the officers did perch to get the fruit. There was a nig mowing the ripe wheat, a scanty crop, for the land is meagre. Then we kept along, on the flank of Barlow's people, who made most rapid and compact marching, being, in sooth, well driven up by a most unmerciful provost guard!— Was sent ahead to caution Miles not to march his brigade so fast; he said he couldn't march them slower, but would mass them, for a rest. Found Barlow in a cherry tree, by the roadside, and in a woman's garden. He invited me in his quaint style, to partake of the fruit also, remarking he knew it would not be long before Meade's staff got there! Not much beyond this, was surprised to see the improved appearance of the farms, which was in reality because we had struck the arable belt lying along the James River. 3.30 P.M. Arrive at the Clarke house, whence Gen. Meade sent me to see the nature of the land further on. Rode with Duane across a wide field, turned a small grove and came in sight of what seemed to me a fog bank, or a grey ploughed field, or a great dust. "There's the river," says D[uane] coolly. The optical cheat cleared up, and I appreciated that I stood not far from the edge of a bluff overlooking a mighty river a mile wide! Six weeks in the Wilderness, and the James River at last! There was Fort Powhattan over against us, and there were the comely farms and the pleasant groves, on either bank. The precise spot was just above Wilcox' wharf—a signal officer was trying to attract the attention of the fort and to open communication with the two steamers there lying. Duane looked out a position to cover our right. At the Clarke's were three or four young women, not very aristocratic to behold. We camped somewhat to the east, in a large field by the house where once lived John Tyler, the big-nosed Vice-President. It was but a moderately good house, with rather a good, ornamented chimney-piece. There was a great cackling among the local negroes at recognizing a friend who had left them as an officer's servant in McClellan's time! By diligence did get not only milk, but even green peas; for we strive after our mess as after a grand battle![191] After a very handsome march the whole 2d Corps got in this evening, and camped; Gibbon's people being behind our headq'rs. Despite their fatigue and notwithstanding permission to go at once to sleep, they insisted on first making a breastwork! Such is the force of habit and such the contrast between the men of today and the men of the beginning, who could hardly be driven to throw a shovelful of earth! This afternoon the cavalry, under Wilson, advanced on Malvern Hill and were driven back by the enemy's infantry, which pursued till it struck Crawford and then got driven in turn. The whole 5th Corps is in position, covering the right flank towards Malvern hill, above Long's bridge. During the night the 6th Corps (which lead, instead of following the 9th) crossed at Jones' Bridge. Main trains delayed at Cole's ferry by unexpected width of the Chickahominy. Pontoons sent for.

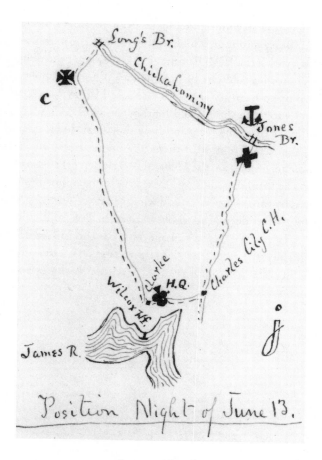

Position Night of June 13.

June 14, Tuesday.

At daylight 9th Corps crosses at Jones' bridge. 5th Corps comes in, to near Charles City courthouse. Wilson's cavalry in observation, towards Malvern hill, ascertained that the bulk of Lee's army was there intrenching. Rode down to Wilcox' Wharf with the General, and saw Birney's people being ferried over to Windmill point. They had repaired the wharf and were using two steamers at once. Beheld there Col. Butler with what remains of the no longer "bloodless" 93d N.Y. On the other side we could descry our men having a fine bath on the beach. The General cut through a wood and came out by a house on the bluff where Barlow had his headq'rs, and stopped a moment to speak to him about (I think) having another wharf repaired, as there would then be more facilities for ferrying. Getting back to our tents, went over to the 20th Mass. near by, and saw Capt. Patten, now in command. He has but two other officers left to help him. Called up Bessy and took a look at him. (He is the man who gloriously distributed lozenges in the cars.) Patten told me they had been obliged to order a court martial on Billy Milton's brother, who was a melancholy coward and could not keep up to his duty (He was dismissed [from] the service—a sad affair).[192] Also he told me about Cold Harbor; how his cook was killed while bringing his dinner from the rear; and how they kept down the enemy's fire by their sharpshooters. I reminded them of Abbott's horse and promised to help get him home. Meantime the General had ridden off to see the laying of the great pontoon, from the point by Douthart's to the opposite side. It was of 92 boats, braced by three schooners, and was over 2,000 feet long, the water in the centre being 85 feet deep. The whole was finished by midnight. Hancock's Headq'rs are at Tyler's. All the 2d Corps is to cross and to advance tomorrow on Petersburg. The 18th Corps passed up the river in boats, this afternoon, and is to advance on Petersburg tomorrow from Point of Rocks, opposite Butler's left on the Appomattox.[193]

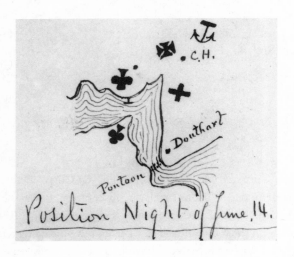

June 15, Wednesday.

Leave at 10 A.M. and stop at Warren's, who is at a house this side of Charles City C.H. I was afterwards sent back to explain to W[arren] about the rations for his men. The General rode to Douthart's—a brick house large and good, standing at the point of a well tilled peninsula which is enclosed by a bend of the river. We camped near by. The General in a sharp humor, though things seemed moving well enough. Admiral Lee reported to Gen. Meade—a simple looking man who seemed not likely to fire the river! He had the "Atlanta" and other vessels to cover the crossing, if need be. He spoke of the sinking of the stone vessels above Dutch Gap and spoke of it as a slur on the navy, as if it could not keep back the rebel war-ships. Capt. Beaumont also paid his respects; a black whiskered party, brother of Beaumont of Wright's staff.[194] Then we rode to the bridge—a great wonder. First, the approach to it, running along the river beach for some distance, where they had to cut down huge cypresses and heavily corduroy bad boggy places, was remarkable. This was prepared by Weitzel who, though a Brig. of Vols. reported to Duane; but, just then, enter old Benham, who took command and carried off all the credit, to the great rage of Duane. Benham was at the bridge in his usual condition of active muddle.[195] The bridge itself was a beautiful specimen, and the artillery and the waggon train were crossing at that moment in an uninterrupted stream. But Gen. Meade ordered it opened, to let up certain vessels. Here the tide makes from 3 to 5 feet but the water is not brackish. 6.30 P.M. As we were at dinner Col. Babcock arrived and reported that Smith was successfully advancing on Petersburg and had taken two or three guns. Immediately Burnside was ordered to cross and march that night on Petersburg and form on the left of the 2d Corps. The waggon train was halted to let him pass the pontoon. Enemy reported leaving Malvern Hill and crossing on a bridge near Drury's bluff. Tomorrow, at 4 A.M. two divisions of the 5th Corps to be ferried from Wilcox' Wharf the other two from wharf near the pontoon; and both to march on Petersburg, taking position on left of

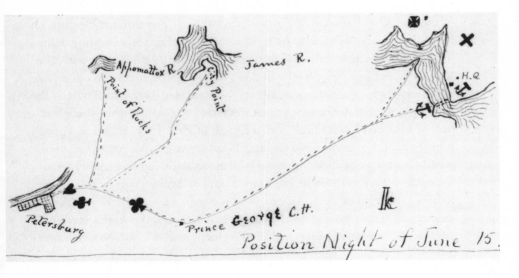

the 9th. Main train to pass the pontoon, followed by Wilson's cavalry. 6th Corps to hold an intrenched position till all are over, and then cross under cover of the gunboats. Bridge then to be taken up and carried to City Point.

June 16, Thursday.

Took a bath in the James, last night, as had done already in the Rapid Ann and in the North Anna. — 5th Corps crossing; waggon train has been moving down since yesterday afternoon and is still crossing by the bridge. 8.30 A.M. Gen. Meade went down to the bridge with Saunders and myself and we signaled for a boat, which carried us in great state on board, when the chief was received with great whistling of boatswains. A contrast, rather, between the smug clean sailors and their officers and our sad trio of dusty soldiers, their clothes torn with the bushes and threadbare with hard use! Truly the Americans are sailors by nature, and look their craft after a three-month turn at it; but the more they soldier it the less military they appear. This "Atlanta" is just like a great, iron turtle, with an angular back, in which there are narrow ports for three or four big rifled cannon, which are handled with surprising ease by a few ropes and pulleys. The inside was like a low attic. We saw where a number of bolt-heads were knocked off by one of our 15-inch shot, when we took her. The shot nevertheless, did not go through.[196] The current seconded by an ebbing tide, was very swift just now. 10.30. Gens. Meade and Humphreys, with Saunders and myself for aides, got on a steamer, to go up the river to City Point. As was going on board beheld Lt. Richard Robins marching on board another steamer, with his regiment. He is not naturally pretty and the dust, fatigue and sickness of the campaign had marred the poor fellow's little pretensions![197] — It is an hour's trip to the Point. On the right we passed Harrison's Landing, famed in McClellan's day, and there is the great brick house with a high roof, called Westover, and belonging to the Seddon family.[198] The shores on either side are pretty high, somewhat resembling Narragansett Bay. City Point is the head of bluff land at the junction of the James & Appomattox. There was a nest of scattered houses here, with a church or two. They still stand, though somewhat hurt by some naval shelling. Near a once pretty cottage, just on the point, Grant had pitched his tents. We landed at the meagre old wharf and walked to the top of the bluff, but found Grant had gone to the front, reported to be a good 7 miles away. An orderly was detailed to show the way, and off we started. Just at the edge of the village, and behind some works, saw a neat camp and some negro sentries. "What regiment?" says I. "5th Massachusetts cavalry"—" Is Col. Russell here?""No Sarr; he's in der hospital, wounded!" It

made me jump! Harry hit in yesterday's fight; but the man said not dangerously. The General had but two aides, so did not dare to halt there! Presently
we met Grant and his staff coming back: "Well," he said "Smith has taken a line
of works there, stronger than anything we have seen this campaign!—If it is a
possible thing, I want an assault made at 6 o'clock this evening!"— Asked Col.
Rowley to have a care of Hal, which he promised to do.[199] We went over an
open country till we turned to the left and crossed the railroad, where we cut
Burnside's column, moving up. It was pitiable to see the men!—without water,
broken by a severe march, scorched by the sun, and covered with a suffocating
dust. Gen. Ledlie was just passing, a well looked young man (but who turned
out a most drunken, incapable wretch). After crossing, we turned sharp to the
right and kept through a wood in which the negroes had had a quite sharp
fight, coming into an open across which was a little breast-work. Here a negro
regiment, under Jack Ames (Class '54) took 3 cannon, very gallantly.[200] There
we again turned left, crossed a patch of woods and a run—a lot of 9th Corps
batteries were just there, and came on the main Coggins' Point (or Telegraph)
road. On the right of the road, below Bailey's house, was Burnside, halted, with
his staff under a tree. Stopping with him a few minutes, the General pushed
ahead, and got to Hancock's Headq'rs at 1.45 P.M. These were in a clump of
tall pines on the edge of an extensive clearing, which the enemy had long ago
made to give a field of fire for their works, which lay some hundreds of yards in
front of us, and were very strong redans, with a continuous infantry parapet, to
connect them. (At this point, where Hancock was, the U.S. Military Railroad
afterwards crossed the Coggin's Pt. Road)— From the swell in front I got my
first sight of the spires of Petersburg (which I was destined to stare at a long
while!). The clump of large hard pines showed marks of a heavy artillery fire and
was much cut; a dead black soldier and a white one lay there. A few yards in the
rear I had seen a dead rebel, behind a little barricade—probably a skirmisher.
3 P.M. Sent to establish our Headq'rs—a difficult matter, for things are as dry
as bone dust. Found Bailey's house all smashed inside and used as a hospital.
There was a field hospital of Birney's Div. just the other side of the run; and
about 50 or 40 wounded there, from the skirmish line. Put our Headq'rs in the
field, below the house. 3.45 P.M. The General earnestly consulting with Hancock
and others about the assault. Humphreys and Barlow made a personal reconnaissance, and of course got vigorously peppered! Birney, Barlow and a part
of Gibbon to attack and Smith (Martindale?) to demonstrate strongly on the
right.[201] 6 P.M. Our batteries opened heavily, chiefly from the captured works
just in our front. The General rode onto the open ground and sat there on

horseback. Sharp musketry from Smith (Martindale?) and from Birney. The cannonade very heavy and grand and, as the sun declined, the air, full of dust and powder smoke, gave a copper color to the scene that was most striking. The General sat there till far into twilight; and had a very narrow escape from a round-shot which bounded just past him and Gen. Humphreys. Capt. Emory was with us—a son of the General E.—and newly came on our staff.[202]—In vain! Birney got their first line, and Barlow secured an advanced position, but the main line was nowhere carried, and our 2d Corps lost 2,500 men. At dusk, got leave to go to City Point to see Hal; and Gen. Meade gave me a despatch to Grant and a verbal message. Changed horses, and, with two orderlies, took my way briskly along the lonely road. A splendid moonlight night! After much enquiry at the Point found the building in which Hal was; and, after sending an orderly with the despatch to Gen. Grant, mounted the stairs and entered a room where some eight or ten beds were occupied by wounded officers. Harry lay there, sleeping lightly; with an ugly case-shot wound on his shoulder-blade. He was right glad to see me, covered though I was with dust, and I passed a few minutes, in quiet talk with him. Then to Headq'rs and found Gen. Grant just going to bed. He sat on the edge of his cot, in shirt and drawers and listened to my report. Told him the General would put in a column of 5,000 men of the 9th Corps, by moonlight. He smiled, like one who had done a clever thing, and said, "I think it is pretty well to get across a great river, and come up here and attack Lee in his rear before he is ready for us!"— He prepared a despatch to Gen. Meade, which took back, after arranging to have a telegraph sent to Hal's people.[203] Got back at 1 in the morning, passing the 5th Corps moving up,

Position Night of June 16.

and meeting Kautz's cavalry returning from covering the left. They had some queer little mountain Howitzers with them. Gen. Butler moved out today from Bermuda Hundred and destroyed a little of the railroad. There arrived one division of the 6th Corps at City Point (Neil's 2d) and relieved (this night?) Brooks, who, with Baldy Smith, went back to Bermuda Hundred; Martindale commanding the rest of the 18th Corps. Admiral Lee reports enemy crossing at Drury's Bluff.[204]

June 17–
August 27, 1864

————⚬⚬⚬————

June 17, Friday.

We were up early, and were met by the news that Potter's division (9th Corps) had carried the works in their front with 4 guns and 350 prisoners! This handsome charge was just at break of day. Potter's horse shot under him.— The works ran by the Shind house and so over by the Avery house. The heat of the fight was near the Shind house, which was riddled like a pepper-castor top! About noon sent with orders to Gen. Patrick to detail 3d Penn. Cav. to picket the left of Gen. Warren. Towards evening, Ledlie's division (9th Corps) attacked and carried a second line, in front of the Shind house, (west) and near the pine wood. Thinking again to advance, they made no proper preparation to hold on, by turning the works, &c. Sent down, at dusk to learn the result. After trouble found Burnside's headquarters, east of Shind house, and near the old rebel main line, we had taken.[1] Saw also many wounded coming back. Remember one fellow, shot in the hand, who exclaimed in great excitement "Oh, crikey! warn't it hot! The bullets they just screamed!" Reported back that we held the line; but soon after, the rebels retook it with a counter charge, forcing our people back on the position they had captured in the morning. Complaint was made (I fancy with justice) that Crawford did not bring up his division promptly in support. In this fight fell Maj. Morton, an excentric but talented engineer officer. McKibbin of the 18th Inf. was badly shot in the cheek. The left of our advance today was near the Shind house, (south of it).[2]

June 18, Saturday.

Last night, the General having blown up about being so far to the rear, Gen. Williams moved the Headquarters across the road, which satisfied the Chief, though he wasn't a foot nearer the front than before!

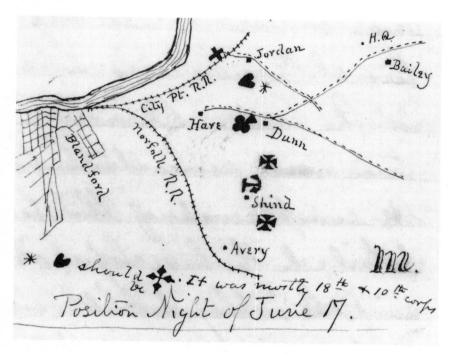

All the camp was down late last night and up early this morning. The General in a tearing humor. "Col. Lyman; go to Gen. Warren, take two or three orderlies and report to me promptly and frequently!" I soon galloped ahead, leaving the General to pitch into poor, clumsy Jim Biddle who, very red in the face, was coming up late! 4.30 A.M. Arrived at 5th Corps headquarters—a couple of tents pitched under a tree, near where saw Burnside, last night. Warren, with his clothes on, was catching a nap in the tent. Burnside sat under a tree and remarked, "he was all ready." He [Burnside] complained of the heavy artillery detailed to his corps. "They are worthless," said he; "they didn't enlist to fight and it is unreasonable to expect it from them. In the attack last night I couldn't find thirty of them!" He afterwards said of Meade (to one of his staff), "He is irascible; but he is a magnanimous man." Near by sat a telegraph operator, with his portable instrument—a characteristic figure in Headquarters, during action. Presently up comes Griffin, in one of his peculiar blusters! and all about a commissary who, he maintains, didn't follow orders. Griffin stormed and swore.—"Now! Now!" said Warren, (who can be very judicious when he chooses) "let us all try to keep our tempers more, and not swear so much. I know I give way myself; but it is unworthy."[3]— We were to have an assault all along the line; but there was a mysterious silence, though the skirmishers were ordered forward. 5.30 A.M. Some shots, but not a great many. They report only a skirmish line in our front. Several little squads of prisoners brought in, who say they were caught asleep and that their line fell back ½ hour before day. One fellow said it was only a very little way to the town and he heard they were going to evacuate it. But another, a fine, sharp fellow, remarked with a quiet smile, "I suppose you think you are going to have a great success; but *I* think you will be disappointed!" He had been taken while out with a party to bury some men.— Our people are now in the rebel works of last night. Still they seem to hold back or not to go on briskly and together. 6.50 A.M. Gen. Meade has ordered the whole line to advance. On the left and in front of the Avery house, Cutler's skirmishers are across the Norfolk rail. 7.15. Roebling rode in, and reported he had observed and reconnoitred the new position of the enemy, which was along the ridge beyond the railroad, and that they had works and batteries in position; in some of which he had counted the cannon. Previous to this the Second Corps people had picked up a rebel order to fall back, and take and fortify a new position, which had been selected. 7.45. Gen. Warren mounted and rode farther forward. He passed the Shind house (where ran the captured pits, just on the bank of a deep waterway) and crossed a large oat field, on the other side of which was the rebel second line of pits which was taken and retaken last night. A great number of rebel dead lay there; two men had lost the tops of their heads, carried away by the same round-shot. Gen. Warren established himself to the right, and in front of, the Avery house, just where a heavy pine wood made a corner into the open land. In our rear was the oat field; on the left, open, untilled land; and in front we could see the ridge whereon the enemy was still busy in digging. Two roads here crossed, where was a large, hollow oak, under which stood the General. As we got there the skirmishing had become quite lively on our right and our left, both of which were in the woods. Batteries also were firing, especially one of ours near the Avery House, "which" quoth Griffin, "might just as well be in New York!"— In return, the enemy sent artillery projectiles wherever they suspected troops, and they unfortunately had a cross-fire just on our big oak, so that we had all sorts of things about our ears, not to mention bullets from Crawford's front! It was extremely hot, there, all the day long, intermittently. At that time Griffin was massed behind the woods, in the neighborhood of the Shind house. Griffin comes frequently to consult, also Crawford. G[riffin] was in his usual loud, confident, reckless humor. He had sent a message that morning to a persistent battery that would fire over his people's heads that "he would do less damage, if he would face about and *fire to the rear!*" Crawford laughed at him for dodging a bullet. Some of Griffin's people now advanced into the oat field, and Phillips coming up with his battery (5th Mass.), Griffin called out to him: "I want you to go in there with your guns; but you will be under fire there." "Well" answered P[hillips], "I have been in those places before!"—and rode on. Griffin went with him to choose a spot, but both were received by an unlooked for skirmish volley from the flank, and came back in a hurry![4] The 22d Mass. and another regiment were sent forward to drive in the enemy's skirmishers, but their first attempt failed, with the loss of several men, as reported by the little adjutant who came in for instructions. All along the line was sharp firing, trying to force back the enemy's skirmishers (who resisted obstinately) and work our troops into a position for an assault. 11.30 A.M. Our batteries partly silence their enemy. Griffin, who was very confident all through, says our guns have driven theirs away, but Roebling the cynical, says they are there, and will fire when needed. Assault ordered for 12 m. by Gen. Meade. None made then by anybody. 1.30 P.M. Crawford is reported too much to the rear and overlapping to the left (he being on the right of the 9th Corps). Think he replied he was *not*; but, all day, there was this trouble in getting the divisions of the 5th and 9th Corps forward simultaneously; or, indeed, of getting them forward at all. Meantime Gen. Meade was getting more and more indignant that he could not get his orders for an attack obeyed; and sent such telegraphs that Warren got very angry, and said corps commanders must have discretion, and he would not stand to be thus bullied! Artillery fire slack. Ayres reported as close in. 3.30 P.M. The batteries all open from our side. "Now" cried Griffin to an artillery officer "Captain I want you just to distribute your water-pots over that side hill!"— We rode into the open plain to see the troops go up. The advance was chiefly by the brigades of Chamberlain and —— on the left. It was as I expected—45 days of death, danger, and toil are no preparation for a rush! The men moved up without spirit, received a withering fire, and fell back behind the first crest. Chamberlain desperately wounded.[5] The railroad cut, which offered protection, was full of our wounded. About us came plenty of minié bullets, cutting up the dust, and of shells & case there was no end. Of the wounded brought past us there was an uncommon proportion of terrible artillery lacerations. Lt. Blake, Phillips' 1st Lieutenant, was brought in on a stretcher, just drawing his last breath, with a bullet straight through the head. I shall never forget one poor artilleryman, his face almost blown to pieces; one of his eyes hanging out and his clothes on fire, apparently from premature explosion of a shell.[6] 6 P.M. Another assault; chiefly on the right by Sweitzer's brigade, Crawford's division and parts of the 9th Corps. Warren drew his sword and, with shut lips, walked a few paces forward to look. He turned back, and, with a sad air, said "It's just the same as before!" Griffin, however, was still confident, and said "I gain a little each time. The next rush I will take those works!" He determined to try once more at 7.30. Rode in at 7.10 to tell Gen. Meade, who already had countermanded the attack: "for" said he "he can but take a point, and he will be driven out again." During the day, Birney, (who commands the 2d Corps, because Hancock is disabled by his old wound) made a very strong attack, with 7 brigades, but was repulsed, to his bitter disappointment, as they said, for it was a chance for great distinction. (The lines, as determined by the advances of this day, remained afterwards, as those of investment on this side of the town.) At supper, Meade was extremely brave and cheerful, though much disappointed. "I had hoped," said he "all alone to have entered Petersburg this

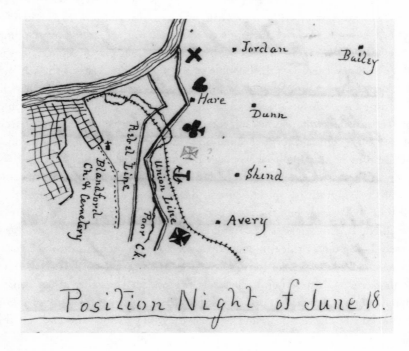

Position Night of June 18.

day." I felt extremely depressed by what I had been through and seen, so that the General cried out, "Why, Lyman, you are demoralized!" Gen. Humphreys had been down in person to our tree, during the day. One round shot skipped directly over son Harry's legs, but valiant papa seemed only fearful for his horses, having no such thing as personal fear. By the kindness of Mr. Dana and Col. Dent, Harry was sent home yesterday. The troops, many of whom were much exposed, covered their front during the night.[7]

June 19, Sunday.

Lively sharpshooting along our whole front, as customary when troops first face each other. The divisions of Russell and Ricketts which had been over at Bermuda Hundred to assist Butler (under Wright) relieved the 18th Corps on our right. 11 A.M. Ordered to carry a flag and try to get an armistice for burial of the dead and removal of wounded between the lines. Got a sprig bugler and a tall sergeant armed with Gen. Williams' white table cloth on a staff. Rode down the road past the Dunn house to Gen. Birney's Headq'rs, which were pitched in a little hollow of a run. The covers and holes showed the spot had been a dangerous one. Gen. Mott was there, commanding the division. Birney returned soon and said it was too hot in his front to get out a flag; but gave me an orderly to show the way to Barlow. Passed a part of the intrenchments on the way. There were some graves close to them, so as to be almost uncovered. It was woods all the way, but, at one spot, the orderly showed where the attack of the 16th had been; and in another was a gap, where could see the rebel line very nicely, across an open field. My guide exhorted me to come on, as "they were generally pretty free with their bullets." One came past my head near Barlow's camp. Found my classmate stretched at length and taking it easy. He pressed me to stay and talk, but was already late, so he gave me a guide as far as the oat field of last evening. Gen. Warren was at the Avery house, a well to do Virginian mansion with lots of little outbuildings and a very nice box hedge. It had been pelted by the light twelves. One solid shot had lodged between the lathing and the timbers after describing most curious angles in the wall. "They are firing there all the time," said Warren, shaking his head unpromisingly. He sent for Major Walsh of the 3d Penn. Cav.—a goodly Pat, and a promoted sergeant of regulars; and he undertook to guide me through the picket line. We crossed the rail, went into the woods, and, passing a cavalry picket reserve, kept the wood road to the right, which brought us soon to a field, and a meagre house, where was another picket reserve, and a cavalry subaltern, in a state of profound ignorance! Here we faced north, passed a mounted vidette at the corner of a field, with his carbine ready; floundered through a bushy swamp, and suddenly descried an infantry man of sinister air; but he was only one of our pickets which here ran through the wood. Capt. Thatcher and Lt. McKibbin came up presently and sent off to stop the fire of a battery on our right, so that we could get the flag out.[8] Meantime we sat down in a narrow wood-road, and Walsh regaled us with an account of how, with a squad of men, he made a push up the main road, near us, (Jerusalem plank) and how, to his surprise, he caught a volley which disabled several of his horses! Putting the flag three or four paces ahead, Capt. T[hatcher] & I walked carefully along the wood road till we saw the open through the trees, and one grey-back, looking suspiciously at the waving flag. The bugler sounded and, at once, there started up some 50 or 60 men, as it were from the ground! They had been lying in pits, concealed on the hill side. A private coming forward was sent for an officer, and presently came a flushed Captain, waving a spotted brown handkerchief, in token of peace! He took the enclosure; also a bundle of letters for rebels, which had brought with me; and promised a prompt answer. Presently came Maj. Crow, of an Ala. regiment, and Harris' brigade. A lithe, pleasant, cheery man, who gave an account of how he had gone on a leave to North Ala. and our cavalry rushed into the town, and he had to take refuge in the belfry of the court house! Then came Col. King, stout and polite, but with a defiant dark eye. He was curious about colored troops and said he would not be afraid, one against two of them! We were on the Jerusalem plank road, looking up which, we had woods in our rear and right, but open ground in front and on the left, rising in a gentle slope. Along this ran their picket pits, and their sharpshooters were in a house on the crest, close to the road. Beyond seemed a redoubt—part perhaps of the old works of defence.[9] McKibbin came along the wood-road and told Capt. Thatcher, who remained, that the enemy were employing the time of the truce to take an advanced position for their skirmishers. Major Crow thought this could not be so, but sent to correct it; and the officer said they were only putting up bough covers against the sun. 4.15 P.M. Came a sulky looking young staff-officer, in very great spurs, and brought a message that answer would be returned by showing a flag from their works, and, that, meanwhile, the Union staff officer should retire and hostilities should recommence. Thereupon went back to a poor, one-room house, in a little clearing, and waited. It was deserted but there were a few old school books &c. lying about. Sent in my trumpeter to ask how long I should wait. The skirmishing had begun again vigorously, and the battery also. Trumpeter came back and brought a note saying I could at once come in. But there came, just then, the answer from the enemy, which carried to Gen.

Meade (7 P.M.). It was signed by Beauregard, and was a specimen of his mean creole blood.—"He did not know there had been any fight of consequence and should therefore refuse. After any engagement of real moment, he should be glad to extend the courtesies of war!" He lied; for he knew full well that there had been heavy fighting and that we at least had lost some thousands. But he wished to show his dirty spite. Lee does not such things.[10]

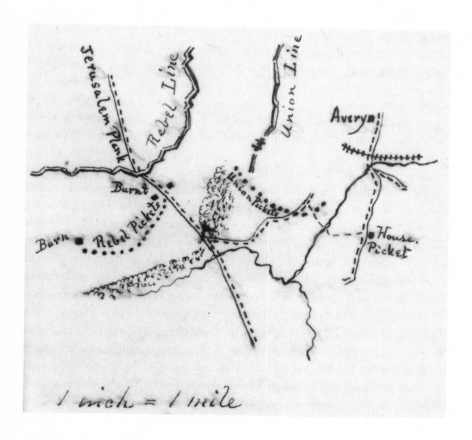

June 20, Monday.

Artillery and musketry still continued. Smith relieves 2d Corps which is to march to the left tomorrow. A negro waggoner executed for rape. They put the scaffold in rear of the works, too near, and it narrowly missed but that more died by shells than by the rope! Grant is still at City Point. Charles Paine was over; he is Volunteer Aide on Butler's staff.[11]

June 21, Tuesday.

I was ordered to go to Gen. Birney and report progress of 2d Corps. 11.30 A.M. To 5th Corps Headq'rs where was Capt. Arthur McClellan, who is going to learn the road, so as to guide Ricketts' division of his corps. Hadyn was there too.[12] The 2d Corps is today to go, by an unseen road, and form line west of the Jerusalem plank. Griffin's division is to move to the left and make connection with the 5th Corps. And Ricketts' Div. (6th Corps) is to follow later. The road was narrow and full of troops, and led by several clearings where young corn was growing—small, it seemed to me, for the season (it was the road past the "white" or Southwell house). — We go on very slowly. Mott's division was on the march—but came out at last on a wide road, at right angles to ours, which they said was the Jerusalem plank. Before us, to the left was a big cornfield, and a white, wooden house, of good size, and with several out buildings. There was Birney who told me Barlow had been sent along the road, which ran west, in front of the house, to reconnoitre and hit, if possible, the Weldon R.R. The house was deserted, but belonged to one Williams—"Maasa dun gone ter Petersburg; but kirry mos all um furniture with him."—But he left the ice which was the essential; also were there several milch cows and numerous astonished negroes.[13] This was 12.45 P.M. Barlow struck a heavy force of dismounted cavalry, which, at 3 P.M. opened two guns on him. He had a brisk skirmish and drove them back. He had a small force of mixed cavalry with him, which was probably rather in the way. He then received orders to come back. Gen. Meade came also to the Williams' house. He had passed the Cheevers house, where he found Griffin's people massed in rear of their skirmishers. The General asked G[riffin] if his orders were not to form continuous line of battle. Griffin replied, doggedly, that he could at any time form line. "Those were not your orders, Sir!" quoth Meade. "Shall I change the disposition?" asked Griffin, gruffly. "No Sir" replied the General severely "I give you no orders; you may get those from your corps commander!" All this was characteristic of both men. Griffin is always kindly to his inferiors; gruff and fault-finding to his superiors. Rode out to meet Barlow coming back. A little beyond the Browder house descried him coming along at the head of his column, arrayed in a checked shirt and lolling about on his horse, *more suo!* "Hullo! See here!" shouted he "I've caught a Cambridge man!"—Sure enough, there was a stout, handsome man, mounted on a fine white horse, and daintily dressed, with the 3 stars of a Colonel on his collar and a fanciful sort of helmet of grey felt. It was a certain Baker, in the law school in the time of Daves &c. His effect was spoiled by Barlow's quaint device of mounting a most scaly looking Adjutant, *en croupe*, behind him![14] The wounded were carried to the Williams house, and laid on the grass in the shade. There was a rebel cavalry private, badly shot in the shoulder, who was a man of good education & had traveled in Europe. This N.C. regiment was very full and seemed to have good material. There too lay one of our sharpshooters desperately shot through the lungs, and dying fast. He was breathing, with the characteristic quick, sobbing expiration, and in a feeble, wandering voice, asked for more morphine. "We have just given you some," said the attendant. "Yes; but it don't do no good!" he replied. Nothing could do *him* good. I came also upon my little Lieutenant, who got communication for the flag of truce at Cold Harbor. Here he was, hit in the ankle—just one of those slight wounds that are exquisitely painful. "Oh," he said between laughing and crying: "it hurts awfully,—smoked beef?—certainly! I'm as hungry as a bear!"— Orders for the line to form, with Griffin extending to the plank road; then Gibbon, Mott and Barlow, prolonging to the left. Rode up the Jerusalem plank, past the house of "Maasa Billy Jones" and towards where I had carried out the flag. Struck our new breastworks (about where Ft. Davis was after). There was there a battery of light twelves. Dense woods on each side and in front; but could see, perhaps 800 yards in front, the house occupied by the rebel sharpshooters. There was more or less skirmishing going on. Barlow did not get into position, because the enemy returned, along the Williams house road, driving Ben Crowninshield's mixed cavalry before them. Ben, however, made a stand near the Browder house and held on, with much shooting and small loss. As Duane and I were riding home, about dusk, we met Ricketts' division coming along near the Jones house. "I don't know the country," quoth R[icketts] "I wish you would put me in position." But Duane couldn't see it. He has no extra enthusiasm, the Major, and doesn't propose to do extra duty. Ricketts marched on to cover the left and set Barlow free. At the Cheevers house—a rather tasty little place—was Griffin, with whom Duane stopped to speak. He wanted to be sent south, on a railroad breaking expedition, and expatiated grandly on what he could do, and how fast he could march. Joe Hayes is back from his Wilderness wound and has the regular brigade of Ayres division, a great compliment to a volunteer officer![15]

June 22, Wednesday.[16]

Start at 8 A.M. General and 2 staff officers, Wilson's cavalry and Kautz sent south to break the railroad at Burkesville Junction.[17] 10 A.M. We arrive at Birney's Headq'rs in rear of Jones' house, Gen. Williams going with the staff to new camp on the Jerusalem plank, opposite and below Jones.

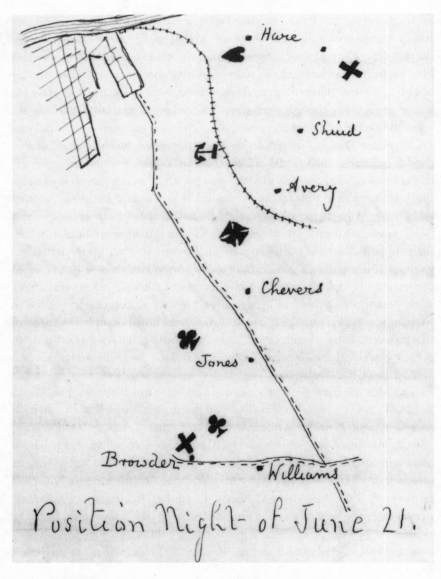

I was ordered, at once, to ascertain and report the position of the 6th Corps (9.45 A.M.) Passed through a wood, and, S.W. of Jones house, found Upton's brigade and his division (1st) in a line, running north and south, and joining Barlow on the right. He asked me to ask Gen. Williams if his Commission as Brigadier had got along yet.[18] The pickets were well out, and all was quiet. Found nearly all the troops in a pretty dense wood, on the east side of a swampy run, for part of the way.— The soldiers were digging holes in the bog clay, for water. 10.30 A.M. Reported accordingly to Gen. Meade, who was exceeding snappy, & told me to *stay* with Gen. Wright and to report back by orderlies. Again followed the troops to find Gen. Wright, but found Ricketts instead, just continuing Russell's left with his division. It was in a briary open in the N.W. corner of the Williams farm. Wendell Holmes was there and offered to show the way back to Wright, whom found near Upton's brigade. He was talking with Barlow. Gen. Meade came presently and was in great haste to get out cavalry on our left flank, and 11.15 A.M. sent me to direct Gen. Patrick to send all his cavalry under Col. Jones. Meantime Ben Crowninshield had reported and imprudently had told the General he was out of ammunition. Whereupon Meade burst out upon him, told him he was unfit for his command and would see that he was relived! Poor Ben! who thought he had been so efficient.[19] At Gen. Patrick's found the once splendid Col. Baker, dusty & exhausted under a tree. Barlow had relieved him of his horse, and he pathetically appealed to me for an ambulance, saying he had been march[ed] 12 miles in the dust & had an affection of the heart! Had seen him last night at Gibbon's Headqr's, by Jones ice-house. About noon got back to Wright's Headq'rs, but nobody was there, except Halsted, who rode out with me, till we struck the 6th Corps picket line, which we followed to the left till we got to the Browder house opening, in rear of which we saw Ricketts' people putting up a breastwork, and there too were Gens. Ricketts & Wright. All took their post under a walnut tree; and, pretty soon, the skirmishers were ordered forward. They soon struck the enemy—first on the right by Russell, then on the left by Ricketts.[20] A heavy skirmish followed, the stray bullets coming spitefully about us. At first Ricketts' skirmishers came back a little, but they went on, a little after, and forced back the rebels to a hollow full of underbrush, where they made a stand. The fire then slackened, and we waited for news from the right but heard not a shot—which was singular, for do remember that the firing in our front made a great noise. Did lie under the tree and take a doze, putting a branch over my face, to avoid the intense sun. 4.30 P.M. Capt. Jay came with intelligence that the 2d Corps had been driven in, with the loss of 4 guns and many prisoners! The orders by him, were to fall back to the breastworks, which ran N. & S. across the west end of the Williams farm. (The fact of this mysterious route, which caused so much discussion, was, that Barlow and Gibbon undertook to march out by two wood roads [between Forts A. Hays, and Davis] supposed to be nearly parallel, but which really diverged, the right hand one northward, the left southward. Thence resulted that Barlow's right and Gibbon's left, lost connection, and, through the gap, came Mahone's men, who were marching the other way, and were probably quite accidentally in this position. All this was in dense woods; and thus Mahone's people suddenly appeared on Gibbon's flank and rear. A disgraceful stampede followed and all of Gibbon's left was swept away including the 19th & 15th Mass. taken entire! To show how much surprised *both* parties were, Patten changed the front of 20th Mass. to the rear, fired a few shots and stopped the whole thing on that part of the line. It would seem that Mahone's men were filing to their left, and thus wedged in between. Gibbon got very angry and ordered an impossible charge to recover the guns, and put Col. Peirce and little Gen. Owens in arrest, the latter a slow but brave man.[21] In this disgraceful affair the enemy's force could not well have exceeded 8,000 men, while our own must have been 30,000. But, with hesitating corps commanders, exhausted troops, and a dense and unknown country numbers went for nothing.) Before we fell back Wheaton's division (2d) came up and was ordered in reserve near the Williams house. General Meade very indignant, ordered an advance along the whole front at 7. Wright said his men were tired & could not

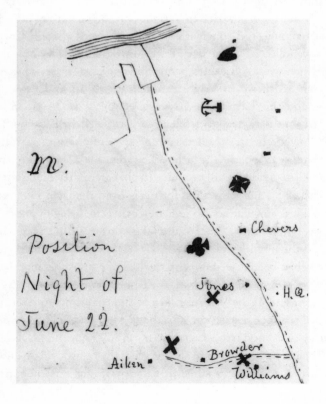

m.

Position
Night of
June 22.

foresee a good result and asked me to ride in and inform General Meade, which did. Found him at the Jones house. He heard my message and said: "Ask Gen. Wright, what I am to do tomorrow if I do not advance tonight?" I rode back with this question. "Ah" said W[right] "that I do not know!" 7.15 P.M. Ricketts' people jumped over the breastworks and disappeared in the scrub pines. We followed, and, on emerging into the clearing where was our walnut, we beheld Ricketts gallantly galloping up & down behind the advancing line, which swept into the next wood, and we anxiously awaited a heavy volley, but, instead, there was a brisk skirmish fire, then a loud cheer as our men charged and then—silence! The enemy had fallen back to Petersburg, leaving out only a strong picket line. Our troops were halted about ¼ mile east of the Aiken house.[22]

June 23, Thursday.

4.30 A.M. Gen. Meade goes to Williams house, where is Gen. Wright. 7. I am ordered to remain with Gen. W[right] and to report frequently. 7.40. Gen. Wright rides out to Gen. Ricketts, who is close to the edge of the woods, by the Aiken farm, and on the wood road from the Browder house. We had presently an arbor constructed, to keep off the sun. Wright then rode, with Russell, into the wood to examine the direction of the line, which wasn't straight and didn't face properly—a chronic trouble in our army, and a natural, where many thousand men are in a dense wood that nobody knows about. But so is the cry: "the divisions have lost connection—they cannot cover the ground designated—their flank is in the air—their skirmish line has lost its direction, &c. &c." — A little lad, whom they call "Upton's boy," who rides all about on a lank horse, came in and reported that Barlow's skirmishers were directly *facing* those of Russell (!) and not far off. Paine gave a very good account of the trend of our lines—and was, as usual, the only man who had much *general* information.[23] A prisoner was brought in, taken singularly. He was sent in last night, as guard over some prisoners, and returned this morning, ignorant that his people had gone off. Consequently he fell into the hands of the Yanks, but not till he had fired on his captor and hit his gun-stock. He described the retiring of the two rebel divisions, the night before. 10.30 A.M. A little Vermont captain came in and reported, that with 80 sharpshooters, he had penetrated to the Weldon railroad and driven back easily a number of cavalry that opposed him. He brought a piece of the telegraph wire. A picket line was thrown out to them, and the cavalry ordered to go & help tear up the rails.[24] Gen. Wright then examined the front and rode out into the extensive clearing of the Aiken farm. The house, which is of good size, stood in the midst of a large oat field.

The pickets were in this field, and the men had put up little bough covers, or their shelter tents, to keep off the sun. There was a group of three or four slatternly women in the doorway, of whom Wright asked some questions. The signal officers reported (and we were telegraphed) that a force of say two divisions, with a certain number of ambulances, was marching out over the Weldon railroad. This looked like work ahead. 12.20 P.M. Gen. Wright arrived at Birney's camp to try and rectify the line and get a simultaneous advance. I went into the Jones house, hard by, to tell General Meade. He sat there, chafing, with an eye like a rattlesnake and a nose that seemed twice as sharp and long as usual! The three Generals conferred a long while.[25] Wright rode back through the pine woods, dreary & black with the fires that had run through them. 2.15 P.M. Back at Ricketts' Headq'rs. Part of Wheaton is in reserve on the left. The skirmishers are at once to advance. Now then, at last, all together! 3 P.M. A sharpshooter came in and reported that our working party had been driven from the railroad, and that the enemy were advancing. "We drove their cavalry easy" he said, "but their infantry came on saucy, I can tell you!" "Stop the advance!" orders Gen. Wright, "Wheaton, strengthen that skirmish line, and tell them to hold on." It was probably then his idea (it was mine certainly) that all A. P. Hill's Corps would be thrown here on our left flank, which was in the air. We could hear the skirmish shots, which grew nearer and more frequent. All began to make breastworks, and the balance of Wheaton's people, connecting with Ricketts near the Browder house road, made a return on our left flank, parallel with that road and towards the Williams house, making a rear defence; for most of the front faced N.W. Afterwards, two brigades came from Russell, and two from the 5th Corps, and the return was continued to within 800 yards of the breastworks fronting the Williams house. Meantime Gen. Meade urged Gen. Wright to attack, telling him not to let the enemy dance around him. The division officer of the day, a Lt. Col., came in and said he had got a view of the main body of the enemy; halted in an open, and they seemed no more than a division. This, with their behavior, convinced me that it was not a grand movement; and, when Gen. Wright asked me, I told him I thought he ought to attack. Pretty soon the cavalry appeared, coming back in a hurry into the corner of the open, to our left. This exposed the flank of the skirmishers, but they, being reinforced to the strength of about 700 (Vermont men) made a hard fight in the edge of the woods by the Lenear house. The same division officer came back, not long after, and reported that they had broken his skirmishers and were advancing in line of battle! (This must have been when they came down the Lenear house road, flanked and took in rear the line, and captured a large number of the brave Vermonters). There was then a pause, as the enemy did not venture to come across the open, but began to work round a strip of woods on our left. The coolness meantime—or indifference—of the troops in line of battle was singular. One fellow absorbed his whole soul in boiling a kettle of beans! "Ho!" growled another, "don't let's stay here; let's go out there, and each man pick his tree!"— It was now getting towards sunset and the enemy began vigorously to press our new skirmish line, and, as we stood in the loop of the works we got the balls from two sides. Maj. Whittier said to Wright; "When the musketry begins you will get all the bullets here, sir"—"When we get them we will move," replied W[right].—Whittier raised his brows at me, as much as to say "Snubbed!"[26]—A force of the enemy was reported moving along our rear, towards the Williams house, and I could hear them whooping. I telegraphed it to Meade, who was much stirred and sent word to Wright he would hold him responsible if the enemy got to the plank road! Thus continuously spurred Wright began to prepare a column of attack (of all things in the world!) but dusk had come already, and he was not sorry of the excuse. The skirmishers, however, fired a good deal, long after dark.— Mounted, and, picking my way over a line of battle that was lying down to avoid the shots, rode in to the Jones house. Gen. Meade there in a tearing passion at Wright and at everybody (and small blame to him!). He undertook to pitch into me, but, as I had a headache, I didn't care, and replied up & down to everything proving that what the rebels last moved along was our "rear" and not our "flank." (I look on June 22d & 23d as the two most discreditable days to this army that I ever saw! There was everywhere, high and low, feebleness, confusion, poor judgment. The only person who kept his plans and judgment clear was Gen. Meade himself. On this particular occasion Wright showed himself totally unfit to command a corps. When he had provided a good pit, to fall back on in case of reverse, and when he found that there was no indication of a grand movement, he should have marched out and vigorously attacked with every man, as Meade constantly urged him to do. As it was, he allowed himself to be tied up and bullied by a force that was probably nothing but Mahone's division! Though I am not *sure* that the force was not two divisions, and those Pickett's and Kershaw's.)[27]

June 24, Friday.

Last night Wright withdrew to the former breastworks on the Williams farm. He considered the position faulty and in the air, unless another advance was immediately proposed. He was over and pow-wowed with Meade, and parted on good terms, for the General respects him, though grievously disappointed this time. Sheridan is at Wilcox' Wharf, waiting to be ferried over. His expedition and attempt to reach Hunter was entirely foiled. At Trevilian Station he had a very severe action, and, though he gained advantages the first day, the enemy (Hampton) turned the breastwork system against him, and stopped the whole advance.[28] A commission is to sit on the 2d Corps disaster of the 22d which has caused plenty of recrimination. (The commission never *did* sit.) This morning arrived Gen. Grant, with two French officers in tow, a commission sent by the French Emperor to watch the war. They were turned over to us and messed at the General's table, having a tent together alongside. The elder, Lt. Col. De Chanal, had the regular, middle-aged Frenchman's air, with those nervous legs! He was a thorough man of the world, and eminent as introducer of rifled artillery in France. Capt. Guzman was small, black-eyed, bright, showing his creole blood. He spoke several languages. Grant remarked that, "if his class had been turned the other end to, he should have graduated high in French!" Hunter 60 miles west of Lynchburg. Weather still exceeding dry; the air full of dust, fine as twice bolted flour.[29]

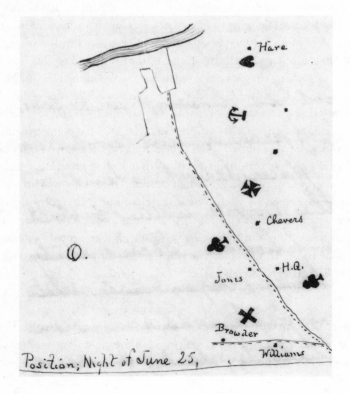

June 25, Saturday.

Gibbon's division is massed to the left of rear of this camp. Showed the French officers about. Went to Wright's, in the woods, to the right of the Williams house. Then out by the Browder house, beyond the pickets. Saw a burying party who had been out by the Lenear house, and seen no enemy, only one of our sharpshooters being there, in a tree.

June 26, Sunday.

(95° in the coolest shade!—and in some of the tents, 104°.)

June 27, Monday.

Our cavalry crossing at Windmill point. Gregg got into a fight with the following force and got roughly used. There fell a few scattered drops of rain, which was so remarkable as to merit note. On the 23d we moved our camp a short way more to the north.[30]

June 28, Tuesday.

Rode over to Gibbon's division and saw Patten, who commands the 20th Mass. though but a Captain, for Abbott is killed, and Macy and Curtis wounded. Patten complained bitterly of Gibbon, saying that his former gallantry was all gone, and that now he refused to expose himself, so that his conduct was a matter of comment, and the officers laid traps to get him under fire, for joke! The division is much run down, especially since the mishap of the 23d. But it is looking up with the present rest. It was sad to see a man of education, thus, under a wretched shelter tent and with no means to keep himself clean, or to get a change of garments.[31]

June 29, Wednesday.

With the General and Gallic officers to see Gen. Burnside, whom we found on the edge of a pine wood, not far N.E. of the Shind house. He had made a bough fence round his tents, in a brave attempt to exclude the pitiless dust! The Frenchies were happy as they found Cutting, Leidig &c. ready to talk the vernacular with them. Presently came Grant, and Ben. Butler with him, an astounding figure on a horse! Short, fat, shapeless; no neck, squinting, and very bald headed, and, above all, that singular, half defiant look! With him rode no less person that Col. Billy Greene! He is Col. of a regiment enlisted from rebels; but, as he has carefully abstained from getting mustered in, he has neither pay nor authority, and is now a sort of hanger on to Butler's staff.[32]

Butler delivered long disquisitions on the strength of the rebel army, which he put extremely low, and boasted much of his secret service, to the amusement of Meade. When we got back, we found the whole 6th Corps had marched down the Jerusalem plank to rescue, if possible, Wilson and Kautz, who had been cut off near Ream's Station, after their expedition to Burkesville Junction, where they destroyed 30 miles of rail, and many stores. But it was too late! The enemy's infantry attacked and routed them, capturing over 1,000 prisoners, and all their wheels, including 12 cannon. It was a shabby affair; and extremely discreditable to Wilson, whose men did not stand at all; for the loss in killed & wounded in the whole expedition was absurdly small out of his force of 6,500! Sheridan ordered up.[33]— Now this arid country is studded with soldiers wells; for, luckily, excellent water may ever be found, at a small depth. In the low places three or four feet suffice; and then the hole is cased with a cracker box; but, usually, they sink from 8 to 12 feet; and commonly they dig steps, to lead down. Adams' headquarter squadron has a magnificent well, some 8 feet across and 18 deep. From it he daily uses 800 gallons; and he has hewed him a notable trough from a great log of hard pine. The driness is in truth a blessing to the troops, it compels them to seek good water, by digging.

June 30, Thursday.

Meade anxious for Wilson, and in a fume over Sheridan whom he thinks slow to get, and over Wright, who intrenched himself at Ream's Station and showed a desire to come back. Getty returned today, well of his wound, which, however, has given him great suffering. With him Capt. Stanhope, of the Regular inf. He once had a room with me, when I was coming to the army.[34]

July 1, Friday.

Wilson coming in, by a detour, without more loss. Took De Chanal to see Ferrero's nig' division, of the 9th Corps, which held part of the ground of the 6th Corps in its absence. He ordered out a regiment which manoeuvred a little to the great delight of De Chanal. There was such a dust you couldn't see the nigs except when they stood still! Ferrero, whom the darks call "Boss Fero," is of Italian (Milanese) extraction; and was once dancing master at West Point—a handsome man—people laugh at him rather—too much perhaps.[35]

July 2, Saturday.

The 6th Corps is back in position, as before.

July 3, Sunday.

There appeared Lieut. Sedgwick, come, fresh from Fair Harvard, to join the 20th Mass. Poor buck! with his new sword, clothes, havresac & patent fixings. He was dropped 7 miles away by the cars, and tramped hither, getting lost, going to sleep in the woods, and finally piloted hither by two of our Zoo-zoos.[36] Owing to the difficulty of getting money and of purchasing food, an order was issued allowing every officer to draw two rations in kind. The bands came round and gave a Gettysburg serenade, tonight.

July 4, Monday.

More band this morning, in honor of the Glorious Fourth. The Sanitary Commission, not to forget us, sent a waggon of many good things, *atque ice.*[37] Gen. Hancock solemnly dined with Gen. Williams. The Rebels looked for an attack today; but Grant does not deal in such theatricals. When the Maryland Brigade band played "Hail Columbia" in the trenches, a N. Carolina regiment opposite rose and cheered! Now we have made our camp comparatively comfortable, with what the Frenchies call "Gourbis," an Arab word for a bower over a tent. Forked posts are first planted, and a gridiron of poles is supported by them. On this gridiron are laid plenty of cedar branches, and others are hung round the edges. Thus we avoid the sun but keep the breeze. The natural position of the camp is villainous—a flat, barren, field with the dust of the neighboring road blowing over it. We strive to make cool drinks—especially lemonade, with tea, instead of water, and well iced. It is admirably refreshing!

July 5, Tuesday.

There is no picket firing, save on the 9th Corps front. Crawford going with an opera-glass to look at the picket line of the enemy, they threw over a paper, wrapped round a pebble, telling "that feller with the spyglass" to leave, or he would be shot at. We made a party of four to City Point, distant 12 or 13 miles, De Chanal, Guzman, & "Rosie." Taking back roads, to avoid dust, we stopped at Epp's house and saw there an old negress, who said she had "double grandchildren," and was mighty glad that "you 'uns" had come round and she had no more work to do! Guzman was much edified at this first specimen of slavery he had seen. He is, secretly, a bit inclined to the Southrons, by reason of some fair dames he saw in Paris; but, being a violent anti slavery man, he is coming round union pretty fast! Near City Point we passed, on our left, a huge, canvas town—a great hospital suited to 7,000 patients, though now there are but

3,000. Its head is capable classmate Ned Dalton. At the Point there was plenty of improvement; a long plank quay, storehouses, and lots of shipping, among the latter 3 barges, side by side, of the Sanitary Commission; and therein all sorts of comforts for the sojers. Entered thereon and was treated to lemonade by dried up friend Johnson, head functionary. Delivered some despatches to Grant and we came back with speed, fearing to be late at dinner.— That night I heard the officer of the day go to the General's tent with a despatch; he read it and said: "Very well, tell Wright to send a good division. I suppose it will be Ricketts," and turned over & went to sleep again. Thus easily are large bodies moved in a drilled army! Ricketts was at once to embark for Baltimore, at City Point. I recollect thinking, at the moment: Why don't they send a corps and make a sure thing of it?—[38]

July 6, Wednesday.

A Headache—rare for me! Engineers hard at work, planning and consulting, which resulted—

July 7, Thursday.

in a proposal to swing back our left now resting near the Williams house. Rode over to see Barlow, not far in front of Jones house. Found him lying in his tent, in his shirt and drawers, listening to his band which is reckoned the best in the army. He hospitably besought me to "take off my trowsers and make myself comfortable!" Truly, as De Chanal says: "*Il a l'air d'un gamin de Paris!*"[39] He discoursed on the loose discipline of the troops (and he has true ideas about this) & the advantages of the assault in column. He said he was ready for another assault and would lead the men himself, and have "no more trifling." The French officers went over and saw the "Mine," a tunnel that the 9th Corps are driving from a gulley, just behind their most advanced point, to a battery of the enemy, opposite. The distance between the lines at this point, which lies west of the Shind house, is but little over 100 yards. Our cavalry horses are now refitting on the James, but they are in very bad condition. News of the sinking of the "Alabama" by the "Kearsarge." *Bon!* Gen. Patrick appointed Prov. Ml. of the Armies operating against Richmond.[40]

July 8, Friday.

There appeared a tall man, with bushy eyebrows and a nervous manner, who looked like an excentric Irishman who was about to tell a funny story. This was Gen. Ord, of Drainsville memory. He has been in command at Baltimore.[41] Suddenly there was a great waking up of musketry on the 18th Corps front!

All the batteries there opened. It was a feint, or an attempt to charge. Some supposed the officers tried to get their men forward. At any rate, they got on their works and yelled and fired. Duane's intense love of McClellan is curious! He thinks him perfection; and indeed McClellan would have placed him very high had he stain in. Now Duane is a disappointed man, and rather listless in consequence, though capable. Old Josiah Quincy dead. Over to see Adams, who has camped his squadron in the edge of the woods just back of us. He is sick—yellow and cross, as everyone round has a right to be. The steady Flint and Higginson ordered a pail of lemonade brewed in my honor and some put a "stick" in it, viz. a dash of peach brandy, captured by our outposts in a demijohn sunk in a pond! *Me judice* a poor drink.[42]

July 9, Saturday.

The remainder of the 6th Corps left for Washington, at 11 this night. Continued heat, dust and drought. Had some diarrhoea, which got a little quinine and whisky for. They are at work now, putting up a large, square fort, just on the left of the Jerusalem road, and near where I carried the flag.[43]

July 10, Sunday.

Little Gov. Sprague, with his rabbit incisors, that make him look like a boy, was over with Birney. The latter seems rather downcast which is natural, considering the sad work he made of commanding the corps on the 18th and 22d of June.[44]

July 11, Monday.

As the advance of the 6th Corps makes a return of our line necessary, which would leave our Headquarters outside, I was sent to look up a new spot in a central position. Guzman and De Chanal came with me, and kept on till they got tired. It was an unpromising hunt! The fields are beds of dust; the woods are run through by fire. Then water is scarce and swamps are plenty. At last found a good pine ridge, a mile N. & E. of Shind, and left a guard there, till the infantry detail should arrive to clear it.— Wallace & Ricketts have been beaten at Monocacy river by Early, who is advancing towards Washington. "Lew" Wallace amounts to nothing, and they say Ricketts' people did all the fighting.[45]

July 12, Tuesday.

Moved camp. While the waggons were en route Gen. Meade rode to see Hancock whom he found in an ambulance, near Finn's house, on the Jerusalem road. Immediately the two began greatly to confab, as usual! Introduced De Chanal to Barlow, whom De Chanal compared to a *gamin de Paris!* The ruins of this little house had been inscribed "Stragglers Rest," by some facetious coffee-boiler. The 2d Corps was here massed, as we thought of making a try for the Weldon road, and Gregg's cavalry even pushed out a reconnaissance; but nothing was done for some reason or other. When we got to camp, we found tents pitched and all pretty comfortable.

July 13, Wednesday.

Part of 2d Corps massed near the "deserted house." Maj. Patten was over and Folsom, their Qr. Mr. to speak about getting Abbott's horse home. It was a day of visitors. "Whisky Mitch," Starr, and a brother of Harry Windsor were all over from the cavalry. Mitchell had a bullet hole in his hat. Starr is nicely over the bullet through the jaw. Likewise there appeared Lieut. Ward Frothingham, in whom anybody may recognize the Brooks rusticity. He is in the 9th Corps and is in hospital for sickness. He said he didn't get any "nutricious food" there, so gave him some whisky and he retired with a further gift of canned chicken. He is almost simple witted, but deserves great credit for his good service.[46]

July 14, Thursday.

We determined today that Heth's division was still opposite us, which determined that Hill's Corps had not left for Maryland. Rode and took a view from a big pine, where Hancock's Headq'rs were, the first day. The signal corps had put up a ladder from which could see the spires and other points of Petersburg and parts of the rebel line. The rebel skirmishers are reported outside Baltimore and Washington. Tonight the Second Corps were destroying their old line, beyond the plank road, to take up the new line which trends S. E. from the new fort on that road, and past the Cheevers house. Also they are leveling the old rebel lines, which we took in the first operations, whereby a number of bodies, in a terrible state, were uncovered; though, of course, again interred.[47]

July 15, Friday.

Rebels reported falling back from Washington.[48] The General rode over to see the new fort, on the Jerusalem road. It is protected by a brush screen, though still the enemy suspect something and occasionally fire over. This work is well nigh done, as is also the new flank line from it past the Cheevers house. South of the Cheevers house is a redoubt having a tremendous sweep towards the Jones place, and here the line makes a turn to the east.[49] We rode to Warren, at the Avery house. He has a great heap of projectiles in his front yard, mostly rebel, fired on the 17th & 18th,—spherical case for 6-, 12-, and 32-pounder guns. Parrott, Hotchkiss and Shenkl shells, solid shot, &c. &c. From these De Chanal eagerly selected a specimen of each to forward to France.[50] From the roof, where the signal people have a good glass, is an excellent view of the enemy's position, opposite. Where the 9th Corps line was, on the right, the men were lying close; but, on the 5th Corps line, they were moving round freely, as were the rebels. Two men were hanged for rape; one had been under Coxe, and came to bid him farewell, on his way to execution. Coxe, who is rather weak, was thereby much shaken, and strengthened himself from his commissary whisky! They endeavored to show some connivance of the woman, but the court decided she acted under fear and violence, and they were hanged. Meade is determined such crimes shall be duly punished. There is but little of this thing; for most cases reported have proved to have no foundation.[51] The Headquarter troops are digging wells, in one of which the Zoo-zoos have struck a stratum of shell marl; from which have secured some good tertiary fossils. Moreover we have our "gourbis" nearly done making a continuous shade on 3 sides of a parallelogram, and producing a fine [. . .]. For once and for a wonder, we have the best camp in the army. Likewise have we a little ice cellar and the heart of cook Mercier is glad.

July 16, Saturday.

The enemy have repaired the Weldon road, (never much damaged) and have been running trains these three or four days. With the General to Martindale's, who is on the extreme right, at the Jordan house, which overlooks the river bottom. Hence we could see the lower part of Petersburg reminding one, with its trees & brick houses, of the corresponding portion of Salem. Across the river bottom ran our intrenchments and those of the enemy, pretty close together; and we watched the puffs of smoke from the opposing sharpshooters. On the opposite bank of the river they have placed a Whitworth battery with which they pelt this house sometimes, but do little or no damage. De Chanal remarked on the defects of our artillery, saying our rifled ammunition was uncertain,

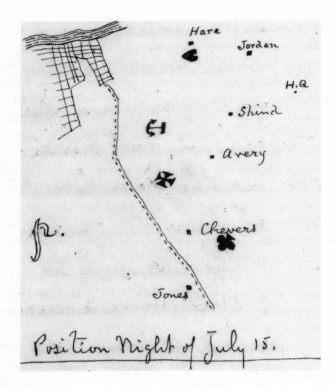

and straining to the gun; whereas the French methods of buttons that slid in the grooves, gave space to ignite the fuse, did not strain the piece, were more accurate, and could be applied to bronze guns—*peutêtre*—in sooth our rifled shells have much to ask for. Did not see the General when he rode off, and so lost him. He rode along the river bank some distance. Am struck with the want of detail, even in our regular engineers. They don't seem to care whether approaches are properly laid out, or not, and neglect a great many useful details. They are overworked, to be sure, and the weather is infernal. — A pretty account from home of James Lodge, who has taken to drink and attacked his wife, who had to run from the house! Once he was the most amiable of bachelors, whose chief pleasure was to go to concerts. It is incomprehensible![52]

July 17, Sunday.

Had my first home letters in 15 days; for the rebs stopped the mails. 6th Corps reported at Poolesville. Barlow and his favorite Brigadier, Miles, were over, and partook of iced lemonade, refusing anything more potent. Many deserters came over and reported that at daylight next morning a sortie would be made and Hill's Corps would attack our left. The object being to cover reinforcement, to Johnston, who is hard pressed by Sherman.[53]

July 18, Monday.

Slept in part of my clothes and had my horse ready by daylight—but no musketry—nothing! The thing was given up, so said more deserters, because so many had come over and given information. Probably some sort of attack was intended. So the General rode forth to view our new flank defences. These begin with a redoubt, near the Spicer house, on the McCann Station road and trend nearly west to the redoubt south of Cheevers house. In an open, near Spicer's we found "Boss Fero" camped; for his colored division are detailed to construct and guard these works. Already they have made a good parapet and a very extensive slashing in front of the wooded portions. We rode down the Jerusalem plank to visit Gen. (or Col.) Devin who commands the picket line. We found him just riding out to reestablish his picket line which had been driven in by the enemy, near the Gurley house. He was attired in a blue man-of-war shirt, trowsers with high boots, and a slouch hat, and, brave simple man, looked much better than in the regulation dress.[54] Wm. Waud is here, a brother of Alfred and likewise an artist. He is with 18th Corps. Out of some blue clay from the wells, A. Waud made me a pipe, like to a turk's head, very pretty.[55] For the first time, have now a bed raised from the ground, made with stakes and a sacking of oat bags. In general, prefer to sleep on the ground. Gen. Meade has received a public gift of a sword and asked me to compose an acknowledgment for him, which did and he copied and sent it off! Good joke. — Col. Sharpe has been to Washington where all were sweating with fear! He told them Early had not over 25,000 men; they swore he had 92,000 including all A. P. Hill. He offered a heavy bet they would all fall back the moment the 6th Corps appeared in front of Washington; and it came so to pass!

July 19, Tuesday.

Rain! actually rain!! the first for 47 days!!![56] It rained nearly all day and soaked the dust to the hard pan. Rode out with Riddle—my roan mare lame from an interfering cut.— Plenty of reb' projectiles still lying loose in the field near Avery house; in front and to left of which they are beginning a covered waggon road, to carry up ammunition to the batteries; it is 12 feet wide and 4 deep and the sand thrown up towards the enemy makes a parapet that will cover a waggon top.

July 20, Wednesday.

Sudden irruption of Butler with Charlie Paine. B[utler] is a sight to behold, on horseback! After a sharp encounter he has driven Baldy Smith to "await orders in New York." Butler was to command the *Department*, with Headq'rs at Fort Monroe; Smith to command "forces" in the field. Not so! Butler stuck at Bermuda Hundreds and remarked "Department" and "forces in the field" were inseparable; so he should stay there. Baldy wrestled and got thrown. Halleck, whom Butler hates, sent him an aide. "I have nothing for you; you may go back. By the way, Gen. Halleck is translating Jominy at 9 cents a page. If you put those 9 cents in a box and rattled them you would get an idea of Gen. Halleck's brains!" President's proclamation for 500,000 more men. Col. Weld was over bringing his Lt. Col. Jarves, who lost a leg in N.C. and was hit again in the Wilderness.[57]

July 21, Thursday.

Ord to have the 18th Corps; and Birney promoted to 10th Corps; a loss as a division commander. "Whisky Mitch" over again, with a Paddy cavalry Captain, Whiteford, probably another "Papal Zouave," like Keough, O'Keefe and Coppinger. Rode out and got some specimens of reb' projectiles to send home. Crawford dined with us off his own tomatoes! What with Club and Sanitary Commission friends he gets good *provant*. Hood has relieved Joe Johnston. Sherman near Atlanta. Lee said to be sending men west.[58]

July 22, Friday.

Appointed to conduct Col. De Chanal to Butler's; and Rosie accompanied. We steered a straight course to Point of Rocks, (which has a fort on this bank) descended a steep way to the river, here divided by an island, and crossed the pontoon. Butler's camp was to the right, not very far away. Saw there, Bob Davis (who seems in the last stage of lazy indifference), Charlie Paine, and Col. Kensel.[59] Butler mounted and carried us to see a negro regiment drilled by its sergeants—well done. Then along the lines, stretching from James to Appomattox. These works for revetment and finish are the coquetry of field fortification; each soldier has his sand-bag loophole. Again at his H'dq'rs Butler showed a new doubled-shelled schrapnel; a rebel cask torpedo; and a new time fuze. During dinner he said to me: "They spoiled a good mechanic when they made me a lawyer, and a good lawyer when they made me general." He delivered a long exposition (which I translated) on the virtues of a huge *powder-boat*, which he would explode between Moultrie, & Sumter, by clock-work, and not only flatten both forts but Charleston into the bargain! De Chanal replied (citing examples) that no such result would follow and that the effect would be limited to a very small radius. "No effect!" cried B[utler] suddenly bursting into French, "*mais pourquoi* non?" "Ah" said De C. with his sharp French eye; "*mais pourquoi si?*"[60] Part of the 19th Corps has arrived from N. Orleans and was camped within Butler's lines. News of a heavy sortie by Hood, who turned Sherman's left, and took some guns and prisoners and killed McPherson, (a great loss)—but was finally driven away in confusion. Maj. Platt, (an insufferable snob, though a regular) was relieved as Judge Advocate, by Major Hastings, a pleasant man.[61]

July 23, Saturday.

Jack Ames (Class '54) was over with Col. Russell, a bald headed and extremely funny man and a good officer, though coarse. Ames is Captain of regulars and Col. of a negro regiment which distinguished itself in the fight where Harry was wounded.[62]

July 24, Sunday.

The General rode over and pow-wow'd with Hancock; where were Gibbon and his brother-in-law aide Moal; who groaned at the way they *seized horses* in Baltimore, but I could not chime in, for the owners are all rank Secesh. Saw Henry Higginson who is trying to serve again, though his health is shaky and plainly his thoughts are on his Ida![63]

July 25, Monday.

De Chanal is pathetic over cutting down wood—"Oh! When I think what labor I have been at, on the little place I have at home, to plant, only for my grandchildren, such trees as you cut down without reason!"—"*Ah! Un chêne; encore un beau chêne!!*"[64] To look at the refused flank line again, which is garrisoned by Gibbon and Mott. Barstow with one of his malarial attacks. He lies on his bed and rolls from side to side, like a polar bear; rather funny to all but *himself.*

July 26, Tuesday.

Two divisions of cavalry and whole 2d Corps moved to the rear, and the division of Cutler (5th Corps) now holds the flank line. On our right in rear of the 9th Corps, the negro division is camped. Mimi has moved from Mrs. Cabot's at Beverly to Cora's [on Beacon Hill].

July 27, Wednesday.

Hancock had crossed at Point of Rocks and had passed Bermuda Hundreds and crossed the James on a pontoon at Deep Bottom. Today he advanced, hoping to break a hole for the cavalry to go through and destroy railroads north of Richmond. He captured 4 20-pdr. Parrotts and a few men; but, beyond, found 7 brigades intrenched. Grant, who was there, did not favor a further advance.[65] About 4,000 of 19th Corps, now with Butler, ordered to Washington. Col. Pleasants has been a long time at work on a tunnel, 410 feet long, beginning in a water gully, 1 mile west of the Shind house, and running under a rebel bastion, of 4 guns, opposite. The shaft ended in 3 diverging chambers as magazines, above which were 18 feet of earth and the parapet. The whole was known as *"the Mine."*[66]

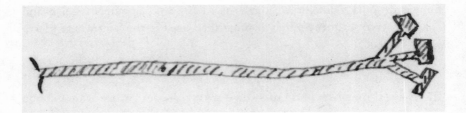

The undertaking, when first begun, received little attention, because it was uncertain what our future moves would be. Afterwards, when it seemed as if we should lie there, the engineers were ordered to report on it, and reported the point of assault unfavorable because it lay in a reentrant angle, flanked on either side. Burnside vehemently maintained it was a *salient*, and quarreled with all the engineers sent to work for him, viz. Turnbull and Harwood. Duane and he already hated each other.[67] But now happened a most favorable combination of circumstances; for, by the creditable perseverance of Col. Pleasants and his regiment of Penn. miners, the mine was finished, and, at the same moment Hancock's move to Deep Bottom had called away a considerable part of the troops in our front, having, it would seem, alarmed Lee. Therefore, although the spot was unfavorable for assault, and especially unfavorable for bringing up supports, yet the want of reserves seemed to lay the enemy open to a surprise, by which we could crown Cemetery ridge, just in rear of the Mine, with a strong force, and thus take in reverse a good part of the rebel line, and command the town. Duane had sent for the mining records before Sebastopol & got me to read them to learn the proper charge; for, what with malaria and sunstroke, and quinine, whisky and arsenic, he can hardly see, but clings to duty to the last! Finding nothing there, he said the book was a humbug, and determined on 8,000 lbs. as the charge, which was put in today, the powder being carried in in kegs, and their heads knocked out in the magazines. From these a water-tight boxing was laid to the outer end of the tunnel, the further part of which filled simply with loose powder, and the outer portion held a time fuze. The charge was tamped with 25 feet of sand bags and the mine was ready. The rebels, either from suspicion or precaution, had sunk shafts and run listening galleries, but had failed to go deep enough, though our men could hear them overhead. — Crook has been driven out of Winchester.[68]— Today our left refused line was held by the negro division, and by a mixed division of 9th Corps.

July 28, Thursday.

The enemy at Deep Bottom advanced on Gregg's division of cavalry, and got one gun by shooting the horses, after a heavy fight; but Torbert's division of cavalry coming up in support, the enemy were driven in confusion and lost 3 flags, the 2d S.C. and the 18th & 28th N.C.— Got a log from a tall hard pine, in which a spherical case had *burst*, making a split up & down in the tree, which stood on the Coggin's Pt. road just where Hancock had his Headq'rs after. The shot came from the Dunn house battery (700 yds.) and struck 8 ft. from the ground. Gen. Meade went to City Point, and thence to Deep Bottom. Gen. Humphreys expressed himself displeased with the clumsiness of the Deep Bottom "surprise," the information given to the enemy, &c. Barlow's wife has died at Washington of malignant typhus. As he was in presence of the enemy Meade could not, at first, grant him a leave; but did grant it hearing she had died without friends about her. The soft-hearted General glad of the excuse! Anyway, Barlow was entirely incapacitated by this sudden grief.[69]

July 29, Friday.

Hot; 95° in the shade. Last night heavy guns and 10-inch mortars were put in position in batteries that had previously been prepared for them. Gen. Hunt very busy with his artillery against tomorrow. Hancock was to lie still all day; then to withdraw and relieve the 18th Corps by one division holding two in the reserve. The 18th Corps to concentrate on right of the 9th to assist in the attack. Ayres division of the 5th to mass in the railroad cut, on left and rear of 9th Corps and support if necessary. Gen. Meade had had consultations with Burnside, who wanted to lead the assault with the negro division of Ferrero. Meade replied that these negroes were green and had never seen a great action;

he had no right to run risks; if they failed people would justly say "Oh! you put forward the negroes to sacrifice them for nothing!"— Grant being referred to decided for Meade's view. Gen. Humphreys then drew up the orders with great care: Burnside to clear away abattis (most were destroyed already by artillery), cut down his parapet for a division front so as to make it passable for a column doubled on the centre. Put his *best troops* to *lead* the assault; and the supports so formed as to advance promptly. The mine having exploded, the artillery would all open and the 5th Corps would fire, to keep down the enemy's reply. The leading column of assault would seize the crest; the supporting columns would face to the right and left, so as to make connection with the advance, cover the flanks, and sweep the enemy's breast works. The 18th Corps would assault in conjunction; and all other troops be ready to act in concert, &c. &c. The moment is opportune; only 3 divisions are opposed to us; for 5 have gone to keep back Hancock.— In the magazines are 100 rounds per gun, ready for the salvo.

July 30, Saturday.

The hour appointed to spring the mine was 3.30 A.M. At 2.30 we all were up and horses saddled. It was so dark that Meade telegraphed permission to Burnside to delay the firing for 30 minutes, if he chose. About 3.30 we got to B[urnside]'s Headq'rs. All his baggage was packed, ready *to go into Petersburg!*[70] Burnside had gone forward to the "Taylor house battery" about on a line between this and the Mine. This was in a pine grove and a bad place for us to see anything, though something might be seen from near the Shind house. There we waited in queer suspense—some thinking the 8,000 lbs. of powder would make a small earthquake, tear up trees, and knock distant people down; but I had concluded there would only be a local effect and no great noise. Presently (after 4 A.M.) arrived Gen. Grant, "What is the matter with the Mine?" he asked. "Don't know," replied M[eade]—"guess the fuze has gone out."—A true guess, as it proved.—It had failed at the splicing, upon which an officer & sergeant boldly went into the passage till they found the spot and again fired the fuze! A gallant act! At 4.40 A.M. I heard a dull, heavy explosion, not louder than the distant sound of a siege gun; and, instantly, as if by magic, the entire artillery on our side burst forth and the air rung with the hum of shells! Someone, from the opening beyond, cried out "Yes! its gone!"—and this was the springing of the mine.—there was no trembling of the ground about us, or shock; and only the muffled sound above mentioned. Those who could see said, that a vast mass of earth was lifted straight perhaps 130 feet into the air, looking like the pictures of the Iceland geysers. The explosion took place under and rather on one side of the bastion, buried the 4 guns, and left a vast "crater," about 120 feet long, 25 deep, and 50 wide, with steep sides, round the edges of which were piled masses of clayey earth not pulverized by the fall.— So astounded was the enemy and so covered was their position by our augmented artillery that their reply was weak indeed and was soon almost silenced. Meantime, after incomprehensible delay (usually described as at least 20 minutes) the assaulting column moved forward, in a loose manner. This was Marshall's brigade of Ledlie's division, a brigade composed of dismounted cavalry and demoralized heavy artillery (!) the whole good for nothing, over which Marshall, a severe, courageous man, had been put, in the vain hope of beating in some discipline! Ledlie was a wretched, incapable drunkard, not fit to command a company, and was the ruin of his division.[71] And yet Burnside, with inconceivable fatuity, allowed the troops for leading the assault to be *selected by lot!* The corps was enough run down to make it hard to get a good forlorn hope with the most careful picking. Then no gap had been made in the parapet, which, next the mine, was at least 8 feet high—all in disobedience to orders. Presently there came in a knot of a dozen or more prisoners, who had been dug out of the mass! Their hair, ears and pockets had been filled with yellow sand. All were more or less bruised & bleeding, but cool and composed to a wonderful degree! They were of the 18th & 22d S. Carolina, and were in support of the battery, in a rear breastwork, like this:

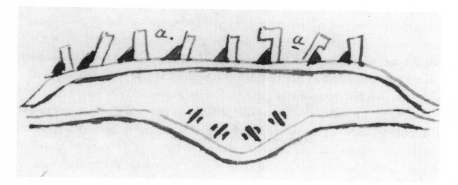

with a number of irregular bomb proofs (a. a.). One man, a sergeant, talked a good deal. He said he was asleep, and thought a caisson had exploded. He was presently struck down by the falling masses of earth, from which he extricated himself: "I could have got off" he said; "it was some time before your people came up; but I stopped to help out another man." All this time there was more or less cannon & musketry.— Orders were sent to take the crest—to push on at once!

But plainly there was a hitch! Col. De Chanal, who was standing with me, was frantic over this loss of precious moments! "*Mais, cette perte de temps!*" he kept saying.[72] In fact Marshall's brigade had gone into the crater and had filled it, and now were utterly immovable and sullen! The supports, brought up by the flank in bad order, crowded into the crater and the neighboring bomb-proofs and covered ways. There was some fighting and the rebel breastworks for 200 or 300 yds. were taken, with a few prisoners, but advance to the crest the men would not. Our own covered ways were jammed with supporting troops that could do no good to anyone. 7 A.M. A lull.—Dr. Mc —— told me, about this time, that no bullets now came round his ambulances at the front, while, at the first, there were a good many.[73] At a few minutes after 8 A.M. the troops of the 18th Corps and the black division of the 9th attempted a charge. Saunders, who saw it, said the troops would not go up with any spirit at all. The negroes came back in confusion, all mixed with the whites in and about the crater. Their officers behaved with distinguished courage, and the blacks seem to have done as well as whites—which is faint praise—. This attack was over 3 hours after the springing of the mine. Meanwhile, of course, the enemy had strained every nerve to hold their remaining works and had made all preparations to retake the lost ground. They got guns in position whence they could play on the assailants without fear of getting silenced; and they brought a heavy musketry to bear in the same direction. The space between our line and the crater now was swept by a heavy fire, and made the transit hazardous. 9.15 A.M. or thereabouts; a charge by a brigade of the 18th Corps and a regiment of blacks; a part of one white regiment got to, or nearly to the crest, but of course could not stay. During the morning a despatch had come, by mistake, to Gen. Meade, directed to Gen. [Burnside]. It was from Lt. Col. C. G. Loring Insp. of 9th Corps, who reported that the troops [were] jammed in the crater and *could not be made to advance*. Loring had himself gone into the crater. This was the first news from the spot that showed M[eade] the hitch in affairs; because Burnside's despatches had been of a general and a favorable character. Hereupon Meade telegraphed Burnside that he wanted the full state of the case, which B[urnside] took to mean that *he had not told the truth*! and at once flew into one of his singular fits of rage. Grant mounted his horse and rode down towards the Taylor battery to try and see something. Meade remained, receiving despatches and sending orders. Grant is very desirous always of seeing, and quite regardless of his own exposure (as at Spottsylvania &c.). 10.30 A.M. Burnside and Ord came in. The former, much flushed, walked up to Gen. Meade and used extremely insubordinate language. He afterwards said he could advance, and wished of all things to persist; but could not show how he would do it! Ord was opposed to further attempts. Meade ordered the attack suspended. As Ord & Burnside passed me, the latter said something like: "You have 15,000 men concentrated on one point. It is strange if you cannot do something with them." Ord replied angrily, flourishing his arms, "You can fight if you have an opportunity; but, if you are held by the throat, how can you do anything?" Meaning, I suppose, that things were so placed that troops could not be used. Burnside said to one of his staff officers: "Well, tell them to connect, and hold it." Which was easy to say, but they seem to have had no provision of tools, and, at any rate, did not connect with the old line. Poor B[urnside] remarked, quite calmly: "I certainly fully expected this morning to go into Petersburg!"— I was directed to show Gen. Ord a camping ground for his corps, which I designated near the "deserted" house. At 11.30 A.M. Headquarters mounted and rode sadly to camp. Went over to 9th Corps hospitals, near our camp. They were full of wounded and their condition was disgraceful! There were not half enough tents, or even bough shelters for the wounded, who lay on all sides, in the broiling sun. While one man lay on the amputating table I saw an officer and another man lying on the bare ground, close by, with no protection whatever, waiting their turn! It was more striking as a contrast to our other hospitals even under most disadvantageous circumstances. I was so shocked that I reported it to Gen. Meade; and the Sanitary Commission afterwards did the same. The General ordered an inspection; and Dr. McParlin was detailed. 3.30 P.M. Harwood, of the Engineers, said to me: "They have retaken that point and captured a brigade of our people!" Indeed the rebels had made a bold charge upon the huddled mass of demoralized men and retaken the crater, killing some, driving back others, and capturing most. They captured Gen. Bartlett with his wooden leg; and Col. Stephen Weld of the 56th Mass. I sent a telegram to Weld's father, saying he was all right, for Loring had so told me; and I never found the truth till next morning; but it turned out the mistake did good rather than harm. And so ended this woeful affair!— "If you ask what was the cause of this failure . . . I could answer with many reasons from many officers. But I can give you one reason that includes and overrides every other—*the men did not fight hard enough*" (T. L. letter July 31st, 1864).[74]

July 31, Sunday.

Hot again, very. So was yesterday. Our losses, as near as I can find by close enquiry, are K. 400, W. 1,650, P. 1,000; Total—3,050. The rebels lost 220 prisoners. I doubt if their loss altogether is ½ our own. Surveys going on for a rear line, to shorten the old one, and, with the redoubts, to be held by much fewer men. Rebels reported at Chambersburg.[75] The Inspector could not help blaming the 9th Corps hospitals somewhat, but made a weak diversion against the sanitary, which, he said, by supplying stores *gratis* gave temptation to the surgeons to neglect the regular army supplies, for which they had to make requisitions, and for which they were *responsible*. In other words, when corrupt officers abuse a charity, the Charity is to blame and not the officers. However, the effect was right, and the hospital was brought up.

August 1, Monday.

Happening to wake early, heard the General direct a truce to be held from 5 to 9 A.M.—Rosencrantz & I saddled and proceeded to the front. Passing to right of Shind house we kept through the pine wood, at the corner of which I was, June 18th. There were advanced camps there; and the tents protected by banks of earth, showed that projectiles were common. At the front edge of this wood we dismounted and went on foot along the covered way that there begins—a poorly constructed affair, often enfiladed and usually covering me only to the shoulder. Crossing the open field, and leaving on our left Ft. Morton (the Taylor house battery) which occupies the site of that house, we descended to the railroad cut; on the other side of which we ascended a little, passing a spring, which was protected by a gabionade, then again descending, we came to a deep water-cutting, with steep sides, whereof the bottom was dirty mud & water (Poor Creek). Scrambling up the high bank, opposite, we stood behind the parapet opposite the crater. Crowds of our soldiers were standing on top, and we, climbing up, at once saw one of the most awful spectacles possible. In the moderate space between us and the enemy—some 110 yards—lay perhaps 200 bodies. The heat and intense sun of 48 hours had so swollen and blackened them that negroes were not to be told from the whites, save by the hair! The faces and hands of many were actually white with a moving layer of maggots! From the field rose a sickly stench. Over against us were the jagged outlines of the crater, with heaps of gravel and sand, and irregular masses of clay; ill crowned by groups of rebel soldiers, who, in their ghostly gray uniforms, and heavy slouched hats, stood out in exaggerated figures against the sky, like malevolent spirits. Both parties had out lines of sentries, who permitted only officers and the burial party, on the ground. The rebels were meanly employing their negro prisoners in this work.[76] In the midst stood an officer with the white flag. Most of the bodies in the centre were negroes; one rebel lay there, perhaps blown over by the explosion or accidentally shot while coming in as a prisoner. Col. Thomas told me these blacks were killed when they were driven out of the mine, and rallied just outside the entrenchments. This whole space, by much sharpshooting, was almost paved with bullets, mixed with pieces of shell. We returned by another covered way, to our left, and saw them bringing in one or two blacks who had actually survived the exposure for two days. They looked as if they might recover, though extremely exhausted.— The General went to City Point by rail from a station in rear of Jordan house. Took us 20 minutes. Everyone at Grant's of course much disgusted. Grant said it was a "Fizzle." Col. Duff, who is a boastful empty-pate of the Western stamp, said that the trouble was: "there was too much of this damned *science!*" which was ingeniously far from the true reason. We saw Ord when we returned; against whom and Burnside, there is complaint. The latter had prepared a note regretting his hasty language to Gen. Meade, but received just then a notice that his conduct in the whole affair would be looked into by a court of inquiry.[77]

August 2, Tuesday.

Two telegraph operators tried for taking off messages and giving them to Burnside, who now fought hard to defend them. The court martial acquitted them for want of evidence, but, as they had confessed already to Gen. Meade, he ordered one or both out of the army.[78]— Report that rebels are mining Fort Hell—we countermine but find nothing. Everybody *now* thinks that everyone else is mining him! —Young Sedgwick, of the 20th, got taken at the Deep Bottom affair, the other day. Rather a short military experience!—[79]

August 3, Wednesday.

Grand medicine pow-wow over the "second line" by the Engineers. Humphreys, Warren, Duane, old Barnard, Michler, and Mendel, all dabbing on maps with their fingers. Heavy guns sent to the rear, which had been brought up for the mine. Torbert's cavalry went yesterday to Washington.[80]

August 4, Thursday.

Poor Jim Higginson! Miss Grace Heath, to whom he was engaged, has died of diphtheria. Interceded with the General to get him a leave. Flint got one at the same time, because his father is reputed dying. The General's kind heart gave it them, but his military conscience was wounded at giving leaves to two officers from the same squadron; so he pitched into me to relieve his feelings.[81] —The Lieut. General has gone to Washington, whither Wilson's cavalry has gone also. The General started to visit Ben. Butler, with Frenchies and staff officers. We rode to his Headq'rs and got on board Ben's fine steamer "Greyhound," on the Appomattox. Sailing down, we turned into the James, which at once becomes narrower, though still of good width, with the left bank high and wooded. The channel runs close to this bank and there lay two small gunboats, their men at quarters and their guns run out. "The left bank is lined with sha-arpshooters!" roared one gunboat captain, from his paddle box. "Stop her!" rung *our* Cap.— Ben got very mad and ordered the boat to proceed, while we all got with dignity into the cabin! except Ben who stuck out his stomach on deck! Bang! went the boat behind us, sending a huge shell into the bushes; while the other paddled ahead and fired also.— Query: *were* there any sharpshooters? They fired into a foolish excursion boat, the other day, and killed two peaceable persons. Hence, perhaps, this excitement. Ahead we could see the wooded ridge of Malvern Hill. The river doubles on itself in a most singular way, thus the Bermuda Hundreds line, which runs from a loop in the river near Dutch Gap to the Appomattox at Pt. of Rocks, is say 3½ miles, while it is 15 or 16 to go round. Deep Bottom is on the left bank, a high wooded rise in a bend of the stream, and opposite a submerged tract, where the trees have been killed by the water breaking in. There we have a lodgment and Foster's brigade holds it with works. At Dutch Gap both banks are high, but the left is the lower. Several monitors here lay and among them the "Onondagua" with two turrets. We went aboard. Everything moves, as easy as a coffee mill, by machinery. Seven boilers and 19 steam engines on board! Even currents of fresh air are pumped by steam. 92° in the cabin. The big 15-inch gun looks just like a red hippopotamus! From the high bluff on the right bank of the river there is a fine view towards Richmond, over some well cultivated land along the stream. By the Howlett house, in the bend of the river next above, is a rebel battery of 19 heavy guns, to sweep the reach towards Deep Bottom. In one of our bluff batteries which reply to this one we saw a Sawyer gun, where the projectile has a spiral lead flange which fits in a corresponding groove in the bore. We rode back by the line of defensive works. At Butler's saw the cheerful Hutchins, now a Quartermaster.[82]

August 5, Friday.

About 6.30 P.M. We heard several volleys of musketry on the right, followed by the batteries, which opened heavily. Two divisions were ordered at once to march in support, but were halted when we heard the case, which was, that a small mine had been sprung about 40 yards in front of the works, on the bottom land. What was the object, nobody could say. Some thought it a miscalculation, others that it was to blow in a supposed mine of ours. We continue to get countermining rumors from Fort "Hell," &c.[83]

August 6, Saturday.

Rode along our flank line, and met with this incident, instructive though extreme. [TL quoted the following anecdote from his letter of August 12, 1864.] "Discovered a patriotic sentry sitting with his back to where the enemy might be supposed to come, and reading a novel! He belonged to the 7th Indiana (3d Div. 5th Corps—old 1st Div. 1st Corps) 'What are your instructions?' say I. 'Haint got none,' replies the peruser of novels. 'Then what are you here for?' 'Well, I'm a kind of an alarm sentinel,' said the literary militaire. 'Call the corporal of the guard,' said I, feeling very much disposed to laugh. The sentry looked about a little, and then, singling out a friend, called out: 'Oh! Jim, why won't you just ask Jeremiah Miles to step this way?' After some delay Jeremiah appeared. He was in a pleasing state of ignorance. Did not know the sentry's instructions—did not know who the officer of the guard was—did not know much of anything. 'Well,' said I: 'Now suppose you go and find the sergeant of the guard.' This he did with great alacrity. The sergeant, as became his office, knew more than the corporal. He was clear that the sentry should not read a book: also, that his conduct in sitting down was eccentric; but when it came to, who was the officer of the guard, his naturally fine mind broke down. He knew the officer *if he saw him*, but could *not* remember his name. This he would say, the officer was a Lieutenant. 'Suppose you should try to find him,' suggested I. Of course! that he would do; and soon the 'Lootenant' appeared. To him I talked like a father, almost like a grandfather, in fact; showed him the man's musket was rusty, and that he was no good whatsoever. Lootenant had not much to say; indeed, so to speak nothing, and I left him, with a strong impression that you can't make a silk purse out of a sow's ear." All this is ludicrous, but, yet more, it is sad!— Sultry and less breeze than formerly.— Sent application to Massachusetts for a further leave of absence from my arduous duties as A.A.G. of that state!—[84]

August 7, Sunday.

The good, musical Dr. Derby to see Barstow. He hath been ordered, from a soft "posish" under Butler, to be Chief Surgeon of the 3d Div. 5th Corps. The 18th Corps men, on the alluvial bottom, are getting sick. Home papers growling. Old Gen. Patrick has given over getting us preachers, this summer. He used to be enthusiastic.[85]

August 8, Monday.

Adams is to have the Lt. Colonelcy of the 5th Mass. nig. cav. Gen. Meade testified before the Court of Inquiry on Gen. Burnside.[86]

August 9, Tuesday.

Rumor that Butler is to be Secretary of War. This morning we heard a heavy explosion towards City Point, and there came a telegraph in few minutes that an ordnance barge had blown up with much loss of life. "Rosie," Worth, Cavada and Cadwalader were in a tent at Grant's Headq'rs when suddenly there was a great noise, and a 12-pdr. shot came smash into the mess-chest! They rushed out—it was raining shot, shell, timbers and *saddles* (of which there had been a barge load near)! Two dragoons were killed near them. They saw just then a man running *towards* the explosion—the only one—it was Grant! and this shows his character well. About 35, mostly negro lumpers, were killed, and 80 wounded. (The cause of this was never known. It was commonly thought, after, to have been a rebel torpedo.) Rode to Dalton's hospital and dined, Adams accompanying. It is a town of tents, with regular streets—easy accommodation for 8,000 patients!—Steam engine to pump water from the river—every one of the 4,000 patients on a cot—best food and neatness for all. When Ned heard the explosion, true to his instincts, he called out; "Harness the ambulances!" Introduced to Drs. Smith & Phelps.[87]

August 10, Wednesday.

Poor Riddle sick, as he often is, "malarial malaise," and very mal at his aise indeed! Bully Farragut has captured, in splendid style, the Mobile forts & fleet! Sheridan appointed to command all the troops of the upper Potomac. Do not know that Meade quite likes this; one of his corps, and most of his cavalry is taken and added to other troops and the command of the whole given to his chief of cavalry, while he is left in this now rather negative spot.[88]— Rode to beyond the Dunn house, that eve, and watched the camp fires and the flashes of the picket firing.

August 12, Friday.

2d Corps suddenly picked up its duds and marched off! Rode out and saw Patten, riding at the head of his men, and keeping up appearances with a pair of cotton gloves! He was very chipper, as he understood they were going in transports to Washington.— That Col. Thomas got taken by mistake, on the day of the truce, and was carried to Petersburg, but was liberated afterwards.

He described the look of the streets and said he saw bird cages in the windows, which sounds queerly. He also discovered a bawdy house! Bravo! I wish the rebs' had kept him. He is a low-minded, scheming fellow.[89]

August 13, Saturday.

Hancock embarking at City Pt. Hancock to be followed by Gregg, who marches this afternoon. We had visitors in person of Messrs. Otto, Assist. Sec. of Interior, a stout, well spoken, and well educated man; & Prof. Mathile, an examiner at the patent office. He is a Swiss, a friend of Agassiz, and was compromised in the ridiculous Neuchatel affair of Pourtalès' Steiger. Also a chatty Mr. Falls, apparently Otto's "striker."[90] Butler has started a canal across the Deep Bottom loop, to cut off the Howlett house battery; just as if the enemy would not put batteries to enfilade it, when done! He has called for volunteers, with extra pay, to work on it, and now the rebel rams come down and pitch mortar shells into and about the trench. We often hear the distant booming of their pieces. Going over to ask Loring about Weld, found Burnside's Headq'rs in a state of pack up, and a band, and Gens. Potter, Willcox and Ferrero taking a drink. Pell greeted me with, "Any commands for Newport?" Which all means that B-sides has, with his staff, 30 days leave, which I fancy will be extended so far as this army is concerned!—[91]

August 14, Sunday.

Hancock having, after delay, disembarked at Deep Bottom, attacked in conjunction with Birney's 10th Corps, which latter took a battery of 4 heavy cannon and two mortars. Macy's brigade advanced to the assault, but Macy's horse was shot and fell on him and the attack was repulsed. We took some prisoners. Poor Patten was hit in the leg, and amputated at the thigh. Parke has got back from sick leave and takes the 9th Corps. We now occupy our new line, holding the old with the pickets. The 5th Corps is taken out and massed in reserve.[92]

August 15, Monday.

A thunder storm burst on us in the afternoon, deluging all things. The dry weather had made us negligent of trenches, so now we were flooded! Officers were shouting frantically for their servants and for spades, and grabbing small articles floating on the tide. De Chanal grubbed manfully with a stick and I helped him to rescue his traps. "Long" Craig was seen standing in his tent on a cracker box with a mop in his hand![93]

August 16, Tuesday.

Sharp fighting at Deep Bottom in which we got the best of it and took a lot of prisoners. Gregg went up the Richmond road to 6½ miles of the city, but met a crowd of infantry and had to come back. The rebs had two Generals killed. Chamblis, of the cavalry (on whom was found an excellent map of the country and works round Richmond) and Gherrard (?). Enemy sending more troops to the north side. They have also recalled troops from their way to help Early.— Barlow is with Ned Dalton at City Pt. sick. Bartlett is sick too.[94] 5th Corps was to move this night, but order was countermanded.

August 17, Wednesday.

Carried a sealed order to Gen. Warren, who has had his tents pitched for two months in the yard of Col. Avery's house—a longer time, he said, than ever before in the war, when on active campaign. Rode back and had him a map prepared with the latest information, which took to him midst a brisk thunder storm. The negroes of the 10th Corps today repulsed a heavy assault, with much credit.

August 18, Thursday.

Somewhat before 1 o'clock this morning, we were wakened by the sudden bursting forth of a tremendous cannonade from the enemy to which our guns moderately replied. For two hours the still, damp, night air reverberated with the roar of mortars and guns and the hum and bursting of shells. The camp was alive with officers in aerial dress, discussing this sudden uproar. In the midst comes a telegraph from Grant to ask what it is. Officer of the night takes it to the General's tent and finds him fast asleep! He sleeps heavily and just now, has a deafness from cold in the head. Now it happened that the officer scratched just in a partial lull of the cannonade; so the General, after reading the telegraph, asks, very innocently: "Is there *more firing than common* tonight?"— We fired some 1,500 rounds, and the enemy much more, yet, on our side there were only 6 killed and 24 wounded! So much for artillery, when men are covered. It was exceedingly grand, indeed. All this was intended to keep us from moving, but the 5th Corps moved, all the same, at 4 A.M. and took the route to the Gurley house, via the Jerusalem plank. There Warren formed his line, and, at 8.20 advanced and moved up the Weldon rail, towards Petersburg. At 1.30 P.M. heard heavy musketry from him and some cannon. Near the junction of the Vaughan road with the rail his advance came on the division of Heth. The Maryland brigade, always a poor lot, gave way, exposing the left of the regulars who were much cut up, and were forced back. It is just to remark that the 13th N.Y. Heavy Artil. all behaved well and fired steadily.—They are Germans.— Reinforcements coming up the line was reestablished, but in the rear of the ground of the fight, viz. about ⅓ mile north of the Globe Tavern. Not for the first time, it occurs to me that our infantry is inferior to that of the enemy. The troops intrenched and began destroying the rails, and so the day's operations ended. Mott is ordered back from Deep Bottom to relieve part of the 9th Corps in the lines. Willcox, being relieved by an extension to the left of the 18th Corps, goes, late at night, to Warren.

August 19, Friday.

Steady rain. Mott got along about 7 A.M. and began to relieve the 9th Corps people, a ticklish matter in broad day, for the covered ways were waist deep in water, and the troops had to move over open ground, more or less exposed to the enemy's batteries. 12.15 P.M. The General started for the left, where all was quiet. We went slop, slop, woefully through mud and puddles. Not far this side of Cheever's we came on a damp brigade of Potter's people. I was ordered to tell them to march on; and went after Gen. P[otter] whom found at Gen. White's H'dq'rs near by. White has the 1st Div. 9th Corps, once Stevenson's and, afterwards, that miserable Ledlie's, whom we have at last got "shut" of. Charlie Mills is the A.A.G.—saw him there.[95] Caught the staff, by galloping, near the Williams house. We passed Wright's old breastworks (June 22) and the Aiken house; then kept on through a skirt of wood and emerged on a large open tract, entirely flat in the midst of which stood a ruinous building of brick painted yellow. This was the old "Globe" or "yellow" tavern and stood right on the railroad. This space was dotted with ambulances, spare batteries and squads of troops. We arrived at 1.45 P.M. at the tavern, where found Warren, who had a narrow escape yesterday. A bullet hit his horse just between the eyes, and, had he had his head down, grazing, as is often the case, Warren's body would have received it. Mounted to the roof, to get a view—found a good part of the house had no floors; and such of the plastering as was not peeled off was ornamented by rebel charcoal inscriptions! There were several shells through the gables.[96] Had a good view of the position, which consisted of a flank line (running parallel to and west of the railroad, to at least ⅓ of a mile south of the tavern) and a front line, at right angles, running east along the edge of the woods which bound this farm on the north. It struck me, that, while the left flank was thus refused and strongly intrenched, the right was in the air, and only continued by a picket line. The extreme right rested in the woods lying between the Aiken and tavern clearings, and about two miles from the nearest point of our old lines, say near Fort Davis. 3.30 P.M. The General moved towards home—4 P.M. As we rode through the Aiken farm, we met White's division coming along, with little, bald-headed, White himself riding at the head. He is no soldier, but always ready to fight; a trait that goes far in war! Almost at the same moment I heard dropping shots in the woods on our left, and was surprised the General said nothing. (He was so deaf from the cold that he never heard one of them!) for I expected each moment the pickets would come tumbling in on top of us! Just as we got to the Jerusalem plank we heard the cannon opening, but the woods kept off the sound of the musketry, for the most part. A rapid fire continued a short time and then ceased. "During said short time was enacted one of those disgraceful surprises which we have in such perfection! The enemy, making a front attack, at the same moment threw a strong column down a road leading (north and south) past the Lenear house and outside our right flank. They smashed through the picket line, passed down the road, faced to their right, and rushed, yelling and firing, into the open fields in rear of our right wing." (Letter August 23.)[97] At this moment White, who was approaching the Lenear house from the east, with admirable vigor, charged into the woods, struck the enemy in the flank and rear, and routed them, while Wainwright's batteries were firing canister from the tavern clearing. Thus assailed the enemy rushed into the woods and came immediately upon the rear of Crawford's people and of the regular brigade of Ayres division, who were thus taken between a front attack which they were resisting and a rush in the rear; moreover the canister came among them from our own batteries. A great crowd were swept out as prisoners, mostly of the regular brigade and the consolidated Penn. Reserves, many of whom were armed with repeating rifles. Among the taken was Joe

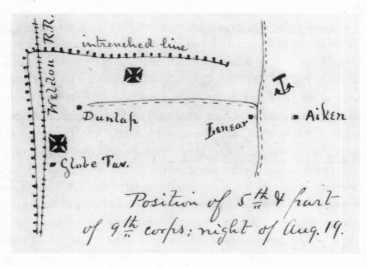

Hayes; and the whole number of prisoners was not less than 2,000! And so, though the enemy was actually driven off, we made an immense loss, that *should* have been a gain. The position was faulty; Warren should have corrected it, and Meade should have known it![98]

August 20, Saturday.

Last night a cavalry brigade, from Deep Bottom, passed our Headq'rs on their way to report to Warren, to cover his flank & rear. Young McKibbin, of the regulars, was brought in an ambulance, badly hit in the shoulder in yesterday's combat.[99] Rain still today, making the roadless country so deep that no waggons were allowed west of the plank, whence all stores were packed on mules. 200 prisoners were brought to our place, taken yesterday; among them some of *their* Maryland brigade, well looking men, with remains of a spruce uniform, and little kepis of grey and sky blue. They showed more sensitiveness than the real Southrons, and were loud in their statements that they were fighting hard when taken.

August 21, Sunday.

Hancock returned from Deep Bottom with the remaining two divisions and took position on the left, convenient to Warren. His men now call themselves "Hancock's cavalry."— At a halt, one of the men explained that "we were only stopping for the staff to git fresh hosses!" 9.30 A.M. Heavy cannonade again opened from Warren, which disturbed me because feared a repetition of yesterday. 1.10 P.M. The General once more rode to the left, and, as we were crossing the little run below Avery's there came a despatch from Warren, saying he had repulsed the attack, which was made chiefly on his left refused line by troops of A. P. Hill and of Beauregard; for a concentration had been made by the rebels from Deep Bottom. Warren had put up an *advanced* line, on his left, shorter than the one behind it, thus:

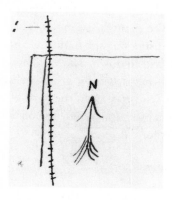

They began with a heavy artillery practice throwing a concentric fire chiefly into the angle of the position and about the tavern. Meantime the enemy appeared from the woods, in three lines of battle, and at once attempted to charge across the open beyond the railroad, but were met by such a volley from Griffin's people that they at once broke and fell back. Haygood's S.C. brigade, issuing from a point in the woods, came on the end of the front line, and rushed forward, thinking the game theirs, when, to their dismay they received the canister and bullets of the rear line, in their right flank! They began to throw down their arms, and Capt. Daly, a division provost marshal, ran out to receive their surrender, when Haygood rode up crying "Shoot him! shoot him!" at the same moment discharging his revolver at Daly, who fell, but still clung to the flag he had seized. Haygood then cried "Face about!" and the entire brigade ran for it, midst a shower of projectiles. Some 400, however, fell into our hands. The men vowed that *next time* they would go on shooting! (Daly was supposed mortally hit; but recovered.) We took also 4 flags.[100] The General stopped at the Jones house to confer with Hancock and then kept on to Warren, who was in good spirits and wanted to make a counter attack; but Meade thought not, as there seemed little to be gained, since we already had the railroad—a great point truly; for to touch this has been like touching a tiger's cubs; and, this time, Lee has concentrated all available force to recover it. The ground on this flat is treacherous; sand with a little clay, and, when wet, as now, your horse will suddenly flounder to the girts! What is curious is, that a little trampling, as by an occupying body of troops, soon renders the surface sure in all weathers. When we got to the tavern, the stretcher bearers were out in a big cornfield, west of the railroad, burying the dead and bringing in the wounded rebels. One of them, a handsome youth, lay, stone dead, close by; and another was there, with a great hole in the top of his head, and the brains protruding. He had been left there as of no account. (Yet, next morning, he had recovered enough to feel the flies on his face and brush them away, and he was put in hospital.) The enemy's loss in the day's work cannot well be less than 1,500. They had sharpshooters still in the distant trees, so that our people near the Blick ruin had to keep down. The men, however, defiantly stood on the parapet and amused themselves by firing back. We lost Col. Dushane com'd'ng Maryland Brig. who was hit in the head by a cannon shot. A good deal more intrenching had been done; some too on the right flank, and plenty of scattered epaulements for batteries.[101]

August 22, Monday.

Last night we connected from the Weldon road to the old works and strengthened our position generally. The enemy concentrated near the Leadworks (looking for an attack from us) and left Warren's front. Miles division of 2d Corps marched to Ream's Station on Weldon road (say 5 miles below Yellow Tavern) to tear up the track, Gregg's cavalry with.— They had new fangled machines to twist rails, but, it unfortunately proved that the rails twisted *them!* As we came home from visiting Warren again, we were caught in the biggest kind of a thunder storm—rain in sheets.—Poor Biddle's horse, clumsy like his rider, slipped down and plunged B. in the mud!

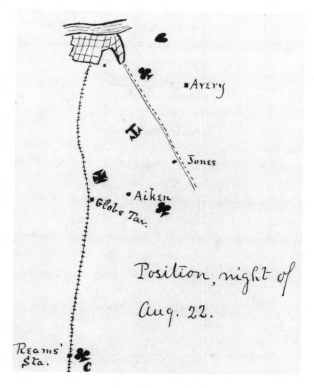

August 23, Tuesday.

A pretty time to be one and thirty!—riding over a quicksand country and looking at muddy troops!— The General rode along the new part of the breastworks, beginning at the Strong house clearing (to which Mott's men stretched) and coming out above the Globe Tavern. He was in a mood to "rake" people and he began on a 2d Corps Colonel, commanding a brigade,—a rather sulky specimen. He was blown sky high, for not having his men ready and belts on—all proper. Then he left a polite message for "Boss Fero" to move his headquarters nearer his line of battle (!) from which they were distant about 700 yards. He ordered me to inspect the 9th Corps brigades, and ascertain the state of preparations and the orders. Found that they had no particular orders and that most of the men had their belts off. Most, or all, were ordered under arms at 15 min. before daylight. The negroes were in the best condition for defense, on the average; also they had put up a great deal of good breastwork. The men were still at the slashings in front; for much of the line runs through thick woods. When we got near the Smith house (S.E. of Aiken) on our way back, we found Hancock with his tents up, in the clearing. The woods were full of Gibbon's men. Maj. Mitchell and the rest of the staff were on the ground thoroughly tired. The servants were getting them some dinner. Presently Hancock said he would start at once for Ream's Station. "Pack up!" roared Mitchell, in comic despair "Won't I get the dinner?" said the aghast dark.—"No-o-o!"— Sent $15. to Maj. Bob Davis, Butler's A.A.G. to get some coffee &c. to Hayes & Sedgwick, by Flag-of-truce boat. (Note. He never sent it and never returned the money!)[102] We visited also Parke today, camped in a field south of the Aiken house. Potter invited us to his tent and told us about the siege of Knoxville, and several good defensive fights he made in falling back on the town.— About the 21st Dr. Ghieslin was ordered away, a quiet man and a good, who has been much in New Mexico. He was in Canby's early fights there. Capt. Cavada, also, is mustered out—a Cuban, but a man of character. He speaks English perfectly, having been a good part of his life in this country.[103]

August 24, Wednesday.

The General went to City Point. Two boys came in from Petersburg. Enemy reported moving troops south.

August 25, Thursday.

The 10th Corps changed with the 18th. Ord has been holding 3½ miles of line with 7,500 men—rather slim work! 12.30 P.M. General left for the new positions. Stopped at Mott's and after at Parke's. We heard some guns from Hancock—plainly the southward move of the rebels yesterday was on Ream's Station! Arrived at Yellow Tavern, Gen. Meade ordered Saunders to go to Hancock by the Weldon road. S[aunders] came back quite flushed, having been briskly shot at by A. P. Hill's skirmishers, whom he reported advancing on Hancock, together with cavalry. Crawford was massed, close to the tavern, ready to march down the railroad to Hancock's aid. (Meade was always sorry he did not send Crawford; but Hancock *asked no reinforcement*, and afterwards frankly said he would have needed none, had his men fought properly. Nevertheless he had an almost sharp talk with Meade about it, and, in his defence, said; "I would *never* ask for reinforcements!—a brave but not a soldierly remark.)[104] A force of the division of Mott, under McAllister, ordered to march down the Jerusalem plank and hold the junction of the Ream's Station road. Willcox' division of 9th Corps ordered to march down plank road and report to Hancock. The engineer troops ordered to supply the place of Mott's men. At 4.30 P.M. we left the tavern to go to Ream's Station. Hancock already had fighting but had repulsed a vigorous attack, placing his men behind the intrenchments in shape of a horse-shoe, which the 6th Corps made when they went to bring in Wilson (June 30). We took the plank road, because the route by the Weldon rail was cut off.— Some distance down, we passed Willcox' division. Of all barefaced straggling this was the worst!! Rapid artillery had begun from Hancock (5.30) and the men deliberately fell out in squads! Some sat eating by the wayside; others crowded round wells and springs; and others went to sleep in the bushes. At the head of the column rode weak Willcox himself, as placidly, as if his people were marching with well closed ranks! When the division halted that eve, in rear of Hancock, it boasted 800 men!!! It is one of Gen. Meade's faults, that, in these matters of detail in discipline, he does not at once interfere and cause severe punishment to be meted out. At the junction of the Ream's Station road was McAllister—a middle-aged, dried up, Puritanical man, not brilliant of intellect, but an indomitable fighter. He was setting his command in order to hold the roads.[105] Meanwhile the cannon, 3½ miles west of us, were going almost continuously and so they kept on till dark. Some ambulances were coming back, full of wounded, among them one load of Sleeper's men, showing his battery had been exposed. Gen. Meade had thought of going to Hancock, but it was so late by the time he had given the necessary orders here, that he determined it would be useless, as the way was blocked, and it was over 4 miles by the road. We therefore returned to Headq'rs. Sleeper; sure enough, was brought there, shot through the upper arm. He was somewhat weak and feverish from loss of blood, but sat awhile in my tent, and talked manfully. Presently came Capt. McIntie, with the mean news that, in a final charge, about sunset, the enemy had broken through and had captured a part of the line which however, H[ancock] hoped to get back with the reinforcement that was coming up. The rebels preceded the attack by a furious cannonade, which, owing to the defective form of the works took many points in reverse. 11 P.M. Bah! Miller in, with intelligence that we were driven from a part of our works with the loss of Sleeper's battery and another, 8 guns in all. They were foolish enough to tell Sleeper, and spoil his rest. Capt. Bronson, of Hancock's staff, was shot dead while rallying the men, and Hancock's horse was shot through the neck. Bronson was son of Prof. B.[106]

August 26, Friday.

Early to Jones' house, where was Hancock, who had marched back during the night. He had buoyed up his spirits with the story of a safeguard who had remained at the house he was guarding, and, early this morning went on the field, which he found deserted, except by one or two Confederates looking for dead friends. They respected his neutrality; and said their loss was tremendous! Also he gave great accounts of the rebel dead he there saw. Therewith Meade & Hancock greatly did comfort themselves, and further were gratified to find that they had marched off one way while the enemy marched off the other! A double retreat! The earnest De Chanal got quite enthusiastic; particularly as H[ancock] thought he could hardly have lost prisoners of any consequence. But, when it came to returns, there were 1,700 men missing, against 700 killed & wounded! And still the enemy's loss was extremely heavy in killed & wounded. The assault broke through Miles' line, in which a Heavy Artillery regiment scandalously gave way. Gibbon's people, being called on to recover the ground, behaved wretchedly:—the guns were lost, and it was only by the great bravery of Miles and other officers, that the rout was arrested by a handful of men. The Corps commander & his staff rushed to the front & labored like subalterns. "You should have seen the old man get right down to his fighting!" cried Mitchell, in admiration—"The rebels licked us; but a dozen more such lickings and there will be nothing left of the rebel army!" Dr. Doherty, the faithful follower of Hancock, was seen with a large stick banging stragglers! He had a bullet through his rubber coat, which was rolled behind his saddle. Lt. Col. Walker, A.A.G. was taken prisoner.[107] The dismounted cavalry behaved with a courage that shamed the infantry, and, with their repeating carbines, repulsed the enemy several times. This disgraceful affair was the weak effort of the dregs of what had been two splendid divisions, now worn to a shadow by fighting, privation, climate, and marching. Gibbon's had greatly depreciated through the want of confidence that many officers & men had in its commander; and now, to complete its ruin, the greater part of the sad remnant of the 20th Massachusetts with its colors and Lt. Col. Curtis, fell into the hands

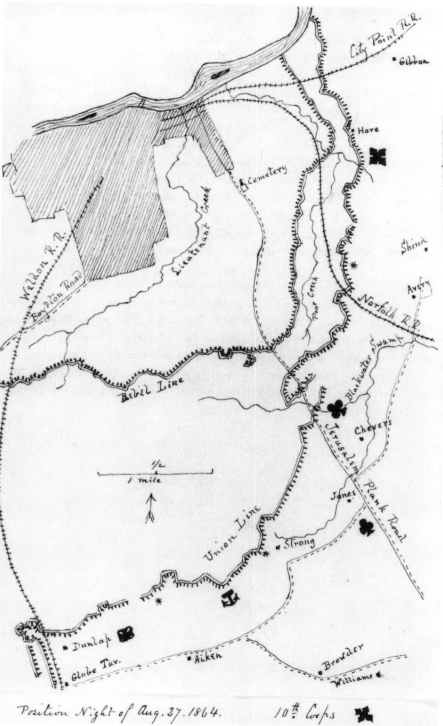

City Point R.R.

· Gibbon

· Hare

Cemetery

Lieutenant Creek

Weldon R.R.

Boydton Road

Shind ·

Poor Creek

Avery ·

Norfolk R.R.

Blackwater Swamp

Rebel Line

Cheveys ·

Jerusalem Plank Road

½
1 mile

Jones ·

Union Line

Strong ·

Dunlap ·

Globe Tav.

· Aiken

Browder

Williams ·

Position Night of Aug. 27. 1864.   10ᵗʰ Corps

of the enemy. However, Miles (Barlow's) division maintained a good spirit to the very last, through the energy and gallantry of its commanders. Col. Beaver, just from a leave of absence, joined his command as the fight began, was almost immediately struck, and lost his leg close to the hip joint. (The surgeons, much interested, had him carried all the way to City Point by hand; and he survived.)[108] We visited Warren, who certainly means to stay, for he has now made a complete intrenched camp, front, flank & rear. Old Barnard had been snuffling round and has decided on a bastioned fort on the railroad, in front and in rear (afterwards Forts Wadsworth & Dushane). Ambulances, with a cavalry escort, were sent to Ream's Station, but found the field in possession of the rebel cavalry. Guzman got back from a visit to Washington.— The signal corps reported the enemy's column marching back into Petersburg.— Thus was Hill revenged for the Wilderness, and Heth for Bristoe Station![109]

August 27, Saturday.

Petersburg papers jubilant. "The guns are very nice ones and just what we want."— Grant was up and rode to the extreme left. He was joined by Hancock & Parke as we passed their Headq'rs. Got a 15-day leave for home!!! (See next Vol.) whereupon we got off a sell on Biddle, to the effect that I was going on a secret mission to Richmond! He was very mad when he found it out, but finally got again good natured and took one of old Rosie's sempiternal brandy (vel whisky) cocktails.

August 28–
October 31, 1864

Having accumulated a quantity of notes on the campaign which
I have not had time to write out. I will, for convenience,
continue from this date in this book. The diary from May 3d will
be found in Vol. 13A.

August 28, 1864, Sunday.

Camp, ¾ of a mile to the westward of Burchard's (Burkett's?) house, before
Petersburg.[1] Said the General to me yesterday; "I think I must order you home
to get me some cigars, mine are nearly out!"— This was a great surprise, but it
is hard to surprise a man out of going home, after a 5-month campaign. Gen.
Williams gravely prepared a 15-day leave & the aides tendered their congratulations. Poor Biddle! We persuaded him that was going to Richmond on secret
service! He got very mad when undeceived, having talked about it all over
camp; but soon recovered and we prepared for him a friendly cocktail. There
was packing of valise, and instructions to Albert the Silent. Then up betimes
this morning, breakfast, and so to City Point per 7 A.M. mail waggon. There we
must needs wait for the boat that leaves at 10. Took a second small breakfast
with Comstock at Grant's mess. The mail boat was jam up with soldiers, baggage, horses & sundry freight, besides a sprinkling of Officers, among them
Lt. Col. Kensel of Butler's staff. And a Capt. Todd, brother of the staff officer
of Hancock who recently died. There was the *triste* spectacle of half a score of
cases—the bodies of some slain at Ream's Station. Among them that of Capt.
Brownson, Hancock's Commissary of Musters.[2] Nothing can more show the
effects of a long war than the sight of an infantry soldier, stretched fast asleep
on one of these cases! We passed the familiar Wilcox' Wharf and Windmill
Point, and Fort Powhattan. The banks of the river vary a good deal, in some
places high but in other places, low and marshy. There are no rock cliffs in this

tertiary formation. At Wilson's Wharf is the narrowest point of the lower river; opposite is the extensive Kennon's Marsh. On the wharf side, there is a moderately high bank, now occupied by a work, Fort Pocahontas. Gunboats patrol the stream, especially near Wilcox's Wharf. Below this (Wilson's Wharf) the ~~Pamunkey~~ [TL corrected to] Chickahominy comes in and the river gets very wide. As we approach the mouth there is a notable sandbar, stretching nearly from the left bank to the right. At Newport News you are shown the wreck of the Congress, and the place of the fight between Merrimack & Monitor. Here the river-mouth makes a bend to the N.W. On the south run up the estuaries of the Nansemond, leading to Suffolk, & of the Elizabeth, going to Norfolk. Shores low & sandy. At Fortress Monroe there is a tolerably large wharf. The houses are limited to a few refreshment places & officers' houses. Had no time to go in the fort; but Louis Stackpole came out and saw me. Here took the Baltimore boat that started an hour after (5 P.M.). Got a stateroom along with Pease who got a leave to see a conveniently sick grandmother. The sea smooth; jelly fish very numerous. Chesapeake Bay is so wide in its lower part that you see the two shores only in patches. The Rip-raps, over against Fortress Monroe, have a work begun, which, it is said, will be of 5 tiers with a barbette. The Baltimore craft crowded; but a shade better than the City Pointer; the supper cooked in a universal frying pan.[3]

August 29, Monday.

We got at 5.30 A.M. to Baltimore. To the Eutaw House, a great advance on Barnum's, which have discovered is Secesh. Got a very comfortable bath, shave & breakfast. Except for abundant soldiers, Baltimore looks quiet. At 9.40 A.M. got on a very crowded train. Mr. Seward had a car to himself; a man with a face & eye that looked as if they had been trying to measure and see through intriguing men for many a year. His expression is a pleasant one, and not far from genuine in its character.[4] Of all things in the world, there was an old lady, from Yankeedom, who kept a boarding house in Norfolk—they go everywhere! The rail now saves time by going round Philadelphia; first up the Schuylkill, past Fairmount Waterworks, then cross & back on the other side of the city. At 6.15 P.M. New York, where had time to tea at the Astor before the 8.30 train for Boston. In the sleeping car there was of course, Staunton Blake. He always is. He enlivened me with a banker-like account of the national debt, in all its horrors, whereat was amused. It is always strange to suddenly be cast into money and politics in coming away from the army.[5] Rumble-Bumble all night—you think you don't sleep at all, but you do a good deal and—*August 30*, [Tuesday]. 6 A.M. behold the Back Bay and the new houses and the gravel banks thereof! Ah, *Che bella!* And did not a practical & neat Bostonian expressman undertake to convey my valise unto the Eastern depot, while I walked and contemplated the familiar common, getting along in time for the Beverly 7.15 train. Had sent a telegraph from Baltimore, so that they should expect me. At the Beverly station, behold Master Bob Russell, grown straight & better looking. He was mildly glad—had come with a small waggon for "me and two other fellers"—who proved to be *par nobile* Felton boys. We trotted along & passed the Bancroft house, with its old trees, and there was small Sallie, a picture of plump, brown health! So pull up & hop out to see her, when forth came Mr. & Mrs. Russell and with a rush of welcome!— Then on to Witch Lane, and up *çi-devant* Aug. Lowell's Avenue, to Howland's house, when his familiar voice greeted me from the front door! and Amie too who conducted me upstairs and pointed, with a theatrical air, to a room door. For there was my Mimette, as blooming as a rose, and so surprised and glad to see her Ted! What could have brought me?— Official business, to buy cigars for the Major General Commanding! And then appears quite a young lady, Miss Cora Lyman! who said "Papa" with becoming bashfulness. She has grown larger and has good, active, legs of her own, and composes long sentiments; as well she may, being two & a half years old. Her light hair is now cut off short. Cora, the greater, is looking very well & G. H. S. too; so also the children, Amie really quite a grown lady, to wit: nearly 14, and very well looking. *Sapristi!* How comfortable did the breakfast seem! The house a large improvement on their other one, near by. It is on a high, piney ledge, and commands a fine prospect of Salem & Marblehead harbors, and of the bay. In front, below, a parlor & dining room & a small room back; above two large & two small bed rooms on the second floor & the same on the third; besides a large wing for kitchen & servants. There are some 15 acres, including a cow pasture. If the house were a little more on the sea it would be all that could be asked. Not much done today, surely, but talk & take it easy.[6]

August 31, Wednesday.

Something or other the matter with me; small appetite; weak, sort of nausea. We took tea at Co's great crony, Mrs. Brimmer; who lives with her Martin in the former house of "George B—upton." There were Mrs. & Mr. "Tot" Peabody, very nice people indeed, who temporarily dwell in a small house, hard by. Indeed, it is a perfect nest of one's acquaintances. There is Dick Parker on the point, John Cushing & his elle at Ober's (?) house; Dr. Hooper with Nellie &

Miss Clover at Ober No. 2., (the bobolitionist [*sic*] Ned, with his wife, is in N. York)— The "martyr" Rogers dwells in a house on Ch. G. Loring's place. Beyond the crossing is Mrs. Cabot—t'other way, towards Beverly, the Russells, and so they string along, occupying the good situations to the profit of the natives. How amazingly neat everyone looks! Just out a bandbox seem they.— Dad Sohier the *invalide* is staying at the Brim[mer]s. He stays about with his friends, tells them of the damp corners of their houses & other defects; and departs to stay elsewhere. A very good fellow, with the brightness of his family. He goes to Europe each winter and returns usually towards the summer months. The Brims' house is a really nice one and furnished with good taste; much *meuble* from the well known Salem Fellows; he who remarked, that Frank Peabody had been in his shop "amplifying round."[7]

September 1, Thursday.

Must needs to Boston, for there are to be bought cigars, a saddlecloth, and sundries for the General and some things for myself. Called on & found Palfrey who looks well. He & I discussed the war & the news generally; of gossip there is little stirring. Frank is a mystery—three years engaged and not married. I don't see it; there must be money enough for a modest start. Got a waggon & drove to Brookline. How pretty it looked! And what a waste it seemed—nobody to see those flowers and the well cared for trees—nobody to live in the old house, at this the best season of the year, when the autumn fruits are ripening. There was the faithful Silas with his fine barnful of hay, whereof he is proud. But Mimi shall not go back there again till the day that the Lord sendeth peace on Israel. It's too lonely—too much responsibility. Back to Beverly in the afternoon. Little Mrs. Badger now is staying with us; very glad to see me. Really a remarkable woman; she seems no older than when she came, six and twenty years since. Little Co-co comes down to dessert, each day, and has a mouthful of pudding, if there be a plain one! If not, she sits up very good and says: "Pudding not dood for Cowa; give her a fit."—She is a child of most excellent disposition and Mimi has a great faculty of making her obedient & reasonable without anything more in way of discipline than firmness. It is not a little strange to see how very small children perceive whom they may set at naught and who must be obeyed.

September 3, Saturday.

The children had a Sanitary Fair in the billiard room today, for which great prepa-rations have been making for some days. Great was the excitement of Amie, as to who should take tickets & who stand behind the tables, and who sell cake and ice-cream! They made $330 just from this little affair. We have the brave news of the capture of Atlanta; *tandem!*[8]— To Boston. Very weak—all my bile running the wrong way, and getting worse. To Dr. Cabot, who said the northern air, with the late cool change had brought to the surface the malaria in the system. He told me to take some rhubarb & magnesia and follow it with wormwood tea.[9]

September 4, Sunday.
Rather better. Took to low diet, and to the tea, which conceive to be a humbug.

September 5, Monday.
Lay abed; headache; mean generally; nausea. In the afternoon, good Dr. Torrey, a pleasant man, sensible, and of the Jackson school. He gave a blue pill, which went down & came plaguey near coming up again.

September 6, Tuesday.
Blue pill is a good man—better, but still abed. Dr. T. made me a certificate to Gen. Meade, saying I should probably not be fit for duty for 2 or 3 weeks. The Medicus recommended white of egg as a helpful specific.

September 7, Wednesday.
My liver is not to be scared by white of egg; so was worse again today—: Queer feeling very, don't take an interest in any thing; jocose remarks especially, strike me as idiotic!

September 8, Thursday.
My Mimette says with high satisfaction, "Oh, you do look *so* yellow," for she sees therein promise of my staying at home, poor child! "You must pitch into me a little harder," says I to the Doctor. Therefore the apothecary made me liver pills, and there was a trifle of quinine also each day; for my gums are sore with the malaria.

September 9, Friday.
Better again—Liver! you must give it up; I shall fire two pills at you every evening till you go back!—

September 12, Monday.
Steady improvement, but nothing to say these last days. Sit still mostly, with Mimi, and see little Co-co go out to take her walks and come again. Show the child the pictures in Pickwick, wherein she recognizes Mr. P. also Weller and

"Weller's Papa" and "Snoggrass." This eve came Marry to take tea, bringing fair Emilee and Tintie. The latter in elegant long dresses is quite the grown up damsel. She is small but has a very fine figure. I call Em "Conversation" and her "Figure." Harry is up from Naushon, his wound improves but the suppuration indicates another piece of bone yet to come out. Otherwise he looks finely.[10] N.E. rain.

September 13, Tuesday.

More rain; despite which the restless Em' was off to Naushon with Hal. You have to sail there for a good bit in a yacht; bah!

September 14, Wednesday.

Felt so much improved that walked to see Lt. Col. Loring, about a mile off, taking Winthrop on the way. Bob, with pa & sis, lives in the house a wee beyond Joe Gardner's. He is an awful Copperhead is Bob and scruples not to associate with Slidel's Secretary, Eustis, at Paris. He told me various stories of the sufferings of the Baltimoreans, at all of which I took care to laugh and said it served them right. Dick Codman, late Dep. M.P.C. is engaged to the younger sister of Kittie Sargent (Mrs. Goodwin) whose husband, by the way, saw down here. Mr. & Mrs. Russell back last eve from Naushon, in a damp condition. The weather fine after the northeaster.[11]

September 15, Thursday.

Prof. Agassiz, Mr. Burckhardt and Mrs. Agassiz drove over & dined with us. Agassiz is pretty well, but can do no work of any consequence. I fancy there has been a gradual physical failure in him for, say the last eight years—within the last two they say his mind has at times shown signs of decided loss of power, but I cannot say I see it. He is the same brilliant & versatile man, though not able any longer to pursue severe study. Mrs. Agassiz is, as always, a most charming and devoted woman, a satisfaction to look on. Old Burkhardt is *toujours bien*, though he too is less young than when he used to come to see me in college. The Prof. what with his students at the Museum and his grand Academy of the national science (which seems to be a bull-ring for learned combatants) has managed to fight with everybody; a bad trait which he shares with most savants.[12]

September 16, Friday.

Went a perch fishing, off the rocks; the amusement of mine youth. Do I not remember, over twenty years ago it must have been, by Jingo! how Charlie Eliot & I had our poles and our clams and did successfully fish off Castle rock, when

Nahant was less peopled than now, and when good Uncle Eliot dwelt in the Greek temple cottage and had the best of chowder in a flat tureen with a yellow dog for a handle! Greatness is all stuff; it is much better to be boyish—upon my word I believe I like to catch perch as well as ever! Ned Browne, my good croney, called; he's a model of neatness & round comfort is Ned. We asked him to come, with us two, to the family dinner at Mamma's, to which he gladly did assent. Have a slashing appetite at present to make up for past starvation. Alex & Annie were over, both looking extremely well; a most tender and domestic couple are they; and Annie is much prettier again since she is not obliged to nurse her baby. Got a very kind letter from Gen. Meade, wherein he spoke of his short visit home, where he found his son Sergeant very ill with his lungs, and must go to a milder climate. He was received at Washington in a flattering manner by the President and Stanton; so much so that he offered to get me a Lt. Colonelcy in the Adj. Gen's. Dept. if I wished it; which took as quite a compliment, but declined it, for various good reasons. The Bancroft house, where dwell the R[ussell]'s is some 200 yrs. old, with low ceilings and beams of oak therein, quite quaint.[13]

September 17, Saturday.

To town. Having seen that poor Patten would be buried from the college chapel today, drove first to Cambridge. There was a collection of friends at the library, Profs. Child, Lowell, Wyman & Lovering; Jack Adams; Frank Palfrey; Col. Macy; Herbert Mason, Wendell Holmes and many others; among the strangers was Mr. Stanley, under the wing, perhaps, of Charles Norton, who thanked me for my pains in regard to his brother-in-law, Arthur Sedgwick. We walked in procession to the chapel, where were Drs. Walker, Hill & Peabody, to perform the services. The coffin lay in the chancel, and, with the railing, was beautifully covered with flowers. The services were impressive, especially Dr. Walker's reading of the scriptures, and the singing; I thought I recognized the voice of Langmaid in the choir. He must have been a classmate of Patten. The last time I saw Patten he was riding at the head of his men, when the corps was going to embark, as he believed, for Washington. They were going to Deep Bottom, where he lost his leg, and died after a couple of weeks in the Philadelphia hospital. He was an intrepid & excellent officer of the pattern which the 20th makes.[14] Drove thence to Brookline, where was surprised to find Albert sent home sick by Gen. Meade. He is very weak with diarrhoea, but will doubtless soon mend here. Then in town where had invited Browne and Burkhardt to dine at Parker's. The dinner was very good, but, as to the price, $5.00 a bottle for champagne is a specimen! Coming down in the cars, found

Dr. Bill Thorndike, home on sick-leave from the army. Happy feller, going to see his wife and babby![15]

September 18, Sunday.

Dr. Hooper paid us a morning visit, the entertaining man. He related how a philanthropic person brought a Sunday-school of blackguard children to Nahant, and how they suddenly began to run about crying, "Oh, Jim, what a good place to fish, if we can find where a sewer comes in!" His daughter Nellie appeared soon after, very pleasant and nice. Wonder she don't marry some chap. But they say there are 100,000 too many women in Massachusetts. Mr. & Mrs. Russell came to tea. They both seem remarkably well. Their great thorn now is, to get the new house, corner Louisburg Sqr. and Mt. Vernon St. furnished and in order.

September 19, Monday.

Mimi & I performed perch-fishing feats today, on Parker's point and on a little wharf by Dr. Hooper's. Mimette did catch a sculpin—then the little perchlings would run away with her bait, and caused great indignation in her mind. But she was gratified when at last she got a good sized "chogsit" as we used to call 'em at Nahant.

September 20, Tuesday.

Little wife & I made a travelling day of it, going to town and thence to Brookline where we spent some time. Bought a gold chain for her, at Bigelow's, to put her locket on, which she wears always round her neck. We made preparations for shutting up the house and paying off the "help."— Intend also to sell the horses, which are not particularly valuable. Went about actively with Walt and marked out what trees were to be cut or transplanted. Then we went over and dined with dear old Mrs. Cabot, who looks remarkably well, bless her soul! Miss Saidie was there too; and we were very cheery, for Dr. Cabot, who had come out with his wife, brought the good news that Sheridan had completely defeated Early at Opequan Creek and driven him in confusion with a loss of 5 guns. Rhodes was killed, also Goodwin & Fitz Lee wounded. On our side we had the irreparable loss of Gen. David Russell, an admirable & an honorable soldier, commanding 1st Div. 6th Corps. Gen. Upton was wounded. Russell was a man of extraordinary personal courage and, at the same time, a very plain and retiring man; one of his peculiarities was, that, when wounded, he never would make it public, but sought to conceal it.[16]

September 21, Wednesday.

Mimi went again to town to the Sanitary. She is much troubled now with lame back, as she strained it last summer, trying to wind a clock. We all took tea at the Russells, the deuce Howland appearing in a post-prandial manner. We have a bit of fire nearly every day, now, because it is cool, morning & evening.

September 22, Thursday.

Little Sallie's birthday, she is 13, only to think of it! A most lovable and sweet-dispositioned little girl she is. Hal goes tomorrow. He came to bid goodbye, and Mimi shed sisterly tears over him, though he is only going to Pt. Lookout, to remount his regiment. It's hard for his wife, who is but weakly and has eyes good for nothing.[17]

September 23, Friday.

Paid a last visit to Brookline, for shall go next Monday to w, a, r, war; you'll find it a damnable bore. Went with Watt over the nursery and also among the trees generally and marked a good many that must come out. Left Albert to come out again when able and if he chose still to remain with me. We went, all hands, to dine at the Brims.' A very good dinner they gave and Martin said he thought that Sheridan's victory justified a bottle of champagne, a sentiment that found further confirmation from the news sent in the eve' by Dr. Hooper, that Sheridan had gained a second victory, at Fisher's Hill, near Strasburg, where Crook turned the rebel left, and we took 20 cannon & a large number of prisoners. Bravo![18]

September 24, Saturday.

Dine at the Russell's, which is like the old Jube's Lane days, when we had peace & quiet, which, of course, we didn't appreciate; we never appreciate anything till we lose it and get something worse. Gold has been down as low as 185 or so; it *had* been to at least 290, during the summer. Miss Edie Forbes was married last night to her Perkins.— That cub of a brother of hers, Bob, went to a neighbor's to stay away during the ceremony. Really the cur ought to be turned out of decent society. Annie and Alex were with us; but the vagrant Em' at Lenox. They have a good croquet ground where the enthusiastic Alex disported himself most vigorously.[19]

September 25, Sunday.

Wrote a letter to Heywood, from whom had an epistle the other day. Poor old H! Despite his ridiculous, vain & long winded ways, he is a man of sterling worth. What surprises me is, that he, with his unusual perseverance and good head has made so little progress; for, I fear he gains no more than a livelihood. With half his ability a man of address & skill would have gained an important position.[20] It was a raw day, this, with a cold northerly wind. We drove to see Harry Lee. His place, beyond Mrs. Cabot's is a monument of perseverance. He bought it perhaps 16 years ago, a barren little headland, looking out to sea; but now he has made green grass and goodly trees to grow and the place is truly striking. Old Mr. Lee, so long a bright, cranky, old statistician has quite lost his mind, and must have a man to care for him. His remarks are most singular at times. *e.g.*, His son Harry calling to see him, he said, "Well, now that Higginson (Harry's partner) what a pity it is he drinks so!" The friendly Bullards were at tea when got there. Good Stephen, who looks always as if he had the mumps, did bid us welcome, and we took a seat at the fire, with comfort to ourselves. Lizzie's children have her brightness, and more even, but look like their papa. Mary was over to see Co, one day last week, and looks very well indeed. It is pleasant to think how C.G. has now a good post as President of an Ins. Co. for Mary has lived a pinched life that she was not brought up to.[21]

September 26, Monday.

Black Monday, and be hanged to it! Poor Mimette walked with me to the Russells whom I bid adieu to. The day was passed, *au reste*, in packing and getting ready. Howland to whom had bid a tender farewell, last night, unexpectedly returned from town and ate dinner with us. He has been low in spirits rather, of late, good man; rather irritable from the vexed question of Bob Oliver's going to the war as 2d Lieut. in Hal's regiment. He was bent on it, and really lost appetite at the prospect of refusal. Howland & Co were against; Hal, Mr. R. and Quin seemed for. But go he will.— The standing joke now is that Aunt Eliot received the $1,000 left her by Aunt Pratt less the war tax!—A performance I presume of the astute Philip H. Sears.[22] It was not so tough as usual for little Wife to let me go, because she has had a longer visit than she expected. But she cried a good deal, poor child, and was sad to look upon. Good bye small woman! It may always be for the last time, but we won't think of it. Things are too uncertain for such talk. I kissed wee Co-co and she said "Good by papa; yoo go 'way and not come back no more." And so, after *vive valeque* all round to the train that landed me in Boston in good time for the 8.30 express for N. York. In the sleeping car found Geo. Dexter, who is going back to his business, and who came to see me at Beverly. He looks very well & but little changed, from his college days.[23]

September 27, Tuesday.

Got the Astor a little before 7 A.M. It is a pleasant break in the journey to have an hour there for wash & breakfast. To straighten my legs, started to walk to Jersey City Ferry, in the Astor entry stood a tall Major General, whom recognized, from photographs, as Hooker. Was much disappointed in his appearance; there is a great want of character about his mouth, and, in addition, he was shaky about the legs, red in the face and had a boiled eye, like one who had been on a great spree.[24] The 8 A.M. train brought me at 4.30 P.M. to Baltimore. A Dr. Brockenbrough? (D.D.) sat by me, a Christian Commission man &c. &c. who, like many of his cloth, has studiously worked himself up by the study of rebel enormities. However, the treatment of our prisoners, by the enemy, is beyond all shadow of doubt, most outrageous, and not in keeping with their military conduct in general.[25] Had just clever time to get by a carriage to the boat, hard by. There was a great jam of freight & soldiers & civilians on board, but the weather was fine and it made no difference. Had a chance, before sunset, to look at the river & upper bay, which are quite pretty with moderately high banks, wooded or cultivated.

September 28, Wednesday.

After an early breakfast from the universal frying pan, landed at the Fortress [Monroe] at 7.15 A.M. Here was a long wait for the very slow Washington mail boat, appropriately called the "Express." Loafed about the street, or the road, and noticed pomegranites and figs nearly ripe, in one of the little gardens. At 10 we got off again and paddled wearily up stream. There was an accession in form of a strong detachment of Christian Commissioners, nearly all Methodists; a singular, and curious body; to most of us seeming very narrow & bigoted; yet possibly mainly right without, and, at any rate, quite justified in having their own opinions. They had an intense desire to obtain dinner and to sit all together at table!—also justifyable. They were going to relieve other delegates, the rule being that none should volunteer for less than 6 weeks service. We were late at City Point, and so the mail waggon never got me to the camp till after dark. Gen. Meade received me very kindly as did Gen. Humphreys to whom presented two scent-bags of Mrs. Lyman's manufacture; also there were useful gifts from her & Co to Simon Barstow. Cadwalader & Christiancy have gone—mustered out. The two French officers also have departed. The fact is, old De Chanal wrote some pretty Union letters, officially, whereof one fell into the paws of the Minister of Marine, who married a secesh. Thereat he raised a row and it was implied to M. le Colonel that he might as well inspect the gun manufactories, and not write so much politics. Otherwise all goes as usual, but have come just at the nick of time; for orders are out that the army should be ready to move at 4 tomorrow morning. The staff to be prepared at 6, but tents not struck till further orders.[26]

September 29, Thursday.

The move now proposed consisted of an advance both on the right and the left flanks. On the right, towards Richmond, taking the north side of the river; on the left towards the Boydton plank road and South-side rail. The strategic object was two-fold; first, to effect threatening lodgments as near as possible to these points, gaining whatever we could by the way; and, secondly, to prevent Lee from reinforcing Early.[27] Accordingly Ord, with the 18th Corps, crossed at Aiken's landing advancing towards Chaffins' (Chapin's) farm, where he stormed a fort (Harrison) getting 16 cannon and 200 or 500 prisoners. Birney, crossing with the 10th Corps, near Deep Bottom, advanced on the New Market road and joined on Ord's right. They then endeavored to carry the line on Chaffin's bluff, but were repulsed, Gens. Ord & Stannard being wounded, and Gen. Burnham killed. But they held their ground first captured and turned the fort & works against the enemy.[28] This day, we on our part, were not to advance in force, so as to leave time for the enemy to get over towards their left. About 9.30 to Hancock's, where of course the General talked a long while—they were all packed over there and Mitchell and the rest were fast asleep on the boards that had been used for tent-floors. Dr. Doherty, bright & awake, was very proud over a bullet hole he had discovered in his rubber coat which had been rolled up on his saddle and was punctured at Reams Station. They have at last stopped the Whitworth bolts by putting the railroad, between Meade's & Hancock's stations, in a *covered way*. This railroad, 8½ miles long, was completed in 9 days.[29] Then to Jones' house, where was Gen. Parke, now in command of the 9th Corps. About 1.30 we got to Globe Tavern. Gregg had pushed his cavalry out west of Reams Station and had had some skirmishing. Two divisions of the 9th Corps were massed near the Gurley house (these are the 3 white divs. consolidated in two, under Potter & Willcox). In a short time, Gen. Baxter, with 700 men, was ordered to reconnoitre towards Poplar Spring church. He advanced and got as far as the church and drove in their outposts upon which they fired shells into the church road. He returned without loss.[30] At 4.40 the enemy's cavalry in strong force, fell on Gregg, with brisk carbine firing and a good deal of cannonading. They drove in his outposts and blew up one of his caissons, but he held with his main body, with small loss. This ended the day's reconnaissance and we returned to camp, after dark. It is different now from those long June days when you could see to shoot till going on for 9 o'clock!

September 30, Friday.

Engaged a solemn, & very black boy John, during Albert's sickness. He used to work for Biddle and is reputed honest. We were all up and saddled early, again, but did not ride out till 8.30 when we went to Hancock, still at Deserted House, of course. He holds from the river to the Jerusalem plank, then come the negro division, then Crawford's extending to the Weldon R.R. There is a bastioned fort on the site of the Blick house, close to the railroad (Wadsworth), and another corresponding, on the rear line (Dushane).— Potter & Willcox had been massed as before mentioned, and Griffin and Ayres were taken out of the line and moved out towards Poplar Church early supported by Parke with his two Divisions. At 12 we got to Globe Tavern. Gen. Warren was at the front, Griffin had the lead, Ayres moving so as to be in his rear in moving out, or on his right if faced towards Petersburg. Parke moved out keeping more to the south. There was already some artillery firing on part of the rebels. At 12.45 there was brisk musketry beyond the church, which, however, was not prolonged. About 2 we had news that Griffin had handsomely taken a line & redoubt, getting a piece of artillery also. 2.45. The General rode to the scene of action; some 2½ miles off. The farm was that of Peeble, whose house stands on a ridge, not high but commanding—a little to the north of it, by a log barn is the captured redoubt with a very well made infantry parapet forming part of a new, exterior line, running from the Lead works in a general S.W. direction & intended to cover the Boydton plank road and the South-side R.R. This line was defended by Archer's brigade and by dismounted cavalry. The principal attacking force was a brigade commanded by Col. Gwynne, whom met at dinner given by Joe Hayes. He got up from a sick bed to go out and was now lying down in the Peeble house, his horse having fallen on him and bruised him seriously.[31] The house was shot through by a good many bullets and hit by some shells. Our loss was but small in the attack, not over 100, because the men went up handsomely. We got 60 prisoners. Inside the redoubt lay two dead rebel artillerymen, at least one was of that arm, having bright blue pantaloons with a red cord. In front they were burying two or three of our men and a corporal was marking their names on a headboard, copying from letters found in their pockets. There was a provost guard line along the breastwork to keep back stragglers. The General took a stand at the redoubt and issued orders to have the 9th Corps form upon the left and advance with "Griffin." Ayres had already taken the continuation of the line to the right of G[riffin] finding only a number of pickets; close to the Chapel house they had a redoubt, not yet done. At 4.15 the General went to the Peeble house, to wait developments. To the north of this farm, beyond a narrow fringe of wood, was the extensive, open, Pegram farm; then another skirt of wood, and then, to the N.E. the Boswell farm.[32] On this the enemy massed and, as Parke advanced, fell diagonally on Potter's right flank; for Griffin had failed to advance in line of battle with Parke. This attack was announced by cheers and heavy musketry in the wood beyond the Pegram house. Potter's people were thrown into complete confusion and came back, followed by the enemy and losing over 1,000 prisoners. Griffin, too late to turn the defeat to victory, but in time to restore the line, advanced and drove back the rebels of whom some even crossed the Pegram farm and were only stopped at the wood this side of it. Griffin then advanced a battery and this, as well as the infantry, continued to fire till after dark; our line being then about the Pegram house. Griffin was in favor of throwing up works there, and then connecting to the right (as being shorter); but it was decided to withdraw to the captured line, leaving Hoffman's brigade at the Pegram house. Griffin proved right, afterwards. Our loss in killed and wounded was not large, but in the 9th Corps, and that chiefly in Potter's division. The total loss of the day could not fall short of 1,900, a large proportion prisoners; that of the enemy must have been much loss; but the strategic success was an important one. Potter's horse was wounded in four places. Gen. Meade remained in consultation till 9 P.M. From the Globe Tavern we took the train to near our Headq'rs—a novel thing for a General to return to his tent after a battle, by a rail-car!

October 1, Saturday.

Rain, everything sloppy; the roads beyond the Globe Tavern threatening to get very deep; luckily there is an unusually good corduroy from near Avery house to the tavern. At 9 A.M. Hoffman's brigade was withdrawn. Mott's Div. ordered to the left by R.R. in case of a strong attempt to retake our ground. Indeed the enemy felt all along our line, pretty sharply in the morning, and finally made a real attack on Ayre's which he readily repulsed killing & wounding a great number of them. The extension is now nearly connected with Fort Wadsworth by Bragg's brigade of 3d Div. 5th Corps entrenched on the plain west of Fort Wadsworth.[33] We left H.Q. at 10.30 and, stopping a long time at Hancock's and at the tavern, got to Peeble's at 3. Here were Gregg, Warren, & Parke, with whom was much confab. It was sloppy & cold. Poor Potter was there, silent as usual, but looked disconsolate, as he well might after his mishap, which was not his fault withal. We left for Headq'rs at 5.30, and met the last of Mott's people moving to the left. This eve Gregg was attacked on the Vaughan road, but repulsed them. Strategically this day was marked by a series of feelers, all round on part of the enemy, to find what ground we really held, and perhaps also, to make us concentrate along that front. The General undertook to save time by telegraphing for a train at the tavern, of which it resulted, that, by a series of delays, we got back at 11.30, instead of 7.30! Meantime we built a rousing fire in the brick fireplace and went to sleep. At my tent was my first letter from Mimi, whereat was content.

October 2, Sunday.

Butler has a stampede on—he sent one of his theatrical despatches, saying he had a rebel deserter, an officer whom he had "put on his life," to give a correct account, and who made out pretty much all Lee's people were over there, sworn to crush Gen. B[utler] "if it took every man they had!" "Be it so!" says B. "I accept the alternative!"—"They are my equals in numbers with the *advantage* of attack!"— They did make strong assaults to retake Fort Harrison (yesterday?) but were repulsed with loss of 200 prisoners & 2 flags; also many K & W.[34] To relieve Butler, we had Washington orders, to demonstrate along our left today. Accordingly it *was commanded* that the whole skirmish line of the 5th and 9th Corps should be pushed vigorously forward, and the enemy followed up to near his works. [TL's note: Refer this to Oct. 8.] This morn—Mott should advance on the left, and Gregg should attack any cavalry in his front at daylight, but it turned out the enemy's cavalry had gone back. We left H'dq'rs at 8 and stopping on the way at Hancock's got to Globe Tavern at 10.15 where the General sent me to look for a new camp. Griffin had been ordered to move out, at the same time with Parke & Mott, and reoccupy the line by Pegram house. At 10.45 heard considerable artillery and musketry near the extreme left. This was principally from Mott, who, having driven the enemy's outposts from the continuation (to the left) of the captured line, had advanced on a redoubt in their main line, but came back without any strong attack, or much loss. The rest of the advance occupied the ground designated, with skirmishing & artillery firing, and proce[e]ded to connect to the right with Ayres. Having, with difficulty found a tolerable camping ground near Aiken house, rode to the front, and, at the Peeble house, met the General coming back from the Pegram farm (1 P.M.). While there they had a wonderful escape from a shell, which came into the staff when crowded together, took a bit out of Gen. Humphreys' horse's tail, scraped the leg of Gen. Meade's boot and buried itself between

Gens. Griffin & Bartlett who were talking together. It was one of those rebel Parrott's, with raised rings. It came butt-end formost and did not explode. They seem a poor shell, which fails often to take the grooves, and often does not explode. Orders were given to connect the lines through and refuse from just to the left of the Pegram house. Loring & Leidig were back today and remain on the staff of Gen. Parke.[35] We went to the new camp after dark. This whole country is rather redolent from having been camped over so much, but will improve with cleaning.

October 3, Monday.

It was pleasant to have a quiet day; for, since have been here, have had no time to settle myself and look after my horses; or write a decent letter home; moreover am not yet quite strong from the sickness, and a rest don't go bad. The front was quiet, though there is always a certain amount of sharpshooting between the Jerusalem plank and the river, which, at night is increased by mortar shells.

October 4, Tuesday.

The General today rode along the new line where the shovel was everywhere busy. There will be redoubts as well as the present infantry parapet and good slashings are already made & will be increased. The line is as straight as the lay of land and the necessary flankings will allow, from Ft. Wadsworth to the Pegram house, whence the refuse begins, running to the Clemens house, then the return of contravallation, running by Widow Smith's house across the Vaughan road to Ft. Dushane. The land is open west of Wadsworth; then oak woods to Pegram farm; then pine woods with openings to beyond the Vaughan road, and thence open again to Dushane. Fifth Corps has orders to hold from Fort Howard (north of Aiken) to Pegram farm, when comes the 9th Corps. A redoubt rapidly going up near Pegram house is the point nearest the enemy, apparently, & their lines may be clearly seen thence in good cannon range. There was a slight skirmish & our pickets, just there, were driven in and again drove the enemy back, and a battery opened. Otherwise, all quiet.[36]

October 5, Wednesday.

Gregg covering rear I left on Vaughan road. Went out to look for a new camp, as the General would fain move more to the left. Found a pretty spot near the widow Smith house. Here a redoubt is begun; another close by on the Vaughan road, and a third near where Forey's house was on the way to Fort Dushane. (TL: Met Mott's men going back to the 2d Corps, they having been relieved by the nigs.) No country could be more favorable to works; a soil light & sandy, and an abundance of hard pine, which is excellent for revetment.[37]

October 6, Thursday.

Gen. Humphreys sent out Aides today to inspect the picket line, throughout the army. Biddle—poor Biddle!—was selected for the 2d Corps line, nearly the whole exposed to fire. Now of course B[iddle] did it the worst way. Hancock gave him a Captain, who either from ignorance or deviltry, conducted him, mounted, straight up the Jerusalem plank; in consequence the sharpshooters opened on him as soon as he was well clear of the first crest! Naturally, to his dismay, he was shot at all the way to the lines. The General wanted a camp more removed from the rear breast-work, and succeeded in finding one, within three hundred yards of Poplar Spring Church. Two Britishers are here; Lord Mahon, son of Earl Stanhope, whom heard at the Literary Fund dinner, and Capt. Hayter. The former rather a soft subject, with a feeble aquiline nose. The latter rather dull, apparently, and good natured, with a certain air like Peel—both in the guards.[38]

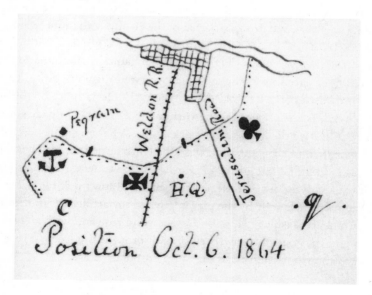

October 7, Friday.

The broad-faced Gen. Benham, in a highly unbrushed state, as usual, was up to consult about a line of works to cover City Point. He brought a lot of pro-files &c. which seemed not greatly to interest the Commander. Between 7 &

10 A.M. the Rebs made an attack on Butler's refused right, defended by Kautz' cavalry, surprised K[autz] and drove him back in confusion, and took his 8 guns. Birney (who was quite sick at the time) advanced to cover the flank & rear, repulsed the enemy, with heavy loss, and drove him back, recovering the position. The General rode to the left, accompanied part way by Gen. Bartlett, he of the gorgeous jacket, who got back a few days since from a sick-leave. The General approved the new camp-ground but said he would not yet move there; which is like him. He is always uneasy in a new camp for a day or two, and then won't move out of it. On the extreme left and rear we found the negroes, now working at redoubts & breastworks. We rode out from the Clemens' redoubt to the outer cavalry vidette, whence we could see the continuation (S.W.) of the rebel line we took, and now apparently very feebly held, as their present line runs back of this, near Boisseau's house, and about parallel to the Boydton plank.[39]— Warren has gone on a leave and Crawford is in command. Grant at Washington.

October 8, Saturday.
[TL's note: See Oct. 2.] The skirmish line was pushed forward considerably, according to orders, and drove back that of the enemy, with more or less dropping musketry. The skirmishers went forward, as far as was safe, without a real attack on the enemy's works. On the left, Parke found the continuation of the captured line deserted, except by some men who were digging it down. Towards evening orders were issued to take & burn the W. D. Davis house, on the Squirrel Level road, as it was a nest of sharp-shooters. For this, a brigade advanced and took & burned the house, after a brief fight. What is singular is, that this Davis, a Captain of rebel infantry, was killed and buried on his own farm, a few days since!—Poetical justice— During the movement our zou-zous and the 68th Penns. were put on the line between forts Howard & Hays; for there was a gap there, held only by the picket line and the artillery of the redoubts, aided by a dense slashing. This evening the wind rose and we had a sudden, frosty, night; the first since have been back. It brought the scenes a year since at Wallach's house, when we had the camp fires of evenings.

October 9, Sunday.
Took a ride to visit the three rear redoubts; they are nearly done. It is interesting to see the progress of revetting; and sloping the Scarp &c. Wrote home for my buffaloes, winter clothing &c. &c.

October 10, Monday.

Gen. Humphreys left on a week's leave. The General took a look at my camp-ground, now cleared & cleaned, but would not move there. Then he continued on, and inspected the progress on extreme left. In the 9th Corps a number of men were under-going punishment, standing on barrels on top the breast-work, with placards on their backs, as: "Coward & Shirk": "I skedaddled!" &c. In another place was a perch supported on two forked posts, 10 feet high; on which men were made to sit with a sentry over them. Gen. Parke showed us the Clemens house work, which is a swallow-tail lunette looking down two roads very nicely. Also he showed us the proposed rear line, and where he would run the slashings; there is no parapet, on the rear, as yet. Rosencrantz & Craig had a funny experience today. They took a stroll, just at evening, to Fort Davison, where they asked some questions about the place, Rosie having on his Swedish coat with three stars on the shoulder! Word was presently sent to Gen. Crawford, that two suspicious characters, one in a rebel overcoat, had been in the lines! Gen. C. telegraphed to Gen. M[eade] who sent a regiment to secure the place!

October 11, Tuesday.

Gen. Doyle, commander in Nova Scotia, came to visit the General. He is an Irishman and favorably disposed to us—wore a uniform, like the undress of the Guards, and, in his little gold-laced cap, looked like a military *punchivello*. He was very jolly & bluff, and rode about most untiringly, with his dyed moustache, though they have it that he is between 60 & 70. We took him about & showed him about 3 ½ miles of parapet and 8 redoubts made in a week's time, which astonished him mightily, not to mention the slashing. Then, after giving him a bite, we rode to the Avery house, whence he could have a view of the rebel line. They were, as usual, throwing shells and sharpshooting.[40] News today of Torbert's cavalry victory near Strasburg, where he completely routed the enemy's horse under Rosser & took 11 guns, headquarter waggons, &c.[41] There were a parcel of citizens, who were tacked on to our cavalcade, some of Grant's numerous and very common friends. The losses of the Army of the Potomac proper up to Oct. 1 in this campaign are killed ____ wounded ____ missing ____ making the astounding figure of ____, to which must be added the losses of the 6th Corps in Maryland and the Valley, making a grand total of ____. From the missing are to be subtracted many killed & mortally wounded left on the field & deserters; but the largest portion, by far, must be prisoners.[42]

October 12, Wednesday.

In camp all day, writing up my diary &c. There came a Norwegian, Balling (Clinton Hall; Astor Pl.) who has an order for a picture of "Grant & his Generals" from one Benoni Howard, a N.Y. gent, who, having made a fortune on Lucifer matches, now proposes to found his collection of paintings with this as a basis. Mr. B[alling] seems to have a knack at a rapid water-color likeness, but he is not always happy, as his attempt on Gen. Meade looked like a highly intoxicated Jew. We must fear that Benoni will not get a very high work of art, though good enough for him, possibly. The weather is now magnificent; clear, warm by day, though not hot, and cool, not cold, by night. There were rumors this eve that the Penn. election had gone 5,000 democratic![43]

October 13, Thursday.

Alas & Alack! There came to me a box of pickles, but so delayed had they been at Washington, that they were nearly all mush! It is said that the 6th Corps is on its way to rejoin this army.[44] The Richmond Examiner has a despairing & desperate article on the state of affairs and complains of the immense number of absentees (deserters); so it would seem that they have a like trouble with us. The General rode over to Gen. Parke's where there was a report that the rebs were going to attack the nigs, on the left. A couple of sharpshooters, with telescopic rifles were asked by an officer if they had found good places. "Ah, good places; but *no shooting!*" On the 2d one or more rebel shells (3 inch) were found to have a filling of dust with only a little powder—query, cheating contractors?

October 14, Friday.

Rode with the General to Fort Stevenson, which now is not far from done, a work of large relief, capable of sheltering near 1,000 men, and with a bastion front. The Williams house has disappeared and the country is hardly to be recognized, so much timber has been felled and slashed.[45] There are rumors of a move by & bye, and a ridiculous story that Grant said he would be in Richmond in a couple of weeks. Some officers having been seen intoxicated, an investigation showed that over 5/6 of all the officers bought whisky of the Commissary; and of these, the average purchase was 3½ gals. pr. month!—A good deal of course goes to the men.

October 15, Saturday.

Did not ride out today, but, taking a stroll, saw Dr. Derby at his hospital (2d Div. 5th C.) He looked seedy though smiling and told me Charlie Eliot had concluded *not* to come back from Europe.[46]

October 16, Sunday.

Rode over to see Gen. Miles (now comd'ng Barlow's Div.) at the Jordan house, on the extreme right. Found him sick—feverish. Introduced to Dr. Barton. Went to enquire after Corp. W. Gilson, Co. I, 5th N.H. Vols. whose wife asked after him; he was wounded & taken in Haygood's charge at Cool Arbor. Miles said a very poor class of substitutes were now coming to the army. He had to put them in enclosed works.[47] As many as 12 deserted in one day, *to the enemy*, from the 2d Corps. Returned by our old camp. All is deserted near there. The amount of good farm manure about this country is now very great, camp sweeping &c. &c. The General sat over my camp-fire this eve and growled a little. He said of three brevet Brigadiers sent down, only one was of his nomination (Gregg's brother) and all were Pennsylvanians. The two others were Gregory & Gwynne (both brave soldiers). They have also brevetted a Col. Brown. No men may be expected, till after election, from Indiana or Ohio. The Richmond papers speak of their "victory" last Thursday. We made a reconnaissance, and, when they came out, turned & drove them back. Our loss 350. The whole somewhere near the Darbytown road. Hood with an army has suddenly turned up at Dalton![48]

October 17, Monday.

There was a perfect eruption, from City Point, of the *militaire* and the *bourgeoisie*, in carriages & on horseback. Grant, Gens. Meigs, Barnard; Eaton, Dr. Barnes, Surgeon Gen'l. Also Stanton, Fessenden, Sam Hooper! (of all men in the world), Sim Draper, & old Barney. Meigs (Qr. Mr. Gen.) is a handsome man with dark eyes, a hooked nose & a beard now getting gray; as self satisfied a looking party as ever saw!— Eaton is Com. Gen'l a stout man, nothing particular. Dr. Barnes is an uncommonly nice and intelligent gentleman, well looking also. With Secretary Fessenden (an acute, sarcastic, common sense old peep) was his son the general, who lost a leg in the Gulf department, and has a patent substitute. Stanton looks like his photographs, short, very stout with a big head & beard; a face expressive of large intelligence, but coarse. The distinguished "Sim" is very tall with a large "pot" and an expression bright, sly, & good natured. Barney didn't look like a man of much force, which fancy he is not. We toted the crowd out as far as Fort Wadsworth and showed the glories thereof, in which they seemed not much interested. Old Sam Hooper looks more like Mike Kennedy *in dies*. He even has the same shaky hands and lips.[49]— Gen. Humphreys got back this eve; luckily in time to miss his very dear friend Stanton. Gen. Meade went to City Point with them and there met Admiral Porter, Mrs. P. &c. and, returning as far as Hancock's had a high jinks there for some time. The joke was, that Biddle was entrusted with a bundle of cigars, to carry for the General, but, with his usual *à tort et à travers* style, construed it into *distributing* them broadcast among the staff. Therefore when the General asked for them, they were all gone but one! Great horror of the innocent B. and mirth inextinguishable of the staff.— The country has an idea that this army has been tremendously increased, whereas, owing to mustering out, the losses at Hatcher's Run, &c. it actually was smaller Oct. 10th than Sep. 30th.—Col. Wells, of the 34th Mass. was killed in a reconnaissance near Strasburg, a day or two since. He was brother of Mrs. Lothrop Thorndike and a most gallant & rising officer.[50]

October 18, Tuesday.

They mustered McMahon out! That's because he was noisy in favor of Mc-Clellan: a very good soldier who has fought alongside kind "Uncle John" in all the great battles. But that little Paddy Collis, because he leaves his command and runs about Pennsylvania getting election returns, is allowed to do as he chooses. Rode along left, with Gens. Meade and Humphreys. The 5th Corps has taken to cheering the general. New redoubts and batteries are going in along the line.[51]

October 19, Wednesday.

We took cars to near City Point, to see Gen Benham's new line, which stretching from near Old Court House, on Bailey's Creek, runs about north and strikes the Appomattox at a ravine. Gen. B[enham] was in waiting, with a fat horse and a huge, antiquated saddle, all just like himself. He's an old red faced, stampeded porpoise! This line, which has 7 redoubts on it, is calculated to enclose a space for the trains. Phleg Clapp came out to see me, which was kindly of him. 4,700 men, down here on sundry duty in the lines, were put at Meade's disposition. At Grant's H'dq'rs we had news that Sheridan was fighting today. Sherman was moving after Hood. There was there a Lt. Preston, taken over a year since in a boat expedition to capture Fort Sumter, and just now exchanged. He had been in the best southern prison at Columbia S.C. and had fared tolerably, but looked pale & unhealthy. Gen. Williams & Dr. Pyne dined with us. The latter is a merry priest, Irish by extraction and very conversational and bright, tinged also with a bit of vain affectation. He is somewhat noted in Washington. Charlie Mills went over to the 2d Corps, as A.A.G.[52]

October 20, Thursday.

Completed a goodly chimney in front of my tent, to which it is partly connected by a side-wall of logs and by slipping forward the tent fly. This is the first brick chimney in camp and persons deride me for so much pains, when we shortly shall move; *mais nous verrons.*[53] News of Sheridan's victory of Cedar Creek, where his army under Wright, surprised by Early, was driven back some four miles, when Sheridan, coming up, restored the day, drove the rebels in confusion and captured 23 cannon, besides recapturing 20 he had lost. The rebel General Ramseur fell, mortally wounded, into our hands. On our part, Gen. Bidwell was killed, Gens. Wright, Ricketts & Grover wounded, Cols. McKenzie & Kitchen wounded. And, lamentable to state, Charlie Lowell, commanding Reserve Brigade of cavalry, fell, mortally wounded in the spine! This last is a blow that could scarcely hit more than it does—His mother's only son now left; James was killed on the peninsula;—then his young wife, so soon to be confined—and poor Mrs. Shaw who might have leaned on him, with Bob dead and gone. It is a tragic thing![54]

October 21, Friday.

Gen. Grant came up, and with Gen. Meade, rode round the lines, with an object doubtless, for Hunt has orders to put the redoubts in condition, as to artillery, and we have rumors of a move. The goodly & argumentative Hunt gave me a disquisition on the duties of chief of artillery, about which there is so much bickering with corps and division commanders. He considers the artillery of an army as a corps command, and the batteries detailed to corps commanders, as detached brigades under the corps chief of artillery and subject to the like governance with any other detached brigade. That division commanders should give discretion to their artillery officers in the placing and use of batteries, as their interference continually is productive of damage. This is one of the general's sore points, about which he has had endless discussions with everyone, from Gen. Meade downward.[55]

October 22, Saturday.

Raw & blustering. Dined with Crawford. He is a strong anti McClellan, and, of course, powerful for the Administration. Don't know exactly what to think of C.—brave, perhaps dashing, untiring in his endeavors to introduce order and discipline, but specious, & talkative; unpopular with his officers also. He gave a funny description of the retreat of Banks from Stonewall; how news came to Strasburg that Jackson was crossing the river on the flank and how Banks said, in his measured way, "Gen. Crawford, what had we best to do?" and finally concluded not to be in a hurry. Then the battle of Winchester; the flight through the town; the grand retreat in a waggon of Capt. Collis, the commander of the body-guard; and the poetical peculiarities of Mr. Adj. Gen. Copeland, keeper of the General's brains![56]

October 23, Sunday.

Clapp was up and spent a while with me, going to dine to the squadron. The General rode to City Point, to consult, probably, on the coming move. Took a ride with Barstow—slow work, as that hero exercises at a walk. The Reb papers have a purported reprint of one of Custer's letters to a young woman, a coarse production, intended to show the .norals of our officers.[57]

October 24, Monday.

The happy Barstow departed on a leave. Macy has been breveted Brigadier and was anxious to know what had become of his letter of appointment. Told him the recommendations had been duly forwarded and he would be appointed. Gen. Hunt told me a variety of stories of the Scott & Worth imbroglio where Hitchcock played a leading part. Hitchcock he accused as a coward and said that once he was ordered on an expedition against the Indians, whereat he wrote a private letter to the wife of the Secretary of War, asking for some more intellectual position than a frontier post, surrounded by low-toned officers! Letter got returned to his comd'ng officer by A.G. with endorsement "Application of Capt. Hitchcock for change of post, respectfully returned to be forwarded through the proper channels!" Whereat awful endorsements from Com'dn'g officer and many others! There have been quite sharp allusions against Meade lately in the papers (the Cropsy affair injured him) and a most savage and abominably untrue attack in Beecher's paper, the "Independent."[58]

October 25, Tuesday.

Gen. Meade complained to Gen. Grant, who said the article was bad and assured the General that he would show his private despatches to him and he there would see the invariable tone of praise. This was kind but was not the General's point, who wanted something published. He read me the correspondence; told him not to mind, that he had Grant and Stanton on his side and a good record, and history was not based on newspapers; upon which he laughed.— Writing up my diary all day—.

October 26, Wednesday.

There was a long, confidential, order of march out today—to corps commanders. The sense was: Hancock, with 2d and 3d Divs. to march at about 2.30 at night down the Vaughan road and cross Hatcher's run, then keep north to the Boydton plank, and, if the other moves were successful, keep on & strike the Southside R.R. Gregg's cavalry, on Quaker road, to cover his left, 9th Corps, leaving 1,500 men on the line, march at the same hour and pass out of our left line of works on the Squirrel Level road, and, if possible, force the enemy's line near Hatcher's run (it being supposed that the continuation of their line, running N.E. & S.W. had not been fully completed near the run), 5th Corps to support & form on their left, marching out at same place & time and bearing a little to the left (south). Waggons all to go to City Point. No waggons to the front but ambulances (also a few of Gen. H'dq'rs.) Three days [rations] on the men and 60 rounds. 5th Corps to leave 2,500 men of Crawford's Div. on the line. 1st Div. 2d Corps to hold the lines in presence of the enemy. If the direct attack did not succeed, the 5th Corps to work to the left across Hatcher's run and try to turn the works and form junction with Crawford.[59] At 11 we broke camp near Aiken's, and went to one close to Poplar Grove church, stopping to confab at Warren's. Then the General rode over and confabbed with Parke, and finally inspected the place where they were cutting a double way for the troop to march out, by Fort Cummings—wasn't satisfied and sent me to tell Gen. P[arke] to look out for it. We were back at camp at dark, where we had tents & baggage in light marching order.

October 27, Thursday.

Up at 4.15—very dark and some little rain—at 6 we heard shots to westward, denoting some little skirmishing, probably outposts. 6.15 A.M. the General rode out to Peeble's house and thence to Fort Cummings, where he waited developments. As we rode along we cut the rear of the 5th Corps near camp and found it passing out on the left of Fort Cummings while the negro div. of the 9th Corps was marching out on the right. At 7.30, 8, and 9.30 there was brief, but brisk musketry from the W. & S.W. This came in part from Hancock (who forced Hatcher's run, capturing 50 prisoners and took in reverse such of the enemy's works as were parallel to & on the west side of the run)—in part from Warren & Parke, the former of whom put in two new regiments against the line of works they had discovered, which regiments came back in confusion, on being fired into. It was found that the line was finished and too strong to carry. At 8.10 A.M. the enemy began to throw spherical case from two guns, doing little or no damage, in the woods. 8.40. Gen. Grant with some staff officers and Gen. Barnard, also a couple of cits, arrived. At 11 both Generals rode to the Watkin's house, where was Gen. Parke (a little beyond). A few minutes after we continued to Warren, who was not far from N. Clemens house. Here came Ayres & Griffin—of Griffin's 4,400 men, 2,800 never fired a musket in battle! Crawford was ordered to move to the left, cross Hatcher's run and try to get round on the rear of their line. As we sat there an unexploded spherical case came near taking off the hind legs of Grant's 4,000-dollar horse. Roundabout here was a good bit of cleared land, the Watkins, Clemens and Armstrong farms. Passing the latter house we crossed the run at 12.30 P.M.—a narrow, deep, miry brook, mostly impassible for infantry. Here was an old dam, & opposite was an epaulement for guns; from this, or even from below this, ran a rifle-pit, which passed along the bank of the stream till it got to a point opposite the line running from them north-east, which it joined by crossing the run. Warren was there and Crawford's men were advancing, their right resting on the run. Here the woods, filled with tangled underbrush, were fearful; as bad as any portion of the Wilderness. On the other side of the run the rebel works were also in woods, but less thick. Continuing on a narrow wood road, past Dabney's steam sawmill, we came on the tail of the 2d Corps, moving.[60] We kept on with difficulty for some time, & finally halted, while an aide was sent on to find Gen. Hancock. Meanwhile heavy firing rose to the southward, or, as it were, in our rear. This turned out to be Davies' brigade fighting, on the Quaker road, with the enemy's cavalry. However, Gen. Meade ordered a brigade of infantry halted, against emergencies. Meantime word came back that Hancock was on the Boydton plank road and wanted to keep on to the railroad; but orders were at once sent to halt him, while we kept on and got to him at 1.30, under a big oak, on the road, and close to the site of Wilson's steam mill. Hence quite to the run, on the right of the road, the land was open, much of it corn field; on the left the woods straggled as far as the road in some places. There were some cross undulations of ground, the most notable, one that covered the run from our view and where stood a house within about 500 yards of the stream. On the left of the road was Gregg's cavalry, also Gen. Mott with part of his division. The 2d Div. (today under Egan) was near the run and skirmishing briskly. Several of our batteries were firing and the enemy were replying, some of the stray shot coming over our way. Egan was preparing now to force the bridge, and had asked for one more brigade, which was given. Already he had got the head of the bridge and planted a flag on it. Meantime the enemy sensibly placed a battery to enfilade the plank road and soon gave us a tremendous dose, killing a man and a horse and forcing us generals to get to the opening of the woods, on the Dabney mill road. Before we went it was whimsical to see the two cits & not a few officers form a "queue" behind that big oak! This was 3 P.M. Hancock & Gregg were here all the time; Grant (who is noticeably an intrepid man) had ridden alone down the road to look a little; got into a hot place, got his horse's legs tangled in a piece of telegraph wire and ran much risk, man & horse. He returned, quite red, and said sharply "Some damned fool had thrown telegraph wire in the road." "Yes," quoth Hancock in his high voice, "Yes—great many damned fools in this army!"— (We feel the want of officers severely now; so many disabled or slain, or mustered out on expiration of service.)— Soon after we rode back to camp, established near Armstrong house, getting there at 4.15. Grant left for City Point, but left orders for Hancock to withdraw at 9 A.M. tomorrow; for he saw the game was blocked, and that he could not break their line and drive them up their works so as to establish a short line to Southside Railroad, from the Pegram house angle. At 5.30 P.M. came news that Hancock had had a severe fight. A. P. Hill crossed a heavy column over the run, between Crawford (whose progress was very slow through the woods) and Hancock and fell on Mott, part of whose division was covering the right of Hancock and formed along the east edge of the corn field. Mott's lines were broken and came back, still fighting. A battery put in the edge of the field was overrun, and Egan's rear was exposed. The latter, with gallantry, faced by the rear rank & charged the rebels on the flank, driving them in confusion back into the woods. He then received in turn and repulsed several attacks. Meantime Gregg was attacked violently by Hampton's whole force but held on manfully. Hancock had the best of it, but, when the dusk closed his men were much scattered & exhausted, & were short of ammunition. Gen. Meade therefore sent by Maj. Mitchell, the choice either to withdraw in the night, or to receive Ayres & Crawford & fight it out in the morning. Hancock chose the former, though Warren was eager to fight it out. Had been sent about 4.30 P.M. to ask Gen. Griffin if he found any point for an assault, to which he replied, no; that Gen. Bartlett had reconnoitred with a skirmish line and had found the works complete even to a log on top to shoot under, and an abattis in front. Hancock determined to withdraw, and accordingly the Dabney's Mill road, now choked with straggling pack animals, was cleared; and Egan's division fell back to Dabney's Mill, where it took position to cover the passage of Mott's people. Ayres had already moved at nightfall to the same neighborhood. A heavy rain which increased the difficulty of movements or of getting up ammunition assisted in determining Hancock's course. He was obliged to leave some 250 wounded behind, in a house, having no ambulances to remove them. Many strange escapes occurred today, & recaptures. Lt. Woolsey rode straight into a dozen reb cavalry on a wood-road—two shot at him, and one seized him round the waist; but he hit his captor between the eyes & broke away at a gallop. Bingham was taken & slipped away; Dresser (having on a rubber coat) rode right up to a rebel brigade, which had just crossed the run to attack Mott, and covered his retreat by asking some indifferent questions. Capt. Mills riding down to Gen. Egan, on the Boydton road, came on a rebel battalion which had got cut off. He rode back & told Mitchell, who took a regiment and went & captured the whole lot.[61] Many squads of the enemy, having our men as prisoners, fell into Crawford's line and were taken. There was a strong disposition to blame Crawford for not getting up to attack the enemy on the west side of the run in the rear; but others said that the thickets prevented, & certainly they were very bad. *Had* he attacked, the enemy must have been cut to pieces on that part of the field.

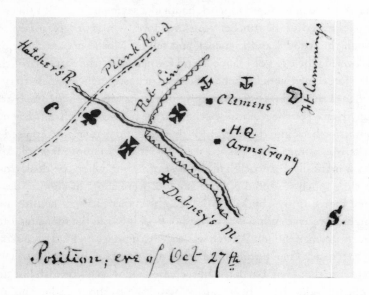

October 28, Friday.

As soon as it was light Griffin's skirmishers opened heavily. It was a misty morning, & Headquarters were already packed to pull out. The whole force had orders to fall back by the way they came, and Mott had already taken position on the Vaughan road to cover Egan's withdrawal. Gen. Meade having cautioned Parke, the day before, to look out for his right, he had refused it, carrying an entrenched line to within about a mile of Fort Cummings, running north of & parallel to Squirrel Level road. After consulting with Warren & Hancock, the General rode to the Watkins house, in front of which they were preparing a breastwork for one of the successive lines of battle by which the 9th & 5th Corps were to fall back; this was about 9; at 10.15 A.M. we got to Peeble's house passing some of Ayres people halted on the way. The flank line was still manned as we passed. Our losses in this move were nearly 1,900, of whom 650 taken. We took over 900 prisoners.[62] At the same time Butler moved to his right, & about 3 P.M. yesterday attempted to storm a line, with part of the 18th Corps, under Weitzel, and was driven back with heavy loss. His move consisted in the 18th Corps going via Varina & Deep Bottom, up the Williamsburg stage road, past the field of Fair Oaks (beyond which they found the enemy's line); while the 10th Corps moved to the right from their Chaffin's farm lines & demonstrated.[63] As we waited at Peebles up rode a motley set, Gen. L. Thomas, A.G., U.S.A.—an old womanish, smiling old fellow, with a big nose; a lot of staff officers, and two figures of fun, who were presented as *Chef de batallion* de Boissac, *sous* Lieut. Anatole Viscompte de Monthurthe; also a fat young man, who turned out to be Col. Darling holding the perilous position of aide to Gen. Sanford com'dn'g. N.Y. militia! De Boissac, Monthurthe and Darling seemed to be travelling on their cheek, which was immeasurable. De B. was a little chap, chunky and done up in a tight jacket covered with braid and medals. De M. had on a black dress coat and red trowsers and fez, and was as vulgar & gabbling a Frenchman as ever saw—the other was of more wit, though likewise a gabble-pate (Gen. De Trobriand since said these were only sergeants in the army; but fancy they were what they professed, risen from the ranks). Darling (who had come down to electioneer for the Republican candidate for Governor, Fenton, in N. York—in case of his election D[arling] was to be Qr. Mr. Gen.!) afterwards dined, slept, & breakfasted at H'dq'rs without a shadow of invitation. His cheek was the more admirable for being so quiet! Last night Miles' men ran into the "crater" & grabbed a couple of field officers and 20 men. My good Rosie returned very tight at eve, a fault of his; sometimes he will be quite straight, at others he will be sprung once a week or so. The two Frenchies lived with Gen. Meade and amused our evening by rhodomontade. Our camp, as before, near Aiken house.[64]

October 29, Saturday.

Carefully bowed off the Gauls, with an orderly, implying they were to stay off. (*N.B.* Showed them the lines yesterday). Col. Church, Editor of the Army & Navy Journal, was in my tent, a little man, from "Hubville" apparently; sufficiently intelligent.[65]

October 30, Sunday.

A certain Capt. Alden A.A.G. came from Washington with a large lot of brevets for meritorious officers; Crawford, Barlow, Griffin, Ayres, Miles, Gregg, Potter &c. to be brevet Maj. Gens. Cols. Macy, Gregg, Wainwright &c. Bvt. Brig.

Gens.— The enemy flanked our pickets, while Mott's men were relieving by Miles' & gobbled 50 or more, which gave rise to considerable musketry. Duane was back tonight, looking poorly. The General [Meade] is ordered to hand in a report on the whole campaign, at which he is despairing.[66]

October 31, Monday.

Busy writing out my own notes for the General's report, to help the gaps in his memory and his papers. He drives like a steamer, when he once takes his pen! All the Regulars—about 1,200 only—are to go to N. York to recruit & rest. Macy was over, anxious over the brevet.[67]

November 1–
December 31, 1864

Private Note-book before Petersburg, Dec. 3d, 1864
In case of my death, I ask that this book may be
sent *unread* to my wife!

———— ⛬ ————

November 1, 1864, Tuesday.

We were favored with my chief Brig. Gen. Schouler, A.G. Mass. He smiled about, feebly, and agreed with everybody. We represented to him the troubles of the army, especially the sending of Germans to fill our regiments. Sleeper was over: he is well of his wound and has a pretty full battery, but no officers. Both his Lieutenants were killed at Hatcher's Run. Louis Cabot was over, also, from the distant Terry. He described their move to me (at the same time as Hatcher's run). Now he is the Headq'r guard of the 10th Corps, which Gen. Terry commands, Weitzel having the 18th. Cabot spent the night with the squadron, where Flint has a big chimney, lined at the bottom with brick, and the rest of wood & mud. Maj. Hastings left today, to be mustered out & Lt. Col. Brinton reigns in his stead as Judge Adv.[1]

November 2, Wednesday.

Birth-day of my Mimette, who is 28, *par bleu*. She has a way of saying that it is very lucky I am bald, because it makes up for only three years between us! Capt. Wistar came to be on Gen. Humphreys' staff. He is a blackeyed Philadelphian—a very good fellow, and belongs to the regular infantry. Dr. Bill Thorndike was over to see me, and was a cheering light, as the day was varied with rain & hail. His health is restored by his visit home, where they are feeling very depressed over the death of Col. Wells, Lothrop's brother-in-law.[2]

November 3, Thursday.

Flocks of election commissioners, scurvy looking fellows, are coming down here to look after the presidential vote. Voting is a state matter; from some states there is no permission for soldiers to vote. Those who can, vote either by proxy or by commissioners. By proxy, they publickly declare that they wish to give to a certain person at home the power to vote for them, and to him a proper document is duly forwarded. By commissioner, they appear before this officer and their vote is registered and given to him, in a sealed envelope.

November 4, Friday.

Channing Clapp appeared, escorting two gentlemen, one Cunningham who married Fanny Cary, the other a cousin of John M. Forbes and looking not unlike him. Both very pleasant gentlemen and so brought back real Boston with their stories of China & Japan and their talk about "taking a little run down to Calcutta." They dined with the General, after having visited the lines. There are rumors of an expedition against Wilmington by Porter, who, with a big fleet, has been lying some time at Fort Monroe. The rebel ram Albemarle lying near Plymouth, N.C. has been very gallantly blown up by a torpedo boat under Lieut. Cushing. Rode with Miles as far as 2d Corps H.Q. He told me what a miserable man Gen. Ledlie was; how he was drunken and entirely incapable.[3] The soldiers are now making winter quarters, to enjoy them while they can.— Ledlie, when Gen. Bartlett came to him, before the mine went up and told him the parapet & abattis were still in the way, replied, "Well, they must get over them as well as they can!" That is the way things are managed in the 9th Corps. What I fear is, that Parke, a fine officer and charming man, is not stern & rough enough to bring their loose ends into shape.

November 5, Saturday.

Taking a ride to the left noticed that the railroad is extending in that direction, having already passed Ft. Wadsworth. We are favored now with the usual rumors, that accompany lying still in camp.—Hancock to enlist a veteran Corps—Parke to take the 2d.—Humphreys to take the 2d—Gibbon to take the 9th, Hancock to have Butler's command—Thomas to relieve Meade—Both armies to be commanded by Meade, &c. &c. It was cool this night, with a little ice. The enemy attacked our picket line by night and got several of the pits, but were driven out with a loss of between 100 & 200, including 40 prisoners.

November 6, Sunday.

Had numerous Sunday visitors, including Gen. Warren, Roebling, Sleeper, &c. but heard nothing very new except that Roebling will leave the service this winter, to help his father in the great bridge over the Ohio at Cincinnati; also, *peutêtre*, to marry Warren's sister.[4]

November 7, Monday.

Warm showers—muggy. Mimi has been for some days at Aunt Mary's who is very kind to her and looks upon little Cora as a paragon. Wifekin has written me that she wants *buttons* from distinguished Generals.[5] Gregg was down to reconnoitre over the Nottoway, and found no forces, of any account. He gobbled a number of the enemy's scouts. Up to Nov. 1 the *heavy* guns and mortars, alone, have cast 890 tons of shot & shell at the defences of Petersburg! Boarded up the open front of my fly leaving a door, and, to Rosie's indignation, a large opening over it for ventilation:—the frigid Swede would have everything tight and a big fire.[6]

November 8, Tuesday.

Election day, and one of the most momentous—indeed the most momentous since the days of Washington. Ben. Butler is in New York, with the regulars, &c. &c. to keep order and has issued a proclamation, to the effect "if you don't keep quiet, I'll make you!"— Out of some 19,000 votes which were cast in this army, Lincoln's majority was over 8,000. Having got some buttons for Mimi from Gen's. Meade, Humphreys &c. rode over to Gen. Hancock to beg of him. The valiant one, with his big face, like that of a Dutch admiral of Rembrandt, was steaming away in a tide of discussion with Gibbon, and plying the fire from a small flask. He drinks too much for his health, though never saw him at all tipsy on any occasion. He told me he expected to leave the Corps, under new orders, and would go tomorrow. He was in a great state about the brevets that had been sent back to Washington for revision. Endeavored to explain to him that Gen. Meade had done it only to prevent gross injustice to various officers, in the matter of seniority. There was a flag of truce sent by the enemy this morning to ask to bury their dead from the night attack. There were 16 bodies lying outside our line, on Gibbon's front not far from the Mine. They belonged to Holcom's S.C. legion, who had been "spoiling for a fight," and now had all they wanted. Being fresh troops, they were much interested in their comrades, and were particular even to carry in their hats that had fallen off.

There was much curiosity to know about our election; in fact Grant looked for an attack from them, but all was quiet. News came of the capture of the rebel privateer "Florida" by the "Wachusett" in the Brazilian port of Bahia—a plainly illegal act, though a welcome one to ship owners.[7]

November 9, Wednesday.

Went to Gen. Warren & Parke for more buttons. Warren, who employs his mind incessantly about something, had a microscope with which he was examining the little water animals. Showed him a Cyclops with its egg-bags, which he had not before seen. There was a south wind and it was summer warm. At Parke's saw Gens. Bartlett & Potter, who contributed buttons also. In the evening the cannon & mortars on the Jerusalem plank could not be heard at Headquarters, though usually they make a loud noise. These detonations spreading, or stopping, are not easily explained. There was the case of Raccoon Ford, of Locust Grove, &c. &c.[8]

November 10, Thursday.

Enough news has come to confirm Lincoln's election.—No rows any where, and everything very creditable. A grand spectacle of order in the midst of most terrible war! Rode out with Gen. Humphreys and saw some dress parades, by brigades of the 9th Corps—very creditable. The nigs went through their evolutions in handsome style.

November 11, Friday.

The Republicans are in a great fuss over alleged distribution of fraudulent votes; and, on the representation of some commissioners, Gen. Meade has arrested several persons, among others a McKibbin, brother of the two who are in the regular infantry. Stanton was evidently in high excitement as he sent down a Lt. Col. & a boat expressly to bring up the culprits.[9] Our mess nigger Anderson who has a grave clerico-military air, did disturb the public peace by suddenly threatening to punch the head of Chef Mercier! And, after confinement in the guard house, further menaced a smashing of our crockery! Whereat he was again clapped in durance for the night.

November 12, Saturday.

Heard that Fannie Foote had a little girl—*bon!* and doing well—*bon! bon!*[10] Rode over and visited friend Sleeper in rear of Fort Stevenson. He was in the usual neat hut, with a black walnut mantel, which he had constructed from a leaf of an old table. Also he boasted a pair of tongs, which a prevoyant private had picked up for him last summer and carried ever since, in the battery waggon! The papers published a contraband piece of news that Sherman had let go connections, left Thomas to look after Hood, destroyed the Atlanta & Chattanooga rail, and was marching on Charleston S.C.! Orders from Grant to seize the papers & allow none to get over the lines.[11]

November 13, Sunday.

Lt. Col. Commandant in New Brunswick, came up with Comstock and we showed him as far as Griffin's line. The day was raw and do think the gallant Colonel was cold & not much interested. His only remark, of a military nature was of the corduroy road."Oh! Ah! Very good *now* you know, but what will you do in *wet* weather?" which was rather funny. The railroad is now done to near Poplar Spr. Ch. where the terminus will be. Barstow was back from his leave looking very lively. Gen. Gibbon dined with us, and was much overcome at our raw oysters. He has two brothers in the Secesh army and his sister came only the other day from the south. Weighed today, in ordinary clothes 169 lbs.[12]

November 14, Monday.

The Quarter Master got some of the Engineers to put up a flag staff for the Headquarters. It is of a single stick of hard pine, elegantly tapering, and 70 feet high—a remarkable stick of timber. Col. Russell, of the colored troops, was over and told some funny stories of his nigs—e.g. how some of them put, for experiment, a shell on the fire—one party holding that it wouldn't "splode," cause "er gone done shot out er cannon," the other, that it would—which it did! Likewise how a Yankee cast an empty shell he had filled with wet powder, into a group of gamblers of both colors, and, when the party, stampeded by the fizzing, scattered, stepped in & picked up the greenbacks![13] It was a raw day, and, as rode out with the General (to see about a tiff between the hospitals & the Qr. Mrs. concerning putting down a railroad platform at the terminus), began to feel cold and rather sick. At Gen. Parke's, Loring gave me some whisky but that didn't do, so rode home, by which time had a regular malarial chill. It is very disagreeable—cold; pain and sickness at stomach; general prostration. Dr. McGill (a very well educated young man) gave me some sugar of lead and opium and, in two or three hours was all over the worst of it.[14]

November 15, Tuesday.

Gen. Humphreys boiled over on the exaggeration of the importance of some cavalry fights; e.g. Wilson, on the Burkesville raid, had 5,000, he had 4 distinct fights, and was finally routed with loss of all his artillery. His loss was 13 k.

110 w.!!— In directing some works on his front, by moonlight, Gen. Egan got a bad wound in the arm.[15]

November 16, Wednesday.

Sheridan has been appointed a Maj. General in the regular army in the same order that accepts McClellan's resignation. This is a *coup de théâtre*, appointing a man for gallantry in the field in contradistinction to one who resigns. Meade is cross over it, and no wonder, as he has been completely passed over, after hard labor in a department of little honor. Gen. Canby has been dangerously wounded by a guerilla, in going up the Arkansas River. Sherman reported at Kinston Ga. Gen. Burnside was down and spent the night at 9th Corps headq'rs. Got a pair of trowsers of the Qr. Mr. today for $3.10. They are made for officers and are really pretty good.[16]

November 17, Thursday.

Orders were suddenly issued to prepare rations and trains for a move—all corps to be in readiness. We concocted an excitement on the strength of this; but after all it proved only to be one of Butler's mare's nests that the enemy were certainly about to evacuate Petersburg! Rode with the General to Hancock. They have some new men there—Maj. Cairncross, A.A.G.—a Bull, *çi-devant* private soldier, and Dr. —— a very gentlemanly man, acting medical director. It finally has been arranged to transfer the negroes all to Butler, giving him thus a corps. He will return us nearly as many white troops (new regiments) which will be better from all sides. Two negro regiments have gone. The evening train brought back Albert looking as fat as possible; whereupon the faithful nig John will retire, with a small present and a certificate.[17]

November 18, Friday.

There appeared Messrs. Kirkpatrick & Herbert, both Britons; the former a diplomatic party, the other a former officer and now an Oxford person. What *is* the reason that Englishmen, whether they know anything or not, always succeed in looking more or less idiotic? This Herbert was especially successful in the attempt and simpered like a weak school-girl. Either from folly or courage, he insisted on going all over the ticklish places on the lines, where his curiosity might have been rewarded by a ball in the pate. This morning—no! night—we had a desertion—47 head of cattle got a stampede, rushed up the Halifax road, and slammed through our picket line; greeted by the enemy's picket, they dashed on and were only brought up by the main line, whose scare was turned to the gladness of fresh beef! Warm rain in the eve. There arrived Major Smythe, Royal Artil. and Mr. Lunn from Montreal. The former a gentlemanly, bald, florid Britton, the latter a solid pleasant, blue-nose bourgeois.[18]

November 19, Saturday.

A driving northeaster, which delayed the mail, so that it didn't arrive during the whole day. Have not yet got over the chill that had the other day—bowels still out of order. Some officer of the guard got it into his head he would have the sentinels call the hours, so all the camp stayed awake, as well as the guardians, which brought down a torrent of eloquence against them the next morning!

November 20, Sunday.

Still rainy. The politician Wilson and that zero demagogue Gardner were down in a train. Verily I turn my back on such.[19]

November 21, Monday.

Quiet, drenching rain, *voila tout.*

November 22, Tuesday.

As Smythe and Lunn were guests of Gen. Humphreys, Gen. Meade turned out some cavalry for them. The weather was clear at last and we all rode along the rear line, (the cavalry being on the Jerusalem road) visiting Fort Stevenson, where was a small garrison of Germans—a proper dirty set! They are most certainly very inferior to our natives. There was one in a moustache, spectacles and long hair, with the slovenly devil-may-care of an unmistakable German Bursch—an odd figure to put in a blouse & sky blue trowsers! We saw the brigades of Brev. Brig. Gen. Gregg and Davies. They had been turned out hastily but looked hardy & well, men & horses. After which we returned to the General's headq'rs on the road.— Saw there Capts. Treikle, Arrowsmith &c. and enjoyed a couple of real Newton pippins. It had begun now to blow up fresh, and, by the time that got to Hancock's (whither the General had sent me, to say that the gentlemen were coming) it was right cold. Hancock has not yet his orders, and Gen. Humphreys is fussing and fuming, afraid that he shan't have any fighting this autumn—as he is to command the 2d Corps. We all were in after sunset, the grave Lunn bringing up the rear in a[n] ambulance. Kershaw has left the Valley and is over opposite Butler, whereat Benjamin makes excuse, with that and the weather, not to send any white troops yet, in exchange for the nigs. Dr. Milhau, medical director of the 5th A.C. has left—an excellent man and a loss to us.[20]

November 23, Wednesday.

Cold last night; ice this morning. Capt. Dallas, Prov. Ml. has gone to Washington and is relieved by Phil Schuyler—who is back from a long sick-leave. Dallas is no loss. "Sandy" as he has been nicknamed, is a kind of Micawber; his something never turns up and meantime he plays the valetudinarian military. There is a pimply faced youth, Fairchilds down here, a dull chap of the English rifles.[21]

November 24, Thursday.

Thanksgiving day—a New England festa made national this year by the President's proclamation. With that sudden prodigality that is so characteristic of our people there was a grand subscription for turkeys and they were sent to this army at the rate of one half a turkey per man; by shiploads they came and commissioners with them whom we dubbed "Turkeys." Rebel deserters state that Sherman has taken Macon. Took a ride beyond the plank road where the cavalry hospitals now are. In the undisturbed, sunny thickets little birds were twittering, and there too was a pompous *Picus pileatus* clattering away on the dead trees.[22]

November 26, Saturday.

Gen. Humphreys has at last the command of the 2d Corps, and departed this morning, to relieve Gen. Hancock, who has orders to proceed to Washington and recruit a corps of 20,000 men, of those who already have seen 2 yrs. service, to be called the 1st Corps. A large number of the officers at these Headquarters accompanied him (Gen. Humphreys) to his new headquarters at Deserted house; for he is very popular, both for his bravery and urbanity.[23] Unfortunately could not make one crowd, as the General went on a grand expedition to see Gen. Butler's curiosity shop, 'tother side of James river. We took a train at 8 A.M. and found Gen. Grant dressing in his tent. There was a large gathering to go up the river; Lt. Cols. Comstock and Porter, Gen. Ingalls; Senator Nesmith; "Pet" Halsted, who is a blower of the Greek Fire; a lot of "Turkeys" from New York among them Mr. King and Benson; one Leary, son of hatter, and patriotically intent on selling a steamer to government; old Col. Monroe, once on Scott's staff, now on drinking and card playing duty. "Nes" is a rough stick—very—once a borderer and quartermaster carpenter for the outposts—now a senator from Oregon, with plenty of brains & energy and a thoroughly humorous and coarse disposition. He is distinguished for ability and dirty stories, and is a great friend of Ingalls, who is not himself extremely refined. "Pet" is a man with flowing gray beard, Quixote face and long hair and a disreputable politician and low schemer. He was a great friend of Kearney and it was to him that the letter was addressed, criticising McClellan and beginning "My Dear Pet." Mr. Benson was a mild, New York club man, and made me think how complete was the atrophy of brain caused by that life.[24] After a pleasant sail we reached Aiken landing, between Deep Bottom & Dutch Gap about 11:30, where Capt. DeKay received up and took us about a couple of miles to Butler's H'dq'rs by Cox's house, north of the landing. They had good log houses there and brick chimneys withal. Butler, who had no officer to receive Gen. Grant, came forth, looking in all directions at once and saluted the Generals (Crawford & Warren were also along). Found there Amos Binney, Maj. & P. Master, who had come to settle with Butler about his quarters at Norfolk, but had had nothing but talkee, talkee, when we arrived and knocked his prospects for that day. Was introduced to Maj. Michie, chief engineer, a young man of great intelligence and most pleasing manners. Also to Col. Piper chief of artillery (?) and to Gen. Turner a pale-faced youth who did not look to have great force of character. There passed a one-armed General with straggling hair and a wild blue eye, whom they told me was Wilde! In truth I should not have recognized the easy-going Dr. Ned Wilde whom have not seen for years. Fancy he is somewhat cracked.[25] Butler is getting sued for $50,000 in gold he forcibly took from a man in N. Orleans, under pretense of government property. He said it was all right, because he had "*charged himself* with it in his accounts." (!) "Well" said Nesmith, "but how about that actual bullion?"—"I tell you" quoth Butler "I *charged* myself with it." The fact is it is the duty of an officer to turn over to the U.S. Sub-treasurer all monies he may thus obtain. Then all mounted and proceeded to Fort Harrison which is on a low hill, the first high land of Chaffin's farm. This was the key of the rebel position, which ran from the river about E. & W. having a good infantry parapet, a battery on the river, and this fort. In front of the line was a clean sweep of a mile for artillery and then woods. It was a very handsome thing the taking of it. Our present line, to avoid enfilade from the river, is refused S.W. and terminates in Fort Brady, near Cox's ferry. On the right, the line runs to somewhere about the Newmarket road, then turns and goes to Deep Bottom. Standing in Ft. Harrison we could see, right opposite, the rebel line, distant only 800 yards. The pickets were close to each other but entirely friendly; there was no firing anywhere in the neighborhood. We had turned the work and added to it and had a good lot of field pieces there. Gen. Weitzel joined us, an intelligent, Saxon looking man with light eyes and beard. He was negligent in dress and I venture to guess, is better at his trade of engineer, than as a field fighter. We all went to Fort Brady next, standing on a bluff overhanging the river.[26] Then across the fine farm of Aiken, back again to Dutch Gap, to see the canal, a sight worth the journey. The loop of the river is here reduced to a neck of land, 50 feet high and 135 yards wide, the tour made by the stream being over 5 miles! Through this they are cutting a canal some 70 feet deep (18 feet below water level) and perhaps 100 wide. The soil is gravel, sand and indurated blue clay. They have found lignite, pyrites, and a fossil leaf impression in the clay, which Ludlow gave me. That amiable Brevet Brigadier received us and explained the work.[27] The whole neck was sprinkled with bits of mortar shell, which the rebs throw from "Gopher holes" on the opposite flat. They did not bombard us while we were there. At the mouth of the canal was a dredging machine, sunken by a bomb that fell in it two nights since. There have been some 50 men killed and 200 wounded in the work. Getting back to Butler's, Maj. Michie invited me to dine and entertained me with Ben Butler's numerous projects for the destruction of rebs. A fire engine to squirt down their earthworks; a petard to blow up their abattis; an iron net, thrown by mortars, to net them; and finally an auger, 5 feet in diameter, to bore under ground to Richmond! Of this last there were complex drawings. But Butler's grand splurge we were kept till dark to see, to wit, Greek fire. This, in shells, seems now to be a success; they have so improved the fuze that it ignites the fluid, and they have successfully burnt several houses near here. But this exhibition was a sort of 4th of July affair, whereby an ignited jet was thrown by a garden engine and made to set on fire barrels & lumber; then they played water on it, which only made it worse. Then they exploded some of it in a shell, and fired a pile of brush. All very pretty. Butler said 5 men, with a squirter could hold an enclosed work. "Good thing" quoth Meade, "then I can leave my entire line in charge of 100 men and move on the flank with all the rest of the army!" And so we departed quite convinced that, in his own words "when they made him a lawyer they spoiled a good mechanic; when they made him a general they spoiled a good lawyer!"[28]

November 27, Sunday.

Gibbon is mad, considering the appointment of Humphreys, to *temporary* command of the corps, a slight. He's a fool! Gen. Meade has done everything for him, and now he sulks and asks to be relieved. Roger A. Pryor, once noted as a brawling congressman, was captured while trying to exchange papers on the picket line. He is only a private soldier, having fallen from his high estate as general.[29] Grant has promised Meade a Major Generalcy in the regular service.

In fact Meade went to him & said: "When you came first down, I said I was willing to resign and give my position to some other; but you replied you wished me to stay. I have been overshadowed here by you, doing hard work; the success has always been laid to you, the failure on me. You promised me long ago a Major Generalcy. When Sherman was made you said you wished him to rank first—that was all well. Then you wish to give me the Middle Department. It slips through your fingers and Sheridan has it. Then he is made Major General and I am left out. You continually profess to be my friend, but your friendship is the ruin of me. You allow the papers to heap lies on me, when a word from you would set it right; you allow honors to fall to others while I am left to work obscurely. This will debase me before my own army & if it is to go on I wish to be relieved." Grant was much moved thereat and went to Washington and had the matter arranged. There dined with us a funny old man, Dr. Maceuen who came to get a sick son of his, a Major. The Doctor is a dried up, white haired little man, sort of cracked, but very bright and well educated. His son Malcolm, also a cracked coon, was my classmate. His excentricities so increased, that, after sundry disreputable scrapes, he conceived the idea of running the blockade, to become a Brigadier in the rebel service (!)—was captured and now resides in Ft. Lafayette.[30]

November 28, Monday.

My wedding day—I wish I were at home!— A parcel of naval officers came up to look over the lines, from the fleet at Ft. Monroe. Gregg made a reconnoissance to Rowanty Creek, going down the Jerusalem plank and bearing westward.

November 29, Tuesday.

The 9th Corps is to relieve the 2d in the trenches and the 2d takes the place of the 9th on the left. While the pickets were relieving, near Fort Cummings, Wilcox sent in a flag of truce, very likely to see what was going on—having a request that Roger A. Pryor should be returned—which was refused. The negroes are now all exchanged for 6 regiments of whites. My Thanksgiving box at last arrived, quite a choice affair with mince pies, preserves, and many luxuries, which we will eat in honor of the ladies. Sent some to Flint &c.

November 30, Wednesday.

The whole 2d Corps line relieved last night by the 9th. Gen. Humphreys stopped, on his way to the Peeble house, changing headquarters. Gibbon's division is camped outside the works, west of the Vaughan road. Gregg was over to get orders. Gen. Warren paid me a visit and told of his experiences on the Platte R. in the west. He said if you got among buffalo and killed one the smell of the blood made the rest mad and you could kill several. The bulls graze on the outside of the herd. In the midst in came Rosie, having been to a St. Andrews' eve dinner, and very drunk. He disgraced himself by his performances, so told him next morning that would not have him in my tent if he couldn't behave like a gentleman, which afflicted him much; for he is tender in pride, the good Swede. Maj. Duane has taken to making me visits, most frequent and lengthy. His eyes are but poorly and so he seeks amusement in visits and has taken an extraordinary shine to me. He enters with a brusque "Don't I look ill? I wish to be entertained!"—"Busy, Major?"—"Don't care if you are!" and down he sits, and I run him and he runs me.[31]

December 1, Thursday.

Gregg went off this morning for Stony Creek with nearly his whole cavalry. He made a surprise of it, captured, with small loss, two forts, two guns and 170 prisoners. He destroyed some 3,000 bags of corn, a number of new tents and a great variety of small stores & ammunition. Channing Clapp with Lt. Col. Washburn, 3d Mass. Cav., were over together with Lt. Col. Spaulding of the Engineers.[32]

December 2, Friday.

The General went to City Point where Grant told him Thomas had fallen back to Nashville, which vexed the Lt. Gen. who telegraphed to attack. General Meade said he joked Admiral Porter on the sinking of the *Florida* and told him he had to get out of the scrape by getting an *army* transport to run into her! The greatest boodle of nigs, mostly women & children, were marched to the Prov. Ml's. One old creature over 90 years old. The desire of the negroes to get away is certainly striking; at every sacrifice they come off and follow the troops. There was one scoundrel, Maj. Fitzhugh of Hampton's cavalry, who had formerly taken Captain Lazell of the 2d (?) cavalry, put a pistol to his head and compelled him to give him his boots! They did wrong not to force him to walk in barefooted.[33]

December 3, Saturday.

A warm day. Rode down the Vaughan road, where Gibbon's division is camped, outside the rear line. Passed the Davis' house, turned to the east along the Church road and cut across to the Weldon railroad. Very interesting to see a bit of new country. Effie Lowell has a daughter and is doing well. Got a board floor on my tent.[34]

December 4, Sunday.

Gibbon has gotten over his mad, on a complimentary endorsement from Grant, and will continue with his division. Meade is rather indignant that *his* endorsement would not pacify Gibbon, who owes everything to him. A telegraph came from Stanton announcing to the General that he had been made a Major General in the regular army, to rank next Sherman. Whereat he was right content.[35] Duane is to have two brevets in the regular service which make him Colonel. Again rode down the Vaughan road quite to our infantry picket line which is extended to beyond the ruins of the McDowell house. This is not far east of the Armstrong house, by Hatcher's run. There, on the picket line, saw a rebel flag of truce, sent in with letters to Gregg. The stupid Captain had allowed the flag to come in to his reserve (!) and was put under arrest for it. A part of Wheaton's division (1st) of the 6th Corps arrived this eve, coming direct from Winchester by rail & boat.— George Blagden is married to Miss Dexter.[36]

December 5, Monday.

Crawford's division was relieved on the right of the 5 Corps' line, by Wheaton's, and went into camp on the west of Jerusalem plank, outside the works. Wheaton visited H'dq'rs with Maj. Lincoln & Capt. McClennan. He is the same as of yore, excellent for a brigade, but probably hardly up to a division. Col. McKenzie also was over to visit us, with his two fingers off. He says he has been hit 6 times this campaign, but "only three hurt." From all these learned much of the valley fighting; how they could see the whole rebel army running for it, across a wide plain, at the battle of Cedar Creek; how at Winchester our cavalry came in on the enemy's flank and made a regular sabre charge, driving their infantry before them. The troops had a good time there; a healthy country, with pigs, chickens and turkeys, and no fighting except in the set battles.[37] They were very regretful to return, though they will be content to find no fighting and neat, ready made huts, whereas the 5th Corps will be wroth to go; in particular Ayres has an elegant head quarters, arranged with a fence and evergreen ornaments. Part of 3d Div. 6th A.C. got up in the evening; the 2d Div. is somewhat delayed in the valley, by reason of reported movements of Early. Congress met.

December 6, Tuesday.

Still warm. The 1st Div. 6th Corps relieved Crawford who camped on the Jerusalem plank, near where Temple's house was. There appeared Gen. Crittenden, with two aides, who all dined with us. He is a good, brave man, though transcendental looking and no great soldier. They only have ordered him here to make him resign, for he can get nothing higher than a division, which he won't take.[38] An additional excitement was the illiterate friend Alden, with a trifle of 253 brevets for this army! All the aides at these h'dq'rs are breveted one grade, except Emory & Stryker. The latter is a plain injustice, as he is a very efficient officer. Gen. Williams cannot get a brevet (so they decide) because old Thomas A. G. is only a Brigadier. Though in sooth they put up Barnard, when his superior, Delafield, was only a Brigadier: but then B[arnard] is a stout administration man! Fisher is made full Col. & chief of the Signal Corps, *vice* Myers. Rosencrantz is a happy man with his brevet of Major, and now the thing is for each superior to hand down his shoulder-straps to his next below. Sleeper is made brevet Major which pleases him, and he has earned it. Old Schriver is Brev. Brigadier, for which he will have to be hooped! Gen. Hunt a Brev. Maj. Gen. which pleases us all. A printed letter of presentation accompanies many of the brevets, which most officers count better than the commission as it is signed by Gen. Meade.[39] Gen. Seymour, now commanding 3d Div. 6th Corps, visited the General. He relieved the divs. of Ayres & Griffin, on the line, this night. Gen. Grant was up with a Capt. De Marivault com'd'ng a French corvette. Showed him Ft. Wadsworth and found him an intelligent man and a gentleman, who had had excellent chances to see both sides, at New Orleans, Charleston &c. &c. From Griffin & Bartlett who came just at dark, learned that their corps would march tomorrow morning. Ho! ho![40]

December 7, Wednesday.

This morning the 5th Corps & Mott's division of the 2d, preceeded by Gregg's cavalry, marched down the Jerusalem road bound for parts unknown. Warren kept straight on to the Nottoway, which he crossed by pontoons and his leading division got that night to Sussex C.H.

By next morning all his troops were over and the bridge taken up. All, this at Freeman's bridge. In the eve, as our information ran, Mahone's Div. of A. P. Hill's Corps marched down the Boydton plank and Wilcox was held also under arms. We had orders to be ready to move camp and expected an attack all day. South-west warm rain.[41]

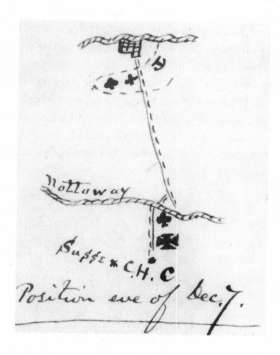

December 8, Thursday.

Fine & cooler. There is a British engineer Lieutenant here, one Satterthwaite, a hulking creature, to entertain whom is like rolling a barrel of apples up hill.[42] Gibbon's people, having erected log huts just outside the works, have been ordered inside, as such would be a cover for an attacking force. It is a stupid piece of business and one that many officers should each have prevented. Col. Kirwin, with what cavalry Gregg had left, some 700, made a reconnaissance to Hatcher's run, on the Vaughan road, where they were stopped by the enemy, who had dammed the stream and made it difficult of passage. It being already dark, they came back, after a skirmish. About this time a perfect brigade of stragglers was brought in from Warren, who had taken up the pontoon and left a squad of cavalry to bring in the coffee-boilers thus cut off. There were 850 of them; showing an average of 4½ per cent in a march of 17 miles, and rather hard going.[43]

December 9, Friday.

The reconnoissance was again pushed out, supported this time by Miles' division. Though the day was very cold & windy, the infantry took to the water, and forced the passage, losing 32 men of whom two or three were drowned. Among the cavalry, the Lieutenant who brought in the stragglers yesterday was killed, poor young man! The cavalry then kept on to within sight of the Boydton plank road where the enemy was found in works, which have been made since our visit there. They took a rebel mail carrier who said that A. P. Hill's Corps was yesterday at Dinwiddie C.H. Miles took a threatening attitude, on the stream and remained there. At evening the reserves of the 1st & 3d divs. 6th Corps, under Wheaton, marched out to support Miles, also Spaulding's engineers. It was a hard night for them, cold with a heavy, drifting snow & sleet.— Ames' division (white) & Paine's (black) are on shipboard, under Weitzel, at Fortress Monroe, waiting for good weather to sail for Wilmington with Porter's great fleet.

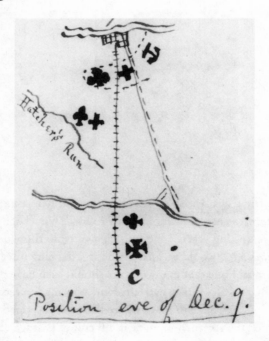

Position eve of Dec. 9.

December 10, Saturday.

Same cavalry that went far out on the Vaughan road reported heavy artillery fire in a southerly direction. This report gave such uneasiness to Grant that he ordered Potter, with 8,000 of the 9th Corps, to march to the Nottoway.

He started this evening, with all the remaining cavalry. To help hold our lines, Benham, with 2,000 engineers, was ordered post haste from City Point, to the infinite horror of that much-telegraphing officer!— Weather foggy & thawy. (Miles & Wheaton were withdrawn, having some near skirmishing.) Riddle has resigned on account of ill health & will go tomorrow, a good officer and a man of independent & sensible character. Woolsey invited all hands to eat of oysters, at a newly established log house, over the way, in his honor. We had some good songs & stories; and that Rosencrantz got so disgraceful again, that it brought the matter next morning to a crisis, and he promised, with many repentances to be straight in future. Col. Thomas the fat, has lobbied himself into a Brigadiership, by going to Washington; an outrage, as Meade doth think.[44]

December 11, Sunday.

All day we still remained rather in doubt about the position of Warren, but, at 6 P.M. came Capt. Paine from the expedition having left the 5th Corps on the banks of the Nottoway. On Wednesday the advance got to Sussex C. H. On Thursday they struck off westward and reached the railroad in the afternoon, and worked at destroying track from then till midnight, beginning at the Nottoway bridge & working down. On Friday the work was pushed south till they got to the Meherrin, where the other bank was held with 10 guns in earthworks, in reconnoitering which & skirmishing with some cavalry, Maj. Manlius Sargent was killed by a shell. As it would take some time to flank the works and there were only 6 days on hand at the start, Warren left the Meherrin bridge untouched; the rest of the road (18 miles) with two bridges was thoroughly destroyed & the rails twisted. Except some cavalry skirmishing and bushwhacking, there was no fighting. Some of our men were killed & stripped, in return for which the troops (some of whom got drunk on the applejack of the country) burnt houses by wholesale. Saturday the home march began. Hill probably went down somewhere by Stony Creek & took position. Gen. Potter put his best leg foremost & marched back today, getting in by 7 P.M. The night was a terrible one for troops, extremely cold, with a high cutting wind.[45]

December 12, Monday.

All of Getty's division but one brigade arrived. Gen. Wright also with his staff got here. Saw Whittier, McClellan, Kent, and Tomkins, all looking well and natural. They were full of the glories of the valley and the fatness thereof. Poor Gen. Wright looks well but is in poor spirits—his luck has been hard. Rode out to see the 5th C. march in. It is cold & disagreeable yet. The men showed

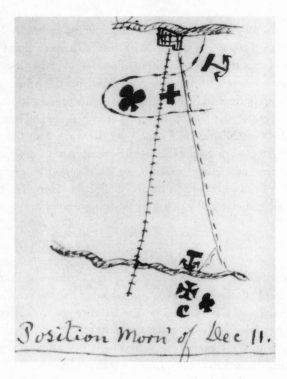

the effects of their 6-day hardships in their look of slack discipline & many too seemed to feel cold. The corps camped ¾ mile outside the works, stretching from east of the Jerusalem plank, more than half way to the Weldon road.[46]

December 13, Tuesday.
Gen. Wright ate breakfast with us and then repaired to his new quarters at the Globe Tavern, Warren having moved to pretty near the Smith house. Gibbon was relieved on the line by Getty and camped in the rear, on extreme left and in a line with the 5th Corps. Mott comes next extending to Halifax road.

December 14, Wednesday.
A fine, mild day. Rode along our picket line, from Col. Wyatt's house, along the Church road, to the Weldon R.R. W[yatt]'s is a quite large house and there is a big corn field by it, many acres in extent. Berlin was back with a Lieutenancy in the artillery reg. of Brev. Brig. Gen. Wainwright. He is highly pleased with his brevet Captaincy. A certain rather self-sufficient but fairly agreeable young Lord Newry is here, and paints quite well in water colors.[47]

December 15, Thursday.

There was a medal presentation at the 2d Corps—medals voted by congress to certain men of distinguished gallantry. There were near 20 in all, but two or three had been since killed in action. Detachments of troops were on the spot to witness the ceremony and were drawn up on three sides of a square, in front of Gen. Humphreys' headq'rs which now are on the Squirrel level road, south of the Peeble house. Gen. M[eade] with many general & staff officers, stood on the fourth side, and the recipients came & stood opposite. He then made a very good address & handed the medals to the men, several of whom were already promoted to officers. After which the band played gaily and such of the generals as wished it had some punch. The medals are in form of a star, of bronze. The die-work is well done, but the finish is commonplace.[48] Talked with Summerhayes & Macy about the battle of the Wilderness; for there is great dispute between the 2d Corps & Wadsworth's division of the 5th about the fighting on the plank road. Macy said the regiment lay parallel to the road for 2 hours & then changed front forward and was very hotly engaged on the right of the road. They lost 200 men & 10 officers and yet he *never saw a single rebel*! Summerhayes said the same; also that he saw other troops beside his corps, while M[acy] only saw 2d Corps, but Gen. Wadsworth, who rode violently about giving orders.[49]

December 16, Friday.

There were hanged three men, of the 1st Div. 2d Corps, for desertion to the enemy. Think it well to be prepared to witness anything, so made a point to ride over & see it. A portion of the division was under arms, round a high gallows. At the stated time the three men were brought, in an ambulance, preceded by the band playing a dead march, and followed by a waggon carrying their coffins. The condemned had each a white cap on; two were in rebel uniform, and one in our own. On the scaffold a clergyman decorously read a service and the men kneeled to pray. This took some time, and there was a good deal of delay in putting on the ropes and tying the culprits; but, at last, the caps being pulled down, they were all thrown off at once, and hung so many bundles of clothes twisting round & round! The most painful part of the spectacle was when the ambulance passed, carrying them to execution. That very night & from this very division, five men deserted to the enemy! At the 9th Corps h'dq'rs at Deserted house, Gen. Meade gave medals of honor to some 8 or 10 deserving men. The troops could not be withdrawn from the lines, so there was no parade, but the General, as before, made some fitting remarks.[50] The enemy opened a 100-pounder on the Avery house, but without damage. News that Sherman had taken Fort McAllister by storm, securing his communication with the fleet on Ossabaw Sound. At the same time a brief telegraph announced that Thomas yesterday attacked Hood in his works and routed him entirely, taking a great deal of artillery & many prisoners. Burbridge & Stoneman have made a raid into S.W. Va. in Breckenridge's rear, destroying much railroad & government property, and now are going towards Saltville. The rebel papers give also an account of the fight at Franklin in which they lost in General officers 7 killed, 5 wounded & 1 made prisoner!—a most unusual loss in a fight of that magnitude. Among the killed was Cleburne, a serious blow to them. Was surprised to see Waud here; he is well again & is on a visit.[51]

December 17, Saturday.

From particulars of Thomas' victory, it would seem that he took some 5,000 prisoners and 50 cannon. This is fortune indeed! It was *the* point of the whole campaign, and crushes completely any rebel hopes of success to cheer them. Rode with the General to Crawford, who has his h'dq'rs on the Sturtevant Mill road, at the McCann house. C[rawford] had carted his log house, all the way from his old place, by us, down here. Saw Mead, who, though mustered out, stays as a volunteer to wait for a new commission he expects.[52]

December 18, Sunday.

There arrived a glorious hat for Gen. Humphreys, a present from Mimi and with a corps badge thereon worked by herself. Then there was a box of cigars a Christmas present for Gen. Meade. Rode to see Gen. Bartlett, camped near the Smith house. He gave me a lot of photographs of reb' generals.

December 19, Monday.

That good man Gen. Meade said to me; "I have a Christmas present for Mrs. Lyman—a certain worthless officer whom I shall send home to her!" Excellent Commendatore! And that very evening he gave me a 30-day leave. Rode along the 5th Corps pickets on their right (facing to rear) and came by the Halifax road back to camp.

December 20, Tuesday.

A fine frosty morn' to leave. Gave my blessing to all the camp (mostly still abed) and took the 8 A.M. train for City Point, Rosie & Worth coming with me to see me off. There were some 6th Corps officers going down, with whom had a talk. They agreed Wright was very unpopular, looked on as not capable of commanding. They accused him of allowing one brigade to do all the fighting outside Washington. It is extraordinary how a man may seem to have every requisite for a good soldier—courage, coolness, education, fine disposition—yet fail after all! Getty they spoke highly of—said he "ran the corps." Another curious instance; for he is a man who courts nobody, is rather laissez faire, & rarely speaks to anyone, but he has an intrepidity and a judgment on the field that win confidence for him. The 10 A.M. boat took me by 4 P.M. to Ft. Monroe whence the Baltimore boat started an hour later. Was lucky to have Gen. Mott as a companion, by whose favor got a stateroom, and went first into supper. He is a very kind gentleman, and do always regret that his men have done so seldom well; but in fact he has not the stern energy needful. There too was Gen. "Lew" Wallace, who looks like a second rate opera singer with his huge moustache & theatrical air. There too was a certain burly Col. Markland, who has been to carry the mails to Sherman and who wouldn't set them afire were he to fall among them. Also Col. Kensel, of Butler's staff, newly married & voyaging with bride and papa-in-law, the distinguished "Col." Newell A. Thompson of my ilk. A poor boy, who had lost his leg at Chaffin's farm, got the stump hurt coming on board, and was in much pain; therefore gave him my berth and took meekly to the floor. Col. M[arkland] had all the last news to tell of Sherman;

how his infantry had scarcely even seen an enemy, and the very cavalry had had but little fighting. Also how many of Sherman's men had never seen the ocean, and went at once to fishing, with ridiculous little line, in deep water.[53]

December 21, Wednesday.

A heavy snow-storm greeted our arrival at 6.30 A.M. in Baltimore. After break-fast at the Eutaw, where bid adieu to Gen. M[ott] took the 9 A.M. train for New York, where got at 5.30, the snow having now changed to a rain, making a charming slush! What was my surprise at seeing the names of G. R. Russell & Daughter on the Astor book. Marched upstairs & surprised them! and we had a gay tea together. They have been (in company of a box of mince pies) to see Harry & Mary & the baby, at Point Lookout. There Harry's regiment guards, with small assistance, 15,000 rebel prisoners—a nigger guard over rebs (!)—They are well fed, with as good white bread as the soldiers have. As to *our* poor prisoners, I saw some of them going on furlough, and one Ver-monter told me the sufferings were beyond description—as many as 160 died in one day. When I spoke of retaliation "No!" said he "if *we* did such things we should never prosper!"—That man was a Christian.— Took the 8 P.M. train for Boston ha![54]

December 22, Thursday.

It turned right smart of cold last night, making the neat villages of mine native N.E. frosty & full of icicles. The snow & ice so impeded the track that we were 3 hours late and were not in till 9.30, which after all was more handy than an earlier hour. It didn't take long to go in a "booby" to 1 Louisburg Square. And who should personally open the front door but Mimi herself, blooming in a nice morning dress! And there was a little voice, saying quite modestly "papa," in the entry behind, and this was small Cora grown in size and much more in brain, for she talked like an old head, and is as bright as can be, while at Beverly she had not that sequence of thought that gives power of conversation. Very glad were they all to see me Mimi & Baby, Madre, Tintie & Sallie. All very well & natural; only Tintie grown and broadened into a complete young lady of 18. How happy am I to get once again home; when we think of the many, many officers who had just as much to lose, and who have lost it.— This is an excellent house & well furnished withal, in part with new and in part with old. On the right, entering, a dining room where is that tune-playing clock under which I used to sit so long in my lover days, at the Jube's Lane house, in the little study.

In the 2d storey, two excellent drawing rooms, and one small & two large bed rooms in each of the next two storeys. The views from the upper windows, over back-bay are most pleasant. Cora came round pretty soon to see us, looking very well & natural; also saw Howland for a moment as he sat with Frankie in the sleigh. In very good spirits is that model man,—an improvement from last autumn. In at the faithful Sparrell's, the *barbiere di Boston*, encountered Bob Winthrop, and we went together to visit Chas. Thorndike & Mrs. who are at the Parker House, where also beheld, to my surprise, Mrs. Badger's daughter Rebecca, whom have not seen these years, but who looks quite as of old, and now is visiting the excellent Harvey Parker. Chas. T[horndike]'s boy is a likeness of mamma and is Augustus *gennant*.

December 23, Friday.

Took Mrs. Mimi out a shopping, partly for Christmas presents. Very cold viz. -2°. Annie Agassiz, the active, appeared from Cambridge at breakfast. My name having been put down by excellent Ned Browne at the Union Club, went there to meet Col. Stevie Weld, who has got paroled from a southern prison. He wanted to know something of the Mine affair, as he expects perhaps to be summoned before the Committee on the conduct of the war. He gave me an account of his own capture, and said the trouble was that they rushed a lot of negroes in with the whites and there they all were, jammed up together, between the main rebel line and a rear line made to cover the supports of a battery. He said they killed many of the negroes in cold blood.[55] Jack Reed was in, looking fat & full of whisky. Also, to my surprise, young Fearing who in Rome was engaged to Miss Peters. Engagement since *vompu*. Aunt Mary called at the house; and, that Evening, came Padre & Em', followed in a later train by master Bob, coming from his school at Sing Sing with a rank of sixth, which is right smart.

December 24, Saturday.

Called on Frank Palfrey, in his new office, 16 Court St. There came in Col. Pearson, who is well enough of his severe hit, to go about on crutches. We all adjourned and took a Tom & Jerry but they do seem to me more watery than in the good days of college. That eve went round with Mimi & helped Co & Howland to dress a Christmas tree, which was quite a labor—so many candles, spangles & odds & ends. Was fortunate enough to find Aunt Eliot on calling at Lizzie's; to think of her, with a full head of black hair & nine grandchildren![56]

December 25, Sunday.

To hear cousin Foote at Stone Chapel. We hire a part of Dr. Hooper's pew. Tom Appleton came home with us. He is funnily serious in his belief in spiritualism.—He told us Mrs. Greeley Curtis had lost her little baby; if sick men get children, they too will be sick. The church was well decked with greens, for it was Christmas Sunday.[57]

December 26, Monday.

Our Christmas was made really merry by the news that Sherman had taken Savannah! Hardee, deeming the place untenable, evacuated and escaped to the northern side of the river, and our troops marched in, taking a large number of heavy guns, and finding a great amount of cotton stored in the town, which contains, it is said, some 25,000 people. The dinner at Co's was a fine affair with nearly a dozen youngsters and twice as many oldsters. Park Shaw's two eldest boys are good looking, well grown lads, one of them with a turn for drawing; but little Park and the two girls are puny. Sat between "Aunt Pauline" and Lou Shaw, with Aunt Anna for'nenst me; the Colonel Greene came not. A sprig of holly from Petersburg decked the plum pudding. After the dessert the tree was lighted by the combined labors of Alex, Howland & self, in the little library and the crowd was admitted to an admiring gaze. Thereat the numerous presents were given about. Cora gave me the psalms of David very finely bound & Mimi had already given me a new dressing gown. And so *adieu* Santa Claus![58]

December 27, Tuesday.

It turned about and was thawy. Mimi & I walked to Cambridge for to see the Professor, Alex &c. We there took a lunch and greeted the civil Burckhardt and the always delectable Mrs. Agassiz. Ida & her Henry were in town. The Prof. goes to Washington on Friday to attend his conventicle of quarrelers, called the Scientific Academy.[59]

December 29, Thursday.

Ned Browne gave in honor of Charlie Thorndike & self, a dinner at the Union Club. Present Gus Perkins, Bill Otis, Bob Winthrop, Ned Codman, Fred Bradlee, Sales and Geo. Chase, 10 in all. George Chase looks like a yellow shadow, a big change from when he weighed 180 lbs! Still they say he's better. Gus Perkins said, quite sentimentally, and referring to the house being that of the late "great A"; "the last time I was in this room, I *slept* in it!" which was greeted with ironical laughter. The dinner was very good & expensive withal. There was a centre basket of fruit & flowers which Ned gallantly sent to Mrs. Thorndike.[60]

December 30, Friday.

Visited Fanny Foote in her wee house, t'other end of this slanting square. She looked very well and is strong enough to walk out. The baby we didn't see. Never much of a loss!— Our dinner was at John Cushing's, in his new house on the milldam. Had the distinguished honor to conduct in mine ancient young friend Miss Mary Bowditch. Besides we had Bob Cushing, Mr. & Mrs. Chas. Thorndike, & Mr. & Mrs. Dick Parker. So it was a very merry dinner, for Mrs. Dick is a fund in herself. John's house is very handsome; the dining room especially is ornamented with a beam roof, painted in an Etruscan style. The good Sue is fatter than ever and has an enviable double chin.[61]

December 31, Saturday.

There was a lively snow, midst which drove Mimette to see old Mrs. Cabot in Brookline; for have Robin & a sleigh in town. Saw also Miss Saidie & Mrs. Edward. A most pleasant house it is out there, to be sure. Maj. Bowditch, of Hal's regiment, son of Mr. Ingersoll came to dine. At Mine Run he was wounded as a Lieut. in the 1st Mass. Cav. A very good fellow, like most of the blood.[62] News this morn of the flumux of the Wilmington expedition. After a month or two of delay the expedition sailed, some 7,000 land troops and an immense fleet. Porter exploded his powder ship, which did no damage, at all, as might beforehand have been known; for De Chanal told Butler the scheme was impracticable as long ago as last summer, when we went to see that worthy and he refreshed our minds with a long plan for blowing Charleston out of water! The fleet then opened a terrific fire, shutting up the fort (Fisher) but doing no great damage. Under this cover a division was landed; but Weitzel, who commanded, reported 14 guns bearing on the beach and an assault impracticable. So the land troops were reembarked and went back to James River! This is like to kill off Butler, who had a quarrel with Porter before. If it has that effect, the expedition will not be without good.[63] Though the year ends with a bungle in North Carolina, yet the progress in the twelve months has been very great. In the west, Gen. Sherman, with forces to those of the enemy about as 5:3 drove Johnston, by a series of flanks, to Atlanta; where Hood, taking command, attempted sorties on a great scale, in which he lost largely. Sherman again flanked, and Hood had to retreat to Macon, whence he issued to make his foolhardy march on Nashville leaving Georgia & Savannah an easy prey to Sherman, while he himself was utterly routed by Thomas. The Eastern campaign, far more bloody, was less decisive. While Grant with forces about as 3:2 by a series of left flanks and with combats of unprecedented severity, marched from the Rapid Ann to the James, Butler made an impotent attempt on Fort Darling, was defeated & fenced in at Bermuda Hundreds. Then followed operations before Petersburg & threatenings of Richmond. Lee tried a diversion with Early against Washington, which drew from us only 1 infantry corps & 2 cavalry divisions, and ended in the complete rout of Early in the Shenandoah. Banks' grand expedition up the Red River was a most complete botch work, ending in his retreat, with great loss. On the whole, the western armies of the rebels are *hors du combat*, their eastern army, severely worn, is closely confronted, while Sherman, with a free foot, threatens every disaster in the south.[64]

January 1–
July 1, 1865

(With selected entries to July 25, 1865)

———∞∞∞———

January 1, 1965, Sunday.

Boston. Cold. To church at Stone Chapel, Mimi & I called on Uncle George & Aunt Nancy, who now live entirely alone, poor folks, though they look very well and Uncle George is quite a wonder for a man within three or four years of eighty. Cora sent me, the mindful creature, a pencil case for a present. Dined with her, and Howland entertained us with an account how he went to New York and moused over the old Denning suit and was surprised at the complex rascalities of the ancient Wm. Denning.[1]

January 2, Monday.

We drove to Milton in a sleigh and visited Aunt Amelia Russell, who there dwells with Aunt Rose. Then to John Forbes, where we saw *toda la casa,* including Willie, newly returned from a compulsory residence in Columbia S.C. Malcolm is grown a young man. Ma'am F. is as kind and as weak as ever; and John's nose is more & more stupendous & intelligent looking. The New Year was celebrated today, and the Horace Grays were kind enough to invite us, as usual. We hoped to see John, who came to Washington the other day, with news of Sherman from Foster; but it seems he had not the time to come on. Judge Horace was there, gratified plainly at his Supreme Court position. Co & Howland, Mr. & Mrs. Gray completed the company, for Bessie had a headache, & Hattie has actually gone to Europe.[2]

January 3, Tuesday.

Bob's holidays being over, he returned to school. As to Em' she was off on a cool pic-nic to Naushon! John Forbes with his daughter & two sons, Henry & Ida, Annie & Alex make the party. I prophesy they will be friz!— Drove to Brookline.[3]

January 4, Wednesday.

Whether it be change from tent to house, or a fag end of malaria, or what not, do feel very weak and no nervous energy here. A little walk makes me tired & sleepy & do not feel like taking hold of any work. Had a most jolly dinner at Jack Adams, Mrs. A. being present at the courses. There were Bob Winthrop, Bill Otis & Frank Palfrey. We got running the gassy Bill, who observed that he had never served in the field. "For which" said Bob gravely "a long suffering country is profoundly grateful!"[4]

January 5, Thursday.

Arthur had asked me to a quiet family dinner; Bob Paine & Lydia were there to meet us. And he gave a very good spread with a variety of wines, among others a sweetish California wine, very much like Lacrima Christae, grown on the sides of Vesuvius. He has three chicks now Julia, Arthur and the baby. Arthur will be younger when he gets to be 50. At present he wears a felt hat, of quaker cut, on the back of his head, and has a generally venerable & country air.[5]

January 6, Friday.

After a hospitable dinner at Co's, we went to see Faust—Mephistopheles, Bellini; Margherita—Miss Kellog; Faust—Lotti who sung as if he had a corn-cob in his throat, and acted, like all tenors, as if he had stiff sticks in all his limbs. Bellini had no conception of his part, but sung well. Em' returned from Naushon with great accounts, though she confessed there was but one fire in the house when they arrived! They went a-hunting and Henry shot a doe.

January 7, Saturday.

Collected quite a lot of dividends—this boarding with one's friends is a money saving arrangement! So shall be able to lay up quite a sum this January. Cora & Howland added their company to our family dinner, today. Howland is in excellent spirits this winter, whereas he was quite low last autumn.

January 9, Monday.

Drove out and went to Alex's lecture at the Museum. Mimi, Annie, Mrs. Russell and the Museum students and employees were there. Alex gets on very nicely and is very condensed & instructive in his mode of handling; though he has none of the poetry & eloquence of his father. I had asked the Terrapins to dine with me at the Union Club; and there assembled Frank Palfrey, Fred Bradlee, Jack Adams, John Cushing, and Mr. Burkhardt (guest). We had an elegant dinner and kept it going till 11.30, during which we got through two bottles apiece, neatly; but were all decorous, as became grave Terrapins.[6]

January 10, Tuesday.

The hock, sherry, champagne, madeira, claret, maraschino & brandy did not make a harmonious company and laid me up during the fore part of the day, but, at eve, revived & went with Mimi to see Don Sebastian, a double distilled tragedy, & spectacular opera, with a good deal of noise & not much music. Saw mine ancient friend Lorini, who grows huskier & huskier; he sang "that Turk who had one only daughter." Susini (grown very fat) was the bad inquisitor. On the whole it was rather pleasing, though the guns scared Mimi who braced herself to the peril![7]

January 11, Wednesday.

Ben Butler has been relieved & ordered to Lowell! Ho! ho! ho! That is brave—Fort Fisher was the handle. Now with Banks and Butler tied up, we have the field clear for a good spring campaign.[8] Dined at Mrs. Turner Sargent's, in company of Mrs. Winthrop S.; Mr. Frank Parker; Mrs. Wadsworth, Mr. & Mrs. John Sturgis & Mr. Edw. Boott, who is as gentlemanly & fine looking as ever. Poor Mimette! She thought it a "high neck" and it was a "low neck" and so she hadn't on the right dress! Behold what awful things trouble us, from Wars to Woman's dress! The house is a gem; such a crowd of little objects of art & nice books; such a pretty, inlaid dining room; and so much taste in the Prague glass & French porcelain. And a very nice woman is Mrs. Turner.[9]

January 12, Thursday.

They had a whist club, which meets at the members' houses. There is the Dr. Hooper lot & the Agassiz lot, and Miss Nina Lowell, &c. &c. So we played and played, having at my table Dr. & Miss Nellie Hooper and Mrs. Dr. Sam Parkman. After which they are allowed salad & oysters.[10]

January 13, Friday.

Devoted this evening to visiting good Mrs. Browne, with whom took tea. Showed her the maps of Petersburg, &c. Miss B. was at table also Frank, who seemed very bright & lively. While Ned dressed for the party sat & talked in his room. He has still another old, tall, family clock, more gorgeous than its predecessors.[11]

January 14, Saturday.

The newspapers had the unwelcome intelligence that Meade's confirmation was deferred while Sheridan, Sherman and Thomas were confirmed as Maj. Gens. in the regular army! Bah! Drove to Brookline with Mrs. The Miss Burbank who has taken care of Eben's children (his sister-in-law) has been suddenly attacked with violent lung disease which threatens a fatal end. Poor woman! she was engaged to a farmer down east. Our Saturday dinner was augmented by Aunt Rose, and by William & Malcolm Forbes.[12]

January 15, Sunday.

Everyone was astonished to hear that Mr. Everett died this morning, early—apoplexy. Visited Jim Lawrence, after church. He is always bright, despite his constant pains & sickness. We went to Lizzie Bullard's in the evening to see Aunt Eliot who is staying there.[13]

January 16, Monday.

In the sleigh to Cantabridge. While Mimi listened to Alex's lecture, was engaged with Burkhardt in correcting the coloring of the plates for my Ophiurans, which he is to color by hand. They will be very handsome & well done. We went to hear, for the first time, Fra Diavolo. It was a great success, even Lotti, as Fra, was goodish; Bellini was most comic in Lord Rocburg, and Morensi was an admirable my Lady. There are many familiar airs and all together it was by far the best thing they have done. The two brigands, by Dubrueil & Weinlich, were excellent in acting.[14]

January 17, Tuesday.

We got the famous & unlooked for news of the fall of Fort Fisher! Assaulted by Terry, of the old 10th Corps, with Ames' division, while Paine, with his negro division occupied a line across the narrow peninsula and kept off Hoke, who tried to make a diversion. An assault by sailors & marines, on the sea front failed, but the land troops got in after 7 hours hard fighting taking all the garrison, said to be 1,200 to 1,800. (Note: There were 1,800 prisoners & 400 killed & wounded.) Lt. Preston of the navy, whom saw last summer at City Pt. as a returned prisoner, was killed; also Lt. Col. Lyman (Luke, formerly of the 27th Mass.?)[15]— We went to a charming dinner at Jim Codman's in Brookline. Mrs. Sargent does the hot house for flowers, Mrs. Codman the cold house for fruits. The roses & other flowers were most pleasant to see. Company, Miss Mary Bowditch, Ben Crowninshield, Mr. & Mrs. Frank B[owditch] (she a charming young woman, with a remarkably handsome mouth) & Mr. & Mrs. Dick Parker. Jim opened, in my special honor, a bottle of his first chop "Codman" madeira whereof he has but 16 bottles left. After dinner we all got talking and laughing at a great rate about old times and the time went fast till nearly 11, when we drove home in a hard snow storm. Yea, Parker's coachman went off the avenue & meandered over the lawn, & finally came back to the house & got a lantern.[16]

January 18, Wednesday.

Got a letter from Gen. Meade, permitting me to stay as long as I liked, good man!— He is low in spirits, being anxious about his confirmation, and what is worse his eldest son is very low, and he himself was ordered back from his leave, and all on some frivolous secret service gossip. It went to my heart and I wrote a letter to John Forbes & got Mr. & Mrs. R[ussell] to write to Wilson & Sumner. To hear La Figlia; it's but a weak opera, after all. Susini as the Sergeant; Kellog as the daughter of the regiment.[17]

January 19, Thursday.

We paid an evening visit to good Mrs. Cabot, who is temporarily on a town visit at Mrs. Perkins' boarding house. What a horror is a boarding house! Wall tent much better—such smells of departed fish & soup! I really think I could smell Sam Lawrence's last dinner, when he smashed up and went under in '57! Mrs. Cabot was entertaining old Mr. Clark Cabot, who looks, in face, like an amiable, spectacled, cranium.[18]

January 20, Friday.

Went to see the Governor, whom could not find yesterday, as he was preparing for Mr. Everett's funeral, which took place with unusual solemnities. The remains were escorted to Chauncy St. Church by the Cadets and a band of music. Chief Justice Bigelow, Mr. Winthrop and other well known persons were pall bearers. Behind followed, as chief mourners, two of the ugliest people that could have been found, Wise and William the Phenomenon.[19] After these religious services, the hearse was escorted by a force of infantry & of cavalry and many citizens, as far as the bridge, while minute guns were fired from the common.— The Governor received me kindly and promised to write to Wilson & Sumner, if I would address him a letter, on this topic, stating my views of Meade's claims for promotion—did so.— He went on to talk with interest on our troops and said he was for recruiting in our state by putting the town Selectmen to work & interesting the people. He is a polite and intelligent man. Suggested to him not to send more Germans, and he said there were sent only 900, mostly Belgians. Being told that Gen. Williams was in town, went to call on him at Mr. Lombard's, 9 Marlborough St. The Gen. was arrayed in a suit of black & was happy as a lark at the idea of his leave & his new position as Inspector Gen. of the Armies in the field. He goes Sunday night & so couldn't go to dine with me. Saw his father & his step-mother, also Mr. Lombard.[20]

January 21, Saturday.

Gen. Williams called in the morning and much pleased Mimi et al. Took him round also and introduced him to Howland. Gave a snug dinner to Channing Clapp, who returns to City Point on Monday. There were Ned Browne, Burkhardt, Channing, Ch. Thorndike & Alex. We had a nice dinner & chat, & behaved with praiseworthy sobriety—only 5 bottles among us all. It is to be noticed that if wine be really fine, nearly double the quantity will be drunk than when simply good. The claret was $5. per bottle and was truly not above fair. Champagne $5.50 per bottle; so that dinner giving is no joke now. However, it is surprising to see how prices follow the fall of paper, and how gold follows the inflation of the currency. Thus, though gold tumbled 20 or 30% after the successes of Atlanta, Savannah and Fort Fisher, it crawled steadily up, after each, till it got to its present norm, say 220, i.e. 120 per cent premium. The same is true of the unfounded rise during the dubious campaign of the summer; it could not hold at that height, because it was above the norm.[21]

January 22, Sunday.

Dined at Cora's, having previously made my Sunday visit to Jim Lawrence. Having told Howland it was very bad to wax Madeira corks, he did disagree and would fain prove his point by opening an exceeding old bottle of Santa Cruz wine—the soundness of which I admitted and was glad of the result of the discussion.

January 23, Monday.

Silas went for a visit down East. Drove to Cambridge & got all the proof sheets of my catalogue, to prepare an index. The day was abominable, rain & blow & slip and slush, which grew wus as the eve drew on. We were to have a Charade enacted; for the "Social Club" (called "Mind" by Dick Parker) meets at our house. It is composed in chief of tabs, yea! ancient ones—The word Mary Stuart—viz. "May" (a tableau of children in the May Queen—Amie, Sallie &c) "Rye" (a scene between Mr. & Mrs. Panny, Em & T.L. She tells Mr. P. he is all awry; he presents a straw bouquet saying this is also "a rye") "Stew" (Irish scene between Quincy & Miss Putnam, who is cooking a stew) "Art" (Mr. & Mrs. Crowell of West Yarmouth, Miss Putnam & T.L. come to get their portraits from Michael Angelo Bellini, Quincy). "Mary Stuart," (a scene from the Abbot by Annie and Miss Dorr & Alex). The tabs were highly pleased and all things went off with éclat. But many were our trials, first. They had forgot to send for Alex' dress, so must needs trudge for it to Curtis. Then, one hour before the company was to come, all the gas went out!! So away to the office and got a man who soon put the pipe in condition, with a drink of whisky. The supper & some of the arrangements were rather topsey turvey; for mamma is not given to taking much pains about such things, and the horror of her precise daughters may be easily conceived! Saw (when descended with my face washed) at supper, Prof. Rogers, Edw. Whipple, Mrs. Edwards, Mrs. R. B. Forbes, and lots more, including Mr. & Mrs. Andrew.[22]

January 24, Tuesday.

Alex left for a three-week tour in Missouri, a sort of secret "oil" Expedition, under the auspices of John Forbes and Nat. Thayer, & he to have 10% of profits, if any. There was a sleigh ride of a bowling club, to go first to Mr. Nat Bowditch's, Jamaica Plain and then return to a town supper. Mimi & I were to go as patrons of Em' & the young fry, but Mimi had a sick headache, poor bird, and even I had a pate ache too, so we stayed at home, to Mimi's great remorse, for she thought it her duty to gang.[23]

January 25, Wednesday.

The quarterly & annual meeting of the Trustees of the Museum of Comp. Zool. being holden today, did make my first appearance as Trustee. It was a solid affair in the lordly Council Chamber, under the picture of Mr. Higginson, first minister of Salem. There was his Excellency in the chair; also these

Trustees; Mr. Ticknor; Ch. Justice Bigelow Pres. of Senate; Wm. Gray; Dr. Jacob Bigelow; Dr. Walker, Prof. Agassiz, James Lawrence. Reports of last meeting; of the Finance Committee; of Com. on Museum. The permanent fund is $100,000. Other investments $100,000. Land & buildings $78,000. Collections, valued $61,000. = Interest on permanent fund $7,000. Catalogue fund $7,500. Prof. Agassiz said the Emperor of Brazil had prepared a large collection of fishes for the Museum, and that Milne Edwards had forwarded many excellent things, and would continue so to do. We discussed the fireproof nature of the Museum and appointed a Committee to look after it, in view of the partial destruction of The Smithsonian, the morning of yesterday. We also showed the progress made on the catalogues. N. Thayer was chosen Treas. Wm. Gray. Sec., L. Agassiz Curator, as before. Agassiz got home yesterday from his long Washington trip.[24] Then to Brookline where repacked & arranged some of my wine, wherewith do love to dabble; a learned amusement! Got too a suit of London gray, which, with a new hat, will make me a cit for a time; for do hate to wear the buttons when am so long off duty. We had, in the eve, the biggest kind of a spree; to wit, a party of 12 to see the Morris & Pell nigger minstrels & after to sup with me at Parker's. There were Mr. & Mrs. Dick Parker, Jim Codman; Frank Bowditch; & John Cushing; and Miss Mary B. & Col. Stevie Weld. The minstrels have a new little theatre, fitted in what was the Province house. They were quite amusing and our good spirits filled any gaps in their wit. At Parker's we had a moral orgy and made enough noise for a class supper! Mrs. Dick Parker & her husband were too funny for anything and we had a regular lark, in which ale assisted. Finally we retired nearly at one o'cl. Mrs. P. fainting at once, on being told the hour! It was cold today & yesterday. Sleighing excellent.[25]

January 26, Thursday.

Met Charlie Whittier in the street. He said, rather scornfully, that Gen. Wright had fallen from his horse & so he [Whittier] had a leave of a day or two. Poor Wright, do hear, from various sources, that he drinks sometimes and vacillates between extreme confidence and a sense of insufficiency—a melancholy case of too much responsibility! In the evening Mimi drove with me to Quin's in Jamaica Plain, to a whist. The faithful Ely took our sleigh & we went in & took off our furs, for it was right smart of cold. The house is really pretty, finished with chestnut. Quin has a number of excellent pictures, e.g. one by Troyon. We had about enow for 5 tables. Co & Howland; Ida; Mrs. A.; Nellie & Clover Hooper; Mr. Burkhardt; & Ned Perkins, that fresh gentleman, came later, &c. &c. There were flowers disposed about with Pauline's good taste, and the supper was ditto, though no champagne is allowed in these times, very proper.[26]

January 27, Friday.

The other day met Roebling in the street, with his bride who is Gen. Warren's sister. He is out of service and will go to superintend the great suspension bridge at Cincinnati. Today the two came to dine, and after to the opera with us and Em! She is an "army belle," as Tom Appleton says; very bright & plucky but not burdened with refinement. Roebling looked curiously in a good long-tail & a white tie. Fra Diavolo was excellent with a crowded house also. Saw Capt. Graham of the artillery there. Last night was a curious party given to, or for, Mrs. Sparks' daughter by her mother & Mrs. Whitwell. It was called a "*thé dansant*" and was much dancing, no supper, and little tea. On the same card was put "also May 1st, 12 to 4." Nobody but Mrs. Sparks could have invented sich! Since the first two weeks (when got over my malarial touches) have certainly enjoyed myself as much as ever in my life.[27]

January 28, Saturday.

Mimi drove with me to see the greenhouses of old Mrs. Cabot. We hoped to see all the acacias in bloom, but only a part were out. However, there were plenty of fine flowers whereof Thomas cut a number which we brought in, to Mimi's contentment. Drive now Howland's motley mare, because Robin was took bad and sent to Brookline.

January 29, Sunday.

Called with Mimi on Mrs. Roebling, after church. She received us, in camp style, in a small bed room, a good deal encumbered with her trunks and his boots. Ate a private Sunday dinner with Jim Lawrence. Mrs. Prescott was there, of course and his children Jim, —— & Prescott. He is wonderfully cheerful & talked most agreeably—described how he dined in state once, when pa was minister, at Duke Norfolk's—in a hall 70 feet long & 30 high, encrusted with mirrors, that cost, furniture & all, £10,000.

January 30, Monday.

Went to Mr. Robt. Apthorp's office and saw 15 bottles of very old, private Madeira. Took the whole at $8 paper per bottle! Ah, my besetting weakness—just as some people collect snuff boxes! Having bought 4 doz. of expensive wine the other day, shall feel sheepish about this and not tell Mimi! ho, ho; a secret down cellar! Took the whole out to Brookline and carefully rebottled and corked it.

January, 31, Tuesday.

Met a gentleman in the street, to whom was introduced by Frank Peabody and who turned out to be Charlie Greene, brother to Nat, and my *quondam* playfellow as a boy! Have not seen him in say 18 years. He expressed surprise at my height and age; as if one stopped growing at 13 years old! Little babe Cora has a touch of canker in the mouth, now very prevalent so had Dr. Bigelow to her, who recommended a little oil and a mouth wash of borax.[28]

February 1, Wednesday.

Yesterday the House passed the amendation to the Constitution forever forbidding slavery on the soil of the United States! It now remains for the President to sign and the States to ratify. This news is unexpected, important and good. 1st. It abolishes a great curse & drag upon us. 2d. It shuts the door against premature and degrading compromise with the Rebels.[29] Went to see Mrs. Dr. White, poor Perrin's sister. She reminded me of him. We talked some time of him and she promised to send me a book of his. She has his simple, straight forward way and is plainly permanently affected by his death. Then called on Dr. Henry I. Bowditch to find where could get a large photograph of his son, Nat, who fell near Kelly's Ford. For am now collecting the photographs of officers that have personally known, who have fallen in active or died from disease, in this War. He showed me an album beautifully ornamented with twining flowers, painted on the title page, and with patriotic sentiments in the hand of the Doctor himself. Katie Putnam, who was engaged to his son, did the flowers. It is a pleasure to see a man of his purity of character.[30] Took advantage of being near at hand to take a look at the new hall of the Nat. Hist. Soc. on the new land. The hall is imposing, with open space quite to the roof and lateral galleries and some rooms entering therein. On the ground floor is a good sized library. Also took 50 cents' worth of the Big Organ which is a striking structure indeed, with a heavy carved wood front, comparable to a large house. The tones are grand, though the heaviest chords are too loud for the hall, for this organ is one of the largest in the world. In the eve we went to tea at Mrs. Cabot's. There came Mr. & Mrs. Walter, ditto Eliott, ditto Charlie Gardner with his sister Loulie. Sadie & the resigned Louis were already there. Charlie Gardner is getting a corporation & looks really fatherly at his tender age. He has a pretty little wife.[31]

February 2, Thursday.

They rung & fired for the Emancipation Clause. To my great joy Gen. Meade was confirmed yesterday, 32 to 5, despite a malicious speech by Wade of Ohio, of an hour and a half's length. Wrote a note of congratulation straightway to him. A very pleasant dinner chez Brimmer, Mr. & Mrs. Charlie Thorndike, ditto Aug. Perkins, ditto Dick Parker, then Bob Winthrop & Miss Augusta Thorndike. Mimi resplendent in a new dress of cherry silk. The friendly Martin (who is getting quite grayish) honored us gents by a bottle of White Top madeira, which was a work of art! (Note: Vide 7th)[32]

February 3, Friday.

After a dinner with Co & Howland, Em called and we three went to the French theatre, on Co's tickets. It was in the little theatre they have made in the Tremont temple; and the play, "La Joie de la Maison" amused me, though there were inexcusable faults—parts not learned, carelessness in detail. It was a treat to see the solid men of Boston, who didn't understand a word, smiling away blandly at the most scandalous passages!

February 4, Saturday.

Worked on the index for my Catalogue of Ophiurans. Mrs. Dr. White kindly sent me, with a note, a book of Perrin Ellis', with his name on the title and the date 1854.— This afternoon, or evening rather, the children had a play, Sally & Frank and Amy Shaw.—"A Soldier's Courtship"—very successful and the charade "Out-rage" was still better. Frank appeared in female characters and Amy & Sallie in male, to our great delight; little Sallie looking much like a small edition of her papa! Mrs. Carrie Tappan & her two shapeless young daughters, and Quin, Pauline, Co & Howland were of the audience.[33]

February 5, Sunday.

A Smart snow, just in time to keep up the sleighing. Again dined by invite at Jas. Lawrence's. Miss Annie Motley also honored us. After dinner came Messrs. Arthur Devens, Wm. Amory and Wm. Rives. The latter asked questions about the war, without which would not have mentioned it, seeing his unfortunate position as a Virginian. They spoke of Capt. Payson, who was on Devin's staff, was shot in one of the lower leg bones in the attack at Cool Arbor, and has been bed ridden ever since—now, poor lad, he is improving and hopes to be about soon.— The peace negotiations are all gone up: they produced no impression on my mind. The President went to Fortress Monroe (with Mr. Seward also) and saw Stevens, Hunter and Campbell on ship-board. They talked together and separated— Ah! the beginning of the end; but that end not very near, unless we beat them hard first.[34]

February 6, Monday.

Took Mimette, in a sleigh, to visit Mrs. Amos Lawrence at Longwood and Mrs. Sue Dabney at Jamaica Plain—neither at home—*tant mieux*—left cards. Got from General Meade a letter, in good spirits over his confirmation—He saw & talked frankly with the reb' peace commissioners.— They did not seem to mention the necessity of their *independence*, but hinted at more protection of *state rights* by the constitution; did not regard slavery as material; thought that the matter might well be left to the good judgment of the generals in the field—Significant![35] Cora took us to the "*théâtre français*" again. Play, "Les Alliés"—very good indeed; and much better than before. Thereafter, a little supper chez Co, to which came Mr. & Mrs. Brim', Mr. & Mrs. Gus. Perkins and Em! Mrs. Brimmer declaring she could not eat anything & had a headache, and then consuming quail, salad, ice cream, cake and punch!—a kindly woman, but babyish.[36]

February 7, Tuesday.

Went, last Thursday, and saw Dr. Mason Warren's fire-proof building, containing the Mastodon, &c. &c. There is an upper and a lower room, with a collection of parts of mastodons, besides the big skeleton; the Zeuglodon (which the Doctor still persists in labeling "Sea Serpent," though it's a whale!) bird tracks; a good collection of sawed calculi &c. &c. John Bryant's dead—Bryant & Sturgis—both gone now—"Lather & Shave"—what good did *he* do, but pile one dollar on top another? Caleb Chace thrown from a sleigh, fractured base of skull—died also—*aetas* 70—another close handed man. Bought some Harvard Coll. spoons, as a souvenir, 6 big—2¾ oz. each, 12 small, 1¼ oz. each. Driving to Brookline, found Silas back. His Maine neighbors are making money from sheep & lumber. There was a wild time over the confirmed news of Hal's retirement from service! The girls were in the greatest indignation; Mimi saying he was disgraced and crying about it. Their view is extreme; had he stayed, it would have been more to his credit; but, after his service he has a right to retire without disgrace—voila![37]

February 8, Wednesday.

Ned Browne told me Tim Lewis was seriously sick and seriously poor so we both sent him somewhat. News that, on Sunday last the 5th Corps with Gregg's cavalry moved down the Weldon road, struck off to the west, crossed Rowanty Creek and made connection in their right with the 3d div. 2d Corps which forced Hatcher's run at the Vaughan road; which the 2d div. facing to the west, on the east side of the run, repelled several attacks coming from direction of Armstrong's. Losses small. Query: Reconnoissance, demonstration, or extension of the line?[38]

February 9, Thursday.

The old story, confound it! On Monday, the 3d div. 5th Corps on the right and leading advanced into the thickets towards Dabney's mill. At first they drove back Pegram's division (he being killed), also another division, but that fellow Mahone struck them on the flank and drove them back in confusion, till they rallied in the breastworks, near the Vaughan road, when the enemy was checked and retired. The cavalry, under Gregg, went as far as Dinwiddie Ct. House. They had brisk infantry fighting, Gens. Davies & Gregg Jr. being hit. In the 5th Corps Gen. ~~Ayres was hit (shoulder)~~ [Struck out by TL], Col. Bankhead (hand) &c.[39] Ah! Do feel ashamed, to be here and my people fighting. But it's not my fault. Hastened to the State House and got Schouler to telegraph to Barstow to ask if there were to be more moves, if so, wished to come on. Then felt a little better. To a whist at Chas. Codman's, where played with Pauline, M. Thoron and Miss Lilie Ward, whom of course called Madame Thoron, whereas *she* is the elder one, Annie! *C'est égal;* we beat 3 of 4 games.[40]

February 10, Friday.

Telegraph from Barstow —No need now. Gen. will advise you.—So I suppose they will be content to fortify and hold this new flank, from Ft. Cummings to somewhere beyond Hatcher's Run, near Vaughan road. Went to Cambridge and ordered at Warren's, Cambridgeport, some photographs, to make up the collection I am making of my friends who have fallen in the War. Then continued to Agassiz whom found at dinner and so took a glass of Yvorne and a cut with him. After which explained to him some corrections to be made in the catalogue and gave him the index for the printer. Pauline, Mrs. A. & Burkhardt dined there, and the latter came with me in town, *à pied.*— On Tuesday Crawford again went out towards Dabney's mill and drove back the rebs into their works, which are said to be near the mill. If so the line is a new one. The Georgia General Sorrell was killed (note: mortally [?] wounded), adding another to their many officers who thus expose their lives.[41]

February 11, Saturday.

Our "family" dinner was naught, for Sallie was at the French theatre, and poor pa Russell up stairs with a twinge of gout. However, M. Burkhardt came and we had several brisk games of whist which enlivened us. Called on Mr. Zerda-helyi, who lives 8 Dix Place, to hear him read a chapter on outposts, from his forthcoming book on campaigning. It seemed a careful compilation, but, after all, an officer who has had next to no military experience like him, can scarcely hope to do much in the book way. A studious, worthy man, but an everlasting, crack-brained talker![42]

February 12, Sunday.

Nothing would do but must again dine with Jim Lawrence. So after hearing a good discourse from Rev. Rufus Ellis (he who told Perrin "as you sow, so shall you reap") and taking Mimi a walk midst the snow storm, &c. &c. did end the day there. Mrs. Prescott was ill up stairs, but James' classmate Arthur Devens came to dessert and helped at a bottle of "Constitution"—a very fine wine of 1837 bottling. Had made a map for Mr. L's edification, to show him the positions round Petersburg.[43]

February 13, Monday.

A kind letter from Gen. Meade, explaining the move, the other day, which, it would appear originated only in a cavalry move to see what trains we could pick up at Dinwiddie C. H.—We got 25 waggons. The infantry supports got naturally into a fight & we have staid on that ground. It was developed that the rebels have moved their line forward—i.e. made an additional advanced line, which takes in the Clement's house and runs a little behind Dabney's mill. Flying rumors of our capture of Branchville and evacuation of Charleston, Mobile &c. &c. All probable, but needing confirmation. Cold & cutting weather, rising from 5° upwards, towards mid-day, with much wind. Drove with Mimi to Brookline, coming round via Cambridge; where went into the fore room to look at a photograph there of a group, that contains Temple, Swan, Herbert Mason & Henry Abbott. It was taken 2 days before the battle of Chancellorsville, where Temple (17th U.S. Inf.) fell. Of those four, two have fallen on the field, and the other two been seriously wounded.[44]

February 14, Tuesday.

Little Cora went on a great spree with papa & mamma, to wit, all the way to Milton Hill, for a dinner with Aunt Amelia & Aunt Rose. It was really pleasant in that quaint old house. They had hoisted a festive flag in our honor and gave a dinner worthy of all praise and enough to eat for a regiment. To my surprise a decanter, too, was put upon the table, and Aunt Rose was much gratified at my discovery that it was first chop old Madeira. Over the door is a picture, left

Aunt Amelia, of "Uncle Otis Ammidon," painted when he was a young man, by Sargent, father of Turner & Winthrop S. Little Co was subdued, at first, by all the novelty, but soon rallied and was highly pleased.— That evening Em' gave a supper to the fiancés Charlie Bowditch & Miss Rockwell; she a lady-like and pretty girl with light hair. There also were 8 more making 12 *in toto* including Em' & Mimi. Was myself to make one, but Mr. Frank Loring was polite and bright enough first to say he couldn't come and then, that he would like to change his mind, so his obtuseness worked well for me and relieved me of entertaining the snipes![45]

February 15, Wednesday.

Visited Mr. & Mrs. Thuolt in the evening, who now board corner of Allston & Somerset, and have better rooms than of yore. Fifteen years have made no change in the intensity of the feelings for his country and against Austria in this honorable and high-spirited man. His wife keeps her good looks, despite much weak health, and has the remarkable black eyes & arched brows of an oriental. Snowing hard, which towards morning turned into rain, and—Annie Smith came, vice Adeline, to take care of the Baby; a great improvement.[46]

February 16, Thursday.

Here was a slushy, sloshy day, so did stay mostly at home, getting up my notes for my diary of the first part of last campaign not yet written. Driving for a mouthful of air to see Burkhardt at Cambridge, where stopped but a few moments, & looked at my plates which he is coloring. Met Jim Emmerton in the street this morn—he is Major, or something in the 2d Mass. Heav. Artil. Mimette with me to dine at Howland's. Thither came Miss Bessie Gray & Mrs. Brimmer. The former is certainly bright, and so entertaining at an argument. She said Ludlow reported that our reb' prisoners were as bad in shape as the reb' union ones. He is the only man that ever heard say so. Mrs. Brimmer has been so babied by Cora and her Martin for a series of years, that she has got thoroughly selfish (in small things) and childish; though she's a good hearted and kindly woman, by nature. Met Capt. Scott, the other day, who has been handed by Butler over to Ord. His former General Gordon is at Fortress Monroe. They seem rather to keep him out of the field.[47]

February 17, Friday.

We got the last of the sleighing by a jaunt to Brookline. Raised Mrs. Woods wages to $16 pr. month. Miss Burbank, who had been so dangerously ill with her lungs is better & hopes to get home, by & bye. It was very melty and the mill dam was pretty nearly bare, by the time we returned. Ever since have been home (and for some days before) there has been sleighing, most of the time very good—quite unprecedented—yet there has been no great snow storm, but the snow has frozen & held, so that we may say of the sleighing, that it seldom has been longer, or less of it. George Curtis was in for a few moments—caught here between two trains.— He reported all the Staten Islanders well, and told us some funny anecdotes of a certain brassy scapegrace Sam Ward, brother of Mrs. Dr. Howe.— To tea chez the Turner Sargents—nice people—you feel more placid after being with them. So pleasant & intelligent & loving of art. Their very tea service, of silver, was different from those of other folks, and more tasteful. Big-eared Greenough, son of Gas-Greenough, was there a few minutes.[48]

February 18, Saturday.

To make up for no outside olive branches at our family dinner, there came Mr. & Mrs. Chas. Dabney. He related the story of his punching the head of the southern law student, Miles, when in college. Out of this affair grew the rumpus wherein Mr. Billy Prescott got his nose pulled in an opera box, without resenting the insult! A young, bleached looking, Mr. Shattuck came at the top of the evening—one of Em's friends.[49]

February 19, Sunday.

Hal surprised us all by his sudden appearance by the night train from New York. Papa & Mama were much pleased to see him; the girls greeted him, all round, with a serious kiss—rather icy! After a sermon from cousin Foote, called on Jim Lawrence, for it won't do to dine there *every* Sunday, and talked a good bit with him. He showed me a letter from "Phenomenon" Wm. Everett to the Lecture Committee of the Mercantile Library, a letter almost inconceivable for its conceit & arrogance. He says the sending of a free ticket to him was truly *meant* as a kindness, but he wished to take a part, not as an auditor, but as a *lecturer*—had had eminent success as a public speaker; and, if he were entitled to a ticket as a compliment, it would be because he was a public speaker, and, *if* a public speaker, *why* was he not asked to lecture there?—It was really comical!— News this morn that Sherman had entered Columbia! He is going pretty fast! The danger lies ahead. Lee must be devoting all his best talents to planning a heavy blow against some separate part of our armies—e.g. of Sherman's troops; and, as our forces converge towards Richmond, the moment of peril draws on.— Of all men in the world, got a letter yesterday from Geo. Webb in Court, in London! more cracked than ever, and a Lieutenant in something. He only wants $100 loan & a commission in our army! Wrote him civilly that couldn't see the point.[50]

February 20, Monday.

After nearly four years of waiting and labor and strife, we got, this day, intelligence that the Nest of Rebellion, Charleston, had fallen into our hands! These men, who swore great oaths to shed their last blood on its ramparts, have ignobly marched out at the prosaic command of "military expediency!" They have reaped the whirlwind.— On the 18th our forces occupied the place, finding 200 cannon and ammunition. Cotton, stores, & railroad bridges burnt.[51]— Ned Browne, Charlie Thorndike & self took a carriage and a basket containing a trifle of cold supper and wended our way to Burkhardt's room, in the Museum "Barrack." Here he had prepared a table and cards and we went at the whist, in true old style. Then followed the little supper, whither came Alex, just back from a fruitless search after "ile" in the lands of west Missouri. He even crossed into Kansas, being sent on an exploration by Nat Thayer, John M. Forbes &c. We drove home feeling almost as if it were still college days.

February 21, Tuesday.

To a very amusing sale of 500 bottles of Daniel Webster's wines, which he had in Washington, the winter he died, and which were there packed & sent to Boston, and have since lain in Mr. Paige's cellar. Of course there was rather a mixture & it was a lottery to go into it! A few bottles were opened, but one could not depend on the rest being like them. It was a study to see how far mere name goes. The "star" pale sherry, worth perhaps $30. per doz. sold at $6.25 per bottle! "Tinta" madeira, scarce fit to drink, was the same price. Bought 2 cases, purporting to be "S" madeira, at $3.50 per bottle.[52]

February 22, Wednesday.

The cannon roused us at sun-rise, a double salute for Washington's birthday and the fall of Charleston. Mr. Russell, in the glory of his heart, has had a flag pole put on the balcony, and had out his stars & stripes. Hal left us last night, to go to N. York, where he has hired apartments and will put Mary under Dr. Elliot's care. (Note: 75 W. 45th St, between 5th & 6th Av.) To Brookline, where opened the two auction cases—result, 20 bottles fine old madeira; 1 do. fine old pale brandys; 2 do. brown sherry—poor; *and* 22 do. Sicily madeira.

Ha! ha! ha!—Well, fancy the rest were about as badly off, on the average. Did get something good, and the Sicily makes *very* fine jelly! At 3 P.M. got on my uniform and, with Annie and Paw & Maw went to pay my devoirs to "Mrs. Washington" (Harry Otis). There was her china & picture house in full bloom with many handsome flowers, gifts from her lady friends (e.g. cousin Mary Pratt). Likewise a huge lot of wedding cake and a modicum of wine. There was Col. Graham, of the engineers, in full tog, even to sword & epaulettes. Also other notables, among whom was introduced to Col. Taylor who had addressed the people in behalf of East Tennessee, one of those concentrated, black eyed, desperately bilious-temperament men who are characteristic of the West.[53] There were Aunts Rose & Geraldine & Miss Mary Rivers. Yesterday, by the way, met Miss Lilie Motley in the street, Lothrop's daughter.— Cannot rest here quiet any more; feel that the army may move at any moment; ergo will go, *Deo volente*, next Monday night! At 5.30 dinner at Uncle Charles! Company Mr. & Mrs. Phil. Sears & Miss Raggio, a half-bred young lady, daughter of a Greek merchant said to be of rather low extraction. Florence appeared to great advantage, being well dressed, and a real lady. She has the kind heart of good Uncle Charles, who was very bright & lively. Mr. Fred also bestirred himself to be entertaining. He looks white and bloated, rather, and still sports those extraordinary floating, tressy whiskers, which are my periodical wonder. Mimi & I kept up the dissipation by going, for whist, to Mr. Sam Ward's house, an elegant new one, on Commonwealth Avenue, with such a feudal black walnut dining room & fire place, that Gain Shaw said he was endeavoring to get up the sentiment of being a baron! Introduced to Mrs. John Bancroft, by John himself who looks & talks just like the J. B. of old. She a modest body great friend of Pauline. Introduced, also, to Mrs. LeFarge, whose husband, the excellent flower painter, is a boyish looking chap, with no muscles, a small head, and protruding eyes. Weather clear & very mild.[54]

February 23, Thursday.

Drove with Mimette to visit Mary Guild in West Roxbury. Glad to see the addition of a stable to the place. They have had a hard time in the by-gone. Passed Wales', going back & ordered some flowers. Went down town and bought a little picture, by Niles, of a wee gal on the ice, with her sled; very clever, and rejoiced Mimi, to whom gave it. Went with her to see Nellie Shaw who goes back to Staten Is. tomorrow. There saw Willie Forbes, who is on for a short visit and not yet exchanged. After that called on Jim Lawrence, where found Mrs. Geo. M. Dexter.

February 24, Friday.

Despatch that Wilmington was taken on the 22d *ça marche!* Scofield moved on both banks of the river, while the gunboats helped by water. The enemy were first driven from Ft. Anderson, and subsequently our people advanced on the city, whence the rebels retreated, leaving 30 cannon & 700 prisoners; besides which they burned vast quantities of resin & much cotton. Hoke was there.[55] Visited many fashionables, with Mimi, e.g. Miss Lilie Motley at the Austen (H. G. Otis) house. She has grown of a bad figure & is by no means so pretty as at Vienna. Perhaps the last time was in this house, was at a mixed party, in the lifetime of old H. G. O.—when wore a jacket with bright buttons & danced with the then Misses Emily & Mary Otis. Do well remember how—enter Mrs. H. G. O. jun. who embraced & kissed papa-in-law! Thus did she gradually extinguish all hopes of the old gentleman's money! Saw there today Miss Cleveland, who charged me, when we entered Richmond, to put a flag in Washington's hand. It's a grand old house, certainly.[56]— Went also to see Mrs. Edwards, & Miss Dorr, the former, with her kindly, mincing ways, grown very old, poor woman, and in a wig now. To Brookline, where put away papers &c.

February 25, Saturday.

Drove with Little Wife to Cambridge, to call on Aunt Hannah [Shaw]. She, good woman, has lost 50 lbs. by virtue of Banting. Aunt Eliot not at home. Saw, however Mrs. Agassiz, and bid good bye. In town purchased various small goodies for the behoof & comfort of Albert. Gen. Meade's son, Sergeant, is dead at last, poor fellow.— Family dinner, unusually large, in all 12; Lou Shaw, Will Forbes, & M. Burkhardt as extra company and then all the children, save, of course, the absent Hal & Bob. After dinner a few games of whist, in which Burkhardt & Mr. R[ussell] rather defeated my side. Saw Palfrey in the morn', who told me Macy had the offer of Prov. Ml. of A. of P. Told him thought M. should take it. Splendid weather lately—clear, mild, bracing.[57]

February 26, Sunday.

Went & saw Jim Lawrence and he bid me bon voyage for my return to the army tomorrow. Called too on Mrs. Barstow who may have somewhat to send by my hand. Cora must needs have us to a farewell dinner, which was very agreeable to our feelings. There was no company beside, and we made it a strictly family affair. Cora confessed (what did not before know) that it was she who wrote the anonymous letter to Mr. Wm. Amory, which said that forty gentlemen had banded together to tar & feather him, if he should repeat such conduct, as shaking hands with Beauregard &c. &c. in Charleston! She wrote it the spring of '61 and did much trouble the spirit of William thereby, insomuch that he bears it, to this day, in mind, though he never rightly knew who sent it.[58]

February 27, Monday.

Over two months at home! Now it seems hardly possible—about two weeks, that is the way it seems. Little wife is very brave, though she has been breaking out in little showers of tears, these last few days. Made a call or two and purchased a few necessaries, & packed that familiar valise. (By the bye, called, the other day, on Mrs. Hooker, at her aunt's Mrs. Brooks and presented her a bouquet; for she was very kind at Rome to us, and we have had no chance, this winter, to return it.)—Then poor Mimette and I drove to Bonny Brookline, where we gave some final orders to Silas the Serious. The train went at 8½ ocl', so, after a cup of tea, went up to kiss my little Co-co, but the small thing was in her crib, and had already toppled off to sleep, looking as cunning as a snowdrop! It was hard to go, & leave Mimi; but I have had more than my share and have no right to complain, for indeed we never were happier than during this visit. So good bye household, and good bye Co & Howland, kindly waiting at the cars, to see me off! Oh, shelf in this sleeping car, you are not equal to that bed at Number 1 Louisburg Square.[59]

February 28, Tuesday.

Those men at the Astor must take me for a restless spirit of travelling; appearing and taking early breakfasts, at intervals of weeks or of months. For companion in the Baltimore train had a foreigner, German possibly, who beguiled the tedium with cigars, sandwiches and cognac. Found a stateroom on the boat, though did not find my valise, which had missed the connection—*Eh! bien*; Adam's Express. There was Mr. Schuyler aboard, going to see Phil, who was a boon in the way of an evening chat. Saw also Capt. Paine of the Signal Corps.[60]

March 1, Wednesday.

Found the Washington boat waiting to go at 8 A.M. which is exceptional, for usually we wait for her. Took breakfast at the "Hygeia Saloon" at Fortress Monroe, not so named, *certes*, by reason of the healthy victual! On the boat bound up the river found the beautiful & entertaining Craig & the young Harry Humphreys. As we drew near the region of City Point, observed numerous great flocks of ducks, feeding near shore. At the Point saw Capt. Beckwith & Gen. Patrick, with whom Mr. Schuyler was to pass the night.[61] We were 6 hours coming up. Took the 3 P.M. train for the front, which however only got under way late and arrived about 5 at H'dq'rs. As descended from the ambulance there of course was old Duane, all ready to "visit" me; also Barstow and Gen. Webb, our new and acceptable chief of staff. Going in to dinner was kindly greeted by the General who, poor man, has just come back from burying his son. He playfully said he should have me courtmartialed for returning without orders. John Ropes at dinner. Old Rosie was delighted to behold me and had a Swedish flag over my bed. Also he has a frame inside and other improvements to the tent.[62]

March 2, Thursday.

Rain all day. Lt. Col. Campbell is Judge Adv. now; an officer whose left arm is disabled by a wound. Capt. Whittemore Qr. Mr. *vice* the card playing Kephart. Sanders, Meade & Bache, off on leave. Stryker replaced as signal officer by Capt. Davis. Col. Ruggles, our new A.A.G., is a young man with a florid face and red moustache; prompt & military in demeanor. Brev. Maj. Sleeper has resigned his battery, under advantage of a misconstruction of the 3-year mustering out law. Had rather have seen him hold to the end, but he is a good officer with a good record.[63]

March 3, Friday.

Cloudy but no rain. Rosie conducted me to view our new line, which starts at Ft. Sampson and runs W. of S. outside the Vaughan road to the crossing of the same at Hatcher's Run. Here is a tête de pont, on the other side, and here the line refuses. There are no enclosed works, but several strong batteries along this new line. At present the 9th Corps holds from the Appomattox to Fort Howard about 9 miles. Then follows the 6th holding about 4½ miles to Fort Sampson, and then the 2d for 5½ miles, making a total of 18 miles. The 5th is refused, on the extreme left, and held in reserve.[64] The cavalry pickets begin on Weldon R.R., ½ m. below crossing of Church Road, run to Sinai Ch. & thence to Bailey's Cr. This army has increased net about 8,000, since left, and now stands: four Corps, having, with artillery, an average for duty of 68,000–72,000; the largest being the 2d, say 20,000; the smallest the 5th say 15,500. Cavalry 6,000, now under Davies, Gregg having resigned. Then the engineer brigade 4,500, Provost Marshal brigade, 2,500, reserve batteries &c. &c. make a total for duty of over 87,000. According to Kensall the army of the James, including those detached to N.C. has 50,000 infantry & artillery and 4,000 cavalry, of whom say 35,000, in all, remain with us.[65] The total strength therefore of the two armies against Richmond may be estimated, at this moment, as 122,000 officers and men in line of battle. Sheridan is estimated at 10,000 infantry and 15,000 cavalry, total 25,000. Sherman, besides his coast garrisons, is thought to have 70,000 in his own column and 35,000 in Scofield's column; total 105,000. This would give the armies converging on Richmond, 252,000. The opposition may be guessed at as, Early 5,000; Lee 60,000; Joe Johnston (who has gathered Hoke, Hardee, most of Hood, and a variety of fragments) 50,000; total 115,000. The new camps both of 2d & 5th Corps, being on sandy ridges, are much better than most of their last camps. The rebel forces are rather concentrated on their right, their forces being engaged in extending their line beyond the Boydton plank, & up the Oak & Claiborne roads to near Sutherland's Station, on the south side R.R. This from deserters whom heard examined at Schuyler's, where, by the way, S[chuyler] senior is staying, and where Babcock & the Captain have artistic cottages, nicely papered within. These deserters show a tone of lowness in Lee's army never before seen—the veterans—men of '61 now deserting, bringing their loaded weapons with them—900 to this army alone, in the month of February. In one day there were as high as 134. And all this with the strongest precautions—an exterior line of sharpshooters, with rewards for every deserter dead or alive. Favorable signs; but there is much blood yet between us & the death of the rebellion![66] There is here now a certain Capt. Botiano, an officer of the Wallachian (Roumanian) forces educated in France and now with us, to study warfare. This Roumania is of Moldavia & Wallachia, and is under Prince Cousa, paying tribute to the Porte and guaranteed his protection; and they seem, indeed to have not only his but that of everybody else—in fact to be rather over protected. The language resembles the Italian, but, to judge from his face, there is an admixture of sundry βάςβαςοι with the blood of Trajan's colonists! He is a man of sufficient intelligence with all a Latin's idea of centralized governments. Speaks French well, but no English as yet.[67]

March 4, Saturday.

Heavy wind & rain last night & this morning. Which held up enough to let me have a ride towards Jerusalem plank. Cavalry still camped there; there is a railroad branch running thither, from near Jones' house.[68] In the evening went with Flint to Col. Spaulding's engineer camp, to hear his nigger minstrels (all enlisted men). He has most excellent rustic quarters, laid out with much taste and made entirely from the wood of the country, without any assistance in material, save nails. The minstrels were in a building used as a church on Sundays and a theatre on days secular. It is a masterpiece of rustic architecture, of hewn logs, and in form of a short cross. The niggers were really excellent, the speech, by an ancient dark, on the state of the country, was side-splitting. After the which pig's feet were served by the hospitable S[paulding] and Flint must needs have a horse raffle, which cost me $10. without result.[69] — A funny anecdote of the conceited Crawford. Artist came here to make medallions of Meade and corps commanders. C. getting wind of it, comes up, wakes artist in the middle of the night and asks him what it would cost to make a *statuette of himself.* Gen. Webb, also, got wind of *this* and, meeting C. said "Have you seen this artist down here?" "Seen him!" cries Crawford "Why he has done nothing but *bore me to have my statuette made!*"

March 5, Sunday.

Had a perfect stream of visitors Gens. Wainwright and McKenzie; then Whittier (now A.A.G. 2d Corps.), Arthur McClellan, Farrar &c. Rode out to see Fort Fisher, now enlarged to be a large, bastioned work, for fear of the enveloping guns. Beyond it they have a new battery with 6 32-p'd'r Parrotts. Also there has been erected a signal tower, 140 feet high, in rear of Ft. Fisher. Deserters from the lines opposite both armies report that Sheridan (who left his lines last Monday) defeated Early on Thursday, occupied Charlottesville, and, as some say, took Early & most of his command.[70]

March 6, Monday.

Deserters say that a number of regiments have been sent from various brigades (probably to cover Lynchburg.) The Gen. invited me to ride and we went past the Wyatt house (Crawford's H'dq'rs) to those of Gen. Humphreys, which are ½ mile north of Cumming's house where is Gen. Griffin. A branch railroad, which is to be altered to run part way on the Weldon, passes in front of this spot and has its terminus near Cumming's house. It has a high trestle work over Arthur's Swamp, the which did much astonish Botiano by its rapid construction. We found Gens. Crawford, Getty, Wright & Wheaton at Warren's H'dq'rs. "Well" said Warren to me, "you are curious. I should think, with your place, you would stay at home and let us fight it out!" Saw there Hadyn who was shot through the body at Cedar Run [Cedar Creek], at the same time as his General, Ricketts. He gave me some account of the fighting up there in the valley.[71]

March 7, Tuesday.

There came up, for a tour of our lines, a boodle of 12 ladies, with a number of gentlemen, distinguished folks, more or less; thus, Mrs. Gen. Grant, Miss Stanton (~~daughter~~ [TL corrected to] niece of Sec. of War), Miss Bradlee (of N. J.), Mrs. Smith, sister to Dr. Grier (who came with new-married Mrs. G.), Miss Woodruff and papa, Judge W[oodruff], Mr. & Mrs. Harding (part proprietor of Philadelphia Enquirer) &c. &c. Rode over to receive them, with ambulances, at 11.30. Mrs. Grant is very even and quiet, with a pleasant expression, though she has a tremendous cast in one eye. Miss Stanton (whom handed about a good deal before knew her illustrious parentage!) is very modest & rather good looking, & reminded me of Miss Lizzie Clark, once a noted Newport belle. Miss Bradlee was the best looking; on the whole they were the comeliest lot we ever have had. Old Bradlee & old Woodruff got bravely on horses, though the latter hadn't ridden since '34! All the Aides being turned out for their entertainment, the party, the General gallantly leading, rode from his Headquarters where he had received them. We showed them the elegant quarters of Col. Spaulding; then the 6th Corps hospitals, which were most nicely arranged, and where met Dr. Holman, for the first time since the corps returned from the Valley. Then we carted them to Ft. Fisher, & showed them the rebs and a review of Keifer's brigade 3d div. 6th A.C. K[eifer] can't use his hand yet. Made the acquaintance of Brev. Brigadier Penrose, not yet fully well of a bad wound in the arm.[72] Nothing put down by their jolting over corduroys & mud holes, the ladies a review. The gallant General received them with fruit, crackers, cider & ale. He has for would now fain keep on, down the Vaughan road and all the way to Warren's quarters there to see his house, the log chateau that Crawford originally framed, close to us, here. Then Griffin's division was reviewed, on a field not far off, and presented a good appearance. Saw there Gen. Bartlett, gorgeous, as usual, in many trappings & much lace. Gen. Humphreys was introduced by me to Miss Bradlee, for which do expect his gratitude. The gallant General had ridden quietly over from his quarters, while Whittier had careered over the country, in a vain pursuit of the ladies! Saw Curtis of the Mass. 20th, & Col. Rice of the 19th. Still better was Crawford's review, near Wyatt's house, the setting sun looking beautiful on the bayonets. It was dusk before the party got to H'dq'rs where a lunch was ready; but as it had been intended for a one o'clock bite, it looked rather meagre for the evening, so the General felt rather peevish, but we got in some hot meats and opened some champagne & restored the equilibrium. Finally we packed them all off, much impressed with the day, and our souls had rest. Rosie, Jay, &c went with, for a dance on the boats they have especially for them, and they wanted me to come but couldn't see *that* point! Gen. Joe Hayes came down and was my guest for the night, after smoking his cigar with the General. He told the circumstances of his capture & how Blatchford the reb Prov. M'l asked him if he knew Tom Appleton! It was really a magnificent day, warm & clear, but—

March 8, Wednesday—

Here was the southerly rain again, coming down heavily. Lent Joe my horse and he went off and had a grand time, all day long, at the 5th Corps, with Ayres & Griffin. Rosencrantz came back from the Point, having done a deal of supper eating & of dancing with the ladies.[73]

[Clipping from newspaper, inserted]

Petersburg Mine Explosion—Important Communication.

A message of the President, sent to the Senate yesterday, communicated the opinion and finding of the court of inquiry instituted by the President in the case of the Petersburg mine. The opinion is signed by Major General W. S. Hancock, president of the court. After narrating the circumstances of the assault, the failure is ascribed to the following officers: First. Major General A. E. Burnside, in not obeying the orders of the commanding general, in the formation of the assaulting column; in not preparing his parapet and abbatis for the passage of his troops, and in not employing engineer officers to lead the columns with the working parties. Yet the court is satisfied that General Burnside believed the measures taken by him would insure success. Second. Brigadier General J. H. Ledlie, in failing to push forward his troops promptly, and in blocking up the avenue designed for the passage of troops ordered to follow, he being most of the time in a bomb-proof ten rods in the rear of the main line, where the movement could not be witnessed. Third. Brigadier General Edward Ferrero, for want of readiness for the assault, not going with his troops, but remaining in a bomb-proof. Fourth. Colonel Z. R. Bliss, 7th Rhode Island, commanding brigade, in remaining behind with one regiment in a position where he could not see what was going on. Fifth. Brigadier General O. B. Wilcox, in lack of energy in carrying out General Burnside's order to push his troops forward to Cemetery Hill. The court concludes the opinion as follows: "Without intending to convey the impression that there was any disinclination on the part of the commanders of the supports to heartily co-operate in the attack on the 30th of July, the court express their opinion that explicit orders should have been given, assigning one officer to the command of all the troops intended to engage in the assault, when the commanding general was not present in person to witness the operations."[74]

March 9, Thursday.

Hayes went home & expects soon to come back for a brigade. Despatches from Sheridan show, that, at Waynesboro, a dozen miles east of Staunton, he routed a small force, under Early, took 12 guns, 1250 prisoners and some 250 waggons, besides cotton & supplies.[75] Last night the General went to the Minstrels at Col. Spaulding's and today there was a Matinee musicale at the same place under the leadership of Halstead, who is quite known as a musician. The band was that of the N. Jersey Brigade and the music was most praiseworthy. A solo by the leader Reinhardt was excellent (on the clarinette) and the other pieces were judiciously selected from Operas, &c. There was a lot of ladies (another batch) among the audience. Mrs. Gen. Webb and Mrs. Emory came to camp, but did not come to the concert. After that was a review of Miles' division near the Peeble house, whereat appeared General Doyle, our New Brunswick friend, who, it appears, wrote the article on the last campaign, in the Edinburgh Review. We rode down the line, the Chief going at full gallop, perhaps to please the ladies looking on. Introduced to Gen. Hamlin (Brevet). Barstow got back from Washington, bringing a certain Chevalier de Karnbeek of the Dutch legation, who slept in my tent. Gov. Clifford came too. Was introduced to Capt. Robert Lincoln, who seemed to me rather pale, sleepy and thick-skinned.[76]

March 10, Friday.

An extremely chilly north-east storm, in the morning, which changed to hail and then partly cleared up. There must needs come again a posse of women (who seem to think this a pic-nic ground!) Gov. Morehead of Penn. was the spokesman. We took them in ambulances to Ft. Welch and showed them a review of Keifer's brigade. Among them was wife of Jay Cooke, who lately has made a noise in selling the 7/30 loan. She was a bourgeoise with a turn-up nose. What a happy country for all is if each class will keep by itself, where they feel at ease; but what a spectacle is any attempt at a public ball, where all classes mingle, or indeed any public entertainment where we seek to produce an imposing effect! Speaking of this, it is painful to think of the degradation of some of our heads. There is the Vice President "Andy" Johnson, absolutely under liquor the very day of his inauguration! He began a debauch the very moment of leaving the West, and has so kept it up since, that some people think he will not recover his mind. It is humiliating! The President said, in his shrewd way, "I shall be very careful of my health, these next four years!"[77]

March 11, Saturday.

Rebel news, that Hoke & Hill (not A. P.) had attacked the advance of some of Scofield's force (under Cox?) and driven them back 3 miles taking 3 guns & 1,500 prisoners. Sorry to hear it; for it seems a useless waste, to prolong this fight by trifling reverses, now that it seems so near its end. Per contra, by advices from Thomas, it would seem that Sherman turned on Cheatham, who was coming up with part of Hood's army, in his rear, and routed him—no particulars.[78] The Lieut. Gen. came by train to the extreme left, with a party of half a dozen ladies and some gentlemen; among them our old friend the Hon. Washburn. Gen. Humphreys turned out the 2d & 3d divisions, near the Cummings house in their honor. The General rode to the left on horseback, stopping to get Gen. Warren, who treated to a little ale, which, in sooth, is no treat for me. The troops made a fine show, the 2d div, looking especially clean & steady. But it went to my heart to see the Massachusetts 20th, a poor skeleton of some hundred and odd men, and to think how I saw them, a year since,—with well filled ranks, marching proudly in review, with Abbott at their head; and how they were called up, afterwards, to drill, as the model of the corps. But they have undermined the rock on which they have been dashed to pieces. The reason of Hon. Washburn's presence appeared that evening, when he presented the congressional gold medal & resolutions to Gen. Grant, for the capture of Vicksburg. Gens. Meade, Webb & Hunt went to City Pt. and the corps commanders, with a few division commanders and Aides de camp. The presentation was in the upper salon of the "Martin," lying at the wharf. Gen. Ord was present and a number of officers from the Army of the James. Mr. Washburn was concise in his observations and was followed by Gen. Grant, in the following burst of eloquence, read from a paper "Sir! I accept the medal. I shall take an early opportunity to write a suitable reply to the President. I shall publish the circumstance to the troops under my command before Vicksburg, in general orders." "Ah!" said Pell "I thought we had him sure on a speech *this* time but now we never shall get one out of him!"— And so home, after a slight collation. The whole presentation was a model, particularly the speeches. As for the medal, the gold (3 lbs) and the mechanical execution were its only merits. Was introduced to Mrs. Griffin, a very nice, pretty woman.[79]

March 12, Sunday.

Splendid day! Walked out and surveyed a part of the "loop" line that Gen. Wright held, the June day that Mahone humbugged him. This line is not laid down on any of the maps.[80]

March 13, Monday.

Rebel news that Wade Hampton had surprised and driven back Kilpatrick, taking some guns apparently. It must be a poor officer that can't get ahead of old "Kil!"— Long telegraph from Sheridan that he was then at Columbia, on the James, having had no opposition since he broke up Early at Waynesboro! He took Charlottesville, destroyed the bridges & R.R. near there. Then struck south to the James at Scottville, destroying the canal as he moved east. He intends to cut across the Va. Central R.R., near the S. Anna, and come out at "Whitehouse, where supplies are to be sent him." Completed my survey of the loop line to Ft. Stevenson. Brev. Brig. Gen. Macy arrived, and will take the post of Prov. Ml. of this army. With him was young Robins (Richard's younger brother) who is on his staff.[81]

March 14, Tuesday.

Summer warm, and the frogs merrier than ever. Telegraph from Scofield that he beat Bragg, instead of Bragg *him*, in the fight of the 10th (or 9th). Fancy the real fact is Bragg attacked him and drove back a part of his force, that then supports came up and repulsed Bragg, who, finding his position a bad one, retreated across the Neuse in the night. The rear of Sherman's column was to get in yesterday to Fayetteville, whence, it is to be presumed, he will march on Raleigh.[82] Today sutlers ordered to the rear and orders out for troops to stand ready at very short notice to move—precautionary probably on the approach of Sherman & Co. Nine 4-gun batteries ordered to each corps, and the superfluous batteries to report to Brev. Brig. Gen. Tidball, who will assign as many to the 9th Corps line as he needs and will order the rest to City Point; this, and the work on the old flank and rear line beyond the Jerusalem [Plank] Road, indicates that the 9th Corps will hold that position, while *nous autres* cut loose entirely and either move to join Sherman and Scofield, or else move round in the rear of the enemy's present lines.[83]

March 15, Wednesday.

Davis has given a message to his congress, saying that Gen. Lee had signified a willingness to have an authorized meeting with Gen. Grant, with an idea of attempting peace; but that Grant had declared he had no power in the premises.

Thus showing, says Davis, the Yankee determination to give no terms save utter subjugation!—Significant! There came another bunch of visitors Senators Wilson, Morrill, Foster, &c. also some women with them; but, for myself, did run away and complete my survey of our lines east of the Aiken house, during the operations of June 22nd & 23d.[84]

March 16, Thursday.

The Hon. Secretary of War favored us with his presence. Was introduced to him and found him as mild as drawn butter. He is short, dark, very thick set, very big-headed; a small, turned up nose; a long black beard, mixed with gray, and a somewhat goblin air. With his party (some 20) were M. Geofrey, the French Minister, another Gaul or so, and Sam Hooper, with no less person then the handsome, though icy, Mrs. Sturgis Hooper, who produced a great impression on all the officers. We went, after lunch & punch for them, to the Cummings house, whither they went in the cars, while some of the Aides rode, to the sweating of my mare, in order to be there in time. Here the 5th Corps was turned out (at a notice of 2 hours, to Mr. Stanton's great surprise).[85] Crawford's division was largest and marched best, the other two needed drill badly, though the men seemed clean and hearty. These reviews do not average, like the great ones of the 2d & 6th Corps, held by Grant last spring, when the ranks counted so many reinlisted veterans, and when the corps were a third larger than now. Considering, however, the unprecedented campaign, (lasting, with varying activity from the first of May to the middle of December and involving a movement & fight in the first of February, and more or less siege duty the whole time) the strength & appearance of the corps is all that could be hoped for. Last year, after the grand battle at Gettysburg, in July, there was no more fighting of moment till October, and then the engagements were but partial, during that month and November, with long rests between. Except the small affair in February (loss 250) scarce a gun was fired all winter. Thus the troops had 5 months rest & drill. This eve played some whist for a novelty in Gen. Webb's tent, with Duane, beat the Ch' of Staff and Capt. Hilt (3d Inf.) three straight games.— Bill Forbes, the Lt. Col. is engaged to Edith Emerson. There was a story that he was after Em', but never saw any symptoms.[86]

March 17, Friday.

St. Patrick, hys day, in whose honor the Irish brigade of the 2d Corps gave races, near the Cummings house. There was a stand, gay with flags; and a band which discoursed sweet music from an army waggon. A large number of soldiers were allowed to be present and behaved most correctly. On the stand were Gens. Humphreys, Mott, Hayes, Warren, Crawford, Ayres, Miles &c. &c. Gen. Meade was also there, and a parcel of ladies; but little Mrs. Griffin, with her G. was on horseback and kept out of the way, afraid perhaps of the Commander, as her presence with the army is rather a smuggling affair. The sports were rather drawn out, and the races too much separated. Still, several were very good; while, in others, the horses baulked at the hurdles and made a real muss of it. Col. Von Schaick's horse fell on him and hurt him rather severely, and one soldier was knocked down and seriously if not mortally injured. Phil Leidig rode a race, & rode it very well, though he got beat by short distance. There was "Ma-a-her of the Sword," sober for a wonder! He insisted on an introduction to *me*; what for who can tell?— The day was warm and fine, after a perfect gale last night, accompanied by rain. Noticed peach blossom buds much swollen, and some leaf tufts just beginning to peep out; the willows also have leaves a third grown; but notice no wild flowers.[87]

March 18, Saturday.

Rode down to City Point, which took a couple of hours—distance by road probably 14 miles. There visited Channing Clapp, at his Engineer camp just inside the inner line. To my surprise Abbott, of our class, was there and made me promise to send him some notes of my occupations since graduation, for we are to have a decennial dinner and a pamphlet about the Class. Rode down to the Point, to buy a saddle-cloth &c, and met our Zoos-zoos marching in; for the gallant 114th hath been relieved at last, by the 11th U.S.[88] Then to visit Ned Dalton, who has a neat lodge, and with him Mrs. D. who looks as kindly & bright as of yore and young, despite the gray hairs that start early in her family. Dined with Channing; company, Old Benham, Mrs. and Capt. Eliot; Miss E[liot], Mrs. Coxe, Col. Michler &c. Old B[enham] is an odd character, of opposites, in some respects a correct & refined gentleman, in others a vulgarian; well taught in his profession yet impracticable in the field; of ready wit & intelligence, yet utterly wrong headed and getting no sort of tact by his direful experiences! He invented the picket shovel lately, a really valuable thing. It is plain that there is somewhat between Channing and this Miss Eliot! A good girl apparently and simple, but not his equal in refinement; and, do fear, she has nothing to amend Channing's impecuniosity. Forgot to say that saw Mr. McBurney at Dalton's, Charlie Howard's father-in-law. Rode home by star light, merrily—a sweet night withal. Sheridan at Whitehouse. Scofield has advanced to Goldsboro.[89]

March 19, Sunday.

Mrs. Meade is to come down by special boat, to visit the army, and, at General's request, telegraphed yesterday noon for Mrs. Mimi to come too! Tonight got reply that she would come with Em' and Howland. What an excitement! There came a raft of mariners today & the General showed them the lines. There was Jenkins, the lighthouse man; Percy Drayton, Farragut's right hand, a gentlemanly and rather slender & retiring person; Capt. Alden & one or two others.[90]

March 20, Monday.

More mariners! Admiral Porter; Capt. Barnes, his Flag officer; Mr. Fox, Assist. Sec. of the Navy, a short, stout man, with a large bald head and a beard mingled with gray. Porter is of middle size, very dark with a black beard, and an eye that denotes courage, and some humbug too; that's his character; he is a brave man, but talks vainly and rather flippantly, and not like a man who was accustomed to great deeds. To my surprise there was also Bob Sturgis, looking very well indeed, and "long Green," whom have always desired to know, as he is a great character in Manila and throughout the East. We took them all to Fort Fisher, of course, and then showed them Wheaton's division, which turned out with the new 60-round cartridge box, slung in front. Gen. W[heaton] himself was on a nice horse, with a gorgeous saddle-cloth, and was a beau, as usual. The division was perhaps the best that have seen lately. Gen. McKenzie has gone to take the cavalry of the Army of the James, which he regrets, but promotion is promotion.[91]

March 21, Tuesday.

More or less of hard rain & a good bit of high wind which do fear will give the pleasure party a seasick turn when they get in the lower bay.

March 22, Wednesday.

At 11 ocl' the General, with General Webb and Jay & Barrows, took a special train for City Pt. there to await the "Collyer" which was to bring our party. Fine, with a stiff N.W. wind, whereby the telegraph was down & we could not tell about the approach of the steamer. The peach & plum trees are just in bloom at the point, and must be about two weeks earlier than last year at Culpeper (the day we went to visit Grant). We lunched and dined and did heavy loafing round the Lt. Gen's H'dq'rs—the mail boat arrived but no excursion steamer.

As, at last, we were about giving her up, there was a message that she might be looked for at about 8 P.M. so we all got on a tug and went down to meet her. Getting on board, there was the goodly company at supper!—near thirty in all.—Small Mimi was smiling away in a nice, jaunty hat, and Emmie too; and the goodly Howland was at their side all bright & pleasant! An out of the way and unexpected meeting certainly—not the less agreeable for that! The grand party was under the lead of Gen. Hardie, and consisted of Mrs. Gen. Meade, Misses Marguerita, Sarah and Henrietta and Masters Spenser & Willie and Maj. George Meade; two Misses Cadwalader, Mr. & Mrs. Jim Biddle; Mrs. Hopkinson & son, Mrs. Norris, Miss Sergeant; Misses McCall & Hunter; Messrs. Craig, Biddle, Wharton & Marcon, Dr. Cumack, Mr. Henry, and Mr. White ex captain in the 6th Penn. Cav. Mrs. Meade has a pleasant and still good looking face, for her age, and very fine hair. She has a little of the languid, half southern way, and is wanting in force, somewhat. The children are in two squads, the eldest daughter and Willie are Meades; the rest Sergeants, dark with small noses. The two Misses Cadwalader are very lively and look like the Captain. Geo. Meade seemed to be making a set at Miss McCall, because, possibly, she is a head taller than he. Old Biddle looked remarkably well, and his wife is a really charming lady, full of sweetness. Mrs. Hopkinson is a friend of the Meades and a remarkably good looking woman for the mamma of a big boy. With the party had also come Mrs. Gen. Webb, who is rather a pretty woman and had two nice children along. After our ship had made fast, Gen. Grant came aboard with Mrs. G[rant] and Mrs. Gen. Rawlins (to whom had been introduced) and we have the band & sundry conversation. The General passed the night on the steamer which gave me a chance to do the same. The boat is a rather dirty affair and Gen. Hardie does not shine in directing the cuisine. That, however, don't count when one can see his wife.[92]

March 23, Thursday.

We all were up betimes, and at 9 A.M. took a train for the front. Ambulances were waiting to take the dames to H'dq'rs, where succeeded a grand introduction of countless officers; also there was a lunch in the General's mess tent, an improvement on the steamer fare, and lo! did find two bottles of champagne in the bottom of the box, and this, with lemonade, gave an abundant beverage. Then some ladies got on horses (of whom Em' was one) and the rest in ambulances, and all started to see Spaulding's camp, including the famed rustic church, and afterwards Fort Welch. Meantime, however, the wind (which had been blowing hard already, though the sky was fair) rose to a furious gale, and in this flat region without turf, and shorn of its wood, swept such clouds of sand and dust as never yet saw in all my army experience. Still, between the gusts, we managed to show them the enemy's line; but, in coming back, the ambulances fairly lost their way amid the whirlwinds of sand, and had to change their course to get to Patrick's Station, where we took the cars for Humphreys' Sta. By good fortune the wind lulled and we had a decent time for the review which was really fine, being the whole corps with four batteries.

March 24, Friday.

We again slept on board, last night and today got better weather, though rather raw & windy. Taking the "Martin" we went up the river, with a band of music & all needful accessories of company, including Duane & other excentrics, also Gen. Humphreys, who flourished round at a great rate and was most gallant. Above Deep Bottom (where now is a trestle bridge) we boarded the flagship "Malvern" and were received with a salute and lunch by the hospitable Admiral Porter. Great chances have these mariners, with their skinning of blockade runners of champagne and cigars &c. &c! Then he put us in boats and ran up with a towing tug to the iron-clads, boarding the "Monadnock" (double-turret) and seeing the torpedo boats with their booms ready for action. The Dutch Gap canal looks singularly, only 150 yds. and then the other bank of the river and the river itself in the foreground. Stopping at Aiken's landing we went up to Ord's (once Butler's) H'dq'rs and took the ladies by ambulance to Ft. Harrison. All of which occupied so much time that we got home to the "Collyer" long after dark.[93]

March 25, Saturday.

There was to be a grand review for the President, but Generals may propose, Rebs dispose! At 4.30 A.M. the enemy having massed three divisions, under Gordon, attacked and suddenly carried Fort Stedman and two open batteries, near the right of our line. The danger was imminent, but the garrisons of Forts McGilvery and Haskall stood firm, on each side, which Hartranft, with the 3d division, most gallantly charged, recaptured the lost position and took 1,900 prisoners. It was perfectly the Mine turned just the other way! Meantime the telegraph having been cut, we got no news till 7.30 A.M. at City Point. Out tumbled the General, followed by me, whom he sent to turn out Collis and order him to march all his force to report to Benham on the outer line of the Point. Presently came word that the line was reestablished; so we ate breakfast with the party before going to the front. This broke up the pic-nic and bid small Mimi adieu after a most pleasant visit from her, with no mishap save the stealing of "Uncle" Howland's pocket-book. We got up to the h'dq'rs about 11.30. Stopping on the way to speak with Gen. Parke who was waiting near Meade's Station. Under orders from the General, Humphreys and Wright were pushing out and, at 12.15 a heavy artillery announced that the 2d Corps was carrying their entrenched picket line by the Watkins' house. Immediately the enemy moved troops to his right and at 5.15 and 7.15, made desperate charges to retake the pits, but was repulsed with very heavy guns, among the rest over 300 prisoners and 2 flags. Wright advanced by Fort Fisher, took their entrenched picket line and held it, with considerable fighting, and much artillery from the opposing forts. The result of the day was 2,800 prisoners and 10 flags. Our own loss about 2,000, of whom 400 to 500 prisoners. The enemy's total loss estimated at 5,000. Everyone in good spirits! At 1 p.m. the President came up & reviewed Crawford's division which chanced to be at Fort Dushane in support of that part of the line. A review, a pleasure party and a battle all in one day. The President is the ugliest man that ever saw, lank and peaked featured, with an expression of comic vulgarity. Yet his face is full of concentrated shrewdness & humanity; and, indeed, the heavy folds of his eye give almost a look of genius. His appearance altogether is that of a highly intellectual and honest Satyr! Mrs. L. common! He saw whole droves of rebel prisoners, who seem as hardy as ever and rougher than ever.[94]

March 26, Sunday.

Rode down to Gen. Humphreys and told him of Botiano's admiration of his fight. Also of the departure of the ladies.— A week ago departed our familiar red-leg orderlies, whom did regret, for they were cleanly quiet lads.

March 27, Monday.

Sanders has gone to command the 2d Penn. Cav—Good luck to him!— Sheridan's cavalry has come via Deep Bottom & Pt. of Rocks, & now for stirring times! The General rode out & confabbed with Wright, Humphreys and Warren. Humphreys is confirmed to his corps, *Bon!*—(Saw Richard Barlow and his wife, pretty little thing.)[95]

March 28, Tuesday.

The General took me with him by early train to City Point, to see no less than the redoubtable Sherman! who has arrived for a conference. A remarkable looking man as he stood before Grant's hut, on the grass. Anatomically we might say, an elongated, bifurcated ganglion, covered by a wrinkled integument. A

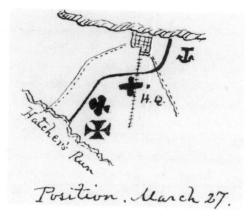

Position. March 27.

tall, sinewy, spare man, with a great forehead, large, thick nose, sunken gray eyes, and a wide firm mouth. As he earnestly talks the deep wrinkles of his face & forehead work and play. The back of his neck from his build, would be thin and hollow, is, on the contrary, swelled; a fighting neck! A glance shows that his head is made up of lines seldom seen together. The expression of his face is homely but pleasing. There were together Grant, Sherman, Meade and Sheridan, a sight for remembrance! The latter more stubby than ever and much sun-burned. As we returned in the cars there was Ord's command (2 white div's under Gibbon, and a black) marching, under Rosencrantz' lead towards the left of our line, which they are to hold, relieving Humphreys. They came by night from over the James. Reducing baggage and ready now to move tomorrow. Maj. Smythe again turned up, to go with us on this move.[96]

March 29, Wednesday.

Order of march; 2d Corps cross Hatcher's Run, march down Vaughan road, face to right and form line with its right connected by pickets with our entrenched left. 5th Corps move south, cross Hatcher's Run at W. Perkins, march along Church road to Quaker road, move up this and form on left of 2d Corps. Cavalry to move to Dinwiddie and thence strike to come in on the enemy's right flank, also to destroy South Side Railroad. 9th and 6th Corps to stand fast, Ord's troops to occupy line held by 2d Corps.[97] Warren got across at 5 A.M. At 7.15 we left our sandy knoll we had occupied since October of last year. Adieu brick chimney, built of clay and bats, thou hast given me much comfort! Going down the Vaughan road and passing Gen. Humphreys' H'dq'rs (where now was Gibbon) we crossed the run at 9.15 and halted a mile beyond. There was 2d div. 2d Corps putting up a breastwork facing north. A couple of English

Greenies were along, Lieuts. Reginald Talbot and Abercrombie.[98] About noon we started for the junction of the Quaker road; getting on the wrong path met Flint and the escort, who had the honor to draw "first blood" having been sent on a reconnoissance by Humphreys, charged a picket breastwork, lost one wounded and one prisoner, and taken one—all this somewhere between the Quaker and White Oak roads. At 12.30 got to junction of Quaker road, where was a large part of the 5th Corps. Griffin's division was marched up the road to join Humphreys left, which rested near the Quaker meeting house. 1.45. Got to the crossing of Quaker road over Gravelly Run, where they were making a bridge as the brook, though not over 25 feet wide, is impassable for artillery. There are stones in this part of the country and the land begins to be a red clay, like the soil round Culpeper. Having got Griffin across, with 2 batteries, an advance was ordered, with Humphreys on the right and a little to the rear, and Ayres and Crawford coming up as fast as possible. Having started the line, Gen. Meade rode back to the Vaughan road, whither Grant had come. Had the satisfaction of shaking hands with Gen. Williams, who related to me his experiences at Charleston & Savannah. To my great surprise he spoke in high praise of the drill of the negro troops. The enemy attacked Griffin heavily, on the Quaker road, about 5 P.M. but he handsomely repulsed them, losing some 400 k. & w. and inflicting a much heavier loss on them. The lines were then halted and we camped near Gravelly Run a little off the Vaughan road. That night at 10.30, the enemy opened their batteries on Parke and demonstrated against his pickets.[99] Heavy rain.

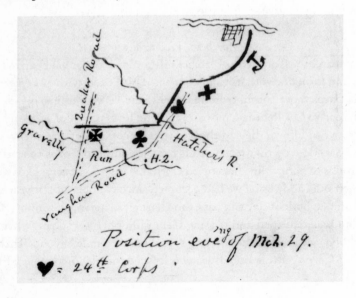

March 30, Thursday.

Heavy rain, which reduced the roads, already poor, to a hopeless, sandy pudding! Gravelly Run was swelled to treble its usual size, and Hatcher's Run swept away its bridges and required pontoons. Notwithstanding this the lines of the 5th & 2d Corps were advanced so that our left rested at the junction of the Quaker & Boydton roads, and the right at Armstrong's mill, the line passing through the Crow house. Turner, on the left of the 24th Corps, made a right half-wheel, drove the enemy into their lines and connected Humphreys' right with our old works, by an east & west line. The cavalry, meantime, had got to Five Forks. No hard fighting, but a good deal of heavy skirmish. The peach trees, which are numerous here, are loaded with blossoms, making the farm houses look as if in a pink cloud. So terrible were the roads and so questionable the possibility of getting up supplies, especially forage for cavalry, that the Generals began to speculate on the necessity of drawing back.

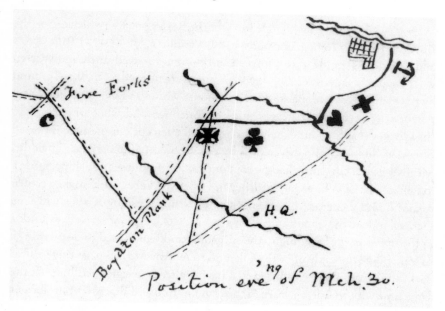

Position eve^{ng} of Mch. 30.

March 31, Friday.

The sun came out about 10, just before which we left camp and moved to the front over corduroys and through seas of mud. (It took 1,000 engineers 56 hours to get a train of 600 waggons 5 miles!) Brisk skirmishing was heard running along Humphreys' front, and, about 10.30, heavy musketry from far out on our left. The General pushed on and got to Warren's H'dq'rs at 11.— W[arren] was at the front, but we soon learned that Crawford and Ayres, being pushed out towards the White Oak road, had been attacked and driven back in confusion; but Griffin had stopped the stampede. Keeping up the Quaker road, we found Humphreys at its juncture with the Boydton (Mrs. Rainie's). The General ordered Miles to attack on the 5th Corps right, which had been already directed by Gen. H[umphreys]. From this point may be seen, say ⅓ mile to the front, the great oak, under which we stood at the first fight of Hatcher's Run. With Gen. Humphreys were all his staff, among them Charlie Mills, who nodded and smiled at me, poor boy! Just then (11.30) a battery of light twelves, on the Boydton road, opened on us with solid shot, but hurt no one. A few minutes after Gen. Meade, having given his orders, rode back, a couple of hundred yards, to a small rising ground, while Humphreys rode into the open field, in front. Just then, Mills was struck by a cannon-ball, and fell dead from his horse. A gallant, capable little fellow, the favorite child of his parents![100] A little before noon, Miles charged into the pine woods, west of the Boydton road, with heavy firing, and drove back the enemy, taking one or two colors. 1.30. Rode over to Warren, whom found say ¾ mile N.W. of the Butler houses (which are on the Boydton road) in some oak woods across a tributary of Gravelly Run. Ayres and Crawford's people were reformed and going again to advance; and Warren was personally superintending. Griffin's guns were planted on the open ground by the plank road. 2.30. Back to J. Butler house whither came Grant, just then. About 4.30 we could hear heavy firing from Sheridan, and, when we got back to the Quaker road we found an officer, who had been cut off, and who reported Sheridan cut in two and driven back by a heavy force of infantry to Dinwiddie. Meanwhile the 5th Corps had pushed out and, with some skirmishing, made a lodgment on the White Oak road, beyond where the rebel works make a return to the N.W.[101] Went to 2d Corps hospitals to see after the body of Mills, while the General rode to those of the 5th Corps, to visit Col. Sergeant severely wounded in the upper part of the thigh. The surgeons kindly promised to do all things, to send home the body of Maj. Mills, and so returned to camp, getting in after dark, and wrote a letter to his father, having already telegraphed him. At the same time with this death, learned those of Grafton and Storrow of his former regiment, the Mass. 2d, who fell in North Carolina. Natie Appleton came down this evening, and is to be a sort of volunteer aide on Gen. Wainwright's staff. The N. Y. Herald has got hold of that suppressed order on Fort Stedman, and published it, with *Grant's* signature. Upon which Meade wrote a letter, explanatory and corrective. This night Griffin's division was ordered down the Boydton road, to the assistance of Sheridan, by Grant, but, on the advice of Meade, the whole corps was sent—with the happiest fruits, as it proved.[102]

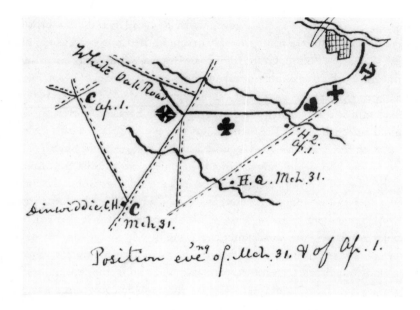

Position eve'ng of. Mch. 31. & of Ap . 1.

April 1, Saturday.

Enemy reported as retired from Sheridan's front. 6.30. To Grant's Headq'rs, near Dabney's mill, with its well remembered pile of sawdust. At this time it is proper to record, verbatim, two orders of Bvt. Lt. Col. Biddle, which are such models and so truly Biddelian as to demand immortality.—(No. 1) "Capt. Flint—Maj. Gen'l Meade directs that you take your escort and assist in getting battery waggon to Gen'l. Grant's H'dq'rs. It is stuck in the mud between here and our Head Quarters. J.C. Biddle, Bvt. Lt. Col. A.D.C." (No. 2) "Capt. Flint—I made a mistake. Assist to take battery waggon to our new Hd. Qrs. J. C. Biddle, Bvt. Lt. Col."—(!) Whereat rose to Flint these mental queries: "When & where did B. write? Where is this battery waggon? *What* is it? What is the spot called between "*here*" and "our H'dq'rs?" "Where are new H'dq'rs?" *It* ended in his riding up to the nearest battery and ordering them to harness their waggon; whereas *the* waggon contained the *telegraph* battery! At 9.30, the General rode, by the Dabney's Mill road, to Gen. Humphreys. The same way we marched to the first fight of Hatcher's Run; now, despite hasty corduroys, the going was awful with the mud of late rains. We found H[umphreys] near the junction of the Plank & Quaker roads. There were there Messrs. Campbell ("Archie") and Brown, the latter once of Boston. The former a friend of H. and having a son on his staff.[103] All was quiet in his front, and we hold with our pickets out towards the White Oak road where the 5th Corps was. Back to Grant's, where we staid some time and where, at 1.30, we got news that Sheridan and 5th Corps had "driven" the enemy to 5 Forks (probably driven in their outposts, as the main fight was later *at* 5 Forks). Grant folded the despatch, and said "Then I want Wright and Parke to assault tomorrow morning, at 4 o'clock!"— It further was determined that the 24th Corps should participate. We camped between Dabney's mill & the Vaughan road crossing at Hatchers run, with a fine view of our old entrenched left. The General was this evening taken with a malarial catarrh, with fever, and coughed a good deal. 8 P.M. News that Sheridan and the 5th Corps had completely smashed the enemy, at 5 Forks, and taken 3 guns, a number of waggons and over 4,000 prisoners! It seems that the enemy, Pickett and Fitz Lee, foolishly halted at 5 Forks, where the 5th Corps struck and overlapped them from the east, while the cavalry attacked them from the south. After a vigorous resistance they were utterly routed, and those not taken were scattered. Grant thereupon got hasty to have an attack at once by the 6th Corps, whereat Wright expostulated and said, if they would hold to the original 4 A.M. he "would make the fur fly!" Meade could not go against Grant's order but implied that he agreed with Wright, who made, perhaps, the necessary delays. Parke, meantime, opened a heavy cannonade, and we had this and all sorts of skrimmaging in front of the 24th Corps, all night long. Ord was putting up a battery wherewith he proposed to take in reverse the "Crow house" battery of the enemy, near Hatcher's Run. At midnight came Warren. Went out to congratulate him, when observed he looked depressed, and his Aide, young Wadsworth, whispered that he was *relieved!* Poor Warren! A man of marked ability and valor, too rapidly promoted, and now cast down at the turning point of this great war. In his day he was wont (like many young men) to make severe criticisms on others, but this humiliation he did not deserve. Warren's military ability, which was great, did not exactly take the direction of command of troops. He seemed unable to "spread himself" over more than one division, and he had the incorrigible error of trying to do each thing *himself,* putting no faith in his subordinates. It was this that ruined him; for Sheridan (who disliked him before) seeking to give him some orders for the attack by his corps, found he had gone off to look after the 3d division, and, after the fight, relieved him. His great strength was as a field engineer and perhaps chief of staff; to discern proper routes, put troops in position; discriminate points of attack and of defence. He was a man of sleepless energy, activity and study—his mind never still; a master of his art, and of a daring spirit; but promotion was too rapid and in the wrong direction.[104]

April 2, Sunday.

A memorable day, on the morning of which, at 4.15, the fate of the Army of Northern Virginia was sealed, when the 6th Corps broke the rebel centre! General Wright, who had minutely arranged all things, had formed his three divisions for the assault in columns of battalions, leaving only minimum garrisons in his redoubts. Seymour on the left, Getty in the centre, and Wheaton on the right. They all advanced at once, rushed over the line and took all the redoubts in their front. They then swept up the line in the direction of Petersburg and the river.— Continuous heavy fire from Ord's left (musketry) where he tried the enemy's line but could not get through. 6 A.M. News that Parke had carried two batteries and two lunettes in their line, with the connecting curtain. Gen. Potter wounded, reported mortally; this is the second General officer, for the gallant Winthrop fell yesterday at the fight of Five Forks.[105] 7.30. Despatch that McCallister of 3d div. 2d Corps had captured the picket line in his front—a good deal of cheering from the right of the 2d Corps—Seymour said to be on the South Side track. 8.15. A.M. Despatch that Ord & Hays (2d div. 2d Corps) have taken the line in their front. (The 19th & 20th Mass. took a work with several guns and some hundreds of prisoners.) In fact the enemy were abandoning this part of the line as fast as possible, and moving to their right. At this time the General rode off to the left, with myself alone, so that for some time, I wrote his orders & despatches. 8.45 A.M. Sent telegraph ordering Benham to move up at once to Parke, from City Point. We found Gen. Grant in an open field, in front of Dabney's mill, and, after a few moments of conversation, Gen. Meade kept on to the left and followed our line of breastworks, the men of Mott's division cheering him loudly. 9 A.M. Having notice from Mott that the enemy were double-quicking to their own right, Humphreys was directed to move with caution, as we had no supports to send him. At the Rainie house found Gen. Humphreys. Miles division having been down the Plank, was returning, and was ordered up the Claiborne road, while the rest of Humphreys force was to move by the left flank and pass up the Boydton road. It was presumed (10 A.M.) that Sheridan & 5th Corps would be moving along the Cox & River roads, towards Petersburg, and would join our left (Miles' div.). So a despatch was sent saying that Wright was moving down (south) on the Boydton plank, with Ord covering his left, while 2d Corps was moving *up*. Sheridan, however, turned N.W. and followed that part of the enemy along the Namozine road, the 5th Corps being still detached under his orders. Meantime Wright, finding that no enemy lay between him and the advancing 2d Corps, faced about and moved on Petersburg, so that his left might swing to the Appomattox, while his right should touch the left of the 24th Corps that was reaching towards the 9th. Now we started for the most interesting ride that perhaps ever had, a ride straight up Boydton plank road, where hitherto none might go, save as prisoners of war! We passed the battery, whence came the fatal shot for poor Mills, and the entrenched line, with its abbatis. Then descended to Hatcher's Run bridge, where our men planted their flag at the first fight there. We crossed, rode up the ascent and came on the wide space of open land that surrounds the town. As we struck the rear of the column marching onward, the men broke into loud cheers, which were continued all along. It was grand!— We halted, at 12, by the Harmon house, where was Gen. Grant already. Hence was an excellent view; to the S.E., 2 miles off, was the high signal tower and Fort Fisher; between us & that we got a rear look at the rebel entrenchments. To the N.E. were the noted chimneys of the "Lead Works," surrounded by field works and entrenchments, a part of the inner line of the town.[106] The batteries were firing on both sides pretty briskly. The 2d div. 2d Corps was brought up and put in line, while Mott was held in reserve. Meantime Parke's men were holding on gallantly to their captures, while the enemy knew their only safety lay in disputing to the utmost. One lunette was retaken by them, but the rest remained with us. Gen. Hamlin's brigade was sent to his support, and these troops, with the brigade of the noted Collis, made Parke quite easy. Our old friends the Zoo-Zoos were put in, behaved gallantly, and lost a large number of men. 1 P.M. Gibbon took two enclosed redoubts by assault, after a desperate resistance, he losing heavily. They were near the [Boydton] plank road and were important.[107] 1.45 P.M. Word having been received that Miles had encountered the enemy entrenched at Sutherland's Station, Humphreys moved down the Cox road, with Mott, to his assistance. Miles, however, at 3.30 attacked; flanked & routed the enemy and took 3 guns.[108] We took up our camp at Well's house (on map) at the point where the Boydton plank turns east to go towards the town. Preparations were made to plant artillery, to cover the throwing of a pontoon over the Appomattox early tomorrow; at the same time orders were issued for an assault, in case any weakness should appear at daylight; and Parke was ordered to open his batteries on the bridge. To my surprise there appeared Dr. Le Conte, who is a Med. Inspector and hath turned from bugs. Also Joe Hayes and Bache. The former will have a brigade of the 5th A.C.[109]

April 3, Monday.

About 5 in the morning, heard Duane say, outside my tent, "They have evacuated the town!" And, sure enough, they had; as indeed we expected. Actually
a free entrance to a place that for nine and a half months was tabooed to us by
cannon & musketry. At 6 A.M. we rode in, by the Boydton road, the General
at the head, followed by his staff & escort. Passing formidable redoubts and
breastworks, and leaving those "lead-work" chimneys on the right, we entered
the outskirts—shabby, tumble-down houses of blacks & poor whites. As we
got to the heart of the place we came on Market St. where dwell the *Haute
Noblesse*; a street for all the world like one in Salem, with the same good, square,
brick houses and trees about them. Then, near the water, was a compact business street, whose lower part was much hit by shells. The town lies in fact in
a great water-gulley, next the river; so that you mount a short hill, to get to
Cemetery Ridge, the noted rise that overlooks the Mine. There is a very large
graveyard there and the ruins of an old chapel.[110] We examined the site of the
mine, and the bomb-proofs of the enemy, and then it became more than ever
apparent what a short distance, lay between the "crater" and that wished for
crest! Returning to town, we had confirmation of the death of A. P. Hill, who
was shot by a straggler of the 6th Corps, whom he tried to take.[111] Grant was
halting at the large house of Mr. Wallace where we too rested awhile. There
was a large tobacco warehouse near, where one could see the various forms of
chewing & smoking weed. There were little leaves on the tulip trees as big as a
dollar, also the strawberries were in bloom. Crowds of nigs came about selling
Confederate money for whatever we would give. They were all as plainly pleased,
as were the whites *not* so. Leaving the place by the river road, we halted to rest
at one Morton's house, and then, continuing west, came up with Wright at 2,
where the cross-road leads to Sutherland's Tavern, on the railroad. There were
almost acres of our coats and blankets, wherever our brigades had halted; for
the weather waxes warm now. Crossing to the tavern we found the ground of
Miles' fight covered by large army trains. The Reb works were still to be seen,
hasty breastworks. Grant was camped here, and we chose our camp not far off.
He gave us official information that Weitzel entered Richmond this morning
at 8.15 A.M.! That is what may be called long-range strategy! Sheridan, with
the 5th Corps is moving on Amelia C. H. He has taken guns & many hundred
prisoners today and reports much ammunition abandoned by the enemy. Abercrombie & Talbot go tomorrow back.

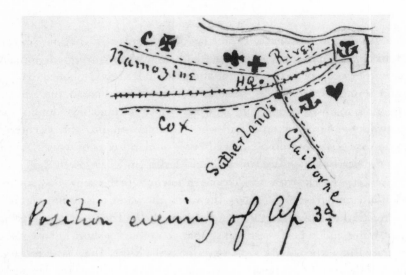

April 4, Tuesday.

Up at 4. The road full of trains (among them that of the cavalry) going slowly to the front. At 7.15 left Grant, at his camp, and rode on, taking the Namozine road. Passed Weld, on the cross-road. He is just down and was hunting after his regiment.[112] 9 A.M. Found Wright halted on the road, near Mt. Pleasant Church. The comic Capt. Barnard said "this news would knock gold to 75 cents on a dollar!"— A funny incident occurred when Paddy Walsh, Lt. Col. of the 3d Penn. Cav. passed with his regiment. The troops mistook him for Grant and cheered him; all of which he took with great dignity! 10.30 met Gen. Barringer of the rebel cavalry, coming to the rear, having been taken by the scouts of Sheridan.[113] 10.45. Halted a little at Namozine church, which is just by the way side, and then kept on to Mrs. Cousins, which lies about ⅓ of a mile from the road, and opposite Mount Poplar Church. There we had some lunch & iced water and then on again as far as Jones (4.45) to the east of Deep Creek. Old J[ones] couldn't hear at all, though he could speak, and went about poling a bit of slate at you to make you write on it. The head of the Second Corps was beyond the creek. They had had a hard time all day getting forward the trains, which were essential for the troops ahead who, like themselves were pretty much out of rations. Gen. Meade rode out to Gen. Humphreys and did not get in till dusk, when he was found to have a malarial chill. We made a bed for him in the house and built a fire. The chill was succeeded by a high fever which excited his nervous system greatly though it did not affect the clearness of his mind. Good Gen. Humphreys gave us some supper, after which was up nearly all night, writing and receiving despatches. At 9.30 P.M. came a despatch from Sheridan announcing that he was at Jetersville and the whole rebel army in his front, to the north, and might be taken could our infantry be hurried up. This excited Meade to move, not only by its real importance, but because he suspected Sheridan of manoeuvring to get to himself all the credit of success, but preparing to shift the blame, in case of failure. He at once ordered the 2d & 6th Corps to move at 1 that night and to march on Jetersville, 13 or 15 miles distant, hoping to attack the next morning. He issued an order also (since called the "starvation" order) which encouraged the troops to make a fresh exertion to capture the enemy, and was all good except the last clause, in which they were exhorted to face starvation &c. in order to accomplish this great end. Meade would not have put this in had it not been for his high fever, which made his language excited. Everybody worked hard. Col. Bachelder was up all night getting up the supply trains, and Gens. Humphreys & Wright had no sleep. The movement of the army today was: Part of cavalry with 5th Corps to Jetersville, 2d, followed by 6th Corps, to Deep Creek, on the Namozine road; 24th Corps along Cox road (i.e. 2 div's 24th & 1, black, of 25th) followed by 2 div's of 9th Corps.[114]

April 5, Wednesday.

The 2d Corps duly moved at 1 at night, but, after going a mile, found the road blocked by Merritt's cavalry which had got there in some unexplained way, and which barred the way for 6 or 7 hours.

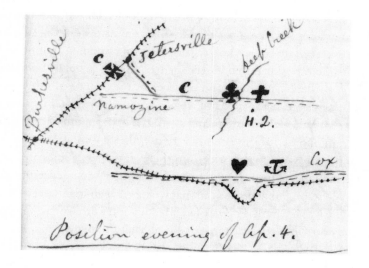

However, the men meantime got rations, which was some consolation for the delay.— Jef. Davis went to Danville on the 3d. Today we took the General in his spring waggon, in which we made him a bed, and left at 9.15 A.M. At 10 got news that the enemy was still near Amelia Court House. We were with the 2d Corps, which was marching. To get to Jetersville we struck from the main road to the N.W. and, passing the 2d div. got to Perkinson's house, where was Gen. Humphreys. Near there were some hundreds of rebel prisoners, the feeding of whom was a rather hard question. They talked of giving them some mule meat, till they could get to the waggon train. Hence we saw an explosion, in the direction of Amelia C. H. which was explained afterwards. Davies had gone out with his brigade, and struck their train, capturing 5 very handsome Armstrong shunt field-pieces, and destroying a large quantity of waggons.[115] Gen. Sheridan's headquarters were at the Childres house, near the railroad, and the 5th Corps was well entrenched across the railroad, ½ mile S. west of Jetersville. Gen. Meade still badly, and troubled, with, cough, fever, and sickness at the stomach. He consulted with Gen. Sheridan and said we must attack, if we could get up the 2d & 6th Corps in time. He treated S. very handsomely, and refused to take command of him, only resuming the 5th Corps.[116] 2.10 P.M. Head of 2d Corps gets up. 2.45 Sheridan, having passed nearly all of his cavalry to the left, rode off himself, to look after helping back Davies, who was pressed by the enemy after he took the train. 3.30. The guns brought in, with 4 flags, one of them that of a Medical Purveyor, very gay! With them also a crowd of lean mules and their negro drivers, a most comical sight! 4.20. Increased reports that the enemy were coming down on our left.— Some of the cavalry gentlemen rather stampeded. Did not believe a word of their talk, for certainly they would only demonstrate and reconnoitre, under the circumstances. And so it turned out; they smashed up some small cavalry force on our flanks, but never came even to the infantry skirmish line. The General now rode out to Sheridan and Griffin, on the Jetersville road, and returned at 6.30. Head of 6th Corps up. Gen. Sheridan came back soon and we had supper with him. His scout Maj. Young took a rebel Colonel today, and also got Barringer, the other day. These scouts, 40 in number, are apparently very useful. They are volunteers, have a sort of rebel dress, and boldly ride into the enemy's outer lines and pick up such information and prisoners as they can. The enemy do not venture to hang them if caught, probably because so many of their own men wear a made up dress. Young was formerly a private in 1st R.I. infantry 6th Corps. We camped at a house near Childres; waggons not up till near midnight.[117]

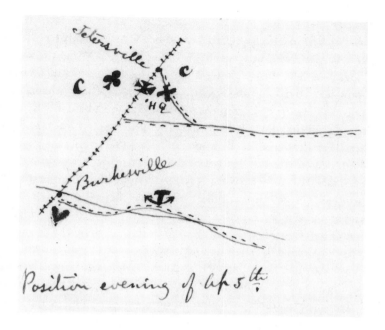

April 6, Thursday.

Grant got up last night and staid with Sheridan. This morning the whole line moved forward on Amelia C. H. At 7 we saw Grant at Childres, & there saw Barlow, just down. He is to have the 2d div. 2d Corps, Hays (of reg. artil.) being relieved for slowness.[118] Sheridan moved off to the left to try and cut into their waggon trains, while we moved straight out on the Amelia C. H. road. At 8 A.M. the information was positive that the enemy were all moving off to our left, making a westerly detour, to gain, if possible the road to Danville (so it seemed).— Therefore Sheridan's information that they were at a stand-still was inaccurate; they had been moving continuously, as some then thought, on Stony Point Bridge. Meade ordered the 6th Corps to face about and move off to the westward, to try and strike the column in flank; & the 2d Corps was put on the Deatonsville road. 9 A.M. Got to the fork, beyond Jetersville, where the road goes north to the upper Amelia C. H. road, and thence west through Paineville; here the 5th Corps was moving out; a portion passing then. There was firing in a westerly direction. 10. We rode back and halted at Jetersville, a collection of half a dozen houses & a church. The house where we were was once a combination of store & residence. The woman a dried up, most bitter secesh, ready to cry with despair over her cause. 12.20. Despatch to Grant (who was here) from Sheridan, that he had headed the enemy from the road to Burkesville. Renewed orders sent to Humphreys & Wright to attack as soon as possible. The former, indeed, conducting a vigorous direct pursuit, was keeping up a sharp running fight the whole time. Whereby had a curious panoramic view of part of it from the upper piazza, on a bald hill, lying N.W. At 11.30 had seen the rebel trains passing there, along the Deatonsville road. Then their cavalry come out of the woods and our batteries shelling them. Then their infantry emerge, build a breastwork; the artillery go into position, and, at last, the hill taken by our troops at 1.15 P.M.—all quite like a puppet show! The main trains are to park at Burkesville; Ord, who is there, is to march to cut off the enemy, and to send an expedition to Farmville, to destroy the bridges over the Appomattox. Our H'dq'rs train having been sent along the Deatonsville road, I was despatched to pull it up and make it go into camp. Put after it at a gallop for some 9 miles, to the blowing of Col. Bachelder's horse, who was along! Country hilly and picturesque, with many brooks in deep gulleys. Beyond that bald hill the way was strewn with ammunition, waggons, tents, camp baggage, muskets and, above all, with little Dutch ovens! Plainly the Rebel animals were giving out. About sunset, halted the train 2 m. south of Deatonsville. At this time there was sharp artillery not far beyond us. The General came in after dark, and at the same time, about 8.30 P.M. came a staff officer of Gen. Sheridan with a despatch which said "I attacked with two divisions of the 6th Corps &c. &c." The General supposed it was from Wright; but, when the name was read, P. H. Sheridan; he exclaimed; "And so Wright *was not there!*"—"Oh, yes!" replied the officer. Meade was thoroughly vexed at this combination of fine news and borrowed (yea pilfered) glory. The despatch of S[heridan] was a selfish piece of trickery—it was not even true; for Wright made the decisive attack in flank, which resulted in the capture of Ewell, Custis Lee, Kershaw, and other generals, and of 8,600 men, with 14 guns. All near Sailor's Run. The cavalry had headed them and obstructed the road; Humphreys crowded on their rear, and Wright broke in their flank. Wright did have nothing at all to do with Sheridan, being in immediate communication with Meade. Humphreys this day took several hundred prisoners, by himself, and a large quantity of waggons & ambulances. Meade sent in a report with those of Humphreys & Wright; but of course the wide awake Sheridan had his in first and on its way to the press! All this did not prevent great rejoicings on our part over this news so glorious for the cause.— Griffin has orders to pass in rear of the 2d & 6th Corps and to strike for Prince Edward C. H.[119]

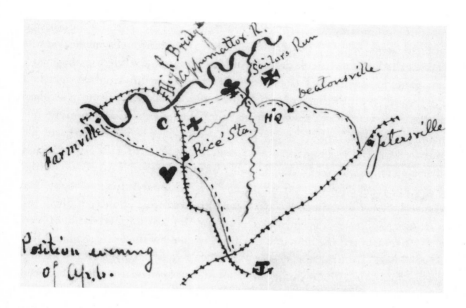

April 7, Friday.

Started at 8.20 A.M. and kept on, westward. The General in his waggon again having got worse by riding yesterday. The road still strewed with rebel debris, till we came to Sailor's Run, a stream in the gorge between two steep hills. This hollow was quite filled with abandoned waggons, ambulances, caissons & guns, and the hill-side was white with papers from some office boxes that had been broken open. They had got pinched at a small bridge here, and were left, a sight to behold!—On the hill opposite we found a part of the 5th Corps, moving across the road, to pass in the rear of the 2d & 6th. Hence may be seen Willis Mt. lying N.W., which increased the resemblance of the country to Culpeper. 10.30. Despatch, that 2d Corps has crossed at "High Bridge," whither we turned also our horses. At 11 we came upon the river, here only about 70 feet wide, running prettily between high steep banks. Following along we came to High Bridge, a most surprising structure for this part of the country, being nothing less than a vast viaduct 2,350 feet long, supported on brick piers, of which the tallest must have been 140 feet. It spans the bottom land, in which the Appomattox runs, and which is about a mile wide at this point. At either end, the rebels had made a strong enclosed work, in which they had abandoned 18 disabled guns, & had blown up the magazine in one, throwing a cannon clean over the parapet into the ditch. At a poor house hard by we halted for some time, to get news from the pursuit. At 12.40 P.M. the General sent me to find where Wright was and what doing. Crossing a deep run (Briery River) found the general at the crossing of Bush Creek, some 2½ m. off. He said he was marching on Farmville and was then at the head of the column. He said he did not know whither the enemy had gone but was moving to find them. Meade seemed to think Wright had progressed very little that day. Intermittent rain. 4 P.M. Heavy firing of artillery and musketry, to the westward, at first thought to be from Humphreys, but turning out to be Crook's (Gregg's) div. of cavalry, which had forded at Farmville and attacked the rebel infantry, who easily drove them back.[120] Afterwards a sharp, distant fire from N.W. *did* come from Humphreys, who now reported the whole rebel army in his front intrenched and apparently full of fight. The General at once sent me to Wright to order him to cross at once, or direct the 24th Corps (already at Farmville) to cross and attack as soon as possible. Overtook & transferred the despatch to Farrar, who knew the exact road and had a fresh horse. The bridges however were all destroyed at Farmville and neither corps could cross! (Plainly pontoons should have been nearer—it lay between Meade & Duane.)[121]— Meantime there continued more or less musketry in the direction of Humphreys, who, at 7 P.M. reported that he had attempted an assault on a point with one brigade, but had been repulsed with heavy loss. Gen. Smythe of 1st div. 2d Corps mortally wounded, by a skirmish shot, in the neck; a valuable officer, Irish by descent. Gen. Mott was shot through the leg, a day ago. The rebels are marching towards Lynchburg by the Stage road, and

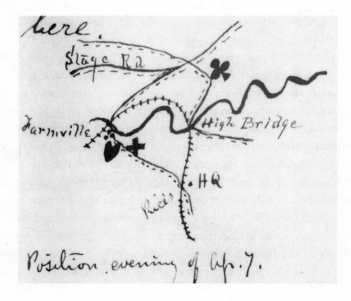

were covering their rear today, near the junction of this road with the Farmville one. We went back 4 miles and camped at Rice's Station, where the country was beset with rebel breastworks, thrown up against the 24th Corps. Heard after, that Gibbon was thought rather to have fooled round yesterday, instead of pitching into them. An expedition of a couple of regiments, under Washburne of the 4th Mass. Cav. yesterday had a fight near Farmville, whither they had been sent to destroy the bridges, but the enemy were there first, caught them in the forks of Bush River and killed or took a large part of them. Washburne himself got a wound of which he finally died.[122]

April 8, Saturday.

We begin to get now the fine air of the mountains and this morning early, the ground was white with frost. Off betimes at 5.45 A.M. Returned to and crossed at High Bridge, whereof the rebels had burned the last 3 spans; the rest was saved only by the vigor of Maj. Livermore, who ran, with some pioneers, and cut away the burning part. Then turning to the right we kept along a poor wood road, and then, bearing to the left, we came on the rear of the 2d Corps marching out, on the stage road. At the fork of this into the upper & main stage road we came on Gen. Humphreys, just where there is an ill-worked coal pit (oolitic) called Piedmont Coal Mine.[123] 8. He had had some trouble in finding by which road the enemy had retreated, but decided finally that it was by the main stage route. There was important news, viz: that Grant, incited by the tone of Ewell's staff officers, had sent out a flag, last night, to demand Lee's surrender! A response had come in, and now Gen. Williams had just ridden forward with a second note. This showed that the idea had been entertained—a most important fact! As we kept along the road we came on Gen. Williams, whom the enemy had fired on, when he tried to go forward with a flag, and wounded his orderly. He soon after succeeded in getting the letter in. 11.30. Got to house of one Elam, where we rested the horses and then kept on as far as Stute's house, over a wide road full of boulders & holes—evidently neglected these years.[124]— Before halting this time, Grant had caught us. He was in good spirits and said "How are you, old fellow?" to Meade. Stute's was a good house with a piano &c. Grant was taken with one of his severe headaches; and it is a singular sign of forbearance that he allowed the staff officers to go on for a long time pounding the piano and singing choruses, without objecting. Saw Lee's autograph there in a pencil note to Grant. He had asked an interview to treat of "*Peace*" to which Grant had replied that he had no authority in the premises.[125] His waggons could not get up, so we gave him dinner. There was a queer fellow along, a Col. who has been over Europe with contrivances for mining; especially for the simultaneous discharge of many magazines at great distances. He was in the Danish war and spoke of the great slowness of the Danes; e.g. that the 2d Corps made more works in a day than the Danes in several months. About sunset we could hear vigorous artillery from Sheridan, in the direction of Appomattox Station. The 24th Corps, followed by the 5th, are en route to support him.

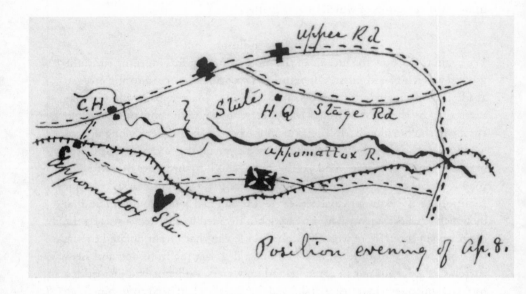

April 9, Sunday.

Lee had proposed an interview with Grant at 10 A.M. and had staid in rear for the purpose, *but* received the refusal above mentioned, from Whittier who carried it. Gen. Meade better but keeps still to the spring waggon. Off at 6.35. 7.30 A.M. arrive at junction of upper road, where the 6th Corps was coming in. 7.45. Much artillery from Sheridan. Road here much better. 8.30. Found Wright by the roadside at the H'dq'rs of Humphreys, who, however, had gone on. The rear of the 2d Corps was just then moving out. Halted here same time. 9.45. A negro came in, who said our troops entered Lynchburg at 10 yesterday. (This proved a mistake.) Another negro followed with the very important information that Sheridan had stopped their train, the night before, near Appomattox Sta. and that the artillery (of which the train chiefly consisted at that point) was falling back when he left.— Grant today rode across country to join Sheridan, and did not continue with us. A staff officer was sent ahead, to press on the 2d Corps and to order the waggons out of the road, that the 6th might close up on it. 10.30. We moved briskly forward and cleared the road very successfully by means of a trumpeter. 11.45. Got to Gen. Humphreys at the head of his column, about 4½ miles east of Appomattox C. H. His skirmishers had struck those of the enemy a short bit ahead.—No firing. 12. Orders were given for them to push on, but, just then, a white flag was reported. Gen. Humphreys ordered it received and the line still to advance. An officer then brought in a note from Lee, asking a suspension of hostilities, as Gen. Ord had agreed to one, at the other end of the line, until Gen. Grant could be found. Gen. Meade replied he had no authority for such suspension, Lee having got no agreement from Grant. Just then, however, came Gen. Forsyth, from Sheridan, who said that the cavalry attacked the head of their train, last night, near Appomattox Station, and took 20 guns (probably of their artillery reserve) and near 1,000 prisoners, that the 24th & 5th Corps had come up in the night and formed across the road. Sheridan had likewise taken several railroad trains, loaded with provisions, at the station.[126] As Gen. Forsyth had to return, and, as he reported the enemy with their arms stacked and plainly about to surrender, Gen. Meade agreed not to move forward till 2 P.M. 1.30. While we sat there waiting, a negro came in, who said their skirmish line had thrown down their arms and walked leisurely back to the main body. 2. No answer coming, Gen. Humphreys sent word for the skirmishers to advance; but they had only begun when (2.20) there arrived Col. Kellogg, Ch. Commissary to Sheridan, with Maj. Wingate of Lee's staff, bringing a note from Grant to suspend hostilities. Wingate said they burned their baggage, last night, meaning to cut through today. He remarked "It would have been better to have burned our train, some days ago; then you would have seen no more of us; but, in trying to save a train we have lost an army!"—Which was quite true.[127] Gen. Humphreys sat on a stump and gave $100 Confed' notes to such as wanted a souvenir; for they had captured a barrel full the day before! 5 P.M. There came Bvt. Maj. Pease with a note—official news that Lee had surrendered to Grant the Army of Northern Virginia!!! Led by Gen. Webb the staff gave three cheers; then three more for Gen. Meade, who got on his horse and rode through the ranks of the 2d and 6th Corps. This patient, silent, old army now for once burst forth! In a frenzy of excitement, the troops rushed to the sides of the road and shouted till my very ears rung with the noise. Hats & caps flew in the air; flags waved; cannon fired; and one fellow cast his full havresack under the horses' feet, crying:

"Charge over *that*; charge over anything I've got!"—After all this excitement we were glad to go into camp, near the road (some 5 miles east of the C. House). Plainly all was up, for this day I lost my pill-box & the only remaining rowel of one spur! The bands and the cheering lasted late that night. An eventful Palm Sunday.[128]

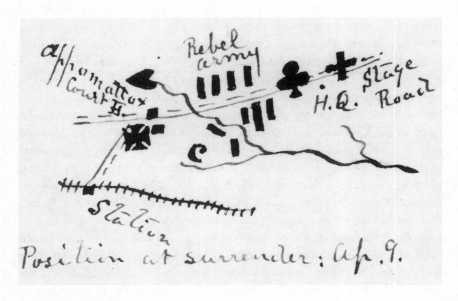

April 10, Monday.

Intermittent rain. Gen. Meade determined to go through the Rebel army, and see Lee on the way, also see Grant, on the other side. He would take only Gen. Webb, George & myself, as intercourse was strictly forbidden between the armies. Passing our picket line, and continuing on the main stage road we came among groups of rebel soldiers, standing listlessly about. The country here is most open, on either side of the way, and deeply cut by several brooks, the headwaters of the Appomattox. Being sent forward by Gen. Meade, found Gen. Field whom took to the General. He is dark eyed man, with a long face and full cheeks,—rather good looking; and, at first, very sullen.[129] He guided us to Lee's H'dq'rs, in a small wood, and consisting only of a ply, with a camp fire before it. His baggage had perhaps been burnt, the night before, along with much more; as we saw many burnt waggons here and there. Saw only one or two waggons at his place. The rebel infantry was camped, or rather bivouaced, along the road, with their muskets stacked and the regimental colors planted.

They appeared to have very little to eat & very few shelter tents. The number of men actually organized seemed small, their bivouacs did not appear larger than those of a weak corps. Lee was away, but, as we rode along, we met him returning. He looked in a brown study, and gazed vacantly, when Meade saluted him. But he recovered himself and said "What are you doing with all that gray in your beard?" "That *you* have a good deal to do with!" said our General promptly. Lee is a tall, strongly made man, with a florid but not fat, face. His thick hair and beard, now nearly white, are somewhat closely trimmed. His head is large & high; the eye dark, clear, and unusually deep. His expression is not that of genius, or dash; but of wisdom, coolness, and great determination. His manners are courtly and reserved (now unusually so, of course). Though proud & manly to the last, he seemed deeply dejected. Meade talked with him some time.[130] Lee said he had only some 10,000 men actually left for duty, though there were many unarmed and extra duty men beside. He stated he had looked for a break all through the spring as he had but 40,000 muskets to hold his entire line! By this he must have meant infantry in the trenches, excluding cavalry, reserves in rear, rear pickets, artillery &c. because our captures, added to his losses and his probable desertions during his retreat, would indicate an army of 55,000 or 60,000 officers & men equipped for duty, previous to Fort Stedman. Our forces actually taking part in this last campaign of 12 days, must have outnumbered his somewhat more than 2 to 1. Saw there Lt. Col. Marshall, his Aide—a very moderate and sensible man—and Col. Baldwin, Chief of Artillery. Also a Dr. Hunter, brother-in-law of our Harwood of the engineers—and plainly a secesh dyed in the wool. Talked a few moments to Lee, who said he remembered Mrs. Eliot & Uncle Charles. Just then up came old Wise, to see his brother-in-law, Meade. He was a forlorn spectacle, and ludicrous too. An old man, with spectacles and a short, white beard; a stooping, sickly figure, with his legs tied round with gray blankets. A son of "Paris" Faulkner was on his staff. We sent him some food.[131] And so we left the forlorn group and continued to Appomattox Court House, hoping to find Grant; but he already had left. In the McLane [McLean] house (there is a cluster of houses here) a good sized building of brick, there was a meeting of commissioners. Among them, saw Longstreet (a stout, large headed man, with a full beard) and Gordon who has a thin, martial face, straight hair brushed behind his ears, and a cruel looking, blue eye, set above high cheek bones. As turned to speak to Gibbon, a voice behind me said "How are you Ted?" It was "Roonie" Lee! all buttoned up in his general's gray coat, and looking better than of yore. Shook hands with him and said was glad to see him. Poor Roonie! you lost that boat-race in college by careless training, and now you have lost a four-year race, & with it everything!¹³² Col. Halifax, of Gen. Longstreet's staff took us back, past their pickets—a tall and pleasant looking man. Who should turn up there, with Gen. Wainwright & Natie Appleton, but Botiano! He got left by foolishly going to Washington. And has been wandering round in rear of the army ever since! And so rode we back through the wreck of the Army of Northern Virginia, an army that thrice has carried the war into the enemy's territory and, by its skill and valor, has foiled five great attempts for the capture of Richmond. 3.15 P.M. We got back to camp. Mr. Ould was there, on his way to Richmond. He has been Rebel commissioner of exchange, and got caught in the lines of the 6th Corps. A fat, worldly looking man, with plenty of whisky & cigars in his ambulance.¹³³

April 11, Tuesday.

At 6 A.M. H'dq'rs were off en route to Farmville. The 5th & 24th Corps would stay, to look out for the capitulation; while the 6th & 2d would go back, by the same road. Bache was in arrest last night for going into the rebel lines against express orders. He is the only officer that have ever seen in arrest at these Headq'rs.¹³⁴— We passed Stute's house at 9.45 and watered the horses at Elams an hour later. Near the Piedmont mine we struck off to the south by the Farmville Plank road, (very bad) and got to the town at 12.45 crossing the Appomattox, on the banks of which it lies, by a pontoon bridge. The place is like Warrenton in look, but not so well built or large; it is the centre of the tobacco region and had much tobacco stored. There is a large brick hotel on the main street. The place has been full of refugees from various parts, as the land about there is arable, and board cheap. The General had a room in the hotel, with a fire of Piedmont coal, which burns well. A brigade of the 9th Corps is in the town. At 7 P.M. a group of officers rode in; one dismounted and, going to Gen. Meade's room, said: "I have come to give myself up. I *was* Gen. Fitz Hugh Lee; I suppose I am *Mr.* Lee now!" Sure enough there he was, with his staff. One of them, Col. Pickens, was wounded. Meantime the indomitable Spaulding had got up his "Minstrels" in the great dining hall, and the Reb staff went down to hear. A strange sight in the midst of our officers! Our waggons not being up, accommodated myself on a sofa with a piano cover for a blanket.¹³⁵

April 12, Wednesday.

The rear of the main supply train was clear of town this morning, en route for Burkesville. 9.45 A.M. Head of the 6th Corps passing. At 10.45 we started for Burkesville, recrossing the river and again crossing at High bridge, and passing

Rices Station. Arrived at Burkesville (following the R.R.) at 3 P.M. There is no town, only a big way-house at the junction, but the country all about is open & dotted with farm houses. It has high rolls and is abundantly watered, but the soil is an exhausted clayey sand supporting no turf. The immense trains were parked all about, making acres of white waggon tops. We called on Gen. Parke, whose corps runs along the railroad from Sutherland's to Farmville; but repairs are going on only as far as this point. The brigade at Farmville will be drawn in so soon as the rear of the army gets through. Greeted Loring & all the 9th Corps' staff. Was surprised to see Gen. Ricketts, looking as well as ever, and come now to take his old division again (which won't please Seymour much!).[136]

April 13, Thursday.

We camped last night near the house of one Fowlkes ¾ mile N. of the Junction; but, a heavy rain coming on, our field was turned to mud and flooded some of the tents and I was soundly abused for the selection. Went out to pick out another, and circled the whole country round, to find, at last, close by a nice spot in the edge of a pine wood; a lovely camp it made, my last gift to Headquarters.

April 14, Friday.

Fine. The cherries are as big as green peas. Moved to new camp. Mimi is staying at Annie's at Cambridge. There came yesterday a Reb' Lt. Col. Smith (a civil soldier & son of "Extra Billy") with another man and delivered a note from the Governor of Va. to the President.[137] It was understood to ask if permission would be given for rebel leaders to go to Europe. Also there were other points, about amnesties, &c, probably. Duane is very wroth at being deprived of his battalion of regular engineers, which is directed to report to old Benham who is now here with his troops. The northern papers tell us of the great rejoicings there. The railroad gauge is already changed from Petersburg here, but such is the condition of the track that it takes 23 hrs. to go the 62 miles to City Pt.

April 15, Saturday.

Heavy rain. I heard the General say, as he stood by his campfire and read a telegram: "Bless me! This is terrible news!"— It was the announcement that President Lincoln was assassinated last night at Ford's theatre—shot through the head—and that Mr. Seward also was attacked and dangerously, if not mortally wounded! The intelligence spread everywhere the utmost consternation, even with the entire want of details. General Meade prepared a very beautiful order about it, to the Army. This is a most serious event for us, even in our present comparative safety. We have only to pray that Johnson will take a lesson from his experience and from the responsibilities of his station and use the powers he unquestionably has by nature.[138] We heard that night of the death of Col. Sergeant, on his way to Washington. We had hoped the best for him; but his wound turned badly.— A man of superior abilities & of a remarkable wit. The 6th and 2d Corps are camped, the first N.E. the other S.W. of the Junction. Major Smythe who has followed us thus far, and messed with the General, has left us—a very gentlemanly man, and of sound sense though *poco a poco*.[139]

April 16, Sunday.

5th Corps has got to Farmville on its way here. The paroled at Appomattox C. H. amounted to 26,000, of whom only about 10,000 had muskets. The rest were artillery, a few cavalry, extra duty men, and men who had thrown away their arms. 600 vehicles, 1,700 animals (most very poor) and about 130 guns. The amount of artillery lost on the march is great—taken, abandoned or buried. Griffin's management of the corps has been satisfactory and Grant now has a quite different opinion from when, at the Wilderness, he asked: "who is this man *Gregg?*"[140]

April 17, Monday.

Visited the 6th Corps H'dq'rs, near Petersburg R.R., with Gen. Meade. Gen. Wright had been much poisoned by dogwood, but is pretty much over it. It would seem that a second-rate actor, a brother of Edwin Booth, named J. Wilkes Booth, is the assassin of the President. This morning Farrar, with detachments of the regiments, presented to Gen. Meade some 20 colors, taken by the 6th Corps; among them I recognized the flag of the 18th N.C.—the regiment of my truce friend, Maj. Wooten![141]

April 18, Tuesday.

We had as guest, Mr. Faulkner, who was our minister at Paris, when the war broke out. He was some time in Fort Warren, but was released, and has lived at his place, quietly, a sort of Union man. He considered Virginia would easily come back if treated judiciously, that she now was badly represented &c. &c. He spent some time in Stonewall Jackson's camp and wrote some official accounts of his campaigns, and had a great admiration for him. F[aulkner] is a small, civil, political looking man, with gray hair brushed behind his ears. He came with Gibbon who is about 15 miles ahead of his corps and dined with us.[142] He, Gibbon, said the reb' generals, the night of the 8th agreed to attack, before light, at Appomattox Sta. & C. H. and, if only cavalry were found, to cut through, but to retire if they came on infantry. Accordingly, while Gibbon was getting his two divisions into line, early, the cavalry was attacked and driven in confusion, but, as soon as they came on his line, they returned without a shot. Andy Johnson has been inaugurated as President and his address was dignified, and his bearing is said to have been excellent.[143]

April 19, Wednesday.

Had thought to go, with Gibbon's column, to Richmond; but today came telegraphic order to send the 9th Corps to Washington, *de suite*, via Petersburg; so determined to go too, for it is a chance to get home at once, and certainly do not earn my daily forage *here*. The General was most sorry to lose his old mess-mate, and indeed all expressed themselves sorry at my determination. The General gave me a special Order accepting my resignation, and the following letter, which to me is more than pay for what little I have done.

[Transcribed by TL]

> Burkesville Va.
> Headquarters Army of the Potomac
> April 19, 1865
> Lt. Col. Theo. Lyman A.D.C.
> Col:—In parting with you after an association of over twenty months, during which time you have served on my staff—I feel it due to you to express my high sense of the assistance I have received from you, and to bear testimony to the zeal, energy and gallantry you have displayed in the discharge of your duties. Be assured I shall ever preserve the liveliest reminiscences of our intercourse, and wherever our separate fortunes may take us—I shall ever have a deep interest in your welfare and happiness, which, by the blessing of God, I trust may be long continued[.]
> Most truly your Friend, Geo. G. Meade, Maj. Gen. U. S. A.

Packed up my effects, part to go by express & part by the waggons of the 9th Corps. And so lay down to my last sleep at the Headquarters of the Potomac Army.

April 20, Thursday.

Really felt quite choky to go round & shake all by the hand for a farewell! Old Duane was quite hearty, and so indeed was everybody. My tent-mate for this year and more, good Rosie, shook me by the hand and said "Adieu, my benefactor!" I have made him heir to all my camp furniture that do not take home. And there even was Albert shaking hands with *his* friends, John &c. 10.45 A.M. Mounted and left the camp for—the North. Gen. Parke had gone already from his H'dq'rs near the Petersburg R.R. but overtook him, some 7 miles out, following the route that lies nearly parallel with the rail. Passed the 5th Corps on the march to relieve the 9th; also saw Gens. Griffin & Ayres; and Gen. Bartlett who is just ordered to take a division in the 9th, to the indignation of the staff of that body, though B[artlett] is a good man.[144] The General received me with his usual kindness as did the aides. There was Capt. Goddard a good Rhode Islander, & jolly, Loring with his brevet star, Pell, Van Buren, Ned Dalton, Dr. Adams &c. &c. Only Phil Leidig was away, but Cutting was along, a Tidball Ch. of Artillery, most of the time. We halted at one Dr. Campbell's, at Nottoway C. H. an arrant Secesh and completely broken by his ill luck. He was a very old man & steeped in gall. In his garden was the first rose that have seen; strawberries in flower; and the luxuriant yellow jasmine. Took a couple of strawberry plants, hoping to make them grow at home. At Wellesville (22 m.) which consists of a house & barn, we slept in the house. Gen. Hartranft was there with his division. He is a modest soldierly man, and has won an excellent name for himself. The girls had been very secesh when we moved west, but now had recanted! Heavy thunder shower.[145]

April 21, Friday.

Left at 6 A.M. At Ford's, Gen. Parke left us, intending to wait for the train & get directly to City Point. We got to familiar ground at Sutherland's and camped 2 mls. beyond it, on the Cox road, at a house whose owner, a woman was exceeding fussy & seemed to think we ought not to be anywhere near there! It was a thing to be remembered, to hear her say "please" to her slaves, who understood very clearly their position! The 5th Mass. cav. are picketing here, but Adams was away. Young Pat Jackson, a Lieutenant, came to see his uncle Loring.[146]

April 22, Saturday.

A short 8 miles, by the Cox road, took us to Petersburg. Many troops, chiefly cavalry & blacks, are still camped about it. We rode to a handsome house in Sycamore St. which "Boss Fero" has appropriated to himself; and rested our horses. For City Pt. we took the road next the river, leaving Fort Stedman on our right. The works on the alluvial flat next the water, are very near together and heavily traversed on both sides. We had hardly got to our own lines when we were assailed by the characteristic dust, which continued to the Point, where we found Gen. Parke ready to go by "River Queen" a fine steamer that will take us & our horses—good luck! Leaving at 2.15 P.M. we paddled rapidly to Fort Monroe, where Col. Badeau got out (he had come from Richmond) for he heard that Grant had gone suddenly to North Carolina, and he would fain follow.[147]

April 23, Sunday.

There were two "bridal" staterooms on board, of which Parke had one, and Loring and I the other, wherein we were in clover. By delay in coaling &c. we did not get to Washington till 2 P.M. The Potomac, with its banks already green and the trees in leaf, was very fine. To Willard's on horseback, and put my horses at Nailor's opposite; where they will stay in charge of Albert, till Silas (to whom telegraphed) comes, to help them home. Called on John Forbes, who has a large house in I St. and was most kindly received by Mrs. F. & all of them. Dined there. Mr. & Mrs. Sr. Cunningham and Sam Ward appeared as guests. A certain Lieut. of the 2d Cav. was there, wounded. The same that was at Milton Hill with a previous wound. A brave little fellow. Got there the information that Mr. & Mrs. Russell were to be at New York, with Hal at the Clarendon. The city is hung with mourning for the President and people wear crape or badges. It is looked on as ill affected not to do so.[148]

April 24, Monday.

Called on Gen. Hunt and was introduced to Mrs., a brunette, quite well to look on. They live in I St. as does Gen. Humphreys, whom did not find at home. The city really looks much better than usual, just in spring, with the fresh leaves. There are some good houses, and one, the Corcoran, is somewhat of a palace, with garden, stable, greenhouse &c.[149] To Gardner's, 511 7th St. and ordered some photographs. Took the 4.30 P.M. train for Philadelphia getting in at 11.15. Observed that Baltimore also was much hung with black, and with little draped flags at the windows. Had a room at the Continental a town of a place and very clean & good *and* expensive.

April 25, Tuesday.

Failed not to go at once and see Mrs. Meade (1838 Delancey Pl.). The house was heavily and handsomely draped with flags and black. Poor, good lady! She is somewhat weak, and having been preyed on by the deaths of her son and brother, and much wrought up by the injustice done the General by the papers, during these last movements, she was quite hysterical, but plucked up a good deal, after some pleasant & encouraging talk. Her daughter Marguerite was there, also there came her brother-in-law Mr. Smith (who visited us at Brandy Sta.) and Mrs. Biddle.[150] Then went to Wenderoth —— Chestnut St. and ordered a large photograph of the General; very good. Then to —— Chestnut St. & ordered a pair of riding boots (the real stiff-legged Hessians; and only $45!) The talk of everyone is Sherman's "surrender to Johnston" as it is called, which first heard of from Col. Bowers at Washington. Overbalanced by the power he so long has had, misled by a certain degree of leniency shown to Lee, and persuaded by the specious statements of the rebels, Sherman concluded a convention with Johnston, by which the rebels could retain their arm's in their own arsenals; convene their old legislatures; receive to a great degree a general amnesty, and even (by implication) continue to hold slaves! The revulsion of public feeling against Sherman was, in its suddenness and intensity, one of the most remarkable instances in our history, of the intense sensitiveness and perception of the mass in all questions of vital public importance.[151] Crossed to Camden and took the Amboy train at 2 P.M. getting to N. York at 7. The Jersey country is well worth seeing for its fine market gardening,—having a fertile soil of its own, & lying between N. York & Philadelphia. Took the steamer at "Amboy" and went through the Kill van Kuhl past Staten Is. to the city, the men-of-war firing their evening gun as we passed up the harbor. The President's funeral procession had gone through the city that day, with much pomp; and all Broadway was hung with mourning, and with many devices. Found Mr. & Mrs. Russell with Hal & Mary at the Clarendon—all much surprised at my sudden advent! Mary's eyes seem to me stronger. Their boy Jim is sturdy, walks a little, and seems to have appropriated all his mother's strength.

April 26, Wednesday.

Bob R[ussell] was on from spending the Easter holidays in Boston. He is improving in looks. Went to Brady to order some photographs. Left by the shore-line at 12.15 getting to Boston at 9 P.M. Home, to go no more back! Mrs. Mimi, wreathed with pleasant smiles, was at the head of the stairs to welcome me. For all mercies we should be thankful to God; especially when we think of the poor women to whom Peace brings no husband, or son, or brother!—Oh stranger, tell it in Lacedaemon, that they died in obedience to her laws.

April 27, Thursday.

In these two months past little Cora has grown a good bit bigger and amazingly older. Now she talks almost in an argumentative way! She put her little arms out to papa very sweetly, as she sat up at her porringer of bread & milk. Cora the greater welcomed me with tears in her eyes, and Howland was rejoiced also. Reported, according to orders, to the Governor, and was received with this military saying: "How are you; and how is Simon?" (to wit, Barstow!) Visited goodly Ned Browne; and, after, Palfrey, the newly married swain. News today that Booth has been shot near Port Royal Va. in trying to escape. It is best so. The other conspirators has [*sic*] mostly been arrested.[152]

April 28, Friday.

Johnston has surrendered; same terms as Lee. This includes all troops east of the Chattahoochee; with Beauregard, Hardee, Semmes, &c. Davis a fugitive, said to have a lot of specie with him. To bonny Brookline. The spring is a wonder for earliness! Two weeks ahead at least. The grass under full growth and the little leaves of the earlier trees peeping out. Saw the faithful Watt delving in the garden. There will be endless caterpillars this year, which Flynn is directed to vigorously annihilate. Mr. Haynes was up and to him gave some directions for repairs & improvements. Oh! This moving a family is far ahead of moving a corps!

April 29, Saturday.

Once again our "family dinner," at which Annie & Alex greeted me. They are housekeepers at Cambridge, with the Professor & Mrs. on their way to Brazil. Went about to order carpets & the like for our Singletree. Of course met lots of people in the street; who are very kind in their welcome to me.

April 30, Sunday.

Mr. & Mrs. Russell home by the shore-line this morn, early. To the Stone Chapel to hear our cousin Foote. We did dine at dear Co's, *en famille.* Rowland has sent me his pledge of 6 bottles old madeira, on the fall of Richmond. Saw Jim Lawrence, who is said to be engaged to Annie Motley! Too bad. But Jim is a kind, generous man. We all have our errors.

May 1, Monday.

Going to Brookline we dined at good Mrs. Cabot's, who looks extremely well. Louis was there, inert and funny as usual. Miss Sadie also, and one of the Doctor's boys, Sammie, now grown a big chap. Louis feels badly over the death of Col. Washburne, of whom they had good hopes. A raw May Day (as is invariable) after our almost summer weather.[153]

May 2, Tuesday.

They printed in the Advertiser an article that wrote, to show Meade's services in the last campaign. It was called *Suum Cuique*. Out to Exhib. dinner at the Porc. These boys have run a huge debt, despite our warnings at the meeting a year since. It arises from their keeping a wine list in the rooms. Made a big row about the same, and scared their bad consciences; they promising to set it straight. Present Hon. Bros. Billy Howe, Gus. Perkins; Geo. & Theo. Chase; Browne; Mifflin; H. Hunnewell; Fred. Lyman &c. And Immediates, Deputy L. Tucker, Sec. Greenleaf; Mifflin, Chadwick, Wells, &c. &c.—in all a large table full. Walked in thereafter, to my benefit, for the night was fine.[154]

May 3, Wednesday.

Letter from Gen. Warren, with a map, showing his action at 5 Forks. It was explanatory. He feels deeply his removal, poor man! Also Humphreys "Delta" from that chivalric man of science. To a meeting of the Nat. Hist. Soc. in their new building. An annual meeting taken up entirely with reports (of which a tremendous one from laborious Scudder!) and elections. It was catching to one's breath to hear them calmly talk of $100,000 when formerly we were wont to scrape hard to get the needful, to keep expenses of a few hundreds up. In addition to the large sums subscribed they have a legacy coming in from that eccentric surgeon, Dr. Walker, which is estimated at $175,000! It is quite wonderful. Wyman is still President.[155]

May 4, Thursday.

To Brookline, where saw the contented Albert, who, after many delays, has got on with Silas & the horses. The latter look well & will look still better. Alex in a peck of trouble about the De Koninck collection, of which a balance of $7,000 stands unpaid! And Agassiz has left the plan to give De K. U.S. gold Bonds for it, which De K. *accepts*; and now whence will the money come? The old Borneau, "Marcus" came up on one of his visits. A strange man! with Americans from his childhood, forgetting his savage tongue, yet not able to speak good English.[156]

May 5, Friday.

Mr. Russell's birthday—65—Mimi & I gave him Leech's caricatures.

May 6, Saturday.[157]

Hal on, for a day. He will soon come *en permanence*. The girls still have rather cool politeness to him. Mary & Mimi had a correspondence on the subject. Mary is rather a weak girl, though with a deal more headpiece than her mamma.

May 10, Wednesday.

Ah! Master Hal! So you resigned your colonelcy on account of your wife's weak health, and now she proves *en voie!* That is no way. No more will I defend you.[158]

May 13, Saturday.

Summoned to see the Governor, who wanted me to be a commissioner about getting shad and salmon over the dams in the Merrimack & Connecticut.— Accepted.[159]

May 14, Sunday.

That secular print, the Sunday Herald, announced that Jeff. Davis was taken, by Col. Pritchard, 4th Mich. cav. at Irwinsville Ga.—Here is a poetical justice to end this war with!! Everyone asking for that "sour apple tree."[160] We dined at Howland's, and paid an evening visit to Uncle George & Aunt Nancy who go tomorrow to Waltham. There were Arthur, Lydia, Sarah &c. The worthy Sears was very earnest to ask if a visit now to Richmond was in no wise fraught with danger from disease or violence! This desire to go south is of sudden & rather tardy growth!

May 16, Tuesday.

Got a huge document appointing me a "Fish" commissioner.

May 18, Thursday.

To State House, got qualified by Councillors Bird & Talbot as commissioner & had some talk with them on the authority and the question at large. Boys crying ballads & caricatures of "Jeff" taken in his wife's gown! Being recognised by his boots, one wag observed "his last shift was bootless."[161] Drove with Mimi to Brookline, to make preparations, as we move out tomorrow. The air was very cool today—at least 30° lower than yesterday!

May 19, Friday.

This morning talked to Mr. Storrow & Edmund Dwight on the dams & their effects on the fish in the rivers.[162]

May 21, Sunday.

Took a ride on "Culpeper" (my black mare). She is a link with the past, coming, like her rider, from the field to a quiet stall! The roan "Petersburg" takes happily to harness.

May 22, Monday.

In town & saw John A. Loring who said Tisdale had refused the "fish Commission." L[oring] wished to see me again & undertook to look up all legal points about the passage of salmon &c.[163]

May 23, Tuesday.

Saw Wyman, who gave me some fish information, and told me he was going to Richmond next Friday. So promised him notes. The grand march in review today of the Army of the Potomac, through Washington, was a grand success, Meade leading the whole.[164]

May 24, Wednesday.

Harry Lee called, pregnant with the soldiers' celebration. What a cheery man!—a family of sick children at home, servants going away—but cheerful to the last![165]

May 25, Thursday.

For the first time, put Mimi on the black mare "Culpeper," who carried her finely, to my satisfaction. This being a success she has the finest saddle horse in the state for a lady!

May 30, Tuesday.

This day, the Old Army of the Potomac marched in triumph through Washington, past the President, the Lieutenant General, the Cabinet, and all the foreign ministers and chief persons of the country, assembled on a great platform in front of the White House! Meade rode at their head. A glorious day for these poor troops! If those who have fallen could pass tonight before that platform, what an array of regiments it would be! Passed the day at Lowell to investigate further this matter of a passage for fish up our rivers.[166]

May 31, Wednesday.

A more distant expedition to Holyoke, above Springfield.

June 1, Thursday.

In the first train. Charlie Heath was in it. He is in business now in N.Y. which separates him from his family, poor, tall man!— There was a grand procession, auspice Frank Palfrey, and we all witnessed it from Aunt Mary's house in Beacon St. It was like most such—day fine, and all things respectable— The military under Gen. Bartlett, looked well. It was strange to see the City Greys &c. still in their old fashioned uniform, while the rifle-clubs &c. were in the modern blouse & cap. Steam fire-engines were a new feature. Pudding-head Sumner was thereafter to deliver the eulogy on the late President. We had quite a flood of company at dinner (no! tea). Loring came first and left with 2 cigars, a bouquet & some lettuce. Then came deaf R. B. Forbes with his daughter, Edie Perkins & Em'; finally Bob Winthrop appeared. He said that Pinckney Alston was killed before Richmond, as also Wm. Pringle, & that the father Wm. Bull Pringle, was living at Charleston in the deepest destitution. What a whirlwind to these misguided sowers of the wind![167]

June 3, Saturday.

Ha! ha! ha! Loring was so sure that he had control of the Governor's appointment of the other fish commissioner, and now the Lt. Gov. has appointed Mr. Rice of Worcester, whereas L. wanted Mr. Alfred Reed! Family tea at 1 Louisburg Sq. Bob Oliver has gone to Texas with his regiment.[168]

June 7, Wednesday.

Called on Abbot to consult on the class-supper of which I am to be president. He lent me his brother's report to Adj. Gen. Conn. on the siege train before Petersburg & Bermuda Hundreds. Whole number of rounds fired on Bermuda Hundred's front & Petersburg front from the beginning to March 1, 1865—55,450 = 1,118 tons of iron. This only from *mortars & siege pieces*, as he was only over the siege train. The field artillery fired a great deal beside. The average of firing before P'b'g was greatest in September, viz: 7.8 tons per day. At the Mine assault 5,835 rounds were fired from 81 siege guns & mortars = 75 tons iron. After that 29 siege guns & mortars only were left.[169]

June 8, Thursday.

Ned & Mrs. Dalton dined with us, and Browne came also to support the symmetry of the table. We had a *grand succès*; Mrs. Dalton told us funny anecdotes of the manners of Eugene Bachelder's mother; & Ned tempered our enthusiasm for the Sanitary Commission, with anecdotes of *that*.

June 17, Saturday.

Real "Bunker Hill Day"—*id est* thermometre 90°. We drove in to take the usual family tea. Called on Mr. Geo. Tichnor, who said that my mare ran off with Russell! ho! ho! ho!

June 23, Friday.

A fair, & cool day for Class-day. Drove over & (Mimi wouldn't go) and spent a couple of hours. Saw & talked with Cac Chase. He is to be supper toast-master. At the Porc saw new side-board given by Bro. George Mifflin. Staid a few moments at the spread of Bros. Tucker & Chadwick—very handsome—in second house beyond the Brattle. Saw there Mrs. Turner Sargent and Mrs. Tucker, Miss Bowditch. They had a tent in the yard—all in good taste. Found Ludlow in the crowd, to my surprise. He has a new graduating. Took him back with me and dined him. He much pleased with my place. He said Roonie Lee was down and got 6 mules of him at Williamsburg, and was now living at White House in a small cabin, with his brother and cousin, & tilling the soil! We live in an age of romance & wonders and we don't appreciate it! The negroes he said, had pretty much all the ready money there.[170]

June 27, Tuesday.

By the 8 A.M. Lowell train, with fellow commissioner Alfred A. Reed, to testify before the Select Committee of the N. H. Legislature, on the Fish-way question; all at Concord. Getting there at 3 P.M. Mr. Bellows met us & gave us a dinner at the Eagle Hotel. After which he brought round 4 fine blacks in a light barouche (which he had driven over from his 800-acre farm at Walpole) and took us a drive up the river then crossing & coming back the other side. The elms are here splendid, and the distant hills and fine grass lands make an excellent *coup d'oeuil*. Was introduced to Governor Smyth, a long-bearded, cleanly country politician. He invited us to sit on the platform, while he received 3 returning regiments, the 10th, 12th & 13th, under Bvt. Brig. Gen. Donahoe. They formed line in front, and the Gov. & sundry Honorables said a few words, sensibly not keeping them too long from their supper which waited at the hotels.[171] Then we had our little meeting at the Representative Hall, which is a temporary thing, in the City Hall, while the Capitol is building anew. Explained what action the Mass. Commissioners had taken; the disposition of the State, &c. Mr. Reed spoke of the value of trout & salmon, and the ease of taking and rearing spawn. Judge Bellows then spoke a long while as advocate of fish-ways. He is an old-fashioned, sensible & well informed gentleman, of an agreeable sort; one of the

Websterian school, plainly. Then there was some talk of "land-locked salmon" from a Mr. Fletcher and of black basse from Mr. Wills and so we separated; after a vote of thanks to us for our pains. We talked awhile in the room, at the hotel, of one Mr. Bingham, an ultra Democrat, and so to bed. They are discussing the Constitutional Amendment (forbidding Slavery) and the Copperheads, who abound in some parts of the State, are airing their sentiments.[172]

June 28, Wednesday.

The Oriental Reed was up by 4.30 A.M. –ἐγωγε —It took me right back to the army to see the "Doughboys" lying asleep, in the green, covered with their shelter tents, just as in bivouac![173] Mr. Bellows kindly gave us a cup of coffee at Mr. Stearns' house—which we had visited the day before and see Mr. & Mrs. S. and Mrs. Bellows a quite pretty woman. By 8.30 we were in Boston, and did breakfast at Mr. Russell's—so much for early rising! Ran about town and also looked up some books at the Athenaeum—on fisheries; and, after a town dinner, drove out with Mimi, who has done her last day at the Sanitary. Drove in state with Mimi & visited Mr. & Mrs. P. S. Van Rensselaer (the ones we saw at Rome) who are staying at Mrs. Gen'l. Sumner's.

June 30, Friday.

A hot day, for this last of June; about 89° in the shade; and 80° in the bed-room that night. This evening called on Charlie Appleton, where we were nearly eaten by skeeters. His wife, poor woman, is better of her illness, and he is in good case, though they are a dismal couple, as they have cause! Old, deaf pa Mason was there, and stupid Mr. Amory.

[Newspaper clipping, inserted]

FAREWELL ORDER OF GENERAL MEADE TO THE ARMY OF THE POTOMAC.—The following order of General Meade to the Army of the Potomac was published yesterday in Washington—

HEADQUARTERS ARMY OF THE POTOMAC

June 28, 1865

Soldiers: This day, two years ago, I assumed command, under the orders of the President of the United States. Today, by virtue of the same authority, the army ceasing to exist, I have to announce my transfer to other duties and my separation from you. It is unnecessary to enumerate all that has occurred in these two eventful years, from the great and decisive battle of Gettysburg, the turning point of the war, to the surrender of the Army of Northern Virginia at Appomattox Court House. Suffice it to say that history will do you justice; a grateful country will honor the living, cherish and support the disabled, and sincerely mourn the dead. In parting from you, your commanding general will ever bear in memory your noble devotion to your country, your patience and cheerfulness under all the privations and sacrifices you have been called on to endure. Soldiers: Having accomplished the work set before us, having vindicated the honor and integrity of our government and flag, let us return thanks to Almighty God for His blessing in granting victory and peace, and let us earnestly pray for strength and light to discharge our duties as citizens as we have endeavored to discharge them as soldiers.

GEORGE G. MEADE,
Major-General U. S. A.

July 1, 1865, Saturday.

Was today at the State House to see the Governor who said he wanted to consult me on entertaining Gen. Meade when he should arrive for Commencement for he would specially write the General a note.

July 2, Sunday.

A deluge of rain this afternoon; in midst of which took a ride; and was reminded in my rubber of the army.

July 4, Tuesday.

All hands nearly, off to the "Glorious Fourth." It is in truth a Fourth of glory— and we have a right peace at last. My flag on the barn was raised accordingly, and the little silk one of Florence was displayed on the balcony. We took the baby to a pyrotechnical display that eve, chez Mrs. J[ohn] Sturgis, and she stood the crackers with much valor, but, overcome by the late hour, fell asleep on "Paapsy's" shoulder going home. We have all her curls razed, the which makes her look more practical though less pretty.

July 6, Thursday.

Rode horseback with Mimi as far as Mary Guild's to ask her to tea tomorrow. Coming back, overtook Capt. (now Bvt. Maj.) Flint and his Lieut. ——How-land. Invited both to dine tomorrow.[174]

July 7, Friday.

This day were hanged in the prison yard at Washington, four conspirators against the life of Abraham Lincoln, to wit: Mrs. Surratt; Payne (Powell); Atzerodt; and Herrold—a solemn & eminently fitting vindication of justice!— Dr. Mudd & Arnold are imprisoned for life; also McLoulin. Spangler has 6 years in prison.[175] Flint & Howland dined with; the latter a promoted sergeant but intelligent and discreet. Flint was with the engineers on their recent trip to survey the Wilderness (a rare chance to envy him!). They went as far as Cold Harbor. He brought me a valuable gift, a section of the red oak which was cut down by bullets at the "salient" or "death angle," May 12, 1864. The actual part cut off is in the War Dept. and is 23 inches through; this section, taken 5 feet below is 25 inches. They spoke of the many bodies still lying unburied (now skeletons) on the field of the Wilderness, especially just on each side of the Plank Road. (Burial parties have since been out there.) The rebel works were everywhere better built than our own. At Spottsylvania, they had three lines and flanking lines besides! At the "salient" the trees are killed by bullets over a space of several acres. On either side of the Wilderness plank road, in front of the rebel pits the saplings were all cut down by musketry, so as even to make a real "slashing." In the 6th Corps front there were not marks of heavy fighting, comparatively. Chas. and Mary Guild and Fanny Foote came to tea and made up quite a Cage company with the modest Flint. They had promised to bring Bates, but could not find him, so the militaires had to come without him. He had gone probably to report at Ft. Warren.[176]

July 9, Sunday.

By the way, Flint says Duane is at Willet's Pt., having charge of the N.Y. fortifications; Rosie & Berlin are going west of far west with Gen. Hunt, who is thither ordered.

July 11, Tuesday.

Bothered about in town about Meade's entertainment next week; also Class supper; also fish question. Gen. Meade will stay with me. In afternoon Frank Parkman called & told me of his visit to Richmond, &c. He went out to Cold Harbor, and saw the way our poor men burrowed into the earth, to avoid the enfilade fire; and saw the partly buried bodies and the many broken muskets and every sort of military debris. What a time was that![177]

July 14, Friday.

Had a meeting for determining about the Meade dinner. As walked up the steps of 1 Louisburg Sqr. beheld mine "Uncle" Jonathan Russell in company of

Mr. Upton. He looks much as when, some 11 years since, we partook together of cocktails, only stouter and still more lazy. There were only Wendell Holmes & Mr. Weld at the meeting and we settled the dinner question presto; it being all left to me.[178]

July 16, Sunday.

Major Lincoln's secretary out, in a heap of excitement about Meade's advent, and wanting to have some civic honors thrown him; so sent him a note explanatory.

July 17, Monday.

Was down and ready at the cars at 5 P.M. to receive the General who soon arrived in a special car, and accompanied by George Bache and Barstow. The General was in plain clothes and looked very well. We at once drove to Brookline, and gave the twain straightaway some dinner. Barstow took Bache & Geo. Meade under his wing. Barlow & Dr. Palfrey came and added their company to our dinner, which was set forth with flowers by way of welcome. After all had gone, Meade had a long talk about the affair of Sailor's Run, and the reports of Sheridan. He said it was hinted that Wright was not quite straight at Cedar Creek and thus held S[heridan] in fear, which might account for his supineness.[179]

July 18, Tuesday.

As a beginning of festivities we had prepared a reception briefly at the neighbors. There were flowers from Wales all about; the big room was set in best order, and with the "Bacchus & Panther" on the new pedestal and the fresh gilding on the bookcases, looked quite palatial! An excellent collation was spread in the dining room & thither we directed the overflows from the reception parlor. Howland came all the way from Beverly and Uncle George from Waltham. We had a big lot of people, say 150, all of whom were introduced to the General who was most affable. Had my section of the tree from the "death angle," the shell that nearly hit the General, the tree with a spherical case in it, and Lee's chair to entertain the company withal. Got along famously except that called Aunt Geraldine "Mrs. Rivers" to her manifest indignation—*mais ma foi,* if these old women will get married again.— In the afternoon was our dinner to the Gettysburg warrior at the Reveres. Thither came as hosts: Capt. Brigham; Surg. Gen. Dale; S. M. Weld; G. H. Shaw; Harry Lee; Jas. Lawrence; Geo. M. Barnard; Wendell Holmes; Dr. Mifflin; Wm. Gray; Maj. John Gray; John Ropes; Ingersoll Bowditch; Alfred Reed; Hal Russell & Mayor Lincoln. Prof.

Holmes, J. R. Lowell, & Gen. Meade & staff (including Macy & Col. Bachelder) were the guests with the Governor who presided. The dinner, graced by some private madeira, was excellent. In the midst came the 11th Infantry Band and serenaded us, and the officers were asked in to take a glass of wine. Then the crowd gathered and cheered for the General, who went on the balcony and said a few words. The Governor then proposed in fit words, the General's health, and he replied in a pretty speech. Prof. Holmes gave us a neat little "pome," quite unexpectedly, and so the evening went on most cheerily, which was a wonder, considering the mixed class of the company. As I looked on this as a grand occasion—a sort of celebration of the Peace, did open, to the health of the Guest, a bottle of White Top. The first since my wedding![180]

July 19, Wednesday.

We gave Meade a sweater today!; viz: mealing him through Commencement *ab ovo usque ad malum*, beginning even with a breakfast chez Barstow at 7.30 A.M. They are again in their old house, 33 Charles, and cozy it is. Mrs. Barstow did the honors in a distinguished manner and so did sons Simon & John. Thereafter all of us, in full tog & swords got us to the State House, where we were honorably put in carriages and wended solemnly to Cambridge under corpulent escort of the Lancers. This is probably the last year of the procession, as the college is now detached from the State. There we went in grave files, led by John Albion, to the church; where did devote myself to keeping seats for Mrs. Meade & Mimi, who arrived at 12. The parts were rather above the average but were soaked in politics—such grave advice as we all got on the rights of the negro and reconstruction! Abbot had got out his history of the Class for the decade, a creditable & interesting pamphlet. The last of the performances was the presentation to George Gordon Meade of a degree of L.L.D. *honori causa*; the Latin sentence being a very neat allusion to Gettysburg! Turned the General over to Simon & hied in town to the Grand Class Supper at Parker's. It was a big thing—a great success—whereat did preside. Present: Abbot, Agassiz, Arnold (much improved with a big beard), Barlow, Bliss, Brooks (P), Browne, Brown (E.J.), Chase, (Toastmaster) Clark (R.M.), Dalton, Edgerly, Emmenton, Fiske, Gibbons, Green, Heywood (well, and of a conceit most astounding, and that grows yearly. He was out last Tuesday and said he had a prospect of a share in a silver mine!), Hosmer, Johnston (Old Sam looks very well, and as natural as ever), Jones, Longfellow, Lyman (B.S.—He has never shaved and has a huge downy beard that doesn't look badly.), Lyman (T.), McKenzie, Mitchell, Paine, Reed, Ropes (He has grown very *fat*, and is the same good, wild Westerner), Russell

(Ed. G.), Sanborn, Thwing, Tileston, Walker, Waters, Willard, Wright.— The supper was really cheery & flagged not. We had a nice ode from Reed, and he wrote besides a clever, humorous song. There was a good bit of sharpshooting which kept up till 1 in the morning when I drove Barlow out to Brookline, in a heavy rain squall.[181]

July 20, Thursday.

The Mayor took possession of the Lion [Meade] this morning and trotted him round to various schools, finally bringing up at Faneuil Hall, where Mimi & Mrs. M[eade] were in the gallery ready to behold the "reception." The floor was about ¾ full and the General was handsomely greeted with cheers, after which he had to shake hands for an hour, with a nearly continuous stream of people. The entertainment of that eve was more quiet & agreeable; viz: a very handsome dinner at Mr. Dehon's, where were some 24 seated. The 2 Baches, Martin Brimmer, Mr. Frank Bacon, old Peter Harvey, Judge Thomas, Governor Clifford &c—altogether a good deal, of course, of mild "copper." Miss Dehon, who is a smart gal, was the only female, and was flanked by Gens. Barlow & Meade. At dessert was much lively sparring between Thomas & Clifford on age; T. avowing that, at a college centennial celebration when he was a boy, Clifford was shown him as the man who remembered all about the very beginning! Dehon proposed Gen. Meade's health and the General, in a few touching words, proposed "the sacred memory of Arthur Dehon."— At dark, we had music and a reception of some thirty ladies and gentlemen. Mrs. Barlow was there, also Mrs. Tom Motley. Charlie appeared looking much better than expected. He is on the mend, after dangerous illness. Altogether, Dehon did the thing most handsomely. The house was Bacon's.[182]

July 21, Friday.

The long looked for Celebration, called the "Commemoration for the returning soldiers" at Harvard. The sky smiled on the anxious Chief Marshal, Harry Lee, who has almost turned into a "Commemoration" with thinking of it! To begin betimes, the Porcellian had asked the General & staff to breakfast at 9 A.M., a breakfast in my official honor and in honor too of the military Bros. It was in excellent taste and the table was filled with blue-coats, to discuss the cold fowls, salmon, & woodcock. Afterwards the Club elected the General an Honorary, whereat he was much gratified, and we gave him three cheers.[183] And so to Gore Hall, where the uniforms gathered thick, with many a familiar face! Of our class there were noteworthy Maj. Gen. Barlow; Bvt. Maj. Gen. Hayes; Lt. Col. Dr. Dalton; Corporals Hosmer & Waters &c &c. Then there were Admiral

Davis, Bvt. Maj. Gen. Devens, Bvt. Maj. Gen. Force &c &c. Ayres was there, among the guests, and Joe Smith, Commissary of the old 2nd Corps. Hal's class mustered strong, and there was Phillips the Battery officer. In fact there were too many to mention.[184] The Class of '60 has lost most, to wit 12. The soldiers when formed in files, make a long line. We marched to the church, where the gallant Jackson had seated Mrs. Meade & Mimette, and there had exercises of about 2 hours; viz: prayer by our P. Brooks (now the most noted Episcopal clergyman of Philadelphia) and an address by Dr. Putnam, which was good, but overstrained, rather. The music was most capital, from a full orchestra and choir. Then all the ladies to Harvard Hall, where they had a collation, while the men, again forming a procession, marched to a huge tent, pitched round the Liberty Tree, and extending from Harvard Hall to Holden. There was a large balcony where the ladies sat to hear the speeches. Against the draped side of Hollis was hung the roll of names of those who have fallen from among the graduates, amounting to near 100. Those who have served, in one capacity or another, are over 500, as recorded in a little book laid on each plate. The dinner was the only good one of the sort that ever saw. There was fun in the class of '60, which Harry Lee going to quiet, they turned on him and cheered him vociferously. Of speaking there was surely enough, a long, rather good overture from Mr. Chas. G. Loring who presided; then lots of others, Devens, Meade, Davis, Holmes (a poem), Lowell (ditto). In fact, with big & little we kept on till dusk, and then home, having witnessed the greatest fete old Harvard ever saw. Poor Charles Mills! He came up and shook my hand and thanked me for what I had done. There have [been] four pairs of brothers killed from among the graduates: Reveres; Lowells; Abbotts; and Dwights. At the table of honor was the Marquis de Chambron, grandson of La Fayette, an intelligent but not very neat Frenchman.[185]

July 22, Saturday.

A special car took us to Beverly. On the road there was quite a small rush at Lynn and at Salem, the crowd fain to shake hands with the Double-star. Also at Beverly, where Howland waited with his barouche, there was a gathering which cheered as we drove off. The General was handsomely welcomed by Co, and handed, in all honor, into the house, whence he admired the goodly Marblehead. The dinner was of "Bobby Win," Dr. Hooper, Mr. & Mrs. Brimmer, Mrs. Wadsworth, and Miss Bessie Gray; 12 all told. Bobby did rather air a mild copper, while Dr. Hooper was not slow to fire from the other line, so that there was no lack of excitement. After dinner, Annie, Sallie & Frank arrived from a visit to Nahant and gazed with silent awe at the Great Commander.

After a delightful day we had an extra train, at 8.30 P.M. to take us back, not escaping a small ovation at Salem.[186]

July 23, Sunday.

Took the two to Church, at St. Pauls. Coming home did plague Mrs. M[eade] by telling her that Mimi was a Unitarian and said that "all the stupid men went into the Episcopal church!" To which the General cried out, "And so they do!"— His honor Judge Gray dined with us, and, in the afternoon, who should appear but good Gen. Doyle! as funny as ever.

July 24, Monday.

As the Southrons say, "we were shut" of the General today, who went to Nahant with Mrs. & George and Gen. Doyle, of all men in the world (!) for his brother Percy had a love affair with Mrs. Mountford that now is. He first went to the Historical Society where Bob Win[throp] showed him sundry old clothes of sundry big men. Meade came back that evening, to the great disappointment of Mifflin, who had prepared a reception for him. Col. Graham (Capt. Willy's father) came out to see his brother-in-law, the General, and brought Miss Putnam, the daughter of the boarding house with him. The old Colonel has a fine white beard, and was loquacious on his wrongs in the lake survey at the hands of Chandler, who in good sooth, is a scoundrel.[187]

July 25, Tuesday.

We got the General and Mrs. to the 8.30 A.M. train, for nothing will do but that they should go, and go through in one day to Philadelphia. Barstow stays behind, but George and Bache accompanied him. They all seemed very gratified at their reception in Boston, as they well may be.

Suum Cuique by Theodore Lyman
Boston Daily Advertiser, May 2, 1865 and May 4, 1865.
To the Editors of the Boston Daily Advertiser:—
In view of the great fact that the Army of Northern Virginia has been annihilated, and with it the first and the last hope of the rebellion, it may seem a matter of almost too much detail to call attention to the merits of any of the chief actors in this final and most important scene. Yet the gratitude due to these men, not less than a proper spirit of justice, demands that each should have his full share of honor.

It is safe to say that many officers of the old Army of the Potomac were considerably surprised on being informed by the newspapers that General Sheridan (with apparently some slight advice from General Grant) had broken, routed, surrounded, and finally captured Lee and his forces. They had before believed that General Meade, who had led them to the crowning victory of Gettysburg, still commanded them, when, for the last time, they confronted their ancient adversaries. Perhaps a candid view of this short campaign may show that they were right in their belief.

When General Sheridan arrived near Petersburg from his well-conducted raid on the Richmond Canal and the Virginia Central Railroad, he was intrusted with the command of all the cavalry then in that neighborhood, making, with what he had brought with him, some 12,000 mounted men. General Meade had the Army of the Potomac, except the division of cavalry detached; and General Ord commanded the Army of the James, except its cavalry, amounting to a large brigade. Of this army only three divisions, two white and one black, participated in the subsequent operations.

In the grand movements that followed, we may pick out five actions which may be called the essential blows that produced the result. These are (1) the battle of Five Forks; (2) the storming of the rebel works around Petersburg; (3) the barring of the road at Jetersville; (4) the battle of Sailor's Run; (5) the hemming in of Lee near Appomattox Court House. The general features of these may be understood without referring to a map, and without explanation of movements in detail.

(1) On the 31st of March, General Sheridan had orders to sweep round the extreme left of the army, with his cavalry, and attack the right and rear of the enemy. He had advanced but a little way, when Pickett's infantry and "Fitz" Lee's cavalry attacked him, cut him in two, and drove him back to Dinwiddie. Here his position was so precarious that General Grant determined to send him a division of infantry, as a support. General Meade however advised that, not a division, but *a whole corps* should be sent. The advice was taken and it was this change that turned the fight of the next day to a victory, when it otherwise would have been a drawn battle. Sheridan, reinforced by the Fifth Corps under Warren, advanced, struck the enemy in front and flank, took over 4000 prisoners and nearly destroyed Pickett's noted Virginia division. This was a brilliant success

over a detached force; but the formidable intrenchments and batteries of Petersburg still stared our troops in the face. These once carried, and Lee's defeat was certain—his capture possible.

(2) On the 2nd of April, the day succeeding the battle of Five Forks, General Meade had, by order of General Grant, directed a strong assault to be made, by the Sixth and Ninth Corps, on the works on their front. The assault was delivered a little before daylight. The Ninth Corps, under Parke, carried the first line, despite the most formidable opposition, and held it. The Sixth Corps broke through the enemy's line like an avalanche, swept the breastworks in both directions, swung round to the Appomattox River and, with part of the Twenty-Fourth Corps under Gibbon, completed the investment of Petersburg on that side. The strategic importance of this day's work has been scarcely appreciated. The enemy's centre being crushed, one wing was driven into the inner defences of the town, while the other, hopelessly rolled up, was hotly pursued by the Second Corps, and a portion of it completely routed by Miles's division, at Sutherland's Station. The Army of Northern Virginia had received its death-blow. Petersburg and Richmond were untenable and were evacuated that night. Could that army have escaped even the capture that awaited it, its destruction would have been but a question of days.

(3) Richmond and Petersburg abandoned, the enemy with his forces now reunited, and with his heavy trains, was straining every nerve to make good his escape to Danville. On the 4th of April, Sheridan, with excellent sagacity, pushed a portion of his cavalry in all haste to Jetersville. The Fifth Corps, temporarily detached to give stability to his column, came up soon after, and the enemy was cut off from his direct march southward. It was after dark when news came to General Meade that the enemy had been brought to a stand. Although the infantry had been fourteen hours on their feet, and had but just gone into bivouac, he ordered the Second and Sixth Corps to move at one o'clock that night, and to march on Jetersville, hoping to attack next morning. But a division of the cavalry, which had mistaken its way, blocked the road and detained the infantry more than six hours; so that the opportunity was lost. Still, the enemy was forced to make a considerable detour to the west, and thus experienced, two days after, the disastrous rear-guard fight at Sailor's Run.

(4) As soon as the exact line of retreat was discovered, on the morning of the 6th, General Meade directed Wright, with the Sixth Corps, to move in a westerly direction hoping to intercept the enemy and strike him on the flank, while the Second Corps, under Humphreys, continued the direct assault. Sheridan, who now had only his cavalry, had already moved rapidly to the left, to cut off the head of the column. The result of these admirable dispositions was, that the enemy's rear guard under Ewell, being hemmed in by the cavalry in front, the Appomattox on the right, the Sixth Corps on the left, and the Second Corps in the rear, surrendered, after a stubborn resistance, near a brook known as Sailor's Run. It was on this occasion that General Sheridan so far forgot himself as to write, in an official despatch: "I attacked them with two divisions of the Sixth Corps, and routed them handsomely." Whereas, General Wright was the officer who attacked; and he was under the immediate orders of General Meade, and had nothing whatever to do with General Sheridan, whose entire command numbered not over 7000 mounted men, while the Second and Sixth Corps had together not less than 25,000 men actually in the fight.

(5) Without a moment's delay, the direct pursuit was conducted along the Lynchburg stage road, while the cavalry, followed by three divisions of the Army of the James under Ord, and by the Fifth Corps, took the shortest roads to cut off the retreat. On the afternoon of the 8th of April, the cavalry struck the head of their train, feebly guarded, near Appomattox Station, captured a number of pieces from their artillery reserve, and brought their column to a halt. During the night the enemy made preparations to break through the cavalry before daylight; it was agreed, however, by their generals, that the attempt should be given up, if infantry were encountered. The rebel infantry accordingly attacked our cavalry and drove them back, but, coming upon the troops of Ord and Griffin, they in turn retreated. Knowing that Meade, with two army corps, was close on his rear, Lee now demanded a suspension of hostilities, which was granted by Ord, and was followed by the formal surrender to General Grant.

It is the object of this brief review not to depreciate the unquestioned merits of General Sheridan, but to show that the whole credit by no means belongs to him. In no one engagement did General Sheridan handle one-half as many troops as were commanded by General Meade.

It was Meade's troops that carried the rebel lines by assault, and it was his troops again that made the decisive charge at Sailor's Run. At no period during the toilsome pursuit were they wanting in the right place and at the right moment. But General Sheridan is fortunate in his arm of the service, the swift-moving cavalry; and the cavalry are fortunate in their music—the trumpet. —T.

Notes

⸺⸺⸺⸺

Abbreviations

AAG	Assistant Adjutant General
ADC	Aide-de-camp
ANV	Army of Northern Virginia
AoJ	Army of the James
AoP	Army of the Potomac
CM	Commissary of Musters
CoS	Chief of Staff
CS	Commissary of Subsistence
IG	Inspector General
LC	Library of Congress
Lyman Papers MHS	Lyman Family Papers, Massachusetts Historical Society, Boston
Meade Papers LC	George Gordon Meade Collection on Microfilm, Manuscripts Division, Library of Congress
Meade's Headquarters	George R. Agassiz, ed., *Meade's Headquarters, 1863–1865: Letters of Colonel Theodore Lyman from The Wilderness to Appomattox.* Boston: Massachusetts Historical Society, 1922
MHS	Massachusetts Historical Society
MHSM	Military Historical Society of Massachusetts
NARA	National Archives and Records Administration
OR	*The War of the Rebellion: A Compilation of the Official Records of the Union and Confederate Armies,* 128 vols. Washington, D.C.: GPO, 1880–1901. All citations from series one, unless otherwise noted.
PC	Porcellian Club
QM	Quartermaster
TL	Theodore Lyman III
USCT	United States Colored Troops
USMA	United States Military Academy
Warren Papers NYSL	Gouverneur Kemble Warren Papers, New York State Library, Albany

INTRODUCTION

1. Duncan, *Blue-eyed Child of Fortune*, 292.

2. Seaburg and Paterson, *Merchant Prince*, 181–82, 241–42; Morison, *Maritime History*, 277–79.

3. Nahum Sapen to Theodore Lyman III (hereafter TL), June 21, 1879, Lyman Papers MHS, box 20.6.

4. Account book of G. H. Shaw, Samuel Atkins Eliot, and Geo. Williams Lyman, executors of the estate of T. Lyman, Jr., Lyman Papers MHS, bound vol. 9.

5. Newspaper clippings and a draft of the oration in the Lyman Papers MHS, box 12.6.

6. Bache to Lt. T. A. Craven, Feb. 9, 1856, Lyman Papers MHS, box 3.2.

7. In 1853, Meade invented a hydraulic lamp for use with European Fresnel prismatic lenses, a design that so improved the brilliancy of the light and economy of whale oil consumption that the Lighthouse Board adopted the pattern on the Atlantic coast. A bust of Meade sits at the base of the Barnegat lighthouse, Long Beach, New Jersey, a tribute to his lighthouse skills.

8. TL to Gardner Howland Shaw, Feb. 8, 1856, Lyman Papers MHS, box 12.6.

9. Coleman, *Genealogy of the Lyman Family*, 367; Forbes, *Rich Men*, 45.

10. TL to Howland Shaw, Sept. 30, 1856, discussing the 1856 election. His views had changed little by 1860. Lyman Papers MHS, box 12.7.

11. TL to Howland Shaw, June 25, 1861, Lyman Papers MHS, box 13.3.

12. TL to Howland Shaw, Aug. 13, 1861, Lyman Papers MHS, box 13.4.

13. TL to Howland Shaw, July 13, 1862, Lyman Papers MHS, box 13.14.

14. Maj. Henry Jackson How (Harvard 1859), 19th Massachusetts Infantry. TL to Howland Shaw, Aug. 3, 1862. Lyman Papers MHS, box 13.14.

15. Anna Curtis to Mimi Lyman, Sept. 1, 1862; TL to Cora Lyman Shaw, Sept. 20[?], 1862; TL to Howland Shaw, Sept. 7, 1862, Lyman Papers MHS, box 13.15.

16. TL to Cora Lyman Shaw, Oct. 7, 1862, Lyman Papers MHS, box 13.16.

17. TL to Howland Shaw, May 8, 1863, Lyman Papers MHS, box 14.4.

18. Meade to TL, Dec. 22, 1862, Lyman Papers MHS, box 3.3. One word is illegible.

19. TL's notebook, vol. 11, July 14, Lyman Papers MHS. Col. Paul Joseph Revere (Harvard 1852), 20th Massachusetts Infantry, a member of the Porcellian Club and a Terrapin. Lt. Sumner Paine, Co. F, 20th Massachusetts Infantry. Lt. Col. Charles Redington Mudge (Harvard 1860), 2d Massachusetts Infantry. Lt. Henry Ropes (Harvard 1862), 20th Massachusetts Infantry. Brig. Gen. Francis Channing Barlow (Harvard 1855) was wounded July 1 and left in enemy hands. The *Harvard* was the PC team's rowing shell.

20. TL's notebook, vol. 11, July 24, 27, 1863, Lyman Papers MHS. Col. Shaw transferred from the 2d Massachusetts to command the 54th Massachusetts (Colored). He was killed leading his regiment in the assault on Ft. Wagner, July 18, 1863.

21. Entry dated Aug. 10, 1863, TL's notebook, vol. 11, Lyman Papers MHS.

22. Meade to TL, Aug. 12, 1863. TL's notebook, vol. 11, Lyman Papers MHS, box 14.5.

23. Meade, *Life and Letters*, 2:276.

24. TL's notebook, vol. 11, Aug. 15, 17, 1863, Lyman Papers MHS.

25. Adams, *Theodore Lyman*, 160.

26. Henry Adams to Charles Adams, Oct. 16, 1863: "Ted Lyman had apparently been sounding your praises largely. It is well to have friends at headquarters." Ford, *Cycle of Adams Letters*, 94.

27. *Meade's Headquarters*, 256. These notes for Meade were subsequently expanded in "finished" form into TL's notebook vols. 13A and 13B, Lyman Papers MHS.

28. Dana, *Recollections*, 189; Sumner, *Diary*, 279; Warren entry dated June 2, 1864, Warren Papers, NYSL, box 1.7.

29. Carleton, "The May Campaign in Virginia," 127. Sauers, *Gettysburg*, 160.

30. Halleck to Meade, Mar. 20, 1864, NARA, RG110, Letters Sent by HQ of the Army M857, roll 7. For a definitive analysis of Meade's difficulties with Dan Sickles and the Committee on the Conduct of the War, see Sauers, *Gettysburg*.

31. Thomas, *Three Years with Grant*, 255.

32. Capt. George Meade to his mother, May 16, 1864, Meade Papers LC, Microfilm Reel 11.

33. *Boston Daily Advertiser*, May 2, 4, 1865. In 1887, Humphreys's ADC, Carswell McClellan, published *Grant versus the Record*, a rebuttal of Sheridan's role as recounted in Grant's and Badeau's writings.

34. Hagerman, *American Civil War*, 265; Meade, *Life and Letters*, vol. 2: 107–8.

35. Meade to his wife, Apr. 20, 1865, *Life and Letters*, 2:274.

36. *Atlantic Monthly* 22, 208–11.

37. Bail, "Harvard's Commemoration Day," 260.

38. TL to Mimi Lyman, Apr. 17, 1866, Lyman Papers MHS, box 18.8.

39. Adams, *Theodore Lyman*, 171.

40. TL to Mimi Lyman, Feb. 3, 1881, Lyman Papers MHS, box 20.7.

41. TL to Mimi Lyman, Jan. 27, 1882, Lyman Papers MHS, box 20.7.

42. TL to Mimi Lyman, Jan. 8, 1883, Lyman Papers MHS, box 20.11.

43. TL to Miss Clark, May 4, 1887, Lyman Papers MHS, box 20.12.

44. TL's description of symptoms, the age of onset, and his clarity of mind until death suggest that he suffered from amyotrophic lateral sclerosis or Lou Gehrig's disease.

45. Charles L. Peirson to Mimi Lyman, Mar. 20, 1910, "On returning Theodore's letters written during the War of the Rebellion," Lyman Papers MHS, box 20.13.

August 31, 1863–March 9, 1864

Lyman labeled this Vol. 12; it is assigned Lyman Papers, bound vol. 14, in the MHS.

1. TL married Elizabeth "Mimi" Russell in 1858. Her parents were George Robert Russell, a merchant and historian, and Sarah Parkman Shaw. Mimi's uncle, Gardner Howland Shaw (Harvard 1838) married TL's sister, Cora, in 1848. TL and Mimi's first child, Cora "Co-Co," was born in Florence, Italy, and named after TL's sister. The Somerset

Club at the corner of Somerset and Beacon streets was frequented by textile mill owners, cotton buyers, and merchants—the "Cotton Noblesse"—and had long been considered Boston's most prestigious club. Many of its members had close economic and political connections in the Southern states. Textile manufacturer and Somerset member Enoch Redington Mudge. Mudge's son, Lt. Col. Charles Redington Mudge (Harvard 1860), 2d Massachusetts Infantry, was mortally wounded at Gettysburg. Capt. Montgomery Ritchie (Harvard 1846), 1st Massachusetts Cavalry. Likely TL's Porcellian Club brother, Edward Dexter of Beverly (Harvard 1845). The exclusive Harvard Porcellian Club (the "Porc" or "PC"), founded in 1791, admitted the elite of East Coast society. TL served as grand marshal of the club (as had his father before him).

2. Mimi's uncle, Francis George Shaw of Staten Island, father of Col. Robert Gould Shaw. Lt. Col. Edward Needles Hallowell, 54th Massachusetts Infantry, was wounded during the assault on Ft. Wagner on July 18, 1863, where Col. Shaw was killed; Hallowell succeeded to command of the regiment. A lawyer with literary pretensions, Joseph Converse Heywood graduated from Harvard with TL in 1855; his dramatic poem was titled "Salome, the Daughter of Herodius."

3. Maj. Gen. Samuel Porter Heintzelman commanded the defenses of Washington. Capt. Charles Paine Horton (Harvard 1857), 2d Massachusetts Cavalry. Maj. Edward J. Mallet of New York, paymaster. Conrad not identified. Capt. Walter Curtis of Massachusetts, in charge of railroad transportation for the Quartermaster Department in Washington. Lt. Col. Charles Fessenden Morse (Lawrence Scientific 1858) of Roxbury. Capt. William A. Amory of West Roxbury, 16th Massachusetts Infantry. Silas Langley, a farmer on TL's Brookline estate. TL's groom, Albert H. Woods, sixteen-year-old son of housekeeper Sarah Holmes.

4. TL's PC brother, Stephen Henry Phillips (Harvard 1842), Massachusetts attorney general, 1858–61. Bostonian John Henry Devereux superintended the Orange & Alexandria Railroad (O.&A. RR), which ran at this time from Alexandria to the Rappahannock River Bridge, a distance of about 54 miles. The O.&A. formed the principal line of operations and supply for the AoP from Aug. 1863 until it was abandoned in May 1864.

5. On Aug. 27, 1862, during the Second Manassas campaign, Confederate major general Richard Ewell's division delayed the advance of Hooker's division at Kettle Run near Bristoe Station. Amory's regiment fought in the engagement. From Alexandria to Warrenton Junction (modern-day Calverton) by rail was forty-five miles. A branch line ran eight miles west to the town of Warrenton. "Warrington" reflected local pronunciation and was a common misspelling in reports of the period. TL later corrected himself.

6. As was true of most of his class, TL did not hesitate to express his sense of superiority over ethnic groups. He acknowledged that the "Paddies" would fight if well led but had little use for Germans in the ranks. Mimi's cousin, Col. Robert Gould Shaw, referred to his own 54th Massachusetts as a "good nigger concern." For historic context, TL's language throughout this volume has been retained.

7. Army HQ had been established near the hamlet of Germantown.

8. Lt. Frederick "Rosie" Rosencrantz, a Swedish army officer and veteran of AoP HQ, carried dispatches for McClellan, Burnside, and Hooker before joining Meade's staff.

9. Maj. Gen. Andrew Atkinson Humphreys (age 52, Philadelphia, USMA 1831), Meade's CoS from July 1863 until November 1864. Humphreys was a regular army engineer, who specialized in river hydraulics; his son, Lt. Henry Hollingsworth Humphreys, 112th Pennsylvania Infantry, served as his ADC. TL's PC brother, Maj. Simon Forrester Barstow of Boston (Harvard 1837), joined army staff under Gen. Hooker in January 1863. Col. Edward Russell Platt of Vermont, 2d U.S. Artillery, the army's judge advocate. As CoS, Humphreys stated that it was his duty "to form an opinion respecting everything of importance that takes place in the Army." Humphreys, *Biography*, 207. The modern equivalent of CoS is executive officer or XO.

10. Crawford's HQ were near Rappahannock Station (modern Remington) on the O.&A. RR. Brig. Gen. Samuel Wylie Crawford (age 33, Pennsylvania, Univ. of Penn. Medical School 1850) commanded the Pennsylvania Reserves, Meade's first divisional command. Gov. Andrew Curtin of Pennsylvania visited the army on Aug. 28 to present a sword to Meade in recognition of his victory at Gettysburg.

11. Regular army veteran Maj. Gen. George Sykes (age 40, Delaware, USMA 1842) commanded a division in Porter's Fifth Corps during the Peninsula campaign and was brevetted for his gallantry at Gaines Mill. Sykes succeeded to Fifth Corps leadership when Meade was appointed commanding general of the AoP. Lt. Col. Frederick Thomas Locke of New York, adjutant, Fifth Corps. An adjutant, formally an assistant adjutant general or AAG, was a unit's chief administrative officer in charge of orders, records, and personnel.

12. Brig. Gen. John Newton (age 41, Virginia, USMA 1842) served in the corps of engineers before the war and taught engineering at the USMA. He commanded a division in Sixth Corps during the Fredericksburg and Chancellorsville campaigns. Meade personally selected him to command First Corps after the death of Reynolds at Gettysburg, making an enemy of Maj. Gen. Abner Doubleday, who was senior division commander. Ohio-born physician Maj. Benjamin Chambers Ludlow, 4th Missouri Cavalry, ADC and acting inspector of artillery. On Sept. 1, Kilpatrick's division of cavalry rode to Port Conway, a landing on the Lower Rappahannock River opposite Port Royal, where the captured gunboats *Satellite* and *Reliance* were docked. After a brief skirmish on the north bank, Kilpatrick's artillery fired across the river to sink the gunboats. *OR*, vol. 29, 1:9. Richmond newspapers reported the gunboats as "lightly damaged."

13. Maj. Gen. Oliver Otis Howard (age 32, Maine, USMA 1854) taught mathematics at the USMA. He led Eleventh Corps at Chancellorsville, where it was routed on May 2, 1863; the corps was outflanked and collapsed again at Gettysburg on July 1. Howard's failings were attributed to the many Germans he commanded. Catlett's Station on the O.&A. RR, two miles north of Warrenton Junction.

14. TL's cryptic abbreviations are spelled out in the text for clarity. Chief of artillery Brig. Gen. Henry Jackson Hunt (age 43, Michigan, USMA 1839); provost marshal Brig. Gen. Marsena Patrick (age 52, New York, USMA 1835); Maj. James Cornell Biddle of

Philadelphia, 23d Pennsylvania Infantry, ADC; Capt. Henry Page of Massachusetts, asst. QM; Capt. Charles E. Pease of New York; Capt. Addison Gordon Mason, 5th Pennsylvania Reserves; Captains James H. Starr (Harvard 1857), Charles E. Cadwalader, and George Meade of Philadelphia, all detailed from the 6th Pennsylvania Cavalry; Lt. John Rufus Edie of Pennsylvania; Lt. Charles W. Woolsey, 164th New York Infantry (Seth Williams's ADC). Lt. Col. William G. Le Duc, chief QM, Eleventh Corps. Gen. Meade's oldest son, Capt. George Meade, age 20, completed two years at West Point before entering the service in 1862. Biddle and Cadwalader were from "old stock" Philadelphia. Capt. Cadwalader's father, John, was a U.S. District Court judge, his uncle George a brigadier in the Mexican War, his grandfather a brigadier in the War of 1812, and his great-grandfather a staff officer during the Revolution. Cadwalader was competent and cool under fire. Biddle, trained as a civil engineer, also came from a distinguished military family but did not always meet expectations. He could be something of a buffoon and was the target of much good-natured camp humor.

15. Brig. Gen. Gouverneur Kemble Warren (age 33, New York, USMA 1850) taught engineering and mathematics at West Point; he led a brigade of Fifth Corps and was wounded on the Peninsula before joining AoP staff as chief of engineers. In this role, he diverted troops to defend Little Round Top at Gettysburg. Warren commanded Second Corps for a time after Hancock's wounding at that battle. Warren was an energetic officer who believed he possessed solutions for most military problems and did not hesitate to let his superiors know it. In his early months as army commander, Meade relied heavily upon Warren, but the relationship grew increasingly antagonistic.

16. Brig. Gen. Seth Williams (age 41, Connecticut, USMA 1842) was a mainstay of the army's staff, serving as AAG successively for McClellan, Burnside, Hooker, and Meade. Before the war, Williams was Robert E. Lee's adjutant at West Point. Maj. Gen. Quincy Adams Gillmore commanded Union forces besieging Charleston. Gillmore's engineers had mounted a massive 300-pound Parrott rifle to fire upon Ft. Sumter. The "300-pounder" with a ten-inch bore could throw a projectile weighing 250 pounds nearly five miles.

17. Maj. Gen. William Henry French (age 48, Maryland, USMA 1837) succeeded to command of Third Corps after Maj. Gen. Sickles was wounded at Gettysburg. French's performance as a corps commander had been lackluster, and Humphreys and Warren urged Meade to replace him.

18. TL referred to the colors of divisional HQ flags and corps badges worn by the troops. Colors were assigned to the first three divisions as red, white, and blue in order; a fourth division would be green. Corps badges were: First Corps, orb; Second Corps, trefoil; Third Corps, diamond; Fifth Corps, Maltese cross; Sixth Corps, Greek cross; Eleventh Corps, crescent; Twelfth Corps, star; and Cavalry Corps, crossed swords. TL used corps badges in his sketch maps of the army and depicted the locations of the cavalry with a "c."

19. The artillery batteries of the AoP used smoothbore bronze twelve-pound Napoleon "howitzers" and rifled guns—iron three-inch Ordnance and ten-pound Parrotts—in about equal numbers. The Napoleon was designed primarily for close-range, antipersonnel use. Rifled guns were more accurate at longer ranges.

20. French's division commanders: Philadelphia lawyer Maj. Gen. David Bell Birney (age 38); Brig. Gen. Washington Lafayette Elliott (age 38, Pennsylvania, attended USMA); and Brig. Gen. Henry Prince (age 52, Maine, USMA 1835). Elliott and Prince were regular army officers who served in Mexico. Prince was captured at Cedar Mountain in Aug. 1862, exchanged, and reassigned to AoP in autumn 1863. Birney lacked a West Point education but had proven himself in battle in the AoP's major campaigns. He was a favorite of the Radical Republicans. Before the war, Birney's father, outspoken abolitionist James Gillespie Birney, was chased from Kentucky for his views and published an antislavery newspaper in Cincinnati.

21. Capt. Jacob Henry Sleeper, 10th Massachusetts Battery, of Boston; his father was a founder of Boston University. Lt. Col. Waldo Merriam, 16th Massachusetts Infantry, of a Boston merchant family. After Gettysburg, some units from Third Corps were diverted to New York City to quell violent anticonscription riots.

22. Lt. Albert Ordway, 24th Massachusetts Infantry, was detached for service as Prince's ordnance officer; he made captain in June 1864. Ordway studied natural science at Harvard under Prof. Jean Louis Rodolphe Agassiz and in 1860 graduated from the Lawrence Scientific School. After the war, Col. Ordway settled in Richmond and served as provost marshal during Reconstruction. In a postwar notation, TL wrote that Ordway married "a Secesh girl, big enough to eat him." TL's mare "Culpeper" was the gift of his sister and mother-in-law, Mrs. Russell. Lt. Col. John B. Howard of New York, chief QM, Third Corps.

23. TL first encountered regular army officer William Montrose Graham on the Florida coast in 1856 while collecting specimens for the Museum of Comparative Zoology. Graham commanded Second Brigade, Horse Artillery, Cavalry Corps, consisting of one volunteer and seven regular batteries. Graham's father, Col. James Duncan Graham, was overseeing work on facilities in Boston Harbor; his mother was Charlotte Meade, sister of Gen. Meade.

24. Samuel Cabot Jr., a partner in Perkins & Company, a China trading firm, and one of the wealthiest men in Boston, died at age 78. Cabot and his wife, Eliza, had an estate near TL in Brookline between Clyde and Heath streets. TL visited Mrs. Cabot on a number of occasions when home on leave. Capt. Edward William Hooper (Harvard 1859), ADC to Gen. Rufus Saxton in the Beaufort Military District, South Carolina. Dr. John Jeffries Jr., cofounder of the Massachusetts Eye and Ear Infirmary; his sons John and Edward Payson Jeffries (Harvard 1856, PC).

25. Provost marshal Marsena Patrick had access to stockade labor. Patrick was an effective, opinionated, and often downright grumpy officer as revealed in his published diary, *Inside Lincoln's Army*, ed. by David S. Sparks. Maj. James Chatham Duane (age 40, New York, USMA 1848) was appointed chief engineer of the AoP by McClellan. Duane took a "shine" to TL and often sought his companionship. Lt. Col. Charles Kingsbury Jr., of New York, AAG, First Corps. Capt. John Redman Coxe of Pennsylvania, asst. CS, AoP.

26. Gen. Lee's HQ were on the railroad at Orange Court House, about seven miles south of the Rapidan River.

27. Meade served on Zachary Taylor's staff in the Mexican War. Some detractors attributed Hooker's dazed state at Chancellorsville to alcohol. In this case, there seems

ample evidence that he was dazed by an exploding shell. TL, however, did encounter a rather "shaky" Hooker at the Astor Hotel on Sept. 27, 1864. See his entry for that date.

28. Henry Timmins, related to TL by marriage, died Sept. 6 in Newport, Rhode Island. Louisa Powers died in childbirth. Lt. James Amory Perkins (Harvard 1857), 24th Massachusetts Infantry. *Tandem triumphans,* "victory at last!" Ft. Wagner and Ft. Gregg, Confederate forts defending the approaches to Charleston, had fallen. Former AoP commander Maj. Gen. Ambrose E. Burnside occupied Knoxville with the reconstituted Army of the Ohio on Sept. 3. In Aug. and Sept., Maj. Gen. William Stark Rosecrans led the Army of the Cumberland into northern Georgia and maneuvered Confederate general Braxton Bragg out of Chattanooga with little fighting. As TL wrote this, Rosecrans's army was overextended.

29. "Shindy," a brawl.

30. Maj. Gen. Alfred Pleasonton (age 39, Washington, D.C., USMA 1844) commanded Cavalry Corps, AoP, from June 1863 until Mar. 1864. His hard-fought battle against Stuart's troopers at Brandy Station, June 9, 1863, was said to have made the Union cavalry. Capt. Robert Walsh Mitchell, Co. B, 6th Pennsylvania Cavalry, earned the sobriquet "Whiskey Mitch" at HQ. William Scott Worth, 8th U.S. Infantry, son of Mexican War general William Jenkins Worth. Others identified.

31. Fauquier White Sulphur Springs, ten miles upriver from Rappahannock Station; the Old Carolina Road crossed at Kelly's Ford, four miles downriver from the railroad bridge.

32. Brig. Gen. John Buford (age 37, Illinois, USMA 1848), the army's most efficient cavalry officer, excelled during the Gettysburg campaign and was marked for promotion. Buford commanded First Division, Cavalry Corps; his brigade commanders: Col. George H. Chapman, First Brigade; and Col. Thomas C. Devin, Second Brigade.

33. Roads from Beverly and Kelly's Ford converged on the railroad at Brandy Station about midway from the river to Culpeper Court House.

34. Brig. Gen. George Armstrong Custer (age 23, Michigan, USMA 1857) had abundant raw courage and a flair for publicity that brought him promotion. Brig. Gen. Hugh Judson Kilpatrick (age 27, New Jersey, USMA 1861) commanded the cavalry's Third Division. Brig. Gen. David McMurtrie Gregg (age 30, Pennsylvania, USMA 1855) commanded Second Division, Cavalry Corps.

35. Lt. Col. Charles Ross Smith, CoS, Cavalry Corps; surgeon George L. Pancoast; ADCs Lt. George W. Yates, 4th Michigan Infantry, and Lt. Benjamin T. Hutchins, 6th U.S. Cavalry. Signal officers: Lt. Aaron B. Jerome, 1st New Jersey Infantry; Capt. Davis E. Castle, 19th Indiana Infantry.

36. Pony Mountain, a steep round hill two miles southeast of Culpeper.

37. As a green campaigner, TL was justifiably proud that he could produce food, tea, and a candle out of his saddlebag, but one wonders how many such "souvenirs" the farmer had sold to other army officers.

38. Officers of the 2d Massachusetts Infantry killed or mortally wounded at the battle of Cedar Mountain, fought Aug. 9, 1862: Maj. James Savage Jr. (Harvard 1854), Capt. Richard Cary, Capt. Richard Chapman Goodwin (Harvard 1854), Capt. Edward

Gardiner Abbott (Harvard 1860), and Lt. Stephen George Perkins (Harvard 1856). Savage was a prisoner of war for five months before succumbing to his wounds. All were upper-class Bostonians and TL's acquaintances. Mimi's brother, Henry Sturgis Russell (Harvard 1860, PC), called "Harry" or "Hal," was captured at Cedar Mountain and later exchanged.

39. Col. Horace Binny Sargent (Harvard 1843) and Capt. Charles Francis "Charlie" Adams Jr. (Harvard 1856), 1st Massachusetts Cavalry. Adams was son of a diplomat and grandson of Pres. John Quincy Adams.

40. Brig. Gen. Alexander S. Webb (age 28, New York, USMA 1855), son of a wealthy New York newspaper publisher. Webb was CoS, Fifth Corps, during the Peninsula campaign and a brigade commander at Gettysburg. The competent Webb would replace Humphreys as Meade's CoS in Jan. 1865.

41. Two divisions of Lt. Gen. James Longstreet's Corps were detached from the ANV on Sept. 9 and sent by rail to Georgia where they would fight at Chickamauga, Sept. 19–20, 1863. "Stewart" was Confederate major general J. E. B. Stuart.

42. William Douglas Wallach, newspaperman and publisher of the Washington *Evening Star* from 1855 to 1867. Meade and his personal staff posed for photographer Timothy O'Sullivan on the steps of the Wallach house (house no longer extant). Two catalogued views are in the LC: sitting Meade—TL wears an officer's hat and stands on the far right (LC-B8184-7098); standing Meade—TL has donned a forage cap and stands second from the right (USZ62-133286). Internal photographic evidence suggests that the less successful and previously unpublished sitting Meade view was taken first. Also pictured with the general: Humphreys, Ludlow, Biddle, Cadwallader, Capt. Meade, Bates, Bache, Mitchell, and Rosenkrantz.

43. Honorable John Minor Botts, age 61, lawyer and three-term U.S. representative from Virginia. Botts, an outspoken critic of the Confederate government, had been arrested under martial law in 1862 but was eventually released on his parole. Botts was a bipartisan haranguer. On Sept. 30, he directed a letter to Pres. Lincoln complaining that the "despotic hand" of Secretary of War Stanton had "rudely refused permission" for food and clothing to be forwarded to him from Washington. He added, "Through the courtesy of Gen. Meade I have obtained supplies of provisions for present use." John M. Botts to Abraham Lincoln, Sept. 30, 1863, Lincoln Papers, ser. 1, General Correspondence, LC. Capt. Boleslawski of the Military Geographical Institution of Vienna. Stevens not identified.

44. Maj. Gen. Henry Wager Halleck (age 48, New York, USMA 1839) coordinated three armies in a successful campaign to capture Corinth, Mississippi, in May 1862. Lincoln called him to Washington to serve as general-in-chief of all Federal armies, displacing McClellan in the position. Based on his treatise *Elements of the Art and Science of War* (1846) and his translations of the writings of Jomini, "Old Brains" had a reputation as a theoretician. Halleck's policy that "Lee's army, not Richmond, was the object of the campaign" is often thought to have originated with Ulysses S. Grant. Meade and Halleck's relationship was combative at best. The Aulic Council managed the war department of the Austrian Empire. The councilors were noted for their

knowledge of military science, but in the war against Napoleon often hamstrung their field armies by issuing outdated orders from Vienna. *Plein pouvoir,* "full authority."

45. Pres. Lincoln, Halleck, and Secretary of War Edwin Stanton were then debating whether to detach troops from the AoP to reinforce Rosecrans at Chattanooga. Lincoln's reasoning was sound. The Eleventh and Twelfth Corps were ordered to Tennessee on Sept. 24 in the war's largest and most efficient movement of troops by rail.

46. Brig. Gen. Horatio Gouverneur Wright (age 43, Connecticut, USMA 1837), regular army engineer, commanded First Division, Sixth Corps.

47. Prof. Henry Lawrence Eustis (age 44, Massachusetts, Harvard 1838, USMA 1842) taught engineering at West Point and at Harvard. Maj. Henry Lee Higginson (attended Harvard 1851), 1st Massachusetts Cavalry, was shot and saber-slashed during a melee near Aldie, Virginia, in June 1863, as described in Perry, *Life and Letters,* 196–98. Higginson was engaged to Ida Agassiz, daughter of Prof. Louis Agassiz. Ida's brother was Alexander Emmanuel Rudolphus "Alex" Agassiz (Lawrence Scientific 1858, PC), director of and lecturer at the Museum of Comparative Zoology. Alex married Mimi's sister Annie. Mimi's sister, Emily "Em." Col. Francis Winthrop "Frank" Palfrey (Harvard 1851, Harvard Law 1853), 20th Massachusetts Infantry, wounded and captured at Antietam, paroled and discharged for disability in April 1863. Lt. Edward Bromfield Mason (Harvard 1858), 2d Massachusetts Cavalry, died of injuries from a riding accident at the Readville Camp.

48. Chickamauga ranked among the worst defeats of Federal arms, but it was a costly Confederate victory. Bragg's Army of Tennessee lost fully 25 percent of its strength. Bragg pursued Maj. Gen. William Rosecrans's Army of the Cumberland to Chattanooga and occupied Missionary Ridge and Lookout Mountain overlooking the town, thereby closing off the main routes of supply. As events would prove, the Confederates had not "carried their point."

49. Sir Henry Holland (1788–1873), physician to Queen Elizabeth and six prime ministers. Maj. Gen. Henry Warner Slocum (age 36, New York, USMA 1852), lawyer and former state legislator, commanded Twelfth Corps after Antietam and performed well at Chancellorsville and Gettysburg. Transferred west, Slocum would command Twentieth Corps during the Atlanta campaign. Two of Slocum's brigadiers: Alpheus S. Williams (age 53, Connecticut, Yale 1831), lawyer and engineer officer; and Joseph F. Knipe (age 40, Philadelphia). Williams had commanded a division in Banks's corps at Cedar Mountain, where so many of TL's friends were killed.

50. "From the Rapidan we learn that all is quiet. Meade is making 'I would' wait upon 'I dare not.'" Richmond *Sentinel,* Sept. 22, 1863. It is noteworthy that Meade was reading a newspaper printed in Richmond forty-eight hours earlier.

51. Maj. Sidney Coolidge, 16th U.S. Infantry, director of the Harvard Astronomical Observatory and a surveyor, astronomer, and ethnographer of international repute.

52. G. K. Warren waxed impatient over the political wrangling. Although TL was tactful, in this context Warren's statement appears critical of Meade's "I dare not."

53. Slocum's brigadiers: Williams, Knipe, George Sears Greene (age 62, Rhode Island, USMA 1823); and Thomas Howard Ruger (age 30, Wisconsin, USMA 1854). Greene, the grandson of Revolutionary War general Nathanael Greene, was a prominent civil engineer before the war.

54. Fifth Corps divisional commanders: Romeyn B. Ayres (age 37, New York, USMA 1847); Charles Griffin (age 37, Ohio, USMA 1847); and Crawford. These three capable officers would hold divisional command through the end of the war.

55. French's ADCs: Capt. Harvey Y. Russell, 10th New York Infantry, and Capt. William Henry French Jr., General French's son. Capt. Emeric Szabad was a professional soldier who fought in Hungary's 1848–49 War of Liberation, served on the staff of "Pathfinder" Frémont in 1862 and found a place on Warren's staff in 1863. Hill not identified.

56. Brig. Gen. Henry Washington Benham (age 50, Connecticut, USMA 1837) commanded the engineer brigade of the AoP. Col. Joseph "Joe" Hayes, 18th Massachusetts Infantry, and Capt. Channing Clapp both graduated from Harvard with TL in 1855. Clapp was Benham's adjutant.

57. Maj. Gen. George Henry Thomas (age 47, Virginia, USMA 1840) won the nom de guerre "Rock of Chickamauga" for his Fourteenth Corps' tenacious stand on Snodgrass Hill. Maj. Gen. Alexander McCook's Twentieth Corps and Maj. Gen. Thomas Leonidas Crittenden's Twenty-first Corps had been driven from the field at Chickamauga. The two corps were consolidated on Sept. 28 to form a new Fourth Corps, leaving McCook and Crittenden without command. Crittenden reappeared in Virginia, May 1864, to lead First Division, Ninth Corps for a brief time.

58. In 1862, Napoleon III of France with the backing of Mexican conservatives overthrew the republican government of Presidente Benito Juarez. In 1864, Napoleon III installed Archduke Maximilian as emperor of Mexico. The Degollado family fell into disfavor during the reign of Santa Ana, and Mariano Degollado had been living in exile in the United States; he married Ortilia Jordan, a Virginian, and in 1865 Maximilian appointed him chamberlain in his court. Gen. Jose Cortez and Senor Francisco deP. Suarez were members of the conservative faction that supported Maximilian.

59. Lt. Col. Thomas Sherwin (Harvard 1860), 22d Massachusetts Infantry, classmate of Mimi's brother, Henry Sturgis Russell.

60. Likely Dr. John Foster of Hermitage Plantation, Natchez; his son, John Sanderson Foster of the Jeff Davis Legion. LSU Special Collections, Mss. 2184.

61. William Sturgis Hooper (Harvard 1852), volunteer ADC on the staff of Maj. Gen. Nathaniel Banks, died Sept. 23 in Boston. His beautiful but "icy" widow visited the camps of the AoP in 1865 and caused a stir among the younger officers.

62. Dr. Jonathan A. Letterman (age 39, Pennsylvania, Jefferson Medical College), regular army surgeon, appointed medical director of the AoP by McClellan. Letterman instituted reforms of diet and sanitation for the troops and introduced the first modern system to treat battlefield casualties. See TL's entry for May 19, 1864, where he described the Letterman system. Mitchell's Station on the O.&A. RR south of Culpeper near the battlefield of Cedar Mountain.

63. Regular army officer Col. Nelson Henry Davis, asst. IG for McClellan and Hooker, was transferred to the Department of New Mexico.

64. Brig. Gen. Robert Ogden Tyler (age 31, Connecticut, USMA 1853) commanded the Artillery Reserve. Other officers identified. The citizens of Warren's hometown, Cold Spring, New York, presented him an engraved sword in a rosewood case. TL wrote to Mimi that Warren seemed so nervous that he expected Dr. Young, the presenter,

to say, "Warren, will you have this sword to be your lawful, wedded wife?" *Meade's Headquarters*, 27.

65. Humphreys's ADCs, Capt. Carswell McClellan of Maryland and Adolphus F. Cavada of Philadelphia. John Minor Botts resided at "Auburn" (which today overlooks Rte. 29 about two miles west of Brandy Station). Botts's four unmarried daughters attracted steady visitation by young Federal officers.

66. TL's Singletree estate is today within a residential Brookline neighborhood, bounded by Boylston, Heath, and Pound streets. The Christian Science Benevolent Association owns the site of the house, which TL's friend referred to facetiously as "Brookline Castle" (no longer extant). At the time of the war, TL's uncle, George Williams Lyman, a Boston merchant and a partner in the Waltham and Lowell textile mills, occupied the Lyman family estate. The Vale, in Waltham, today is a house museum. Gillie "the talking devil" unfortunately remains unidentified.

67. Humphreys commanded Second Division, Third Corps, at Gettysburg. Several of his supporting batteries were overrun by Longstreet's attack on July 2. Maj. Gen. David Bell Birney, who assumed command from the wounded Sickles, implied that Humphreys had abandoned his guns. Hancock's Second Corps recaptured one battery. Little of this behind-the-scenes rancor made it into the pages of the OR.

68. William Riddle of Philadelphia, 5th Pennsylvania Reserves, was Meade's ADC along with Addison Mason when Meade was a division commander. Riddle moved to John F. Reynolds's First Corps staff and was at that general's side when a sharpshooter felled him at Gettysburg.

69. Famed orator, former U.S. congressman, four-term governor of Massachusetts, U.S. senator, and Harvard president, the Honorable Edward Everett spoke for two hours at Gettysburg on Nov. 19, 1863, elaborating on TL's résumé of the battle. Pres. Lincoln followed with a brief, but more memorable address. Everett credited TL and Henry Halleck in the published version of his Gettysburg oration. Everett, *Speeches and Orations*, 4:659.

70. TL's casualty figures are acceptable for the AoP but much too high for the ANV. He appears to have double counted Confederate wounded and captured wounded and added extra stragglers for good measure. Estimates of casualties in Lee's army range from 20,500 to about 28,000. The Federal army captured 12,227 wounded and unwounded soldiers.

71. Official returns for the AoP "equipped for duty," including officers, dated Oct. 10, 1863: 59,018 infantry, 12,126 cavalry, and 5,989 artillerymen, for a total of 77,133. *OR*, vol. 29, 1:226. TL likely deducted "extra duty men," those detailed for noncombat roles, which in the AoP could run as high as 20 percent.

72. Maj. Gen. John Sedgwick (age 50, Connecticut, USMA 1837), commander of Sixth Corps, was a veteran of the Seminole and Mexican wars and a stalwart of the AoP. He commanded a division in Second Corps during the Seven Days' Battles and at Antietam, where he was severely wounded. During the Chancellorsville campaign, he led Sixth Corps to capture Marye's Heights while Hooker crossed the Rappahannock upstream with the bulk of the army. The president considered Sedgwick, who outranked

Meade, as a possible replacement for Hooker. Sedgwick declined and suggested Meade for the command. Lt. Col. Jacob Ford Kent, IG, Sixth Corps. Brig. Gen. Albion Parris Howe (age 45, Maine, USMA 1841), commanded Second Division, Sixth Corps.

73. The Anderson house stood north of the O.&A. RR halfway between Rappahannock and Bealeton stations.

74. CoS Humphreys wrote of Lee's movement: "Lee's army was pouring over the Rappahannock, a few miles above us, while we had three corps halfway to Culpepper Court House. No time was to be lost; our army was at once set in motion, and it was too late for us to occupy, as we had intended, Warrenton, or any other points between this and there; Lee was within a hair's breath of getting between us and Washington. We beat him, however, in the game." Humphreys, *Biography*, 210. According to Henry, his father's diligent staff work was responsible for the skillful withdrawal from the Rappahannock and "saved" the army, in spite of its commanding general. Humphreys, *Critical Examination*, 7–8. For Marsena Patrick, the situation seemed all too familiar. He fretted that the army was due for its "annual Bull Run flogging." Sparks, *Inside Lincoln's Army*, 295.

75. Brig. Gen. Rufus Ingalls (age 45, Maine, USMA 1843), the AoP's chief QM served on McClellan's, Burnside's, Hooker's, and Meade's staffs. If there is an unsung hero of the AoP, it is Ingalls; by 1863, he was a master of the science and art of logistics.

76. Army HQ did not sanction random violence against the local populace and their property. Many of the rank and file, however, appeared to have different ideas and likely welcomed Gen. Grant and his "western" concepts of justice when he came east in Mar. 1864.

77. Auburn Mills on Cedar Run halfway between Warrenton and Catlett's Station. Confederate major general J. E. B. Stuart and two brigades of cavalry were cut off by the rapid approach of Second Corps on the road behind them and bedded down in the woods within hearing of surrounding Federal camps. Stuart extricated his troopers after a brief firefight at dawn.

78. Col. James E. Mallon, 42d New York Infantry, commanding Third Brigade, Second Division, Second Corps. Union losses at Bristoe Station totaled 546. Confederate losses in the brief but bitter fight were reported as 1,378. *Battles and Leaders*, vol. 4, 84n.

79. Officers of the 2d Massachusetts Cavalry: Col. Charles Russell Lowell (Harvard 1854); Maj. Caspar Crowninshield (Harvard 1860, PC); and Capt. William Hathaway Forbes (Harvard 1861, PC). Capt. Henry Winsor Jr. (Harvard 1860), 6th Pennsylvania Cavalry. Lowell was the grandson of the "Old Judge," John Lowell of Roxbury, and nephew of textile magnate Francis Cabot Lowell. Forbes was son of industrial titan John Murray Forbes.

80. Starr's HQ detachment of the 6th Pennsylvania Cavalry was replaced by a battalion of the 5th U.S. Cavalry led by Capt. Julius W. Mason. The Reserve Brigade, commanded by Col. Alfred Gibbs, included the First, Second, and Fifth regiments of U.S. Cavalry. Halleck to Meade: "Is [Lee] not trying to bully you, while the mass of the rebel armies are concentrating against Rosecrans? I cannot see it in any other light. Instead of retreating, I think you ought to give him battle. From all the information I can get, his force is very much inferior to yours." *OR*, vol. 29, 2:328.

81. Maj. Gen. Daniel E. Sickles (age 44, New York), Tammany Hall lawyer, former U.S. congressman, and War Democratic, rose to command Third Corps through his political influence and a symbiosis with Joseph Hooker. Sickles disregarded Meade's orders in the placement of his corps at Gettysburg on July 2 and lost his leg in the battle. TL thought the meeting cordial, but Sickles departed with an understanding that Meade was not eager to return him to command. The combative Sickles took his case to the Joint Committee on the Conduct of the War and the *New York Herald*. Sears, *Controversies and Commanders*, 197–224.

82. Meade's comment to TL was very personal and reveals the nature of their relationship. This was not the type of sentiment that would inspire confidence if broadcast among the staff at large.

83. Lincoln to Halleck, forwarded to Meade: "If General Meade can now attack him on a field no more than equal for us, and will do so with all the skill and courage which he, his officers, and men possess, the honor will be his if he succeeds, and the blame may be mine if he fails." *OR*, vol. 29, 2:332. Brig. Gen. Wesley Merritt (age 29, Illinois, USMA 1860), one of the cavalry's rising officers.

84. Confederate major general Robert E. Rodes. Brig. Gen. John R. Cooke's North Carolina brigade of Heth's Division bore the brunt of casualties at Bristoe. Gen. Lee chastised Hill for not conducting a proper reconnaissance but did not arrest him. Cooke of Virginia attended Harvard. On Oct. 17, Pres. Lincoln issued a call for volunteers to fill vacancies in existing regiments with the implied threat that those failing to volunteer would likely face conscription.

85. Meade advanced the army in two wings: Second and Third Corps marched along the O.&A. RR and First and Sixth on the Warrenton Turnpike with Fifth Corps in reserve. The site of Groveton is within the Manassas National Battlefield Park. At the beginning of the war, Warrenton Turnpike was one of the finest macadamized highways in Virginia with a crushed stone surface and cut-stone culverts and bridges.

86. The two battles of Bull Run or Manassas were fought west of Bull Run along the Warrenton Turnpike; a large portion of both battlefields is preserved within the national park. Lt. Carl L. Berlin, 8th New York Cavalry.

87. Kilpatrick's division was attacked front and flank by two divisions of Confederate cavalry and pursued for five miles along the Warrenton Turnpike. Some regiments rallied at Buckland Mills where the pike crossed Broad Run. Confederates termed the affair the "Buckland Races." Brig. Gen. Henry Eugene Davies (age 27, New York City, attended Harvard, Columbia 1857).

88. Halleck's communication and Meade's response in *OR*, vol. 29, 2:346. Bunsby, a character from Charles Dickens's *Dombey & Son* (1847–48), chap. 39: "Bunsby ... with his stolid mahogany visage, as usual, appearing to have no consciousness of anything before it, but to be attentively observing something that was taking place in quite another part of the world." This anecdote quoted in *Meade's Headquarters*, 35–36.

89. Georgetown was two miles west of Thoroughfare Gap, Greenwich halfway to Warrenton from Bristoe, and Auburn four miles southwest of Greenwich. Thoroughfare Gap was the "back door" to Manassas, through which a Confederate column could turn Meade's flank.

90. Ζεύς Βροντίζων, "Zeus Thunderer." Capt. Francis Markoe Bache, 16th U.S. Infantry, joined HQ only a few days before TL arrived; his father, Hartman Bache, married Gen. Meade's older sister Maria del Carmen Meade in 1829. On Oct. 24, Meade asked for War Department confirmation of Lyman as volunteer ADC. Lyman's appointment was approved by order of the Secretary of War Oct. 31, logged Nov. 1, and received AoP Nov. 4. NARA, RG94 box 39, War Dept. Orders and Endorsements, 12 (Ms Pub, roll 6, item 4230).

91. Stanton Blake (Harvard 1857), investment banker with a New York firm. Likely surgeon Edward Swift Dunster (Harvard 1856), inspector of hospitals in Washington.

92. The Invalid Corps, subsequently renamed the Veteran Reserve Corps, was organized under the War Department in 1863 to enable officers and soldiers who had been partially disabled to finish out their terms of enlistment. The much-maligned powder blue uniform was scrapped for conventional military dress. For a concise history of the Invalid Corps, see *OR*, ser. 3, vol. 5:543–68.

93. Areopagus, the ruling council of elders of ancient Athens. In this case, TL likely referred to Lincoln, Stanton, and Halleck. Meade, who no longer anticipated a threat via Thoroughfare Gap, transferred First Corps from the far right to the far left of the army. William F. Sturgis of the trading firm Bryant & Sturgis died Oct. 21 at the age of 81. At one time, the Boston firm handled much of the trade with the Pacific Northwest and China.

94. Unfortunates captured by partisans were described as "gobbled" or "gobbled up." Capt. Emeric Szabad was exchanged in Mar. 1864; his journal of captivity was published in 1999 as *The Libby Prison Diary of Colonel Emeric Szabad*, edited by Stephen Beszedits. Hooker appointed Col. Edmund Schriver IG of the AoP in Mar. 1863.

95. Prof. Agassiz and his students were compiling what was intended to be a ten-volume *Contributions to the Natural History of the United States of America*. Only five volumes were published. Volume 5, illustrating starfish embryology, finally appeared in 1877. Prof. Henry James Clark, noted scientific artist and microscopist, complained that Prof. Agassiz did not give him proper credit for his work and eventually resigned from the project.

96. Lt. Nathan "Nate" Appleton Jr. (Harvard 1863, PC) of Cambridge, 5th Battery Massachusetts Light Artillery, son of wealthy textile manufacturer Nathan Appleton, co-developer of the Waltham and Lowell mills.

97. Three-mile Station on the Warrenton Branch RR (modern-day Casanova). Col. Murray's house stood on the south bank of Turkey Run on the road from the station to Auburn (modern Rogues Road); its absentee owner was Lt. Col. Edward Murray, who was serving as Gen. Robert E. Lee's IG.

98. During this period, Meade told TL, "I do wish the Administration would get mad with me, and relieve me; I am sure I keep telling them, if they don't feel satisfied with me, to relieve me; then I could go home and see my family in Philadelphia." *Meade's Headquarters*, 38–39.

99. Col. Charles Russell Lowell commanded an independent cavalry brigade that included the 2d Massachusetts Cavalry. Lowell married Josephine "Effie" Shaw, sister of Robert Gould Shaw, and brought her to live at his HQ in Vienna, Virginia. Lowell

became the nemesis of John Singleton Mosby and his partisan rangers. Lt. Theodore M. Sage, brigade QM. "As he was riding through a wooded road, in the discharge of the duties of his office . . . the party were fired upon by cowardly murderers concealed in a thicket by the roadside, one of the shots striking Lt. Sage in the lower part of the back and proving almost immediately fatal." Gracey, *Annals of the Sixth Pennsylvania Cavalry*, 202. Lt. Lewis Stackpole Dabney (Harvard 1861), 2d Massachusetts Cavalry. Edward Grew (Harvard 1863). "R. M." was Capt. Randolph Marshall Clark (Harvard 1855), 1st Massachusetts Cavalry, discharged Aug. 1863. Harrison and Smith not identified.

100. Sedgwick, commanding the right wing, was to cross the Rappahannock River at the O.&A. RR bridge. French, commanding the left, was to force a passage downstream at Kelly's Ford.

101. Atkinson was secretary to the royal governor of Prince Edward Island. Victor Yorke, a lieutenant in the Royal Artillery. TL and family returned from their European tour aboard the steamship *Africa* in May 1863.

102. Two brigades of Brig. Gen. David Russell's First Division, Sixth Corps, led by colonels Peter Ellmaker and Emory Upton, overran the entrenched Confederate bridgehead established on the north bank of the river. In the stealthy twilight assault, Sixth Corps suffered fewer than 350 casualties but netted more than 1,650 prisoners from Jubal Early's division, Ewell's Second Corps. *OR*, vol. 29, 1:619.

103. Lt. Henry Howard Sturgis, 20th Massachusetts Infantry, discharged July 1862. In an inventory of family artwork compiled sometime after the war, there is noted: "Alibaster Urn. Dug up outside Rome by T.L. 3rd in a clandestine manner."

104. Welford's Ford was on the Hazel River or Gourdvine Fork, a tributary of the Rappahannock. The Welford house, "Farley," today is a private residence.

105. Lt. Oscar Hagen, asst. QM. British military observers: Lt. Col. William Earle; W. Ulrick O'Conner, Lord Castlecuffe; Capt. Sussex Vane Stephenson; and Capt. Cecil Lennox Peel, son of Sir Robert Peel.

106. As ranking corps commander, Sedgwick directed the army in Meade's absence.

107. One of those acoustic shadows often reported during the Civil War. Stevensburg is five miles closer to Raccoon Ford than Brandy Station.

108. Joseph Bradford Carr (age 35, New York), a tobacco merchant, replaced Elliott in command of Third Division, Third Corps. Although Carr had distinguished himself at Gettysburg, the Senate would not confirm his appointment as brigadier.

109. Capt. James Madison Robertson, a regular army officer of the 2d U.S. Artillery, commanded seven batteries organized as First Brigade, Horse Artillery, Cavalry Corps. Lt. Gustav von Blucher, 29th Battery New York Light Artillery, served as Brig. Gen. Robert Tyler's ADC. Tyler commanded the Artillery Reserve. Capt. Henry R. Dalton.

110. Sixth Corps officers: Wright, First Division, and Howe, Second Division, identified; one of Howe's brigadiers, Thomas Hewson Neill (age 37, Philadelphia, USMA 1847). Brig. Gen. Henry Dwight Terry (age 51, Connecticut) commanded Third Division; his brigadiers were Alexander Shaler (age 36, Connecticut), Prof. Henry Lawrence Eustis, and Frank Wheaton (age 30, Rhode Island).

111. Likely William Page of Boston (Harvard Divinity School 1850), active in the Sanitary Commission, with charge of a military hospital in Washington, D.C.

112. On Oct. 17, 1863, Maj. Gen. Ulysses S. Grant was elevated to command of the Military Division of the Mississippi, which unified the Departments of the Ohio, the Cumberland, and the Tennessee. In one of his first actions, Grant replaced Rosecrans at the head of the Army of the Cumberland with Maj. Gen. George H. Thomas. Upon reaching Chattanooga, Grant organized an effective supply line and gathered reinforcements—bringing Gen. Sherman's command from Alabama, and Eleventh and Twelfth Corps from Gen. Meade. On Nov. 24, Eleventh and Twelfth Corps under Hooker seized Lookout Mountain and, on Nov. 25, Thomas stormed and captured Missionary Ridge, lifting the siege and sending Braxton Bragg's army on a precipitous retreat into North Georgia.

113. Gen. Lee's HQ were on the railroad at Orange Court House with his army deployed behind the Rapidan River on a front of about twenty miles. From the O.&A. RR bridge downriver to the convergence of the Rappahannock, the Rapidan fords were Robertson's, Somerville, Raccoon, Morton's, Mitchell's, Jacob's, Germanna, Culpeper Mine, and Ely's, each a few miles apart. Robertson's Tavern at Locust Grove was on the Orange Turnpike about five miles west of Wilderness Tavern en route to Orange Court House, with Verdierville six miles farther. Parker's Store and New Hope Church were on the Orange Plank Road, which ran roughly parallel to the turnpike but two miles south of it. From Richardsville roads led southeast to Chancellorsville via Ely's Ford.

114. Adj. Seth Williams issued preparatory orders for the movement that opened the Mine Run campaign on Nov. 23. See *OR*, vol. 29, 2:480. French's Third Corps with Prince's division in the lead had the shortest march to the fords of any of the army corps. With time to prepare, getting lost *before* reaching the river was inexcusable.

115. Capt. John G. McBlair, ADC, described his staff duties during the campaign in some detail. *OR*, vol. 29, 1:748. Capt. Henry Pickering Bowditch (Harvard 1861) of Jamaica Plain and Lt. Charles Appleton Longfellow of Cambridge, 1st Massachusetts Cavalry. Bowditch was son of prominent Bostonian Dr. Henry Ingersoll Bowditch and grandson of Nathaniel Bowditch, the mathematician; he was a student at the Lawrence Scientific School at the war's outbreak. Longfellow was son of poet Henry Wadsworth Longfellow. Both men would be discharged for disability in Feb. 1864.

116. The Confederate divisions of Maj. Gen. Robert Rodes and Maj. Gen. Jubal Early of Ewell's Second Corps delayed Warren's advance at Robertson's (also called Robinson's) Tavern. Ewell's third division under Maj. Gen. Edward Johnson attacked French. With Ewell ill, Early commanded the corps during these operations. Early's report, *OR*, vol. 29, 1:830–36. Lee meanwhile was bringing up A. P. Hill's Third Corps from the far left flank.

117. Capt. George Middleton Barnard Jr. (Harvard 1857), 18th Massachusetts Infantry, CM and acting ADC for Fifth Corps. Barnard's father was a well-to-do cotton agent for the Boston textile firm Maury & Wilder. Brig. Gen. Joseph Jackson Bartlett (age 29, New York, lawyer), commanding First Division, Fifth Corps.

118. Col. John Egbert Farnum, 70th New York Infantry, a wealthy New Yorker, was implicated in a scheme to traffic in slaves. Farnum's 260-ton yacht *Wanderer*, sailing

under the flag of the New York Yacht Club, landed in the Savannah River in December 1858 with a cargo of 750 African males. The ship's captain and other principals were later arrested, and a congressional inquiry followed. Farnum, a founder of the yacht club, claimed that he had sold the vessel and was unaware of its activities, which was unlikely. Farnum was in any case acquitted. Sometime during his stay at Brandy Station, Farnum scrawled his name on the wall of the "Graffiti House" where it can be viewed today.

119. Lt. Washington Augustus Roebling (age 26, Pennsylvania), Warren's ADC; his father, John A. Roebling, designed the longest suspension bridge then conceived (more than 1,000 feet) over the Ohio River at Cincinnati. Construction of the bridge was interrupted by the war.

120. Orders issued Dec. 1, *OR*, vol. 29, 2:531–32. Col. Joe Hayes identified.

121. As a leader of the Young Ireland movement, Thomas Francis Meagher extolled the "sword" as the only means of ending British domination of Ireland. "Abhor the sword? Stigmatize the sword? No! I hail the sword as a sacred weapon." Escaping exile in Tasmania, Meagher made his way to New York City. He organized the Irish Brigade, which he led with distinction at Antietam and Fredericksburg. Meagher had political influence within the Lincoln administration because of his ability to recruit Irishmen for the army. *Çi-devant* in TL's usage translates roughly as "of former repute as."

122. TL's cousin Arthur Theodore Lyman (Harvard 1853) was treasurer of the Appleton Company and the Hamilton Mills in 1862 when he moved to James W. Paige & Co., selling agents for these and other mills. By this point in the war the supply of Southern cotton had all but dried up, and mill owners fought among themselves over what trickled through. Paige was accused of undercutting others and forced out of his directorship, causing the dissolution of the company.

123. TL included some of his most finished maps in his letters home, many of which have not been published. On Dec. 3, Gen. French was informed that there would be an official inquiry into his performance during the Mine Run campaign. French responded, "So far as my own conduct is concerned I have no apprehensions of the result." *OR*, vol. 29, 1:747.

124. Likely PC brother Capt. Louis Cabot (Harvard 1858), 4th Massachusetts Cavalry. Louis was the youngest son of Samuel Jr. and Eliza Cabot, TL's Brookline neighbors.

125. Gordon's brigade of Hampton's cavalry division overran the 1st Massachusetts Cavalry on Nov. 29 at Parkers Store. Gordon reported that his attack succeeded in driving Adams's men "out of their camps, and scattering them through the woods, capturing a number of prisoners, some horses, overcoats, blankets, guns, and their camp equipage." *OR*, vol. 29, 1:901–2.

126. Officers of 1st Massachusetts Cavalry: Capt. Adams, Capt. Edward Austin Flint (Harvard 1855), and Lt. Benjamin William Crowninshield (Harvard 1858, PC). TL knew Flint as "Ducky" at Harvard. Perry, *Life and Letters*, 214. Meade's report, Dec. 7, 1863: "The unnecessary delay in the progress of [Third] corps, and the failure to attack the enemy as soon as he was encountered, deploying to the left, and allowing the Sixth Corps to pass and continue the line to Warren, was the cause that a junc-

tion of the center and right columns was not made early on the morning of the 27th, and was one of the primary causes of the failure of the whole movement." *OR*, vol. 29, 1:12–19. On Dec. 8, Gen. Warren wrote his brother, "I did all I could & if Gen'l Meade had done as I have wished him ever since Gettysburg, change some of the corps commanders, especially Gen'l French, we should have succeeded. My efforts to have these men removed made them all enemies of me, and they are trying to shift blame in the newspapers to my shoulders. . . . I do not feel very kindly toward Gen'l Meade under all the circumstances." Warren Papers NYSL, box 3.5.

127. Ida Agassiz married Maj. Henry Lee Higginson on Dec. 5. Dr. Samuel Cabot (Harvard 1836, PC), son of Samuel Jr. and Eliza, married Hannah Lowell Jackson. Samuel and Hannah would be TL's neighbors in Brookline.

128. The Benjamin Bennett house stood a short distance west of the Botts house, "Auburn," on the old main road that is modern Rte. 648. On Dec. 8, Provost Marshal Patrick wrote in his diary that the soldiers "have robbed every citizen of his forage and subsistence, have torn down good houses for the lumber and bricks, and where they could do nothing in the way of carrying these things off, they have burned houses, barns, outhouses & meat houses. . . . I was sent for by Gen. Humphreys, to talk this matter over with him—not this particular case, but the general relaxation of discipline, the disposition to plunder, burn & commit all sorts of depredations & vandalism, by our troops—I told him what were the causes of this terrible conduct—that Gen. Meade had taken no steps to check this conduct until the evil had become too great to be borne." Sparks, *Inside Lincoln's Army*, 321–22. Only a few days earlier, Patrick had floored his tent with "refuse lumber" and secured a window sash and pair of andirons. Scavenged bricks were highly prized to build officers' chimneys.

129. *C'est mauvais!* "It's wrong!" Mimi's brother Henry Sturgis Russell accepted a commission as colonel of the 5th Massachusetts Cavalry (Colored). The perception at the time was that Negro soldiers would not be used in combat, and in TL's opinion, Hal seemed to be shirking his full duty.

130. The attacks against Marye's Heights at Fredericksburg, Dec. 13, 1862, demonstrated for many officers in the AoP the futility of a frontal assault against a well-entrenched position. Secretary of the Treasury Salmon Portland Chase published his annual report on the state of the economy.

131. Bache's apology could be read as a measure of TL's accepted status at HQ. Bostonians Nate Appleton and Lt. George F. Barstow, 3d U.S. Artillery.

132. "Sclavic," variant of Slavic.

133. Capt. Bootekoff of the Russian steam-frigate *Osliaba*. Czar Alexander II, the first head-of-state to recognize the United States as indissoluble, dispatched a flotilla of the Imperial Russian fleet on a diplomatic mission to American ports. The unexpected arrival of Russian warships in New York harbor in Sept. 1863 ignited a flurry of banquets and parades. Afterward, several ships steamed to Washington, D.C., where the officers were treated like royalty by the press. The czar had ulterior motives in sending the fleet to America: first, Poland had revolted against Russian rule; second, England, France, and Austria threatened to intervene on the side of the Poles; third, if war was

imminent, it was essential that Russian warships escape ice-locked Baltic ports for the winter. The presence of these warships in American waters further muddied the issue of European recognition of the Confederacy. On Sept. 16, 1863, Capt. Bootekoff entertained Mrs. Lincoln and other dignitaries aboard his ship in New York. A *New York Herald* article, dated Sept. 17, 1863, described the visit and named Bootekoff's officers, many undoubtedly included among TL's visitors.

134. Buford died at Gen. Stoneman's residence in Washington, D.C., attended by his ADC, Capt. Myles Walter Keogh.

135. TL's Harvard classmate, PC brother, and close friend, Payson Perrin Ellis. Ellis was an agent of Augustine Heard & Company, a firm heavily involved in the China trade.

136. Blackmoor not identified. Maj. Charles Albert Whittier (Harvard 1860), ADC and acting AAG, Sixth Corps; Lt. Henry Weld Farrar (Harvard 1861), 7th Maine Infantry, ADC; Col. Lewis A. Grant commanded the Vermont Brigade.

137. The Major house, "Presque Isle," stood on the north bank of Hazel River.

138. Likely Capt. Henry Page, asst. QM. Capt. George H. Mendell commanded a battalion of regular engineers attached directly to army HQ.

139. Capt. Montgomery Ritchie, 1st Massachusetts Cavalry. Col. Daniel C. McCallum, superintendent of military railroads.

140. Brig. Gen. Michael Corcoran, commanding the Irish Legion, was captured at First Bull Run and remained a prisoner of war for more than a year. Exchanged, he assumed command of King's division, headquartered at Fairfax Court House. Dr. George Hinckley Lyman (age 54, Boston City Hospital) served as medical inspector of military hospitals after combat duty during the Peninsula campaign. Dr. Lyman was distantly related to TL.

141. Howland and TL's sister Cora lived at 8 Mount Vernon Street on Beacon Hill with their three children and six servants. The Massachusetts State House complex now occupies the site. TL's Brookline estate "Singletree."

142. Eliza Perkins Cabot, "Old Mrs. Cabot," inherited the main Cabot property (and its extensive greenhouses), and two of her sons, Dr. Samuel Cabot and James Elliott Cabot, occupied adjoining parcels. Neighbor Henry Lee married one of the Cabot daughters. TL described works of art purchased and shipped from his and Mimi's European trip; TL commissioned "Infant Bacchus on a Panther" from William Wetmore Story (Harvard 1838, PC) whose studio was in Rome; the sculpture is in Boston's Museum of Fine Arts, gift of Mrs. Henry Lyman. The paintings of Sassoferrato, a 17th-century Italian artist, were much in vogue in Boston at the time.

143. TL's brother-in-law Howland and sister Cora hosted the party at their home on Beacon Hill. Howland and Cora's children (TL's niece and nephews) were Amy, Francis, and Henry. Howland's nephew Frederic Sears Jr. and niece Marian "Min"; Howland's sister Anna Blake Shaw and husband, William Batchelder Greene; their children Elizabeth "Bessie," Robert, and William. Howland's brother Samuel Parkman "Uncle Park" Shaw, wife Hannah, and two of their children, Samuel "Parkie" Jr. and Mabel. TL's Aunt Mary Lyman Eliot, widow of former Boston mayor Samuel Atkins Eliot. Mimi's parents George Robert Russell and Sarah Shaw Russell; sisters Emily, Marian "Tint," and Anna with husband Alex Agassiz; brothers Robert Shaw Russell with daughter Mary Louise "Loulie" and Henry Sturgis Russell with wife Mary. Mimi's

cousin Robert Shaw Oliver. Alexander's sister Pauline and husband Quincy Adams "Uncle Quin" Shaw; Quin's niece and Col. Robert Gould Shaw's younger sister, Ellen "Nellie" Shaw. Mimi's youngest sister Sarah had the flu. TL's paternal uncle George Williams Lyman, kept house around the corner at 6 Joy Street, a three-story brick edifice that stands imposingly today. TL's cousin Arthur Theodore Lyman. Two of George's granddaughters, Lillie and Minnie, were gravely ill with diphtheria, probably accounting for the melancholy; his granddaughters would not survive the winter.

144. Hartman Kuhn (Harvard Law 1852) of Philadelphia. TL's PC brother Crowninshield was Robert Gould Shaw's roommate at Harvard. Lt. George Blagden (Harvard 1856), 1st Massachusetts Cavalry.

145. Col. Paul Joseph Revere (Harvard 1852, PC), grandson of the Revolutionary War hero, mortally wounded while leading the 20th Massachusetts Infantry at Gettysburg. His widow was Lucretia Watson Lunt Revere. Palfrey and Revere were fellow Terrapins—TL's social club from college days.

146. Prof. Louis Agassiz, wife Elizabeth Cabot Cary Agassiz, and scientific artist Jacques Burkhardt. Agassiz and his students founded the Museum of Comparative Zoology. Anthony was a junior curator at the museum.

147. Frederic W. Putnam, curator of fishes and reptiles, special assistant to Prof. Louis Agassiz. Edwin Hale Abbot, secretary of the Harvard class of 1855. Harrison Gray Otis (Harvard 1811, PC) became one of the wealthiest men in Boston by developing Beacon Hill; his grandson William Church Otis. Likely Samuel Hubbard Hammond of Brookline, businessman and land speculator.

148. Boston merchant Horace Gray and second wife, Sarah; daughters Elizabeth and Harriet, and son Horace Jr. (Harvard 1845, Harvard Law 1849). Gov. Andrew appointed Gray Jr. as associate justice of the Supreme Judicial Court of Massachusetts in Aug. 1864. The Grays resided at 57 Summer Street.

149. Jonathan Ellis, father of Payson Perry Ellis. The Russells lived at 1 Louisburg Square on Beacon Hill. The elegant townhouse, a private residence, dominates the garden square today. TL's obituary of Payson Perrin Ellis appeared in the *Boston Daily Advertiser*, Jan. 4, 1864. TL's friend Charles Hale was editor of the paper.

150. TL's cousin, Francis Parkman (Harvard 1844), historian and horticulturalist, author of *The California and Oregon Trail* (1849). Parkman suffered from poor eyesight and chronic migraine headaches. Nine-year-old Francis "Frankie" Shaw, Howland and Cora's son. TL's PC brother, Maj. Simon Barstow of Meade's staff, home on leave; the Barstows lived at 33 Charles Street. Massachusetts governor John Albion Andrew.

151. TL was overseeing publication of a catalog of starfish, based in part on his own collections. It would be published in 1865 as an "Illustrated Catalogue of the Ophiuridae and Astrophytidae in the Museum of Comparative Zoology."

152. TL's classmate Clapp. Lawyer Edward Ingersoll "Ned" Browne was TL's classmate, PC brother, and attorney. Maj. Charles Whittier of Sixth Corps staff.

153. TL's cousin Arthur. After the opening ceremony, Gov. Andrew and notables were escorted by the Independent Corps of Cadets to Old South Church for the election sermon and thence to the Parker House for the Annual Dinner to the Cadets. Thomas Amory Dexter (PC) graduated from Harvard with TL's father in 1810.

154. James Lawrence (Harvard 1840, PC), son of Abbott Lawrence, manufacturer and founder of the mill town of Lawrence, Massachusetts. James was a director of the A. & A. Lawrence Company, which imported European goods and was invested heavily in mills and railroads. James and TL were close friends.

155. A wedding gift to Henry Lee and Ida Higginson. TL's cousin Charles William Eliot (Harvard 1853), postwar president of Harvard. Mimi's uncle, Francis George Shaw, and wife Sarah, originally of West Roxbury, lived on Staten Island. Elvira, wife of Brookline farmer Eben W. Reed.

156. William Makepeace Thackeray (1811–63), acclaimed British columnist and novelist. James Perkins Sturgis, acting Master's Mate, U.S. Navy, died Jan. 2.

157. Rev. Cox not identified. Possibly John Hubbard Sturgis of the architectural firm Bryant & Gilman that designed Boston City Hall. Miss Mary Ingersoll Bowditch, age 25, granddaughter of Nathaniel Bowditch. Bob's (Col. Robert Gould Shaw's) sister Susanna married Robert Browne Minturn Jr. Robert and brother John were principals in Grinnell, Minturn & Co., a major mercantile firm. The firm's founder, Moses H. Grinnell, was an influential political ally of Secretary of State William H. Seward.

158. Lanny not identified. Capt. Philip William Stanhope, 12th U.S. Infantry. Parson Samuel Greene's School prepared wealthy students for Harvard and was on par (nearly) with Boston Latin. Likely George Osgood Holyoke (Harvard 1856) and Arthur Amory Eckley (Harvard 1856, PC). Charles Lowell married Josephine Shaw; her sister Susanna married Minturn. John Chandler Bancroft (Harvard 1854). *Peutêtre*, "perhaps."

159. Col. Waldo Merriam, wounded at Gettysburg, was returning to duty. ADC Capt. John Coalter Bates, 11th U.S. Infantry, son of Attorney General Edward Bates. Capt. Craig W. Wadsworth, son of Brig. Gen. James Samuel Wadsworth and Buford's ADC. The 114th Pennsylvania Zouaves, wearing turbans, short Moroccan-style jackets, and baggy red pantaloons, replaced the 93d New York as the army's provost guard. The "bloodless" 93d New York had yet to see combat, but its time would come.

160. Charlie's father, Charles Francis Adams Sr., served as minister of the U.S. to Great Britain, where his mother and brother Henry resided during the war years. Family correspondence for the war years was published in 1920 as *A Cycle of Adams Letters, 1861–1865*, edited by Worthington Chauncey Ford.

161. Frank Palfrey (discharged) on a social visit to the army. Palfrey had just published an analytical article on the army's ambulance system in the *North American Review*. After the war he wrote the Scribner's "Campaigns of the Civil War" volume on Antietam and Fredericksburg (1881). Col. George N. Macy of Nantucket, 20th Massachusetts Infantry. Meade's son John Sergeant was gravely ill with a lung disease. *Pro bono aliorum*, "for the good of the others."

162. Capt. Philip Schuyler Jr., 14th U.S. Infantry, joined Brig. Gen. Marsena Patrick's staff and served as an intelligence officer. Before the war, the 410-ton merchant vessel *Oneida* operated out of Salem in the China trade. In April 1863, the ship was taken and burned by the Confederate privateer *Florida*.

163. Officers of the 20th Massachusetts Infantry: Capt. Oliver Wendell Holmes Jr. of Boston (Harvard 1861, PC), age 22; regimental surgeons Nathan Hayward of

Roxbury (Harvard 1850), age 34, and John Gardner Perry of Boston (Harvard Medical 1863, PC), age 26; Capt. Arthur Russell Curtis of Boston, age 23; Henry May Bond of West Roxbury (Harvard 1859), age 30, regimental adjutant; Capt. Henry Lyman Patten of Cambridge (Harvard 1858), age 27; and Maj. Henry Livermore Abbott of Lowell (Harvard 1860), age 21.

164. Capt. Thomas Wilson (USMA 1853) of Washington, D.C., replaced Col. Henry F. Clarke as chief CS. Dr. Thomas A. McParlin of Maryland replaced Dr. Jonathan Letterman. Rosecrans proffered charges against two of his corps commanders, McCook and Crittenden, for their poor performance at Chickamauga. IG Edmund Schriver of New York (USMA 1833) served as recorder for the Court of Inquiry. *OR*, vol. 30, 1:929–1004.

165. Mrs. Meade to TL, Jan. 25: "Gen'l Meade has been extremely ill. . . . [He] has had a congestion of the lung followed by an inflammation of the liver. The disease has yielded to medical treatment; and I hope he will soon be in his usual good health." Lyman Papers MHS, box 3.4.

166. Carswell and Henry B. McClellan, sons of a prominent Philadelphia surgeon and first cousins to Maj. Gen. George Brinton McClellan. Henry served as CoS for the Confederate Cavalry Corps and in 1885 published his *Life and Campaigns of Major-General J. E. B. Stuart*. Carswell McClellan published postwar volumes critical of the memoirs of Grant and Sheridan.

167. Phillips Brooks (Harvard 1855), rector of the Church of the Holy Trinity. Brooks would write the carol "O Little Town of Bethlehem" after the war.

168. TL's uncle George Williams Lyman's Beacon Hill residence. Historian Francis Parkman's brother, John Eliot Parkman, civilian captain's clerk on *USS Aries*. Rear-admiral Lee reported on Jan. 20, 1864, that "on the occasion of the destruction of the blockade runner steamer *Dare* by the *Montgomery* and *Aries*, on the 7th instant, a boat from each vessel was swamped in the surf, and the officers and men of each fell into the hands of the enemy." "I. E. Parkman" was listed among those captured, likely a misreading of "J. E." *OR*, Navy, ser. 1, vol. 9:392. Abby, wife of TL's cousin William Pratt Lyman; their daughter Olivia "Lillie," age 5, died on Jan. 16. TL's cousin Charles William Eliot; his son, Charles Jr., recovered.

169. Brig. Gen. George Washington Getty (age 44, District of Columbia, USMA 1840) joined army staff as IG and afterward was assigned Second Division, Sixth Corps. Abolitionist Brig. Gen. Edward Augustus Wild (age 38, Harvard 1844) recruited an "African Brigade" from among former slaves in North Carolina. Dr. Wild was TL's Brookline neighbor.

170. Brig. Gen. Gershom Mott (age 41, New Jersey), Third Brigade, Second Division, Third Corps. Brig. Gen. William Hopkins Morris (age 37, New York City, USMA 1851), First Brigade, Third Division, Third Corps.

171. In 1813, Prussian Ludwig Adolf Wilhelm Lutzow organized a partisan unit—the Freikorps—to operate against the communications of Napoleon's army, a prototype for Mosby's Rangers.

172. TL's cousin Mary Ellen Lyman married Charles S. Arnold, a cotton buyer who lived in Wilmington; her sons, George Lyman Appleton, from a first marriage, and

William. Mary's diary in the Southern Historical Collection, University of North Carolina at Chapel Hill, describes running the blockade.

173. As senior corps commander, Sedgwick commanded the AoP in Meade's absence. "Rapid Ann" was an alternative spelling of Rapidan and appeared on many Federal maps. TL's PC brother Jeffries falsely represented himself as a broker for a New York firm and profited on the sale of merchandise that he did not own. The *Boston Daily Advertiser* covered the trial in dramatic front-page fashion. Jeffries's conviction was later overturned.

174. Lt. Henry C. Christiancy, Humphreys's ADC. Others identified.

175. Second Corps commanders: Brig. Gen. John C. Caldwell (age 30, Maine, Amherst College), First Division; Brig. Gen. Alexander S. Webb, Second Division; and Brig. Gen. Alexander Hays (age 44, Pennsylvania, USMA 1844), Third Division.

176. "Trig," tidy, in order. Warren's Second Corps reported 255 killed, wounded, and missing. The cavalry lost about 15 killed and wounded. The army maintained a signal station atop Stony Mountain, a steep-sided round hill southeast of Stevensburg that overlooked the road to Morton's Ford.

177. Brig. Gen. Isaac Wistar, commanding 4,000 infantry and 2,200 cavalry, departed from Williamsburg on a forced march toward Richmond, hoping to make a dash into the city. Before dawn, Feb. 7, the cavalry reached Bottom's Bridge on the Chickahominy, twelve miles from Richmond. There, the Federals probed the weakly manned defenses but withdrew with a loss of nine killed and wounded. Eppa Hunton, the Confederate commander at the bridge, wrote, "I am at a loss to understand why the enemy has retired for the small repulse received." *OR*, vol. 33:143–50.

178. Judson Haycock, Co. K, 1st U.S. Cavalry. Companies A and K were attached to army HQ at this time.

179. Brig. Gen. Joseph Bartlett, First Division, Fifth Corps; Col. Joe Hayes. Lt. James A. Snyder, 3d U.S. Infantry, Sykes's ADC. Surgeon William Holbrook, 18th Massachusetts Infantry. Nate Appleton. Col. James Gwyn and his ADC Capt. Amos M. Judson, 118th Pennsylvania Infantry. Bostonians Capt. L. M. Tucker, ADC, and Capt. William T. W. Ball, brigade CS. Moldan not identified.

180. Capt. John Barclay Fassitt, 23d Pennsylvania Infantry, Birney's ADC, attended Harvard but, according to records, did not graduate. *Qui facit per alium facit per se;* "he, who does for another, does so for himself." Clever Latin quips were widely circulated among Harvard students. Fassitt was awarded the Medal of Honor in 1894 for heroism at Gettysburg. Brig. Gen. Henry Jackson Hunt and his ADC, Lt. Charles T. Bissell, 1st Michigan Cavalry.

181. *Picus pileatus,* pileated woodpecker. *Charadrius vociferus,* killdeer.

182. Likely Lt. George Mifflin Bache Jr., U.S. Navy, assigned command of the gunboat *Lexington,* which would participate in Nathaniel Banks's ill-starred Red River campaign, beginning Mar. 15. Bache had family ties with Gen. Meade.

183. Ulysses Grant, Secretary of the Treasury Chase, Secretary of War Stanton, political general Nathaniel Prentiss Banks of Massachusetts, and former presidential candidate Charles C. Frémont of California were considered as possible replacements

for Lincoln on the Republican ticket in the 1864 election. Maj. Gen. George B. McClellan would head the Democratic ticket.

184. Mary "Minnie," daughter of William and Abby Lyman, died Feb. 9 at age 8. William Lyman would die on April 17 of diphtheria like his two daughters. TL's cousin George Theodore Lyman was eventually institutionalized.

185. Robert Charles Winthrop Jr. (Harvard 1854, PC); his father had been a seven-term U.S. congressman from Massachusetts. Charles Thorndike (Harvard 1854, PC).

186. Surgeon James T. Ghiselin of Maryland.

187. The Confederate army during the Peninsula campaign numbered about 90,000 men, its greatest strength of the war. McClellan's intelligence network nearly doubled these numbers. During the current campaign, Meade's Bureau of Army Intelligence (under Marsena Patrick and Col. Sharpe) accurately estimated the strength of the ANV according to numbers carried on the rolls. There was no way to know how many Confederate soldiers were missing from the ranks due to illness, wounds, and absenteeism. This count typically inflated the number of effectives by a third or more.

188. London-born Alfred Rudolph Waud lived in Boston and New York City before joining *Harper's Weekly* as a special artist and war correspondent. TL and Waud became particular friends. The Library of Congress, Washington, D.C., curates some 1,150 wartime sketches by Alfred Waud and his brother William, who traveled for a time with Sherman's army. "Jim Crow," a stock character of minstrel shows, usually was played by a white man, his face darkened with burnt cork. Waud's practical joke appears directed against radical abolitionists among the clergy.

189. Capt. L. F. Lyttle. Capt. John J. Coppinger, Co. F, First Battalion, 14th U.S. Infantry, served as ADC for generals Torbert and Sheridan and later as colonel of the 15th New York Cavalry. Pope Pius IX recruited an international brigade of Catholics, including an Irish legion, in an unsuccessful attempt to regain territory lost to the Piedmontese and French in the Italian War of 1859. In 1861, Secretary of State Seward sent the Catholic archbishop of New York to Rome to offer commissions to Legion veterans such as Coppinger and Myles Keogh. Keogh served as Buford's ADC.

190. Biddle and Cadwalader likely resorted on occasion to the saying *au courant* in Philadelphia that "when a Biddle gets drunk, he thinks he is a Cadwalader."

191. In Jan. 1864, the New York *Tribune* quoted Meade as saying that French was "probably too drunk to know or do his duty," a statement which Meade denied making. *OR*, vol. 29, 1:747–48.

192. Maj. Nathaniel Michler of the topographical engineers. Joseph Kennedy, statistician and director of the National Census in 1850 and 1860. Kennedy's opinions of race and ethnicity were typical of the time.

193. Vice Pres. Hannibal Hamlin of Maine, Lincoln's first vice president. Hamlin was a widower; his daughter, Sarah Jane. TL described Hamlin as "one of the most ordinary-looking men that ever obtained the suffrages of his fellow citizens." *Meade's Headquarters*, 75. Gov. William Sprague of Rhode Island resigned his office in 1863 for election to the U.S. Senate; his wife was the attractive Kate, daughter of Secretary of the Treasury Salmon P. Chase. Pres. Lincoln appointed Judge Samuel F. Miller to the

Supreme Court in 1862. Lt. Col. Joseph W. Dickinson, formerly of army HQ, resigned his commission on Jan. 26, 1864. Evidently his visit to the AoP was a social call, or perhaps he was on a "fact-finding" mission for Dan Sickles, who was soon to accuse Meade of wanting to retreat in the face of the enemy at Gettysburg.

194. Col. Samuel Sprigg Carroll (age 31, Washington, D.C., USMA 1856) commanded the Gibraltar Brigade of Ohio and Indiana troops, First Brigade, Third Division, Second Corps.

195. Secretary of War Stanton dispatched George L. Schuyler to Europe as a special agent in July 1861 to purchase arms for the military. Schuyler was a senior partner in the New York City military and sporting goods firm of Schuyler, Hartley, & Graham.

196. Capt. William Henry Paine of the topographical engineers, Maj. Michler's ADC.

197. Prussia and Austria united to seize the Danish duchies of Schleswig and Holstein. In their brief war, the heavily outnumbered Danes were soundly defeated.

198. Capt. Henry R. Dalton, AAG, First Division, Sixth Corps. James City crossroads, modern hamlet of Leon in Madison County.

199. Brig. Gen. Judson Kilpatrick broke the chain of command to meet with Pres. Lincoln and Secretary of War Stanton on Feb. 12 to finalize plans for the Richmond raid. This irregular proceeding suggests that the raid had a hidden agenda. Kilpatrick's superior, corps commander Pleasonton, opposed the operation. Col. Ulric Dahlgren, son of Admiral John A. Dahlgren, served on Hooker's staff and was wounded during the Gettysburg campaign, his leg amputated at the knee. "M.C.'s" (members of Congress).

200. *Nous verrons*, "we shall see."

201. A detachment of the 2d Massachusetts Cavalry, commanded by Capt. J. Sewell Reed, was ambushed near Dranesville on Feb. 24. Reed and about a dozen of his troopers were killed—James Miles among them. *OR*, vol. 33:159–60. TL employed Paschal "Park" Barrell Jr. and Charles Freeman Fernald as farmhands. Both men served with the 2d Massachusetts Infantry, Co. H, and were mortally wounded at Chancellorsville. TL's "fourth," also a farmhand at Brookline, was Alonzo B. Langley, 4th U.S. Artillery, who survived the war.

202. Congress commissioned Grant a lieutenant general in the regular army, and the Pres. placed him in command of all Federal armies in the field. Grant displaced Halleck, who would thereafter serve Pres. Lincoln and Secretary of War Stanton as CoS.

203. Telegram from Kilpatrick, Mar. 3, 9 P.M.: "I have failed to accomplish the great object of the expedition, but have destroyed the enemy's communications at various points on the Virginia Central Railroad; also the canal and mills along the James River, and much other valuable property. Drove the enemy into and through his fortifications to the suburbs of Richmond; made several unsuccessful efforts to return to the Army of the Potomac. I have lost less than 150 men." *OR*, vol. 33:182.

204. Surgeon Edward Barry "Ned" Dalton, TL's Harvard classmate. Ned Dalton reappeared in the Wilderness and later as chief surgeon and administrator of the army's general hospital at City Point.

205. Brig. Gen. William F. Barry, chief of artillery for Washington's defenses, joined William T. Sherman's staff. Barry's ADC Lt. Carl L. Berlin joined Hunt's staff.

206. "This was the first intimation [Meade] had that the committee was even examining into the Gettysburg campaign, let alone that any charges had been made against him." Meade, *Life and Letters*, 2:171–72. Meade's full testimony before the Committee with exhibits may be found in ibid, 354–95.

207. Patrick recorded in his diary that Capt. Charles Stuart McEntee, who accompanied Kilpatrick, said "he thinks the papers are correct that were found upon Dahlgren, as they correspond with what D. told him." Sparks, *Inside Lincoln's Army*, 347–48. Meade "promptly disavowed having ever authorized, sanctioned or approved of any act not required by military necessity, and in accordance with the usages of war." Meade, *Life and Letters*, 2:191. Dahlgren's unfortunate guide, Martin Robinson, led the column to a ford that two days of heavy rain had made impassable. Assuming treachery, Dahlgren hanged him, and the locals left his body to dangle for weeks as an example of how the Federal army treated runaway slaves. Libby Prison in Richmond.

208. Adj. Charles Kingsbury Jr. Timothy Bigelow Lawrence (Harvard 1846, PC). *Hoi polloi*, the common people.

209. Francis Shaw had offices in the Trinity Building on Broadway. Boston merchant Richard Sullivan Fay Jr. wed Miss Mary Bowditch's sister Elizabeth. Possibly industrialist Charles Hammond, originally from Boston. Canterbury not identified.

MARCH 9–MAY 3, 1864

Lyman labeled this Vol. 13, Part 1; it is assigned Lyman Papers, bound vol. 15, in the MHS.

1. Mimi's brother, Henry Sturgis Russell and wife, Mary, named their baby after Maj. James Savage Jr., 2d Massachusetts Infantry. Little Cora was born in "Florence the beautiful."

2. On this date, after meeting with Pres. Lincoln in Washington, D.C., Lt. Gen. Ulysses S. Grant visited Gen. Meade at his Brandy Station HQ. Meade offered to relinquish command of the AoP, if Grant wished to replace him, and to serve in any capacity. Grant declined Meade's offer and later wrote: "This incident gave me even a more favorable opinion of Meade than did his great victory at Gettysburg the July before. It is men who wait to be selected, and not those who seek, from whom we may always expect the most efficient service." Grant, *Personal Memoirs*, 470.

3. TL's uncle Charles Lyman and his cousins Florence and Charles Frederick Lyman. *Mauvaise graisse*, "bad fat." Snelling not identified.

4. TL's aunt Mary Lyman Eliot lived at 31 Beacon Street; TL's cousins Elizabeth "Lizzy" and Charles Eliot with his wife Katherine "Kate."

5. Mimi's father. TL's great-aunt Mary Williams Pratt, widow of William Pratt of Salem, and cousin Frances Ann "Fannie" Eliot, who married Unitarian minister Henry Wilder Foote (Harvard 1858). Foote was installed as pastor of King's Chapel (the Stone chapel) in Dec. 1861. Aunt Mary died in Aug. 1864.

6. Grant at first favored Maj. Gen. William Farrar "Baldy" Smith (age 40, Vermont, USMA 1845) because of his engineering prowess during the siege of Chattanooga. He may have intended that Smith would replace Benjamin Butler. So far as can be determined from the record, Grant did not anticipate Smith replacing Meade.

7. TL's cousin Arthur Theodore Lyman and wife Ella Lowell; their daughter Julia. Col. Charles Russell Codman (Harvard Law 1852), 45th Massachusetts Infantry, mustered out of service in July 1863 and was elected to the state senate in 1864. Charles's brother, Richard Codman (Harvard 1864).

8. In 1863, a group of Somerset Club men, disturbed by Copperhead sentiments espoused by other members, split away to form Boston's Union Club. The conditions for membership were an "unqualified loyalty to the Constitution of the United States, and unwavering support of the Federal Government in efforts for the suppression of the Rebellion." Boston icon Edward Everett served as the club's first president. Although later inducted into the Union Club, TL retained his affiliation with the Somerset, as did many of his friends and associates. Somerset members John F. "Jack" Anderson, Charles H. Appleton, Ives G. Bates, and John D. Bates. Wealthy merchant and manufacturer Abbott Lawrence supported the work of Prof. Agassiz at Harvard and endowed the Lawrence Scientific School. TL was well acquainted with Mr. Lawrence's three sons, James "Jim" (Harvard 1840, PC), Timothy Bigelow "Biggie" (Harvard 1846, PC), and Abbott Jr. (Harvard 1849). Col. George N. Macy. Capt. Henry R. Dalton. James Henry Howe married Martha Slater; his brothers George Marshall Howe (Harvard Medical 1854) and William Edward Howe (Harvard 1852, PC).

9. *Nota bene*, "please notice."

10. Possibly Dr. David Mack (Harvard Medical 1863). Likely Capt. Thomas Lawrence Motley, 1st Massachusetts Cavalry. George Dexter (Harvard 1855, PC), banker and cotton buyer. Likely Richard Frothingham, editor of the *Boston Post* and treasurer of the Massachusetts Historical Society. TL's classmate Brig. Gen. Francis Channing Barlow (age 29, Brookline, Harvard 1855) was recuperating from his Gettysburg wound; Barlow rejoined the AoP in time for the spring campaign, commanding a division in Second Corps. Likely Jacob Crowninshield Rogers. Henry Winthrop Sargent (Harvard 1830, PC). Timothy Lewis was a farmer and caretaker at Beverly.

11. Henry and Ida Higginson. Henry's brother Capt. James Jackson Higginson, 1st Massachusetts Cavalry, had been captured at Aldie in June. Alex and Annie's son, George Russell Agassiz, born in 1862, would edit TL's wartime letters to Mimi for publication in 1922. TL was a cofounder and financial supporter of Agassiz's Museum of Comparative Zoology, thus his election to the board.

12. "Bob" was Col. Robert Gould Shaw. Mimi's brother Col. Henry Russell, 5th Massachusetts Cavalry (Colored), organized his command at the Readville camp, where Col. Shaw trained the 54th Massachusetts. Col. Francis L. Lee (Harvard 1843, PC), 44th Massachusetts Infantry and brigade commander, discharged. Albert Smith Bickmore, discharged from the 44th Massachusetts Infantry, studied under Prof. Agassiz and sought funds to procure specimens for the Harvard collection. Lacedemonian, "Spartan." *Trop doux*, "very soft."

13. Mimi's sister Emily "Miss Emmie" indulged in amateur theatricals. Burnside's victory at Knoxville and Grant's at Chattanooga effectively "liberated" much of pro-Union East Tennessee. During the winter, Bostonians organized charity events to assist destitute loyal Tennesseans.

14. Judge Horace Gray Jr.

15. William Church Otis, Robert Charles Winthrop Jr., John Quincy "Jack" Adams, Edward Ingersoll Browne, and Col. Frank Palfrey.

16. TL's PC brother and relative by marriage, William Batchelder Greene (Harvard Divinity 1845), and children William and Elizabeth. Greene was colonel of the 14th Massachusetts until his resignation Oct. 1862. Confederate deserters were "galvanized" or organized into regiments to perform noncombatant duties. Uncle Quincy Adams Shaw, wife Pauline, and son Louis. Investment banker Augustus Lowell, TL's Brookline neighbor. Beverly on the North Shore was a fashionable location for summer homes for Boston's wealthy families.

17. The Porcellian Club had (and retains) a reputation for exclusive membership, unabashed nepotism, and parsimony (or a deliberate disdain of ostentation). A nondescript doorway surmounted by a boar's head on Harvard Square is today the entrance to the club. Brothers of the Porcellian Club (Honoraries were alumni; Immediates were current students): Richard Codman (1864), William Lawrence Tucker (1865), William Philips Walley (1864), George Harrison Mifflin (1865), Hollis Hunnewell (1858), Jacques Burkhardt Jr. (1856), Ned Browne (1855, Harvard Law 1857), Alex Agassiz (1855, Lawrence Scientific 1857), George Bigelow Chase (1856), William Powell Mason (1856), Henry Parker Quincy (1862), Martin Brimmer (1849), Abbott Lawrence Jr. (1849, Harvard Law 1863), Harrison Ritchie (1845), Augustus Thorndike Perkins (1851), Henry Austin Whitney (1846).

18. Benjamin Foster Whitehouse of Brookline, 2d Massachusetts Infantry. TL's former farmhand, Alonzo B. Langley, sought a commission in the 16th Battery Massachusetts Light Artillery. Gaetano Donizetti's *Lucrezia Borgia* was first performed at the Opera La Scala in Milan in 1834 and became a staple of traveling operatic companies.

19. Charles Gounod's *Faust* premiered in Paris in 1859. Based on the play by Johann Wolfgang von Goethe, the opera follows the story of Dr. Faustus who sold his soul to the devil—Mephistopheles. At the time of the Civil War, Jacob Meyerbeer was one of the most popular composers in Europe. Stock actor Joseph Hermanns played the leading role.

20. Mimi's youngest brother, Robert "Bobbie" Russell. Mimi's sisters, Emily, Marian, and Sarah "Sallie." Mrs. Eliza Perkins Cabot, widow of Samuel Jr. William Gray owned the property south of TL's Brookline estate at Heath and Warren streets.

21. TL's Brookline neighbor, Col. Henry Lee Jr., who served on Gov. Andrew's staff. Lawyer James Elliot Cabot (Harvard 1840, PC) and wife Elisabeth lived three properties down from TL on Warren Street; Cabot attended the Lawrence Scientific School for a time as a student of Prof. Agassiz. Lee was Cabot's brother-in-law.

22. Evidently, TL paid medical expenses related to the carriage accident of Mar. 25.

23. Possibly Harvard professor Phineas N. Brewer. Henry Howard Sturgis resigned his commission in the 20th Massachusetts Infantry in July 1862. Henry's father, Henry Parkman Sturgis, headed a large New York City mercantile firm. Gardner Green Hammond. Reed not identified.

24. TL's father established the Westboro Reform School, later renamed the Lyman

School, to rehabilitate (mostly poor Irish) delinquents. Joseph H. Whittlesey, 5th U.S. Cavalry, served as a recruiter after being disabled during the Peninsula campaign.

25. Brig. Gen. Amiel Weeks Whipple was mortally wounded at Chancellorsville while commanding Third Division, Third Corps. His sons were Charles William, age 18, appointed to West Point in 1864, and David. Spencer, age 14, was Gen. Meade's second youngest son. Meade, *Life and Letters*, 2:183.

26. Maj. Gen. Winfield Scott Hancock (age 40, Pennsylvania, USMA 1844) had recovered enough from his Gettysburg wound to resume command of Second Corps. Maj. Gen. Gouverneur K. Warren was shifted from Second Corps to Fifth Corps command, ousting regular army stalwart Sykes. The senior (Sixth) corps commander, Maj. Gen. John Sedgwick, was known as "Uncle John." New York lawyer and politician Brig. Gen. James S. Wadsworth (age 56) attended Harvard for two years. TL socialized regularly with Brig. Gen. Alexander "Alick" Hays. *Têtu*, "stubborn."

27. Meade wrote, "I tried very hard to retain Sykes, Newton, and even French, as division commanders, but without avail. I had very hard work to retain Sedgwick. As to Pleasanton, his being relieved was entirely the work of Grant and Stanton." Meade, *Life and Letters*, 2:185. Grant's handpicked man, Philip H. Sheridan, replaced Pleasonton. Pleasonton went to Missouri to command William Rosecrans's cavalry. Rosecrans was himself a recent exile to the Trans-Mississippi.

28. Newton was reassigned to divisional command in Fourth Corps, Army of the Cumberland, for the Atlanta campaign. French resigned rather than face an official inquiry into his role in the Mine Run campaign.

29. As Meade's CoS at Gettysburg, Brig. Gen. Daniel Butterfield was subpoenaed to testify before the Congressional Committee on the Conduct of the War. Butterfield, like Sickles, was a Tammany Hall lawyer and a protégé of Joseph Hooker. Sickles, Butterfield, and Doubleday promulgated the story that Meade had planned to retreat from the field at Gettysburg.

30. Col. Samuel Sprigg Carroll, Third Brigade, Second Division, Second Corps, after the reorganization. Capt. Robert Walsh Mitchell.

31. Warren *judice*, "in Warren's judgement."

32. Dabney & Cunningham, a Boston shipping firm. Peel et al., British military observers who visited HQ the previous Nov. TL's cartes-de-visite of Earle, Stephenson, and Peel are in the MHS Photograph Collection 94: 87–89.

33. Regular army officer Brig. Gen. John Oliver Gibbon (age 36, Philadelphia, USMA 1847), wounded at Gettysburg and returning to field command. Gibbon penned the premier handbook for artillerymen in the Civil War, *The Artillerist's Manual* (1860). Sickles's mouthpiece, Historicus, in a second letter to the *New York Herald* dated Apr. 4, quoted Maj. Gen. David Bell Birney at length to support his contention that Sickles and Third Corps saved the AoP at Gettysburg. Birney afterward visited both Hancock and Meade to disclaim being a "partisan of Sickles." Meade, *Life and Letters*, 2:190.

34. Brig. Gen. James Brewerton Ricketts (age 46, New York City, USMA 1839), wounded at Antietam and returning to field command. "Milroy's weary boys" had been whipped by Stonewall Jackson in the Shenandoah Valley in 1862 and routed by

Dick Ewell at Winchester at the start of the Gettysburg campaign. These six Ohio, Pennsylvania, and Maryland regiments were consolidated into a brigade of Ricketts's Sixth Corps division, commanded by Brig. Gen. Truman Seymour. The "boys" would fulfill their lackluster reputation at the battle of the Wilderness. They would, however, redeem themselves at Monocacy Creek in July 1864.

35. TL bought his roan (later renamed "Petersburg") from Maj. Oliver Ormsby G. Robinson, whose battalion of the 3d Pennsylvania Cavalry had been attached recently to the provost guard.

36. This was the first meeting of the generals since TL had returned to the army. Grant and Meade first met on Mar. 10.

37. Capt. William Jay from New York served as Meade's ADC during the Chancellorsville campaign. Maj. William Riddle. *Argal*, "ergo."

38. Brig. Gen. James Clay Rice (age 35, Massachusetts, Yale 1854) commanded Second Brigade, Fourth Division, Fifth Corps.

39. Pres. Lincoln refused Slocum's resignation. Slocum afterward supplanted Hooker as commander of Twentieth Corps in the Georgia and Carolinas campaigns, 1864–65. The Excelsiors were Sickles's old brigade. Dismantling Third Corps eliminated any position for Dan Sickles in the command structure. This may have been an underlying motive for Halleck's and Meade's reorganization of the army, although this was never stated.

40. Famous Prussian astronomer and Russian emigré, Friedrich Georg Wilhelm von Struve (1793–1864), can be readily identified; his relative left few tracks. The younger Struve's carte-de-visite (CDV) is in the MHS Photograph Collection 94: vol. 1, 91.

41. Photographer Timothy O'Sullivan superintended Alexander Gardner's field office with the AoP where he helped develop techniques for photo-reproduction of maps for the topographical engineers. He photographed the Brandy Station winter encampment and on the side produced tintypes (ferrotypes) and cartes-de-visite for individual officers and soldiers.

42. Lt. Otto L. Torslow, Battery G, First Rhode Island Artillery. Czar Alexander II declared Russia's serfs free from indentured servitude in 1861, a European emancipation proclamation. Seeking further reform, the Polish people tried to assert their independence from Russia in 1863. The revolt was crushed, but the implication was that democratic reforms—e.g., Lincoln's Emancipation Proclamation—might have unanticipated results.

43. Nationally noted clergyman and orator Dr. Edward Norris Kirk (1802–74). Likely Brookline Congregationalist Edward S. Tobey (1813–91). "Holy" Sturgis not identified.

44. Capt. Henry Warner Janes, asst. QM. Lt. Col. Cyrus Bellou Comstock (USMA 1855), regular army engineer. Lt. Col. Adam Badeau (age 32, New York City), military secretary. Brig. Gen. John Aaron Rawlins (age 33, Illinois), Galena lawyer and Grant's CoS. When Lt. Col. Horace Porter (Lawrence Scientific School 1855, USMA 1860) joined Grant in Apr. 1864 as ADC, the staff consisted of fourteen officers. These included also Lt. Col. Orville Elias Babcock (USMA 1861), regular army engineer;

Grant's brother-in-law Lt. Col. Frederick T. Dent (USMA 1843); Lt. Col. William Reuben Rowley of Galena, military secretary; Lt. Col. Theodore S. Bowers, 48th Illinois Infantry, AAG.; Lt. Col. William L. Duff, IG; Capt. George K. Leet, AAG; Capt. Ely S. Parker, AAG; and ADCs Capt. Peter T. Hudson and Lt. William McKee Dunn Jr. Porter, *Campaigning with Grant*, 31–34.

45. TL's cousin Arthur eventually recovered from the disease.

46. TL refers to the fighting at Morton's Ford, Feb. 6–7, 1864.

47. Humphreys's ADC Capt. Carswell McClellan. Brig. Gen. Alfred T. A. Torbert (age 30, Delaware, USMA 1855) replaced the deceased Buford in command of First Division, Cavalry Corps. Brig. Gen. John Henry Hobart Ward (age 40, New York City, regular army), First Brigade, Third Division (Birney's), Second Corps. Alexander Hays, Second Brigade, Third Division, after the reorganization.

48. Engineer Capt. Joseph C. Briscoe, 40th New York Infantry, Birney's ADC. Maj. William Galbraith Mitchell had been Hancock's ADC since 1861. Brig. Gen. Philip Henry Sheridan (age 33, Ohio, USMA 1853) was Henry Halleck's ADC in 1862 and transferred to the cavalry where he rose to brigadier. For his role in the battle at Stones River, Sheridan was commissioned a major general of volunteers and assumed command of an infantry division in the Army of the Cumberland. At Chattanooga on Nov. 25, 1863, Sheridan's division stormed up the face of Missionary Ridge and routed the opposition in its front. Brig. Gen. James Harrison Wilson (age 26, Illinois, USMA 1855), formerly an engineer on Grant's staff, was given Third Division, Cavalry Corps.

49. Mimi left Singletree to stay with Howland and Cora on Beacon Hill.

50. Mott would command Fourth Division, Second Corps, in the reorganization. Col. William R. Brewster was not confirmed as a brigadier. Harrison Smith, brother of Col. Charles R. Smith, 6th Pennsylvania Cavalry, married Maria Sergeant, sister of Mrs. Meade.

51. Walter Gale, 15th Massachusetts Infantry. TL's classmate Frank Barlow. Twenty-four-year-old Col. Nelson Appleton Miles of Boston commanded First Brigade, First Division, Second Corps. On Apr. 12, Confederate troops under Gen. Nathan Bedford Forrest overran Ft. Pillow on the Mississippi River, defended by Tennessee "Tories" and soldiers of the 6th U.S. Heavy Artillery (Colored). More than 500 defenders were killed, including many wounded or surrendering ex-slaves and "traitorous" whites. Forrest wrote after the battle, "It is hoped that these facts will demonstrate to the Northern people that negro soldiers cannot cope with Southerners." *OR*, vol. 32, 1:610.

52. Lt. Rosenkrantz's commission had expired but would be renewed by the time of active campaigning.

53. Meade to Grant, April 17, 1864, in *OR*, vol. 33:889–90.

54. Dahlgren's signed address to his men stated: "We hope to release the prisoners from Belle Isle first, and having seen them fairly started, we will cross the James River into Richmond, destroying the bridges after us, and exhorting the released prisoners to destroy and burn the hateful city; and do not allow the rebel leader, Davis, and his traitorous crew to escape." *OR*, vol. 33:178. Kilpatrick was sent to take command of one of Sherman's cavalry divisions, and Prince (fallen from grace after Mine Run) went to garrison duty in Tennessee.

55. Col. J. Howard Kitching commanded First Brigade, Artillery Reserve, consisting of the 15th New York Heavy Artillery under Col. Louis Schirmer, and the 6th New York Heavies led by Lt. Col. Edmund R. Travis.

56. Barlow's First Division, Second Corps, comprised four brigades under Col. Nelson A. Miles, Col. Thomas A. Smyth, Col. Paul Frank, and Col. John R. Brooke. Kalapsa was a former Harvard student from Hungary.

57. Mott's ADC, Lt. William G. Thompson. Lt. Col. Michael William Burns, 73d New York Infantry (4th Excelsior Regiment). The "Bowery Boys" of Dan Sickle's Excelsior Brigade aggressively cultivated their reputation as hell-raisers and street fighters.

58. Capt. Charles Adams Jr. and Capt. Edward Austin Flint with companies C and D, 1st Massachusetts Cavalry, were assigned as HQ escort. Adams confessed that he did not want to return to his regiment after his brief sojourn in England. (See TL entry, Jan. 14, 1864.) Adams wrote: "Theodore Lyman realized my position. In my great perplexity I wrote to him, and he explained the situation to Meade. So my squadron was by special order detached from the regiment and directed to report to the Headquarters of the Army of the Potomac for escort duty. Taken altogether, it saved my army life from utter failure." Adams, *Autobiography*, 155.

59. TL's uncle George Williams Lyman. George's son, William Pratt Lyman, died of diphtheria, April 16. George's granddaughters, Olivia and Mary, died from the same cause.

60. Edward Lyulph Stanley, fourth Baron of Alderley. His father, Lord Stanley, was Postmaster-General of Britain in 1860. Meade described the baron as "quite young (only twenty-four) but highly educated, very smart and clever, and full of information." Meade, *Life and Letters*, 2:191. Stanley's CDV, autographed and dated Apr. 23, is in the MHS, Photograph Collection 94: vol. I, 92.

61. Capt. Ely Samuel Parker, civil engineer by profession, was sachem of the wolf clan of the Tonawanda Senecas of New York. Commissioned a captain of engineers, Parker would become Grant's military secretary. Maj. Gen. Nathaniel Prentiss Banks's army was defeated Apr. 8 at Mansfield, Louisiana. Despite gaining a tactical victory at Pleasant Hill three days later, Banks abandoned his Red River campaign. He was thereafter shunted out of field command.

62. Capt. William Jay. Henry A. Cram was wedded to Margaretta Meade's sister Katherine. John Cadwalader, former U.S. representative from Pennsylvania and U.S. District Court judge. Capt. Charles E. Cadwalader, Meade's ADC.

63. Gov. Dennison and Congressman James A. Garfield of Ohio visited the army, engaged Meade in an "off-the-record" discussion on the strength and condition of the AoP, and promptly returned to Washington, D.C., with "discouraging stories." Secretary of War Stanton chastised Meade for having "unguarded conversations with visitors" and revoked passes for "members of Congress or any one else not connected with the service." *OR*, vol. 60:590.

64. A Confederate division, supported by the ironclad *Albemarle*, captured the Federal enclave at Plymouth, North Carolina, on Apr. 20, 1864, taking some 2,900 prisoners. TL referred to the reported massacre of black soldiers at Ft. Pillow. Lt. Gen. James Longstreet and his First Corps rejoined the ANV after a disappointing winter

campaign in East Tennessee. Maj. Gen. Ambrose E. Burnside brought Ninth Corps, 23,000 strong, east to cooperate with the AoP in the coming campaign. Burnside's Fourth Division, Ninth Corps, comprised two brigades—six regiments of U.S. Colored Troops (USCT) and a detachment of 30th Connecticut (Colored).

65. Officers with talent or connections were habitually detailed from their regiments for staff duties. Returning these officers to their regiments was an attempt to improve combat readiness. Nate Appleton.

66. Hunt, Chief of Artillery, AoP. Col. Henry S. Burton, 5th U.S. Artillery.

67. Maj. Gen. Ambrose E. Burnside (age 39, Rhode Island, USMA 1847), former commanding general of the AoP, outranked Gen. Meade and would for a time hold semi-independent command under Grant's direction. Burnside's IG Lt. Col. Charles Greely Loring Jr. (Harvard 1848). Warren had been reading *A Manual of the Mollusca* (London, 1851) by Samuel P. Woodward.

68. Col. William Francis Bartlett (Harvard 1862) of Haverhill, Massachusetts, 57th Massachusetts Infantry, First Brigade, First Division, Ninth Corps. Burnside's division commanders for the coming campaign: Brig. Gen. Thomas Greely Stevenson (age 28, Boston, *hon. mem.* PC), First Division; Brig. Gen. Robert B. Potter (age 35, New York, lawyer), Second Division; Brig. Gen. Orlando B. Willcox (age 41, Michigan, USMA 1847), Third Division; Brig. Gen. Edward Ferrero (age 33, New York, USMA instructor), Fourth Division. Stevenson was the son of Hon. J. Thomas Stevenson, a prominent (and wealthy) Boston lawyer. Although not a Harvard boy, Stevenson attended the best prep schools in Boston and found his niche in merchant banking. He was inducted into the PC in 1860 as an honorary member. Maj. Gen. T. L. Crittenden assumed command of First Division on May 12 upon Stevenson's death; he would be relieved by his own request on June 9. Maj. Gen. John Grubb Parke (age 36, Philadelphia, USMA 1849) was assigned to Burnside's staff as CoS. Capt. Frederick Winthrop, 12th U.S. Infantry, AAG. Capt. William Willard Swan (Harvard 1859), 17th U.S. Infantry, acting AAG, Second Division, Fifth Corps, and Capt. William James Temple, 17th U.S. Infantry.

69. The manifold writer was a leather-covered dispatch book of tissue-thin sheets headed "Head Quarters, Army of the Potomac. 1864, __ o'clock __ M." with carbon paper inserts. TL's manifold writer, used in the campaign, is in the Lyman Papers MHS, bound vol. 16. The entries in TL's manifold writer provide real-time battlefield reporting but much is illegible. Harvard boys Adams and Flint.

70. TL provided a rather complete listing of the officers who would direct the AoP in the coming campaign. Some of these men have been identified but are listed together for the convenience of the reader. Maj. Gen. George Gordon Meade and his personal staff: Lt. Col. Theodore Lyman; majors James Cornell Biddle and William Riddle; captains George Meade, John Coalter Bates, Addison Gordon Mason, Charles E. Cadwalader, Francis Bache, and William Jay; and Lt. Frederick Rosenkrantz. CoS Maj. Gen. Andrew Atkins Humphreys and his personal staff: Capt. Adolphus F. Cavada, and lieutenants Henry Hollingsworth Humphreys and Henry C. Christiancy. Adj. Brig. Gen. Seth Williams and his personal staff: Maj. Simon Forrester Barstow, Capt.

Charles Elliott Pease, and Lt. Charles W. Woolsey. Chief of Artillery Brig. Gen. Henry Jackson Hunt and staff: Col. Edward Raynsford Warner, Capt. John Neville Craig, and lieutenants Carl L. Berlin, Charles T. Bissell, and William Scott Worth. Chief QM Brig. Gen. Rufus Ingalls and staff: captains William T. Howell, Luther Hills Peirce, and Henry Page. Provost Marshal Brig. Gen. Marsena Patrick and staff: Col. George Henry Sharpe (army intelligence); captains Philip Schuyler Jr., William W. Beckwith, and Henry P. Clinton. IG Col. Edmund Schriver. Chief CS Lt. Col. Thomas Wilson and asst. Capt. John Redman Coxe. Medical director Dr. Thomas Andrew McParlin and staff: surgeons James Thomas Ghiselin and Ned Dalton, and asst. surgeons Morris Joseph Asch and Thomas Grier Mackenzie. Judge advocate Maj. Edward Russell Platt. Chief engineer Maj. James Chatham Duane and staff: captains Nathaniel Michler and William Paine. CM Capt. William Wilkins Sanders. Chief of ordnance Lt. John Rufus Edie. Signal officer Capt. William S. Stryker. Of these forty-eight officers, seventeen were from Pennsylvania, twelve from New York, and five from Massachusetts.

May 3–June 16, 1864

Lyman labeled this Vol. 13a; it is assigned Lyman Papers, bound vol. 17 in the MHS.

1. The Germanna Plank Road ran from Culpeper fourteen miles southeast to cross the Rapidan River at Germanna Ford before continuing to Fredericksburg. The Orange Turnpike extended from Lee's HQ at Orange Court House twenty-one miles on a straight northeast course to intersect the Germanna Road near Wilderness Tavern. The Orange Plank Road followed a meandering course from one to three miles south of the Turnpike. The Brock Road, a north-south connector, ran from near Wilderness Church via Todd's Tavern to Spotsylvania Court House.

2. TL's summary is similar to general orders issued to the army on May 2, *OR*, vol. 36, 2:331–33.

3. Capt. Marshall Independence Ludington, asst. QM, Third Division, Cavalry Corps.

4. Heavy wooden pontoon boats were more difficult to transport but could support more weight. The lighter canvas boats were designed to collapse for transport in wagons.

5. Brig. Gen. Truman Seymour (age 39, Vermont, USMA 1846); his regiments were routed at Olustee during the Florida expedition in Dec. 1863.

6. See G.O., *OR*, vol. 36, 2:370–71.

7. Humphreys wrote: "Sheridan having received some information during the day to the effect that the main body of the enemy's cavalry was near Hamilton's Crossing [south of Fredericksburg], and suggesting that he should proceed against them, the order for movement on the 5th directed him to do so with Gregg's and Torbert's divisions." Humphreys, *Virginia Campaign*, 21. The intelligence proved outdated. Stuart was already moving by a more southerly route to take his station on the right flank of the ANV.

8. Dr. William Thorndike (Harvard 1854, PC). Ewell's Second Corps, ANV, marched on the Orange Turnpike to intercept the Federal army. Hill's Third Corps advanced in tandem with Ewell on the Orange Plank Road. Longstreet's First Corps was a day's march behind them. Gen. Lee had instructed his commanders to avoid a general engagement until Longstreet arrived on the field. Events dictated otherwise. The head of Sixth Corps turned off the Germanna Road at the Spotswood plantation onto narrow Culpeper Mine Road, which angled southeast towards the Orange Turnpike.

9. Of thirty-two cavalry regiments under Sheridan's command, only the 5th New York was in position to screen the army's advance. This unit's stubborn delaying action along the Plank Road likely saved the crucial Brock and Plank Road intersection.

10. The Lacy house, "Ellwood," served as Warren's HQ during the battle; the house has been restored within the Fredericksburg and Spotsylvania National Battlefield Park and is manned during the season by volunteer interpreters. Meade established army HQ near the intersection of the Orange Turnpike and the Germanna Plank Road, less than a half-mile from the Lacy house. Grant's tents were two hundred yards distant.

11. TL published a lengthy description of the fighting in the Wilderness "taken from my contemporaneous notes" as "Addenda to the Paper by Brevet Lieutenant-Colonel W. W. Swan, U.S.A. on the Battle of the Wilderness" in *Papers of the Military Historical Society of Massachusetts*, vol. 4. The wording of this paper and the notebooks is similar, suggesting that TL borrowed from the same contemporaneous source, which has not been discovered.

12. The intersection of the Orange Plank and Brock roads became the crisis point of the developing battle. Getty's Sixth Corps division was brought from the far right flank to plug the five-mile gap that separated Second Corps at Todd's Tavern and Fifth Corps on the Turnpike. Getty's men arrived minutes before the first Confederate skirmishers.

13. TL's Harvard classmates: Surgeon Ned Dalton, asst. medical inspector, AoP; and Col. Joe Hayes, 18th Massachusetts Infantry. TL thought at first that Hayes's wound—a deep furrow across his skull—was mortal. Dalton accompanied the trains of wounded to Fredericksburg and took charge of the depot hospital there.

14. Griffin anecdote quoted in *Meade's Headquarters*, 91n. Brig. Gen. Charles Griffin's First Division, Fifth Corps, attacked astride the Orange Turnpike across Saunders's field and shattered the advance of Ewell's Corps. A Confederate counterattack caught Griffin in a deadly crossfire and captured two guns.

15. The soldiers of Wright's First Division, Sixth Corps, expected to cover Griffin's right flank, were not yet in position. Warren recognized this difficulty and asked for time to perfect the arrangements. Grant's staff thought this an example of the timidity of the commanders of the AoP and demanded an immediate attack, which Meade ordered. Warren was threatened with dismissal if he did not attack, which he did against his better judgment. Jordan, *Happiness is not my Companion*, 132.

16. Maj. Charles Mundee, AAG, Second Corps. Maj. William G. Mitchell, Hancock's ADC.

17. Col. Samuel Sprigg Carroll was lightly wounded. "While [Brig. Gen. Alexander Hays] was speaking a kindly word," recalled Morris Schaff, "a bullet struck him just above the cord of his hat, crashing into his brain." Schaff, *Battle of the Wilderness*, 186.

18. TL's dispatches to HQ from Hancock's front in *OR*, vol. 36, 2:410–11. Wilson's cavalry division was supposed to be minding the left flank of Second Corps.

19. The officer corps of the AoP nursed animosity against Burnside, stemming from his less than stellar stint as army commander.

20. Capt. Charles Gordon Hutton, Burnside's ADC. This incident, as TL pointed out, revealed a flaw in the chain of command—Ninth Corps being under the direct orders of Grant. Meade was unwilling to assert himself to facilitate Burnside's march, which, considering all that hinged on celerity of movement, seems a clear failing on Meade's part.

21. TL's reports from Hancock's front in *OR*, vol. 36, 2:440, 442–46.

22. Getty reported that "Capt. Hazard Stevens received a wound on the 6th, and had his horse killed under him. Lieut. John Faxon, aide-de-camp, was also severely wounded." *OR*, vol. 36, 1:678. Getty would recover from his wound and return to the army. Wheaton temporarily commanded Getty's division, which was then handed over to Brig. Gen. Thomas Neill.

23. Bostonians Thomas Greely Stevenson; 1st Lt. Charles James "Charlie" Mills (Harvard 1860); and Lt. Col. Stephen Minot "Stevie" Weld Jr. (Harvard 1860), 56th Massachusetts Infantry. Weld published his wartime writings in 1912 as *War Diary and Letters of Stephen Minot Weld, 1861–1865*. Weld's father, an overseer of Harvard University, was PC (1826).

24. TL reported at 8:40 a.m.: "Two squads of prisoners from Longstreet have been recently taken." *OR*, vol. 36, 2:442. Hancock's dawn attack routed A. P. Hill's divisions, driving them in confusion back into a clearing at the Widow Tapp farm. The advance of Longstreet's First Corps reached the field at that moment and counterattacked. The Federals, disorganized and disoriented in the thicket, could not stand against these newly deployed formations. Everyone in the army was anticipating the arrival of Longstreet's corps on the battlefield. For several critical hours, the only cavalrymen patrolling Hancock's left flank were wearing gray. Uncertainty prevented Federal occupation of the unfinished railroad cut, which Longstreet afterward exploited.

25. Col. George Macy eventually returned to duty. Maj. Henry Livermore Abbott. Maj. A. W. Angel, 5th New Jersey Infantry, Second Corps topographical engineer. Maj. John Mason Norvell had been on French's staff and transferred to staff of Third Division, Second Corps, during the March reorganization.

26. Four Confederate brigades filed in along the unfinished railroad cut faced left, and lurched into the Federal left, driving all before them. The Confederates, in their turn, were disorganized by success. Attempting to renew the attack, Lt. Gen. James Longstreet was wounded by his own men. Maj. Gen. Richard H. Anderson assumed command of First Corps, ANV.

27. Lt. Col. Weld assumed command of the regiment when Col. Charles E. Griswold was shot dead through the neck. Weld, *War Diary*, 286. Col. William Bartlett. The "raw veterans" were a brigade of six regiments of mixed experience. The 56th, 57th, and 59th Massachusetts Infantry had not seen combat and suffered most of the brigade's 470 casualties.

28. Burnside's "slowness" may be attributed in part to the terrain. The Plank Road and the Turnpike followed relatively high, rolling ground. Between these roads where Burnside was sent, there was an abrupt ravine ninety-feet deep footed by a swampy fork of Wilderness Run. Today, one can stand in a narrow strip of parkland that overlooks the terrain and, despite the subdivision, landscaping, and water impoundments, appreciate the obstacles that impeded Burnside's attack. Grant's engineer Comstock, who accompanied Burnside, should have reported these difficulties to HQ.

29. Hancock anecdote in *Meade's Headquarters*, 96. The Ninth Corps was stopped by Confederate infantry and artillery deployed on the Chewning farm, two miles in advance of Parker's Store. Col. Daniel Leasure commanded Stevenson's "other" brigade (Second Brigade, First Division, Ninth Corps).

30. See TL notebook entry for July 7, 1865.

31. Capt. Emmor B. Cope, topographical engineer and Warren's ADC. Controversy raged for decades among veterans of Birney's division, Second Corps, Getty's division, Sixth Corps, and Wadsworth's division, Fifth Corps. A review of casualties would suggest that all of these units were heavily engaged at various times throughout the day.

32. TL's letter to Mimi describing Abbott's death spared her the more gruesome details. *Meade's Headquarters*, 97.

33. Maj. John Hancock, AAG, First Division, Second Corps. Gen. Lee organized the final Confederate assault of the day, which temporarily breached the Federal breastwork thrown up along Brock Road. Hancock's staff officers had returned the lines to some order, and the attack was repulsed. Capt. William Wilkins Sanders, acting ADC.

34. Sedgwick's IG, Lt. Col. Jacob Ford Kent, and ADC Capt. Eugene Beauharnais Beaumont, 4th U.S. Cavalry.

35. At dusk, three brigades of Jubal Early's division attacked the exposed right flank of Sixth Corps and stampeded Seymour's "Weary Boys" along with much of Ricketts's division. Seymour's bad luck continued. Captured with him was Brig. Gen. Alexander Shaler (age 37, Connecticut), commanding Fourth Brigade, First Division, Sixth Corps. TL confused division commander Edward "Allegheny" Johnson (not engaged) with brigadier Robert D. Johnston. The "bloodless" 93d New York Infantry lost 260 officers and men in the fighting on the Plank Road; their brigadier, Alexander "Alick" Hays, was killed.

36. Col. Francis A. Walker, Hancock's CoS. Grant's patron Congressman Elihu B. Washburne of Illinois. Grant's comment on Joseph Johnston quoted in *Meade's Headquarters*, 102. The cavalry clashed near Todd's Tavern on the Brock and Catharpin roads.

37. Ferrero's Fourth Division, Ninth Corps. This was the first time in the war that colored regiments were aggregated into a division, an experiment that made many observers uncomfortable.

38. Capt. Augustus P. Martin, 3d Battery Massachusetts Light Artillery.

39. Asst. Secretary of War Charles Anderson Dana of Boston (Harvard 1843), formerly a correspondent for the *New York Tribune*, sent regular dispatches to Secretary of War Stanton, assessing developments at the front. Dana accompanied Grant throughout the Vicksburg campaign and would remain at HQ through the Virginia

campaign of 1864. Dana had been an instructor of Latin and German at the transcendental Brook Farm Institute in West Roxbury.

40. Meade ordered the arrest of Col. Samuel J. Crooks, 22d New York Cavalry. Maj. Peter McLennan replaced him. *OR*, vol. 36, 2:509.

41. Maj. Gen. Benjamin Butler's thrust up James River toward Richmond and Petersburg was anticipated to play a crucial role in Grant's design for the spring 1864 campaign. In theory, Butler's occupation of City Point at the confluence of the James and Appomattox rivers would force Gen. Lee to detach troops to defend Richmond. Pres. Jefferson Davis instead brought up reinforcements on the railroad from the Carolinas.

42. J. E. B. Stuart's troopers sparred with Sheridan over the intersection of the Brock and Catharpin roads at Todd's Tavern. Fitzhugh Lee withdrew a mile south of the tavern on the Brock Road, covering the direct road to Spotsylvania Court House, leaving Wade Hampton's division astride the Catharpin Road to the west. Sheridan retained control of Todd's Tavern—crucial for the AoP's next advance.

43. Orders issued by Meade's AAG, Seth Williams, May 7, at 3 p.m. *OR*, vol. 36, 2:483–84.

44. Grant quoted in *Meade's Headquarters*, 102.

45. The site of Todd's Tavern (intersection of rtes. 612 and 613) is today preserved and interpreted.

46. Capt. J. P. Ash, 5th U.S. Cavalry. Capt. Emlen E. Carpenter, 6th Pennsylvania Cavalry. Sheridan would afterward claim that Patrick's provost guard, not Custer, delayed the march.

47. Piney Branch Church was three miles east of Todd's Tavern at modern Paynes Store. From Todd's, the Brock or Todd's Tavern Road (the main route of advance) continued three miles farther southeast, where the road split to cross the Alsop farm. The forks rejoined a mile north of Spotsylvania Court House. Modern Brock Road (Rte. 613) follows the western fork of the road; the eastern fork is a farm lane that passes the antebellum house site. Alsop's was a prominent location mentioned in many Federal accounts of the battle.

48. Maj. James H. Starr would recover. Brig. Gen. John Cleveland Robinson (age 47, New York, attended USMA 1835), Second Division, Fifth Corps.

49. Sheridan incident in *Meade's Headquarters*, 105–6. Lyman either did not witness or else glossed over the importance of this meeting. Sheridan reportedly claimed he could "whip" the Confederate cavalry if given the chance. According to Horace Porter, Grant told Meade that Sheridan "generally knows what he is talking about. Let him start right out and do it." Porter, *Campaigning with Grant*, 83–84; Sheridan, *Personal Memoirs*, 200. From the beginning, Sheridan viewed his cavalry corps as a semi-autonomous command. Provost marshal Patrick noted in his diary that a raid on Richmond was contemplated as early as May 3. If true, Sheridan was chafing for the raid to begin. Sheridan left at dawn, May 9, taking all three of his divisions, nearly 10,000 troopers. This decision left the AoP with little cavalry support for nearly two weeks.

50. Catharpin Road ran west from Todd's Tavern then southerly to cross the Po River at Corbin's Bridge.

51. The J. C. and T. Hart houses stood about two miles southeast of Todd's Tavern.

52. Brig. Gen. Neill's nickname "Bean" likely derived from his stint at Harvard.

53. Capt. Augustus P. Martin. Warren reported that Lt. Col. Frederick T. Locke was "badly wounded in the face." OR, vol. 36, 2:540–41.

54. Chief engineer Duane.

55. Warren and Sedgwick continued to exercise caution in direction of their corps with some justification. Charles Dana reported from Grant's headquarters on May 9 that "General Hobart Ward is under arrest for running away in the Wilderness battle." OR, vol. 36, 1:65.

56. Schriver, Meade's IG.

57. The "Gate" (evidently little more than a barred opening into a field) was three miles northeast of Spotsylvania Court House on the Fredericksburg, Court House, or "Gate" Road (modern Rte. 208).

58. Brig. Gen. John C. Robinson lost the leg; his division was subsequently broken up, its brigades redistributed within Fifth Corps.

59. Sedgwick's CoS Lt. Col. Martin Thomas McMahon. Ricketts (Third Division) outranked Wright, but his troops had not performed well thus far in the campaign. Brig. Gen. David Allen Russell (age 43, New York, USMA 1845) replaced Wright commanding First Division, Sixth Corps.

60. Brig. Gen. William Hopkins Morris. Butler entrenched his AoJ at Bermuda Hundred and probed westward to cut the Richmond & Petersburg RR.

61. A sharpshooter, reputedly firing a .45-caliber English Whitfield rifle fitted with a telescopic sight, struck Sedgwick below the left eye from about 800 yards.

62. Likely asst. surgeon Jeremiah Bernard Brinton, medical purveyor, AoP. Maj. Charles Albert Whittier of Boston, Sedgwick's ADC, escorted his general's body back to Cornwall Hollow, Connecticut, for burial.

63. Sherman's army group maneuvered Johnston's Army of Tennessee out of its heavily entrenched position at Dalton, Georgia, after fighting on Rocky Face Ridge on May 9. Butler fought an inconclusive engagement at Swift Creek, north of Petersburg, on the same day.

64. TL's honorary PC brother Brig. Gen. Thomas Greely Stevenson. Stevie Weld noted in his diary: "We all of us felt dreadfully today on account of Tom Stevenson's death. Was with him when he died. Had some of my men make a coffin for him." Weld, War Diary, 290. Col. Leasure temporarily assumed command of Stevenson's division. The Brown house (Mott's and afterward Hancock's headquarters) stood one and three-fourths miles east of Alsop's. From Brown's fields, a two-hundred-yard-wide corridor opened through the woods to the "Landron" or Landrum farm beyond, which was the Confederate position dubbed the "Salient" or "Mule Shoe." The range from Landrum's to Brown's was nearly 1,000 yards.

65. Lt. Col. Kent, IG, and surgeon Silas Atherton Holman, medical director, Sixth Corps.

66. Hancock initially put three divisions—Barlow, Birney, and Gibbon—south of the Po River to probe for a weakness in the Confederate left flank. Finding no

favorable point for attack, he ordered the troops withdrawn with Barlow acting as rear guard. Heth's division attacked Barlow in the vicinity of Waite's Shop, and Heth considered the action a "considerable victory." Humphreys, *Virginia Campaign*, 80–81. The smoothbore twelve-pound Napoleon had less range and accuracy than the three-inch ordnance rifle, thus the artillerists' amusement.

67. Col. Emory Upton (age 24, New York, USMA 1861) led a column of assault, consisting of twelve handpicked regiments, against a portion of the Confederate line called "Dole's Salient." The 121st Pennsylvania Infantry, Capt. William W. Dorr's regiment, spearheaded the attack; Dorr was killed. Upton's breakthrough was temporary, as he received no support. Mott, on Upton's left, seemed paralyzed by conflicting directives—to support an attack, while simultaneously reaching out a mile and a half to connect with Burnside. He tried to do both and accomplished neither. Warren's and Hancock's attacks on the right went in late and were repulsed.

68. Congressman Washburne. Burnside's Ninth Corps, still under Grant's direct command, had entrenched in a semicircle astride the Fredericksburg (or Court House) Road with both flanks anchored on Ni River. With no cavalry to cover flank and rear, Burnside was in a precarious position.

69. Criticism of Warren quoted in *Meade's Headquarters*, 110. Beaverdam Station, a depot on the Virginia Central RR, about thirty-five miles northwest of Richmond. Brig. Gen. James Clay Rice from Massachusetts.

70. Ashland Station, a depot on the Richmond, Fredericksburg & Potomac RR (R.F. & P. RR), fifteen miles north of Richmond; Yellow Tavern, on the Telegraph Road, barely eight miles outside the city. Maj. Gen. James Ewell Brown Stuart (USMA 1854) was mortally wounded and died in Richmond on May 12. A stone monument in a residential neighborhood near the site of the Yellow Tavern marks the location of the battle and of Stuart's wounding. This quarter-acre lot is all that remains of the battlefield.

71. TL persisted in calling Kitching "Kitchen."

72. Rawlins died of consumption in 1869.

73. Maj. Gen. Edward "Allegheny" Johnson, commanding a division in Ewell's Second Corps, ANV and one of his brigadiers, George H. "Maryland" Steuart.

74. Explosive bullets, filled with a fulminate that exploded on contact, were available to the Confederacy in limited quantities. Many reports during the war of the use of such bullets were spurious, but in this case it appeared that sharpshooters were attempting to detonate the artillery's ammunition chests. Wright's ADC, Capt. Arthur McClellan.

75. Col. Charles H. Tompkins, 1st Rhode Island Light Artillery, chief of artillery, Sixth Corps. Lt. Robert L. Sawin, 1st Battery Massachusetts Light Artillery.

76. The Mrs. Armstrong house, on what is today called Gordon Road, is a private residence.

77. The Landrum house ruin is preserved within the battlefield park. As TL reported, there is an entrenched position for a battery in the edge of the woods just west of the house site.

78. "Death-angle" passage, abridged, quoted in *Meade's Headquarters*, 113–14. The struggle here constituted the longest, most concentrated firefight of the Civil War. Union

soldiers, lying in some places forty ranks deep outside the captured entrenchments, loaded muskets and passed them to the front for firing. The toppled oak tells but part of the story. When TL returned to the site in 1866, he observed that the "background of oaks" were all dead—killed by "girding" by bullets and probably lead poisoning.

79. Lt. Col. Waldo Merriam of Boston. Brig. Gen. Alexander Webb would return to duty as Meade's CoS in Jan. 1865. Birney's ADC, Capt. Joseph C. Briscoe. Maj. Charles Mundee, AAG, Second Corps. Capt. Henry Harrison Bingham, judge advocate, Second Corps, shot in the thigh. *OR*, vol. 36, 3:295.

80. Lee's new front, built to cut off the base of the salient, was the work of chief engineer Martin Luther Smith, the architect of Vicksburg's fortifications. Upon a return visit to the field in 1866, TL wrote: "The high parapet was not only traversed as often as every 10 or 12 feet, but was enclosed in the rear, so that the line was divided into a series of squared pens, with banks of earth heavily revetted with oak logs. From space to space was what looked like a wooden camp chimney, but in truth an elevated post for sharpshooters, with a little loop-hole in front. I never saw any like them." Entry for Apr. 15, 1866. Lyman Papers MHS, bound vol. 21. The earthen portion of these entrenchments is preserved within the battlefield park.

81. Meade: "Soldiers, your work is not over, the enemy must be pursued, and, if possible, overcome. The courage and fortitude you have displayed renders your commanding general confident your future efforts will result in success. While we mourn the loss of many gallant comrades, let us remember the enemy must have suffered equal, if not greater, losses. We shall soon receive re-enforcements which he cannot expect." *OR*, vol. 36, 1:197.

82. Stanton to Meade, May 13: "This Department congratulates you and your heroic army, and returns its cordial thanks for their gallant achievements during the last seven days, and hopes that the valor and skill thus far manifested will be crowned with the fruits of ultimate and decisive victory." *OR*, vol. 36, 2:654. Grant to Stanton, May 13: "General Meade has more than met my most sanguine expectations. He and Sherman are the fittest officers for large commands I have come in contact with. If their services can be rewarded by promotion to the rank of major-generals in the regular army the honor would be worthily bestowed, and I would feel personally gratified. I would not like to see one of these promotions at this time without seeing both." *OR*, vol. 36, 2:695. Earlier in the day, Grant believed that Lee was withdrawing from Spotsylvania, but a reconnaissance-in-force convinced him otherwise. It was then decided to attempt another flank march and surprise dawn attack against Lee's right. Order of March issued May 13, 5:45 P.M., *OR*, vol. 36, 2:700.

83. The road followed by Fifth Corps was a simple farm lane leading from the Landrum house, across the Ny River by a difficult ford to the Stevens farm, then south to join the Courthouse Road. The S. Beverly house is today a private residence and working farm. None of the battlefield south of Courthouse Road is within the battlefield park. The surroundings are populated by subdivisions with names like "Gunnery Hills Estates" and "Battle Park Lakes."

84. Likely regular army surgeon Samuel Adams, medical inspector, Ninth Corps.

85. The Addison account read by TL appeared in Samuel Johnson, *The Lives of the Most Eminent English Poets* (1793), vol. 2. The Harris farm, focus of Ewell's assault on May 19, is a private residence and (for the moment) a working farm.

86. Secretary Stanton to Grant, May 14: "General Wright was nominated two days ago, and confirmed by the Senate for major-general. General Humphreys, General Schofield, General Wilson, and all before the Senate have been confirmed, except General Carr, whose nomination was not acted upon." *OR*, vol. 36, 2:746.

87. "Culpeper" regained her strength. The roan, "Petersburg," proved a durable animal and survived the war.

88. The Anderson house is a private residence near the end of Leavells Road (Rte. 639), overlooking Ny River.

89. Brig. Gen. Samuel Sprigg Carroll returned to duty in Dec., assigned to the Department of West Virginia. TL's friend Capt. Montgomery Ritchie was Wadsworth's son-in-law. Ritchie retrieved the general's body from the surgeon and accompanied it to Boston after which he resigned his commission. Ritchie died of disease contracted in the service in Nov. 1864.

90. Withdrawing from his Richmond raid, Sheridan reached Haxall's Landing on James River and replenished his stores from Butler's depot. Maj. Gen. Butler, in his advance on Richmond, scored a temporary success at Wooldridge Hill on May 13, driving Confederate defenders from an outer line of earthworks. Sherman forced Gen. Joseph Johnston to retreat south of the Oostanaula River after three days of fighting at Resaca, Georgia, May 13–15.

91. William Sprague, governor of Rhode Island from 1859 until 1863 when elected U.S. Senator. Senator John Sherman of Ohio, brother and patron of Gen. William Tecumseh Sherman. Baker not identified. Chief medical officer Dr. Thomas A. McParlin.

92. Special Orders No. 136: "Each six-gun battery in this army, except the Horse Artillery and Taft's New York Independent Battery, will at once be reduced to four guns, retaining all its caissons." Batteries in the Reserve were assigned to artillery brigades within the army. *OR*, vol. 36, 2:813. Fewer guns meant fewer horses and a reduction in feed and forage requirements. Thus far in the campaign, the Reserve Artillery had been excess baggage. Col. Henry S. Burton, 5th U.S. Artillery, joined Meade's staff as inspector of artillery. *OR*, vol. 36, 2:843.

93. Maj. Gen. Crittenden had remained with the army since the start of the campaign, awaiting a command commensurate with his rank.

94. Lt. Col. Samuel E. Chamberlain, 1st Massachusetts Cavalry. Brig. Gen. Robert Ogden Tyler, Fourth Brigade, Second Division, Second Corps. Col. James Powers McMahon, 164th New York Infantry.

95. Sigel's forces were defeated in the Shenandoah Valley at the battle of New Market, May 15. A column commanded by Gen. George Crook penetrated southwest Virginia and severed the Virginia & Tennessee RR after a severe fight at Cloyd's Mountain. Butler's AoJ, 25,000 strong, probed north from its Bermuda Hundred

enclave to threaten Richmond. Beauregard, with about 18,000 troops drawn from the Carolinas and Richmond's defenses, attacked on May 16 at Proctor's Creek near Ft. Darling and drove the Federals back into their fortifications.

96. Capt. Arthur Russell Curtis and asst. surgeon John G. Perry, 20th Massachusetts Infantry. Curtis would return to duty as a lieutenant colonel in June. "Keltzer," likely Capt. John Kelliher of Bridgewater. Kelliher "had been struck by a shell and fearfully mangled.... His arm and shoulder blade had been torn off, three of his ribs displaced, and his jaw broken in several places." Bruce, *Twentieth Regiment Massachusetts*, 384.

97. In the brief report, delivered by Kingsbury, Sheridan stated, "If I could be permitted to cross the James River and go southward I could almost ruin the Confederacy." *OR*, vol. 36, 1:778. Sheridan had a vision of the weakness of the Confederacy but felt little responsibility toward the army that sustained him. Capt. Carswell McClellan, formerly Humphreys's ADC, was serving on Torbert's staff.

98. Guinea Station, a depot on the R. F. & P. RR fifteen miles south of Fredericksburg.

99. Washington A. Roebling. "Ryan" may have been Irishman Patrick Hart, whose 15th Battery, New York Light, was ordered into action about the time TL rode forward.

100. Confederate Lt. Gen. Richard Ewell led his depleted Second Corps on a turning movement against the right flank of the Federal army. Ewell had been forced to leave his artillery behind by the condition of the roads, and the attacks at the Harris farm were poorly coordinated. The story of negro troops repulsing the attack appears to have been conflated with a skirmish at the Aldrich farm, about five miles north. Humphreys, *Virginia Campaign*, 115n. The 1st Massachusetts Heavy Artillery lost nearly 400 casualties of 1,600 engaged; the 1st Maine Heavies suffered 524 casualties of 1,800 engaged. The 1st Massachusetts erected their monument near the Harris house, where a small plot of land is preserved and interpreted in the midst of a modern subdivision.

101. Confederate generals Braxton Bragg and Joseph Johnston.

102. TL to Mimi: "People must learn that war is a thing of life or death: if a man won't go to the front he must be shot; but our people can't make up their minds to it; it is repulsive to the forms of thought, even of most of the officers, who willingly expose their own lives, but will shrink from shooting down a skulker." *Meade's Headquarters*, 117.

103. Maj. William Cutting from New York, Burnside's ADC and TL's honorary PC brother. *Harper's* special artist Alfred Waud. Judge Josiah Abbott of Lowell, father of Henry Livermore Abbott, killed at the Wilderness. Grant and Meade had determined to cut loose Hancock's Second Corps a day's march from the army—to steal a flank march on Lee and perhaps to entice the ANV into open combat. Hancock was to march along the north bank of the Mattoponi River to Bowling Green and thence to Milford Station. *OR*, vol. 36, 2:910.

104. Photographer Timothy O'Sullivan captured a series of three images of Grant and Meade and their staff officers in the Massaponax churchyard, described in Frassanito, *Grant and Lee*, 116–22. In all three images, TL is seated next to Meade on the church pew, his six-foot-two-inch frame and stylish hat unmistakable. Massaponax Church has an active congregation in the original building, eight miles south of Fredericksburg on Telegraph Road (U.S. Rte. 1).

105. The site of Guinea Station on the R. F. & P. RR and the "house where Jackson died" are included as a unit within the Fredericksburg and Spotsylvania National Battlefield Park, anachronistically dubbed the "Stonewall Jackson Shrine."

106. Col. Charles H. T. Collis, commanding 68th and 114th Pennsylvania Infantry, assigned to army provost guard. Capt. Charles N. Turnbull, Co. D, Engineer Battalion. As elsewhere noted, Charlie Adams commanded a detachment of the 1st Massachusetts Cavalry that served as headquarters escort.

107. Gen. Meade was anxious for the return of his son, Capt. George Meade.

108. Adj. Seth Williams's orders for May 22 in *OR*, vol. 36, 3:80. Williams had it correctly as Harris's "Store" rather than "Station." Meade quoted in *Meade's Headquarters*, 118. Lee directed the ANV south from Spotsylvania, east to Mud Tavern (Thornburg), then south on the Telegraph Road (U.S. Rte. 1) to concentrate behind the North Anna River ahead of the Federal flanking columns. Meade had several opportunities to intercept Lee's line of march but was blinded by the lack of cavalry intelligence.

109. Army HQ were established at Bethel Church (built in 1858), which stands today at the hamlet of Paige, five miles west of Bowling Green.

110. Confederate major general Robert Hoke's division from North Carolina helped defeat Butler's army on May 16 at Proctor's Creek. Hoke reinforced Lee at Cold Harbor, June 1.

111. In a diary entry for May 22, Provost Marshal Patrick reported, "We had a time . . . in overhauling marauders & house plunderers. I went to Meade, who told me he was unable to help me, that Grant had expressed himself strongly against protecting these people at all, and I learned that his staff were themselves engaged in sheep stealing, fowl stealing and the like." Sparks, *Inside Lincoln's Army*, 375. Patrick opposed looting because of its debilitating effects on army discipline (although in this case his own scouts were implicated).

112. Capt. Thomas Lawrence Motley, 1st Massachusetts Cavalry, nephew of diplomat John Lothrop Motley and friend of Henry Lee Higginson. Description of Burnside in *Meade's Headquarters*, 149.

113. Maj. James St. Clair Morton (age 34, Philadelphia, USMA 1851), regular army engineer, assigned chief engineer of Ninth Corps on May 18; his father, Dr. Samuel George Morton, measured skulls from various nations to demonstrate that Caucasians were more intelligent than Asians, American Indians, or Africans and proposed a theory of polygenesis—that God created each race separately.

114. Polecat Creek, eight miles south of Bethel Church. Riddle and Mason, ADCs, and Paine, topographical engineer.

115. Moncure Corner is just south of Polecat Creek on the old stage road (Rte. 652).

116. Warren's Fifth Corps crossed the River at Jericho Mills on pontoons four miles upstream from the Telegraph Road crossing. Wilcox's Division of A. P. Hill's Third Corps assaulted Warren on the Fontaine farm and routed Cutler's division. Warren stabilized his lines with artillery and repulsed the attack. The Sixth Corps moved in support to Quarles Mill, a mile downstream from Jericho Mills, but did not cross the river until morning. A brigade of Hancock's Second Corps advanced astride the Telegraph Road and the R. F. & P. RR, forced back skirmishers, and overran an entrenched

tête-de-pont to capture the Chesterfield Bridge intact. (The Confederate earthwork survives on private property.) The railroad bridge was burned. Burnside and his Ninth Corps moved to Ox Ford, halfway between Quarles Mill and Chesterfield Bridge, but was surprised to find the crossing there held in force. Brig. Gen. Lysander Cutler (age 57, Massachusetts and Wisconsin) commanded the Iron Brigade at Gettysburg and, as ranking brigadier, rose to command Fourth Division, Fifth Corps, after Gen. Wadsworth was killed in the Wilderness.

117. Mt. Carmel Church, four miles north of North Anna River. The brick church is in use today as a Christian academy. Lt. Col. Briscoe G. Baldwin, chief of ordnance, ANV.

118. The cipher dispatch does not appear in the *OR*, but Sherman expressed a similar opinion to Secretary of War Stanton on May 23. Sherman to Stanton, *OR* vol. 38, 4:294. Grant had expressed no dissatisfaction with Meade or with the AoP's performance. On May 20, Grant telegraphed Halleck: "About one week ago, I recommended Generals Sherman and Meade for promotion to major-generals in the Regular Army. . . . I wish you would urge this again." *OR*, vol. 36, 3:4. Having witnessed more than 30,000 of his soldiers rendered *hors de combat* within two weeks, Meade's outrage seems justifiable. If one compares casualties alone, Sherman's men were having an easy time of it.

119. Torbert's ADC, Craig W. Wadsworth. Sheridan's cavalry were en route to the AoP.

120. The attack was directed by Brig. Gen. James Hewitt Ledlie (age 32, New York, civil engineer), First Brigade, First Division, Ninth Corps. Lt. Col. Stevie Weld wrote: "General Ledlie made a botch of it. Had too much ____ on board, I think." Weld, *War Diary*, 296–97. Hanover County preserves a segment of the Confederate lines, which includes the focal point of Ledlie's assault.

121. Special Orders No. 25: "To secure the greatest attainable unanimity in co-operative movements, and greater efficiency in the administration of the army, the Ninth Army Corps, Maj. Gen. A. E. Burnside commanding, is assigned to the Army of the Potomac, Maj. Gen. G. G. Meade commanding, and will report accordingly. By command of lieutenant-general Grant." *OR*, vol. 36, 3:169. This order was a vote of confidence in Meade's skills and an acknowledgment that Grant's staff were not up to the task of coordinating a detached corps involved in combined operations.

122. The Virginia Central RR ran from the Shenandoah Valley via Gordonsville to Richmond, crossing the R.F. & P. RR at Hanover Junction (modern Doswell).

123. Maj. William H. Long, AAG, Third Brigade, Second Division, Sixth Corps. A "sangler" was a minstrel. The E. Anderson house stood south of modern Verdon Road about one mile east of the hamlet of Noel.

124. Capt. Thomas C. Case, ADC.

125. Weld wrote: "I was turning, calling some of my men back at the moment the volley was fired, and got a bullet through my coat that scratched my side for about three inches and drew blood and raised an enormous welt, from which I was sore for a week or ten days. . . . At the moment I was hit it felt like a red-hot iron on my side." Weld, *War Diary*, 297.

126. Criticism of Warren quoted in *Meade's Headquarters*, 146. Artillerists during the Civil War generally were limited by the need to see their targets. Warren was at-

tempting to deliver indirect fire (to strike unseen targets) by using artillery spotters, a useful concept that was not fully developed until World War I. Capt. Julius W. Mason, commanding Cos. B, F, and K, 5th U.S. Cavalry, brother of ADC Addison Mason.

127. The Telegraph Road (U.S. Rte. 1) becomes Brook Pike as it approaches Richmond. Sheridan's corps returned to the AoP from its Richmond raid after being detached from the army for more than two weeks.

128. Lt. Col. Charles G. Loring, IG, Ninth Corps. Capt. Duncan A. Pell, Burnside's ADC. Chesterfield Station on the R. F. & P. RR, about two miles north of the North Anna.

129. By holding fast a salient angle at Ox Ford and withdrawing both wings of his army from the North Anna, Gen. Lee effectively split the AoP into three parts, the right and left wings separated by a five-mile march and two river crossings. Once the strength of Lee's position became apparent, Grant and Meade had little choice but to disengage and attempt another flanking march.

130. The army's AAG, Seth Williams, issued the orders for movement at 10 A.M., May 26. *OR*, vol. 36, 3:211.

131. Burnside's telegram: "My information as to the position of the troops is necessarily obtained from officers in charge of the movement, and deem it quite as reliable as that received by the commanding general from like sources until the certainty is established. I am not in the habit of making reports inconsistent with the facts of the case, and cannot permit any person to make such insinuations." *OR*, vol. 36, 3:256–57.

132. Sheridan reported: "My total loss in horses will not exceed 400, including killed in battle and abandoned on the road shot." *OR*, vol. 36, 1:781. This was likely an understatement. Dr. McParlin's report: "The Cavalry Corps had by this time returned from the Richmond expedition, and two divisions moved in advance. A large number of the horses had become so much exhausted as to die on the road, along which they were scattered at tolerably regular intervals of from 50 to 100 yards, and the infantry following had the full benefit of the results of their putrefaction." *OR*, vol. 36, 1:242.

133. Col. George H. Sharpe, Bureau of Military Intelligence.

134. Mangohick Church, built in 1732, has an active, preservation-minded congregation. The severity of Grant's migraines is generally understated in the sources.

135. The Nelson Ford Road (county Rte. 615) continues south of the Pamunkey to Haw's Shop (modern Studley). The imposing Nelson house, "Wyoming," overlooks the ford from the north bank. It is today a private residence, occupied by descendents of the Nelson family.

136. Raccoon Ford on the Rapidan, Sept. 13, 1863. Correspondent Charles Carleton Coffin of the *Boston Journal*. The Mrs. Newton house "Summerhill" stands north of Summer Hill Road (Rte. 644) about one and one half miles west of the Pamunkey. Mrs. Brockenbrough's house survives south of the road. Both are private residences. For those interested in pursuing Confederate iconography (with permission), William Latane is buried in the Newton family cemetery.

137. Lt. James I. Christiancy, Custer's ADC. Capt. Craig W. Wadsworth. The stubborn fight at Haw's Shop or Enon Church, May 29, pitted Gregg's and Torbert's cavalry

divisions against the divisions of Wade Hampton and William Henry Fitzhugh Lee and resulted in 800–900 casualties. The troopers of both sides primarily fought on foot from behind barricades and hasty entrenchments. For the first time in the campaign Sheridan was operating closely with Meade and the AoP, screening the advance of the army, protecting its flanks, seizing vital intersections and river crossings, and providing intelligence to headquarters. The fighting at Haw's Shop and Old Church (May 30), and Hanover Court House and Old Cold Harbor (May 31), suggest how the campaign might have developed had Sheridan cooperated consistently with the AoP. TL's Porcellian Club brother was William Henry Fitzhugh "Rooney" Lee.

138. Totopotomoy Creek, a swampy tributary of the Pamunkey River. "Tolopotomoy" was a common misspelling on Federal maps, perhaps deriving from the Tidewater Virginia dialect, which tends to swallow consonants. Dr. Pollard's is a private residence off Gould Hill Road (Rte. 645).

139. Five roads intersected at Salem Church or Haw's Shop, giving the location strategic value in the Federal advance south of the Pamunkey River.

140. After withdrawing from North Anna, Lee's ANV marched south on the Telegraph Road to interpose between the AoP and Richmond. The Confederate army entrenched a strong line south of Totopotomoy Creek in fewer than twenty-four hours.

141. TL's PC brother, Capt. Wendell Holmes Jr., now served as Wright's ADC.

142. Aenon, Enon, or Ena Church stood one mile west of Salem Church, which still stands. The Haw's Shop battlefield, for the moment, is pristine. Frank Barlow's younger brother, Richard D. Barlow.

143. Charles Dana to Edwin M. Stanton, May 30: "Very serious mismanagement exists in the affairs of the Ninth Army Corps. The quartermaster's and commissary departments and the artillery alike suffer for want of necessary administrative authority. Animals are without forage and men without rations. It was today ascertained that the artillery horses of the whole corps have not had their harness taken off for the last nine days. . . . General Meade has today appointed Lieutenant-Colonel [J. Albert] Monroe to serve temporarily as chief of artillery for the corps." *OR*, vol. 36, 1:83. The corps had been without an artillery chief since the wounding of Lt. S. N. Benjamin, 2d U.S. Artillery, at Spotsylvania.

144. Longstreet's wounding placed First Corps ANV in the hands of Richard H. Anderson on May 6. From May 8 until May 21, Lt. Gen. A. P. Hill was confined to an ambulance and unable to direct his Third Corps. Lee replaced him temporarily with Maj. Gen. Jubal A. Early. Lt. Gen. Richard Ewell broke down under the rigors of the campaign, and Lee assigned Early to permanent command of Ewell's Second Corps on May 29. In his first foray as corps commander, Early assaulted Warren's Fifth Corps with two of his divisions near Bethesda Church. Despite some initial success, the offensive was stopped at the Shady Grove Road. Warren lost 750 men in the fight; Early suffered more than 1,100 casualties and did not noticeably delay the Federal movement. The battleground today is largely occupied by housing subdivisions.

145. Grant detached Eighteenth Corps from Butler's command at Bermuda Hundred and directed it to White House Landing on the Pamunkey River as reinforcement for

the AoP. Grant brought regular army engineer William Farrar "Baldy" Smith east to command Eighteenth Corps, AoJ. On May 30, Smith's three divisions, numbering about 12,500 men, began to disembark from transports at White House Landing. The 24-pound coehorn mortar lobbed its shell in a high trajectory into the opposing trenches. Weighing but 165 pounds, it could be readily shifted from place to place by a crew of four.

146. Brig. Gen. John Joseph Abercrombie (age 66, Maryland, USMA 1822) coordinated campaign logistics for the AoP, at Aquia, Belle Plain, and Fredericksburg. On May 22, Abercrombie was ordered to break up the supply depot and hospital complex and reestablish it at Port Royal on the Rappahannock. On May 28, he was directed to move the depot to White House Landing. The massive undertaking appears to have gotten out of his hands. On June 7, Dana reported that "General Abercrombie seems bewildered," and he was soon relieved. Abercrombie informed Grant on May 30 that 7,500 new arrivals, detachments, convalescents, and stragglers were on their way to the army. *OR*, vol. 36, 1:67, 3:364.

147. Sheridan occupied the crossroads of Old Cold Harbor on the afternoon of May 31 and was ordered by Meade to hold it "at all hazards." Roads converged there from Bethesda Church, Old Church, White House Landing, New Bridge on the Chickahominy, and from Mechanicsville. As Wright's Sixth Corps toiled to complete its grueling night march to their support, Sheridan's troopers repulsed an infantry assault from behind earthworks "by the fire of repeating-carbines and artillery." Humphreys, *Virginia Campaign*, 173.

148. Grant's Special Order No. 25 placed Smith under Meade's command. *OR*, vol. 36, 3:466.

149. James Lawrence, son of Abbott Lawrence, married Elizabeth Prescott, daughter of historian William Hicking Prescott; their children, James, Gertrude, and Anthony Prescott. Elizabeth's mother lived with the family at 38 Beacon Street adjacent to the State House. Somerset Club member H. Gardiner Gorham died at age 49.

150. Cold Harbor was named for its precedent—a village in southern England. The soldiers also called it "Coal Harbor." In his letters home, TL preferred the variant "Cool Arbor" because it was so "hideously inappropriate." TL quoted here his description of "Cool Arbor" from his letter to Mimi. *Meade's Headquarters*, 136, 140. Fewer than 200 acres of Cold Harbor are protected by Richmond National Battlefield Park.

151. *Meade's Headquarters*, 141. Lt. Col. Cleveland Winslow, 5th New York Infantry (Duryee's Zouaves), mortally wounded at Bethesda Church. On June 2, Warren wrote his wife, "A rupture is probable between me and Meade. Gen'l Meade who has become very irritable and unreasonable of late and with whom I had a square understanding today to the effect that I was no creature of his. I am so well satisfied with my efforts and [...] that I would not fear to run against Gen'l Grant if necessary." Warren Papers NYSL, box 1.7.

152. Grant's ADC, Capt. Ely Samuel Parker.

153. In an article for the *New York Times*, correspondent William Swinton referred to Burnside as *vox et preterea nihil*, "a loud voice but without substance."

154. Col. Henry Clay Bankhead of Maryland, IG, Fifth Corps.

155. Capt. William Latham Candler, Hooker's ADC, resigned his commission when his chief was relieved of army command.

156. Brig. Gen. Robert O. "Bob" Tyler was struck in the ankle by a solid shot and permanently disabled. TL's sister's friend, Col. Peter Porter, 8th New York Heavy Artillery, assumed command of Tyler's brigade and was killed. Col. John R. Brooke, Fourth Brigade, First Division, was mortally wounded. McMahons, see TL's entry for June 7 and note.

157. TL cited here his letter to Mimi: "Possibly it has no parallel in history." *Meade's Headquarters*, 147–48.

158. Officers and members of Smith's staff: Capt. Samuel S. Elder and Lt. Edward A. Duer, 1st U.S. Artillery, acting ADC; Capt. Francis Ulric Farquhar, chief engineer; Capt. Preston C. F. West of the U.S. Coast Survey, volunteer ADC; and Brig. Gen. William Thomas Harbaugh Brooks (age 43, Ohio, USMA 1841) commanding First Division, Eighteenth Corps. Brooks would be assigned command of Tenth Corps on June 17, but poor health forced his resignation in July.

159. TL's observations on assaulting entrenchments quoted in *Meade's Headquarters*, 148.

160. Patrick reported, June 5: "Wainwright has been here, greatly disgusted, as is everyone else, with Warren—a very loathsome, profane, ungentlemanly & disgusting puppy in *power*. It seems as if he & Meade were trying to see how much their officers will bear in the way of injustice and insult." Sparks, *Inside Lincoln's Army*, 381.

161. Shaw was the manservant who kept Hancock supplied with clean, white shirts.

162. Maj. William G. Mitchell. Capt. Clayton McMichael, Birney's ADC. The 5th New Hampshire Infantry under Col. Charles E. Hapgood was assigned to First Brigade, First Division, Second Corps on June 1.

163. Lt. Col. John S. Hammell, 66th New York Infantry.

164. Maj. Thomas J. Wooten, 18th North Carolina Infantry. Hancock's report: "Found considerable difficulty in getting the flag out as the pickets were firing at each other and were close together (about 200 paces), sheltered behind trees, but after considerable delay succeeded in getting the flag out by calling to the enemy. Major Wooten, Eighteenth North Carolina Infantry, met Colonel Lyman and myself; a truce arranged by us to continue for one-half mile on right and left of us during the time we were out with the flag." *OR*, vol. 36, 1:367–68.

165. Capt. Haswell C. Clarke (Harvard 1863).

166. Capt. Alexander M. McCune, 74th New York Infantry. Hancock's report: "I heard a furious cannonade and musketry about a mile to our right, on the Second Corps line, and upon my return to headquarters found that a round shot had struck Captain McCune, assistant provost-marshal, Second Corps (who was standing at the door of General Hancock's tent at the time), and mortally wounded him." *OR*, vol. 36, 1:368.

167. The Second Corps entrenched its flank at Barker's Mill Pond, two miles south of Old Cold Harbor. Extensive portions of Second Corps' entrenchments survive (as of this writing) on private property. Allen's Mill (Beatties Mill on modern maps) is

two and a half miles northeast of the crossroads. The Federal lines extended at this time about six miles.

168. Corp. Cornelius D. Smith of Needham, 18th Massachusetts Infantry.

169. Maj. Benjamin Ludlow, formerly Meade's ADC.

170. Sheridan with Gregg's and Torbert's divisions embarked on a new raid to break up the Virginia Central RR between Hanover Junction and Charlottesville. Maj. Gen. David Hunter, who replaced Sigel in command of forces in the Shenandoah Valley, won a decisive victory at Piedmont on June 5, but continued south toward Staunton, rather than turning east toward Charlottesville. Lee detached Early and his Second Corps on June 12 to prevent the capture of Lynchburg.

171. Sixth Corps CoS, Martin Thomas McMahon's brother, Col. James P. McMahon, 164th New York Infantry, was killed during the assault; a second brother, Col. John Eugene McMahon, also with the 164th, died of disease contracted in the army in May 1863. Their father Patrick died of disease.

172. Col. Stevie Weld and Charles Greely Loring Jr. Brig. Gen. John Gross Barnard (age 49, Massachusetts, USMA 1833) was chief engineer, AoP, under McClellan, and oversaw construction of the defenses of Washington, D.C. Grant brought him onto his staff as chief engineer of the armies in the field.

173. Edward Crapsey of the *Philadelphia Inquirer.* Meade was angered by Crapsey's portrayal of him in his hometown newspaper. Sickles et al. accused Meade of ordering a retreat from Gettysburg; the newspapers criticized him for the Mine Run withdrawal; and now there was libel over his role in the current campaign. There seems little question that Meade (or his provost marshal, Patrick) overreacted.

174. TL was among the few staff officers who spoke well of William Swinton, correspondent for the *New York Times.* Swinton had been expelled from the army during the battle of the Wilderness for eavesdropping on a conference between Grant and Meade but returned as part of Congressman Washburne's retinue. On June 11, Burnside demanded that Swinton receive the same punishment as Crapsey, and Meade expelled him with Grant's blessing on July 6, 1864. *OR,* vol. 36, 3:751; vol. 40, 2:559. Swinton was spared the humiliating mule ride through the army.

175. Col. Henry G. Thomas, 19th USCT, commanding Second Brigade, Fourth Division (Ferrero), Ninth Corps.

176. Marlbourne plantation (extant) was owned by Edmund Ruffin. Ruffin, a noted antebellum horticulturalist, preached secession and pulled the lanyard on one of the first guns to fire upon Ft. Sumter in Apr. 1861. Depressed by the downfall of the Southern cause, Ruffin committed suicide in 1865 and was buried at Marlbourne. The Old Church Tavern still stands.

177. News of Hunter's victory at Piedmont in the Shenandoah Valley, June 5, took three days to reach the AoP.

178. The Trent house survives today as a private residence.

179. George Barnard mustered out Sept. 2, 1864.

180. The York River RR ran from the confluence of the Pamunkey and York rivers at West Point into Richmond. McClellan had located his general hospital at Savage's Station

in 1862 and abandoned several thousand wounded there upon his retreat to James River. Despatch Station was the first depot east of the Chickahominy River crossing.

181. Gibbon's promotion ranked from June 7. Sixth Corps staff officers: Thomas Lloyd Haydn, 7th Connecticut Infantry, and Henry Weld Farrar. TL's tentmate Rosie.

182. Gen. Parke, Burnside's CoS. Marsena Patrick's diary entry, June 9: "Today, trying a negro for a rape on a white girl, Colonel Sharpe being assigned, by the court, to defend the prisoner." Sparks, *Inside Lincoln's Army*, 381.

183. Brady photograph, "General George G. Meade and staff of thirty-four." LC-B8184-B-59. TL is the tall man standing in the rear, five faces to the right of Gen. Meade behind Ingalls and Duane. TL identified most of the officers on his print of this photograph, filed among his war memorabilia at the MHS.

184. Col. Henry S. Burton formerly commanded the army's Artillery Reserve, which was disbanded May 17.

185. Jube's Lane in Jamaica Plain.

186. Charles A. Dana wrote that Gen. Eustis "is relieved of his command and ordered to Washington. He is to be informed that if he does not resign, charges of neglect of duty and general inefficiency will be preferred against him. He is said to eat opium." *OR*, vol. 36, 1:96. Eustis resigned his commission and resumed his professorship at the Lawrence Scientific School, a position that he held for many years. Gideon Forrester Barstow (Harvard 1834) was an asst. surgeon at Ft. Warren in Boston Harbor, where he committed suicide June 5, 1864. Barstow's youngest brother, Nathaniel, 24th Massachusetts Infantry, signals officer.

187. Crook and Averell broke up the Tennessee RR and joined Hunter at Staunton for a move up the Shenandoah Valley toward Lexington and Lynchburg. Congressman Washburne of Illinois had a political motive for denigrating Meade's reputation: as Grant's star rose in the field, Washburne's rose in Washington, D.C.

188. Lt. Col. Frederick Thomas Locke, AAG, Fifth Corps, shot through both checks at Spotsylvania.

189. CoS Humphreys's very detailed orders for disengaging the AoP and moving toward James River were issued by army AAG Seth Williams on June 11. *OR*, vol. 36, 3:747–49.

190. Col. Paul Frank commanded Third Brigade, First Division, Second Corps.

191. The Pres. John Tyler home, "Sherwood Forest," still in the Tyler family, is open to visitors. Also preserved by Mr. Harrison Tyler are the earthworks at Wilson's Wharf, called Ft. Pocahontas, where USCTs, commanded by TL's Brookline neighbor Dr. Edward Augustus Wild, repulsed a determined Confederate assault on May 24, 1864. Ft. Powhatan survives on private property two miles upstream on the south bank of the river.

192. Capt. Henry L. Patten. Lt. Thomas S. Milton, Co. B., 20th Massachusetts Infantry, was dismissed from service on July 11.

193. Of the great pontoon bridge across James River, Humphreys wrote: "The site of the bridge was between Windmill Point and Ft. Powhatan, where the river was 2,100 feet wide. The depth in mid-channel was from twelve to fifteen fathoms. The tidal current was strong; the rise and fall of the tide four feet. The number of pontoons was one hundred and one. In the channel the pontoons were anchored to vessels above and

below, moored for the purpose. Here there was a draw for the passage of vessels. The bridge was commenced from each end and built by successive pontoons and by rafts. After considerable progress was made under Major Duane, Gen. Benham arrived and took charge of the operation." Humphreys, *Virginia Campaign*, 203n. Four hundred fifty pioneers completed the bridge in about eight hours.

194. Acting rear admiral Samuel Phillips Lee directed the U.S. Navy squadron that was cooperating with the armies on James River. Grant had ordered Gen. Butler to obstruct the river, which Lee found objectionable. *OR, Navies*, vol. 10, 149–50. Capt. John Colt Beaumont commanded the USS *Mackinaw* then anchored below Ft. Powhatan; his brother Capt. Eugene B. Beaumont, Wright's ADC.

195. Brig. Gen. Godfrey Weitzel (age 30, Ohio, USMA 1855), chief engineer, AoJ. Duane, chief engineer, AoP. Benham, regular engineer brigade, AoP.

196. The Confederate ironclad *Atlanta* was run aground and captured trying to break the blockade of Savannah in June 1863. She was afterward pressed into Federal service as the USS *Atlanta* and stationed in James River.

197. Lt. Richard Robins of Boston, 11th U.S. Infantry.

198. Westover is a private residence; the grounds are open for public visitation.

199. Mimi's brother, Henry Russell. Brigadier Hinks's report: "Among the wounded were Col. H. S. Russell and Maj. Z. B. Adams, of the Fifth Massachusetts Cavalry, who fell while gallantly leading their regiment in the charge at Baylor's farm." *OR*, vol. 40, 1:723. Russell recovered from his wound. Grant anecdote quoted in *Meade's Headquarters*, 164. Lt. Col. William R. Rowley of Grant's staff.

200. Col. John Worthington Ames (Harvard 1854), 6th USCT.

201. Smith's Eighteenth Corps, but Martindale, Second Division, was given direction of two divisions of Eighteenth Corps and one of Sixth Corps in the assault on the far right flank of the army. *OR*, vol. 40, 2:157. The area of these initial assaults is mostly within Petersburg National Battlefield.

202. Brig. Gen. William Hemsley Emory commanded a division in Nineteenth Corps that would see service in the Shenandoah Valley; his wife, Matilda Bache, a great-granddaughter of Benjamin Franklin was related by marriage to Gen. Meade; their son, Capt. Campbell D. Emory, 9th U.S. Infantry.

203. TL quoted Grant in a letter to Mimi. *Meade's Headquarters*, 166.

204. Brig. Gen. August Valentine Kautz (age 36, Ohio, USMA 1852) commanded a division of Butler's cavalry. Neill received the order to relieve Brooks on June 17 at 4 P.M. *OR*, vol. 40, 2:133. The Confederates maintained a pontoon bridge across James River at Drewry's Bluff above Ft. Darling. Lee finally understood that the AoP was south of James River and moved reinforcements to counter the attacks on Petersburg.

JUNE 17–AUGUST 27, 1864

Lyman labeled this Vol. 13B; it is assigned Lyman Papers, bound vol. 18, in the MHS.

1. Brig. Gen. Robert Brown Potter, Second Division, Ninth Corps. Brig. Gen. James Hewitt Ledlie, as senior brigadier, assumed command of First Division, Ninth Corps,

on June 9 when Crittenden asked to be relieved. Crittenden outranked nearly everyone in the eastern armies except Grant and Burnside and evidently was peeved that his three brigades had been consolidated into two. The Shind farm stood a few hundred yards south of modern Hickory Hill Road (the battlefield park boundary). Avery house stood a mile farther south off modern Poe Lane; neither structure survived the war. The Federals afterward leveled most of these captured Confederate earthworks.

2. Engineer Michler reported that Maj. James St. Clair Morton "exposed himself to the unerring shot of one of the enemy's sharpshooters. He was killed instantly, the ball penetrating his left breast." OR, vol. 40, 1:290. Staff officer Lt. Robert Peebles McKibbin, 4th U.S. Infantry, CM for Ledlie's division. Ledlie reported McKibbin "seriously wounded in the neck" on June 17. OR, vol. 40, 1:534.

3. Agassiz quoted an abridged entry in Meade's Headquarters, 168, beginning with "Everyone was near the breaking point." This sentence is not in the notebooks and was either inserted as a gloss by the editor or culled from a different source than this editor has seen.

4. Capt. Charles Appleton Phillips (Harvard 1860), 5th Massachusetts Light Artillery, Battery E. TL quoted Phillips in a letter home in Meade's Headquarters, 169.

5. Col. Joshua Lawrence Chamberlain (age 34, Maine, Bowdoin 1852), 20th Maine Infantry, commanding First Brigade, First Division, Fifth Corps. Chamberlain was shot through the hips, a wound that many thought mortal. Chamberlain was promoted a brigadier to rank from June 18. He returned to duty by mid-November. Second Brigade, commanded by Col. Jacob Sweitzer, went in on Chamberlain's left. OR, vol. 40, 1:455–56.

6. Wainwright's report: "First Lieut. Peleg W. Blake, of the Fifth Massachusetts Battery, and First Lieut. Thomas Goodman, serving with B, Fourth U.S. Artillery, were either killed in action or died of wounds received shortly after." OR, vol. 40, 1:483.

7. Two "Harrys": ADC Lt. Henry Hollingsworth Humphreys and Mimi's wounded brother, Henry. Charles Dana and Grant's aide Frederick Dent helped secure Russell's leave at TL's behest.

8. Maj. James William Walsh, commanding provost detachment, 3d Pennsylvania Cavalry. Capt. Horace K. Thatcher and Lt. Chambers McKibbin, 14th U.S. Infantry, Warren's staff officers.

9. Maj. James M. Crow and Col. J. Horace King, 9th Alabama Infantry, of Sanders's brigade. Harris may have been the ranking brigadier present. See OR, vol. 42, 2:1217n. (King transcribed as "Ring" in Meade's Headquarters, 172.) Following TL's description, sketch, and historic maps, the place where the flag of truce went out can be located fairly reliably near the intersection of Crater Road (old Jerusalem Plank Road) and Morton Avenue.

10. Beauregard still technically commanded the defenses of Petersburg. Description of Beauregard in Meade's Headquarters, 173.

11. Patrick wrote, "The execution [of Johnson] came off this morning. I went out early & examined the gallows . . . then went back for the troops & prisoner. They arrived, just after a shelling commenced, upon the very place where the gallows was

erected so that I had to form the troops below the crest & leave as few exposed as possible." Sparks, *Inside Lincoln's Army*, 386. Boston Brahmin Col. Charles Jackson Paine (Harvard 1853) served as Butler's ADC. Butler secured Paine's promotion to brigadier to rank from July 4, whereupon Paine assumed command of Third Division, Ninth Corps, which had a large role in the Chaffin's farm operations.

12. Sixth Corps staff officers: Capt. Arthur McClellan, AAG, and Capt. Thomas L. Haydn, ADC.

13. The Williams house stood southwest of the modern Birdsong Road and Crater (Jerusalem Plank) Road intersection.

14. Col. John A. Baker, 3d North Carolina Cavalry, reported captured on this day, attended Harvard. Likely TL's acquaintance lawyer Edward Graham Daves (Harvard 1854). *More suo*, "in his usual manner."

15. TL's classmate Brig. Gen. Joe Hayes assumed command of First Brigade, Second Division, Fifth Corps (which consisted of regular army regiments) on June 20. *OR*, vol. 40, 1:224n.

16. On this date, Grant wrote from City Point: "Gen. Meade on no occasion advised or counseled falling back toward, much less across, the Rapidan. There has been no word or act of his from the beginning of this campaign which indicated even a belief on his part that such a step would ever become necessary. Such rumors as you speak of are entirely idle and without the shadow of foundation." The *New York Times* published Grant's endorsement of Meade, July 10, 1864, one of the few newspapers to do so.

17. Wilson and Kautz with 5,500 troopers left to strike the Southside and Weldon railroads, continuing Grant's strategy of directing cavalry raids against Richmond's supply lines. These raids were disruptive but inflicted mostly superficial damage to the railroads.

18. Col. Emory Upton was promoted for directing the assault at Spotsylvania on May 10, 1864.

19. The cavalry of the provost guard at this time consisted of detachments from the 1st Massachusetts, 1st Indiana, and 3d Pennsylvania Cavalry. *OR*, vol. 40, 1:218. Capt. Benjamin Crowninshield, 1st Massachusetts Cavalry, was not relieved of his command; his report on this action in *OR*, vol. 40, 2:310. Lt. Col. Edward S. Jones, 3d Pennsylvania Cavalry.

20. Wright's ADC, Capt. Richard F. Halsted, rode with TL.

21. TL's astute assessment of the fighting is quoted in *Meade's Headquarters*, 176. The attacking force was the division of Brig. Gen. William Mahone, a Petersburg native. Careful scrutiny of the Michler maps (NARA RG77 G204, 32–40) reveals two diverging woods roads in the area indicated by TL, bisected by a third road leading south from the main Confederate line. Mahone may have been marching on this road under the impression that he was beyond the left flank of the AoP but instead penetrated the gap between the two Federal corps. Gibbon's First Brigade (Col. Byron Root Pierce) and Second Brigade (Brig. Gen. Joshua Thomas Owen) together gave up nearly 1,000 prisoners in this operation. Gibbon relieved Pierce of command on the field, but he was later reassigned to Second Brigade, Third Division (Birney's).

22. Alexander Gardner photographed the Aiken house in Feb. 1865. Gardner, *Photographic Sketch Book*, plate 71. The house stood near the middle of what is now the Petersburg Country Club.

23. Capt. Paine, engineer and Duane's acting ADC.

24. According to Getty's report, the captain was Beattie of the 3d Vermont. *OR*, vol. 40, 1:495.

25. Meade's temper continued to provoke his subordinates. Provost Marshal Patrick recorded in his diary this day: "The despicable selfishness & indifference of Meade, causing him to set aside all the *rights* of his troops . . . insulting all who approach him, makes me very sick at heart." Sparks, *Inside Lincoln's Army*, 388.

26. Wright's AAG, Maj. Charles Whittier.

27. Mahone's and Wilcox's divisions were engaged.

28. The two-day battle of Trevilian Station in Louisa County was the most sanguinary all-cavalry engagement in Virginia. Nearly 2,000 troopers, 20 percent of 10,000 engaged, became casualties. Hampton was not averse to fighting from behind earthworks and barricades to preserve his precious horses. Sheridan's attempt to reach Charlottesville was stymied. According to Wittenburg, Sheridan requisitioned 1,900 remounts in July, but these did not make good his losses for May and June. "The Army of the Potomac's entire Cavalry Corps remained combat ineffective for weeks as a result of the Trevilian Raid." Wittenburg, *Glory Enough for All*, 303.

29. Lt. Col. François De Chanal and Capt. Pierre Guzman were the principal French military observers dispatched to America by Emperor Napoleon III. De Chanal typically handled the social obligations, while Guzman produced detailed reports on the organization, armament, and equipment of the AoP. De Chanal and Guzman stayed at army HQ for three months under TL's charge. Luvaas, *Military Legacy*, 91–97. Early defeated Hunter's forces at Lynchburg, June 17–18. Hunter retreated into western Virginia.

30. On June 24, Gregg lost 350 casualties when attacked by Hampton near Samaria or Saint Mary's Church north of James River.

31. Henry Lyman Patten, soon promoted to major. Abbott killed and Macy wounded at the Wilderness; Capt. Arthur Russell Curtis wounded at Spotsylvania. Gibbon's stock at headquarters had been in steady decline since his hesitation to commit troops on the left flank at the Wilderness, May 6.

32. Ninth Corps staff officers: Maj. William Cutting, ADC, and Maj. Philip Meseir Lydig, AAG. TL's PC brother and relative by marriage, Col. William Batchelder Greene. Butler appears to have offered Greene's services as inspector of artillery to "Baldy" Smith. Smith declined, declaring that he preferred "an old officer of great experience, scientific attainments in his profession, and of activity." *OR*, vol. 40, 2:427.

33. Shadowed and harassed by Confederate cavalry, Wilson's and Kautz's exhausted troopers reached Reams Station, ten miles south of Petersburg, on June 29 to find their route back to the army blocked by Mahone's infantry division. The Federals abandoned wagons, artillery, many of their wounded, and a horde of following contrabands, and fought their way out of the trap.

34. Brig. Gen. George W. Getty resumed command of Second Division, Sixth Corps. Capt. Philip William Stanhope, 12th U.S. Infantry. See TL's entry, Jan. 11, 1864.

35. Brig. Gen. Edward Ferrero, commanding Fourth Division, Ninth Corps; he was indeed a dancing instructor at the USMA, charged with developing the social skills of young cadets; and many likely owed him some acknowledgment for a successful courtship.

36. Lt. Arthur George Sedgwick (Harvard 1864), 20th Massachusetts Infantry. See TL's entry for Aug. 3, 1864. The nickname of the headquarters guard, 114th Pennsylvania Infantry (Collis's Zouaves), may have derived from their characteristic "zoo zoo zoo" chant when going into combat.

37. *Atque,* "and especially."

38. Ricketts's movement was in response to Jubal Early's threat against Washington and Baltimore. After defeating Hunter's forces at Lynchburg, Early turned north and with hard marching reached the Potomac River on July 4. While the bands played at Petersburg, Early's 14,000 veterans were splashing across the Potomac River into Maryland to make mischief.

39. "He has the manner of a Parisian street urchin."

40. The USS *Kearsarge* sank the famed Confederate raider *Alabama* off the coast of France on June 19. On June 18, Grant tapped Rufus Ingalls for chief QM of the armies operating against Richmond. Grant and Ingalls were classmates at West Point. Meade reacted bitterly to Grant's "borrowing" of Patrick. Meade, Patrick wrote, "became very angry not—as he *said*—with me, or with Grant, but with every body & thing.—He has learned that his Staff would, all, gladly, leave him, on account of his temper, and he has become desperately cross." Sparks, *Inside Lincoln's Army*, 393. Meade replaced Ingalls with Lt. Col. Richard Napoleon Batchelder, chief QM of Second Corps. Patrick's position continued in dispute, as recorded in his diary and in Comstock's.

41. Maj. Gen. Edward Otho Cresap Ord (age 45, Washington, D.C., USMA 1839). Ord's last appearance in the Eastern theater had been at Dranesville, Virginia, in Dec. 1861, where he bested a foraging party led by J. E. B. Stuart. Subsequently, he commanded Thirteenth Corps in the Vicksburg campaign. Grant suggested Ord to temporarily head Eighteenth Corps, during Smith's leave of absence; Smith objected as he suspected he was being supplanted. Grant afterward requested Ord for Tenth Corps. *OR*, vol. 40, 3:118, 144. For the moment, Ord was dispatched to aid in organizing the defense of Baltimore and Washington against Early's threat.

42. Josiah Quincy, former mayor of Boston (1823–28) and president of Harvard (1829–45).

43. The remaining two divisions of Sixth Corps (under Russell and Wheaton) were sent on transports to Washington, D.C., to repel Gen. Early's Maryland incursion. The "square fort" was Ft. Davis. Ft. Davis, owned by the City of Petersburg, survives at the intersection of Crater and Flank roads.

44. Sen. William Sprague, former governor of Rhode Island. Maj. Gen. David Bell Birney was being considered for command of Tenth Corps.

45. Maj. Gen. Lewis Wallace with a patched-together force of 5,800 attempted to stop Early's advance at the Monocacy River, outside Frederick, Maryland, on July 9. Ricketts's two veteran Sixth Corps brigades bore the brunt of combat. Wallace, who had been unfairly stigmatized for his performance at the battle of Shiloh, did a creditable job

of pulling together enough reserve units to delay Early for twenty-four hours—enough time for the rest of Sixth Corps to reach Washington, D.C., from Petersburg.

46. Maj. Henry Lyman Patten. Capt. Charles William Folsom (Harvard 1845), QM, First Brigade, Second Division, Second Corps. Capt. Robert W. "Whiskey Mitch" Mitchell and James Starr, 6th Pennsylvania Cavalry. Capt. Henry Winsor Jr. served on Torbert's staff, First Cavalry Division. Lt. Ward Frothingham, 59th Massachusetts Infantry. Frothingham had been "rusticated" at the Brook Farm Institute, a transcendentalist commune supported for a time by Mimi's father and uncle. Frank Barlow also studied at Brook Farm. Asst. Secretary of War Charles Dana taught Latin and German there.

47. On this date, the *New York Times* printed Meade's order expelling its correspondent, William Swinton, from the AoP for "forwarding for publication incorrect statements." The editors added: "Judging from Gen. Meade's previous action in similar cases, and from the general temper he exhibits toward the press, Mr. Swinton is quite as likely to have been excluded for being too accurate as for any other offense."

48. Marching from the Monocacy, Early's army reached the outskirts of Washington, D.C., on July 11 and probed the capital's defenses for two days before withdrawing south of the Potomac. The Sixth Corps, two divisions of the Nineteenth Corps newly arrived from the west, and troops of the Middle Military Division pursued Early back to the Shenandoah Valley.

49. Forts Davis and Prescott.

50. De Chanal reported that the Shenkl was the most accurate American projectile but caused great wear on the artillery piece. Luvaas, *Military Legacy*, 95.

51. The hanged men were Ransom S. Gordon and Daniel Geary, both of Co. E, 72d New York Infantry.

52. James Lodge was a founding member of the Somerset Club and a highly respected member of Boston society.

53. In North Georgia, Gen. Joseph Johnston continued to retreat in the face of Sherman's relentless flanking movements. Nelson Appleton Miles was commissioned a brigadier general of volunteers in June.

54. Col. Thomas Casimer Devin, Second Brigade, First Division (Custer's), Cavalry Corps. Despite two years of efficient service, Col. Devin would not receive his commission as brigadier until Mar. 1865 (the delay likely due to his lack of a West Point education).

55. The Dr. Gurley house stood north of Statesman Hall on the campus of Richard Bland College. William Waud sketched for *Frank Leslie's Illustrated Newspaper* and joined his brother and *Harper's* staff at Petersburg.

56. See TL's entry, June 2, 1864.

57. On July 20, Grant informed Butler, "I have relieved General Smith from command of the Eighteenth Corps: and shall place General Ord in his place." *OR*, vol. 40, 3:355–56. Grant had raised "Baldy" Smith to corps command with high expectations. Smith proved a disappointment and was at odds with Butler from the beginning. Butler wanted rid of the ambitious Smith, while Grant sought placement for Ord. Grant and Butler appear to have struck a deal. Lt. Col. Horatio Deming Jarves, 56th Massachusetts Infantry. Stevie Weld.

58. Maj. Gen. David Bell Birney moved from Third Division, Second Corps, AoP, to command Tenth Corps, AoJ. Brig. Gershom Mott assumed Birney's position in Second Corps. Captains Robert Mitchell and Edward Whiteford, 6th Pennsylvania Cavalry. Whiteford later served as Merritt's ADC. Lt. Gen. John Bell Hood replaced Johnston as commander of the Confederate Army of Tennessee on July 17. Sherman's forces were across the Chattahoochee River and closing on Atlanta from the north and east.

59. Butler's ADCs: Col. Charles Jackson Paine, Lt. Col. George Ames Kensel, and Maj. Robert S. Davis.

60. "No effect! But why not?" "Ah, but why *so?*"

61. Hood launched the first of a series of offensives at Peachtree Creek, July 20. On July 22, Hood initiated the battle of Atlanta in which Maj. Gen. James Birdseye McPherson, commanding the Army of the Tennessee, was killed. Both of Hood's attempts to destroy isolated Federal columns in front of Atlanta failed. Maj. George G. Hastings replaced Maj. Edward Platt as judge advocate.

62. Col. John Worthington Ames, 11th U.S. Infantry and 6th USCT. Lt. Col. Charles S. Russell, 28th USCT.

63. Capt. Edward Moale, 19th U.S. Infantry. Henry Higginson returned to duty on Francis Barlow's staff. On July 24, G. K. Warren wrote his wife, "I believe Gen'l Meade is an august and unfeeling man and I dislike his personal character so much now that it is improbable we shall ever have again any friendly social relations. I have also lost all confidence in his ability as a general. He has quick perceptions but does not know how to act with patience and judgment. He would expect to hatch a chicken from the egg in the same time you could boil it." Warren Papers NYSL, box 1.7. Patrick wrote the same day: "The jealousy on the part of the Corps Commanders against each other and against Meade—especially the bad blood between Meade & Burnside—prevents any unanimity of counsels, or concert of action, even among the troops belonging to the Army of the Potomac." Sparks, *Inside Lincoln's Army*, 403.

64. "A tree; another beautiful tree!"

65. A pontoon bridge connected the entrenched enclave at Deep Bottom north of James River to the south side. Hancock's operations in cooperation with the AoJ, known as first Deep Bottom, grew out of Grant's two-prong strategy—first to strike against Richmond north of the James, drawing off Southern troops, then, several days later, to gain ground south of the James in "bite and hold" operations. Politically, Lee could not afford to leave Richmond vulnerable even though he anticipated the counterpunch at Petersburg that was to follow.

66. Lt. Col. Henry Pleasants and his Schuylkill County coal miners from the 48th Pennsylvania Infantry constructed the tunnel.

67. Captains Charles N. Turnbull and Franklin Harwood, U.S. Engineers Battalion.

68. Paragraph quoted in *Meade's Headquarters*, 196. Duane likely referred to Col. Richard Delafield's *Report on the Art of War in Europe in 1854, 1855, and 1856* (Washington, D.C.: George H. Bowman, 1860), which contained descriptions of the siege of Sebastopol during the Crimean War. At Kernstown on July 24, Jubal A. Early and his Army of the Valley routed a Federal force led by Brig. Gen. George R. Crook. Crook had been left to hold the Lower Shenandoah Valley, while troops of the Sixth and

Nineteenth Corps marched toward Washington, D.C., expecting to take transports to the Petersburg front. Early's victory impelled Grant to send both corps back to the Shenandoah Valley.

69. Barlow's wife, Arabella, before her death had been serving as an army nurse in the hospitals in Washington, D.C.

70. Burnside paragraph quoted in *Meade's Headquarters*, 201.

71. Col. Elisha G. Marshall, Second Brigade, First Division, Ninth Corps, consisting of the 14th New York Heavy Artillery and the 2d Pennsylvania Provisional Heavy Artillery. Ledlie had been accused of drunkenness on the North Anna. Although many such wartime accusations were spurious, the Ledlie case seems sufficiently documented. Agassiz quoted extensively from TL's July 30 notebook entry, but excised the pointed judgment of Ledlie and the graphic description of dead and wounded, among other details. *Meade's Headquarters*, 198–201.

72. "But this loss of time!"

73. Ninth Corps medical director John Ellis MacDonald. TL did not name the man, perhaps because of the criticism that followed.

74. TL's schoolmates, William Bartlett and Stevie Weld were captured in the Mine assault. Bartlett, who had returned to duty after being wounded at the Wilderness on July 22, was exchanged within a few weeks. Weld was the subject of intense War Department negotiations and was eventually paroled in December. *OR*, ser. 2, vol. 7:1159, 1198. The last two sentences were taken from TL's letter home.

75. McCausland's Confederate cavalrymen burned Chambersburg, Pennsylvania, on July 30 in retaliation for Federal depredations in the Shenandoah Valley.

76. Sentence quoted from the notebook in *Meade's Headquarters*, 203.

77. CoS Humphreys to Burnside, July 31: "The major-general commanding directs me to say that the order for withdrawal did not authorize or justify its being done in the manner in which, judging from your brief report, it appears to have been executed, and that the matter should be inquired into by a court." *OR*, vol. 40, 3:707.

78. Burnside responded to Meade: "I am entirely responsible for this and am to blame if any one is. [The operators] have been active and efficient during the campaign, and should not be made to suffer for what they could not help doing." Humphreys responded that the commanding general "is surprised to learn that you had given them such orders after the conversation he had with you upon the subject, in which he declined to authorize your doing so." *OR*, vol. 40, 3:703.

79. Ft. Sedgwick, built astride the Jerusalem Plank Road, was dubbed "Ft. Hell" by the troops. The fort was leveled in the 1960s to make way for a shopping center that today stands mostly empty. "While performing picket duty, Lieutenant [Arthur] Sedgwick and thirty-two men were captured." Bruce, *Twentieth Massachusetts Regiment*, 414.

80. On this date, the War Department ordered an investigation of the Mine disaster: "By direction of the President, a Court of Inquiry will convene in front of Petersburg at 10 A.M. on the 5th instant, or as soon thereafter as practicable, to examine into and report upon the facts and circumstances attending the unsuccessful assault on the enemy's position on the 30th of July, 1864." *OR*, vol. 40, 1:42–43. The court convened on Aug. 6 and met for two weeks.

81. James, brother of Henry Lee Higginson. Capt. Edward Austin Flint.

82. The left flank of the Confederate Bermuda Hundred defenses was anchored at the Howlett plantation overlooking James River. The 1,250-ton double-turreted monitor USS *Onondaga* was one of the Navy's newest ships. The *Onondaga* is shown in the NARA Brady Photographic collection by negatives 111-B-368 and 111-B-1961. The Sawyer gun was an experimental steel-barreled, rifled cannon that threw a lightweight round for a long distance. Capt. William Vincent Hutchings of Massachusetts, asst. QM, Tenth Corps.

83. Mining and countermining were standard siege warfare operations and were probably more pervasive at Petersburg than history has recorded, as mining was a secret affair. In recent years, a Confederate mine several hundred yards long was discovered near the area known as the Lead Works when a portion of it collapsed.

84. Agassiz included this story from TL's notebook under his entry for Aug. 6 though it was written days later; as editor, Agassiz attempted a chronological narrative and did not always retain the correct dates for TL's letters. *Meade's Headquarters*, 206–7. TL was commissioned by Gov. Andrew and appointed asst. adj. general for the state of Massachusetts. He was granted a leave of absence from his "official" duties to serve on Meade's staff.

85. George Derby (Harvard Medical 1843) of Boston was appointed medical inspector for Butler's Department of Virginia and North Carolina.

86. Charlie Adams was assigned the 5th Massachusetts Cavalry (Colored), temporarily replacing Mimi's brother Col. Henry Russell. The proceedings of Burnside's court of inquiry are documented in *OR*, vol. 40, 1:42–163.

87. Recent research has speculated that the blast at City Point was caused by agents who laced the charging coal with explosives fashioned to resemble lumps of coal. TL's classmate Ned Dalton in charge of the main hospital at City Point. Surgeon A. J. Phelps. Asst. surgeon J. Sire Smith.

88. Low camp humor at Riddle's expense. On Aug. 5, Rear Admiral David Farragut's squadron of monitors and wooden gunboats steamed through a torpedo field and past the guns of Ft. Morgan into Mobile Bay. Farragut there defeated a Confederate naval squadron that included the ironclad *Tennessee*. Ft. Gaines surrendered on Aug. 8, but Ft. Morgan held out until Aug. 23. Following the confusion generated by Jubal Early's Washington raid, Grant appointed his man Sheridan to command the newly formed Middle Military Division, which encompassed the Shenandoah Valley. The Sixth Corps and two divisions of cavalry (under Torbert and Wilson) were transferred from the AoP to Sheridan's command. On Aug. 10, Meade wrote: "The Washington papers of yesterday announce Sheridan being temporarily assigned to the military division which Grant told me was intended for me. Grant has been back [at City Point] two days, and has not vouchsafed one word in explanation, and I have avoided going to see him, from a sense of self-respect, and from the fear I should not be able to restrain the indignation I hold to be natural at the duplicity someone has practiced." Meade, *Life and Letters*, 2:220.

89. Col. Henry G. Thomas, Second Brigade, Ferrero's division.

90. Asst. Secretary of the Interior William Tod Otto of Philadelphia. Louis

Françoise de Pourtalès was Prof. Agassiz's colleague at the University of Neuchatel in Switzerland. The nature of the affair involving Steiger remains unexplained.

91. Grant relieved Burnside and did not inform Meade until after the fact. *OR,* vol. 42, 2:142. Burnside would not return to active duty. His ADC, Capt. Duncan A. Pell, and other personal staff were granted leave, although some would return to serve under Parke. Maj. Gen. John Grubb Parke, Corps of Engineers, had served as Burnside's CoS since June. A competent officer, Parke labored throughout the campaign in relative obscurity. TL sought details from Lt. Col. Charles Loring Jr. of the capture of Stevie Weld, July 30.

92. Hancock's movement north of James River evolved into a sprawling seven-day affair intended to draw Confederate troops away from Petersburg. Lee transferred five brigades from south of James River to the defense of Richmond. Henry Patten died of complications from the amputation, Sept. 10, 1864.

93. Capt. John Neville "Long" Craig of Gen. Hunt's staff was a tall man.

94. Confederate brigadiers John R. Chambliss and Victor J. B. Girardey were killed. Butler used the captured map to plan future operations north of James River (the attack on Ft. Harrison). Brig. Gen. Francis Barlow relinquished command of First Division, Second Corps, on Aug. 17, due to illness (possibly emotional prostration due to the death of his wife) and went on extended leave. *OR,* vol. 42, 1:249. Brig. Gen. William Bartlett returned to the army after being exchanged.

95. Brig. Gen. Julius White (age 47, Illinois) replaced Ledlie in command of First Division, Ninth Corps. White soon resigned due to ill health. Lt. Charlie Mills.

96. Globe Tavern stood on the eastern side of modern Halifax Road (the original Weldon RR bed), one-third mile south of its intersection with modern Flank Road. When winter closed in, soldiers dismantled the abandoned building for bricks to build chimneys for their huts.

97. TL quoted this paragraph from a letter to Mimi. *Meade's Headquarters,* 220.

98. Brig. Gen. Joe Hayes was exchanged in early 1865 and returned to the army on Apr. 3. This was one of TL's rare criticisms of his commanding general.

99. Maj. Gen. Romeyn Ayres's report: "Lieut. C. McKibbin, Fourteenth Infantry, temporarily serving on my staff, was severely wounded." *OR,* vol. 42, 1:473.

100. Brig. Gen. Johnson Hagood. Captain Daily, provost marshal for Fourth Division, Fifth Corps. This incident is treated at some length in Powell, *Fifth Army Corps,* 717–20.

101. Col. Nathan T. Dushane, commanding Second Brigade, Second Division, Fifth Corps.

102. Maj. Robert S. Davis. TL actively sought the exchange of Joe Hayes and Arthur Sedgwick.

103. Potter fought a delaying action against Longstreet's troops at Campbell's Station, Nov. 16, 1863. Capt. Frederick Cavada's family had been established among moneyed Philadelphian society for a generation.

104. This is a telling observation on Hancock's approach to command.

105. Col. Robert McAllister, 11th New Jersey, Third Brigade, Fourth Division, Second Corps.

106. Capt. Charles Stuart McEntee, asst. QM. Hancock's ADC William De Witt Miller. Capt. Edward P. Brownson, son of noted philosopher Orestes A. Brownson. The Conservation Fund has preserved 210 acres of the Reams Station battlefield.

107. Surgeon Alexander N. Dougherty. Hancock's report: "Lieut. Col. [Francis Amasa] Walker, assistant adjutant-general, was sent to the front with an order just before the troops were withdrawn, and owing to the darkness rode into the enemy's lines and was captured." *OR*, vol. 42, 1:228. Walker was highly critical of Meade's command decisions at Reams Station, writing, "If Meade did not intend to fight, Hancock should have been withdrawn. If he did intend to fight, Hancock should have been powerfully reinforced." *History of the Second Army Corps*, 585. In hindsight, the criticism holds weight; Meade was lulled by Hancock's bravado.

108. Lt. Col. Arthur Russell Curtis. Hancock's report: "Col. James A. Beaver, One hundred and forty-eighth Pennsylvania Volunteers, desperately wounded, his thigh shattered by a minie-ball." *OR*, vol. 42, 1:245.

109. The Second Corps had ambushed Heth's division from behind a railroad embankment at Bristoe Station and routed Hill's corps at the Wilderness. Ft. Wadsworth, built astride the Halifax Road, is preserved within the battlefield park. Ft. Dushane survives on private property one mile south of Ft. Wadsworth.

August 28–October 31, 1864

Lyman labeled this Vol. 13, Part II; it is assigned Lyman Papers, bound vol. 15, in the MHS.

1. Burchett's house on the main road from Petersburg to Prince George Court House. This distance west placed headquarters just within the battlefield park near the boundary with Ft. Lee. This would afterward become Meade's Station on the Military RR.

2. Grant's ADC, Cyrus Comstock, a Massachusetts man. Kensel identified. Lt. Charles Hodge Dod, AAG, was killed Aug. 26; Capt. Albert Baldwin Dod resigned his commission in the 15th U.S. Infantry earlier in the month and likely had come to retrieve his brother's body.

3. Boston attorney, Maj. Joseph Lewis Stackpole (Harvard 1857, Harvard Law 1859), judge advocate, Department of Virginia and North Carolina, and afterward on Butler's and Ord's staffs. Construction of Ft. Wool on the Rip-Raps began in 1826; engineers completed only two tiers of masonry gun casements because the fort's artificial island began to subside. Capt. Charles Elliott Pease of HQ staff.

4. Eutaw House Hotel, located at northwest corner of Eutaw and Baltimore streets; Barnum's Hotel at Calvert and Fayette streets was a favorite haunt of actor John Wilkes Booth. Secretary of State William H. Seward of New York.

5. Investment banker Stanton Blake.

6. In the late 1840s, Boston's elite began summering along Beverly's "Gold Coast." Gardner Howland Shaw purchased a summer home from Augustus Lowell in Beverly, where the Shaw and Russell families were gathered. Mimi's younger brother, Robert, met TL at the depot. Mimi's youngest sister, Sarah "Sallie." TL's niece Amy Shaw.

7. TL's PC brother, Martin Brimmer and wife Marianne Timmins. In 1915, essayist John Jay Chapman described Brimmer as the "perfect Brahmin." "Tot" Peabody, likely Lt. Col. Oliver W. Peabody, mustered out of the 45th Massachusetts Infantry in 1863; his brother, investment banker Francis Howard "Frank" Peabody. George Bruce Upton (Harvard 1849). Banker Richard S. Parker. John Gardner Cushing (Harvard 1855, PC). Prominent Boston physician, Dr. Robert William Hooper (Harvard 1830, PC), his daughters Elizabeth "Nellie" and Marian "Clover"; his son, Capt. Edward William Hooper (Harvard 1859), was instrumental in organizing the Freedmen's Bureau in South Carolina. Clover married writer Henry Adams in 1872. State senator, the Honorable Charles Greely Loring (Sr.) owned a large property near Pride's Crossing in Beverly and leased a house to Henry B. Rogers. TL's Brookline neighbor, Mrs. Eliza Perkins Cabot. "Dad" Sohier possibly the father of William Davies Sohier who owned a house at Beverly and was related to the Brimmers by marriage. *Meuble,* "household furnishings."

8. In late August, Sherman cut loose from his supply line and marched his army group to cut the railroad south of Atlanta. Two days' fighting at Jonesborough (Aug. 31–Sept. 1) severed Hood's last rail connection and forced the evacuation of Atlanta. Sherman's famous communiqué to Washington, D.C., on Sept. 3 stated, "So Atlanta is ours and fairly won." *OR*, 38, 5: 777.

9. TL's neighbor and PC brother, Dr. Samuel Cabot.

10. Characters from Charles Dickens's *The Pickwick Papers:* Mr. Pickwick, his manservant Samuel Weller, father "Tony" the coachman, and would-be poet Augustus Snodgrass. Mimi's brother Henry was recuperating from his wound of June 15.

11. Adj. Lt. Col. Charles G. Loring Jr., on furlough from Burnside's staff. Robert Charles Winthrop Jr. (Harvard 1854, PC). Confederate envoy to England and France, John Slidell, and his personal secretary, George Eustis. Richard Codman (Harvard 1864, PC), deputy marshal of the Porcellian Club.

12. Prof. Agassiz and his associate Jacques Burkhardt. Agassiz and his colleagues in the National Academy of Sciences argued about Charles Darwin's book *Origin of Species,* published in 1863. Agassiz disputed Darwin's theories; TL was more inclined to agree with Darwin.

13. TL's cousin Charles Eliot. Alex and Annie Agassiz. Meade to TL, Sept. 11, 1864: "My visit home was a most melancholy one—I find my eldest boy now nearly 22 years of age, a confirmed *invalide.* The physicians pronouncing his lungs decidedly diseased, and requiring him to be sent to a milder climate this winter. . . . By the way, I was treated when in Washington with so much consideration by the Presd. and Sec. of War, particularly the latter, that I have no doubt, should you desire such an appt., I could get you appointed a Lt. Col. in the Adj. Gen. Dept." Lyman Papers MHS, box 16.5.

14. Harvard professors: James Francis Child, James Russell Lowell (PC), Jeffries Wyman, and Joseph Lovering. Dr. James Walker (Harvard president 1853–60); likely professors Thomas Hill and Andrew Preston Peabody. TL's fellow Terrapins, Adams and Palfrey. Officers of the 20th Massachusetts Infantry: Col. George Macy; Capt. Herbert Cowpland Mason (Harvard 1862, PC), discharged disability; and Capt. Wendell Holmes (mustered out after Cold Harbor); Mr. Stanley (not identified) with

Charles Eliot Norton (Harvard 1846); prisoner-of-war Lt. Arthur Sedgwick. Likely Samuel Wood Langmaid (Harvard 1859).

15. Meade to TL, Sept. 12, 1864: "I learned that your boy Albert had been quite sick. . . . I found such to be the case, and that he was looking very badly. I therefore advised him to go home for a little while on a leave." Lyman Papers MHS, box 16.5. TL's PC brothers, Ned Browne, Jacques Burkhardt Jr., and surgeon William Thorndike, 39th Massachusetts Infantry.

16. Mrs. Eliza and her son, Dr. Samuel Cabot. On Sept. 19, Sheridan's Army of the Shenandoah defeated Early's forces at the battle of Opequon Creek near Winchester, taking nearly 2,000 prisoners. The desperate, daylong struggle resulted in more than 5,000 Federal casualties. Brig. Gen. David Allen Russell was killed by a shell fragment to the chest; Brig. Gen. Emory Upton assumed command of the division and was, in turn, wounded. Tactically, the battle was a "close-run" affair that might easily have gone against Sheridan.

17. Mimi's sister Sarah and brother Henry, who was leaving to join his regiment, the 5th Massachusetts Cavalry (Colored) on duty at the prisoner of war camp, Pt. Lookout, Maryland.

18. After suffering defeat at Opequon Creek, Early withdrew twenty miles up the Shenandoah Valley to Fisher's Hill, where he hoped to halt Sheridan's advance. On Sept. 22, a column led by Brig. Gen. George Crook maneuvered unseen astride Early's left flank, attacked, and routed the Confederates. For several weeks, Sheridan pursued Early's depleted force up the Shenandoah Valley to near Harrisonburg. He then withdrew whence he came, burning barns, mills, and crops, leaving the Lower Valley a wasteland.

19. Jube's Lane (Forest Hills Street) in Jamaica Plain. Edith Forbes married Charles Eliot Perkins; her older brother, "the cur," Robert Bennett Forbes Jr.

20. TL's friend and classmate and would-be playwright Joseph Converse Heywood.

21. Retired merchant and broker Henry Lee (Lee, Higginson & Co.) and son, Col. Henry Lee Jr., who served on the staff of Gov. Andrew. TL's first cousin Elizabeth Eliot married Stephen H. Bullard. TL's cousin Mary Eliot wed Charles Eliot Gould.

22. Robert Shaw Oliver, TL's nephew, mustered into the 5th Massachusetts Cavalry (Colored), the next day. TL's aunt Mary Lyman Eliot and great aunt Mary Williams Pratt. Attorney Philip H. Sears (Harvard 1844).

23. TL's classmate, George Dexter, a cotton merchant.

24. Former commander of the AoP, Maj. Gen. Joseph Hooker of Hadley, Massachusetts.

25. Dr. Brockenbrough not identified.

26. De Chanal and Guzman returned to France in Jan. 1865. The French government used Guzman's reports to develop a sobering picture of the strength and capabilities of the U.S. forces at a time when France and the United States were at odds over Mexico. In 1872, De Chanal published in Paris *L'armée americaine pendant la guerre de seccession.* An American translation, *The American Army in the War of Secession,* appeared in 1894.

27. Description of the movement quoted in *Meade's Headquarters*, 232–33.

28. Commander of Eighteenth Corps, Maj. Gen. Ord. Brig. Gen. George Jerrison Stannard (age 44, Vermont), First Division, Eighteenth Corps, lost his right arm in the fight and did not return to duty. Brig. Gen. Hiram Burnham (age 50, Maine) was "mortally wounded by a musketball in the bowels. He survived but a few moments." *OR*, vol. 42, 1:799. Confederate Ft. Harrison was renamed Ft. Burnham and is part of Richmond National Battlefield Park.

29. Surgeon Alexander N. Dougherty of New Jersey, medical director of Second Corps. The U.S. Military RR was the logistical marvel that enabled the U.S. Army to sustain its siege of Petersburg. Trains running on published timetables shuttled supplies from the deepwater port at City Point to the rear of the siege works and returned with wounded and sick. Stations with sidings and supply depots were established at regular intervals. Ultimately, the rails would extend some twenty-one miles and support eighteen scheduled roundtrips per day. The railroad was completed from City Point to a junction with the Weldon Railroad near Globe Tavern on Sept. 26. *OR*, vol. 42, 2:1032.

30. Brig. Gen. Henry Baxter (age 43, New York), wounded in the Wilderness, returned to command Second Brigade, Third Division, Fifth Corps. Poplar Spring Church, a simple frame building that did not survive the war, was located west of the intersection of Squirrel Level and modern Fort Emory roads.

31. Col. James Gwyn, commanding Third Brigade, First Division (Griffin), Fifth Corps, led the attack on the Confederate redoubt Ft. Archer. The hexagonal redoubt, reversed and renamed Ft. Wheaton by the Federals, is within the national park; the ground over which Gwyn's troops assaulted is outside the park boundary.

32. Peebles's house stood a half-mile south of Ft. Archer/Wheaton, west of Squirrel Level Road. The site of the Pegram house is within a dense pine thicket northwest of Ft. Fisher. The site has been recently acquired by a preservation group. The Boswell farm is occupied by a steel recycling plant.

33. Bragg's brigade was temporarily attached to Third Division. *OR*, vol. 42, 3:43. This line of earthworks is within the narrow strip of parkland that abuts Flank Road.

34. Gen. Lee transferred two divisions from his Petersburg front (Field and Hoke) north of James River for the failed attempt to retake Ft. Harrison on Sept. 30.

35. Meade: "A more wonderful escape I never saw. At first I thought my leg was gone, as I felt and heard the blow plainly, but it only rubbed the leather of my riding boot, without even bruising the skin. Afterwards Colonel Lyman had the shell dug up, and is going to preserve it." Meade, *Life and Letters*, 2:231. Burnside's former aides, Loring and Lydig, returned to Ninth Corps staff after being furloughed over the Mine inquiry.

36. Federal engineers worked diligently to tie the captured ground at Pegram's farm back into the existing line of fortifications. See *OR*, vol. 42, 1:167–68. The redoubt near the Pegram house was named Ft. Fisher and is within the battlefield park.

37. The redoubt near Widow Smith's was named Ft. Emory (extant on private property); at Vaughan Road, Ft. Siebert; near Forey's house, Ft. Clarke. A revetment was a retaining wall, in this case of logs, built into the rear of the earthen parapet to hold it upright.

38. Arthur Philip, Sixth Earl Stanhope, Lord Mahon; his father, Philip Edward Stanhope, a noted British historian and president of the London Literary Fund until his death in 1863. TL attended a literary fund dinner by invitation in London in May 1863 before his return to the states. Capt. Arthur Divett Hayter.

39. The Clements' house redoubt was named Ft. Cummings. The Boisseau house and a section of the Confederate Boydton Plank Road line are preserved within the Pamplin Historical Park.

40. Maj. Gen. Hastings Doyle, commander of British forces in Nova Scotia.

41. Brig. Gen. Alfred Torbert, commanding Sheridan's cavalry in the Shenandoah Valley, routed the Confederate cavalry divisions of Rosser and Lomax at Tom's Brook on Oct. 9.

42. The most reliable source for these casualty figures are the reports of Medical Director Thomas McParlin, who derived his numbers from regimental reports. For the period, May 1–Sept. 30, 1864, McParlin reported 8,010 killed, 45,000 wounded, and 19,258 missing, for a total of 72,268. The Sixth Corps during its time in the Shenandoah Valley lost more than 1,937 killed, wounded, and captured, making a grand total of 74,205. *OR*, vol. 36, 1:265; vol. 42, 1:200–201; vol. 43,1: 112, 120.

43. Norwegian artist Hans Balling was lieutenant colonel, 1st New York Infantry, wounded at Fredericksburg, and mustered out of service. His more successful postwar artworks were portraits of Civil War generals. Howard not identified.

44. Sheridan believed that Early was no longer a threat in the Shenandoah Valley and dispatched a portion of the Sixth Corps to return to the AoP; it was soon recalled.

45. Ft. Stevenson was a major fort on the line of contravallation (protecting the rear of the army). The fort survives on private property adjacent to Southlawn Memorial Park on modern Birdsong Road. The Williams house stood a half-mile east of the fort.

46. Dr. Hasket Derby (Harvard Medical 1858). TL's cousin Charles Eliot was in Paris studying chemistry and avoiding conscription.

47. Cpl. William Gilson was paroled on Mar. 10, 1865, and died on Mar. 22 of disease. Nelson Miles had been promoted to brigadier for gallantry at Spotsylvania; Barlow on sick leave. Dr. Barton (Burton?) not identified.

48. Col. Edward M. Gregory, 91st Pennsylvania Volunteers, and Col. James Gwyn, 118th Pennsylvania Infantry, for gallant conduct on Sept. 30. *OR*, vol. 42, 3:259. Meade recommended Col. John Irvin Gregg for a brevet. Col. (Bvt. Brig. Gen.) Hiram L. Brown, 145th Pennsylvania Infantry, reported for duty at HQ, Oct. 6. *OR*, vol. 42, 3:82. Gen. John Bell Hood and his Army of Tennessee marched into north Georgia in early October with the objective of destroying Sherman's supply line into Atlanta and forcing his withdrawal from the city. Hood captured railroad blockhouses near Dalton and tore up rails, but these breaks were readily repaired. Sherman did not let Hood's belated operations interfere with his planned march on Savannah.

49. Brig. Gen. Montgomery Cunningham Meigs, quartermaster general, and Brig. Gen. Amos Beebe Eaton, commissary general of the U.S. Army. Brig. Gen. Barnard, chief engineer of the armies in the field. Surgeon General Joseph K. Barnes. Secretary of War Edwin M. Stanton. Secretary of the Treasury William Pitt Fessenden;

his son Col. Francis Fessenden, wounded at Cane River. Samuel Hooper of Boston, U.S. representative from Massachusetts. Republican politicians Simeon Draper and Hiram Barney from New York. TL described this meeting to Mimi: "General Meade received them with his usual high ceremony. He walked out of his tent, with his hands in his pockets, said, 'Hullo, how are you?' and removed one hand, for the purpose of extending it to Grant, who lighted down from his horse, put his hands in *his* pockets, and sat down on a camp chair." *Meade's Headquarters*, 249.

50. Adm. David D. Porter. Col. George D. Wells, First Brigade, First Division, Eighth Corps was killed Oct. 13, during a reconnaissance to Hupp's Hill. *à tort et à travers*, "muddleheaded."

51. McMahon, AAG and CoS, Sixth Corps. Col. Charles Collis, 114th Pennsylvania Infantry.

52. Brig. Gen. Benham; his AAG Capt. Clapp, TL's Harvard classmate. Lt. Samuel W. Preston, U.S. Navy, was captured leading an amphibious assault on Ft. Sumter, Sept. 8, 1863, and exchanged. Dr. Pyne not identified. Capt. Charlie Mills, AAG for the disgraced Ledlie, joined Hancock's staff.

53. *Mais nous verrons*, "but we shall see."

54. At dawn, Oct. 19, Jubal Early's Army of the Valley, surprised the Federal army at Cedar Creek and drove it from its encampments. Sheridan, absent when his army was attacked, rode from Winchester to rally his dispirited troops, and organized a counterattack that routed Early's army. Wrote Wainwright: "This evening we can think and talk of nothing but another victory gained by Sheridan in the Valley. His dispatch is hardly as bombastic as some of his others, though the little word 'I' is to be found in almost every line of it." Nevins, *Diary of Battle*, 473. Confederate Maj. Gen. Stephen Dodson Ramseur died in Belle Grove mansion, which is preserved within Cedar Creek Battlefield Park. Brig. Gen. Daniel Davidson Bidwell (age 45, New York). Gen. Wright, Sixth Corps, slightly wounded; Ricketts, disabled by a bullet to the chest; and Brig. Gen. Cuvier Grover (age 36, Maine/Oregon, USMA 1850), Nineteenth Corps, seriously wounded in the arm. Col. Ranald S. Mackenzie. Col. J. Howard Kitching died of his wounds. Col. Charles Russell Lowell, commanding Reserve brigade of cavalry; his widow, Josephine Shaw, was Mimi's cousin.

55. Hunt first outlined his opinions on the artillery command structure in the previous July in a memorandum to army adjutant Williams. His concerns were to prevent unnecessary firing and waste of ammunition. Meade refused to remove all control over the artillery from the local infantry commanders. Hunt then required his battery officers to submit a written justification whenever they opened fire, detailing the need and upon whose orders. *OR*, vol. 40, 3:318.

56. Maj. Gen. Nathaniel Banks's AAG, R. Morris Copeland. Crawford discussed operations of May 23–25, 1862, in the Shenandoah Valley, leading up to Banks's defeat at Winchester at the hands of Stonewall Jackson.

57. The purported letter from Custer to his wife, printed in the *Richmond Inquirer*, Oct. 21, 1864, described an afternoon of bliss with a prostitute at Portentino's Restaurant in New York City. The editors opined: "Gen. Custer has opened to the inspection of

the world an inside view of Yankee society—he has shown it to be a charnel house, fair to view on the outside, virtuous in appearance, but concealing within the rottenness of the most abandoned licentiousness." Custer's cavalrymen had been prominent in the recent burning of barns and mills in the Shenandoah Valley.

58. Generals Winfield Scott and William Jenkins Worth were involved in acrimonious controversy during the Mexican War. Maj. Gen. Ethan Allen Hitchcock (age 66, Vermont, USMA 1817) was among the oldest officers on active duty during the Civil War; he served as commissioner for the exchange of prisoners. The *Independent* article (dated Oct. 13, 1864) is printed in Meade, *Life and Letters,* 2:341–42. This diatribe is a concise summary of the case against Meade that was promulgated before the Committee on the Conduct of the War.

59. Adj. Seth Williams issued detailed orders for the movement on Oct. 25. *OR,* vol. 42, 3:340–41.

60. Dabney's sawmill was located below Hatcher's Run on Dabney Mill Road (Rte. 613) about two miles south of its intersection with the Boydton Plank Road (U.S. Rte. 1). The sawmill had generated large mounds of sawdust that are mentioned in many accounts.

61. Woolsey, Bingham, Mills, and Mitchell identified. Lt. George W. Dresser, 4th U.S. Artillery, inspector of artillery; Dresser's report, detailing his staff duties and experiences on Oct. 27 in *OR,* vol. 42, 1:456–57.

62. The two-day fight, Oct. 27–28, was called the engagement at Hatcher's Run or Boydton Plank Road.

63. Engagement at Fair Oaks and Darbytown Road. Butler's operations continued Grant's two-prong strategy of threatening the Confederate flanks north and south of James River.

64. Brig. Gen. Lorenzo Thomas (age 60, Delaware, USMA 1823), AAG, War Department. French officers not identified. Likely Col. Charles W. Darling. Republican candidate for governor of New York, Reuben Fenton, defeated the Democratic incumbent, Horatio Seymour, by a slim margin. On Nov. 1, Grant ordered Gen. Butler to New York City "until after the election." Butler immediately requested Darling to serve as his ADC. *OR,* vol. 42, 3:481, 488; vol. 43, 2:91, 558. "Rhodomontade," a game in which each tries to out-brag the other.

65. In 1897, Col. Francis Pharcellus Church would pen: "Yes, Virginia, there is a Santa Claus."

66. TL to Mimi: "'Grant says I must write a report of the whole campaign,' says the General [Meade], in the discontented voice of a schoolboy who has been set a long exercise. 'I can't write a report of the whole campaign. I don't remember anything about some of it. I'm all mixed up about the Tolopotomoy and the Pamunkey and the what-do-you-call-'m creek.' Hence it came that I was requested to give him some extracts from my valuable archives, and I since have written a lot of notes for him, extending from May 4th to August 28th. He is very quick with his pen, is the General, and possesses a remarkable power of compressing a narrative and still making it clear and telling." *Meade's Headquarters,* 256. Capt. Algernon Sidney Alden, assistant adjutant general, War Department.

67. The regulars were to accompany Butler to New York City to assist with peace-keeping duties during the election.

NOVEMBER 1–DECEMBER 31, 1864

Lyman labeled this Vol. 14; it is assigned Lyman Papers, bound vol. 19, in the MHS.

1. Brig. Gen. William Schouler, adjutant general of Massachusetts. On paper, TL served on Schouler's staff. Capt. J. Henry Sleeper, 10th Massachusetts Battery, wounded in the arm at Ream's Station; his lieutenants H. H. Granger and Asa Smith mortally wounded Oct. 27. TL's neighbor and PC brother, Maj. Louis Cabot commanded companies F and G, 4th Massachusetts Cavalry, attached to Tenth Corps HQ. Brig. Gen. Alfred Howe Terry (age 37, Connecticut, Yale Law 1859). Brig. Gen. Godfrey Weitzel, Butler's former chief engineer, assigned to command Eighteenth Corps in place of William "Baldy" Smith. Weitzel afterward commanded Twenty-fifth Corps, made up of USCT regiments. TL's classmate Flint, 1st Massachusetts Cavalry. Maj. George G. Hastings, 1st U.S. Sharpshooters, formerly Gen. McCook's ADC. Lt. Col. J. P. Brinton, 2d Pennsylvania Cavalry.

2. Capt. Francis "Frank" Wister, 12th U.S. Infantry, was one of Capt. Meade's messmates. TL's PC brother William Thorndike. Col. Wells was killed on Oct. 13 in the Shenandoah Valley.

3. Edward Cunningham of Russell & Company married Frances Cary; he sought a contract to provide ships for the U.S. Navy. Paul Sieman Forbes, Cunningham's associate and a cousin of Boston shipping magnate John Murray Forbes. The Confederate ironclad *Albemarle* controlled the Roanoke River downstream from Wilmington from Apr. 1864 until Lt. William B. Cushing, U.S. Navy, detonated a spar-torpedo in her side and sank her on Oct. 27. Brig. Gen. Nelson Appleton Miles commanded First Division, Second Corps, in Barlow's absence.

4. Roebling would resign Jan. 21, 1865.

5. TL's aunt Mary Lyman Eliot.

6. Col. Henry Larcom Abbot, commanding the siege train, reported that, for October alone, the heavy guns at Petersburg and on James River delivered 139 tons of iron at the rate of 4.5 tons daily. *OR*, vol. 42, 3:511–12.

7. Holcombe's South Carolina Legion reached the Petersburg front on Oct. 16. The Confederate raider *Florida* captured or sank thirty-seven vessels before being seized by boats from the *Wachusett* inside the neutral port of Bahia, Brazil.

8. *Cyclops bicuspidatus*, a common microscopic crustacean found in pond water. TL referred to the phenomenon of "acoustic shadow," mentioned in numerous battle accounts.

9. Marsena Patrick wrote on Nov. 11: "Last night I was turned out of my bed, about 12 o'clock, by the arrival of Col. J. H. Taylor, with a guard of 25 men, on a special steamer, for the persons of Jere. McKibbin and his two confreres." Sparks, *Inside Lincoln's Army*, 441. Voting commissioner Jeremiah McKibbin was suspected of fraud in recording the votes of the 118th Pennsylvania Infantry.

10. TL's cousin Frances and husband Henry Foote named their daughter Mary.

11. Sherman would cut loose from his supply depot at Atlanta and began what would be called the "March to the Sea" on Nov. 15. In preparation, he destroyed the railroad and telegraph connections and burned everything of military value in the city. Hood's army reached the Tennessee River near Tuscambia by the end of October, where he awaited supplies before crossing. Meanwhile, Gen. George Thomas, with a portion of the Army of the Cumberland, was dispatched to organize the defense of Middle Tennessee against Hood's anticipated movement against Nashville.

12. A corduroy road was made by placing logs side by side specifically to allow use of the road in wet weather. Although originally from Philadelphia, John Gibbon's family had settled in North Carolina before the war. His wife was from Baltimore and her family was strictly "secesh." Gibbon's brothers: Richard served in the Confederate navy; Robert was a surgeon in Lane's North Carolina brigade; and Nicholas served in the 28th North Carolina. Two brothers-in-law were Confederate officers—Richard Lardner and James Humbert. Wright and Magner, "John Gibbon: the Man and the Monument," 120n.

13. Col. Charles Sawyer Russell of Boston, 28th USCT.

14. Surgeon George M. McGill of the cavalry corps, acting medical inspector, AoP.

15. Expedition against the South Side and Danville railroads, or Wilson-Kautz Raid, June 22–July 2. Brig. Gen. Thomas Wilberforce Egan (age 30, New York), wounded while temporarily commanding Gibbon's division, Second Corps.

16. Secretary of War Stanton to Grant, Nov. 13: "McClellan has resigned, his resignation accepted, and Sheridan appointed in his place on account of his great achievement of the 19th of October." *OR*, vol. 42, 3:612. Maj. Gen. Edward Canby commanded the Military Division of Western Mississippi. Sherman rested his armies at Kingston before continuing operations in central Georgia.

17. Maj. Septimus Carncross, AAG, Second Corps. Surgeon J. McNulty, First Division, assumed the position of acting medical director for the corps when surgeon Dougherty took leave of absence on Nov. 6. *OR*, vol. 42, 3:584. The Twenty-fifth Corps was organized in December to comprise the colored regiments in the Department of Virginia and North Carolina. TL's groom, Albert Woods, returned from Brookline after recovering from his illness.

18. Kirkpatrick and Herbert not identified. Henry Augustus Smyth of the Royal Artillery published observations of the siege of Richmond and Petersburg in *Minutes of Proceedings of the Royal Artillery Institution*, vol. 4 (1865), 363. Lunn not identified.

19. Sen. Henry Wilson of Massachusetts, a vocal abolitionist. Likely Henry Joseph Gardner, former governor of Massachusetts, who vehemently denounced Irish immigration.

20. Gregg's CS, Capt. Charles Treichel, and AAG Capt. Thomas Arrowsmith. Kershaw's Confederate division had been with Early in the Shenandoah Valley. Dr. John J. Milhau, medical director for Fifth Corps since before Gettysburg, was relieved on Nov. 14; Dr. Thomas Rush Spencer was appointed in his place. *OR*, vol. 42, 3:668.

21. Capt. Alexander James Dallas, 12th U.S. Infantry. Capt. Philip Schuyler Jr., 14th U.S. Infantry. Wilkins Micawber, a character in Dickens's *David Copperfield*. Provost

Marshal Marsena Patrick took Dallas on his staff in June 1864 as a personal favor to Gen. Meade. "I am thoroughly disgusted with the fellow," wrote Patrick. Sparks, *Inside Lincoln's Army*, 387–88. On Nov. 11, the War Department issued "British officer" Lt. Fairchild a pass to visit the army.

22. Sherman's columns fanned out on various roads after leaving Atlanta but converged on Milledgeville, Georgia's capital, Nov. 23, after defeating a force of militia the previous day at Griswoldville. The movement toward Macon was a ruse.

23. Due to continuing problems with his Gettysburg wound, Gen. Hancock relinquished command of Second Corps, taking with him many of his personal staff.

24. Grant's ADCs Comstock and Porter. Rufus Ingalls, chief QM, armies in the field. Sen. James Willis Nesmith was a harsh Lincoln critic. New Jersey politician Oliver Spencer "Pet" Halsted and former U.S. Sen. Preston King. King was influential in securing War Democrat Andrew Johnson's nomination as vice president. Benson, Leary, and Monroe not identified.

25. Butler's ADC, Lt. Sidney B. De Kay. Amos Binney of Massachusetts, army paymaster. Maj. Peter Smith Michie (USMA 1859), chief engineer, AoJ. Col. Alexander Piper, 10th New York Heavy Artillery, chief of artillery, Eighteenth Corps. Butler's CoS Brig. Gen. John Wesley Turner (age 31, Illinois, USMA 1855). Brig. Gen. Edward Augustus Wild of Brookline, First Brigade, Third Division, Eighteenth Corps.

26. Godfrey Weitzel, appointed major general of volunteers, Nov. 17, commanding Eighteenth Corps. Forts Harrison and Brady are within the national battlefield park.

27. Col. Benjamin Chambers Ludlow, formerly Meade's ADC, assigned to Butler's HQ.

28. Levi Short of Philadelphia developed the Greek fire of Civil War vintage, probably a combustible solution of phosphorus in bisulfide of carbon.

29. As ranking division commander in Second Corps, Maj. Gen. John Gibbon expected to replace Hancock. Humphreys would lead Second Corps until war's end. Former U.S. congressman from Virginia, Roger Atkinson Pryor, resigned his commission as brigadier general in Aug. 1863 and enlisted as a private in the 3d Virginia Cavalry.

30. Col. Charles Izard Maceuen, 198th Pennsylvania Infantry, killed on Lewis Farm, Mar. 29, 1865; his brother, Malcom Maceuen (Harvard 1855). Ft. LaFayette in New York City Harbor housed prisoners accused of treason.

31. In 1855, Lt. Gouverneur K. Warren led a survey party along the Platt River in Nebraska Territory. On St. Andrew's Eve, young women saw their future husbands in a dream, and buried treasure glowed in the dark; evidently the spirits were at work on Rosie, as well.

32. Stony Creek Depot on the Weldon RR, about twenty miles south of Petersburg. TL's classmate Clapp. Likely Lt. Col. Francis Washburn, commanding a battalion of the 4th Massachusetts Cavalry assigned to HQ, AoJ. Lt. Col. Ira Spaulding, 50th New York Engineers.

33. Lt. Gen. John Bell Hood attacked Schofield's army at Franklin on Nov. 30, losing 6,000 casualties and five general officers killed. Thomas ordered Schofield to withdraw within the defenses of Nashville. Hood followed with his crippled army and attempted

a siege, based more on bravado than capability. The *Florida* was towed from Brazil to Norfolk, where it collided with an army transport and sank. Maj. Norman R. Fitzhugh, chief QM of Hampton's division, was captured Dec. 2. Capt. Lazell not identified.

34. Charles Russell Lowell's widow, Josephine; their daughter Carlotta.

35. "If confirmed by the Senate," Meade wrote, "it places me fourth in rank in the army—Grant, Halleck, and Sherman only being my seniors." Meade, *Life and Letters*, 2:251.

36. The Vaughan Road (Rte. 675) and Squirrel Level Road (Rte. 613) run roughly parallel and cross Hatcher's Run about nine miles southwest of Petersburg. The Armstrong house and mill stood near the run just north of Squirrel Level Road. The Sixth Corps was returning to the AoP after serving under Sheridan in the Shenandoah Valley. Gregg placed Capt. James L. McIlhenny, 12th New Jersey Infantry, under arrest. George Blagden (Harvard 1856).

37. Brig. Gen. Frank Wheaton commanded First Division, Sixth Corps. Maj. Rufus P. Lincoln, 37th Massachusetts Infantry, Wheaton's acting IG. "McClennan" was likely Capt. George Clendenin Jr., Wheaton's AAG. Col. Ranald S. Mackenzie, commanding Wheaton's Second Brigade, wounded at Cedar Creek.

38. Maj. Gen. Crittenden had been angling for a corps command since June. Meade offered him a division under Parke, Ninth Corps, but Crittenden declined to serve under a junior officer and tendered his resignation on Dec. 7. *OR*, vol. 42, 1:689, 842–43.

39. Capt. Algernon Sidney Alden, AAG, War Department, delivered the brevets. Capt. Campbell Dallas Emory, 9th U.S. Infantry, ADC. Capt. William S. Stryker, signals officer. Brig. Gen. Seth Williams, Meade's AAG. Brig. Gen. Lorenzo Thomas, adjutant general of the regular army. Brig. Gen. Barnard, chief engineer of armies in the field. Brig. Gen. Richard Delafield, chief engineer of the regular army. Col. Benjamin Franklin Fisher promoted and appointed head of the Signal Corps in Washington, D.C., *vice*, "as opposed to" Col. Albert James Myer, who formerly held the position. Capt. Frederick "Rosie" Rosenkrantz. Capt. Jacob Henry Sleeper. Col. Edmund Schriver, IG, AoP.

40. Brig. Gen. Truman Seymour captured at the Wilderness and exchanged. Viscount De Marivault commanded the French corvette *La Tisiphone* then in James River on a diplomatic mission to evacuate French citizens from Richmond.

41. Warren directed an expedition to destroy the Weldon RR between the Nottoway and Meherrin rivers as far as Hicksford to within ten miles of the North Carolina line; this particularly vindictive raid left a trail of burning houses and barns in its wake.

42. The War Department issued Lt. J. V. Satterthwaite a pass to visit the AoP on Dec. 3.

43. Col. Michael Kerwin reconnoitered to Hatcher's Run with the 6th Ohio and 13th Pennsylvania Cavalry. *OR*, vol. 42, 1:494–95.

44. Col. Henry Goddard Thomas, 19th USCT, assigned command of Third Brigade, Third Division, of the newly organized Twenty-fifth Corps, Maj. Gen. Godfrey Weitzel commanding.

45. Maj. Manlius Sargent, commanding 1st Massachusetts Cavalry. Warren's report: "The country enabled us to forage our animals to some extent. Scarcely a man was to

be found. Many houses were deserted or contained only helpless women and children. We had evidences, however, of the men lurking about in the woods, for on our return it is reported some of our men were found dead along the route; in one instance, with throat cut. Whether this was true or not, it soon became the belief of all the men in the command, and in retaliation almost every house was set on fire. Every effort was made by the officers to stop this incendiarism (which most likely punished only the innocent), and with partial success." *OR*, vol. 42, 1:443–46.

46. Getty's Second Division, Sixth Corps. Wright's staff: AAG Maj. Whittier; IG Lt. Col. Jacob Ford Kent; ADC Capt. Arthur McClellan; and chief of artillery Col. Charles Henry Tompkins.

47. Rosie's friend, Lt. Carl Berlin. Twenty-two-year-old Francis Charles Needham (Oxford 1863), 3d Earl of Kilmorey, Lord Newry.

48. Twenty-one individuals from the Second Corps awarded the Medal of Honor are listed in *OR*, vol. 42, 3:812.

49. Capt. John W. Summerhayes, 20th Massachusetts Infantry, acting asst. IG, 2d Division, Second Corps. The controversy over who did what, when, and where in the Wilderness continues to this day.

50. Eleven Medal of Honor awardees from the Ninth Corps are named in *OR*, vol. 42, 3:815.

51. Ft. McAllister guarded the southern approaches to Savannah. With its capture, Sherman, who had been incommunicado for more than a month as his army trudged across Georgia, established contact with the U.S. Navy. Thomas's attack at Nashville on Dec. 16 destroyed Hood's Army of Tennessee as an effective fighting force. With about 5,700 cavalrymen, Maj. Gen. George Stoneman raided from Knoxville along the Virginia & Tennessee RR into southwestern Virginia. The saltworks at Saltville produced much of the Confederacy's supply. At this point in the war, nearly 2,000 slaves from all over the South were employed there distilling salt from brine wells. Special artist for *Harper's*, Alfred Waud. Gen. Hood's dispatch concerning the battle of Franklin and giving details of the loss of generals was printed in the *Daily Examiner* on this date.

52. Crawford's CM, Lt. James P. Mead.

53. Maj. Gen. Gershom Mott, Third Division, Second Corps. Maj. Gen. Lewis Wallace, Middle Military Department. Col. A. H. Markland, special agent of the Post-Office Department. Newell A. Thompson, volunteer ADC on Butler's staff. On this date, Meade wrote his wife: "Mrs. Lyman has sent me a Christmas present of a box of nice cigars." Meade, *Life and Letters*, 2:253.

54. Mimi's father George Robert Russell; her brother Col. Henry Sturgis Russell, 5th Massachusetts Cavalry (Colored). The Federal prisoner-of-war camp at Pt. Lookout, Maryland, is a state park.

55. Weld had been captured at the battle of the Mine. Ned Browne placed TL's name for consideration in the Union Club, and he was accepted.

56. TL's future brother-in-law (he would marry the elusive Emily), Col. Charles Lawrence Peirson (Lawrence Scientific 1853), 39th Massachusetts Infantry, wounded in August during the fight for the Weldon RR.

57. Thomas Gold Appleton (Harvard 1831), notorious in Boston for his acerbic wit, was quoted at one point as saying, "When good Bostonians die, they go to Paris." Col. Greely Stevenson Curtis, 1st Massachusetts Cavalry, resigned from the army in Mar. 1864 with broken health due to chronic malaria; Curtis studied at the Lawrence Scientific School before the war but could not complete the curriculum because of poor eyesight.

58. Howland and Cora Lyman Shaw hosted the dinner at their house on Beacon Hill. Samuel Parkman Shaw; his sons George, Robert, and Samuel Jr. and daughters Mary and Mabel; Uncle Park's sister, Anna Blake Shaw, married William Batchelder Greene. Pauline Agassiz Shaw, daughter of the professor and wife of Quincy Adams Shaw.

59. Prof. Louis Agassiz was a founding member of the National Academy of Sciences (1863). Against the backdrop of civil war, the members heatedly debated the merits of Darwin's theories.

60. "Ned" Browne (Harvard 1855, PC), Charles Thorndike (Harvard 1854, PC), Augustus Thorndike Perkins (Harvard 1851, PC), William Church Otis, Robert Charles Winthrop (Harvard 1854, PC), Edward Wainwright Codman (Harvard 1854, PC), Frederick Wainwright Bradlee (Harvard 1860, PC), John Simmons Sale (Harvard Law 1855), and George Bigelow Chase (Harvard 1856, PC). The "great A" was merchant prince Abbott Lawrence, whose business partner was Thomas Handasyd Perkins, Augustus's grandfather.

61. John Gardner Cushing of Watertown (*hon. mem.* PC) and wife Susan; his brother Robert. Mr. and Mrs. Richard T. Parker.

62. After discharge from the 1st Massachusetts Cavalry, Maj. Henry Pickering Bowditch accepted a commission in Hal's regiment, the 5th Massachusetts Cavalry (Colored). Bowditch went on to graduate from Harvard Medical School (1868) and became a preeminent professor of physiology.

63. Confederate Ft. Fisher defended the entrance of the Cape Fear River and access to the port of Wilmington, North Carolina, the last haven of blockade runners on the Atlantic coast. In mid-December, Adm. David D. Porter and Maj. Gen. Benjamin F. Butler led an amphibious operation to capture Wilmington with the result described by TL. The fleet returned to Ft. Monroe with little to show for the operation.

64. TL offered here a very astute synopsis of the war situation.

January 1–July 1, 1865

Lyman labeled this Vol. 15; it is assigned Lyman Papers, bound vol. 20, in the MHS; selected entries from Lyman's vol. 16, assigned bound vol. 21 in the MHS.

1. George Williams Lyman would die in 1880 at the age of 93. William Denning was sole trustee of TL's grandfather's William Henderson's estate, and his letters discussing the Henderson accounts are a study in obfuscation. In 1834, the Henderson family sued Denning for misappropriating funds.

2. Mimi's aunts Amelia Eloisa Russell (b. 1798) and Rose Russell. John Murray Forbes, one of Boston's wealthiest men, was instrumental in raising funds to support

the war effort; his son, Maj. William Hathaway Forbes (Harvard 1861, PC), 2d Massachusetts Cavalry, captured near Aldie in June 1863; his youngest son, John Malcolm Forbes. The elder Horace Gray, noted horticulturalist and founder of the Boston Public Gardens, and wife lived at 79 Mt. Vernon Street. Horace Gray Jr. (Harvard 1845, Harvard Law 1849) was appointed associate justice of the Massachusetts Supreme Court in Aug. 1864; Gray shared TL's passion for natural history, being something of an expert on birds and butterflies. Maj. John Chipman Gray (Harvard 1859, PC), Gen. Foster's ADC in the Department of the South.

3. TL's nephew Robert Russell.

4. John Quincy "Jack" Adams. Likely William Church Otis, grandson of Harrison Gray Otis, third mayor of Boston.

5. TL's cousins, Arthur Theodore Lyman and Lydia Lyman Paine; Lydia married real estate lawyer and investor Robert Treat Paine, TL's Harvard classmate. Arthur was treasurer of the Lowell textile mills. Paine was great-grandson of a signer of the Declaration of Independence.

6. Alex Agassiz lectured regularly at the museum. TL's PC brothers: Col. Frank Palfrey, Frederick Wainwright Bradlee, and John Gardner Cushing. Scientific artist Jacques Burkhardt was their guest.

7. Gaetano Donizetti's *Don Sebastian*, first performed in 1843. Domenicio Lorini and Signor Susini were veteran players in the traveling opera company.

8. After Lincoln's reelection, Butler's political usefulness faded, and the failed amphibious operation against Ft. Fisher proved his undoing. Butler, from Lowell, Massachusetts, continued his political career after the war as a U.S. congressman and as governor of the Commonwealth. Ten-term U.S. congressman and former governor of Massachusetts, Maj. Gen. Nathaniel Prentiss Banks, was eased out of field command after his failed Red River campaign.

9. Likely Mrs. John Turner Sargent. Henry Winthrop Sargent (Harvard 1830, PC). Likely lawyer Francis E. Parker, mentor of Robert Treat Paine. John Sturgis. Edwin Boott.

10. Dr. Robert William Hooper and daughter Elizabeth "Nellie" Hooper. Anna Lowell. Dr. Samuel Parkman, an early pioneer in the use of anesthesia at Massachusetts General Hospital.

11. Ned Browne's brother Francis Charles Browne (Harvard 1851).

12. Chairman of the Committee on the Conduct of the War, Sen. Benjamin Wade of Ohio, continued to block Meade's confirmation as major general in the regular army. Maj. William Hathaway Forbes and his young brother, John Malcolm.

13. Edward Everett (1794–1865).

14. Daniel Auber's 1830 comic opera *Fra Diavolo* (Brother Devil) was loosely based on the life of a notorious French highwayman, viewed as something of a Robin Hood. Cast members, Signor Lotti, Signor Bellini, Signorina Morensi, Amati Dubreuil, and Joseph Weinlich.

15. After an unrelenting naval bombardment, Ft. Fisher was taken by ground assault on Jan. 15. Lt. Samuel W. Preston, aide to Rear Admiral David Porter, was killed

leading a landing party in the assault. See TL's entry Oct. 19, 1864. TL mistook Lt. Col. Jonas W. Lyman, 203d Pennsylvania Infantry, killed in the attack, for Lt. Col. Luke Lyman, 27th Massachusetts Infantry.

16. Benjamin William Crowninshield (Harvard 1858, PC).

17. Meade to TL, Jan. 14, 1865: "By the by, perhaps you can be of some service to me, by influencing Senators in my favor, as I anticipate opposition to my nomination in the Senate. If through your friends you can secure the vote of any senators it will be a service." Urging Meade's confirmation as a major general in the regular army, TL and his in-laws penned letters to senators Charles Sumner and Henry Wilson, and to influential financier John Murray Forbes, a close associate of Gov. Andrew. Donizetti's *La Figlia del Reggimento*. Clara Louise Kellogg.

18. Widow Eliza Cabot, TL's Brookline neighbor. Commission merchant Samuel Lawrence, worth $350,000 in 1852, was bankrupted by the Panic of 1857. "Cranium" Clarke Cabot was Mrs. Cabot's brother-in-law.

19. Edward Everett was a Boston institution—doctor of divinity, author, minister, orator, five-term U.S. congressman, Massachusetts governor, ambassador to England, president of Harvard, secretary of state under Pres. Tyler, U.S. senator, president of Boston's Union Club. Edward's son, William Everett. Wise not identified. Hon. George Tyler Bigelow, chief justice of the Massachusetts Supreme Court. Robert C. Winthrop, president of the Massachusetts Historical Society.

20. Grant tapped Seth Williams to be IG of the armies—a promotion for Williams but a decided loss to Meade, who relied heavily on his administrative skills. Mr. Lombard not identified.

21. TL's dinner guests are identified.

22. TL's caretaker, Silas Langley. A charade might be composed of tableaux, in which costumed participants acted out scripted scenes. Sir Walter Scott's *The Abbott* revolved around the imprisonment of Mary Queen of Scots. Although somewhat conjectural, TL's guests included notables: likely Prof. Fairman Rogers, Harvard lecturer, member of the National Academy of Sciences, and associate of Prof. Louis Agassiz; noted essayist and literary critic, Edwin Percy Whipple, a relative by marriage to Howland Shaw; possibly Rose, wife of Robert Bennett Forbes; possibly Gov. and Mrs. Andrew. Mrs. Edwards not identified.

23. The Forbes Group and investors James Forbes and Nathaniel Thayer were developing oil, railroad, and mining interests in Kansas and Missouri during the war. After the war, Alex Agassiz (who trained as a mining engineer) became president of Calumet Mining Company, one of the most productive copper mines in Michigan. He used his wealth to finance a series of zoological expeditions, beginning in 1875. Nathaniel Bowditch, mathematician and investment banker in Boston, and grandfather of "Miss Mary."

24. A portrait of Rev. Francis Higginson of Salem hung on the wall; Harvard professor George Ticknor, founder and trustee of the Boston Public Library; George Tyler Bigelow, chief justice of the Supreme Judicial Court of Massachusetts; William Gray (Harvard 1829), museum trustee and brother of Francis Calley Gray who endowed the museum; Prof. Jacob Bigelow, former president of the American Academy of Arts and

Sciences; Dr. James Walker, Harvard president emeritus; Prof. Louis Agassiz, museum founder; James Lawrence, whose father endowed the Lawrence Scientific School. On Jan. 24, a fire broke out in the Smithsonian building in Washington, D.C., today known as the Castle. The blaze destroyed the second floor and roof of the building as well as part of the museum's collections.

25. Lon and Billy Morris, Johnny Pell, and J. C. Trowbridge were renowned black minstrels, who performed as Pell and Trowbridge's Minstrels and Cowbellogians. Banker Richard S. Parker and wife Martha of Beacon Hill. James Codman and wife Eliza lived in Brookline. Likely John Samuel Cushing (Harvard Medical 1858). TL's special friend Mary Ingersoll Bowditch; her younger brother Ebeneezer Francis Bowditch. Col. Weld identified.

26. Maj. Charles Whittier, Sixth Corps AAG. TL's uncle Quincy Adams Shaw and wife Pauline lived at 241 Perkins Street, Jamaica Plain, overlooking Jamaica Pond. Elizabeth Cabot Cary Agassiz, wife of Prof. Louis, ran a female academy and postwar became president of Radcliffe College; their daughter, Ida. Elizabeth "Nellie" and Marian "Clover," daughters of Dr. Robert William Hooper. Clover was a student at Mrs. Agassiz's academy. Possibly Lt. William Edward Perkins, 2d Massachusetts Infantry.

27. Roebling married Warren's sister Emily and completed the bridge over the Ohio River with his father. Boston wit Thomas Gold "Tom" Appleton. Capt. William Montrose Graham commanded the horse artillery. TL liked to insert bits of army dialect—"sich" for "such" and "wus" for "worse," for example. One of his favorite Virginianisms was "right smart of," which is still used in the Tidewater.

28. Francis Howard Peabody. Charles, brother of Nathaniel G. Greene. *Quondam*, "former, at one time."

29. "Neither slavery nor involuntary servitude, except as a punishment for crime whereof the party shall have been duly convicted, shall exist within the United States, or any place subject to their jurisdiction." The House of Representatives passed the 13th Amendment to the Constitution by the requisite two-thirds majority. Pres. Lincoln signed the legislation on Jan. 31.

30. Dr. Henry Ingersoll Bowditch, professor of clinical medicine at Harvard Medical School; his son, Lt. Nathaniel Bowditch, 1st Massachusetts Cavalry, mortally wounded Mar. 17, 1863.

31. Maj. Louis Cabot, 4th Massachusetts Cavalry, resigned Jan. 17, 1865. Likely Charles Perkins Gardner. Walter and Elliott not identified.

32. TL likely had his news from the morning's *Daily Advertiser*: "Mr. Wade spoke an hour and a half against [the nomination], reviewing Meade's whole military career, denouncing him for his failure to follow up the victory of Gettysburg, expressing the belief that he was mainly responsible for the Petersburg mine affair, showing instances of his arbitrary treatment of junior officers, and declaring that his attempted intimidation of General Pleasanton was cause for impeachment. Meade was nominated on the special recommendation of General Grant, and was finally confirmed by a vote of thirty-two to five." According to TL's tentmate Rosenkrantz, the headquarters staff celebrated Meade's confirmation: "There arrived Gen'l Meade in fine spirit and humor.

He ask me if that was the place to show foreigners the front and the line. I answered that in my opinion it was the savest [*sic*] place near the front, where upon he remarked that if we stood long time on the same mentioned place it would not be very save [*sic*] because the number of drinks were not few—his magnificent band was playing and a kind of a toast was brought out for Gen'l Meade." Rosenkrantz to TL, Feb. 2, 1865. Lyman Papers MHS, box 18.2. Robert Charles Winthrop Jr. (Harvard 1854).

33. TL's niece and nephew, Amy and Francis Shaw. Mimi's younger sister, Sarah "Sallie." TL's uncle Quincy Adams Shaw and wife Pauline. Cora and Howland Gardner Shaw.

34. Widower James Lawrence would later marry Anna Lothrop Motley. Arthur Lithgow Devens (Harvard Law 1843). Lawyer William Amory. Virginian William Cabell Rives (Harvard Law 1847). Capt. Charles Payson, 2d Massachusetts Cavalry, on the staff of Brig. Gen. Charles Devens. After weeks of informal, behind-the-scenes diplomacy, Pres. Lincoln and Secretary of State Seward met briefly with Alexander H. Stephens (vice president of the Confederacy), John A. Campbell (former U.S. Supreme Count justice and Davis's asst. secretary of war), and Confederate senator Robert M. T. Hunter (former U.S. senator from Virginia) to discuss the possibility of peace. Lincoln insisted on three conditions that the commissioners could not meet: restoration of the Union, abolishment of slavery, and the surrender and disbandment of hostile forces. After this meeting Stephens withdrew from the Confederate government and retired to his home in Crawfordsville, Georgia.

35. Meade to TL, Feb. 1, 1865: "Yesterday at City Point I met & conferred with the three distinguished citizens of the Southern Confederacy who have come into our lines on their way to Washington to see if Peace is possible.—I told them frankly upon what terms I thought our people would consent to Peace, but I do not anticipate much from their mission beyond satisfying our people that peace at present is not practicable. They seemed to think slavery would not be an obstacle, but they hinted they ought to have more constitutional guarantees for *state rights*. I told them I thought this would not be countenanced. He was satisfied with the old constitution & would have no change except what was necessary to *finally* settle the slavery question. They were very affable & polite & spoke very freely & after hearing all I had to say regretted the settlement could not be left to the *Generals* in the field—which I thought a good sign. God grant something may come out of their visit." Lyman Papers MHS, box 18.2.

36. Martin Brimmer (Harvard 1849, PC). Augustus Perkins (Harvard 1951, PC).

37. Dr. Jonathan Mason Warren was curator of Harvard's Anatomical Museum, located on Grove Street near Massachusetts General Hospital. The "Zeuglodon" was unearthed in Alabama and toured the United States and Europe in the 1830s, displayed as a "sea serpent." Paleontologists later revealed that the creature had been pieced together, using the vertebrae of five different fossilized whales. The shipping firm of William E. Sturgis (died in 1863) and John Bryant. Caleb Chace not identified. Mimi's brother, Col. Henry Sturgis Russell, resigned his commission in the 5th Massachusetts Cavalry (Colored); he was succeeded in command by Lt. Col. Charles Francis Adams Jr., who wrote: "I got a cool letter from Colonel Russell informing me that he had resigned and

was on the point of leaving the regiment. This makes me full Colonel, and in so far is pleasant enough, but I regard it as decidedly a promotion down stairs as between the command of my regiment and the position I might have held in the Second Corps staff." Ford, *Cycle of Adams Letters,* 2:256. *Aetas,* "at the age of."

38. Meade to TL, Feb. 9, 1865: "On the 4th inst. at 12 M. Gen. Grant sent me word he would like the cavalry to move out on the Boydton plank road & try to intercept some of the enemy's wagon trains, plying between Belfield & Petersburg.—Accordingly at daylight on the 5th, Gregg went to Dinwiddie C.H. which he occupied by noon capturing 25 wagons.—Warren with the 5th Corps moved on the old stage road & took position near Dinwiddie.—Humphreys with two divisions of the 2nd Corps took position on Hatchers run at Armstrongs Mill & the crossing of the Vaughan road." Lyman Papers MHS, box 18.2. Grant's instructions to Meade in *OR,* vol. 46, 2:397.

39. Meade to TL, Feb. 9, 1865: "On the 6th both Humphreys and Warren advanced to give battle. H. found the enemy had retired to his works but Warren found him on the Boydton road & the woods road to Dabneys mill. The fighting was quite spirited till about dark—W. driving the enemy before him & occupying Dabneys mills—when the enemy moved on Crawford & Ayres and after a desperate assault that painful but too familiar spectacle of pack mule bands all caving to the rear, made known the fact that Crawford & Ayres had been broken & forced back. Wheaton was immediately advanced & Gregg withdrawn & the enemy checked & the men rallied & gotten into good order in the lines from whence we started in the morning." Lyman Papers MHS, box 18.2. The AoP suffered more than 1,500 casualties in this operation, mostly from Fifth Corps. Brig. Gen. John Pegram of Virginia was killed. Brig. Gen. D. McM. Gregg, commanding Second Cavalry Division, lost two of his brigadiers slightly wounded: Henry Eugene Davies and J. Irvin Gregg (leg). Col. Henry Clay Bankhead, IG, Fifth Corps. A preservation group owns property at Hatcher's Run battlefield.

40. Likely lawyer Charles Russell Codman (Harvard Law 1852), member of the state senate and former colonel of the 45th Massachusetts Infantry. Codman was related to TL through marriage to Lucy Lyman Paine.

41. Brig. Gen. Gilbert Moxley Sorrel of Georgia, formerly Longstreet's CoS, was shot through the lung but survived to write *Recollections of a Confederate Staff Officer.*

42. Many of the old Boston traders suffered from gout, thought to have been precipitated by impurities in the Madeira wine of which they were so fond. Edward Zerdahelyi appears not to have published his manuscript.

43. Rev. Rufus Ellis, minister of the First Church in Boston. Arthur Lithgow Devens (Harvard 1840).

44. Meade to Lyman, Feb. 9, 1865, as quoted earlier. The junction of the South Carolina RR at Branchville, with lines to Augusta and Columbia, had not been captured by Sherman's forces. Reports of the Confederate evacuation of Charleston were premature. Although Mobile Bay was closed off to blockade runners by Adm. Farragut's fleet in Aug. 1864, the city remained in Confederate hands until Apr. 1865. Temple was killed at Chancellorsville; Abbott at the Wilderness; Mason wounded at Gettysburg and discharged for disability; Swan wounded at Spotsylvania and returned to duty in Jan. 1865 as AAG, Second Division, Fifth Corps.

45. Milton Hill, a suburb of country estates on the Neposet River, eight miles south of Boston. Otis Ammidon (1771–1858) was married to Abigail Russell, sister of Amelia and Rose. Turner and Winthrop Sargent; their father, Henry Sargent, was a noted portrait painter. Charles Pickering Bowditch (Harvard 1863) married Cornelia Livingston Rockwell in 1866. Francis Caleb Loring (Harvard 1828).

46. After the war, Mr. Thuolt returned to Budapest as a member of the Hungarian parliament.

47. James Arthur Emmerton (Harvard 1855), surgeon, 2d Massachusetts Heavy Artillery. TL's PC brother Martin Brimmer. Brig. Gen. George Henry Gordon's former AAG, Capt. Henry Bruce Scott (Harvard 1860), was appointed to Butler's staff in Nov. 1864 and assumed command of the 4th Massachusetts Cavalry in Mar. 1865.

48. Mrs. Woods, mother of Albert, TL's groom. Samuel Ward, brother of Julia Ward Howe, lyricist of "The Battle Hymn of the Republic." The Greenoughs were a well-known Boston family, but their identities in this context are unclear.

49. Charles Dabney (Harvard Law 1853). The southern law student may have been Charles Appleton Miles (Harvard 1853). Possibly William Gardiner Prescott (Harvard 1844).

50. Sherman's forces occupied Columbia, South Carolina, on Feb. 17 and were accused of systematically burning the town to the ground; other accounts blamed the fire that destroyed much of the city on retreating Southern cavalrymen.

51. Sherman's march through the interior of South Carolina isolated Confederate forces on the coast and forced Gen. Hardee to evacuate Charleston on Feb. 18. Union forces had besieged the city since June 1862.

52. The four types of Madeira were named for the predominant grape variety (from driest to sweetest): Sercial or "S," Verdelho, Bual, and Malmsey. "Tinta" was a generic blend best suited for cooking, not sipping.

53. "Mrs. Washington" unexplained. Regular army engineer Col. James Duncan Graham. Col. N. G. Taylor, a commissioner for the relief of destitute loyal citizens of East Tennessee.

54. Samuel Ward previously resided at 20 Louisburg Square, a neighbor of the Russells. Likely Philip Howes Sears (Harvard 1844). John Chandler Bancroft was an artist of the Newport School along with James McNeill Whistler and John Frederick LaFarge. LaFarge married Margaret Perry, niece of Commodore Matthew Calbraith Perry. The Boston Museum of Fine Arts holds several of LaFarge's works, including *Flowers in a Japanese Vase*, completed in 1864. After the war Bancroft forsook art for business and in partnership with Alex Agassiz grew wealthy from his mining investments.

55. Maj. Gen. John McAllister Schofield commanded Twenty-third Corps, transferred by rail and water to North Carolina after defeating Hood's army at Franklin and Nashville. The defiant city of Wilmington had at last fallen, despite the arrival of Robert Hoke's division as reinforcement. Hoke had been at Richmond and Petersburg with the ANV.

56. Harrison Gray Otis lived at 45 Beacon Street until his death in 1848 in a house designed by Charles Bullfinch and built in 1806. The house stands today and is

headquarters to the American Meteorological Society. A famous equestrian statue of George Washington—his upraised arm suitable for holding a flag—was erected on the grounds of the state capital building at Richmond in 1858.

57. Banting's diet, avoiding fat, starch, and sugar, was "published and much discussed in 1864," according to the *Oxford English Dictionary*. Meade's eldest son, John Sergeant Meade, died on Feb. 21, while the general was en route to Philadelphia to visit him. Bereaved but dutiful, Meade returned to the army on Feb. 28. Col. George N. Macy accepted the position, replacing Brig. Gen. Marsena Patrick as provost marshal, AoP, on Mar. 16. *OR*, vol. 46, 3:5.

58. William Amory accompanied fellow cotton manufacturer and former congressman, William Appleton, to Charleston in Apr. 1861 in an eleventh hour bid to avoid war. The men arrived offshore aboard the steamer *Nashville* in time to see Southern guns fire upon Ft. Sumter. Afterward Appleton and Amory met with Confederate officers and officials, some of whom were former associates in the cotton trade.

59. The Russells lived at 1 Louisburg Square.

60. Adams Express was the preeminent private mail and freight delivery company of the Civil War. Col. George L. Schuyler. Capt. Jedediah Chase Paine, signals officer, Ninth Corps.

61. The Hygeia Hotel was a noted antebellum resort. At this point in the war, the hotel's upper floors had been razed to clear a field of fire for the guns of Ft. Monroe. The Victorian-era Chamberlin Hotel currently occupies the site. Captains Philip Schuyler and William W. Beckwith were on Marsena Patrick's staff. Henry Hunt's AAG Capt. John Neville Craig. Lt. Henry Hollingsworth Humphreys en route to join his father's staff, directing Second Corps.

62. Brig. Gen. Alexander Stewart Webb (age 30, New York, USMA 1855), wounded at Gettysburg and again at Spotsylvania, assumed the role of Meade's CoS on Jan. 11, 1865. Meade to his wife, Mar. 2: "Lyman has returned without waiting for my summons, he becoming nervous for fear some movement of Lee's might precipitate matters before he could get notice, and if the army should move, it might be a difficult matter to join it." Meade, *Life and Letters*, 2:265. John Codman Ropes of Boston (Harvard 1857) would become an early historian of the war and active with TL in the Military Historical Society of Massachusetts. On Mar. 31, he wrote: "My visit to the Army was a great success. I went down with Humphreys, staid with him two or three days, living at his table; I had a long and very interesting talk with Meade; I dined and smoked with Wright; I was introduced to Grant. I saw and staid with Jim Higginson, Whittier, Jarves and others." Ford, *War Letters*, 464.

63. Lt. Col. Edward Livingston Campbell, 15th New Jersey Infantry, wounded at Cedar Creek. Capt. Charles B. Whittemore, asst. QM. J. Miles Kephart, 84th Pennsylvania Infantry, mustered out at the end of Dec. On Feb. 2, Col. George David Ruggles (age 31, New York, USMA 1855) replaced Seth Williams as AAG of the AoP; Williams became Grant's inspector general. Grant had an eye for Meade's talent. Maj. Jacob Henry Sleeper, 10th Massachusetts Battery, resigned his commission in February.

64. This was the line established after the fighting at Hatcher's Run in February, segments of which survive on private property. Ft. Sampson is no longer extant.

65. Brig. Gen. Henry Eugene Davies assumed command of Second Division, Cavalry Corps, upon the unexpected resignation of Brig. Gen. David McMurtie Gregg after the Hatcher's Run operations. Lt. Col. George Amos Kensel, IG, HQ AoJ.

66. John C. Babcock, a civilian expert on the organization of the Confederate armies employed by Col. Sharpe, Bureau of Military Intelligence. Babcock was a likely source for TL's estimates of Confederate forces in the field. Capt. Philip Schuyler, asst. provost marshal, would have provided details on enemy deserters.

67. Capt. Botiano not identified. Emperor Trajan conquered the region that would become Rumania and settled it as the Roman province of Dacia. The Rumanian language derives from Latin. The Porte (the Muslim ruler of Turkey) extended protection to the largely Christian population (as did the French and the Austrian Empire). βάςβαςοι, "barbarians."

68. This branch of the military railroad ran due south for a mile to near Ft. Blaisdell to service the rear-facing line of siege works.

69. Lt. Col. Ira Spaulding, 50th New York Engineers, commanding the Engineer brigade. One image of the much-photographed Poplar Grove Church is found in *Gardner's Photographic Sketch Book of the War*, vol. 2, plate 74. The church was located within the grounds of Poplar Grove National Cemetery.

70. Col. (brevet brigadier) Charles S. Wainwright commanded the artillery brigade of Fifth Corps. Brig. Gen. Ranald Slidell Mackenzie (age 24, New York, USMA 1862) promoted to command of the cavalry's Second Division, AoJ. Adj. Charles Whittier. Gen. Wright's ADCs, majors Arthur McClellan and Henry Weld Farrar. Ft. Fisher and Battery No. 27 are within the national battlefield park. The signal tower stood within what is now the Dinwiddie Memorial Park.

71. Col. Wyatt's house stood next to the military railroad. The trestle work crossed Arthur's Swamp ¾ mile to the east of Cummings house, which stood near the intersection of Squirrel Level and modern Plantation roads. Maj. Thomas Lloyd Haydn, Wright's ADC.

72. Julia Dent Grant. As president, Grant would appoint Judge Joseph P. Bradley as a justice to the U.S. Supreme Court. Michigan judge George Woodruff had two sons killed in action with the AoP. William W. Harding took over publication of the *Philadelphia Inquirer* from his father, Jesper Harding, in 1859. William's brother George, a patent lawyer, was lead attorney in an 1855 case over patent infringement on the McCormick Reaper; associates in the case were Edwin M. Stanton and a little-known (at the time) Springfield lawyer named Abraham Lincoln. Surgeon Silas Atherton Holman, medical director. Col. Joseph Warren Keifer, Second Brigade, Third Division; and Col. William Henry Penrose, First Brigade, Second Division, Sixth Corps, both wounded at Cedar Creek.

73. Brig. Gen. Joseph J. Bartlett. Lt. Col. Arthur Russell Curtis. Lt. Col. Edmund Rice. Col. Joe Hayes. Blatchford (not identified) likely asked after Boston wag, Thomas Gold Appleton.

74. The Committee on the Conduct of the War conducted its own investigation of the Mine debacle in January, exonerated Burnside, and predictably placed blame on Meade.

75. Sheridan's 10,000 cavalrymen routed and made prisoner nearly all of Gen. Jubal Early's 1,700 soldiers at Waynesboro on Mar. 2. Early's dogged defense of the Shenandoah Valley, at times brilliant, ended ingloriously with the general and his staff fleeing capture.

76. For Doyle, see TL's entry for Oct. 11, 1864. Capt. George Blight Halsted of New Jersey, Fifth Corps AAG. Former governor of Massachusetts, John Henry Clifford. Brevet Brig. Gen. Joseph Eldridge Hamblin, commanding Third Brigade, First Division, Sixth Corps. The president's son, Capt. Robert Todd Lincoln (Harvard 1864), joined Grant's staff as AAG.

77. Ft. Welch is preserved within the battlefield park. Likely Republican congressman James Kennedy Moorhead. Financier Jay Cooke & Company of Philadelphia rejuvenated lagging sales of the "seven-thirty" loans and raised $830 million for the war effort. Andrew Johnson would be president in little more than a month.

78. A column marching inland from New Bern, commanded by Maj. Gen. Jacob D. Cox, encountered the Confederate divisions of Robert Hoke and Daniel Harvey Hill at Wyse Fork near Kinston, Mar. 7–10. Maj. Gen. Benjamin Franklin Cheatham with two consolidated brigades from the Army of Tennessee was en route to join Confederate forces in North Carolina but saw no action until Mar. 21.

79. Congress bestowed a gold medal to Grant in a joint resolution, passed Dec. 17, 1863. The medal with its ebony and gold-inlaid presentation box is held in the National Museum of American History. Capt. Duncan Archibald Pell, formerly Burnside's ADC.

80. TL referred to the fight at Jerusalem Plank Road, June 21–23, 1864. TL's survey notes not found.

81. Hampton's troopers surprised Kilpatrick's camps at dawn, Mar. 10, at Monroe's Crossroads in Hoke County, North Carolina. With Early's defeat at Waynesboro, Confederate resistance in central Virginia collapsed. Sheridan's cavalry occupied Charlottesville on Mar. 3; Custer's division advanced along the Virginia Central RR and Devin's rode south to destroy the James River Canal. The columns were to meet up at White House on the Pamunkey River. Provost Marshal Col. George Macy and Lt. Edward B. Robins, ADC.

82. TL's surmise was on the mark. On Mar. 8, Confederate forces under Maj. Gen. Robert F. Hoke attacked Cox's column and captured about 1,000 men. After receiving reinforcements, Cox continued his advance on Kinston. Hoke attacked again on Mar. 10 but was repulsed. Sherman was moving on Raleigh

83. Col. John Caldwell Tidball, chief of artillery, Ninth Corps.

84. Republican senators Henry Wilson of Massachusetts, Lot Myrick Morrill of Maine, and Lafayette Sabine Foster of Connecticut.

85. Secretary of War Edwin M. Stanton. U.S. representative from Massachusetts Samuel Hooper; his daughter-in-law, Alice Mason Hooper, widow of Capt. William Sturgis Hooper. Mrs. Hooper was briefly wed to Sen. Charles Sumner after the war.

86. TL referred to the "small affair" at Hatcher's Run, Feb. 5–7, where AoP casualties were 1,539 killed, wounded, and captured. Capt. John McLean Hildt, 3d U.S. Infantry, on "special duty" in camp near army headquarters. Lt. Col. William Hathaway Forbes, 2d Massachusetts Cavalry, would wed Edith Emerson, daughter of Ralph Waldo Emerson.

87. Col. George Von Schack, 7th New York Infantry. Maj. Philip Mesier Lydig, AAG, Ninth Corps. Brig. Gen. Thomas F. Meagher.

88. The 114th Pennsylvania Infantry (Collis's Zouaves) had served as HQ guard, AoP, since Jan. 1864. Meade requested the 11th U.S. Infantry to replace the red-legs, as he wanted to build a reserve of regular army regiments. *OR*, vol. 46, 3:304.

89. TL's classmates Capt. Channing Clapp (Benham's AAG), Edwin Hale Abbot (class secretary), and surgeon Edward Barry Dalton. Brig. Gen. Henry Washington Benham, Engineer brigade. Likely Capt. J. Thomas Elliott, Benham's chief CS. Likely father-in-law of Charles Tasker Howard (Harvard 1856). Sheridan rested and refitted for several days on the Pamunkey River before continuing to Petersburg to rejoin the AoP. Schofield's Twenty-third Corps entered Goldsboro, Mar. 21, and united with Sherman's columns two days later.

90. Thornton Alexander Jenkins, captain of USS *Richmond* at Mobile Bay in Aug. 1864, coauthored with Richard Bache a study on the design and construction of lighthouses. Capt. Percival Drayton served as Adm. Farragut's flag officer, and CoS Drayton was Meade's schoolmate at the American Classical and Military Lyceum in Philadelphia in the late 1820s. Capt. James Alden directed the USS *Brooklyn* during the amphibious assault on Ft. Fisher in January.

91. Rear Admiral David Dixon Porter, North Atlantic Blockading Squadron. Lt. Commander John S. Barnes of the side-wheel steamer USS *Bat*. Asst. Secretary of the Navy Gustavus V. Fox. Robert Shaw Sturgis of Boston retired from the firm Russell & Co. in 1858 a wealthy man. Likely Sturgis's associate, John Cleve Green, the prominent merchant, China trader, and Princeton University benefactor. Brig. Gen. Ranald Slidell Mackenzie.

92. The guests arrived on the steamer *Thomas Collyer*. Capt. William Jay, ADC. Capt. William E. Barrows, 19th Massachusetts Infantry, joined HQ staff with CoS Webb. Col. James Allen Hardie (brevet brigadier), IG of the regular army, War Department. Meade and his wife, Margaretta Sergeant Meade (age 50); their children, Maj. George Meade (age 21), Margaret (age 20), Spencer (age 14), Sarah (age 13), Henrietta (age 12), and William (age 9). ADC Cadwalader had two unmarried sisters, Frances and Sarah. Likely Adj. John Neville Craig. Maj. James Cornell Biddle had been on furlough since January and was returning to duty. Capt. William White of Philadelphia mustered out of service the previous October. Others not identified.

93. Steamer *Lillie Martin*. The iron side-wheel gunboat USS *Malvern*, a former blockade runner, was captured at Wilmington in Nov. 1863 and pressed into service with the U.S. Navy. USS *Monadnock*, the first twin-turret monitor, was built at the Boston Navy Yard and served briefly on James River.

94. The president and his party reached City Point after dark on Mar. 24 aboard the steamer *River Queen*. He was greeted at the gangplank by Gen. Grant. In a letter to Mimi, TL added, "I never wish to see [Lincoln] again, but, as humanity runs, I am well content to have him at the head of affairs." *Meade's Headquarters*, 324. Fort Stedman is within the battlefield park.

95. Meade's CM William Wilkins Sanders, commissioned lieutenant colonel of the 2d Pennsylvania Cavalry to date from Apr. 2, 1865. Richard Barlow, Frank's brother.

96. Maj. Gen. William Tecumseh Sherman arrived at City Point from North Carolina aboard the steamer *Russia* on Monday afternoon. Gibbon commanded Twenty-fourth Corps, which was constituted in December from the white troops of Tenth and Twenty-eight Corps; his division commanders were Foster and Devens. Brig. Gen. August V. Kautz, First Division, Twenty-fifth Corps, consolidated regiments of USCT. Maj. Smythe of the Royal Artillery.

97. Summary of orders issued to the AoP, Mar. 27, by Meade's AAG Ruggles. *OR*, vol. 46, 3:198–99.

98. The War Department issued passes to visit the AoP to Talbot and Ralph Abercrombie on Mar. 23. British rifle regiments wore dark green uniforms.

99. Inspector general of the armies, Brig. Gen. Seth Williams had returned from a tour of troops on the Atlantic coast. The Confederate brigades of Wise and Wallace launched a spoiling attack against Griffin's lead brigade under Brig. Gen. Joshua Chamberlain after it crossed Rowanty Creek at Lewis's farm. Chamberlain was slightly wounded in the fight. Gen. Henry A. Wise was Mrs. Meade's brother-in-law.

100. Humphreys's AAG Capt. Charlie Mills, 56th Massachusetts Infantry, had served generals Stevenson, Ledlie, Hancock, and Humphreys in turn. TL wrote of Mills: "When I rode that evening to the hospital, and saw the poor boy lying there on the ground, it made me think of Abbott, a year ago. It is the same thing over and over again. And strange too, this seeing a young man in full flush of robust health, and the next moment nothing that we can make out but the broken machine that the soul once put in motion." *Meade's Headquarters*, 332.

101. Battle of White Oak Road. A portion of the Confederate defenses are protected and interpreted by a preservation group.

102. Mrs. Meade's brother, Col. William Sergeant, 210th Pennsylvania Infantry, was struck in the thigh by a minié ball and died, Apr. 11, while en route to a Washington hospital. Gen. Meade wrote to his wife: "Willie had established a high character for himself, and was doing so well that it seems hard he should be thus suddenly taken off." Meade, *Life and Letters*, 2:272. TL's acquaintances, Capt. James Ingersoll Grafton (Harvard 1862) and Lt. Samuel Storrow (Harvard 1864), 2d Massachusetts Infantry, were killed when Schofield's force was overrun at Wyse Fork, Mar. 16. Meade's G.O. No. 13 condemned Brig. Gen. McLaughlin, Third Brigade, First Division, Ninth Corps, for a "reprehensible want of vigilance" contributing to the Mar. 25 surprise attack at Ft. Stedman. After examining the evidence, Meade rescinded the order and declared that the Ft. Stedman assault was a *ruse de guerre*, "by which the very best officers may, at times, be victimized." Meade's correction was published in the *New York Times* on Mar. 31, 1865.

103. Lt. Charles Harrod Campbell, ADC to Humphreys.

104. Warren reined in his errant third division and brought it into the rear of Pickett's position, cutting off the retreat of thousands of Confederates. Had he and Sheridan been on friendly terms, Five Forks would likely have been upheld in the history books as a model of tactical cooperation. In this passage, TL seemed to concur with Sheridan's decision to dismiss Warren.

105. Brig. Gen. Robert Brown Potter recovered from his wound. Col. Frederick Winthrop, 5th New York Infantry, commanding First Brigade, Second Division.

106. The Lead Works were located near the intersection of the modern Halifax and Defense roads. Some of these earthworks survive.

107. The 114th Pennsylvania Infantry (Collis's Zouaves) lost thirty-three killed and wounded in a futile assault against the fortifications near Ft. Mahone. The small Confederate garrisons of forts Gregg and Whitworth delayed Gibbon's advance long enough for Gen. Lee to organize an interior line of defense. Ft. Gregg is part of the national park; Ft. Whitworth survives (barely) on the grounds of the Central State Hospital.

108. Four Confederate brigades under Brig. Gen. John R. Cooke had dug in to cover the South Side RR at Sutherland Station but held on for only a few hours. Miles took 600 prisoners.

109. Lt. Col. Joseph L. Le Conte (Lawrence Scientific 1851), a professor of chemistry, mineralogy, and geography. TL's classmate Brig. Gen. Joseph Hayes, captured in Aug. 1864 in the operations around Globe Tavern and exchanged in January, assumed command of First Brigade, Second Division (Ayres), Fifth Corps. Maj. Francis Bache, Meade's ADC.

110. The restored Blandford Church features fifteen stained glass memorial windows executed by master Louis Comfort Tiffany.

111. Lt. Gen. Ambrose Powell Hill, commanding Third Corps ANV, reported to Gen. Lee at Edgehill on Cox Road then rode with a few aides toward Heth's headquarters on the Boydton Plank. The party encountered skirmishers from the Sixth Corps, one of whom shot Hill above the heart, killing him instantly. A rarely visited stone monument in the woods north of A. P. Hill Drive and Sentry Hill Court marks the spot of his death.

112. Weld recorded this meeting: "Saw Theodore Lyman, who is probably home by this time. He was very kind to me indeed, and gave me several articles of clothing which were very acceptable." Weld, *War Diary*, 397. Weld was returning to duty with the 56th Massachusetts Infantry.

113. Lt. Col. James W. Walsh, 3d Pennsylvania Cavalry, army provost guard. Brig. Gen. Rufus C. Barringer led a brigade of North Carolina cavalry in "Rooney" Lee's division.

114. Meade wrote, "The men of this army will show that they are as willing to die of fatigue and starvation as they have ever shown themselves ready to fall by the bullets of the enemy." *OR*, vol. 46, 3:549. Col. Richard Napoleon Batchelder replaced Rufus Ingalls as chief QM of the AoP in February.

115. The accurate British Armstrong rifle was a breech-loading steel gun that used a "shunt" system. When the weapon was fired, projecting studs on the elongated projectile took the rifling of the barrel. Davies's report: "[I brought off] 5 guns, 11 flags, 320 white prisoners, an equal number of colored teamsters, and over 400 animals, captured from the enemy, leaving behind me 200 blazing ammunition and headquarters wagons, caissons, and ambulances." *OR*, vol. 46, 1:1145.

116. Considering the controversy among staff over Sheridan's role in the campaign, the fact that Meade resumed command of Fifth Corps at Jetersville is important.

117. Maj. Henry Young led a contingent of "Jessie Scouts," who wore Confederate uniforms and invoked deep Southern accents when patrolling behind enemy lines. Sheridan used the scouts extensively in the Shenandoah Valley.

118. Brig. Gen. William Hays (age 45, Tennessee, USMA 1840), 2d U.S. Artillery, was a highly decorated officer during the Mexican War. Gen. Humphreys reported: "At General Hays' headquarters I found every one sound asleep.... I learned from General Smyth that no order of precedence had been given to the brigade, and in consequence no one was moving. I ordered him to lead and move at once. I have relieved General Hays from the command of the Second Division and assigned General Smyth to it." *OR*, vol. 46, 3:597–98.

119. In a dispatch directed to Grant, Sheridan wrote: "I attacked them with two divisions of the Sixth Army Corps and routed them handsomely, making a connection with the cavalry. I am still pressing on with both cavalry and infantry." *OR*, vol. 46, 3:610. The battle of Sailor's Creek involved three fairly distinct combats. Sheridan's cavalry cut off the main route of Confederate forces on the road to Rice's Station and fought troops under Richard A. Anderson at Marshall's Crossroads. A mile north, Richard Ewell deployed his infantry to repulse Wright's Sixth Corps, which pressed him closely on the Hillsman farm. Three miles northwest at the Double Bridges, Humphreys's Second Corps overwhelmed Gordon's Confederates when their trains became mired in the bottomland. Wright's losses were 440, Humphreys's 536, and Sheridan's 172 in the afternoon's fighting. Total Confederate losses were 7,700, mostly taken as prisoners. A portion of Wright's and Well's battlefield is within Sailor's Creek Battlefield State Park.

120. Maj. Gen. George Crook, commanding Second Division, Cavalry Corps; his brigadier, J. Irvin Gregg, was captured in the action.

121. Maj. Henry W. Farrar, Wright's ADC.

122. Barlow assumed command of Second Division, Second Corps, from Brig. Gen. Thomas Smyth on the morning of Apr. 6. North of Farmville, a Confederate sharpshooter sent a bullet through Smyth's neck that paralyzed him. He died on Apr. 9, likely the last Federal general killed in combat. Brig. Gen. Gershom Mott was wounded near Amelia Springs on Apr. 6, his third serious wound of the war. Col. Francis Washburn was pistol-shot through the mouth and sabered across the head; he died Apr. 22. Washburn's detachment of the 4th Massachusetts was nearly annihilated in the fight to save the High Bridge.

123. Maj. Thomas L. Livermore, acting IG, Second Corps. The Appomattox was crossed by the railroad bridge (partially destroyed) and a wagon bridge that remained intact. If both bridges had been destroyed, according to Humphreys, Lee could have reached Appomattox Station unmolested ahead of the Federal cavalry, retrieved the rations that awaited him, and reached Lynchburg by Apr. 9. Humphreys, *Virginia Campaign*, 390–91. "Oolitic" coal deposits occur as outcroppings that are mined from pits, rather than from continuous seams.

124. The Elam house survives as a private residence a half-mile west of the intersection of the Richmond-Lynchburg Stage Road (Rte. 636) and the Lynchburg Wagon Road (Rte. 635). The Stutes' house, "Clifton," stands just beyond the Stage Road intersection with U.S. Rte. 15.

125. In response to Grant's note to Lee of Apr. 7, asking for Lee's surrender and stating his wish to avoid a "further effusion of blood," Lee replied the next day: "To be frank, I do not think the emergency has arisen to call for the surrender of this army, but as the restoration of peace should be the sole object of all, I desired to know whether your proposals would lead to that end." *OR*, vol. 46, 1:56. Grant replied that he was authorized to accept the surrender of Lee's army but could not negotiate any broader political issues.

126. Sheridan's CoS, Brig. Gen. James William Forsyth (age 29, Ohio, USMA 1856). The division of Brig. Gen. George Armstrong Custer reached Appomattox Station near dark of Apr. 8, cut the railroad, and cornered the artillery reserve of the ANV. The Confederate artillerymen maintained their position without support for nearly two hours against repeated assaults before being overrun with the loss of more than twenty-five cannon.

127. Maj. Robert Johnson Wingate, IG, Third Corps, ANV.

128. In a letter home, dated Apr. 9, TL enclosed one of Humphreys's Confederate $100 bills. He had scrawled on the back: "My dear Mimi, the Army of Northern Virginia, under Gen. Lee today surrendered to the combined forces of Meade, Sheridan, and Ord, under Lieut. Gen. Grant."

129. Maj. Gen. Charles William Field of Kentucky commanded Hood's old division in First Corps, ANV.

130. Schaff quoted TL's description of Lee in *Sunset of the Confederacy*.

131. Lt. Col. Charles Marshall, Lee's ADC since Mar. 1862. Lt. Col. Briscoe Gerard Baldwin, Lee's chief ordnance officer. Capt. Franklin Harwood, commanding the battalion of regular engineers. C. M. Hunter, asst. surgeon and medical purveyor. Former governor of Virginia, Henry A. Wise. Charles James Faulkner Jr., volunteer ADC to Wise.

132. Confederate generals James Longstreet and John Brown Gordon. Maj. Gen. William H. F. "Rooney" Lee was TL's classmate for three years and a crewmember on the rowing shell "Harvard." Lee was tapped for the PC in 1858 but left Harvard University before graduation to join the regular army.

133. Col. Halifax not identified. Col. Charles S. Wainwright was a brigadier by brevet. Nate Appleton. The Rumanian Botiano. The ANV thrice invaded the North: Antietam (1862), Gettysburg (1863), and Early's Maryland campaign (1864). Every Federal offensive in Virginia was seen as a campaign against Richmond. Only McClellan, Grant, and Butler made direct attempts to capture the capital of the Confederacy. Judge Robert Ould, Confederate agent of prisoner exchange.

134. Bache's discomfiture was temporary; he remained on Meade's staff and soon was promoted to brevet lieutenant colonel.

135. On Apr. 9, Rooney's cousin, Maj. Gen. Fitzhugh Lee, led his cavalry division out of the Appomattox encirclement and made for Lynchburg with the intent of reaching Johnston's army in North Carolina. Recognizing the futility of further resistance, he disbanded many of his regiments on the morning of Apr. 11 and reported himself to Federal authorities.

136. When Brig. Gen. James Brewerton Ricketts was wounded at Cedar Creek in Oct. 1864, Brig. Gen. Truman Seymour assumed command of his Sixth Corps division.

137. Wartime governor William Smith of Virginia served five years as state senator, five terms in the U.S. Congress, and two terms as governor of the state. He was elected a Confederate congressman but insisted on commanding troops in the field from 1861 through 1863 and was wounded five times in battle. Before the war, Smith operated a mail service in the South and from his habit of charging a little bit "extra," he earned the sobriquet of "Extra Billy."

138. G.O. No. 15: "By this army this announcement will be received with profound sorrow, and deep horror and indignation. The President, by the active interest he ever took in the welfare of this army, and by his presence in frequent visits, especially during the recent operations, had particularly endeared himself to both officers and soldiers, all of whom regarded him as a generous friend. An honest man, a noble patriot, and sagacious statesman has fallen! No greater loss, at this particular moment, could have befallen our country." *OR*, vol. 46, 3:789.

139. Mrs. Meade's brother. *Poco a poco*, "little by little."

140. Brig. Gen. Charles Griffin assumed command of Fifth Corps upon Warren's dismissal.

141. Maj. Wooten received TL's flag of truce at Cold Harbor. See TL's entry for June 5, 1864.

142. Charles James Faulkner, four-term U.S. congressman from Virginia, was minister to France in 1859. Faulkner joined Jackson's staff as AAG in Jan. 1863 and penned many of the general's official reports.

143. Pres. Lincoln favored Andrew Johnson, U.S. senator from Tennessee and military governor of the state, as his second vice president to demonstrate his intent to reconcile the Northern and Southern factions. Johnson, from loyalist East Tennessee, backed many of the harsher aspects of Reconstruction for which he was impeached in 1868 for "high crimes and misdemeanors."

144. Bvt. Maj. Gen. Joseph Bartlett, assigned command of Second Division, Ninth Corps, on Apr. 22.

145. Ninth Corps staff officers: Col. Charles Greely Loring Jr., IG ADCs majors James Lyman Van Buren and William Cutting; captains Robert Hale Ives Goddard and Duncan Archibald Pell. Surgeons Ned Dalton and Samuel Adams.

146. Patrick Tracy Jackson Jr., 5th Massachusetts Cavalry.

147. Lt. Col. Adam Badeau, formerly a reporter for the *New York Evening Express*, served as Grant's military secretary from Mar. 1864 to July 1866. The publication of Badeau's *Military History of Ulysses S. Grant* (1868) caused a stir among Meade's former staff officers, who felt that Badeau slighted their general.

148. Boston businessman and industrialist John Murray Forbes, wife Sarah Hathaway, his sister Mary Abbot Forbes Cunningham, and brother-in-law Francis Cunningham. Forbes counseled the Lincoln cabinet on naval affairs and was an early advocate for emancipation. Likely financier Samuel Gray Ward (Harvard 1836, PC).

149. The William W. Corcoran compound at 17th Street and Pennsylvania Avenue expanded to become the Corcoran Gallery of Art, one of the country's finest museums.

150. Mrs. Meade, her daughter Margaretta Meade and husband Charles R. Smith. Meade to his wife: "I am glad Lyman called to see you. He is an honest man and a true

friend. He has a healthy mental organization, which induces him to look on all matters in the most favorable light." Meade, *Life and Letters,* 2:276

151. The text of the "Memorandum of Agreement" signed by Sherman and Johnston near Durham Station, N.C. on Apr. 18 (*OR,* vol. 47, 3:243) reads like a peace agreement between two sovereign countries. The fifth article, presumably referring to slavery, reads, "The people and inhabitants of all the States to be guaranteed, so far as the Executive can, their political rights and franchises, as well as their rights of person and property, as defined by the Constitution of the United States and of the States." Sherman acknowledged that he and Johnston were not "fully empowered by our respective principals to fulfill these terms," but it was a grievous mistake to presume to speak for the new executive, Pres. Andrew Johnson. Secretary of War Stanton disapproved the memorandum on Apr. 21, ordered Sherman to resume hostilities, and immediately dispatched Grant to North Carolina to rein in his subordinate. "I reached here this morning," Grant wrote to Stanton on Apr. 24 "and delivered to General Sherman the reply to his negotiations with Johnston. Word was immediately sent to Johnston terminating the truce, and information that civil matters could not be entertained in any convention between army commanders." *OR,* vol. 47, 3:311. Johnston surrendered his army on Apr. 26.

152. Lincoln's assassin, John Wilkes Booth, was run to ground and shot in a burning barn near Port Royal, Virginia, on Apr. 26. The four men who lost their lives in Booth's pursuit—Carroll, Grosnell, Huntington, and Farley—are interred beneath the flagpole in Alexandria National Cemetary.

153. Louis Cabot. Washburn, mortally wounded near Farmville, Apr. 7.

154. PC Honorables: William Edward Howe (1852), Augustus Perkins (1851), George B. Chase (1856), Theodore Chase (1853), Edward Ingersoll Browne (1853), Benjamin Crowninshield Mifflin (1862), Hollis Hunnewell (1858), and Charles Frederick Lyman (1855). Immediates: William Lawrence Tucker (1865), Richard Cranch Greenleaf (1866), George Harrison Mifflin (1865), James Reed Chadwick (1865), and George Derby Welles (1866).

155. After his abrupt dismissal by Sheridan at Five Forks, Warren spent the rest of his life trying to clear his reputation. He was exonerated by an army court of inquiry in 1879 and died soon after, a bitter man. Humphreys sent to TL a copy of his *Report upon the Physics and Hydraulics of the Mississippi River* "with an apology for asking so much space on your bookshelves." Humphreys to TL, Apr. 26, 1865. Lyman Papers MHS, box 18.5. Jeffries Wyman, Harvard professor of anatomy and president of the Boston Natural History Society, an early proponent of Darwin's theories of evolution. Agassiz's assistant, Samuel Hubbard Scudder, an authority on Orthoptera and Lepidoptera. Dr. William J. Walker, benefactor of the society.

156. Belgian paleontologist, Laurent Guillaume De Koninck, collected fossil invertebrates.

157. Editor's note: from this point on, the narrative has been abridged to include entries that pertain to TL's Civil War experience. TL continued to document his affairs in detail. Researchers interested in Boston's social history should consult the original manuscript.

158. Evidently, Henry Russell's wife, Mary, made a dramatic recovery from her maladies after he resigned his commission, and TL was disgusted.

159. Gov. Andrew appointed TL chairman of the Commission of Inland Fisheries, a position he would hold for seventeen years. TL's scientific credentials and family ties with textile mill owners made him a logical choice for the newly created position.

160. Jefferson Davis and his party fled south in an attempt to reach Texas to reconstitute the Confederate government. A detachment of the 4th Michigan Cavalry, led by Lt. Col. D. B. Pritchard, surrounded and surprised his camp at dawn, May 10, just outside Irwinville, Georgia. Davis was imprisoned in a casemate cell in Ft. Monroe.

161. *Harper's Weekly* printed a caricature of Davis wearing a hoop skirt and bonnet and brandishing a bowie knife at his captors. Davis was wearing a generic waterproof over his civilian clothes and a man's shawl when captured. Secretary of War Stanton kept these items locked in a safe in the War Department. He seemed to prefer the hoop skirt story.

162. Engineer Charles Storer Storrow (Harvard 1829), designer of the dams, locks, and mills at Lawrence. Edmund Dwight, along with George Williams Lyman (TL's uncle), Thomas H. Perkins, William Appleton, Samuel Cabot Jr., and Ignatius Sargent were partners in the Hadley Falls Company that dammed the Connecticut River in 1849.

163. John Alden Loring (Harvard 1843).

164. The AoP paraded down Pennsylvania Avenue on May 23, taking five and a half hours to pass the reviewing stands. Sherman and the western armies marched on May 24.

165. Col. Henry Lee, TL's Brookline neighbor, had taken it upon himself to organize a commemoration of Harvard's military men to coincide with Harvard's commencement.

166. The Grand Review of the AoP was held May 23 as TL previously noted.

167. Capt. Robert Bennett Forbes, former China trade merchant in the firm of Perkins & Co., ship owner and designer. Forbes was a political ally of Gov. Andrew and supported the war financially; his daughter Edith married Charles Eliot Perkins. Mimi's sister Emily was good friends with Edith. Before the war, the Alston and Pringle families were prominent in Charleston's rice aristocracy; at least one Pringle and two Alstons graduated from Harvard and were members of the Porcellian Club. Capt. Thomas Pinckney Alston (Harvard 1854), 14th South Carolina Infantry. William Bull Pringle and wife Mary Motte Alston; their son William.

168. TL sought a place for his nephew, Lt. Robert Shaw Oliver, on Gen. Meade's staff, but Meade had no openings.

169. Edwin Hale Abbot, secretary Harvard class of 1855; his brother, Maj. Henry Larcom Abbot, directed the siege artillery before Petersburg; Abbot's report was published as *Professional Papers Corps of Engineers No. 14: Siege Artillery in the Campaigns Against Richmond* (New York: D. Van Nostrand, 1868).

170. TL's classmate Charles Augustus Chase. PC brothers Mifflin, Tucker, and Chadwick identified. Former AoP staff officer, Benjamin Ludlow. "Rooney" Lee's mansion at White House Landing on the Pamunkey was burned during the war.

171. Gov. Frederick Smyth was elected to the office in 1865. Col. Michael T. Donahoe,

10th New Hampshire Infantry. The regiments were mustered out June 21–22.

172. Henry Adams Bellows of Walpole, New Hampshire, was an associate justice of the state supreme court.

173. A baker's apprentice or doughboy was often dusted head to toe in flour, and it seems a small stretch to refer to an infantryman, his uniform dusted white after a long march, as a "doughboy." The term was first applied to American soldiers during the Mexican War: ἔγωγε, "at least it seemed to me."

174. Capt. Edward Austin Flint's detachment, 1st Massachusetts Cavalry, provided an escort for the topographical engineers engaged in mapping battlefields of the Virginia campaign. His lieutenant, John W. Howland of Amherst.

175. Mary E. Surratt kept the boarding house in Surrattsville, Maryland, where John Wilkes Booth met with his co-conspirators. Lewis Thornton Powell, a.k.a. Lewis Paine, stabbed and seriously wounded Secretary of State Seward. George A. Atzerodt and David E. Herold were assigned to assassinate Vice President Johnson but backed out. Dr. Samuel Mudd set Booth's broken leg; his ancestors have tried since to exonerate him from involvement in the conspiracy. Samuel Arnold and Michael O'Laughlin were brought into a plot to abduct the president but refused to participate in his assassination. Edward Spangler, the stage carpenter at Ford's Theatre, held Booth's horse while Booth shot the president.

176. Capt. John Coalter Bates.

177. TL's cousin, historian Francis Parkman.

178. Jonathan Russell of New York was a relative of Mimi's.

179. Col. Frank Palfrey's father, Dr. John Gorham Palfrey (Harvard 1815, PC), was a Unitarian minister, Harvard Divinity School professor, *North American Review* editor, U.S. congressman, wartime postmaster of Boston, and historian, known for his *History of New England*. Meade and his staff officers considered Sheridan's official reports from the battle of Sailor's Creek as erroneous, deceitful, and self-serving.

180. The guest list for Meade's dinner was dominated by those whose relatives had been killed in the war. The Revere family lost two brothers: Col. Paul Revere, killed at Gettysburg and Dr. Edward Revere killed at Antietam; John Codman Ropes's brother Henry, killed at Gettysburg; Dr. Henry Ingersoll Bowditch lost his son Nathaniel; Alfred Reed lost his son J. Sewell Reed; and poet and professor of modern languages James Russell Lowell lost two nephews, James and Charles. Other participants included Maj. Henry Harrison Bingham, judge advocate and adjutant, Second Corps; Brig. Gen. William Johnson Dale, surgeon general for the Massachusetts state militia; Col. Stevie Weld; TL's uncle Howland Shaw; TL's neighbor Col. Henry Lee; TL's close friend James Lawrence; Capt. George Middleton Barnard Jr.; Capt. Wendell Holmes; Dr. Charles Mifflin; TL's neighbor William Gray; Maj. John Chipman Gray; Col. Henry Sturgis Russell; E. F. Lincoln Jr., mayor of Boston; Oliver Wendell Holmes Sr., professor of anatomy and physiology at Harvard; Col. George N. Macy, provost marshal, AoP; Col. Richard Napoleon Batchelder, chief QM, AoP; and Gov. John Albion Andrew.

181. Harvard Class of 1855: class secretary Edwin Hale Abbot; Alex Agassiz, Museum of Comparative Zoology; Louis Arnold; Brig. Gen. Frank Barlow; Willard

Flagg Bliss; Philadelphia clergyman Phillips Brooks; lawyer Ned Browne; Chicago businessman Edward Jackson Browne; Charles Augustus Chase, Worcester banker; Capt. Randolph Marshall Clark, 1st Massachusetts Cavalry; surgeon Ned Dalton; John Woods Edgerly, clerk in Iowa; Dr. James Arthur Emmerton, 2d Massachusetts Artillery; businessman F. W. Fiske; Edward Augustus Gibbens, teacher in Waltham; Dr. John Green of Brookline; New York City lawyer (and sometimes playwright) Joseph Heywood; soldier and clergyman James Kendall Hosmer, author of *The Thinking Bayonet* (published 1865); TL's good friend Sam Johnston, Chicago businessman; Boston lawyer Leonard A. Jones; architect William P. Longfellow; mining engineer Benjamin Smith Lyman; Rhode Island clergyman William S. McKenzie; Philadelphia lawyer James T. Mitchell; lawyer Robert Treat Paine (husband of TL's cousin Lydia); Boston clergyman James Reed; Cincinnati businessman Nathaniel Ropes; Cambridge clergyman Edward G. Russell; Frank B. Sanborn, a financier of abolitionist John Brown; clergyman Edward P. Thwing; Boston publisher John Boies Tileston; Quincy lawyer Henry Walker; Henry Fitz Gilbert Waters, 23d Massachusetts Infantry; lawyer Joseph Willard; Boston lawyer Smith Wright.

182. Lt. Arthur Dehon of Boston, Meade's ADC, killed at the battle of Fredericksburg.

183. "The Porcellian Club had a breakfast at nine o'clock for its members who had served in the army, of whom over twenty were present. A special guest was Major-General George G. Meade, who 'after the gustatory performances was elected an honorary member of the Club, whereupon he signed the constitution, and is hereafter one of the gods.'" Bail, "Harvard's Commemoration Day," 260.

184. TL's classmates: Frank Barlow, Joe Hayes, Ned Dalton, James Kendall Hosmer, and Henry Fitz Gilbert Waters. Adm. Charles Henry Davis (Harvard 1825), chief of the Bureau of Navigation; Brig. Gen. Charles Devens Jr. (Harvard Law 1840); Brig. Gen. Manning Ferguson Force (Harvard Law 1848); Maj. Gen. Romeyn Beck Ayres; Joseph Sewall Smith; Charles Appleton Phillips (Harvard 1860). After the war Barlow opened a small law practice and married Col. Robert Gould Shaw's sister, Ellen "Nellie" Shaw.

185. TL's classmate Phillips Brooks, relatively unknown in Boston at the time, made a profound impression on his audience. Henry Lee Higginson wrote "on that day, as Colonel Lee said long afterwards, all words, except the prayer of Phillips Brooks, seemed powerless to convey what was felt." Perry, *Life and Letters*, 238. Rev. Doctor George Putnam. John Knowles Paine, instructor in music at Harvard, directed a choir of sixty male and female voices and an orchestra of twenty-six pieces. Charles H. Mills, father of Capt. Mills killed in March. TL made sure that his son's body was embalmed and shipped home to his father. Brothers killed were: surgeon Edward Revere and Col. Paul Revere, Lt. James Lowell and Col. Charles Lowell Jr., Capt. Edward Abbott and Maj. Henry Abbott, and Lt. Col. Wilder Dwight and Capt. Howard Dwight.

186. "Air a mild copper," show a streak of Copperhead.

187. Col. James Duncan Graham directed surveys of the Great Lakes in the 1850s. Chandler not identified.

Bibliography

Bibliographic Note

Considering the number of names recorded on these pages, approaching Lyman's notebooks with an eye to publication was daunting. I attempted in the notes to identify all of the many individuals mentioned. This involved cross-checking military records and compilations with Lyman's pre- and postwar letters and journals and with other officers' published letters and diaries. For civilians, there was nothing for it but to dive into tomes of local history and genealogy, which are in ample supply in the MHS library. I compared sources until satisfied (by name, rank, age, proximity in time and place, context, and association) that I had my man or woman. I was not uniformly successful and resorted to a qualification or "not identified" when necessary. As Joseph Harsh always admonished, "You *must* leave something for other historians to do."

The principal sources for identifying military officers are the official compilations, most notably the *Official Records* of the Armies and the Navies. Access in digital form makes searching these multivolumed sets for hundreds of names a manageable task. Francis Heitman's *Historical Register and Dictionary of the United States Army* (Washington, D.C.: GPO, 1903) provided biographical and service information for thousands of officers, including muster-in and muster-out dates, promotions, commands, and adjunct assignments such as staff positions. William Powell and his collaborator Edward Shippen produced three volumes of detailed information on officers of the U. S. Army: *Officers of the Army and Navy (Regular) Who Served in the Civil War* (Philadelphia, Pa.: Hammersly, 1892); *Officers of the Army and Navy (Volunteer) Who Served in the Civil War* (Philadelphia, Pa.: Hammersly, 1893); and the comprehensive *List of Officers of the Army of the United States from 1779 to 1900* (New York: Hammersly, 1900). Medical personnel at the regimental level are well served by N. A. Strait's compilation *Roster of all Regimental Surgeons and Assistant Surgeons in the Late War* (Washington, D.C.: U.S. Pension Office, 1883). Strait omitted, however, many hundreds of surgeons who served at general hospitals or at levels other than regimental, a decided gap in the documentation.

For biographical information on Union and Confederate generals, I relied on the standard texts: Ezra Warner's *Generals in Gray: Lives of the Confederate Commanders*. (Baton Rouge: Louisiana State University Press, 1987) and *Generals in Blue: Lives of the Union Commanders* (Baton Rouge: Louisiana State University Press, 1992) with some assistance from Roger Hunt's *Colonels in Blue: Union Army Colonels of the Civil War* (Atglen, Pa.: Schiffer Military History, 2001) and Jack Brown's *Brevet Brigadier Generals in Blue* (Gaithersburg, Md.: Olde Soldier Books, 1990). Robert E. L. Krick's *Staff Officers in Gray* (Chapel Hill: University of North Carolina Press, 2003) confirmed the rank, assignment, and presence of Confederate staff officers that were mentioned.

As Lyman was particularly interested in tracking officers from his home state, the adjutant-general's *Massachusetts Soldiers, Sailors, and Marines in the Civil War,* 8 vols. (Norwood, Mass.: AGO, 1937) proved invaluable. These volumes contain full rosters of every Massachusetts regiment. Lyman's immediate commander (on paper), Gen. William Schouler sought to tell the story of the commonwealth's contribution to the war in two volumes, *History of Massachusetts in the Civil War* (Boston: D. Estes, 1868). Schouler focused on the organization and administration of the war effort, which provided background and context for events.

Harvard University's contribution to the war is well documented, and as so many of Lyman's associates were Harvard boys, these volumes were helpful. Francis Henry Brown (Harvard 1857) compiled the *Roll of the Students of Harvard University who served in the Army or Navy during the War of the Rebellion* (Cambridge, Mass.: Welch, Bigelow, 1869) and commemorated the role of graduates in the war in *Harvard University in the War of 1861–1865* (Boston: Cupples, 1886). Thomas Wentworth Higginson compiled eulogies for the war dead in *Harvard Memorial Biographies* (Cambridge, Mass.: Sever and Francis, 1867). For interested readers, these volumes provide detailed biographical information on the lives and service of Harvard men in Federal service. Confederate attendees and graduates of Harvard largely were excluded. In a recent regimental history, *Harvard's Civil War* (Hanover, N.H. and London, Conn.: University Press of New England, 2005), Richard F. Miller offers a social history of the Twentieth Massachusetts "Harvard regiment" in counterpoint to the staid official history penned by George A. Bruce, *The Twentieth Regiment of Massachusetts Volunteer Infantry* (Boston: Houghton Mifflin, 1906). Miller's work reveals conflict between the officer caste and common soldiers, and some of Lyman's associates appear in an unflattering light.

Because so much of Lyman's social life and work revolved around Harvard and its affairs, the *Quinquennial Catalogue of the Officers and Graduates of Harvard University, 1636–1900,* 2 vols. (Cambridge, Mass.: Harvard University, 1900) proved an essential reference. Also useful for information on Lyman's classmates was Edwin Hale Abbot's *Report of the Secretary: Harvard Class of 1855* (Boston: Alfred Mudge & Son, 1865). Lyman's connections among Boston's club society may be traced in a *History of the Somerset Club, 1852–1913* (Boston: N.p., 1913), *Report of the Celebration of the Fiftieth Anniversary of the Founding of the Union Club of Boston, 1863–1913* (Cambridge, Mass.: Houghton, 1913), and the essential *Catalogue of the Porcellian Club of Harvard University* (Cambridge, Mass.: N.p., 1887).

Many individuals known to Lyman were detailed in the pages of James Wilson and John Fiske's *Appleton's Cyclopaedia of American Biography,* 6 vols. (New York: D. Appleton, 1887–89). Mary C. Crawford's *Famous Families of Massachusetts,* 2 vols. (Boston: Little, Brown, 1930) proved an invaluable resource for untangling intricate family ties. Lyman Coleman's *Genealogy of the Lyman Family in Great Britain and America* (Albany, N.Y.: J. Munsell, 1872) adequately addressed the Boston Lymans. The papers of Lyman's cousin Arthur and his wife, published by Ella Lyman Cabot as *Arthur Theodore Lyman and Ella Lyman: Letters and Journals with an Account of Those They Loved and Were Descended from*, 3 vols. (Boston: N.p., 1932) clarified many obscure family details. Two volumes highlight Lyman's connections with his wife's cousin Robert Gould Shaw and expand on the context of Beacon Hill society: Russell Duncan's *Blue-eyed Child of Fortune: Civil War Letters of Colonel Robert Gould Shaw* (Athens, Ga.: University of Georgia Press, 1992), and Marian Smith's *Beacon Hill's Robert Gould Shaw* (New York: Carlton Press, 1986). It was interesting and convenient to access the U.S. census records online at the Library of Congress. The 1860 enumeration revealed that Lyman's peers typically retained between three and eight live-in servants, most of whom were born in Ireland.

Wartime correspondence of many of Lyman's friends and associates has been published, and these men often referenced one another. Charlie Adams and his brother Henry are well represented in Worthington Chauncey Ford's *A Cycle of Adams Letters, 1861–1865*, 2 vols. (Boston: Houghton Mifflin, 1920). Ford also published *War Letters, 1862–1865: John Chipman Gray and John Codman Ropes* (Boston: Houghton Mifflin, 1927). Gray and Ropes were active with Lyman after the war in the Massachusetts Historical Society. Wendell Holmes's letters were collected in a thin volume by Mark DeWolfe Howe in *Touched with Fire: Civil War Letters and Diary of Oliver Wendell Holmes Jr.* (Cambridge, Mass.: Harvard University Press, 1946). Bliss Perry's *Life and Letters of Henry Lee Higginson* (Boston: Atlantic Monthly Press, 1921) is a biography informed by correspondence in the style of the period. Higginson married Ida Agassiz, daughter of the professor. Christian Samito has published *Fear Was Not in Him: The Civil War Letters of Major General Francis C. Barlow, U.S.A.* (New York: Fordham University Press, 2004). Lyman's classmate Frank Barlow offered telling comments on the management of the army. Robert Garth Scott edited *Fallen Leaves: Civil War Letters of Major Henry Livermore Abbott* (Kent, Ohio: Kent State University Press, 1991). Lyman was at Abbott's side when he died in the Wilderness. Stephen Minot Weld Jr.'s *War Diary and Letters of Stephen Minot Weld* (Boston: Massachusetts Historical Society, 1979) presents copious detail on wartime people and events. Weld, like Lyman, was a gifted writer. Lyman's friend, staff officer Morris Schaff published two engaging and often overlooked campaign histories: *The Battle of the Wilderness* (Boston: Houghton Mifflin, 1910) and *The Sunset of the Confederacy* (Boston: J. W. Luce, 1912). Schaff occasionally quoted from the pages of Lyman's notebooks—most notably his description of Robert E. Lee's "brown study" at Appomattox.

In the opinion of the headquarters staff, Grant and Sheridan had marched away with much of George Gordon Meade's credit for the successes of the Army of the Potomac. The ascendancy of Grant and Sheridan in the history books was established early on by war correspondent William Swinton in *Campaigns of the Army of the Potomac* (New York: Swinton, 1866). Meade's name virtually dropped out of Swinton's history after Grant came east to Virginia. Many historians, past and present, have followed his lead.

When it became clear that written history was slighting Meade, his supporters attempted to redress the imbalance. After Grant's memoirs were published in 1885, giving

Meade little ink, aide-de-camp Carswell McClellan jumped to his general's defense enumerating in lawyerly fashion Meade's many contributions to victory in *Personal Memoirs and Military History of U. S. Grant versus the Record of the Army of the Potomac* (Boston: Houghton Mifflin, 1887). Two years later McClellan challenged Sheridan's selective memory in *Notes on the Personal Memoirs of P. H. Sheridan* (St. Paul, Minn.: Banning, 1889). Meade's nephew Richard Meade Bache detailed the general's life and accomplishments in *Life of General George Gordon Meade, Commander of the Army of the Potomac* (Philadelphia, Pa.: Coates, 1897). Isaac Pennypacker's *General Meade* (New York: D. Appleton, 1901) was overly adulatory of Meade and slighted many capable officers. Chief of staff Andrew Humphreys's son, Henry, took umbrage with this narrative and rushed to publication *A Critical Examination [in part] of Pennypacker's Life of General George G. Meade* (Tivoli, N.Y.: Green, 1901). Henry detailed his father's many contributions to Meade's victories and heaped scorn upon Meade. Had Gen. Meade been alive, he would have been among the first to credit Humphreys where it was due. Capt. George Meade published *Life and Letters of George Gordon Meade*, 2 vols. (New York: Charles Scribner's Sons, 1913) hoping to lay at rest all the many allegations against his father. George Meade included extensive documentation of the general's effort to defend himself against the accusations of the Committee on the Conduct of the War.

There is no current biography of Meade, but historians are showing a willingness to reassess his reputation. Ethan S. Rafuse in *George Gordon Meade and the War in the East* (Abilene, Kans.: McWhiney Foundation Press, 2003) provides a very fair and positive view of Meade's modern approach to warfare. Richard A. Sauers has devoted attention to Meade's difficulties with the committee, largely instigated by Dan Sickles, in *Gettysburg: The Meade-Sickles Controversy* (Washington, D.C.: Brassey's, 2003). In this volume, Sauers documented Sickles's campaign to sell his side of the story to the history books at Meade's expense. Sauers reexamined Meade's contributions with a fresh eye in *Meade: Victor of Gettysburg* (Washington, D.C.: Brassey's, 2003) and concluded that a "more balanced picture of Meade has begun to emerge, in spite of the negative literature relied upon by previous historians."

Readers desiring to follow the military operations of the Army of the Potomac more closely while reading Lyman's notebooks should have two books close at hand: *Gettysburg to the Rapidan: The Army of the Potomac, July 1863 to April 1864* (New York: Charles Scribner's Sons, 1883) and *Virginia Campaign of '64 and '65: The Army of the Potomac and the Army of the James* (New York: Charles Scribner's Sons, 1883). Written by Meade's chief of staff Andrew Atkins Humphreys, these volumes (available as reprints) offer a concise account of operations with which he was directly involved. Among recent books on the Virginia campaigns, Gordon C. Rhea's series (published by the Louisiana State University Press) stands out for quality of research and readability: *The Battle of the Wilderness, May 5–6, 1864* (1994); *The Battles for Spotsylvania Court House and the Road to Yellow Tavern, May 7–12, 1864* (1997); *To the North Anna River: Grant and Lee, May 13–25, 1864* (2000); and *Cold Harbor: Grant and Lee, May 26-June 3, 1864* (2002). Rhea is one of the few authors who sought out Lyman's original notebooks as a source, rather than relying on excerpts in the published letters.

Theodore Lyman's Publications

"Addenda to the Paper by Brevet Lieutenant-Colonel Swan on the Battle of the Wilderness." In *Papers of the Military Historical Society of Massachusetts*, vol. 4. Boston: MHSM, 1905.

"Crossing of the James and Advance on Petersburg." In *Papers of the Military Historical Society of Massachusetts*, vol. 5. Boston: MHSM, 1906.

"De Piscium Natura" in *Atlantic Monthly* 22 (August 1868): 208–11 (online at the Cornell University Library).

"On the Uselessness of the Maps furnished to the staff of the Army of the Potomac previous to the Campaign of May 1864." In *Papers of the Military Historical Society of Massachusetts*, vol. 4. Boston: MHSM, 1905.

"Operations of the Army of the Potomac, June 5–15, 1864." In *Papers of the Military Historical Society of Massachusetts*, vol. 5. Boston: MHSM, 1906.

Papers Relating to the Garrison Mob. Cambridge, Mass.: N.p., 1870.

"Suum Cuique." *Boston Weekly Advertiser*, May 2 and 4, 1865.

Theodore Lyman's Scientific Papers

Dredging Operations of the United States Steamer Blake: *Ophiurans*. Cambridge, Mass., 1875.

Illustrated Catalogue of the Ophiuridae and Astrophytidae in the Museum of Comparative Zoology. Cambridge, Mass., 1865 and 1871.

Old and New Ophiuridae and Astrophytidae. Cambridge, Mass., 1874.

Ophiuridae and Astrophytidae of the Hassler *Expedition*. Cambridge, Mass., 1875.

Preliminary report on the Ophiuridae and Astrophytidae dredged in deep water between Cuba and the Florida Reef. Cambridge, Mass., 1869.

Prodrome of the Ophiuridae and Astrophytidae of the Challenger *Expedition*, Cambridge, Mass., 1878–1879.

Report on Ophiuridae and Astrophytidae dredged by Louis F. de Pourtales. Cambridge, Mass., 1869.

Report on the Ophiuridae dredged by H. M. S. Challenger *during the Years 1873–76*. London, 1882.

Manuscript Collections

Harvard Map Collection
Harvard University Archives
    Class of 1855, Secretary's Files
    Class of 1855, Clippings
    Biographical Files
James Foster Family Correspondence
Library of Congress
    Abraham Lincoln Papers

George Gordon Meade Collection
Marsena Patrick Papers
Louisiana State University Special Collections Online Catalog
Massachusetts Historical Society
Lyman Family Papers, 1785–1956
National Archives
Record Group 94, Daily Memoranda for Information of the Maj.-Gen., Commanding, February 1863–January 1865.
Record Group 94, Letters Sent and Received by the Assistant Adjutant General.
Record Group 107, Records of the Office of the Secretary of War, Civil War Passes Granted, 1864–1866.
Record Group 110, Letters Sent by Headquarters Army of the Potomac.
Record Group 393, Army of the Potomac Papers.
New York State Library
Gouverneur K. Warren Papers, Letters
University of North Carolina, Wilson Library Manuscripts Division Online Catalog
Southern Historical Collection, Arnold Family Papers
University Publications of America
Confederate Military Manuscripts (Microfilm Series B, Reel 6)

Sources

Abbot, Edwin Hale. *Report of the Secretary, Harvard Class of 1855*. Boston: Alfred Mudge & Son, 1865.

Adams, Charles Francis, Jr. *Charles Francis Adams 1833–1915: An Autobiography*. New York: Russell and Russell, 1916.

———. *Theodore Lyman (1833–1897) and Robert Charles Winthrop, Jr. (1834–1905): Two Memoirs Prepared by Charles Francis Adams for the Massachusetts Historical Society*. Cambridge, Mass.: John Wilson and Son, 1906.

Agassiz, George R., ed. *Meade's Headquarters 1863–1865: Letters of Colonel Theodore Lyman from the Wilderness to Appomattox*. Boston: Massachusetts Historical Society, 1922.

Bail, Hamilton Vaughan. "Harvard's Commemoration Day, July 21, 1865" in *The New England Quarterly* 15:2 (June 1942): 256–79.

Bruce, George A. *Twentieth Regiment of Massachusetts Volunteer Infantry 1861–1865*. Boston: Houghton Mifflin, 1906.

Carleton, Charles Coffin. "The May Campaign in Virginia" in *Atlantic Monthly* 14 (July 1864): 124–32.

Coleman, Lyman. *Genealogy of the Lyman Family in Great Britain and America*. Albany, N.Y.: J. Munsell, 1872.

Dana, Charles A. *Recollections of the Civil War: With the Leaders at Washington and in the Field in the Sixties*. New York: D. Appleton, 1898.

Duncan, Russell, ed. *Blue-eyed Child of Fortune: Civil War Letters of Colonel Robert Gould Shaw*. Athens: University of Georgia Press, 1992.

Everett, Edward. *Orations and Speeches on Various Occasions*, 4 vols. Boston: Little, Brown, 1885.

Forbes, Abner. *The Rich Men of Massachusetts: Containing a Statement of the Reputed Wealth of about Two Thousand Persons, with Brief Sketches of nearly Fifteen Hundred Characters*. 2nd Ed. Boston: Redding, 1852.

Ford, Worthington Chauncey, ed. *A Cycle of Adams Letters, 1861–1865*, 2 vols. Boston: Houghton Mifflin, 1920.

———. *War Letters, 1862–1865, of John Chipman Gray and John Codman Ropes*. Boston: Houghton Mifflin, 1927.

Frassanito, William A. *Grant and Lee: The Virginia Campaigns 1864–1865*. New York: Charles Scribner's Sons, 1983.

Gardner, Alexander. *Gardner's Photographic Sketch Book of the Civil War*. New York: Dover, 1959.

Gracey, S. L. *Annals of the Sixth Pennsylvania Cavalry*. Philadelphia, Pa.: E. H. Butler, 1868.

Grant, Ulysses S. *Personal Memoirs of U. S. Grant*, 2 vols. New York: C. L. Webster, 1885.

Hagerman, Edward. *The American Civil War and the Origins of Modern Warfare: Ideas, Organization and Field Command*. Bloomington: Indiana University Press, 1992.

Humphreys, Andrew A. *The Virginia Campaign of '64 and '65: The Army of the Potomac and the Army of the James*. New York: Charles Scribner's Sons, 1883.

Humphreys, Henry H. *Andrew Atkinson Humphreys: A Biography*. Philadelphia, Pa.: John C. Winton, 1924.

———. *A Critical Examination [in part] of Pennypacker's Life of General George G. Meade*. Tivoli, N.Y.: Frank O. Green, 1901.

Johnson, Robert, and Clarence Buell, eds. *Battles and Leaders of the Civil War*. 4 vols. New York: Century, 1887–88.

Jordan, David M. *Happiness Is Not My Companion: The Life of General G. K. Warren*. Bloomington: Indiana University Press, 2001.

Luvaas, Jay. *The Military Legacy of the Civil War: The European Inheritance*. 1959. Lawrence: University Press of Kansas, 1988.

McClellan, Carswell. *The Personal Memoirs and Military History of U. S. Grant versus the Record of the Army of the Potomac*. Boston: Houghton Mifflin, 1887.

Meade, George, ed. *Life and Letters of George Gordon Meade, Major General, United States Army*, 2 vols. New York: Charles Scribner's Sons, 1913.

Morison, Samuel Eliot. *The Maritime History of Massachusetts, 1783–1860*. Boston: Houghton Mifflin, 1941.

Nevins, Allan, ed. *A Diary of Battle: The Personal Journals of Colonel Charles S. Wainwright, 1861–1865*. Gettysburg, Pa.: Stan Clark Military Books, 1962.

Perry, Bliss, ed. *Life and Letters of Henry Lee Higginson*. Boston: Atlantic Monthly Press, 1921.

Porter, Horace. *Campaigning with Grant*. New York: Century, 1897.

Powell, William H. *The Fifth Army Corps (Army of the Potomac): A Record of Operations During the Civil War in the United States of America, 1861–1865*. London: G. P. Putnam's Sons, 1896.

Rafuse, Ethan S. *George Gordon Meade and the War in the East.* Abilene, Tex.: Mc-Whiney Foundation Press, 2003.

Sauers, Richard A. *Gettysburg: The Meade-Sickles Controversy.* Washington, D.C.: Brassey's, 2003.

Schaff, Morris. *The Battle of the Wilderness.* Boston: Houghton Mifflin, 1910.

Seaburg, Carl, and Stanley Paterson. *Merchant Prince of Boston: Col. T. H. Perkins, 1764–1854.* Cambridge, Mass.: Harvard University Press, 1971.

Sears, Stephen W. *Controversies and Commanders: Dispatches from the Army of the Potomac.* Boston: Houghton Mifflin, 1999.

Sheridan, Philip Henry. *The Personal Memoirs of P. H. Sheridan.* New York: Da Capo, 1992.

Smyth, Henry Augustus. "Account of the Final Attack and Capture of Richmond by the Federal Army" in *Minutes of Proceedings of the Royal Artillery Institution* 4 (1865): 363–70.

Sparks, David S., ed. *Inside Lincoln's Army: The Diary of Marsena Rudolph Patrick, Provost Marshal General, Army of the Potomac.* New York: Yoseloff, 1964.

Sumner, Merlin E., ed. *The Diary of Cyrus B. Comstock.* Dayton, Ohio: Morningside, 1987.

Swinton, William. *Campaigns of the Army of the Potomac: A Critical History of the Operations in Virginia, Maryland and Pennsylvania from the Commencement to the Close of the War, 1861–1865.* New York: C. B. Richardson Swinton, 1866.

Thomas, Benjamin P., ed. *Three Years with Grant: As Recalled by War Correspondent Sylvanus Cadwallader.* New York: Alfred A. Knopf, 1955.

U.S. War Department. *Official Records of the Union and Confederate Navies in the War of the Rebellion,* 30 vols. Washington, D.C.: GPO, 1894–1922.

U.S. War Department. *The War of the Rebellion: A Compilation of the Official Records of the Union and Confederate Armies,* 128 vols. Washington: GPO, 1880–1901.

Walker, Francis A. *History of the Second Army Corps in the Army of the Potomac.* New York: Charles Scribner's Sons, 1887.

Weld, Stephen Minot, Jr. *War Diary and Letters of Stephen Minot Weld.* Second Edition. Boston: Massachusetts Historical Society, 1979.

Wittenburg, Eric J. *Glory Enough for All: Sheridan's Second Raid and the Battle of Trevilian Station.* Washington, D.C.: Brassey's, 2001.

Wright, Stephen J., and Blake A. Magner. "John Gibbon: the Man and the Monument" in *Gettysburg: Articles of Lasting Interest* 13 (July 1995): 119–27.

Maps

Army of the Potomac, *Petersburg and Vicinity, 1864–1867,* scale of 1:7920. National Archives and Records Administration: RG77 G204-33-40.

Hopkins, G. M. *Atlas of the Town of Brookline, Massachusetts.* Philadelphia, Pa.: Hopkins, 1874.

U.S. Army Corps of Engineers, *Federal and Confederate works during the siege of Pe-*

tersburg, between the Appomattox River and Hatchers Run, June 16, 1864 to April 3, 1865,* scale of 1:7920. LC, Civil War Map Collection 615.

U.S. Army Corps of Engineers, *Petersburg and Five Forks, 1864–1865,* scale of 1:42240. LC, Civil War Map Collection 607.8.

U.S. Army Corps of Engineers, "Map of the Siege of Petersburg, 1864–1865," scale of 1:15840. LC, Civil War Map Collection 617.

U.S. Army Corps of Engineers. *Military Maps Illustrating Operations, Armies of the Potomac and James.* Washington, D.C.: War Department, 1869.

U.S. War Department. *Atlas to Accompany the Official Records of the Union and Confederate Armies,* 35 folios. Washington, D.C.: GPO, 1891–1895.

Index